Between Memory and Power

Handbook of Oriental Studies

Handbuch der Orientalistik

SECTION ONE

The Near and Middle East

Edited by

Maribel Fierro (*Madrid*)
M. Şükrü Hanioğlu (*Princeton*)
D. Fairchild Ruggles (*University of Illinois*)
Florian Schwarz (*Vienna*)

VOLUME 162

The titles published in this series are listed at *brill.com/ho1*

Between Memory and Power

The Syrian Space under the Late Umayyads and Early Abbasids (c. 72–193/692–809)

By

Antoine Borrut

Translated by

Anna Bailey Galietti

BRILL

LEIDEN | BOSTON

Cover illustration: Statue of the caliph on a pedestal of lions, Khirbat al-Mafjar, © "Khirbat al-Mafdjar", Encyclopaedia of Islam, Second Edition [s.v.].

Library of Congress Cataloging-in-Publication Data

Names: Borrut, Antoine, author. | Bailey Galietti, Anna, translator.
Title: Between memory and power : the Syrian space under the late Umayyads and early Abbasids (c. 72–193/692–809) / by Antoine Borrut ; translated by Anna Bailey Galietti.
Other titles: Entre mémoire et pouvoir. English
Description: Leiden ; Boston : Brill, [2023] | Series: Handbook of Oriental studies = Handbuch der Orientalistik. Section. 1: The Near & Middle East, 0169–9423 ; volume 162 | Includes bibliographical references and index. | Translated from the French.
Identifiers: LCCN 2023012050 (print) | LCCN 2023012051 (ebook) | ISBN 9789004466319 (hardback) | ISBN 9789004466326 (ebook other)
Subjects: LCSH: Umayyad dynasty—Historiography. | Abbasids—Historiography. | Syria—Historiography.
Classification: LCC DS94.95 .B6713 2023 (print) | LCC DS94.95 (ebook) | DDC 956.91072/2—dc23/eng/20230403
LC record available at https://lccn.loc.gov/2023012050
LC ebook record available at https://lccn.loc.gov/2023012051

Typeface for the Latin, Greek, and Cyrillic scripts: "Brill". See and download: brill.com/brill-typeface.

ISSN 0169-9423
ISBN 978-90-04-46631-9 (hardback)
ISBN 978-90-04-46632-6 (e-book)

This book is printed on acid-free paper and produced in a sustainable manner.

Contents

Preface to the English Translation (2023) IX
Acknowledgements to the French Edition (2011) XX
Translator's Note XXII
List of Illustrations XXIII

Introduction 1

1 A Time of Writings and Rewritings: Writing History in the Syrian Space 9
1.1 Narrative Islamic Sources and the Question of Their Transmission 9
1.1.1 *The Act of Writing and Modes of Transmission* 12
1.1.2 *Lost Sources and Historical Reconstruction* 15
1.1.3 *Formal Aspects:* Isnād *and* Khabar 18
1.2 Writing History in the Syrian Space under the Late Umayyads and Early Abbasids 23
1.2.1 *On the Origins of Islamic Historiography* 23
1.2.2 *Syrian Historiography in the Umayyad Era?* 29
1.2.3 *Forgotten Sources?* 46

2 A Time of Writings and Rewritings: Historiographic Filters and Vulgates 53
2.1 In Search of Umayyad Historiographic Projects 54
2.1.1 *"Common Link," "Collective* isnāds,*" or Umayyad Historiographic Filters?* 54
2.1.2 *Marwanid Writings and Rewritings* 58
2.2 Toward a Historiographic Vulgate: The History of Syria Rewritten in Abbasid Iraq 68
2.2.1 *Layers of Historical Rewriting under the Early Abbasids* 68
2.2.2 *Al-Ṭabarī: The End of History?* 88

3 A Time of Writings and Rewritings: Sources on the Margins of the Historiographic Vulgate? 94
3.1 Islamic Sources on the Margins of the Vulgate? 95
3.1.1 *Second/Eighth Century Sources?* 95
3.1.2 *Space before Chronology* 103
3.1.3 *Other Perspectives* 108

3.2 Non-Muslim Sources: "External" or "Eastern" Sources? 118
3.2.1 *Intercultural Transmission* 121
3.2.2 *Theophilus of Edessa, the Chronology of Qartamīn and the Syriac Common Source* 123
3.2.3 *Other Christian Sources* 132
3.2.4 *Historical Apocalypses* 140

4 The Second/Eight-Century Syrian Space: Between Memory and Oblivion 145
4.1 *Memoria* as an Object of Study 146
4.1.1 *Islam and Memory* 147
4.1.2 Memoria *outside the Field of Islamic Studies: A Historiographic Overview* 150
4.2 Umayyad Memoria 156
4.2.1 *Umayyad "Realms of Memory"* 157
4.2.2 *The Early Abbasids and Umayyad Memory* 160
4.2.3 *Umayyad Memory and Culture* 175
4.3 Spaces of Memory 178
4.3.1 *The Distorting Prisms of Post-Sāmarrāʾ Historiography* 179
4.3.2 *Syrian-Umayyad* Memoria *versus Iraqi-Abbasid* Memoria: *A False Dichotomy?* 180
4.3.3 *The Syrian Space in Umayyad Ideology: Appropriation of Solomonic Precedent* 189

5 The Creation of Umayyad Heroes: Maslama b. ʿAbd al-Malik, Combat Hero 200
5.1 The Siege of Constantinople: Military Failure, Narrative Success 202
5.1.1 *Epic Tradition and Monumental Legacy* 203
5.1.2 *The Expedition against Constantinople in the Islamic Chronographies* 206
5.1.3 *The Christian Sources and the Construction of Heroes* 215
5.2 From Hero of the Byzantine Frontier to Islamic Hero? 228
5.2.1 *The Competition for Heroisation* 229
5.2.2 *Maslama and the Borders of the World: A New Alexander?* 232
5.3 Eschatology and the Creation of Heroes 238

6 **The Creation of Umayyad Heroes: ʿUmar b. ʿAbd al-ʿAzīz, the "Holy" Caliph** 249
6.1 ʿUmar II in the Islamic Tradition 250
6.1.1 *The Fifth Orthodox Caliph* 251
6.1.2 *A New ʿUmar b. al-Khaṭṭāb* 253
6.1.3 Mahdī *and* Mujaddid*: The Caliph of the Year 100 Hijrī* 256
6.2 ʿUmar II in the Christian Sources 262
6.2.1 *Muslim Apocalyptic and Christian Tradition* 262
6.2.2 *The Caliph's Image* 266
6.2.3 *A Chronology of these* topoi *in the Syrian Space: Propositions and Hypotheses* 270
6.3 Constructing the Image of the Holy Caliph: Stages and Conditions 271
6.3.1 Sunna *and* Sīra*: The Traditionists' Caliph* 271
6.3.2 *The Caliph and the Law: ʿUmar II and Mālik b. Anas* 273
6.3.3 *The Circulation of Elements Related to ʿUmar II: Propositions and Hypotheses* 278

7 **Interpreting the Abbasid Revolution in the Syrian Space** 284
7.1 The Abbasid Revolution: Medieval and Modern Vulgates 287
7.1.1 *The Revolutionary Canon* 287
7.1.2 *A Century of Interpretations of the Abbasid Revolution* 289
7.1.3 *The "Abbasid Revolution" and Modern Scholarship: Questions and Debates* 292
7.2 Syrian Memories of the Abbasid Revolution 299
7.2.1 *In the Workshop of Abbasid History* 302
7.2.2 *History Continues?* 306
7.2.3 *Ibrāhīm al-Imām* 312
7.3 ʿAbd Allāh b. ʿAlī and the Allure of a Syrian Abbasid Caliphate? 314
7.3.1 *Strategies of Isolation* 314
7.3.2 *Confiscation for and by Messianism* 327

8 **Exercising Power in the Syrian Space in the Second/Eighth Century: A History of Meanings** 339
8.1 Patrimonialism and the Creation of a Caliphal Landscape 341
8.1.1 *The Construction of an Islamic Caliphal Landscape* 342
8.1.2 *Patrimonialism and Regionalisation of Powers* 346

8.2 The Mobile Exercise of Power 351
8.2.1 *The Need for Mobility* 352
8.2.2 *The "Umayyad Castles" as an Expression of Mobile Power* 365
8.2.3 *Mobility Lost* 385
8.3 Abbasid Reconfigurations 393
8.3.1 *The Banū Ṣāliḥ and Abbasid Syrian Patrimonialism* 395
8.3.2 *Competition for Mobility and Its Consequences* 399
8.3.3 *Between Damascus and Baghdad: Spaces of Caliphal Power* 403

Conclusion 414

Abbreviations 421
Sources 422
Bibliography 430
Index 496

Preface to the English Translation (2023)

A decade has passed since *Entre mémoire et pouvoir* was first published in 2011. I am delighted that the contribution of the book has been deemed significant enough to warrant an English translation and its inclusion into Brill's prestigious Handbook of Oriental Studies (HdO) series. I am deeply thankful to several people who made this possible. Kathy van Vliet first investigated the possibility of commissioning an English translation, a project brought to fruition thanks to Abdurraouf Oueslati's unparalleled stamina. I am also grateful to Maribel Fierro, M. Şükrü Hanioğlu, D. Fairchild Ruggles, and Florian Schwarz for their support and their enthusiasm in accepting the book into the HdO series.

The translation itself was magisterially prepared by Anna Bailey Galietti, translator extraordinaire. Anna was an ideal choice as a formidable Francophile and a fellow scholar of early Islam. Working with her on the translation was a pleasure at every step of the way even if we both admittedly underestimated the amount of work it would entail.

Being translated is a profoundly enriching experience. It is sometimes also a paradoxical one, as it is quite clear that I would have written the book somewhat differently had I planned it in English from its inception. To overcome that challenge, Anna and I were lucky to be able to workshop an early draft of the translated introduction with Alison Vacca, Sarah Savant, and Matthew Gordon and to benefit from their input to find the right balance between being faithful to the French text and producing an idiomatic translation.

The translated text that follows is the original text, save for a few typos and minor corrections caught by Anna's merciless eye. No effort has been made to update the text or the footnotes as this would have required writing a new book. The only exception was a (quasi) systematic effort to cite books in their English editions when available instead of French originals or translations, already a massive endeavour in itself.

Looking back at *Entre mémoire et pouvoir* ten years later – and sometimes almost rediscovering it in the course of the translation process – proved enjoyable for the most part. Still, some pages obviously did not age as well as others and a few comments are thus in order. First, however, let me briefly reflect on some of the book's contributions and highlight some new developments in the intervening decade.

At the time of the publication of *Entre mémoire et pouvoir*, the formidable boom of memory studies had been largely ignored by Islamicists and there was virtually no scholarship focusing on memory in the field of "medieval Islam".[1] In a way, this wasn't much of a surprise since medieval Islam remains a theory-poor field. The immediate consequence was that if *Entre mémoire et pouvoir* was quite well received, its theoretical framework was at first basically ignored. Things have obviously changed, however, thanks in particular to the important contributions of Sarah Savant and Alison Vacca who both embraced a history of memory approach in their respective work.[2] I have myself pursued this line of inquiry on different occasions, for instance focusing on Karbalāʾ as an early Islamic site of memory and shedding light on the redemption of Alid memory more broadly, to complement the limited comments offered below in chapter four.[3] Moreover, it has been encouraging to see an increased demand for memory studies in the field broadly conceived over the last few years, in terms of both workshops and conferences.[4]

There is still much to be done in light of recent developments, though. It is impossible to do justice here to the last decade of memory studies, but the field is now equipped with handbooks and introductory material that make it more accessible than it once was.[5] In the last few years, some of the most stimulating scholarship on memory – at least from my own perspective – has been produced by Ann Rigney.[6] She notably insisted on the fact that we need to under-

1 See the discussion in chapter 4 below.

2 Sarah Bowen Savant, *The New Muslims of Post-Conquest Iran: Tradition, Memory, and Conversion* (Cambridge: Cambridge University Press, 2013). See the thoughtful review essay of Elizabeth Urban, "Remembering and Forgetting the Persian Past," *Marginalia Review of Books*, August 19, 2014 (https://themarginaliareview.com/remembering-forgetting-persian-past/). See also Savant, "Forgetting Ctesiphon: Iran's Pre-Islamic Past, c. 800–1100," in Philip Wood (ed.), *History and Identity in the Late Antique Near East* (Oxford: Oxford University Press, 2013), 169–86. Alison Vacca, *Non-Muslim Provinces under Early Islam: Islamic Rule and Iranian Legitimacy in Armenia and Caucasian Albania* (Cambridge: Cambridge University Press, 2017).

3 Antoine Borrut, "Remembering Karbalāʾ: The Construction of an Early Islamic Site of Memory," *Jerusalem Studies in Arabic and Islam* 42 (2015), 249–82.

4 I am thinking for instance about the 4th Annual Edinburgh International Graduate Byzantine Conference, held in November 2020, that offered a rich array of papers on the theme of "catastrophes and memory (500–1500 CE)". I am indebted to the organisers for giving me the opportunity to reflect in a keynote address on "Remembering and Forgetting the Past in Early Islam" (available online: https://youtu.be/u-wRi88mX8A?t=36880).

5 See for instance Anna Lisa Tota and Trever Hagen (eds.), *Routledge International Handbook of Memory Studies* (London and New York: Routledge, 2016). The best introduction to cultural memory is offered by Astrid Erll, *Memory in Culture* (London: Palgrave Macmillan, 2011).

6 See in particular her magisterial *The Afterlives of Walter Scott: Memory on the Move* (Oxford: Oxford University Press, 2012); "Cultural Memory Studies: Mediation, Narrative, and the Aesthetic," in Tota and Hagen (eds.), *Routledge International Handbook of Memory Studies*,

stand cultural memory "in performative terms, as a way of recollecting the past and shaping its image using a whole range of media, rather than merely in preservative terms, as a way of transmitting unchanged something inherited from an earlier age."[7] Rigney's many insights would certainly allow for substantial developments if I was to "do over" *Entre mémoire et pouvoir* today. For anyone eager to engage with memory studies, a good starting point is offered by Marek Tamm's thoughtful essay, even though it was published almost ten years ago.[8] Still, Tamm's historiographical survey remains particularly useful, as well as his effort to define concepts that have been sometimes used quite uncritically as memory approaches were trending. Tamm's discussion of "cultural memory" – a central notion in the following pages, indebted as I am to the work of Jan Assmann[9] – is perhaps most helpful to articulate the tension between history and memory:

> In terms of cultural memory, *history is a cultural form exactly like, for instance, religion, literature, art or myth, all of which contribute to the production of cultural memory*. And the writing of history should be treated as one of the many media of cultural memory, such as novels, films, rituals or architecture. The reduction of history writing to a mere medium of cultural history through which a certain social group shapes its relations with the past does not mean that history writing should give up its scientific pretensions or the epistemological attitudes and disciplinary techniques it has evolved over the past couple of centuries. *History writing is simply a very specific medium of cultural memory with its own rules and traditions – one of the most important for as comprehensive an understanding of the past as possible, but certainly not the only or necessarily the most influential one.*[10]

65–76; "Remembrance as Remaking: Memories of the Nation Revisited," *Nations and Nationalism* 24/2 (2018), 240–57.

7 Rigney, *The Afterlives*, 17–8.

8 Marek Tamm, "Beyond History and Memory: New Perspectives in Memory Studies," *History Compass* 11/6 (2013), 458–73.

9 It is worth pointing out that Jan Assmann's seminal *Das kulturelle Gedächtnis: Schrift, Erinnerung und politische Identität in frühen Hochkulturen* (Munich: Beck, 1997), was translated into English shortly after *Entre mémoire et pouvoir* was first published as *Cultural Memory and Early Civilization: Writing, Remembrance, and Political Imagination* (Cambridge: Cambridge University Press, 2011).

10 Tamm, "Beyond History and Memory," 463 (my italics).

As the following chapters demonstrate, I found such an approach particularly fruitful when combined with a history of meanings (*Sinngeschichte*).[11]

Beyond Assmann's scholarship, Patrick Geary's *Phantoms of Remembrance* also proved particularly influential to me.[12] He recently published a reflective essay on his magisterial book more than twenty years after its publication, offering a perceptive discussion of the evolution of the field and of his own thinking on remembrance and oblivion in western medieval contexts.[13] One of Geary's heroes, Arnold of Regensburg, a Bavarian monk writing around 1030 (whom we will meet again below in chapter 1), claimed that it was perfectly legitimate for the old past to "be entirely thrown away" or to "be buried with reverence." And yet, as Geary pointed out, this past often somehow refused to stay "buried" and "was not to be forgotten altogether but rather transformed, both memorialized and commemorated."[14] Listening to those "murmurs" to reclaim "alternative pasts"[15] very much became a guiding principle of *Entre mémoire et pouvoir*. Reflecting on what he would do differently if he was to "do over" his *Phantoms of Remembrance*, Geary concluded that he would focus more on oblivion than on remembrance and that he "would concentrate in attempting to recover not so much the new past that was thereby created, but the old past that was, with only partial success, discarded or buried, but which nevertheless continued to haunt the present as phantoms."[16] I hope that the effort in the following pages to retrieve fragments of forgotten Umayyad and early Abbasid historiographical layers – and their "futures past" (or "former future(s)", *vergangene Zukunft*), to say it with Reinhardt Koselleck[17] – resonates with Geary's insights. In that vein – and building on Koselleck's work – I have

11 Here again, I was primarily indebted to Jan Assmann's work, especially his *Ägypten. Eine Sinngeschichte* (Munich: Carl Hanser Verlag, 1996), translated as *The Mind of Egypt: History and Meaning in the Time of the Pharaohs* (New York: Metropolitan Books, 2002).

12 Patrick J. Geary, *Phantoms of Remembrance: Memory and Oblivion at the End of the First Millennium* (Princeton: Princeton University Press, 1994).

13 Patrick J. Geary, "Remembering and Forgetting Phantoms of Remembrance: Social Memory and Oblivion in Medieval History after Twenty Years," in Sebastian Scholz and Gerald Schwedler (eds.), *Creative Selection between Emending and Forming Medieval Memory* (Berlin & Boston: De Gruyter, 2022), 15–26. I am grateful to Patrick Geary for sharing with me a draft of his thoughtful piece prior to publication and for our many conversations on memory-related topics during my stay at the Institute for Advanced Study in 2016–2017.

14 Geary, *Phantoms of Remembrance*, 8, and below, chapter 4.

15 Geary, *Phantoms of Remembrance*, 21, 177.

16 Geary, "Remembering and Forgetting," 26.

17 Reinhardt Koselleck, *Vergangene Zukunft: Zur Semantik geschichtlicher Zeiten* (Frankfurt am Main: Suhrkamp, 1979), translated by Keith Tribe as *Futures Past: On the Semantics of Historical Time* (New York: Columbia University Press, 2004).

tried to push the discussion further to shed light on alternative periodisations used prior to the Abbasid-era construct that still prevails today as the agreed-upon chronology of early Islam.[18]

Moreover, as the following pages demonstrate, a memory approach is not simply a modern theoretical framework applied to ancient texts, but is firmly grounded in the narrative sources themselves that deliberately frame much of Umayyad and Abbasid history in terms of remembrance and oblivion. Here again, I was indebted to Geary, who emphasised anew in his reflective essay that one of his main interests had been to study "the complex processes of rethinking the past on the part of ordinary clerics and lay persons, less when they were reflecting on memory than *when one could observe them in the act of remembering*."[19]

I should add that early Islamic memory – and singularly Umayyad realms of memory – remains much disputed to this day, as exemplified by the desecration of the (alleged) tomb of ʿUmar b. ʿAbd al-ʿAzīz (ʿUmar II) by the so-called Islamic State (ISIL) in 2020 in Syria, near Maʿarrat al-Nuʿmān.[20]

Another methodological intervention of the book was to challenge the way scholars of early Islam have approached non-Muslim sources, usually in a logic of opposition with Muslim texts.[21] Indebted to both Alfred-Louis de Prémare and Lawrence Conrad, I made the case that we should move away from such a dichotomy and take full advantage of the asynchronous rhythms of transmission across the various near eastern historiographies, in particular to trace and, when possible, to date the circulation of historical information.

Here again, things are now changing and such an approach has been gaining some traction. Robert Hoyland's intellectual trajectory offers a good example: although he started from the premise of a logic of opposition between corpora while writing his *Seeing Islam*,[22] he eventually concluded: "I have become convinced in recent years that this approach is not really valid, since

18 Antoine Borrut, "Vanishing Syria: Periodization and Power in Early Islam," *Der Islam* 91/1 (2014), 37–68.

19 Geary, "Remembering and Forgetting," 15 (my italics).

20 See Omar Ahmed, "Was the 'desecration of Caliph Umar II's tomb' fake news?," *Middle East Monitor*, June 8, 2020 [https://www.middleeastmonitor.com/20200608-was-the-desecration-of-caliph-umar-iis-tomb-fake-news/].

21 Muriel Debié has also pointed out the tendency of Islamicists to regard non-Muslim sources as external, *L'écriture de l'histoire en syriaque. Transmissions interculturelles et constructions identitaires entre hellénisme et islam* (Leuven: Peeters, 2015), xix.

22 Robert G. Hoyland, *Seeing Islam as Others Saw It: A Survey and Evaluation of Christian, Jewish, and Zoroastrian Writings on Early Islam* (Princeton, NJ: Darwin Press, 1997).

the two bodies of material are much more intertwined than had previously been thought."[23]

Moreover, scholars such as Alison Vacca have done much to properly position Armenian sources in this rich historiographical landscape. This view will be reinforced by her forthcoming book, together with Sergio La Porta, firmly situating Łewond's *History* (*fl.* late 2nd/8th c.) *as* Abbasid historiography even though it was composed by a Christian scholar writing in Armenian.[24] Likewise, Philip Wood has recently situated Dionysius of Tel-Maḥre in his proper Abbasid context.[25] It seems to me that this is a much-needed step to rethink our approach to early Islam, one that has been exclusively envisioned in Arabic for too long. Manuela Ceballos, Alison Vacca, and I have endeavoured to complicate the picture in an edited volume aiming to foster a multilingual approach to the early caliphate, very much in line with what scholars of Late Antiquity have been doing for a while now.[26]

---

23 Robert Hoyland, "Reflections on the Identity of the Arabian Conquerors of the Seventh-Century Middle East," *Al-ʿUṣūr al-Wusṭā* 25 (2017), 113–40, at 77–78. Hoyland brought this point home in a separate book: "I do not want to champion non-Muslim sources over Muslim sources; indeed, it is my argument that the division is a false one. Muslims and non-Muslims inhabited the same world, interacted with one another and even read one another's writings. In this book the distinction I make is simply between earlier and later sources, and I favour the former over the latter irrespective of the religious affiliation of their author," *In God's Path: The Arab Conquests and the First Islamic Empire* (Oxford: Oxford University Press, 2015), 2–3. The proximity between Muslims and non-Muslims and the blurred boundaries between religious communities has also been emphasised in several studies, including Antoine Borrut and Fred M. Donner (eds.), *Christians and Others in the Umayyad State* (Chicago: The Oriental Institute of the University of Chicago, 2016); Jack Tannous, *The Making of the Medieval Middle East: Religion, Society, and Simple Believers* (Princeton: Princeton University Press, 2018); Richard E. Payne, *A State of Mixture: Christians, Zoroastrians, and Iranian Political Culture in Late Antiquity* (Oakland: University of California Press, 2015); Michael P. Penn, *Envisioning Islam: Syriac Christians and the Early Muslim World* (Philadelphia: University of Pennsylvania Press, 2015). Not all of these studies implied revising our historiographical categories though, see for instance my review of Penn's book in *Intellectual History of the Islamicate World* 9/3 (2021), 371–75.

24 Sergio La Porta and Alison Vacca, *An Armenian Futūḥ Narrative: Łewond's Eighth-Century History of the Caliphate* (Chicago: The Oriental Institute of the University of Chicago, forthcoming).

25 Philip Wood, *The Imam of the Christians: The World of Dionysius of Tel-Mahre, c. 750–850* (Princeton: Princeton University Press, 2021).

26 Antoine Borrut, Manuela Ceballos, and Alison Vacca (eds.), *Navigating Language in the Early Islamic World: Multilingualism and Language Change in the First Centuries of Islam* (Turnhout: Brepols, forthcoming). The flip side of this conversation, however, is that much remains to be done to properly integrate Arabic sources into the late antique library. The same comment applies to Middle Persian, Hebrew, or Geʿez texts, a point made by Mira Balberg, "Late Ancient Judaism: Beyond Border Lines," *Marginalia, Late*

I should add that several of the non-Muslim sources and/or authors abundantly cited in the following pages have been the object of dedicated studies since the publication of *Entre mémoire et pouvoir*,[27] while Muriel Debié's tome now offers the most substantial discussion on Syriac historiography.[28]

Beyond these broad historiographical comments, a few smaller observations are in order. An obvious starting point is the shadowy figure of Theophilus of Edessa (d. 785), who notably served as court astrologer to the Abbasid caliph al-Mahdī (r. 158–69/775–85), and will be abundantly mentioned in the following pages. Theophilus was famously identified as the *Syriac Common Source* by Conrad, a view subsequently adopted by most scholars.[29] Much has been debated with regard to what should actually be attributed to Theophilus, and Muriel Debié depicted him as the "ghost of Syrian Orthodox historiography."[30] The important work of Maria Conterno should now be added to the discussion as the most systematic challenge to the identification of Theophilus as the "more likely candidate" as once posited by Conrad.[31] I concur with Debié and Conterno that modern scholarship has had a tendency to attribute too much to Theophilus, a trend reinforced by Hoyland's "reconstruction" of Theophilus'

Antiquity and the New Humanities: An Open Forum (2015). (Available online: https://themarginaliareview.com/late-ancient-judaism-beyond-border-lines-by-mira-balberg/).

27 I am thinking in particular about Wood, *The Imam of the Christians*; Marek Jankowiak and Federico Montinaro (eds.), *Studies in Theophanes* (Paris: Association des Amis du Centre d'Histoire et Civilisation de Byzance, 2015); Andy Hilkens, *The Anonymous Syriac Chronicle of 1234 and its Sources* (Leuven: Peeters, 2018); as well as the recent English translation of Dorothea Weltecke's important book, *The "Description of the Times" by Mōr Michael the Great (1126–1199): A Study on its Historical and its Historiographical Context* (Leuven: Peeters, 2021).

28 Debié, *L'écriture de l'histoire en syriaque*. On the significance of her contribution, see Peter Brown's generous review in *Al-ʿUṣūr al-Wusṭā* 26 (2018), 225–31.

29 Lawrence I. Conrad, "Theophanes and the Arabic Historical Tradition: Some Indications of Intercultural Transmission," *Byzantinische Forschungen* 15 (1988), 1–44. For more details on this identification, see below, chapter 3; Debié, *L'écriture de l'histoire en syriaque*, 27–31, 139–43, 556–59, and *passim*.

30 Muriel Debié, "Christians in the Service of the Caliph: Through the Looking Glass of Communal Identities," in Antoine Borrut and Fred M. Donner (eds.), *Christians and Others in the Umayyad State* (Chicago: The Oriental Institute of the University of Chicago, 2016), 53–71, at 66; and *L'écriture de l'histoire en syriaque*, 139.

31 Conrad, "Theophanes and the Arabic Historical Tradition," 43. Maria Conterno, *La "descrizione dei tempi" all'alba dell'espansione islamica. Un'indagine sulla storiografia greca, siriaca e araba fra VII e VIII secolo* (Berlin and Boston: De Gruyter, 2014); "Theophilos, 'the more Likely Candidate'? Towards a Reappraisal of the Question on Theophanes' 'Oriental Sources'," in M. Jankowiak and F. Montinaro (eds.), *Studies in Theophanes*, 383–400.

lost history, and some such "maximalist" approaches are simply untenable.[32] On the other hand, it seems to me that we are still on reasonably firm ground when it comes to the final decades of Umayyad rule, especially in light of a passage in Agapius's *Kitāb al-Taʾrīkh* (*wr. ca.* 942) clearly identifying Theophilus as his main source for the period.[33] From this vantage point, there is still much in support of Conrad's identification of Theophilus as (one element of) the *Syriac Common Source* (now increasingly referred to as the *Eastern Source*) for a specific period of early Islamic history, i.e. late Umayyad times.

Perhaps a broader issue has to do with our modern tendency to always try to identify single individual authors. In that sense Debié is correct in saying that some sources, including part of what has been ascribed to Theophilus of Edessa, have been created by the *Quellenforschung*.[34] Instead we might more profitably approach sources such as the *Syriac Common Source* as literature in excerpts,[35] thinking in terms of text re-use[36] and multi-layered texts with likely multiple authors. A similar trend can be observed in recent scholarship dedicated to the *History of the Patriarchs of Alexandria*, for instance.[37]

---

32 Robert G. Hoyland, *Theophilus of Edessa's Chronicle and the Circulation of Historical Knowledge in Late Antiquity and Early Islam* (Liverpool: Liverpool University Press, 2011). See my discussion in Antoine Borrut, "Court Astrologers and Historical Writing in Early ʿAbbāsid Baghdād: An Appraisal," in J. Scheiner and D. Janos (eds.), *The Place to Go: Contexts of Learning in Baghdad, 750–1000 CE* (Princeton, NJ: The Darwin Press, 2014), 455–501, at 477–81.

33 See below, chapter 3. Agapius's book is isually known as the *Kitāb al-ʿUnwān* in modern scholarship but Michel Breydy has shown that this was a mistake, see his "Richtigstellungen über Agapius von Manbiğ und sein historisches Werk", *Oriens Christianus*, 73 (1987), p. 90–97.

34 Debié, *L'écriture de l'histoire en syriaque*, 27–31. The problem is not restricted to Theophilus of Edessa if one considers, for instance, the many scholarly debates generated by the *Khwadāynāmag*. See now the important study by Jaakko Hämeen-Antilla, *Khwadāynāmag: The Middle Persian Book of Kings* (Leiden: Brill, 2018). See also Robert G. Hoyland, *The "History of the Kings of the Persians" in Three Arabic Chronicles. The Transmission of the Iranian Past from Late Antiquity to Early Islam* (Liverpool: Liverpool University Press, 2018); and the useful review essay of Sebastian Bitsch, "The Story of a Lost Book: Two Recent Studies on the *Khwadāynāmag*," *Iran and the Caucasus* 24 (2020), 92–105.

35 See for instance Sébastien Morlet (ed.), *Lire en extraits. Lecture et production des textes de l'Antiquité à la fin du Moyen Age* (Paris: PUPS, 2015).

36 As best exemplified by the work of Sarah Savant in the framework of her ERC project "Knowledge, Information Technology, & the Arabic Book" (KITAB): http://kitab-project.org/.

37 See in particular several studies by Perrine Pilette: "La recension primitive de l'Histoire des Patriarches d'Alexandrie: Problématique et prospectives," *Acta Orientalia Belgica* 23 (2010), 141–55; "L'Histoire des Patriarches d'Alexandrie: une nouvelle évaluation de la configuration du texte en recensions," *Le Muséon* 126 (2013), 419–50; "Transmission et diffusion de l'historiographie copto-arabe : nouvelles remarques sur les recensions primitive

So, even though I would now frame my discussion of Theophilus differently, I still believe that we do have access to a late Umayyad/early Abbasid historiographical layer with the sections of the *Syriac Common Source* dealing with late Umayyad history. In light of the above discussion with regard to the status of non-Muslim sources, it should be added that Theophilus offers quite a paradigmatic example. Regardless of how much one wishes to attribute to him, Theophilus can hardly be regarded as external to Abbasid historiography and, indeed, to the Abbasid state. As a quick aside, our problem with categories goes even beyond the deceptive dichotomy between Muslim and non-Muslim sources since we still have to reconcile Theophilus's two personae, the astrologer and the historian.[38]

A debate of a different nature now sheds a fresh light on Ibn Aʿtham al-Kūfī, whose death date has generated a fair amount of scholarly discussion. In the following pages, like many other scholars, I adopted the conclusions of Conrad's magisterial study to posit an early third/ninth century date for Ibn Aʿtham, rather than the more traditional option of 314/926–7 that had been rejected as "an Orientalist error" by Conrad.[39] Ilkka Lindstedt and recently Andrew McLaren have, however, produced significant evidence to argue that Ibn Aʿtham flourished in the late third/ninth–early fourth/tenth century.[40] The implications are arguably limited for my discussion below, but it seems to

---

et vulgate de l'Histoire des Patriarches d'Alexandrie," in Juan Pedro Monferrer-Sala and Sofía Torallas Tovar (eds.), *Cultures in Contact: Transfer of Knowledge in the Mediterranean World* (Cordoba and Beirut: Oriens Academic, 2013), 103–140.

38 A point emphasised in my "Court Astrologers," 479–81. See also Debié, *L'écriture de l'histoire en syriaque*, 139–43 and 426–36.

39 Conrad's study was first presented in 1992 and subsequently circulated among colleagues. For various reasons, however, it never appeared in print until Professor Conrad gave Matthew Gordon and I permission to publish his piece in *Al-ʿUṣūr al-Wusṭā: The Journal of Middle East Medievalists* a few years ago. See now Lawrence I. Conrad, "Ibn Aʿtham and His History," *Al-ʿUṣūr al-Wusṭā* 23 (2015), 87–125.

40 Ilkka Lindstedt, "Al-Madāʾinī's *Kitāb al-Dawla* and the Death of Ibrāhīm al-Imām," in Ilkka Lindstedt, Jaakko Hämeen-Anttila, Raija Mattila, and Robert Rollinger (eds.), *Case Studies in Transmission* (Münster: Ugarit-Verlag, 2014), 103–30, esp. 118–123, and "Sources for the Biography of the Historian Ibn Aʿtham al-Kūfī," in Jaakko Hämeen-Anttila, Petteri Koskikallio, and Ilkka Lindstedt (eds.), *Contacts and Interaction: Proceedings of the 27th Congress of the Union Européenne des Arabisants et Islamisants, Helsinki 2014* (Leuven: Peeters, 2017), 299–309; Andrew McLaren, "Dating Ibn Aʿtham's History: Of Persian Manuscripts, Obscure Biographies, and Incomplete Isnāds," *Al-ʿUṣūr al-Wusṭā* 30 (2022), 183–234. On the many challenges of Ibn Aʿtham's manuscript tradition, see Mónika Schönléber, "Notes on the Textual Tradition of Ibn Aʿtham's *Kitāb al-Futūḥ*," in Jaakko Hämeen-Anttila, Petteri Koskikallio, and Ilkka Lindstedt (eds.), *Proceedings of Union Européenne des Arabisants et Islamisants 27, Helsinki, June 2nd–6th, 2014* (Leuven: Peeters, 2017), 427–38, and her review of Qays al-ʿAṭṭār's recent (2017) partial edition of the *Kitāb al-futūḥ* in *Al-ʿUṣūr al-Wusṭā* 28 (2020), 273–81.

me that the content of Ibn Aʿtham's work strongly suggests an earlier historiographical layer than other Abbasid-era sources of the turn of the third/ninth and fourth/tenth century. Whether this has to do with Ibn Aʿtham's sources or with his specific mode of history writing, remains to be investigated.

The death date of al-Yaʿqūbī, often given as 284/897 in modern scholarship, has been amended by Sean Anthony who convincingly argued for pushing it to after 295/908.[41] To avoid confusion, this more correct date has been adopted in the following pages (in one of the few instances where the original text was deliberately updated). My discussion of al-Yaʿqūbī should now be complemented by Anthony's study and by the introductory chapters of the new English translation of al-Yaʿqūbī's works.[42] References to this new translation were not added, given the number of times al-Yaʿqūbī is being cited in the following pages, but this formidable collaborative effort clearly supersedes preexisting translations and should thus be consulted.

The discussion in chapter eight about Quṣayr ʿAmra now needs to be revised in light of epigraphic evidence studied by Frédéric Imbert.[43] And I have had the opportunity to return to the topics of patrimonialism and "itinerant kingship," developed in that same chapter, in a dedicated study.[44] Finally, it goes without saying that much scholarship has been produced on Umayyad and Abbasid history or with regard to Islamic historiography since the publication of *Entre mémoire et pouvoir*. It is impossible to offer a comprehensive overview here.[45]

41 Sean W. Anthony, "Was Ibn Wāḍiḥ al-Yaʿqūbī a Shiʿite Historian? The State of the Question," *Al-ʿUṣūr al-Wusṭā* 24 (2016), 15–41.

42 Matthew S. Gordon, Chase F. Robinson, Everett K. Rowson, and Michael Fishbein (eds.), *The Works of Ibn Wāḍiḥ al-Yaʿqūbī: An English Translation*, 3 vols. (Leiden: Brill, 2018).

43 Frédéric Imbert, "Le prince al-Walīd et son bain: Itinéraires épigraphiques à Quṣayr ʿAmra," *Bulletin d'études orientales* 64 (2016), 321–63; "Califes, princes et compagnons dans les graffiti du début de l'islam," *Romano-Arabica* XV (2015), 59–78.

44 Antoine Borrut, "Pouvoir mobile et construction de l'espace dans les premiers siècles de l'islam," in Sylvain Destephen, Josiane Barbier, and François Chausson (eds.), *Le gouvernement en déplacement. Pouvoir et mobilité de l'Antiquité à nos jours* (Rennes: Presses Universitaires de Rennes, 2019), 243–67. See also the relevant contributions in Alain Delattre, Marie Legendre, and Petra Sijpesteijn (eds.), *Authority and Control in the Countryside: From Antiquity to Islam in the Mediterranean and Near East (6th–10th Century)* (Leiden: Brill, 2019).

45 The most substantial synthesis on the first dynasty of Islam is now Andrew Marsham (ed.), *The Umayyad World* (Abingdon and New York: Routledge, 2021). See also the contributions in Alain George and Andrew Marsham (eds.), *Power, Patronage, and Memory in Early Islam: Perspectives on Umayyad Elites* (Oxford: Oxford University Press, 2018); Alain George, *The Umayyad Mosque of Damascus: Art, Faith and Empire in Early Islam* (London: Gingko, 2021); and Steven C. Judd, *Religious Scholars and the Umayyads: Piety-Minded Supporters of the Marwānid Caliphate* (London and New York: Routledge, 2014). On the "Abbasid Revolution," see in particular Yury Karev, *Samarqand et le Sughd à*

Entre mémoire et pouvoir came out slightly over a decade ago, before Syria was struck by horror. I was incredibly fortunate to spend four wonderful years in Damascus, at the French Institute of the Near East, where I did much of the doctoral work that led to this book. During those years, I had the privilege to get to know and love the country, from the packed streets of the old city of Damascus to those of the souk of Aleppo, from the slopes of Mount Qasioun to the shores of the Euphrates, and from the basaltic landscapes of the Lajā and the Ḥawrān to the vestiges and oasis of Palmyra. While exploring a region filled with Umayyad and Abbasid memories, I unsurprisingly became a historian of memory. As an inadequate gesture, I dedicate this book to my dear Syrian friends and to the courageous people of Syria.

---

l'époque ʿAbbāsside. Histoire politique et sociale (Paris: Association pour l'avancement des études iraniennes, 2015); and Étienne de la Vaissière, "The ʿAbbāsid Revolution in Marw: New Data," *Der Islam* 95/1 (2018), 110–46. Recent studies on early Islamic historiography include Najam Haider, *The Rebel and the Imām in Early Islam: Explorations in Muslim Historiography* (Cambridge: Cambridge University Press, 2019); Tobias Andersson, *Early Sunnī Historiography: A Study of the* Tārīkh *of Khalīfa b. Khayyāṭ*, (Leiden: Brill, 2018); Ryan J. Lynch, *Arab Conquests and Early Islamic Historiography: The Futuh al-Buldan of al-Baladhuri* (London and New York: I.B. Tauris, 2019). Edward Zychowicz-Coghill, *The First Arabic Annals: Fragments of Umayyad History* (Berlin-Boston: De Gruyter, 2021). Several studies dedicated to Ibn ʿAsākir are also directly relevant: Nancy Khalek, "Early Islamic History Reimagined: The Biography of ʿUmar ibn ʿAbd al-ʿAzīz in Ibn ʿAsākir's *Tārīkh madīnat Dimashq*," *Journal of the American Oriental Society* 134/3 (2014), 431–51; Steven C. Judd and Jens Scheiner (eds.), *New Perspectives on Ibn ʿAsākir in Islamic Historiography* (Leiden: Brill, 2017); Paula Caroline Manstetten, "Ibn ʿAsākir's *History of Damascus* and the Institutionalisation of Education in the Medieval Islamic World," PhD. thesis, Department of the Languages and Cultures of the Near and Middle East, SOAS, University of London (2018).

Acknowledgements to the French Edition (2011)

After long years of research conducted over three continents, I have incurred a great many debts. Christophe Picard has been a dominant influence, as he helped guide my first foray into the research that would become my doctoral dissertation (defended in February 2007) and, ultimately, this monograph. He constantly made himself available and gave invaluable advice and support throughout the process of completing this study. Over the years, he has become much more than an academic adviser. The members of my dissertation committee also offered helpful remarks and suggestions, all of which I have tried to put into practice in revising this manuscript. Gratitude is due to Christian Décobert, Fred M. Donner, Anne-Marie Eddé, Gabriel Martinez-Gros and Françoise Micheau.

I am also particularly indebted to André Binggeli, Paul M. Cobb, Denis Genequand and Frédérique Woerther, who willingly read and re-read drafts of the various chapters in this volume. Their advice has been indispensable and saved me many errors; any that remain are, of course, my responsibility alone.

Thanks go out to Wadād al-Qāḍī and Sebastian Günther, who graciously agreed to publish this volume in the series they oversee. Its publication owes a great deal to the editorial team at Brill, especially Kathy van Vliet and Marjolein Schaake. I am grateful also to Anna Olivier of *Index à la page* for her knowledge and expertise in compiling the index.

This study is in large part the result of many productive discussions with friends and colleagues, some of whom I am sure to forget here: Paul M. Cobb, Denis Genquand, André Binggeli, Muriel Debié, Denise Aigle, Fred M. Donner, Christian Décobert, Gabriel Martinez-Gros, Sophie Makariou, Donald Whitcomb, Wadād al-Qāḍī, Alastair Northedge, Christian Robin, Jean Durliat, Alain Ducellier, Louis Pouzet, Alfred-Louis de Prémare, Dominique Valérian, Marie-Laure Derat, Thierry Bianquis, Sylvie Denoix, Hugh Kennedy, Chase F. Robinson, Robert G. Hoyland, Arietta Papaconstantinou, Jens Scheiner, Cyrille Jalabert, Petra Sijpesteijn, Élise Voguet, Wissem Gueddich, Sobhi Bouderbala, Anne Troadec, Emma Gannagé, Marie-Odile Rousset, Yves Gonzalez-Quijano, Peter Wien, Madeline Zilfi, Kenneth Holum, Vanessa Guéno, Nicolas and Magalie Peaudeau, Yvonne Alfonso-Castel, Delphine Roques, Fabienne Landou, Vanina Carcenac and Mathilde Basselier.

Several academic institutions provided ideal conditions for my research, beginning with the Université de Toulouse-Le Mirail, where my academic journey started. I then had the privilege of spending four years in Syria as a scholar at the Institut Français du Proche-Orient. During my time in Damascus, I was fortunate to benefit from the library's rich resources as well as constant contact with other researchers, foremost among them Cyrille Jalabert, who gave me a warm welcome when I first arrived in Syria and served as my guide through Damascus and the Institut. Issam Chehadat was another of my Syrian guides, as were many of the other scholars at the IFPO. I am particularly grateful to Maher Chérif, Sylvia Chiffoleau, and Fanny Lafourcade, with whom I shared a tiny but happy office. Denise Aigle and her invaluable wisdom also accompanied me on much of this Syrian journey, as did Christian Décobert, the director of IFPO at the time, who showed me constant support. These years in the Near East eventually led me to Lebanon, where I taught for several years at Université Saint-Joseph in Beirut and profited from the assistance of Anne Troadec, Emma Gannagé and Lévon Nordiguian. After Syria, I completed my dissertation in Paris during my tenure as a visiting professor at the Université Paris 8. I then revised the manuscript for publication during my post-doctorate in the Arabic department of the Institut de recherche et d'histoire des textes (CNRS), a task completed after I crossed the Atlantic to join the faculty at the University of Maryland.

I was also fortunate to study numerous times at the University of Chicago and its incomparable libraries. These stays were made possible and even more enjoyable with the help of Fred M. Donner, Donald Whitcomb, and Wadād al-Qāḍī. The "Héritages omeyyades/Umayyad Legacies" program I led with Paul M. Cobb between 2004 and 2006 occasioned many valuable conversations over the course of two roundtables held in Damascus and at the University of Notre Dame (Indiana) and during a final colloquium. My gratitude goes out to all those who participated in these discussions. Denis Genequand, Marie-Odile Rousset, Ian B. Straughn, Donald Whitcomb and Alastair Northedge shared their vast knowledge of Near Eastern archaeological sites over multiple trips to Lebanon, Syria and Jordan. Thanks are also due to Naoum Abi Rached and Father Simon Légasse, who patiently taught me Arabic and Syriac.

During a somewhat sudden return to France several years ago, my father, Georges, Florence, and Armand welcomed me back with open arms and provided the perfect environment to write my dissertation. Many thanks as well to my mother, Sabine, my brother, Clément, and my grandparents, who always encouraged me to continue my academic journey to the East. And finally, to Juliette, who generously and with great tolerance shared her husband with obscure Umayyad and Abbasid figures across the Syrian space.

Translator's Note

Wherever possible, we reference English translations and editions of the works cited in this volume. In cases where no English translation or edition for a given primary or secondary source exists, all translations were undertaken from the French (unless otherwise indicated in the footnotes). In a select few instances, English translations or editions of a certain text are available, but we elected not to use them and instead to translate from the French. The reasons for this decision vary with respect to the work in question; foremost among them are the following: the English version of a given source omitted some or all of the material included and referenced in the French, making it difficult or impossible to switch to the English text; switching to the English translation would have involved a prohibitive amount of labour; dissatisfaction with the quality of the extant English version(s). Any errors in translation are entirely my own.

Anna Bailey Galietti

Illustrations

Diagrams

3.1 Circuits of Theophilus of Edessa and the chronology of Qartamīn 126
5.1 Transmission of elements related to Maslama 217
6.1 Transmission of elements related to the caliph ʿUmar II 265

Figures

0.1 Map of major Umayyad sites in Palmyra and Balqāʾ XXIV
0.2 Umayyad genealogy XXV
0.3 Abbasid genealogy XXVI
0.4 Simplified Hashimite genealogy XXVII
4.1 Khirbat al-Mafjar: Statue of the caliph on a pedestal of lions 197
8.1 Location of al-Ṣinnabra / Khirbat al-Karak 360
8.2 Al-Ṣinnabra / Khirbat al-Karak: site map 361
8.3 Inscription of ʿAbd al-Malik (ʿAqaba Afīq / Fīq) 362
8.4 ʿAbd al-Malik's new road in the Golan (based on Elad, "The Southern Golan," 64) 364
8.5 The Banū Umayya 386
8.6 Plan of Raqqa / al-Rāfiqa 405

Tables

4.1 Umayyad *memoria* under the early Abbasids 156
5.1 Main information related to Maslama in the Christian sources 219
6.1 Main information related to ʿUmar II in the Christian sources 263
6.2 Themes associated with ʿUmar II in the *Muwaṭṭaʾ* 276
7.1 Main information related to the "Abbasid Revolution" in the Christian sources 300
8.1 Main information related to Hishām's activities in the Christian sources 383

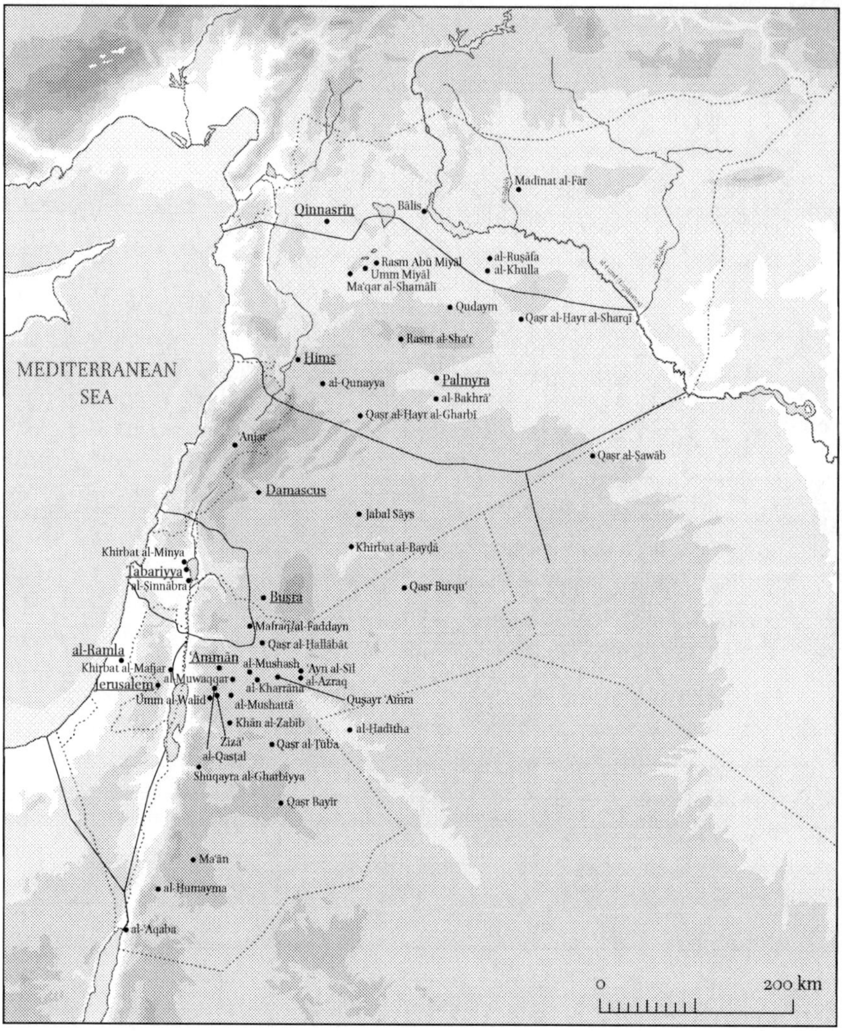

FIGURE 0.1 Map of major Umayyad sites in Palmyra and Balqā'
© DENIS GENEQUAND, *LES ÉLITES OMEYYADES*, FIG. 183

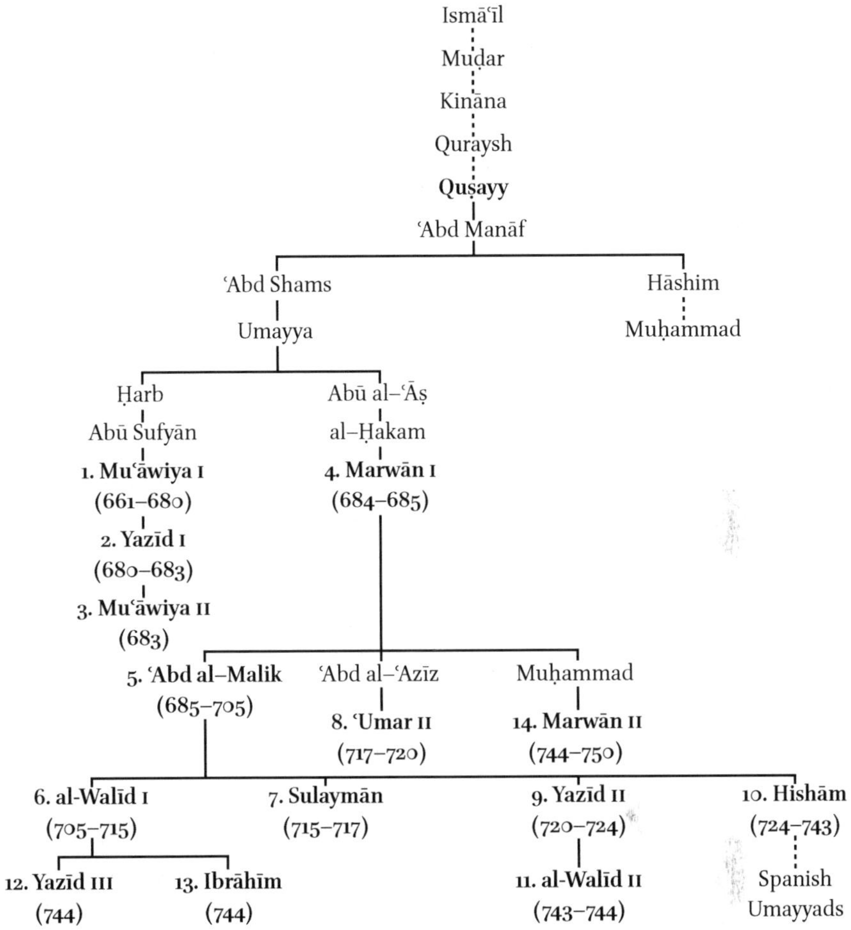

FIGURE 0.2 Umayyad genealogy

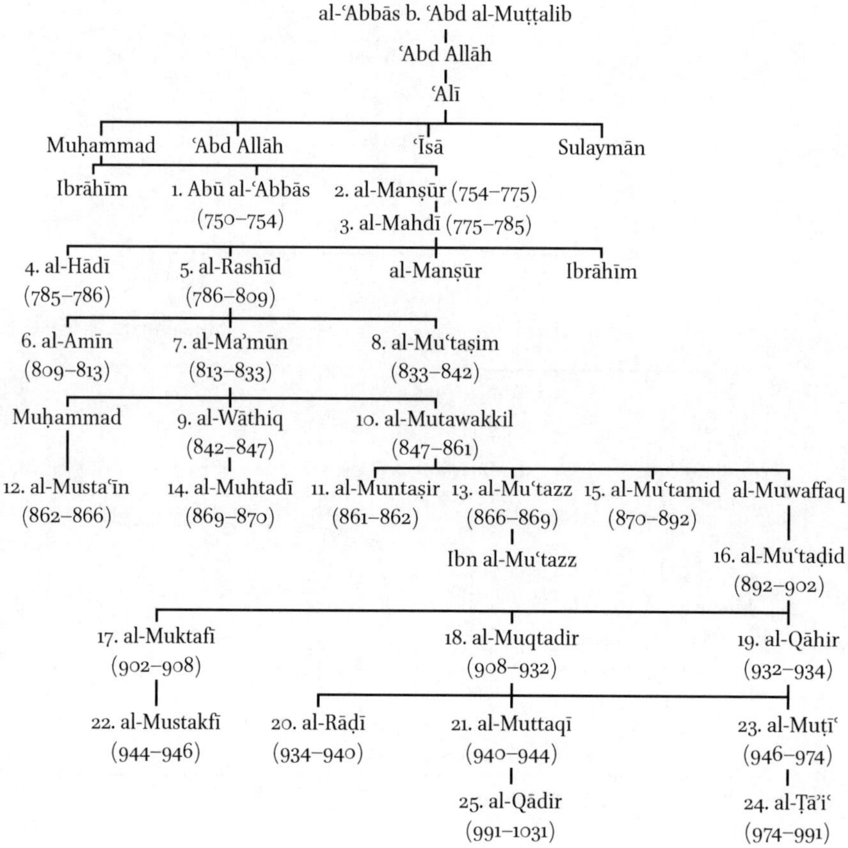

FIGURE 0.3 Abbasid genealogy

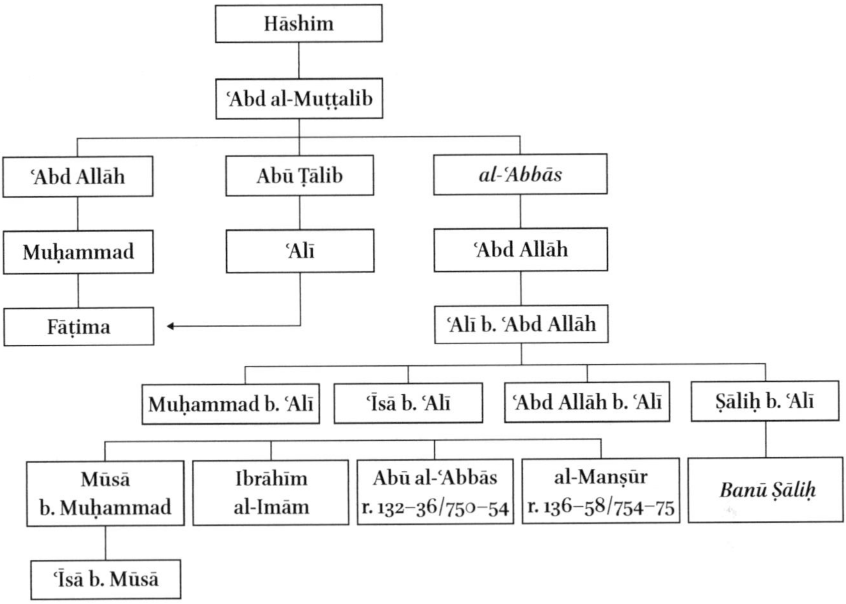

FIGURE 0.4 Simplified Hashimite genealogy

Introduction

> The Syria to which Heraclius bade his moving farewell seems to have vanished, not just from Byzantine rule, but from the face of the earth.[1]

∴

Writing the history of the first centuries of Islam is no easy task. Scholars face a nearly complete lack of contemporary Islamic narrative sources; a limited number of documentary sources; still-fragmentary archaeological, epigraphic and numismatic evidence; and sources regarded as "external" – Christian sources in particular – which are seen as deficient and are too rarely taken into consideration. Such, in sum, is the drastic state of affairs regarding the sources that is so often described in the introductory chapters of books dealing with the rise of Islam. It is undoubtedly at least in part due to the problem of sources that it must still be demonstrated that a history of the first centuries of Islam is possible.[2]

The case of the Syrian space[3] in the second/eighth century, the focus of this study, is particularly problematic: as the above citation suggests, the Syria of early Islam has largely fallen into oblivion. This informational void is principally attributable to the fact that the history of Umayyad Syria was produced in Abbasid Iraq, by historians writing under the very dynasty which had overthrown the previous rulers of Damascus. Crone's statement becomes perhaps even more relevant at the beginning of the Abbasid era. With the transition of the caliphate to Baghdad, Syria seems purely and simply to disappear. The attention of the chroniclers turns abruptly to the East starting from 132/750.

The approach adopted in the following pages takes on the methodological challenge imposed by this unique situation. To borrow Robinson's apt phrase, it aims mainly "to marry history and historiography."[4] Under the circumstances, a simple summary of the sources used in this study would be insufficient;

1 Crone, *Slaves*, 11. So as not to needlessly complicate the footnotes, bibliographic references will be limited to the first words of the relevant article or work. For complete references, please consult the bibliography at the end of this volume.

2 Robinson, *Empire and Elites*, viii.

3 The *bilād al-shām* of the Arab writers. See figure 0.1.

4 Robinson, *Empire and Elites*, viii.

 | DOI:10.1163/9789004466326_002

rather, these sources must constitute the very core of our research. The mechanisms at work in the historiographies of the Near East will be the focus of the first three chapters, which are in a sense the methodological foundation of this inquiry. In the state in which they exist today,[5] Islamic chronographies[6] are a doubly-inconvenient means of approaching the history of second/eighth century Syria: beside the fact that essentially all of these chronographies were produced outside of the region (in this case, in Iraq), the majority were not composed until the end of the third/ninth century, thus in some cases a century or more after the period they describe. The corpus of Christian texts relevant to this study is valuable in part because it minimises this chronological gap; subject to an appropriate methodology, it may allow us to access older historical information in circulation during the course of the second/eighth century.

These brief remarks, which I will further develop in the coming chapters, immediately invite an important observation. The result of these issues with the sources is effectively a spatiotemporal shift between the subject of this study, Syria in the second/eighth century, and the majority of the sources available to document it, in particular where the Islamic chronographies are concerned. This situation inevitably requires certain detours: it is often necessary to turn to Baghdad or Sāmarrāʾ in order to shed light on the historiographic projects which underlie the composition of certain texts. The most obvious example of this issue is, of course, al-Ṭabarī (d. 310/923), around whom the field of Islamic historiography crystallised in Abbasid Baghdad. Although al-Ṭabarī is not the subject of this study, he is nevertheless an unavoidable figure. This is a crucial point, for, as Martinez-Gros remarks:

> The literature of Baghdad did not only claim dominance over Islam, but also to giving coherence to the entirety of the inhabited world, retracing all routes, exhuming the traditions of every kingdom and bending their meanings toward the heart of ancient Mesopotamia and toward

5 The manuscript traditions of the extant narrative sources, and consequently the modern editions of these texts, pose numerous problems. Although the question is largely outside the scope of this study, see A. C. S. Peacock's valuable work dedicated to the particularly complex case of Balʿamī (d. between 382/992 and 387/997), *Medieval Islamic Historiography*.

6 So as not to be overly repetitive, I will alternatingly use the terms chronographies and chronicles. However, it should be noted that the term "chronography" is more pertinent than the traditional "chronicle" (as noted by Robinson, *Islamic Historiography*, 55 ff.), the definition of which poses numerous problems. This fact was notably confirmed by the colloquium "Lectures historiques des chroniques médiévales (mondes arabe, persan, syriaque et turc)," held at the Insitut Français du Proche-Orient in Damascus in 2003. For a deeper reflection on the semantic complexities of the term "chronicle" in the medieval West, see Kooper (ed.), *The Medieval Chronicle* and *The Medieval Chronicle II*.

> the figure of the sovereign Imam, who tied together in his hands all the threads of Creation. To say that this immense intellectual enterprise – which included everything from the translation of classical works to the reconstruction of a Universal History and the development of the field of geography in *Al-masālik wa-al-mamālik* – is "linked" to the caliphate is an understatement. It belonged to the caliphate; it had no other origin or end.[7]

The history of the rise of Islam clearly did not escape the active processes of what I shall call "classical" historiography. For this reason, any work dedicated to this period of early Islamic history must be accompanied by a reflection on how history is written. This question has sustained lively historiographical debates, and certain scholars have defended the idea that Islamic narratives were nothing more than idealised visions of the past composed at later dates, completely lacking any kernel of historical information.[8] The process of historiographical crystallisation was so rapid that it resulted in "a definitive erasure" and "a complete absence of sedimentation between the different stages of writing." However, as Décobert has noted, "a sedimentation may be reconstructed," in particular because the sources do not all say "*the same thing at the same time*."[9] In light of this observation, we may set out in search of an early Islamic historiography of which only fragments now remain. With respect to the fields of history of memory and comparative historiography, it is a question of listening to these "whispers" in order to shed light on "alternative pasts."[10] Analysis of the successive historiographical filters which resulted in the creation of an Abbasid vulgate allows us to identify the different *moments* at which memory solidified through an archaeology of texts. It thus becomes possible to attempt to reconstruct the various meanings that the authors wished to bestow upon the period or a particular event. The stakes were high: mastery of the past allowed one to conjugate power in the present as well as the future. Rulers needed to "have a convincing past at their disposal."[11] Under these circumstances, "memorization ... is not only an activity of organizing knowledge in a new way, but also an aspect of the organization of a new power."[12]

---

7 Martinez-Gros, *L'idéologie omeyyade*, 20–1.

8 Here we have one of the dominant ideas of the historiographical current known as the "skeptics." For a detailed presentation of these different approaches in the sources, see Donner, *Narratives*, 5–31, or Décobert ("L'ancien et le nouveau;" *Le mendiant et le combattant*, 30 ff.), who refuted the arguments of the skeptics in an earlier work.

9 Décobert, *Le mendiant et le combattant*, 34 and 40 (emphasis mine).

10 Geary, *Phantoms of Remembrance*, xiv and 177.

11 Guenée, *Histoire et culture historique*, 345.

12 Le Goff, *History and Memory*, 62.

The relationship between memory[13] and power is the central focus of this study. I shall return to these ideas in detail later, but it is important to emphasise from the beginning that "the past is not a natural growth but a cultural creation," entrusted to "a knowledgeable elite, the specialists in the field [of cultural memory]."[14] Moreover, "one strong incentive for memory (*Erinnerung*) is power."[15] Memory, as it is envisioned in the following pages, is thus a "form of social practice" as well as a "cultural production."[16] The successive rewritings that were willingly orchestrated by a caliphal or otherwise elite power cognisant of the "potential of written culture"[17] must be understood from this perspective. The goal of this rewriting was clear: in many cases, it was advantageous for the ruling classes to weave new threads in the direction of the past in order to make sense of an unexpected present, thereby providing some promise of security and legitimacy for the future. With respect to both the extant documentary sources as well as the successive layers of writing and rewriting that define the period, understanding the history of the Syrian space in the second/eighth century calls first and foremost for a delineation of the history of meanings (*Sinngeschichte*).[18]

Having outlined the major methodological foundations of this study, its contours – and above all its spatial context – must now be defined. The caliphate's division of the provinces is known to us through the authors of the classical period, particularly the geographers studied by André Miquel.[19] It was their vision of the world that was projected onto the first centuries of the Hijra, at a time when the Muslim space was still very much under construction.

In reality, the perception of the Syrian space was still in flux. The Jazīra (Upper Mesopotamia) was gradually becoming an administrative entity during this period,[20] while the outlines of *al-ʿAwāṣim* and *al-Thughūr* were taking shape at the other end of this eighth Syrian century under Hārūn al-Rashīd. Syria's southern borders at this time were equally uncertain, both in the desert

13 Assmann explains the reasons for the relevance of this topic in *Cultural Memory*, especially 2–4. See also the more recent discussion in Cubitt, 1–22.

14 Assmann, *Cultural Memory*, 33 and 40. This work also contains a productive reflection on the concept of "cultural memory" which complements another contribution by the same author ("What is Cultural Memory?"). For more on historians' different approaches to the notion of memory, see below, Ch. 4.

15 Assmann, *Cultural Memory*, 53.

16 Cubitt, *History and Memory*, 128 and 203.

17 McKitterick, *History and Memory*, 22.

18 This concept underwent one of its most transformative developments in the works of the German Egyptologist Jan Assmann. In particular, see: *Ägypten. Eine Sinngeschichte* and *Moses the Egyptian*.

19 Miquel, *La géographie humaine*.

20 Robinson, *Empire and Elites*, 33–62.

leading into Arabia via pilgrimage routes as well as in the Sinai. The internal segmentation of the province, which was divided into *junds* (districts), fluctuated as well. Thus, the *Bilād al-Shām* in the first centuries of Islam truly must be understood as "the Syrian space," in the broadest sense of the phrase. The valley of the Euphrates was not the administrative demarcation line of the Arab authors, but rather a strategic zone whose two banks are inseparable from second/eighth-century Syrian history. The relationship of the major figures of the period to space is one of the central aspects of this study. The eventual cessation of new conquests during this era resulted in the need to define the *dār al-islām*, these immense spaces inherited from the great Islamic expansionist movement and shaped by the policies of the first generations of Muslims. Maslama b. ʿAbd al-Malik, ʿUmar b. ʿAbd al-ʿAzīz, Hishām b. ʿAbd al-Malik and Hārūn al-Rashīd, to name but a few of the major protagonists of the following chapters, subscribed heavily to this logic.

This space was also a political one. The reader will search these pages in vain for an urban or rural history, for example, as those are different topics altogether. In truth, this study is an indispensable first step for any project aimed at writing these other types of histories because it is the path imposed by the nature of the sources. The Syrian backdrop proves a valuable complement to the aforementioned narrative sources through the still-fragmentary evidence provided by archaeology. Both the Umayyads and the Abbasids fostered ambitious architectural programs in the Syrian space: from the foundation of the mosque of Damascus and the "desert castles" built for the former to the projects of immense scale near Raqqa developed by the latter. Archaeology, numismatics and epigraphy are thus indispensable sources as well; a more systematic approach to these last will be proposed in the final chapter.

The chronological limits of this study were determined by the choice of geographical scope. This inquiry begins with the inauguration of the Dome of the Rock by ʿAbd al-Malik b. Marwān in Jerusalem in 72/962 and ends with the death of Hārūn al-Rashīd in 193/809.[21] The first date corresponds with the restoration of Marwanid authority following the turmoil brought about by the second *fitna* and the pretensions to power of Ibn al-Zubayr; this was the true birth of the Muslim State[22] in that it was the assertion of a religious identity that was properly Muslim.[23] Everything was redefined, from the exercise of power to political ideology, both sources of legitimacy. Historiography had

21 For the genealogy of the Umayyad and Abbasid dynasties, refer to figures 0.2 and 0.3.

22 This position was recently defended by Robinson (*ʿAbd al-Malik*, 6), adding to that supported from an archaeological perspective by Johns, "Archaeology and the History of Early Islam." For a dissenting opinion, see Foss, "A Syrian Coinage."

23 See Donner, "From Believers to Muslims," and *Muhammad and the Believers*.

a leading role to play in these processes of redefinition, as it was necessary to create a space of affirmation for the reinstated Umayyad hegemony. The choices made in this regard revealed a certain vision of the world, one in which new heroes were made; these choices also revealed a specific conception of sovereignty, one which I shall elucidate in the following pages.

The other end of the period covered in this study – the death of Hārūn al-Rashīd, the ruler popularised in the *Thousand and One Nights* – marks the caliphate's decision to abandon Raqqa as a place of residence, as well as the outbreak of civil war between al-Rashīd's sons, al-Amīn and al-Maʾmūn. Here, the forces of dissent at work within the Abbasid empire found their first outlet. The return of the caliphate to Baghdad and its subsequent migration to Sāmarrāʾ demonstrated decisively that the geographic centre going forward would be Iraq. The Euphrates had ceased to attract the caliphate.

The infamous Abbasid Revolution (132/750) thus occurred in the exact middle of the period examined here. This monumental event is traditionally presented as a classic caesura in Islamic history, heralding the decline of Syria as the "capital" migrated to Iraq and Baghdad, a city founded in 145/762 by al-Manṣūr.[24] This inquiry aims to distance itself from the approach that favours reductive dynastic division; political machinations aside, the goal of this study is to better comprehend the spatial dynamics that presided over the history of the province during the course of this long eighth Syrian century,[25] and to understand how this rupture formed as a result of the new exigencies that arose in the wake of the coup d'état that had overthrown the Umayyads. However, as previously noted, the sources force us to think on a different level – from al-Zuhrī (d. 124/742) to al-Ṭabarī, perhaps, or from Medina to Sāmarrāʾ – that is, in the context of other temporalities and spaces, namely those of Islamic historiography. To study the Syria of the second/eighth century is thus also to undertake a journey through nearly every work produced by the nascent field of Muslim historiography.

Works of modern historiography specific to each individual question will be covered in detail in the relevant chapters. Here again, a simple introductory survey would not do justice to such a substantial production so rich in debates. I will limit myself in this regard to a few general remarks.

Although it is frequently presented as the apogee of Syrian history, the "Umayyad century" paradoxically suffers from an undeniable deficit of

24 For a recent perspective on the city of al-Manṣūr, see Micheau, "Bagdad."

25 Echoing the work of Hansen and Wickham (eds.), *The Long Eighth Century*.

studies.[26] Since the pioneering works of Wellhausen or Lammens,[27] to name only two of the most significant figures in the field, and in spite of important studies such as those by Crone and Hinds, Hawting, or more recently, Robinson or Humphreys,[28] the first Islamic dynasty has clearly attracted the interest of far fewer researchers than the preceding or subsequent periods. The era of the "foundations of Islam" and grand conquests on the one hand, and that of the "Abbasid caliphate" on the other, have produced a much more abundant bibliography. The last three decades attest to a growing number of studies dedicated to the period of the formation and expansion of Islam: the works of Wansbrough, Crone and Cook, Donner, Décobert, Kaegi, Chabbi, Hawting, or even de Prémare are evidence of this trend.[29] If we limit ourselves to works on the early Abbasids and those more closely related to the subject of this inquiry, the same observation may be made, with the works of Sourdel, Kennedy, Bonner, El-Hibri, Cobb, Gordon, and many others as proof.[30] To oversimplify the issue slightly, it may be said that in the Syrian context, the Umayyad period has largely become the province of archaeologists,[31] while the Abbasid era is the purview of historians.

Syria itself has been the subject of numerous works, in particular in the field of French historiography. The names Cahen, Sauvaget, Élisséeff, Canard, Bianquis, Eddé, Mouton and Jalabert[32] all bear witness to that fact. Moreover, Sourdel has drawn attention to the paucity of studies dedicated to Abbasid

26 This is the same remark that Sauvaget made in 1943! He stated: "cette période d'un intérêt capital reste extrêmement mal connue," *Introduction à l'histoire*, 118. In 1972, Bosworth noted that the situation had changed very little, despite Sauvaget's observations, "Rajāʾ," 36.

27 Wellhausen, *Das arabische Reich*; Lammens, *Études*. For a detailed list of the works of these different scholars, refer to the bibliography.

28 This list is by no means exhaustive. See Crone, *Slaves*; Crone and Hinds, *God's Caliph*; Robinson, *Empire and Elites* and *ʿAbd al-Malik*; Humphreys, *Muʿāwiya*. Hawting's *The First Dynasty* remains the only comprehensive overview dedicated to the Umayyads.

29 Wansbrough, *Quranic Studies* and *The Sectarian Milieu*; Crone and Cook, *Hagarism*; Crone, *Meccan Trade*; Donner, *The Early Islamic*; Décobert, *Le mendiant et le combattant*; Kaegi, *Byzantium*; Chabbi, *Le seigneur des tribus*; Hawting, *The Idea of Idolatry*; de Prémare, *Les fondations*.

30 Sourdel, *Le vizirat* and *L'état impérial*; Kennedy, *The Early Abbasid Caliphate*; Bonner, *Aristocratic Violence*; El-Hibri, *Reinterpreting*; Cobb, *White Banners*; Gordon, *The Breaking*.

31 Sauvaget was one of the great pioneers in this area. Although the field still lacks a comprehensive study of Umayyad archaeology in the Syrian space despite a number of important works, the reader may consult Foss, "Syria in Transition," Walmsley, *Early Islamic Syria*, and Genequand, *Les élites omeyyades*. This issue is discussed in detail in Chapter 8.

32 Cahen, *La Syrie du Nord*; Sauvaget, *Alep*; Canard, *Histoire de la dynastie*; Élisséeff, *Nūr al-Dīn*; Bianquis, *Damas et la Syrie* and "Damas;" Eddé, *La principauté ayyoubide* and "Alep;" Mouton, *Damas*; Jalabert, *Hommes et lieux*.

Syria,[33] a void which Cobb's work has served partially to fill.[34] However, it should be noted that despite the works of the Belgian Jesuit Lammens, Umayyad Syria remains a major gap in this vast panorama.[35] Finally, reflection on Islamic historiography has been the subject of certain very important modern scholarly contributions to which I will return later.

The combination of elements briefly detailed here indicates that our path will often be a tortuous one: our course must adapt to the twists and turns of a historiography rich in meanings. This study is perhaps first and foremost the product of a methodological journey. To write the history of the Syrian space during the second/eighth century in large part comes down to making history in a vacuum. From a historiographic void due to the lack of contemporary narrative sources to a "historical" blank, Syria seems to lose all interest after the Abbasid overthrow of the Umayyads in 132/750, as much in the Islamic sources as, until recently, in modern scholarship as well.

Geary has emphasised the danger represented by the desire to "[listen] to the silences of the past," but he has also demonstrated the great contributions that can be made by studying the "whispers" that mark these texts.[36] Due to the state of the sources, the historian's task often appears to be a balancing act. The reader will be the judge of my ability to walk this tightrope. In any case, the fact that our knowledge of the period rests above all on a canonical history makes it necessary for us to unravel all of its threads so as to try to better weave them anew from the perspective of a history of meanings.

As previously noted, the very existence of an ancient historiographic foundation has been contested. Thus we must begin our inquiry here, as it will require the demarcation of the periods of writing and rewriting that span a historiography split between Syria and Iraq. We may then explore new paths in order to shed light on the prominent figures and events of Syrian history in the second/eighth century. From here, I will attempt to reconstruct the successive meanings given to this Syrian history that oscillates between memory and oblivion. Having somewhat better defined the outlines of this study, it is now time to embark on this Syrian journey, divided between memory and power.

33 Sourdel, "La Syrie."

34 Cobb, *White Banners*.

35 The importance of several histories of Syria should also be noted here, in particular Hitti's classic *History of Syria*. *The New Cambridge History of Islam* also helps to fill this void, thanks to the chapters by Cobb, "The empire in Syria, 705–763" and Humphreys, "Syria."

36 Geary, *Phantoms of Remembrance*, xiv.

CHAPTER 1

A Time of Writings and Rewritings: Writing History in the Syrian Space

> The starting point [of historiography] is not silence (by now irretrievable), but what has been said already.[1]

∴

The sources available today to write the history of the first centuries of Islam are primarily narrative sources composed in Abbasid Iraq; earlier sources did exist, but have not survived. In order to reacquaint ourselves with the second/eighth-century Syrian space, we must look beyond these "classical" texts and aim to fix the contours of historical writing in early Islam, as well as the place that Syria came to occupy therein. This chapter begins with an examination of the emergence of Islamic historiography, followed by an investigation of the conditions under which the narratives of the earliest Muslim historians were transmitted. We shall then turn our attention to Syria, the focus of this study, so as to elucidate a little-known historiographic production. This strategy will allow us to highlight the active role played by the Umayyad caliphs in the development of an Islamic historiography; additionally, it will permit us to shed light on Syria's not-insignificant place in this historiographic development, even though modern scholarship ranks it well behind the production of Iraq and the Hijaz.

1.1 Narrative Islamic Sources and the Question of Their Transmission

The question of transmission is one that properly belongs to the historian's métier. In a recent article, Esch masterfully demonstrated the advantages of a reflection rooted in the source materials when confronting the problems posed by medieval sources.[2] This approach becomes particularly pertinent

1 Rigney, "Time for Visions," 86. Cited in Lorenz, "Comparative Historiography," 34.
2 Esch, "Chance et hasard de transmission."

 DOI:10.1163/9789004466326_003

with respect to early Islam, an era so meagerly endowed with contemporary sources. Specialists in the period have long debated the means of comprehending this extremely fragmentary corpus of documentary sources[3] dating to the first two centuries of the *hijra*;[4] furthermore, one must also contend with the problems posed by the narrative Arab-Muslim sources, all of which postdate this early period of Islam (the oldest extant complete chronography that can be accurately dated is that of Khalīfa b. Khayyāṭ, d. c. 240/854),[5] not to mention – for the time being – the question of non-Islamic sources.[6]

These chronographies are traditionally the first recourse for historians specialising in the period; thus, they require the sort of meticulous analysis with which we shall begin this study. The chronological interval between these sources and the period considered here necessitates a process of "historiographic dismantling" in order to identify the successive phases in which history was rewritten according to the changing purposes for which the past was used and interpreted. This "dismantling" invites us to reconsider the question of historiographic productions antecedent to the early sources that are preserved, both from the Marwanid era as well as under the early Abbasids.

The environment in which the extant narrative Islamic sources were produced – namely, Abbasid Iraq – is another thorny offshoot of the problem concerning the late date at which they were composed. In other words, to study the Syrian space of the second/eighth century is to encounter two major pitfalls: one must make use of sources that are both subsequent to the period under examination and exterior to the geographic area being considered.[7] In these conditions, the full significance of Esch's methodological remarks becomes clear:

> that transmission cannot be integral, of that the historian is perpetually aware. He is less conscious, however, of the inequality of these losses because it is a barely perceptible fact. For this reason, not only is the quantity of our knowledge diminished, but *the proportions of our knowledge are distorted*. We gladly set out with the idea that a little bit of everything has been handed down to us, *as if it were impossible that whole, coherent*

3 I use "documentary sources" here in the strict sense of non-narrative sources.

4 For example, see the diametrically opposed opinions of Humphreys, *Islamic History*, 69, and Koren and Nevo, *Crossroads to Islam*, 1 ff. From Humphrey's point of view, it is simply impossible to reconstruct the history of early Islam on the sole basis of these sources, whereas for Koren and Nevo, these documents are the only means to do so. On these sources, see below, Ch. 3.

5 Khalīfa b. Khayyāṭ, *Taʾrīkh*.

6 Henceforth see Hoyland, *Seeing*, and Ch. 2, below, for more on this question.

7 Sauvaget has previously noted this difficulty, "Châteaux omeyyades de Syrie," 17–8.

> *parts, that entire continents, could have fallen into oblivion*;[8] we also happily assume that what remains to us is a reflection that has merely paled, and that these remnants as a whole are still representative of a past reality, as if, worse still, this image could not also be distorted itself ... However, a much more dangerous risk emerges here: the risk of reconstructing the bits that remain visible to us into a new whole, because we think a great deal more about what we have than about what we do not – if, that is, we are even aware of this absence at all. Let us say that perhaps here one ten-thousandth, there one hundred-thousandth, elsewhere perhaps nothing at all of the reality of bygone eras is transmitted to us, without us still being able to discover it. In sum, it is the problem of the *representativeness* or the *distortion* of that which is transmitted.[9]

In the context of second/eighth-century Syria, the implications of this warning are crucial. The absence of narrative sources written during this period[10] obviously results in a "reduction" of our knowledge, but also in profound "distortions" that give rise to a marked under-representation of Syria in the sources produced in Abbasid Iraq. Furthermore, it should be noted that this distortion is not uniform over the course of the period considered here: overall, Syria is much more present in the sources when the Umayyads are concerned because it was the epicentre of their power, whereas the early Abbasids were fundamentally associated with Iraq. Esch's cartographic metaphor is relevant here: a remarkable and concrete difference exists between the scale of our knowledge of Abbasid Iraq and the scale of our knowledge of Abbasid Syria.[11] Alongside these geographic criteria, consideration must also be given to the ideological stakes involved in asserting the legitimacy of the ruling dynasty. In other words, the question of the Abbasid narratives' tendentious and detrimental discourse concerning the Umayyads[12] must be added to that of the under-representation of the Syrian space, as well as the broader issue of the

8 Italics mine.

9 Esch, "Chance et hasard," 15–6.

10 The questions surrounding the birth of Islamic historiography and the writing of history in the Syrian space are discussed in greater detail below.

11 In a pioneering 1980 article, Sourdel brought attention to the paucity of studies dedicated to Abbasid Syria ("La Syrie"). The important work of Cobb, *White Banners*, has recently bridged a section of this historiographic gap.

12 This question has too often been dealt with in a superficial fashion. See the more nuanced approaches of El-Hibri, "The Redemption," and Borrut, "La *memoria* omeyyade." The place of the Umayyads in Abbasid historiography is analysed in greater detail in Ch. 4.

absence of sources directly produced by the first Islamic dynasty, of which only distant echoes have been transmitted to us today.

The vagaries of transmission offer an astonishing image of the second/eighth century, one largely devoid of source materials. Strictly with respect to the Islamic chronographies, the conclusion for the period under consideration is clear: we do not possess a single contemporary narrative source, neither from the first Islamic dynasty nor from the early Abbasids.[13] In this regard, at least, the Umayyads and the early Abbasids are on an equal footing, even if this state of affairs has not been properly considered until now. The historiography of this period is too often seen as a dichotomy, presenting the Umayyads in an unfavourable light and conversely working in the service of their successors; this situation would seem to guarantee much more reliable information when it comes to the Abbasid period. It will become abundantly clear, however, that the problem is not nearly so simple. Be that as it may, we must examine the later texts composed during the Abbasid period, including those of the great and inescapable al-Ṭabarī, whom Hawting has described as "the most important Arabic source for Umayyad history."[14] However, this situation is itself problematic, particularly with respect to methodology and the manner in which we understand these "later" sources.

Before returning in detail to the classical sources and envisioning what may have become of those that were composed earlier over the course of the second/eighth century, several remarks must be made concerning the writing of history during the first centuries of Islam.

1.1.1 *The Act of Writing and Modes of Transmission*

The existence of any textual source is conditioned by a prior act of writing. Therein lies the initial problem surrounding the licit or illicit nature of the act of writing in Islam, at first with regard to tradition, but also more generally with respect to all written forms, including historical texts. The problem is the concurrence of these other writings with the Qurʾānic text, which some believed should remain the sole written Arabic-Muslim work. This question has been discussed in detail by Cook, whose argument is based on the observation that a later opposition to the act of writing was prevalent in Baṣra in the second half of the second century of the *hijra*.[15] This hostility to writing,

13 Other types of texts do still exist, such as the letters of ʿAbd al-Ḥamīd, the secretary of the last Umayyad caliph Marwān II, the famous epistle of Ibn al-Muqaffaʿ intended for al-Manṣūr, or even the *Kitāb al-kharāj* of Abū Yūsuf Yaʿqūb, written for Hārūn al-Rashīd. The specific problems posed by these sources are discussed below in Ch. 3.

14 Hawting, *The First Dynasty*, 130.

15 Cook, "The Opponents," 441 ff.

datable to the last quarter of the first century *hijrī*, marks the earliest phases in most of the great cultural centres of the Islamic world.[16] Modern research has often proposed a simple hypothesis for this opposition: transmission must at first have been exclusively oral, and it was only later that writing became common. Cook suggests that this Muslim reticence toward writing had Jewish origins, while Schoeler posits that it was the result of challenges to Umayyad attempts to codify the tradition.[17]

The classic example is al-Zuhrī who, in his own words, was "forced" by the Umayyads to proceed with committing the tradition to writing. Having taken this initial step, al-Zuhrī had no objections to other Muslims doing the same: "We disapproved of writing down knowledge [i.e. ḥadīths] (*kunnā nakrahu kitāb al-ʿilm*) until these rulers compelled us to do it. Then we were [i.e. now we are] of the opinion that we should not prohibit any Muslim from doing so."[18] Here we are clearly faced with a *topos* of Islamic literature, one that may be filed in the category of *awāʾil* ("the first one who did this or that was …");[19] among the few extant fragments written on papyrus, some attest to historical writing datable to the beginning of the second/eighth century at the latest.[20] Although al-Zuhrī's confession was sufficient cause for the Umayyads' detractors to accuse them of *bidʿa*, or blameworthy innovation, Schoeler has shown that we can move beyond this question by detaching ourselves from the classic dichotomy of oral versus written. Scholars have for too long focused on the problem of identifying the turning point at which oral transmission was superceded by written transmission, all the while considering these two modes of communication as contradictory and mutually exclusive.[21] These presuppositions, however, do not stand up to the most recent studies on the question,

16 The Muslim authors frequently mention the reed-pen (*qalam*) as the first divine creation, adding that Allah commanded that it write what was predestined. See, for example, al-Ṭabarī, *Taʾrīkh* vol. I, 29 ff., trans. vol. I, 198 ff., who presents different debates and opinions on the subject.

17 Schoeler, "Mündliche Thora," 227 ff.; see Cook's objections, "The Opponents," 474–5.

18 Ibn Saʿd, *al-Ṭabaqāt* vol. II, 389; trans. Schoeler, *The Genesis*, 50.

19 See notably Noth and Conrad, *The Early Arabic*, 104 ff; the remarks of al-Azmeh, "Chronophagous Discourse," 164–5; and Lang, *Awāʾil*. Elsewhere, it is said that ʿUrwa b. al-Zubayr (d. c. 94/712–713) was the first to undertake an act of writing. On this point, see Schoeler, *The Genesis*, 43, and de Prémare, *Les fondations*, 14–6.

20 These attestations relate to the battle of Badr, include the name of the Prophet, and figure in a papyrus of Khirbat al-Mird, edited by Grohmann in *Arabic Papyri*, 82–4; see also de Prémare, *Les fondations*, 12–3.

21 This reflection is closely linked to that on memory, insofar as oral societies were considered to be those with the most excellent memories, whereas written societies made oblivion possible. On these themes, see Ch. 4 below.

which demonstrate to the contrary how closely these two modes of transmission are interwoven:[22] the narrative Islamic sources, filled with scattered "fragments of orality" (*qāla, akhbarna, ḥaddathna*, etc.), offer a striking example of this symbiosis.

Schoeler, rejecting the limitations of this outdated approach, introduced a new typological framework for the analysis of different writings. For this purpose, he borrows the pairing *syngramma/hypomnēma* from the Greek. The former designates a literary work, an actual book, while the second signifies simple notes, an outline or a memory aid.[23] He concludes that a number of titles mentioned in the early Islamic sources refer to outlines or notes rather than to complete texts; until roughly the third century of the *hijra*, the term *kitāb* simply designated "something written." This late date for the appearance of actual books, published and thus transformed from private notes into complete texts, is contested by Elad, who argues for an earlier date located at some point between the end of the first and the middle of the second centuries of the *hijra*.[24]

The nebulous nature of transmission has profound implications. Certain texts remain "open,"[25] in that they had not yet reached the status of true works (*syngrammata*) and thus were susceptible to emendation and reworking. "'Transmitters' were not simply taking liberties with texts: they were *generating* the texts themselves."[26] Historians, not content to merely transmit and record information, reorganised it and, in some cases, completely invented it.[27] Thus, even when sources have survived in the redactions of later compilers, the unavoidable question of the transformations the original may have undergone remains. Landau-Tasseron has recently emphasised this point in an important article,[28] condemning the shortcomings of Sezgin's[29] preferred "method" of reconstructing lost sources by examining the preserved citations found in later works and attested by *isnād*s deemed reliable. Landau-Tasseron warns

22 Among an abundant bibliography, see the important works of Innes ("Memory, Orality and Literacy") and Geary ("Oblivion Between Orality and Textuality"), which contradict, among others, the classic hypotheses of Clanchy (*From Memory to Written Record*) concerning the medieval West. If the question has been less studied with respect to medieval Islam, scholars such as Günther ("Due Results") and Schoeler (*The Genesis*, 8) have nevertheless come to similar conclusions.

23 Schoeler, *The Genesis*, 54.

24 Elad, "The Beginning," 122–3.

25 On this subject, see Hoyland, *Seeing*, 35.

26 Robinson, *Islamic Historiography*, 38.

27 Robinson, *Islamic Historiography*, 18–19.

28 Landau-Tasseron, "On the Reconstruction;" see also Conrad, "Recovering."

29 Developed in the first volume of his *GAS*, otherwise a fundamental work.

against two of the major problems inherent to any attempt to reconstruct lost sources: false attributions (where an authority is cited, but the content of the fragment does not originate therewith), and the metamorphoses of transmitted texts.[30] The implication is that extreme prudence is required when setting off in search of these lost historiographies; one must be constantly aware that even if certain *information* derived from lost sources (the "reliability" of which remains debatable) can be recovered, it is usually impossible to know anything of the *forms* of these texts.[31] The undefined nature of certain texts weakens their position with respect to the transmission process because it necessarily limits their dissemination and consequently their chances of survival as well. An authority is cited and thus transmitted. Under these circumstances, it is plausible to assume that preserving the original text is no longer essential, in the context of a partial oblivion that has now become possible.

Anthropologists have shed light on certain active processes that underlie genealogies, creating the concept of *generative genealogy*.[32] We find ourselves here faced with a similar situation applied to the writing of history; we might even term it a genuine *generative historiography*.[33] Modes of transmission, like the debates that accompany these texts,[34] participate in the active processes that are in and of themselves a writing of history. On this point, we are in agreement with Schmitt, who recently highlighted the fact that "[between] the historian and the document … is layered … all the dense history of transmission (*Überlieferung*) that must be accounted for in order to fully comprehend the document. It is as if, over time, the substance of the document has grown rife with the hazards of transmission, to the extent that the conditions of transmission are henceforth an integral part of the nature of the document that the historian holds in his hands."[35] In order to identify these specific problems, we shall turn to a concrete example.

1.1.2 *Lost Sources and Historical Reconstruction*

The recent editions of two fragmentary works by Sayf b. ʿUmar (d. 180/796) entitled *Kitāb al-ridda wa-al-futūḥ* and *Kitāb al-jamal wa-masī ʿĀʾisha*

30 Landau-Tasseron, "On the Reconstruction," 47; see also Leder, "The Literary Use," 284 ff. and Hoyland, *Seeing*, 32 ff.

31 See, for example, Borrut, "Entre tradition et histoire."

32 This is Lancaster's expression, *The Rwala*, 151.

33 See also the remarks of Spiegel, "Theory into Practice," 2: "… what was the generative grammar that defined historical writing in the Middle Ages, the linguistic protocols that permitted the transformation of the past into historical narrative?"

34 Notably underlined by Petersen in his classic work, *ʿAlī and Muʿāwiya*.

35 Schmitt, "Une réflexion," 43–4.

wa-ʿAlī represent a remarkable advancement in the field of early Islamic historiography.[36] First, these texts are significant for the intrinsic value of the documents – the only known extant works composed by this author – which were previously only accessible through the citations of later compilers; second, they are important because they can be compared with the fragments of these works preserved by later compilers, foremost among them figures such as al-Ṭabarī or Ibn ʿAsākir (d. 571/1176). It must be noted here that the question of Sayf b. ʿUmar's "reliability" and the veracity of the various statements bearing his name in the medieval sources have been the subject of heated debates among modern scholars, especially in the wake of the severe criticisms levelled against him by Wellhausen in 1899.[37] As Landau-Tasseron has noted, this 'anathema' against Sayf resulted in widespread mistrust among modern scholars, many of whom as a matter of course simply reject any *akhbār* attributed to him out of hand.[38] Landau-Tasseron has argued for a reevaluation of the traditions attributed to Sayf by demonstrating the unique character and value of certain of his statements.

However, a close comparison of these texts salvaged from history and the citations attributed to Sayf in the classical sources yields important results regarding the methods and choices that preside over the process of transmission. Al-Ṭabarī omitted 89 of the 196 *akhbār* in the *Kitāb al-ridda wa-al-futūḥ*; of the 108 *akhbār* included in the *Kitāb al-jamal*, he omitted 33 entirely and 8 in part.[39] Al-Sāmarrāʾī, the editor of Sayf's texts, noted that al-Ṭabarī's citations were different than Sayf's and came to the conclusion that al-Ṭabarī felt free to abridge, omit and reorganise his predecessor's material as he saw fit. In comparing the use of Sayf's citations in the works of al-Ṭabarī and Ibn ʿAsākir, Cameron estimates that, in light of the *isnād*s and the biographical evidence, the two authors were working from the same recension, and that it was al-Ṭabarī, rather than Ibn ʿAsākir, who was responsible for the major variations from Sayf's original versions. It is thus clear that Ibn ʿAsākir and al-Ṭabarī did not access Sayf through the same channels, disproving the hypothesis that the *Taʾrīkh madinat Dimashq* relied on the *Taʾrīkh al-rusul wa-al-mulūk* for this purpose.[40]

From the case of Sayf b. ʿUmar, it is evident that the widespread modern scholarly rejection of a transmitter from the late second/eighth century must

36 Sayf b. ʿUmar, *Kitāb al-ridda waʾl-futūh*.

37 Wellhausen, *Skizzen*, vol. 6., 1–7, cited in Landau-Tasseron, "Sayf b. ʿUmar," 1.

38 Landau-Tasseron, "Sayf b. ʿUmar," 1. See also a survey of the critiques against Sayf, 3 ff.

39 Al-Sāmarrāʾī, "A Reappraisal of Sayf b. ʿUmar," 539.

40 Cameron, "Sayf at First."

be revised in light of new questions. The fact that Sayf was the only transmitter to provide certain information aroused the suspicion of scholars, who preferred to agree on *akhbār* that were better supported in the sources. Conrad, however, has cautioned researchers that consensus is not necessarily a measure of historical accuracy,[41] while Landau-Tasseron has insisted on the idea that these different narrations were complementary rather than contradictory and that quite often, Sayf's supposed "errors" or "inventions" were anything but.[42] The complexity of transmission and the modalities of writing history are central to this example.[43] The question of distortion inherent to every process of transmission has generally been analysed by modern scholars in terms of willful falsification or illicit manipulation of the facts in accordance with political and ideological goals; such practices are evident in the sources and well-attested. Nevertheless, a meticulous study of transmission during the first centuries of Islam demonstrates that every "distortion" need not be evaluated from such a negative angle.[44] Beyond simple reflection on an author's reliability, the processes of selection, omission, conservation, or even distortion at work in every act of historical writing or rewriting must be considered, in particular in the case of the Abbasid authors' recompositions of the recent Islamic past, to which we shall return later.

The best way to understand these issues is to let the medieval authors speak for themselves. Ibn Qutayba, the famous ninth-century Sunni polymath (d. 276/889),[45] defined the three matrices of historical writing as follows: establishing chronology; the freedom to select the information included; and respect for truth. The controversial question of establishing dates was one of the central preoccupations for authors of this period, one that extended beyond the bounds of Islamic historiography. The anonymous Christian author of the Syriac chronology of Zuqnīn (wr. 775) echoes this concern: "If he comes across a history that is not similar to this one, he should understand that even former writers do not agree among themselves. One shortens while another lengthens. One writes about the Church while another writes about other matters. It is of no consequence to intelligent and God-fearing people if an event

41 Cited in Landau-Tasseron, "Sayf b. ʿUmar," 12.

42 Landau-Tasseron, "Sayf b. ʿUmar," 12 ff.

43 Numerous other issues could easily be cited as well, such as the relationship between an author and his transmitter(s); for example, Ibn Isḥāq and Ibn Hishām, or even al-Wāqidī and Ibn Saʿd. On these two examples, see de Prémare, *Les fondations*, 362–3, 389.

44 In particular, see the example of Umayyad poetry, analysed by Schoeler in *The Genesis*, 19–20, and below, Ch. 3.

45 On this figure, see Lecomte, *Ibn Qutayba*, and by the same author, "Ibn Qutayba."

is dated one year earlier or one or two years later."[46] The processes of voluntary selection and omission were by no means the sole purview of the Islamic authors; in the medieval West, a Bavarian monk named Arnold of Regensburg, writing around 1030, attests as much in the following statement: "Not only is it proper for the new things to change the old ones, but even, if the old ones are disordered, they should be entirely thrown away, or if, however, they conform to the proper order of things but are of little use, they should be buried with reverence."[47] We shall return later to this "buried" past that, as Geary has noted, "was not to be forgotten altogether but rather transformed, both memorialized and commemorated."[48]

Here we come back to the idea that the compilers "generated" the text themselves.[49] Contrary to modern historians, those of the Muslim Middle Ages were quite comfortable with these multiple reconstructions of the past.[50] As a result, we are confronted with the magnitude of the labor involved in critically dissecting texts in order to identify the successive layers of historical writing and rewriting, in spite of the uncertainties that remain. Before delving into these questions, it will be useful to clarify some of the formal aspects of these texts that were integral to the transmission process.

1.1.3 *Formal Aspects:* Isnād *and* Khabar

Robinson notes that the *isnād/khabar* "couple" (chain of authorities/report) is the most distinctive characteristic of Islamic historiography.[51] This formal aspect has consequently generated an extensive scholarly production that is impossible to treat exhaustively.[52] The union of a content (here, the *khabar*) and a chain of transmission (*isnād*) is familiar to anyone acquainted with *ḥadīth*

46 *Zuqnīn*, ed. 147, trans. Harrak, 139. This concern for chronology among the Syriac authors is important, as it is probably through the lists of the caliphs in Syriac, which were doubtless based on Arabic originals, that our knowledge of the caliphal succession has been preserved. See Robinson, *Islamic Historiography*, 23.

47 "Non solum novis vetera licet mutare, sed etiam, si sint inordinata, penitus abjicere, sino vero ordinaria sed minus utilita, eum veneratione sepelire," cited by Geary, *Phantoms of Remembrance*, 8.

48 Geary, *Phantoms of Remembrance*, 8, and below, Ch. 4.

49 Robinson, *Islamic Historiography*, 38.

50 Robinson, *Islamic Historiography*, 79.

51 Robinson, *Islamic Historiography*, 92.

52 In particular, see Leder's article, "The Literary Use," and the recent discussion of Mårtensson, "Discourse and Historical Analysis," 291–7.

(deeds and sayings of the Prophet), which associate a content (*matn*) with an *isnād*;[53] this practice was then widely adopted in the field of historiography.

The *khabar-isnād* pair is directly linked to the problem of affirming Truth. In a text such as the Qurʾān, Truth is self-evident and indisputable; the revealed word of God needs no external justification to guarantee its veracity and authenticity. Cheddadi summarises the issue:

> the most important problem confronting all procedures for the attestation of the truth … is that of time, with its destructive effects of obliteration, effacement and distortion. The *isnād* is part of the same problem. What is asked of the *isnād* is to guarantee the authenticity of the transmission of a piece of information or *khabar* – which can be isolated sayings, discourse, narratives, texts – by producing the chain of all those through whom this piece of information has been passed down, from its source or origin down through the person who records or reports it at present. There where [the Qurʾān] has the intervention of a supernatural power to assure continuity between its origin and the present moment, the *isnād* in its place uses a formal process … Here, the *matn* or content of the *khabar* is formally distinct from its form, that is, the *sanad*. The process of the attestation of truth is here purely external.[54]

Elsewhere, Robinson insists that the function of history was primarily to give proof of truth and teach lessons;[55] this statement echoes Guenée's studies regarding the primary concerns of medieval Western authors.[56] Donner contends that, beyond the search for Truth, these medieval authors fundamentally sought to historicise piety, and this aim gave rise to the combination of the *matn* (or *khabar*) and the *isnād*: if at first the content was sufficient (that is,

53 I will not address the thorny question of the origin of the practice of the *isnād*, which is the subject of contradictory debates. See notably among recent hypotheses the proponents of a Jewish origin, arguing that the *isnād* had "as a model the process of authentication used in the Jewish schools of the Talmudic period (between 200 and 500 of our era)" (Schoeler, *Écrire et transmettre*, 128, building upon the hypotheses of Horovitz and Cook); this argument is contested by Cheddadi, among others, who refutes the postulation of a rabbinic origin and rather leans toward a reconciliation with the "procedures of argumentation developed in the Christian milieu, emphasising the references to the authorities of the past and the use of citations and anthologies" (Cheddadi, *Les Arabes*, 259.)

54 Cheddadi, *Les Arabes*, 244–5.

55 Robinson, *Islamic Historiography*, 152. On the relationship between history and truth, see also Cheddadi, *Les Arabes*, in particular 47–70 and 244–59.

56 In a fundamental work entitled *Histoire et culture historique*, especially 18–9. More recently, see Given-Wilson, *Chronicles*, 1–20.

self-legitimising), a chain of transmission was added in historicising this content, and thus the individual (that is, the pious transmitter) became the source of legitimation.[57] Khalidi similarly suggests that the Zubayrid anti-caliphate (64–73/683–692) challenge to the Umayyads' authority likely coincided with the wider use and diffusion of the names of transmitters: all available authorities were mobilised in the name of this competition for legitimacy.[58] This format was not exempt from the problems associated with transmission: alongside voluntary distortions, choosing to abbreviate or develop a *khabar* (the practices were by no means mutually exclusive), either entirely or in part, introduced distortions into the text as a result of the changing interests of successive compilers. It is clear that the practice of combining or synthesising *khabar*s, often termed "collective *isnād*s," quickly became common; Donner, however, insists that it was the *matn*, or the content, rather than the *isnād*, that underwent this transformation. These practices were clearly already current in al-Zuhrī's day, if not even earlier.[59]

The use of the *isnād* as a means of authenticating information and identifying transmitters divides modern scholars. Some, such as Elad or Motzki, call for a more immersive investigation of these chains of guarantors, arguing that early *isnād*s are generally authentic and not later inventions.[60] Conversely, de Prémare notes the limitations of this argument:

> This technique of formal presentation aims at providing assurance for an uninterrupted oral transmission by successive individuals of known authority. In fact, the systematic practice of the *isnād* was instituted only gradually. For example, in the middle of the eighth century, the Qur'ānic commentator Muqātil (d. 765) does not mention a single chain of transmitters to support his narrations on the circumstances under which a particular Qur'ānic message was issued [... By limiting themselves to this] traditional Islamic material, [scholars] are compelled to play along with the Muslim clerics of the past, who selected and compiled these elements

57 Donner, *Narratives*, 119–20. Donner situates this process within the context of the emergence of a confessional identity that was properly Muslim: the believers (*mu'minūn*) who gathered around the Prophet progressively defined themselves as Muslims (*muslimūn*). The tipping point occurred around 70/690, especially in the wake of the second *fitna*, as evidenced notably by the inscriptions at the Dome of the Rock. See Donner, "From Believers to Muslims," and most recently, *Muhammad and the Believers*.

58 Khalidi, *Arabic Historical Thought*, 21–2.

59 Donner, *Narratives*, 263–5.

60 See especially Motzki, "The Prophet and the Cat," and Elad, "Community of Believers," 288–90.

> in accordance with the idea they wished to present concerning the origins of their community and the life of their prophet. Consequently, researchers tend to support methods of verification, even while these methods are conditioned by the nature of the material itself. Thus, they concentrate their critical efforts on the meticulous analysis of chains of transmission, or *isnāds*. Despite rigorous precautions, they risk forgetting that these *isnāds* are the very same ones that the Muslim clerics patently selected, validated or invalidated according to their own personal criteria and in the service of their own personal vision of the facts.[61]

De Prémare then proposes a reevaluation of this inordinate attention given to the "knowledge of men" (*maʿrifat al-rijāl*, "men" being the transmitters); he argues that this narrow scholarly focus runs the risk of culminating in "a sort of neo-scholasticism of the Ḥadīth turning round and round in a closed circle [... at the risk] of forgetting to ask ourselves if the global framework of the origins of Islam, within which these traditions were originally selected, collected and categorised, is in many ways an artificial construction? Furthermore, this schema is effectively a structure of consensual orthodoxy, organising a sanctified and already-interpreted history through the reception and presentation of historical documents."[62] Without delving further into the details, the specific problems posed by this Islamic historiographic format seem generally clear. Moreover, as de Prémare notes, the danger of limiting ourselves to adopting the authentication methods imposed by medieval authors invites us to not be satisfied with simple analysis of the *isnāds* preserved in later compilations. As we shall see below, even though the merit of *isnad*-centric methodologies is undeniable, it is worth checking them against complementary approaches, particularly ones that make use of non-Muslim sources.

The *isnād/khabar* format also creates an attenuated image of the great Abbasid authors, who often appear more like mere compilers rather than true historians.[63] These *akhbāriyūn* played an important role in a "complex process

61 De Prémare, *Les fondations*, 12, 27.

62 De Prémare, *Les fondations*, 28–9.

63 Keaney, *Remembering Rebellion*, 4. See also Hoyland, "History, Fiction and Authorship." Among the most severe critiques addressed toward these "compilers" is that of Crone, *Slaves on Horses*, 13: "But the Muslim tradition was the outcome, not of a slow crystallisation, but of an explosion: the first compilers were not redactors, but collectors of debris whose works are strikingly devoid of overall unity; and no particular illuminations ensue from their comparison." For a critique of this idea of a "complete lack of sedimentation between the different stages of writing" and a "definitive erasure," see Décobert, *Le mendiant et le combattant*, 30 ff.

of reactive transmission;" this process included unacknowledged paternity for certain texts, that could be attributed to other authorities, even when the original was completely remade along the way.[64] However, the second half of the eighth century corresponds precisely with the professionalisation of *akhbār* transmission:[65] the period examined in this study is thus also that of the codification of a method of transmitting information, historical information in particular.

These elements of method and form illuminate the numerous pitfalls of using classical Islamic sources in an attempt to better understand the early years of Islam. The composition, transmission,[66] and inherent risks of manipulation and distortion in these sources – to say nothing of the successive phases of historical rewriting that occurred – all give rise to numerous questions. It is useful here to note, as Schmitt has done, "that nothing has been left to *chance* in the degree of preservation or disappearance in any particular genre of documents – not only textual, but also, I would add, iconographic or archaeological – because their transmission, as much as their initial production, is not due to fate, but rather to a 'social act,' or, more precisely, a 'historical act,' with each era adding its own individual reasons for preserving or destroying the documents that had been handed down to them from the past."[67] The widespread adoption of the *isnād/khabar* historiographic format was aimed at alleviating – and often masking – these difficulties. This historiography offers a "consensual orthodoxy," an "official" vulgate of early Islam and the Umayyad and Abbasid caliphates. In order to present the mechanisms of this historiography and attempt to access these alternative pasts – that is, alternative historiographies – we must first try to date the beginning of this historical production before excavating the successive layers of rewriting that span the period studied here; only then can we return to the more certain ground of the preserved sources.

---

64 Leder, "The Literary Use," 278–9.

65 Leder, "The Literary Use," 314. While Leder focuses on the emergence of the *akhbāriyūn*, it is worth noting that a similar and concomitant process is at work in poetry with the appearance of a new genre known as *ruwāt*. On this point, see Drory, "The Abbasid Construction," and above all Schoeler, "Writing and Publishing," and *The Genesis*, 19–20.

66 As Schoeler noted in "Foundations for a New Biography," 21: "Therefore, it is not sufficient to weigh the sources critically against each other; rather, a fundamental criticism of the transmission itself is necessary first."

67 Schmitt, "Une réflexion," 43.

1.2 Writing History in the Syrian Space under the Late Umayyads and Early Abbasids

The absence of contemporary narrative sources from the Umayyad period poses numerous questions. Did these sources actually exist? Were they destroyed or suppressed? What sorts of texts were they? Were they complete, or "published," to use Schoeler's expression? Before we address these issues, we must first broadly examine the emergence and early development of Islamic historiography. This series of questions related to the contemporary historical sources of the first Islamic dynasty cannot be properly understood without the preexistence of a historical consciousness that alone was able to spark a written or oral production. The lack of preserved narrative sources does not mean that the Umayyads were uninterested in history. Rather, it appears that the first Islamic dynasty played a large role in the formation of Islamic historiography. Alongside narrative sources, we will make use of other written works, including various documentary sources (papyri,[68] letters, particularly those of ʿAbd al-Ḥamīd, the secretary of the last Umayyad caliph, Marwān II), and collections of poetry; epigraphy and numismatic evidence round out the list of writing practices firmly rooted in the Umayyad era.

1.2.1 *On the Origins of Islamic Historiography*

Prior to any attempt at writing history, various questions relative to the very conception of the nature of history arise. How, when, and why does a given community decide to produce a discourse on its own past and/or present history? The nascent "Muslim civilisation" is not exempt from these questions; indeed, they are the subject of constant debate in modern scholarship aiming to precisely determine the chronology of Islamic historiographic development. This is an important observation, as it aids our understanding of the highly influential role the "Umayyad moment" played in this historiographic genesis.

The first series of questions is linked to the emergence of an Arab-Muslim historical consciousness. The absence of contemporary narrative historical sources from the first centuries of Islam considerably complicates the task of responding to this fundamental question. Indeed, the problem is not limited to "historical" sources; it applies more broadly to the entire scriptural domain, and particularly the Qurʾān. Scholars have rightfully investigated the place of history in the Qurʾān and the relation of this text to the gradual development

68 For a recent example on this rich production, see Sijpesteijn and Sundelin (eds.), *Papyrology and the History of Early Islamic Egypt*, and Sijpesteijn, Sundelin, Torallas Tovar and Zomeño (eds.), *From al-Andalus to Khurasan*.

of an "Islamic historical consciousness".[69] This debate must be our starting point, although it should be noted that the question of the date of the Qur'ān's composition is one that also divides modern scholars; the arguments of those who claim an early date for the composition of the Qur'ānic corpus are the ones that interest us here. Those who readily call themselves "skeptics" and argue for a later redaction of the Qur'ān in a "sectarian milieu" (in the second or even third century AH), such as Wansbrough,[70] have no place in this discussion precisely because of the date they ascribe to the composition of the Qur'ān;[71] in an important work, Donner has reevaluated this decidedly pessimistic approach.[72] Proponents of the first hypothesis, who offer various dates for the appearance of a closed Qur'ānic text – either under the so-called "orthodox" caliphs, especially ʿUthmān, or during the Umayyad era – are divided over the question of the place of history in the Qur'ānic text. Two radically different points of view on the connections between the Qur'ān and history exist. The question is essential, as it immediately orients any reflection on the emergence of a proper "historical" genre with respect to the Qur'ān. Historicity in the Qur'ān – or the lack thereof – must be considered when attempting to date the origins of Islamic historiography.

Cheddadi has recently asserted that a "historical spirit" can be detected in the Qur'ān. Per his analysis, the Qur'ānic text "proposes a global vision of the history of the world and mankind, using a metahistorical reflection constructed on the basis of a constant recourse to attestations of past acts and events … History [in the Qur'ān] is essentially a history-memory, a history-register (*une histoire-mémoire, une histoire-registre*)."[73] Furthermore, "the Qur'ān is without doubt the text in which the distinction between history and religion, law and history is pushed to its farthest extent. In the Qur'ān, history is clearly manifested as a divine affair."[74] However, "the Qur'ān does not recognise the idea of time as a progression, proposing in its stead the idea of discontinuous time; in place of the doctrine of the organic unity of history, it substitutes the idea of

69 The influence of the biblical tradition on Islamic historiography has been studied by Rosenthal, "The Influence of the Biblical Tradition."

70 Wansbrough, *Quranic Studies*, and *The Sectarian Milieu.*

71 This debate is largely outside the scope of this study. See the recent investigation of de Prémare, *Aux origines du Coran*, 15 ff.; the remarks of Whelan "Forgotten Witness;" and the contributions of McAuliffe, *The Cambridge Companion to the Qur'ān.*

72 See Donner, *Narratives*, 20–5, for a presentation of this "skeptical approach," and 25–31 for his criticism thereof. This approach has been the subject of very important debates that are impossible to fully summarise here. A survey of these debates can be found in Décobert, "L'ancien et le nouveau," and *Le mendiant et le combattant*, 30–40.

73 Cheddadi, *Les Arabes*, 101, 104.

74 Cheddadi, *Les Arabes*, 156.

an absolute history eternally inscribed in the divine Book, a history essentially conceived as a timely communication of Truth to mankind".[75] According to Cheddadi, the Qur'ān possesses preexisting – and favourable – conditions for the development of historiography. While Humphreys considers it difficult to demonstrate a Qur'ānic influence on the interpretive frameworks of the Islamic tradition, he nevertheless suggests that the Qur'ān shaped a consciousness of the past; Rosenthal, on the other hand, sees Muḥammad's interest in history as a powerful stimulus for the emergence of Islamic historiography.[76] Al-Azmeh insists that the corpus of Arab-Muslim writings, the Qur'ān included, attests to a preoccupation with the past,[77] while Neuwirth has highlighted the complexity of the relations between history and the Qur'ān.[78]

De Prémare, however, emphasises "the lack of proper historical data in the text," and notes the rarity "of any historical precision with respect to specific events, including those particular to Muḥammad and the stages of his life." On the basis of this observation, he is surprised by the status of "fundamental historical document" that orientalists conferred upon the Qur'ān and remarks on "the fact that the Qur'ān is the opposite of a 'history' as it was conceived in the nineteenth century."[79] In contrast to Cheddadi, Donner presents the Qur'ān as a text fundamentally dedicated to presenting pious values and mores, subjects that he considers ahistoric by nature.[80] Donner sees the prophets as interchangeable in Qur'ānic discourse, unlike those of the Old Testament;[81] Khalidi agrees, noting that the Qur'ānic prophets are examples of moral lives who reveal essentially the same message.[82] Thus, for Donner, the roots of a historical conscience should not be sought in the Qur'ān – which he considers an early corpus that was closed following the first *fitna* (656–661)[83] – but rather in the link between communal identity and historical writing: the development of history did not arise from a sudden interest in the past, but was the result of a process of identity formation in which believers gradually began to conceive of themselves as Muslims and sought to legitimise themselves as the recipients

75 Cheddadi, *Les Arabes*, 307. On the idea of continuum, see also Khalidi, *Arabic Historical Thought*, 8.
76 Humphreys, "Qur'anic Myth," 274; Rosenthal, *A History*, 39.
77 Al-Azmeh, "Chronophagous Discourse," 163.
78 Neuwirth, "Qur'an and History."
79 De Prémare, *Aux origines*, 19.
80 Donner, *Narratives*, 75 ff.
81 Donner, *Narratives*, 80, 83–4.
82 Khalidi, *Arabic Historical Thought*, 9.
83 Donner, *Narratives*, 46.

of the word of God.[84] The internal and external challenges to the legitimacy of the Believers made historical narration a necessity for them: writing history is at its core a response to the need for legitimation.[85]

Donner states that the documentary evidence does not bear the traces of historicisation earlier than sixty or seventy years after the *hijra* (*c.*685–700).[86] Based on this thesis, he establishes four successive phases in the Arab-Muslim relationship with history:[87]

1) The *Pre-historic phase*, until roughly 50/670, during which the community of believers focused on pious values and had no real historical self-conception.
2) The *Proto-historic phase* (*c.*25–100/645–719), which takes place in the context of the theological debates and political rivalries that helped reinforce the believers' sense of identity. Certain historiographic themes began to appear, perhaps supported by the Umayyads, who played a major role in recording these events.
3) The *Early literate phase* (*c.*75–150/694–768), which was marked by a decisive transition to writing and the crystallisation of the great themes of Islamic historiography.
4) The *Late literate phase*, or classical Islamic historiography (*c.*125–300/742–913), when the texts of earlier eras were collected, reworked, edited, or even suppressed. Most of the elements affirming the legitimacy of the Umayyads and Zubayrids likely disappeared during this period.

In a recent article, Elad strongly disagrees with Donner's central argument, contesting the idea that piety was the unifying force among the first community of believers and defending the notion that a historical consciousness

84 Donner, *Narratives*, 282; on the specific question of the evolution of a "community of believers" to a "community of Muslims," see Donner, "From Believers to Muslims," and *Muhammad and the Believers*.

85 Donner, *Narratives*, 114: "The writing of history, then, is a profoundly legitimizing activity, and one enmeshed in time-bound irony. History is our way of giving what we are and what we believe in the present a significance that will endure into the future, by relating it to what has happened in the past. Or, to be more precise: to write history is to write about events in relation to their own past, in order to provide those events with significance that makes them worthy of being remembered in the future. The function of history is not only 'to provide a specific temporal dimension to man's awareness of himself;' it is indeed to authorize a community's very claim to legitimate existence. The creation of historical narratives is always, ultimately, an exercise in legitimation." Khalidi, *Arabic Historical Thought*, 14, also suggests this connection between the painful birth of the Islamic empire and the emergence of Islamic historiography.

86 Donner, *Narratives*, 120–1; on this critical period comprising the first seventy years of Islam, see also Johns, "Archaeology and the History of Early Islam."

87 Donner, *Narratives*, 276 ff.

among the Arab-Muslims arose earlier, meaning that the first written histories must have appeared earlier as well.[88] The rivalries and conflicts that proliferated from the era of the Prophet on would have been sufficient for creating a sense of truly Muslim identity among believers. The crux of the disagreement between these two scholars is Donner's central argument – that believers were the bearers of ahistoric pious virtues – but this issue is largely outside the scope of this inquiry; however, their chronologies of historical writing are not as different as Elad implies. Donner's "proto-history phase" (phase 2) extends from around 25/645–646 until 100/718–719, while Elad situates it in the middle of the first century following the *hijra*.

Other authors have carefully examined this subject as well. Khalidi also detects the emergence of a "proto-historical consciousness" during the Umayyad – or more precisely, the Marwanid – period:[89] the Zubayrid anti-caliphate (64–73/683–692), the first major challenge to the Umayyads, required the mobilisation of scholarly authorities in the name of this competition for legitimacy.[90] Here we return to Donner, for whom legitimacy and historiography are intrinsically linked. Schoeler agrees, stating: "It is not difficult to see why the Umayyad caliphs preferred to have knowledge accessible in their palace libraries. There, they could easily consult not only the collections containing the traditions of Muḥammad and the accounts relating to his life, but also information about the Arab past."[91] Robinson situates the emergence of Islamic historiography slightly later, although still in the Marwanid period, dating its appearance to between 730 and 830.[92] However, as we shall see, the first "historians"[93] of Islamic historiography were already active well before 730.[94]

Yet another element relative to the connection between history (*taʾrīkh*) and the question of dating with respect to the *hijra* merits more attention than it has previously received in modern scholarship. The act of dating (a letter, an event, etc.) is the first meaning of the root "*ʾ-r-kh*," and the term *taʾrīkh* indicates

88 Elad, "Community of Believers," 246, 251–2; see also Lewis, "Perceptions musulmanes," 79, for whom Islam and historiography are inextricably connected.

89 Khalidi, *Arabic Historical Thought*, 29; Robinson, "The Study," 201.

90 Khalidi, *Arabic Historical Thought*, 21.

91 Schoeler, *The Genesis*, 54.

92 Robinson, *Islamic Historiography*, 30.

93 We will set aside the debatable question of the "conceptual horizon" that accompanies the birth of Islamic historiography. Some, such as Robinson, support the idea of numerous influences (see *Islamic Historiography*, 43), while Cheddadi has recently argued for situating Islamic historiography within the continuity of the Hellenistic tradition, noting its deep roots in the space that gave rise to Islam. See Cheddadi, *Les Arabes*.

94 On this point, see Borrut, "Entre tradition et histoire."

first and foremost the date of an act or deed and thus, by extension, history.[95] The introduction of *hijrī* dating, which represents a properly Islamic absolute time,[96] plays a decisive role in the development of a Muslim historical consciousness. As the use of the *hijrī* calendar is attested at an early date in papyri dating to between 20 and 30 AH,[97] the aforementioned historical consciousness may be dated to this period as well. The oldest completely preserved chronography – that of Khalīfa b. Khayyāṭ – offers an eloquent example of this link between dating and the beginnings of history: the author adopted an annalistic method, and designated year one as the "first year of history" (*sana iḥdā min al-ta'rīkh*) rather than the "first year of the *hijra*."[98]

In modern scholarship, an abundant corpus has grown around the question of the birth of Islamic historiography. Despite the debates and disagreements between different specialists, all recognise the critical role that the Umayyad era played in this regard. Islamic historiography emerged under the caliphs of Damascus. All of these scholars – from the proponents of the early appearance of a historical consciousness (Elad), to those who argue for the eventual later emergence of historiography (Donner), as well as those who insist on the continuity of earlier historiographic traditions (Cheddadi) – name the Umayyad period as the origin of this process. Donner has rightfully highlighted the connections linking legitimacy and historical writing; this point is critical, and forces modern scholars to contend with the fact that the political goals at work in this control over the past have too often been neglected in studies concerned with early Islamic historiography.[99] Yet if the Umayyad period played such an important role in the genesis of an Islamic historiography, how is it that this first Islamic dynasty became the victim of the very processes it inaugurated?

---

95 See Humphreys, "Ta'rīkh."

96 Computing dates of the *hijra* establishes an absolute time by replacing relative dates based on the name of a given year: for example, "the year of the farewell pilgrimage" (*ʿām ḥijjat al-waḍāʿ*, which corresponds to year ten of the *hijra*) or "the year of Yarmūk" (*ʿām al-Yarmūk*, which corresponds to year fifteen of the *hijra*). On this point, see Donner, *Narratives*, 230–54, along with an exhaustive list of these "named years," 249–54.

97 Donner, *Narratives*, 237; Hoyland, *Seeing*, 687–703. On the use of *hijrī* dating in Syriac sources, see Debié, *L'écriture de l'histoire en syriaque*, 281–7.

98 Khalīfa b. Khayyāṭ, *Ta'rīkh*, 13. It should be noted that the older use of the term "*hijra*" poses certain problems, although this use in no way detracts from the explicit link established between the beginning of this dating system and history.

99 This question has been widely discussed in the context of the medieval West. See Spiegel's article, "Political Utility," which already in 1975 emphasised the "political utility" of medieval manipulation of the past, insisting that the past itself constitutes the ideological structure of an argument. More recently, see Geary, *Phantoms of Remembrance*, 7–8, and McKitterick, *History and Memory*.

1.2.2 *Syrian Historiography in the Umayyad Era?*

In addition to the chronological problems, the question of where this emergent Islamic historiography was produced has long occupied modern scholars. By focusing on the identities of the transmitters mentioned in the chains of guarantors, researchers have also attempted to establish a geography of historiography. We will begin with an analysis of the role of the Syrian space in this process.

1.2.2.1 The "Theory of Regional Schools" and the Place of Syria

Wellhausen was indisputably a pioneer in studying the locations where history was written. Working from the *isnāds*, he located the principal transmitters used by al-Ṭabarī in his magnum opus. It did not take more, over a century ago, for the so-called theory of "regional (historical) schools" to appear, with famous narrators set forth as representatives of each.[100] The likes of Ibn Isḥāq (d. 150 or 151/767) or al-Wāqidī (d. 207/823), among others, exemplified the Medina school, while Sayf b. ʿUmar (d. 180/796) or Abū Mikhnāf (d. 157/774) personified the Kūfa school. Wellhausen identified other historical schools, in particular those of Baṣra, Khurāsān and Syria; the production of this latter school, however, had been largely lost due to the vagaries of the transmission process.[101] These different schools were not equally valued; the Medina school was preferred by scholars, and certain transmitters were seen as especially suspect of having falsified their accounts. The aforementioned Sayf b. ʿUmar is the classic example; Wellhausen's censure of Sayf has long endured in modern scholarship. The "theory of schools" was widely accepted by Wellhausen's successors, as attested, for instance, by the works of Duri;[102] it was then rejected by Noth in 1973.[103] Noth's remarks have been favourably received in more recent studies, including Donner's, although Donner questions the fact that Noth's arguments tend to obscure the reality of the situation during the first two centuries of Islam, in which historiography was confined to a small number of major cities.[104] In other words, the "theory of schools" imposed a much-too-rigid analytical framework; however, the limited number of historiographic production centres favoured the emergence of "local" histories.

100 See Wellhausen's preface, *Das arabischc Rcich*.

101 Wellhausen, *Das arabische Reich*, xii.

102 Duri, "Al-Zuhrī;" "The Iraq School;" *The Rise of Historical Writing*.

103 Noth, *Quellenkritische*. An expanded version of this work was translated into English in 1994: Noth and Conrad, *The Early Arabic*; on this second point, see Robinson, "The Study," especially 211 ff., and Khalidi, *Arabic Historical Thought*, 16, n. 13.

104 Donner, *Narratives*, 216.

Donner's thesis, acknowledging the existence of multiple orthodoxies, thus has a spatial dimension: any city may, at least for a time, be associated with a given orthodoxy.

Still, it is due to the significance of these dominant paradigms that modern scholarship on early Islamic historiography has long been centred on Iraq and the Hijaz (especially Medina) rather than Syria.[105] Syrian historiography is considered both to be less well-preserved and produced much later than historiography composed in Iraq or Medina.[106] Al-Ṭabarī's œuvre is a good example of this problem, as the author relies very little on Syrian transmitters, even when reporting information related to the Syrian space. Donner has shown that of the approximately two hundred *akhbār* concerning Syria between the beginning of the Islamic conquests (12/634) and the year 100 *hijrī*, nearly 80% are based on *isnād*s originating with Iraqi or Medinese authorities (Sayf b. ʿUmar, al-Wāqidī, al-Madāʾinī, etc.), while the remaining 20% are often derived from incomplete *isnād*s and thus perhaps have similar origins.[107] This observation is easily applied to other authors as well, and, as Wellhausen has previously noted, only al-Balādhurī (d. 279/892) offers a more balanced approach, employing Syrian transmitters alongside the Iraqis and the Medinese;[108] the works of Khalīfa b. Khayyāṭ, which had not yet been edited at the time, must be added to this group.[109] Our knowledge of the early historians based in the Syrian space has progressed considerably in the last few decades. Along with Judd, however, we should note that the biographies of scholars as important as al-Awzāʿī or Sufyān al-Thawrī do not emphasise geographic elements as distinguishing characteristics, which may signify that "regionalism" was not as important a factor as modern scholars might assume.[110]

It should also be noted, however, that these different centres of historiographic production and the transmitters associated therewith must not be thought of as isolated entities; this is one of the classic assumptions underpinning the "theory of regional schools." Conrad highlights these interconnections using the example of the abundant transfer of information, themes, and methodologies between Medina and Northern Syria, particularly via al-Zuhrī, who was active in both Medina and Damascus and then followed Hishām to

105 One of the pioneering works aimed at overcoming this deficit is Rotter's article, "Abū Zurʿa;" see also Donner, "The Problem," and Elad, "The Beginning."

106 Donner, "The Problem," 1.

107 Donner, "The Problem," 1–2.

108 Wellhausen, *Das arabische Reich*, xii; Donner, "The Problem," 2.

109 Khalīfa b. Khayyāṭ, *Taʾrīkh*.

110 Judd, "Competitive Hagiography," 27.

al-Ruṣāfa, at the imperial court in the north of Syria.[111] The mobility of men and ideas must be taken into account, even if it is still possible to arrive at Cook's conclusion that the successive layers of rewriting during the Abbasid period resulted in an under-representation of the Syrian "tradition" in the sources that survive.[112] A striking example of the links uniting these different centres is the existence of a common core of historical information related to the history of early Islam. Mourad has argued that a work such as the *Futūḥ al-Shām* by Abū Ismāʿīl al-Azdī (d. early 3rd/9th c.) was primarily based on information circulating in Kūfa at the time, but that this information was also known to authors in Medina, such as Ibn Isḥāq, as well as those in Damascus, such as Saʿīd al-Tanūkhī (d. c. 167/784).[113] It is perhaps due to the existence of these shared elements that Conrad believed al-Azdī to be Syrian, a native of Homs, rather than from Kūfa, as Mourad has shown.[114] The existence of a common informational foundation in the different centres of historiographic production is a crucial fact, as it is based on a core, a sort of "historiographical skeleton," that the skeptics claim was completely fabricated at a later date (i.e., the ninth century). These skeptics argue that this unanimity is the result of the invention of a myth after the fact regarding the origins of the Islamic community; Donner refutes this theory in light of evidence attesting to the earlier existence of this consensus among historiographers (around the year 100 *hijrī*), for whom this "kernel" was shared because it was real.[115]

The problem of divergences – either minimal or more significant – remains; they occur with respect to the presentation of certain elements of this shared "kernel" of historical information, and they often lead scholars to reject a given version of events, such as has frequently occurred in the case of Sayf b. ʿUmar. Here, the remarks of Petersen are important, as he insists that the texts were in conversation with each other in a sort of historiographic competition that produced and circulated concurrent versions that then became autonomous and evolved independently of the events they described.[116] This observation is a marker of the complexity of the historiographic processes at work; in this light, it is no longer possible to content ourselves with rejecting a certain transmitter on suspicion of falsification. The debates accompanying the spread of these historical writings were an integral part of the successive rewritings performed

111 Conrad, "Heraclius," 152–3; on the connected theme of how letters travelled, see Touati, *Islam et voyage*.

112 Cook, "The Opponents," 471.

113 Mourad, "On Early Islamic," 588.

114 Conrad, "Al-Azdī's History;" Mourad, "On Early Islamic," 579.

115 Donner, *Narratives*, 287–90; see also Humphreys, *Islamic History*, 87 ff.

116 Petersen, *ʿAlī and Muʿāwiya*; Humphreys, *Islamic History*, 88.

upon these texts, to the extent that sometimes they even took precedence over the original event itself. In this sense, early Islamic historiography is fundamentally a *generative historiography*.

The very existence of these debates conveys the high political stakes involved in the ability to narrate the past, and it is impossible that the first Islamic dynasty was unaware of this fact. Logically, it follows that we must now turn our attention to the connections between the caliphs and historiography.

1.2.2.2 The Pen and the Sword: The Caliphs and Historical Writing

Syrian historiography has long been neglected within the emerging field of Islamic historiography; however, several important works shed light on the nuances of this hastily-sketched tableau. Even so, this approach is a balancing act because we lack the texts produced by these early authors, and thus we must focus our attention on the "sources of the sources." The image that appears before us is unavoidably incomplete, yet it nevertheless elucidates the question of historical writing in the Syrian space, the active role played by the Umayyad caliphs in this process, and the prevalence of historiographic activity in Abbasid Syria. The authorities entrusted with knowledge – history being only a single facet thereof – and its transmission were mobilised by the caliphs, for whom power implied control over the past so that it might reproduce itself in the present and future. In the famous words of Ibn Khaldūn, the pen and the sword were thus complementary implements.[117]

In order to clarify these little-known connections, we must first seek out the "historians" and Syrian transmitters who seem to have been "forgotten" by Islamic historiography. "Historians" here is in quotations marks because, as Donner has noted, it is clear that historiography was a peripheral activity for most of these authors, who primarily worked in other fields (*ḥadīth*, exegesis, *fiqh*, etc.).[118] Wellhausen may have suspected the existence of a Syrian historiography that did not survive;[119] however, it was not until much later that scholars began actively searching for the traces of this production. This is especially the case in Rotter's work on one of the oldest extant Syrian sources, the *ta'rīkh* of Abū Zurʿa al-Dimashqī (d. 281/894).[120] Rotter, interested in the sources consulted in the composition of this text, notes that Abū Zurʿa relied on several Syrian authors, notably Saʿīd b. ʿAbd al-ʿAzīz al-Tanūkhī (d. 167 or 168/783–784),

117 Ibn Khaldūn, *The Muqaddimah*, vol. II, 46.
118 Donner, *Narratives*, 256; Leder, "The Literary Use," 313.
119 Wellhausen, *Das arabische Reich*, xii.
120 Abū Zurʿa, *Ta'rīkh*.

al-Walīd b. Muslim (d. 195/810 or 196), Abū Mushir al-Ghassānī (d. 218/833)[121] and Ibn ʿĀʾidh (d. 232/847).[122] Contrary to the arguments of Dahan,[123] it seems clear that Syria was host to historiographic activity more or less comparable to that of Iraq and Medina during the second half of the second/eighth century and throughout the third/ninth century.[124] But what about the preceding period? Donner and Elad have both tried to respond to this question by tracing the infrequent mentions of Syrian historians and transmitters in the sources.[125] Their work has succeeded in uncovering several important figures, to whom we shall now turn our attention for the purposes of the present study.

It should be noted that much of the debate is located outside the bounds of the period examined in this study; nonetheless, it will be useful to briefly establish certain chronological principles here. Elad argues in favour of the existence of historiography covering the rise of Islam starting in the second quarter of the first century after the *hijra*.[126] One of the classical examples used to support this theory is a certain ʿUbayd (or ʿAbīd) b. Sharya al-Jurhumī, who, in the words of Ibn al-Nadīm: "went to Muʿāwiya ibn Abī Sufyān. He [Muʿāwiya] questioned him on ancient history, the kings of the Arabs and non-Arabs, the cause of the confusion of languages and the dispersion of men throughout the different countries of the world."[127] The caliph then ordered that these lessons be written down and attributed to ʿUbayd (*fa-amara Muʿāwiya an yudawwan wa-yunsab ilā ʿUbayd b. Sharya*).[128] This episode indicates Muʿāwiya's interest in history[129] and further poses the question of the fate of this collection

121 He was interrogated at Raqqa by al-Maʾmūn during the *miḥna* and threatened with death. The caliph asked him: "Do you work for al-Sufyānī?" See Sourdel, *L'état impérial*, 103.

122 Rotter, "Abū Zurʿa," 98 ff. Abū Zurʿa did not limit himself to Syrian sources; for example, for the section discussing the lifetime of the Prophet, he used primarily "Iraqi" informants, and of a total of 44 *akhbār*, only 15 are Syrian, originating mostly with Yaḥyā b. Ṣāliḥ al-Wuḥāẓī al-Ḥimṣī (d. 222/837) and Abū Mushir al-Ghassānī (d. 218/833).

123 Dahan, "The Origin," 109: "During the 2nd/8th century not a single historian in Syria is known who was working on the history of his country."

124 Donner, "The Problem," 3.

125 Donner, "The Problem;" Elad, "Community of Believers" and "The Beginning."

126 Elad, "Community of Believers," 269.

127 "*Wafada ʿalā Muʿāwiya b. Abī Sufyān fa-saʾalahu ʿan al-akhbār al-mutaqaddima wa-mulūk al-ʿArab wa-al-ʿajam wa-sabab tabalbul al-alsina wa-amr iftirāq al-nās fī al-bilād.*" Ibn al-Nadīm, *Fihrist*, 132. Here I follow Cheddadi's French translation, *Les Arabes*, 42. See also Elad, "Community of Believers," 270.

128 Elad, "Community of Believers," 270.

129 This interest is widely corroborated in the sources. Al-Masʿūdī reports a similar sentiment in describing the nocturnal activities of the caliph: "One-third of the night was devoted to the history of the Arabs and their celebrated deeds, as well as to those of the polities of non-Arab kings; to stories about the lives, wars, strategies, and governments of the kings

of ʿUbayd b. Sharya's teachings. The *Akhbār ʿUbayd b. Sharya* is preserved in a later compilation, the *Kitāb al-tījān* of Ibn Hishām (d. c. 216/831);[130] the authenticity and dating of this text divides modern scholars, but it likely dates to the beginning of the Abbasid era.[131] In spite of the questions it raises, this anecdote emphasises the fact that, at a time and in a place that remain difficult to determine, someone was trying to portray Muʿāwiya as the initiator of an Islamic historiography, and furthermore, that this initiative took place within the framework of the Syrian space.[132]

This image corresponds to the presentation of Muʿāwiya as the most prominent foundational figure of the first Islamic dynasty, a role he shares with ʿAbd al-Malik b. Marwān, who restored Umayyad authority following the Zubayrid anti-caliphate.[133] Modern scholarship tends to locate the birth of Islamic historiography during the caliphate of the latter, in the Marwanid period, whereas the medieval authors were of the opposite opinion, placing its emergence in the Sufyanid era. The opposing viewpoints surrounding these two inaugural figures in the field of history and historiography are part of the larger classical debate around the two Umayyad moments – the Sufyanid followed by the Marwanid – despite the fact that it is often quite difficult to determine the

of various nations; in a word, to everything that constitutes the history of the nations of the past … Then he would sleep for a third of the night. Upon awaking, he would sit on his throne and have brought to him volumes containing the lives of the kings, their history, their wars, their strategies. Pages were specially responsible for this reading, as well as for the conservation of these documents. Each night, he listened to a series of historical narratives on lives, traditions, and different political treatises." *Murūj*, vol. 5, 77–78, trans. Pellat vol. III, 726–7, edited by Cheddadi, *Les Arabes*, 42.

130 Ibn Hishām, *Kitāb al-tījān*.

131 See the earlier reservations of Krenkow, "The Two Oldest," as opposed to the optimism of Abbott, *Studies*, I, 9–19. Rosenthal, "Ibn Sharya," offers a more nuanced approach. Finally, Cheddadi, *Les Arabes*, 36 ff., has contested ʿUbayd's very existence, considering him to be a fictional character while suggesting that the *Akhbār ʿUbayd* is a text from the Umayyad era, citing "the adoption of the discipline of history by the new Arab-Islamic culture" (40). The only argument set forth by Cheddadi in support of this dating is that of the status of principal protagonist bestowed upon Muʿāwiya, which does invite increased caution. The most in-depth study of this text is that of Khoury, "Kalif, Geschichte und Dichtung," which is oddly absent from Cheddadi's bibliography. See also Elad, "Community of Believers," 270–1, and Humphreys, *Muʿāwiya*, 129–30.

132 This does not preclude the possibility that the first historical writings were produced elsewhere, in particular in Shiite environments, as Donner postulates in *Narratives*, 278. Elad builds on this point in "Community of Believers," 272–3.

133 On these two foundational figures, see Humphreys, *Muʿāwiya*, and Robinson, *ʿAbd al-Malik*.

provenance of any particular initiative.[134] The chronological framework of this study demands that we limit our scope to the caliphate of ʿAbd al-Malik, although it is by no means prejudiced against the earlier existence of Islamic historiography in the Sufyanid era. More than a secure, guaranteed, and doubtless illusory authority, these sources that stress Marwanid achievements are better-attested, including those describing their architectural programs, administrative and financial reforms, and the active role they played in establishing the Qurʾānic corpus;[135] historiographic work could well have been one of the components of these ambitious policies. However, it is clear that historiographic elements were produced at the court of the Umayyad caliphs beginning at the end of the seventh century, and particularly in the Syrian space.[136]

We shall first concentrate on the principal historical writers active in Syria – and, if necessary, those in Medina or Iraq, in cases where it suits our purposes here – during the period under examination (*c.*72–193/692–809).[137] Despite the loss of their works or traditions, a detailed study of these figures is critical because they played a significant role in the transmission of historical information: later historians citing or consulting one of these authors were not only invoking what this particular author had written, but also what he had chosen to preserve and record from his predecessors. These lost sources should above all be studied with the understanding that they then conditioned the historical information that could subsequently be preserved.

ʿAbd al-Malik regained control of the empire in 72/692, a fact that cannot entirely be reduced to the military dimension of the conflict that put him at war with Ibn al-Zubayr.[138] The caliph's architectural and financial policies attest to this state of affairs,[139] as do the efforts made to ensure control over writing and discourses. This last point has generally not received as much attention as those preceding it, although recent studies have elucidated its importance, allowing scholars to understand the policies of ʿAbd al-Malik as a meticulously-planned global project.[140] The perception of the roles played by

134 See notably the opposing opinions of Foss, "A Syrian Coinage," and Johns, "Archaeology and the History of Early Islam."

135 See de Prémare, "ʿAbd al-Malik," and *Aux origines du Coran*, 12.

136 This process was not limited to Syria. See other examples analysed by Donner, *Narratives*, 227.

137 It is impossible to determine precisely the date at which these authors composed their texts; thus, their death dates – when they are known – serve as chronological markers.

138 On this sensitive issue in Umayyad history, see Dixon, *The Umayyad Caliphate*; Rotter, *Die Umayyaden*; Robinson, *ʿAbd al-Malik*, 31–48; and Donner, *Muhammad and the Believers*, 177 ff.

139 On these questions, see below, Ch. 8.

140 De Prémare, *Aux origines* and "ʿAbd al-Malik;" Robinson, *ʿAbd al-Malik*.

certain key figures among the caliph's entourage requires significant revision. This is certainly true in the case of al-Ḥajjāj (d. 95/714), who was well-known for his military talents and his iron fist as the governor of Iraq; de Prémare has recently emphasised his decisive role in the codification of the Qur'ānic corpus.[141] Al-Ḥajjāj's example is a valuable one: it demands that scholars not "catalog" men too quickly in specific categories, but rather try to comprehend them in all their multi-layered complexity. The caliphate's pressing need to control the written word[142] at a moment when it was convenient to impose its own "orthodoxy" in the face of other concurrent projects is also worth noting. The strategies implemented by ʿAbd al-Malik were intended to exceed the strict boundaries of religious writing in order to extend control of the past, the basis of all caliphal legitimacy. Alongside al-Ḥajjāj, Qabīṣa b. Dhu'ayb (d. 86/705), ʿAbd al-Malik's secretary[143] in charge of the seal and the postal service,[144] undoubtedly also played an important role in this process. Other significant figures of the period merit greater attention as well.

ʿUrwa b. al-Zubayr (d. c. 94/712–713) was a member of a well-known family. His father was a Companion of the Prophet, while his brother ʿAbd Allāh b. al-Zubayr revolted against the Umayyads and installed himself as a rival caliph in Mecca until the year 72/692, when ʿAbd al-Malik succeeded in restoring Umayyad authority throughout the empire. Unlike the other members of his family, who were mainly known for their military exploits, ʿUrwa was a distinguished legal and historical scholar who lived most of his life in Medina, although he spent several years in Egypt as well. He was renowned for his authority in *fiqh*, and at the behest of ʿAbd al-Malik, he wrote on the *maghāzī* of the Prophet in an epistolary exchange with the caliph that remains the subject of much debate.[145] His foundational role is what interests us most here, as he was master to numerous disciples, many of whom – like the famous al-Zuhrī – would later become important transmitters. Al-Zuhrī, along with ʿUrwa's son Hishām (d. 146/763), was ʿUrwa's principal transmitter and ensured the diffusion of his work; however, this transmission is not without its own methodological problems.[146]

---

141 See de Prémare, "ʿAbd al-Malik."

142 For a rich comparison with the medieval West, see McKitterick's various works cited in the bibliography.

143 Al-Ṭabarī, vol. II, 837, trans. vol. XXI, 215. On the importance of this figure in the caliph's entourage, see for example al-Ṭabarī, vol. II, 1164–5, trans. vol. XXIII, 108–9.

144 Ibn Saʿd, *al-Ṭabaqāt*, vol. V, 176.

145 De Prémare, *Les fondations*, 14–6.

146 De Prémare, *Les fondations*, 14–6 and 387–8; on the problems and possibilities associated with the traditions of ʿUrwa b. al-Zubayr, see Schoeler, "Foundations for a New Bibliography," and Görke and Schoeler, *Die ältesten Berichte*.

Khālid b. Maʿdān al-Kalāʿī al-Ḥimṣī (d. 104/722–723)[147] lived in Homs but died in Ṭarsūs, where he was *murābiṭ*. An expert in the Qurʾān, law, and *ḥadīth*, he is considered a reliable transmitter and was famous for his piety. He had close connections to the Umayyads, and served them in several capacities: he was *ṣāḥib al-shurṭa* under Yazīd I, and later carried on correspondence with the caliphs ʿAbd al-Malik and al-Walīd, particularly on the subject of *fiqh*. He participated in the siege of Constantinople in 98/716–717 with Maslama b. ʿAbd al-Malik, whose entourage included many Syrian notables (*wujūh ahl al-Shām*), Khālid among them.[148] Al-Ṭabarī cites some twenty *akhbār* originating with Khālid, most of which are connected to the conquest of Syria, but also more broadly offer information spanning from the prophetic period to the Umayyad era. He also transmitted decidedly pro-Sufyanid and pro-Syrian *ḥadīths*,[149] especially traditions with heavily apocalyptic connotations describing the *mahdī* or the Sufyānī.[150] Ibn Qutayba later suspected him of having Qadarī tendencies,[151] although following the conclusions of Wadād al-Qāḍī, this suspicion was probably in error, as Khālid appears on the contrary to have been violently opposed to the Qadarites.[152]

Rajāʾ b. Ḥaywa al-Kindī (d. 112/730–731) was a prominent figure of the Umayyad era and served the caliphate in several important roles, from the days of ʿAbd al-Malik through the reign of Hishām. He is famous for having supervised the construction of the Dome of the Rock in the role of "spiritual counsellor;" he likely received the surname *Sayyid ahl Filasṭīn* during this period, as he was a native of Baysān (Beth Shean). He also played an almost certainly decisive role in the selection of ʿUmar b. ʿAbd al-ʿAzīz as the successor to the

147 Khālid b. Maʿdān's death date is the subject of some confusion, both in the sources and in modern scholarship; the dates given vary between 103/721 and 108/727. Wadād al-Qāḍī has shown that the date 104/722–723 should be given preference because, if we are to believe Abū Zurʿa al-Dimashqī, it appears in the *dīwān al-ʿaṭāʾ* (*Taʾrīkh*, vol. I, 243, n. 282, and vol. II, 694, n. 2144). See also Wadād al-Qāḍī, "A Documentary Report."

148 Al-Ṭabarī, vol. II, 1315; trans. vol. XXIV, 40.

149 Donner, "The Problem," 7–9; Elad, "Community of Believers," 263; al-Qāḍī, "A Documentary Report."

150 On these apocalyptic traditions, see Madelung, "The Sufyānī," 14, and "Apocalyptic Prophecies," 173–5.

151 Ibn Qutayba, *Kitāb al-maʿārif*, 625; Van Ess, *Theologie*, 111–4. It is difficult to know what *qadariyya* meant during the Umayyad period. The idea that this movement basically consisted of affirming mankind's free will and the predestination of his actions is a later development. On this question, see Watt, *Free Will*; Van Ess, *Theologie* and "Ḳadariyya;" Judd, *The Third Fitna*.

152 Al-Qāḍī, "A Documentary Report."

caliphate of Sulaymān b. ʿAbd al-Malik.[153] Presented as a *zāhid* and an *ʿālim*, he was primarily known as a *faqīh* and a *muḥaddith*.[154]

Maymūn b. Mihrān (d. 117/735–736), renowned in the sources for his piety, was a famous scholar. A cloth merchant who owned his own shop (*ḥānūt*), he was also in charge of the *bayt al-māl* of Ḥarrān under the governor Muḥammad b. Marwān b. al-Ḥakām, who would later preside over the Jazīra under ʿAbd al-Malik.[155] ʿUmar II appointed Maymūn *qāḍī* and put him at the head of the *kharāj* in the Jazīra; other traditions state that he was secretary (*kātib*) to ʿUmar II. His son would continue the family tradition of administrative service as head of the *dīwān* (*al-jaysh*?).[156]

ʿUbāda b. Nusayy al-Kindī (d. 118/736–737), a scholar and legal specialist, was the *qāḍī* of al-Urdunn; he was also its governor under ʿAbd al-Malik and ʿUmar II. He was called *Sayyid ahl al-Urdunn* or *Sayyid al-Urdunn*. He was also the *ʿarīf*, most likely as the commander of a military unit,[157] of a tribal group of which Rajāʾ b. Ḥaywa was a member. Despite his close ties to the Umayyads, he did not hesitate to criticise the caliphs, as was the case following Hishām's execution of Ghaylān al-Dimashqī.[158] He was also a transmitter of historical information concerning, for example, the conquest of Qinnasrīn and the division of booty that followed.[159] He also reported other *akhbār* related to the Umayyad era, and seems to have been particularly concerned with certain themes specific to Syrian history.[160]

Sulaymān b. Mūsā (d. between 115 and 119/733–737), a renowned traditionist, was an Umayyad *mawlā* and possibly a close associate of Hishām, if the narratives stating that he died while visiting the caliph at al-Ruṣāfa are to be trusted.[161] Although he is best-known as a transmitter of *ḥadīth*, he also participated in the transmission of historical information; an *isnād* given by al-Ṭabarī

---

153 On this point, see Becker, "Studien," 21 ff.; Barthold, "The Caliph ʿUmar II," 79–80; Bosworth, "Rajāʾ ibn Ḥaywa," 48 ff.; Eisner, *Zwischen Factum und Fiktion*, 213 ff.; Mayer, "Neue Aspekte," 109–15; Borrut, "Entre tradition et histoire," 333.

154 Elad, "Community of Believers," 260; Bosworth, "Rajāʾ ibn Ḥaywa;" Rabbat, "The Dome of the Rock Revisited," 70–1.

155 Donner, "Maymūn b. Mihrān."

156 Elad, "Community of Believers," 260–1.

157 Elad, "Community of Believers," 260.

158 On this episode, see Judd, "Ghaylan al-Dimashqī," and *The Third Fitna*.

159 He is mentioned in twenty *akhbār* in al-Ṭabarī, all related to the conquest of Syria. See Donner, "The Problem," 11.

160 Donner, "The Problem," 9–12; Elad, "Community of Believers," 260.

161 Donner, "The Problem," 4–5.

tracing back to Sulaymān concerning the siege of Constantinople by Maslama b. ʿAbd al-Malik in 98/716–717 is evidence of this fact.[162]

Ibn Shihāb al-Zuhrī (d. 124/742)[163] is probably the most famous traditionist of the period, and as such produced a copious bibliography.[164] His notoriety stems from the principal role he played in the transmission of *ḥadīth*, but also from his expertise in *fiqh* and even history, in particular concerning the *maghāzī*.[165] Al-Zuhrī studied in Medina under the direction of the most respected masters of the day, among them ʿUrwa b. al-Zubayr, and produced numerous notable disciples, the most famous of whom was the great Mālik b. Anas. He was active both in Medina and Syria, circulating frequently between these two spaces. The status of pioneer conferred upon him by the sources as one who committed knowledge to writing has already been mentioned above.

For our purposes, the connections to the Umayyads merit our consideration. The debate over the value of these ties is an ancient one; medieval authors were quick to reproach al-Zuhrī for his ties to the caliphs of the first Islamic dynasty. An example of this disapproval is offered by the ascetic Abū Ḥāzim Salama b. Dīnār, who warned an Umayyad governor in the presence of al-Zuhrī using this clever phrase: "The greatest of rulers (*umarāʾ*) is he who loves the *ʿulamāʾ*, and the worst of the *ʿulamāʾ* is he who loves the rulers."[166] In modern scholarship, this sentiment was echoed early on by Goldziher in 1890, who subjected al-Zuhrī to a severe critique, even going so far as to state that he falsified a number of traditions that presented the Umayyads in a favourable light.[167] Duri later adopted the opposing position and tried to present al-Zuhrī as non-partisan with respect to caliphal authority, arguing that some of the traditions attributed to him contain criticisms of the Umayyads.[168] More recently, Lecker and others have argued for a return to Goldziher's ideas, emphasising anew the clear and unbroken ties continuously linking the scholar to the caliphs from ʿAbd al-Malik through Hishām.[169] A brief summary of this issue will be useful here.

162 Al-Ṭabarī, vol. II, 1315; trans. vol. XXIV, 39–40. On this episode, see below, Ch. 5.

163 Ibn Saʿd, *al-Ṭabaqāt*, vol. II, 388–9; TMD, vol. 55, 294–387.

164 See Lecker, "Biographical Notes," and "Al-Zuhrī;" Duri, "Al-Zuhrī: A Study" and *The Rise*, 76 ff.; de Prémare, *Les fondations*, 321–3, 393; Schoeler, *The Genesis*, 47–50; Motzki, "Der Fiqh des Zuhrī;" Donner, *Narratives*, index; Robinson, *Islamic Historiography*, index; Cheddadi, *Les Arabes*, index; Judd, *The Third Fitna*, 149–53.

165 Schoeler, *The Genesis*, 47.

166 Ibn Manẓūr, *Mukhtaṣar*, vol. x, 67; Lecker, "Biographical Notes," 34.

167 Goldziher, *Muslim Studies*, vol. II, 43 ff.

168 Duri, "Al-Zuhrī: A Study," especially 10–2.

169 Lecker, "Biographical Notes," 22 ff.

Al-Zuhrī's role in the caliphate of ʿAbd al-Malik has received a great deal of scholarly attention, due to an oft-cited passage of al-Yaʿqūbī (d. after 295/908)[170] that exposes how the caliph, hoping to replace the pilgrimage to Mecca with one to Jerusalem – while the anti-caliph Ibn al-Zubayr controlled the holy cities of Arabia – called upon the scholar to unearth some traditions in order to justify this political decision.[171] Although the validity of this anecdote should be questioned, as indeed it has been in several recent studies,[172] the fact remains that the relationship between these two figures is well-attested in the sources, even if the date of their first meeting remains a topic of debate.[173] Al-Zuhrī's ties to al-Walīd, ʿAbd al-Malik's successor, are less well-documented; nevertheless, al-Ṭabarī notes that the caliph interrogated the scholar on the age of the Umayyad rulers, an event which would later motivate his decision to write on this subject as well as on the duration of their reigns.[174] This narrative may explain how and why his *Asnān al-khulafāʾ* came into being; this work is cited in various sources, and al-Ṭabarī precisely relies on al-Zuhrī to establish the duration of al-Walīd I's reign.[175] Mentions of Sulaymān b. ʿAbd al-Malik are fewer; however, it is reported that the caliph, having been warned of the difference between the *ʿulamāʾ* of the past and those of his day and age, tried to minimise his contact with al-Zuhrī.[176] ʿUmar II, who held him in high regard, asked al-Zuhrī to collect *ḥadīth*s and compile them in a volume;[177] he also appointed him *qāḍī*,[178] a role in which he was later confirmed by Yazīd II.[179] However, beyond his ties to ʿAbd al-Malik, it is above all those he maintained with Hishām that secured al-Zuhrī's fame. Here again, debates persist; for example, there is the question of whether he settled semi-permanently in al-Ruṣāfa at the caliph's court or whether he was a tireless traveler, continually circulating

170 This date is more likely than the usual one of 284/897, see above p. xviii. Zaman had already suggested a death date not earlier than 292/905, "Al-Yaʿqūbī".

171 Al-Yaʿqūbī, *Taʾrīkh*, vol. II, 261. This text was translated by de Prémare, *Les fondations*, 462–3.

172 Elad, *Medieval Jerusalem*, 156–7; Lecker, "Biographical Notes," 22.

173 For example, see de Prémare, *Les fondations*, 321–2; Lecker, "Biographical Notes," 41 ff.

174 Al-Ṭabarī, vol. II, 199, 428; trans. vol. XVIII, 211, trans. vol. XIX, 225; Duri, "Al-Zuhrī: A Study," 10.

175 Al-Ṭabarī, vol. II, 1269; trans. vol. XXIII, 218.

176 Ibn Manẓūr, *Mukhtaṣar*, vol. X, 68 ff.: "*wa-la-azhadanna fī al-Zuhrī min baʿd al-yawm.*"

177 Duri, "Al-Zuhrī: A Study," 11; Schoeler, *The Genesis*, 56.

178 Al-Zuhrī was possibly already a *qāḍī* under ʿAbd al-Malik; see *TMD*, vol. 55, 387 ("… *wa-kāna qāḍiyan bayna yaday ʿAbd al-Malik*"), cited by Lecker, "Biographical Notes," 38.

179 Lecker, "Biographical Notes," 37.

between the Hijaz and Syria, and later between al-Ruṣāfa and Damascus.[180] In any case, it was at al-Ruṣāfa at Hishām's behest that al-Zuhrī dictated *ḥadīth*s that were likely written down by Shuʿayb b. Abī Ḥamza al-Ḥimṣī, a secretary of the caliph.[181] The caliph also charged him with the task of supervising the education of his sons;[182] when Hishām entrusted leadership of the *ḥajj* to his son Maslama in 119/737, al-Zuhrī accompanied him.[183]

In sum, al-Zuhrī performed several different functions in service of the Umayyads: *qāḍī*, collector of *ṣadaqa* and chief of the *shurṭa*.[184] The medieval commentators frequently insisted on the fact that he worked in the service of the caliphs (*wa-kāna yaʿmalu li-Banī Umayya*).[185] This collaboration between pen and sword was fruitful for the scholar, who established himself as a loyal supporter of the Umayyads and was generously recompensed as a result, notably in the form of rural estates.[186] In fact, it was in one of these domains – Shaghb wa-Badā in the Hijaz – that al-Zuhrī fell ill and died in 124/742.[187] As noted, these close connections were criticised by medieval scholars; they also provoked the ire of the caliph al-Walīd II, who bitterly hated al-Zuhrī for having sought, along with Hishām, to change the order of succession so as to remove him in favour of one of Hishām's sons, Maslama b. Hishām.[188] The memory of al-Zuhrī was not exempt from the troubles that plagued the

180 The first option is based on al-Fasawī's assertion stating that al-Zuhrī remained at al-Ruṣāfa throughout the entire caliphate of Hishām ("*khilāfat Hishām kullahā*," *Al-Maʿrifa wa-al-taʾrīkh*, vol. I, 636), that is, for nearly twenty years, while others claim it was a period of ten years (in particular Abū Zurʿa, *Taʾrīkh*, vol. I, 432, and Yāqūt, *Muʿjam*, vol. III, 48). See Lecker, "Biographical Notes," 32–3. The second hypothesis is defended by Duri ("Al-Zuhrī: A Study," 11; *The Rise*, 118 ff.), who suggests that al-Zuhrī settled in Damascus under Yazīd II, whereas Lecker, "Biographical Notes," 32 n. 45, argues for an earlier date sometime during the caliphate of ʿAbd al-Malik.

181 On this figure, see below; "*kataba ʿan al-Zuhrī imlāʾan li-al-sulṭān, kāna kātiban*," Ibn ʿAsākir, cited by Lecker in "Biographical Notes," 27.

182 Ibn Kathīr, *Bidāya*, vol. IX, 342; Duri, "Al-Zuhrī: A Study," 11, and *The Rise*, 118.

183 Al-Ṭabarī, vol. II, 1635; trans. vol. XXV, 166.

184 Lecker, "Biographical Notes," 38–9.

185 Lecker, "Biographical Notes," 38.

186 Al-Zuhrī possessed estates on pilgrimage routes where he engaged in trade with pilgrims. On this point, see Lecker, "Biographical Notes," 49–56.

187 Lecker, "Biographical Notes," 54. Yāqūt places al-Zuhrī's tomb there, *Muʿjam*, vol. III, 351. However, there appears to be a certain confusion in the sources as to whether Shaghb wa-Badā designated one location or two. See Yāqūt, *Muʿjam*, vol. III, 351–2, and below, Ch. 4.

188 The order of succession was established by Yazīd b. ʿAbd al-Malik, who named his brother Hishām as his successor, followed by his son al-Walīd b. Yazīd. Hishām allegedly did not seek to modify this decision until al-Walīd began behaving in a reprehensible manner. This change of attitude was said to have provoked the caliphal initiative to try to upend

Umayyad caliphate during this period; indeed, al-Ṭabarī reports that al-Walīd II declared that he would have killed the scholar himself if he had not already died.[189] Al-Walīd b. Yazīd, while still only heir apparent under the caliphate of Hishām, had previously ordered the trees in the aforementioned domain of Shaghb wa-Badā cut down, probably in retaliation for al-Zuhrī's attempts to convince Hishām to remove him from the line of succession.[190]

Several historical works are attributed to al-Zuhrī, among them: a volume dedicated to the *maghāzī*; a genealogy of Quraysh; one most widely known as *Asnān al-khulafā'*; and works concerning *ḥadīth*, which, as Schoeler notes, would later become "official collections."[191] Alongside his written works, al-Zuhrī also trained numerous disciples, many of whom transmitted historical information while in the service of the Umayyads. Foremost among his disciples were:

– Sulaymān b. Dāwūd Abū Dāwūd al-Khawlānī al-Dārānī (fl. first half of the second/eighth century), primarily known as a transmitter of *ḥadīth*; he was either a *ḥājib* or *kātib* under ʿUmar II.[192]
– Muḥammad b. al-Walīd b. ʿĀmir al-Zubaydī al-Ḥimṣī (born during the caliphate of ʿAbd al-Malik, died between 146/763–764 and 148/765–766), a *muḥaddith* and *qāḍī* of Homs; he was one of al-Zuhrī's transmitters, having spent approximately twelve years with him in al-Ruṣāfa, where he was also in charge of the caliph's *bayt al-māl*.[193]
– The aforementioned Shuʿayb b. Abī Ḥamza al-Ḥimṣī, *mawlā* of the family of Ziyād b. Abīhi (d. 162/779 or 163); he was a renowned transmitter of *ḥadīth* and secretary in charge of expenditures (*al-nafaqāt*) in Hishām's caliphal administration. Under Hishām's orders, he attended and recorded oral lectures given by al-Zuhrī.[194]
– Mālik b. Anas, without question the most famous of al-Zuhrī's disciples. The eponymous founder of the Mālikī school and the "imam of Medina," he is best known for his legal writings and his central role in history of *fiqh*. As

---

the order of succession set forth by his brother and predecessor, to the benefit of his son. For a detailed account of these events, see al-Ṭabarī, vol. II, 1740 ff.; trans. vol. XXVI, 87 ff.

189 Al-Ṭabarī, vol. II, 1811; trans. vol. XXVI, 165.

190 Lecker, "Biographical Notes," 54.

191 For the complete list of works attributed to al-Zuhrī, see Donner, *Narratives*, 301; Schoeler, *The Genesis*, 50.

192 Elad, "Community of Believers," 261–2.

193 Elad, "Community of Believers," 262.

194 Elad, "Community of Believers," 262; Lecker, "Biographical Notes," 27, and "Al-Zuhrī."

we shall see below, his *Kitāb al-Muwaṭṭaʾ* comprises significant historical traditions.[195]

These examples incontestably prove the early existence of historical writing in Umayyad Syria, combined with scrupulous transmission practices and the mobilisation of Syrian and Medinese authorities by the Umayyad caliphs. They also show the pivotal role played by the rulers of Damascus in this process: their activities stimulated the development of the emergent field of Islamic historiography. Donner, approaching these questions from a slightly different angle than that taken by Noth and Conrad, attempted to identify certain characteristic themes within this production.[196] He notes that several of these themes were promoted by the Umayyads – such as *nubūwa*, *umma*, worship and administration, *khilāfa* and *futūḥ* – and that the generic theme of "prophecy" doubtless received special attention, based on the evidence provided by the Qurʾānic inscriptions on the Dome of the Rock.[197] This implication of caliphal power at work in the development of historical writing must be understood in the broader context of the Umayyad's global aims, as control over the past was seen as an essential act of legitimation. These efforts to construct a corpus through writings and rewritings touched the entire scriptural domain: the Qurʾān, *ḥadīth* and *sunna* were central preoccupations of the first Islamic dynasty. Moreover, an important labor of codification was also a major concern during this period, particularly with respect to Islamic rituals.[198] Yet this state of affairs has long been obscured by the very nature of the documents that provide access to this epoch, which has likely resulted in the under-representation of the fundamental place occupied by the Umayyads in this process. It should be noted here that any attempt to completely disentangle these various genres of writing would be in vain. The boundaries between "religious," "legal" or "juridic," and "historical" writings are porous. While these different types of texts certainly have their own individual particularities, they follow the same processes and are often composed by the same authors. These are authoritative texts in a process aimed at the "canonisation" of the final, consummate

195 See below the elements related to ʿUmar II, Ch. 6. On Mālik and the *Muwaṭṭaʾ*, see Schacht, "Mālik b. Anas," and Dutton, *The Origins of Islamic Law*.

196 Noth and Conrad, *The Early Arabic*; see also Robinson, "The Study," and Donner, *Narratives*, 125 ff.

197 On these themes, see Donner, *Narratives*, 147 ff., 227, and Johns, "Archaeology and the History of Early Islam," 433.

198 See Donner, "Umayyad Efforts at Legitimation." These initiatives undertaken by the Umayyads were not limited to the written word. They are also represented in the inscription of an Islamic power on space through architectural projects of vast scale, as well as more generally in daily life, as through the monetary reforms enacted by ʿAbd al-Malik.

divine revelation, of an emergent Muslim identity and of an Islamic history that encompassed the legacies of a monotheistic and hellenistic past.[199] Donner notes that it was not only facts that were gathered and organised in this process of historicisation, but also legends and non-historical materials that were situated among the themes of this developing historiography.[200]

The interest of the Umayyad caliphs in history was also a practical one, due to the educational virtues of the discipline as well as the lessons that could be derived therefrom with respect to governance and the exercise of power. For example, Hishām b. ʿAbd al-Malik, who appointed al-Zuhrī tutor to his sons, ordered that a work on the history of the Sasanian emperors and their polities be translated into Arabic in 113/731.[201] These didactic functions of history echo the "mirrors for princes" genre, which later enjoyed widespread success and popularity in the Islamic world. Works composed under the early Abbasids, such as those of Ibn al-Muqaffaʿ (d. c. 140/757) or Abū Yūsuf Yaʿqūb (d. 182/798), are of the same lineage, despite certain differences in their central themes.[202] Ibn Khaldūn highlights these merits of history and historiography by evoking the roles they played in the Umayyad and Abbasid eras:

> Another illustration of the same kind of error is the procedure historians follow when they mention various dynasties and enumerate the rulers belonging to them. They mention the name of each ruler, his ancestors, his mother and father, his wives, his surname, his seal ring, his judge, doorkeeper, and wazir. In this respect, they blindly follow the tradition of the historians of the Umayyad and ʿAbbāsid dynasties, without being aware of the purpose of the historians of those times. (The historians of those times) wrote their histories for members of the ruling dynasty, whose children wanted to know the lives and circumstances of their ancestors, so that they might be able to follow in their steps and do what they did, even down to such details as obtaining servants from among those who

199 See Robinson, *Islamic Historiography*, 45, and Cheddadi, *Les Arabes*, 127 ff.

200 Donner, *Narratives*, 209–14.

201 Gutas, *Greek Thought*, 27; al-Masʿūdī, *Tanbīh*, 106, trans. 151. Gutas also mentions the possible translation of a Greek medical text under Marwān I or ʿUmar II (*Greek Thought*, 24). The great push to translate the Greek sciences and philosophy into Arabic is mainly associated with Abbasid Baghdad, in particular with the *bayt al-ḥikma* of the caliph al-Maʾmūn (198–218/813–833), as Gutas notes. Saliba has elucidated the considerable role played by the Umayyads in initiating this translation project in accordance with the policies of Arabisation enacted by ʿAbd al-Malik (see Saliba, *Islamic Science*, chapters 1 and 2).

202 Ibn al-Muqaffaʿ, *Risāla fī al-ṣaḥāba*; Abū Yūsuf Yaʿqūb, *Kitāb al-Kharāj*; on this literary genre, see Bosworth, "An Early Arabic Mirror for Princes," and "Administrative Literature," 165–7.

> were left over from the (previous) dynasty and giving ranks and positions to the descendants of its servants and retainers. Judges, too, shared in the group feeling of the dynasty and enjoyed the same importance as wazirs, as we have just mentioned. Therefore, the historians of that time had to mention all these things.[203]

The development of historical writing, however, should not be seen as linked exclusively to power. By the end of the Marwanid era, descriptions of historians with uncertain or nonexistent ties to the caliphate can readily be found.

Al-Waḍīn b. ʿAṭāʾ al-Dimashqī (d. 149/767) was born in Bāniyās but lived most of his life in Kafr Sūsiyya, near Damascus, where he died. He had Qadarite leanings and seems to have had no connection to the Umayyads. Rather, he was likely on good terms with the Abbasids from an early date; al-Waḍīn reports having contact with al-Manṣūr before he became caliph. He transmitted mainly stories of conquests, especially those on the Syrian coast, as well as reports on the population displacements enacted by Muʿāwiya. His marked interest in the coast has led Donner to argue that al-Waḍīn was something of a local historian;[204] it is in this capacity that he was used by later compilers.[205]

Thawr b. Yazīd al-Kalāʿī (d. between 150/767 and 155/772) may have been originally from Homs; in any case, he is identified in the sources as a scholar native to this city. His house in Homs was burned and he was expelled from the city due to his Qadarite sympathies. He then settled in Jerusalem, where he would later die in his sixties. He also spent time in Mecca and Medina, where he appears to have taught. Opinions on his reliability as a transmitter are divided because of his Qadarite tendencies; Mālik b. Anas harbored strong reservations against Thawr, although certain versions report that Mālik transmitted *ḥadīth*s on his authority. Nonetheless, Thawr b. Yazīd does not appear as a transmitter from Mālik in the *Muwaṭṭaʾ*, and he had no evident ties to the Umayyads, under whom he seems to have held no official position.[206] He was, however, in contact with the Abbasids.[207]

The Qadarite sympathies (real or imagined) of these two authors could easily be ample justification for their lack of ties to the Umayyads. For this reason, they could not have been integrated into the project of "Marwanid orthodoxy" sponsored by the caliphs; unfortunately, the documentary evidence does not

203 Ibn Khaldūn, *The Muqaddimah*, vol. 1, 62.

204 Donner, "The Problem," 12–5; Van Ess, *Theologie*, 81–2.

205 Later compilers such as Saʿīd b. ʿAbd al-ʿAzīz al-Tanūkhī, for example, subsequently echoed by al-Balādhurī; see below.

206 Donner, "The Problem," 15–8; Van Ess, *Theologie*, 114–7; Judd, "Ibn ʿAsākir's Sources," 81.

207 Judd, "Competitive Hagiography," 28.

allow us to identify the potential roles they may have played when the Umayyad caliphate briefly adopted Qadarite doctrine under Yazīd III. The example of al-Waḍīn b. ʿAṭāʾ al-Dimashqī also draws attention to the fact that the fall of the Umayyad dynasty certainly did not mean the end of historiographic production in Syria. Syrian transmitters even held high administrative positions in the nascent Abbasid empire, sometimes after having played an important role in the final years of the Umayyad era.[208] Their possible Qadarite leanings, which essentially excluded them from the Marwanid ideological project, facilitated their integration into the Abbasid administration without being a necessary prerequisite. It is important here to focus on certain of these figures and trace their movement through the Abbasid era so as to understand why these Syrian historiographies have not survived and, moreover, why these texts were so infrequently employed by later Abbasid-era authors.

1.2.3 *Forgotten Sources?*

We shall begin this section by introducing several of the transmitters active in early Abbasid Syria, followed by a closer examination of their historiographic production.

Hishām b. al-Ghāz (d. between 153/770 and 159/776), a famous *muḥaddith* of Damascus renowned for his piety and virtue, settled in Abbasid Baghdad where he was in charge of the *bayt al-māl* under al-Manṣūr. He transmitted *ḥadīth*s regarding the Companions, Muʿāwiya's campaigns against the Byzantines, and earlier scholars. He reports, for example, Makḥūl's (d. between 112 and 119) visit to the tomb of ʿUmar II.[209]

Al-Awzāʿī (d. 157/774) is undoubtedly one of the most respected and well-known Syrian jurists of the late Umayyad and early Abbasid period.[210] He had close ties to the Umayyads, particularly Hishām, for whom he was a key adviser. He was essential to the Umayyad attempts to establish and impose their orthodoxy, as well as in combatting the heretical movements that rose

208 These continuities are not only the prerogative of historians and transmitters, but are also attested among administrative officials, military professions, etc. On this point, see Bligh-Abramski, "Evolution versus Revolution," and Elad, "Aspects of the Transition." See also below, Ch. 7.

209 Donner, "The Problem," 18–20; Elad, "Community of Believers," 263. On ʿUmar II's tomb and the development of pilgrimages to the site, see Borrut, "Entre tradition et histoire," 351–2.

210 Al-Awzāʿī's doctrinal developments are outside the scope of this study. On this topic, see Judd, *The Third Fitna*, 153 ff., "Ghaylān al-Dimashqī" and "Competitive Historiography;" Conrad, *Die Quḍāt*; Van Ess, *Theologie* and *Anfänge*, 207–13. For more on the general context of the period, see the corresponding chapter in the following works: Laoust, *Les schismes*; Melchert, *The Formation*; and Crone, *Medieval Islamic*.

up in response. Al-Awzāʿī played a central role in this process, especially in the inquisition against the Qadarites, and was directly involved in the trial of Ghaylān al-Dimashqī, who was sentenced to death in 125/743.[211] With his strong connections to the Umayyads, al-Awzāʿī was forced to adapt to a new state of affairs following the rise of the Abbasids. He succeeded in acclimatising himself to these new circumstances without cutting ties with his previous masters or recognising the legitimacy of the Abbasid Revolution. He was interrogated several times, by ʿAbd Allāh b. ʿAlī as well as al-Manṣūr, but was finally allowed to retire to Beirut. His opinion on questions of jurisprudence was occasionally sought, and several of his students became *qāḍīs* under the new regime.[212] In addition to his legal expertise, al-Awzāʿī also composed a volume on the history of Syria that does not survive.[213]

Saʿīd b. ʿAbd al-ʿAzīz al-Tanūkhī (d. 167/784) was an important Syrian transmitter and compiler, notably on the subject of the conquest of Syria. His reports on the "Lebanese" coast were used by both al-Balādhurī[214] and Abū Zurʿa.[215]

Al-Walīd b. Muslim al-Umawī al-Dimashqī (d. 194/810), a descendant of the Umayyads, composed a number of historical works that do not survive, in particular a volume on *maghāzī*.[216] Later compilers relied on this important transmitter – as Elad has recently noted – for accounts of the conquest of Syria.[217] Al-Walīd b. Muslim himself frequently relied on an informant he referred to as "al-Umawī" or "al-shaykh al-Umawī;" Donner proposes that the identity of this latter may have been Yaḥyā b. Saʿīd al-Umawī (d. 194/809).[218]

Abū Mushir al-Ghassānī al-Dimashqī (d. 218/833), born in Damascus in 140/757, was a traditionist specialising in *maghāzī* and genealogy. He was considered one of the greatest *muḥaddithūn* of his day, and in this capacity was regarded as an authority by scholars as prestigious as al-Bukhārī (d. 256/870) and Aḥmad b. Ḥanbal (d. 241/855). Refusing to accept the dogma of the created Qurʾān, he was imprisoned by al-Maʾmūn in Baghdad, where he eventually

211 On this episode, see Judd, *The Third Fitna* and "Ghaylān al-Dimashqī."

212 On the relationship between al-Awzāʿī and the early Abbasids and the use that was made thereof in his biographical notices, see Judd, "Competitive Historiography."

213 Dahan, "The Origin," 109, who unfortunately does not cite the source from which this information was taken.

214 Al-Balādhurī, *Futūḥ*, 126–7, trans. 194.

215 Rotter, "Abū Zurʿa," 100.

216 Elad, "The Beginnings," 99–100; Dahan, "The Origin," 109.

217 He was, for example, an important source for Abū Zurʿa al-Dimashqī; see Rotter, "Abū Zurʿa," 99.

218 Donner, *Narratives*, 245.

died.[219] Abū Mushir is particularly important as a major source for Abū Zurʿa al-Dimashqī.

Muḥammad b. ʿĀʾidh al-Dimashqī (d. 232/847) is a good example of the state of relative oblivion in which certain Syrian traditionists fell during the Abbasid era. This Syrian transmitter, a disciple of al-Walīd b. Muslim and mufti of Damascus, is generally considered reliable, despite his Muʿtazilite or Qadarite views. Ibn ʿĀʾidh has long been known to modern scholars; Rosenthal noted that he was only cited in later sources, which may be explained by the fact that he was the representative of an unpopular Syrian tradition.[220] In a recent study, Elad mentions that Ibn ʿĀʾidh is cited numerous times by Khalīfa b. Khayyāṭ, who died only eight years after his colleague in 240/854. Below, we shall see that Khalīfa b. Khayyāṭ represents a marginal case in the Abbasid-era sources that survive, insofar as his *Taʾrīkh* and *Ṭabaqāt* were composed slightly before the beginning of a phase of intensive historical rewriting that occurred in the post-Sāmarrāʾ period. As a result, here we find ourselves face-to-face with a concrete example of the "oblivion" of a Syrian tradition that was nonetheless well-known and transmitted during or immediately following the author's lifetime. It seems that the traditions originating with Ibn ʿĀʾidh in the works of Khalīfa b. Khayyāṭ were all interpolations traceable to one of Khalīfa's own transmitters, a *rawī* named Baqī b. Makhlad al-Qurṭubī (d. 276/889).[221] Be that as it may, diffusion of Ibn ʿĀʾidh's traditions is attested in the sources in the second half of the third/ninth century, a phenomenon that is not replicated in the works of other later Abbasid compilers; much later authors would eventually recover and disseminate his traditions.[222] One possible explanation for the "oblivion" of Ibn ʿĀʾidh rests on an examination of his informants. It seems that he derived most of his material from al-Walīd b. Muslim, a fact also noted by Elad,[223] although he did employ other sources. Ibn ʿĀʾidh even possessed a copy of al-Walīd b. Muslim's *Kitāb al-Fitan*.[224] This may explain the fact that al-Walīd b. Muslim is cited by authors ignorant of Ibn ʿĀʾidh, while this latter largely fell into oblivion.

219 *GAS*, vol. 1, 100–1.

220 Rosenthal, "Ibn ʿĀʾidh."

221 See Conrad, *Die Quḍāt*, 167, note 155; Elad, "The Beginnings," 74–5; Landau-Tasseron, "On the Reconstruction," 49. Ibn ʿĀʾidh's traditions were transmitted by Baqī via Bakkār b. ʿAbd Allāh; the elements attributed to Ibn ʿĀʾidh cited by Khalīfa b. Khayyāṭ do not progress chronologically beyond the beginning of ʿAbd al-Malik's caliphate.

222 These sources using Ibn ʿĀʾidh, along with what they can tell us about his lost works, are studied in detail by Elad, "The Beginnings," 67–100.

223 Elad, "The Beginnings," 99–100; Baqī b. Makhlad, *rāwī* of Khalīfa b. Khayyāṭ, often cites *isnād*s in which Ibn ʿĀʾidh relies on al-Walīd b. Muslim.

224 Elad, "The Beginnings," 128.

Abū Zurʿa al-Dimashqī (d. 281/894) is exceptional in this list of Syrian authors in that his works have been preserved.[225] Born into a Qaysite environment between 195/811 and 200/815, he is an example of the continuity of historical activity in Syria in the second half of the third/ninth century. For Abū Zurʿa, history proper was the history of Islam and thus begins with the birth of the Prophet. He is almost completely silent on the subject of ʿAlī's caliphate, only briefly mentioning a *fitna* that took place five years after the assassination of ʿUthmān:[226] he even suggests that there was continuity between the caliphate of Muʿāwiya, who reunited the *umma* at the end of this first major conflict, and his grandfather. His *taʾrīkh* is similarly replete with mixed opinions of the Umayyad caliphs, as witnessed by his choice of vocabulary when marking the ascension of a certain sovereign. Although he mostly relied on "Iraqi" *isnād*s when reporting on the lifetime of the Prophet, following this initial phase of Islam Abū Zurʿa mainly called upon Syrian transmitters: al-Walīd b. Muslim al-Dimashqī (d. 194/810) was his primary source for the period between Abū Bakr and Muʿāwiya,[227] while Abū Mushir (d. 218/833), himself often reliant on Saʿīd b. ʿAbd al-ʿAzīz al-Tanūkhī (d. 167/784), fulfilled this role for the Marwanid and early Abbasid eras.

This not-insignificant sampling of Syrian transmitters during the Umayyad and Abbasid eras poses numerous problems with respect to its representativeness, the factors that ensured its transmission, etc. In light of the subjects treated by these authors, in particular the Prophetic period and the age of conquests, another pivotal question arises. These early historians seem to have focused on the recent Islamic past, generally neglecting more contemporary history; Robinson has recently argued this point with respect to the list of works established by Donner that were composed before the end of the second *hijrī* century.[228] Following Elad, who argues that historiography emerged at an early date immediately following the first Islamic conquests in the middle of the first/seventh century, this relative disinterest in the history of the present merits contextualisation.[229] For the period under examination in this study, the problem remains, as works that seemingly focus on the second/eighth

225 This author, along with his works, has not been properly studied. See the pioneering works of Rotter, "Abū Zurʿa," Conrad, "Das Kitab," and al-Qāḍī, "A Documentary Report." See also *GAS*, vol. I, 100–1, and al-Qujānī's lengthy introduction to the edition of Abū Zurʿa's *Taʾrīkh*, 1–94.

226 Abū Zurʿa, *Taʾrīkh*, 187.

227 Rotter, "Abū Zurʿa," 98–9.

228 Robinson, *Islamic Historiography*, 94; the list of these works is appended to that of Donner, *Narratives*, 297–306.

229 Elad, "The Beginnings," especially 116 ff.

century appear in much smaller numbers than those dealing with *maghāzī* or *futūḥāt*. It is difficult to make sense of this question, as we possess only a very limited amount of fragmentary knowledge concerning these works, of which only the titles – which are not necessarily representative of their contents – or scattered references have survived. It is probable that, at least in certain cases, the citations preserved in later compilations offer a distorted version of a given source, as a solitary part of the whole is used (for example, information relative to the conquest of a specific region) to the detriment of the the rest of the work and the broader project of its author. A certain number of works, of which only the titles are known, nevertheless appear to deal with the Umayyad period or specific important events spanning the era. The works of later authors such as al-Masʿūdī (d. 345/956) and Ibn al-Nadīm (d. 385/995) confirm that they consulted these texts.

One of the oldest listed works belonging to this category is al-Zuhrī's aforementioned *Asnān al-khulafāʾ*.[230] It is difficult to know exactly what this text comprised, although it was likely a list of the caliphs composed at a time when it was extremely important to establish the chronology of the history of the caliphate. Al-Ṭabarī relied on this volume for information given by several transmitters concerning the death of Yazīd I: "Yazīd b. Muʿāwiya died when he was 39 years of age. His rule was for three years and six months according to the report of some. It is also reported that it was [three years and] eight months."[231] This predominant concern with chronology continues through the decades following al-Zuhrī's death, as attested by the appearance of the first "chronographies;" in addition to two separate works both entitled *Taʾrīkh al-khulafāʾ*, one attributed to Muḥammad b. Isḥāq (d. 151/768), the other to Abū Maʿshar Najīḥ (d. 170/780), another volume called *Kitāb al-taʾrīkh* composed by ʿAwāna b. al-Ḥakam (d. c. 147/764) also appeared during this period.[232]

Alongside these important efforts at chronological organisation, other works dealing directly with the subject of the Umayyads are also mentioned in the sources. A *Kitāb sīrāt Muʿāwiya wa-Banī Umayya* is attributed to the aforementioned ʿAwāna b. al-Ḥakam.[233] The renowned Abū Mikhnāf (d. 157/774) is also credited with works concerning the first Islamic dynasty, the Sufyanids, the

230 GAS, vol. I, 280–3; Donner, *Narratives*, 183, 239.

231 Al-Ṭabarī, vol. II, 428; trans. vol. XIX, 225; Donner, *Narratives*, 239. See also a different passage from al-Ṭabarī (vol. II, 199; trans. vol. XVIII, 211) in which the caliph al-Walīd interrogates al-Zuhrī on the lengths of the lives of the caliphs, in particular Muʿāwiya's age upon his death. The same source was possibly used for information concerning the length of the caliphate of al-Walīd b. ʿAbd al-Malik (al-Ṭabarī, vol. II, 1269; trans. vol. XXIII, 218).

232 Donner, *Narratives*, 240, 303, 305; GAS, vol. I, 307–8.

233 Donner, *Narratives*, 195, 303; GAS, vol. I, 307–8.

second *fitna*, the battle of Marj Rāhiṭ, and the early Marwanids.[234] Al-Masʿūdī mentions several volumes on the Umayyads in his presentation of the sources used in the composition of his *Meadows of Gold*: ʿAlī b. Mujāhid (d. 182/798) is named as the author of a work entitled *Kitāb Akhbār al-Umawiyyīn*,[235] while Abū ʿAbd al-Raḥmān Khālid b. Hishām al-Umawī is said to have reported "the general chronicle and history of the Umayyads, their virtues, merits, the examples they followed and the innovations they brought about through their conduct."[236] Works of an apologetic tone dealing with the Umayyads were still current in tenth-century Syria, as attested by al-Masʿūdī's consultation in Tiberias in 324/935–936 of a text entitled *The Book of Proofs of the Imamate of the Umayyads* that claims ʿUthmān as the first Umayyad and continues beyond the caliphs of the East to their Andalusian successors.[237]

Historical texts were undoubtedly produced both during and on the subject of the Umayyad period.[238] The Syrian space was an active centre of historiographic composition under the Umayyads as well as the Abbasids. With the notable exception of Abū Zurʿa, these texts have not survived in their original form, but rather in a much more limited fashion: the best-case scenario is the existence of citations in later compilations, which are not without their own difficulties; in certain cases, these texts are only known to us because the name of an author and the subjects or titles of his works were mentioned in later bibliographic works, such as the *Fihrist* of Ibn al-Nadīm. In the vast project of historiographic reconstruction sponsored by the Abbasids following the caliphate's return to Baghdad after a brief interlude in Sāmarrāʾ – to which we shall return in the next chapter – these "Syrian" sources occupied a very limited space. Only the "obligatory passages" were preserved, particularly when no other alternative was available to the compilers. The sources composed in Abbasid Syria were subject to strategies of oblivion in establishing the historiographic vulgate – that is, the main corpus we shall designate here for the sake

234 Donner, *Narratives*, 304.

235 Al-Masʿūdī, *Murūj*, vol. 1, 12; trans. Pellat vol. 1, 5; Donner, *Narratives*, 195, 305; GAS, vol. 1, 312.

236 Al-Masʿūdī, *Murūj*, vol. 1, 14–5; trans. Pellat vol. 1, 6.

237 *Kitāb al-barahīn fī imāmat al-Umawiyyīn*, mentioned in the *Kitāb al-tanbīh*, 336–7, trans. 433. See also Cobb, *White Banners*, 51–5 and "Al-Maqrīzī," 70.

238 From the middle of the eighth century, the existence of texts composed in Arabic was known to societies neighboring the Islamic empire, as attested in the *T'ung tien*, a Chinese source presented by Tu Yu in 801 on the authority of a certain Tu Huan who was taken prisoner during the battle of Talas and was allowed to return to China in 762. In particular, the work offers a description of the barbarians of the West, the Arabs, of whom it is noted that they possess "a literature that is different than that of Persia." See Hoyland, *Seeing*, 245.

of convenience as "classical sources" – although they remained available and were employed by Abbasid compilers up until the exodus from Sāmarrāʾ.[239] These sources were thus either knowingly marginalised or were no longer available to certain authors working in Abbasid Iraq; their use at later dates by al-Masʿūdī or Ibn ʿAsākir, however, attests to their preservation.

Despite its apparent descent into deliberate oblivion, it is nevertheless true that the history rewritten during the Umayyad era left a lasting impression on Islamic historiography: the selections made during the Abbasid age could not always be divergent from those made under the first dynasty of Islam. Although much remains unknown, to a large extent this Umayyad-era historiographic construction still conditions how we approach the first centuries of Islam. In rethinking the history of its origins, the Islamic community, united around the caliphs of Damascus, bequeathed a massive inheritance both to its Abbasid successors as well as to Muslim society as a whole. Below, we shall see that partial access to these successive historiographic projects is indeed possible. In effect, Islamic historiography is not the only means of preserving these sources; analysis of the processes of intercultural transmission at work in the medieval Near East extant in non-Muslim sources, subject to an appropriate methodological framework, may open fertile new grounds for reflection.[240] Before approaching this broader corpus, however, it is essential to attempt to elucidate these successive layers of historical rewriting: only through this archaeology of the texts can we fully comprehend the complexity of these processes of historical transmission. This strategy also affords us the opportunity to identify successive historiographical filters or moments in which selections in the available material were made that would then determine the nature of other possible rewritings. We must now turn our attention to the consecutive crystallisations of dominant ideologies, the establishment of political "orthodoxies" and their accompanying historiographic filters.

---

239 See Rotter's investigations of the possibility of "Syrian" materials having been used in the Abbasid era, "Abū Zurʿa," 102.

240 On the Christian sources and the circulation of historical information in the Near East in the first centuries of Islam, see below, Ch. 3.

CHAPTER 2

A Time of Writings and Rewritings: Historiographic Filters and Vulgates

> We, the Arabs, report [events], present them in order from earliest to most recent, add and omit [as we see fit], but we do not seek to falsify.[1]

∵

This chapter is dedicated to the *moments* of historical writings and rewritings from the perspective of a history of meanings: successive rewritings correspond to an equivalent number of new meanings bestowed upon the past so that it conforms to the needs of an ever-changing present. Rewritings are conditioned by the prior existence of earlier writings; these earlier writings are notably those composed by the authors discussed in the previous chapter. However, the first Muslim sources written under the Umayyads and early Abbasids – many of which were produced in the Syrian space – do not survive. The prototypical difficulty facing any study concerned with the beginnings of Islam is this: we only have access to "later" sources dating to the third/ninth century at the earliest, the majority of which were composed in Iraq. From the strict perspective of the narrative sources, the Umayyads and the early Abbasids are thus on an equal footing, as they are only known to us through later sources.

The sources available today concerning the first centuries of Islam require a specific methodological approach, one that prevents us from merely recycling this history through the distorting prism of the great authors and compilers of the Abbasid era. The foundation of a vulgate in the chronographies, highly political in origin, came about through various historiographic mechanisms and layers of memory sedimentation that must be described. In order to present the full historical complexity of this vast phenomenon, the successive phases of historical rewriting must be elucidated on the basis of a tripartite

1 "… *Inna qawm ʿarab fa-nuqaddim wa-nuʾakhkhir wa-nazīd wa-nanquṣ, wa-lā nurīd bi-dhalik kādhiban*," Ibn Qutayba, *ʿUyūn*, vol. II, 136.

 | DOI:10.1163/9789004466326_004

hypothesis: the vulgate that was ultimately preserved was not the *only* vulgate that existed, but rather was the one whose success guaranteed its survival; earlier efforts, despite not achieving the same success, nevertheless influenced the final product; and other developments on the margins of this dominant vulgate remained possible. In other words, each rewriting was accompanied by selections, additions and omissions that made up these successive *historiographical filters*, filters that were not always possible to ignore. Thus, composing texts using materials selected by one's rivals or contemporaries was sometimes unavoidable.

2.1 In Search of Umayyad Historiographic Projects

It is possible to demonstrate the existence of historical writing during the Marwanid era; thus, it is important to understand the successive demands to which this production responded. Changing political needs during this period required concomitant changes in discourse. The necessary reinterpretations produced reorientations that must be traced so as to illuminate the phases of these Umayyad rewritings.

2.1.1 *"Common Link," "Collective* isnāds,*" or Umayyad Historiographic Filters?*

Scholars have long noted the omnipresence of certain transmitters in the major compilations. The best-documented example is that of Ibn Shihāb al-Zuhrī, to whom we shall return below. The prevalence of a limited number of authors has given rise to numerous different theories; many of these have concluded that a "common link"[2] or even "collective *isnāds*" – that is, a fundamental authority shared by all or most of the later compilers – must have existed. Produced at an early date by a small number of scholars, the tradition itself was responsible for generating these "obligatory passages" concerning certain figureheads: the mechanism was thus internal and, in a way, accidental.

These explanations appear to ignore the imperative necessity of controlling the past and, by extension, the writing of history. The high political stakes involved in this production resulted in struggles for control among the caliphal authorities and other elite groups: writings were succeeded by rewritings, one after the other, in accordance with the changing political winds, while the resulting texts gave rise to "historiographic debates." However, these rewritings

2 See Schoeler, "Mündliche Thora," 226, 230, and Cook's critique, "The Opponents," 465. See also Cook's remarks in "Eschatology and the Dating," 24 ff.

could not escape the problems posed by the available materials, as these materials were themselves the victims of successive attempts to gain mastery over the past. These sources were neither an infinite corpus nor unmarked by previous influences: "the starting point [of historiography] is not silence (by now irretrievable), but what has been said already."[3] Conversely, these rewritings were produced by this series of historiographic filters, and the creation of a new orthodoxy – that is, a new filter – was largely due to earlier processes of selection. The result is a paradoxical situation where efforts to reconcile the political adversaries of yesteryear conditioned the historical writing of their successors. This state of affairs goes beyond the classic opposition between the Umayyads and the Abbasids; the same problem is easily identifiable within each of these dynasties as well, as power struggles among various parties were exceedingly common.

The thorny question of the materials used by these early historians accompanies the problems of political intrigue. Donner suggests that a comparison of the sources demonstrates that al-Ṭabarī relied not on a mass of documents covering every possible subject, but rather on a thematically-organised documentary corpus from which he chose to highlight certain topics while remaining silent on others.[4] The "common kernel" of information shared by texts produced in different locations was discussed in the previous chapter. Beyond the question of whether or not this foundation was common to these diverse texts because it was "true," the "common kernel" linking the works of Abbasid historiography that survive presupposes the existence of earlier historiographic filters put in place by the Umayyads. In other words, this information can be found in the majority of the sources because its inclusion was impossible to avoid; it was not presented because of its qualitative character, but rather because of its exclusivity.

Studying these successive phases of rewriting – a veritable historiographic stratigraphy – is critical, not for rejecting the credibility of these sources, but for illuminating these different layers and juxtaposing them with other historiographies (Syriac, Byzantine, Armenian) as well as various other sources (archaeological, epigraphic, numismatic). Analysing these historiographic strata alongside other sources will allow us to date when certain information was put into circulation; this in turn will shed light on previously-hidden apologetic discourses, ideological programs, and historiographic projects that can be read as fragments of a past that refused to "stay buried."[5] The prevalence of

3 Rigney, "Time for Visions," 89, cited in Lorenz, "Comparative Historiography," 34.
4 Donner, *Narratives*, 129.
5 Here I borrow Geary's expression, *Phantoms of Remembrance*, 180.

certain dominant figures in the chains of transmission can no longer be solely attributed to the tradition itself, but is rather the result of an active process of historical writing that the caliphate tried to control, especially when competing with rival groups.[6] This does not mean that the entirety of the production that survives today – to say nothing of what does not – has passed through the filter of these successive rewritings. These key figures of transmission were also sometimes the victims of their own success: the abuse of the "label" al-Zuhrī is but one example.[7] In addition to distorting prisms, there are many other snares that twist our perception of these sources. More than just a "common link," the existence of common compulsory materials explains the reliance on such a limited number of transmitters.

The excavation of these successive layers is especially important, as it helps us to better understand both what we have and what we do not; it also allows us to comprehend the changing significations of a particular event from the perspective of a history of meanings. Here, the Christian sources play an essential role, not because they are "external" to the Islamic tradition, but because they provide access to lost substrata of historiographic sedimentation due to the history of the composition and transmission specific to these texts. Furthermore, the Christian sources are significant not for their differing viewpoints – which have often been regarded with suspicion[8] – but because they offer elements originating from different historiographic *moments*.

In this chapter, I shall attempt to bring these stages of rewriting that span the Umayyad period to light, although not without first giving due consideration to the risks and uncertainties inherent to such a project. Although I shall try to demonstrate the possibility of identifying multiple phases of writing – of which history is but one, and not necessarily foremost among similar labors undertaken in *ḥadīth*, *fiqh*, or even the Qurʾānic corpus itself – nothing allows us to confirm that this general framework was applied outside the immediate entourage of the caliphs and/or the scholars concerned, nor that it was systematically put into practice within this limited circle. Additionally, the partial or complete loss of sources produced during these different stages prevents the development of any sort of global vision of this phenomenon. Despite these challenges, this analysis is not a futile endeavour, as it allows for the

6 The question of the functions (social, political, etc.) of written culture has been widely studied by specialists in the medieval West. In particular, see Stock's classic study *The Implications of Literacy*; Geary, *Phantoms of Remembrance*; Spiegel, "Political Unity" and *Romancing the Past*; and the works of McKitterick, *The Carolingians and the Written Word*, *The Uses of Literacy* and *History and Memory*.

7 As de Prémare notes in *Les fondations*, 393.

8 For a detailed discussion of this problem, see Ch. 3, below.

elucidation of evolving political needs and changes in how a particular event was perceived.

An archaeology of texts, or more aptly of writings, aimed at establishing a stratigraphy of subsequent recompositions, is also indispensable with respect to "knowing subjects,"[9] namely, the historians who produced these layers. The study of rewritings is not merely that of the political projects that governed it, but also of the stages of different successive interpretations of the past. Oexle has recently emphasised the "historical conditions of historical knowledge, and more precisely of the *imaginarium*, the historians' imagination, these models of interpretation, representations, concepts and images that are the foundation and guide of historical knowledge."[10] We must consider the impact of the great events of the third/ninth century, as well as those surrounding this period, up through the compilation of the classical sources in the Abbasid era. From the anti-caliphate of Ibn al-Zubayr to the *miḥna*, the battle of Marj Rāḥiṭ (64–65/684), the third *fitna* (126–130/743–747), the "Abbasid Revolution" or the civil war that erupted following the death of al-Rashīd (193–198/809–813): how do we ignore the influence of these events upon the mental frameworks and "memorial images"[11] of the producers of narrative sources? The historiographic layers are reliant upon the strata of memory sedimentation and are inscribed in the "cultures of remembrance," of which "there is always a multiplicity ... that intertwine, meet or compete with one and other."[12] This multifaceted *Erinnerungskultur* doubles as a necessary reflection on the "history of meanings" (*Sinngeschichte*), or the histories of meanings later given by a particular epoch to a particular event, culture, or civilisation.[13] These elements are ample justification for this attempt to identify the subsequent phases of historical writing.

A final methodological note: the breakdown proposed below is clearly open to debate. Certain of these supposed layers of historiographic sedimentation provide too few concrete elements to be defined with absolute certainty. The idea of a process of historical stratification, however, is firmly supported by the information presented in the following pages. Ideally, this inquiry would begin with an attested rewriting of history in order to attempt to trace the events that ultimately caused it. However, the impossibility of such a demonstration

9 I borrow this expression from Oexle, "L'historicisation," 31.
10 Oexle, "L'historicisation," 31.
11 To use Assmann's phrase, *Ägypten. Eine Sinngeschichte*, 475 ff.
12 Oexle, "L'historicisation," 39, and by the same author, *Memoria als Kultur*, 9 ff.; these distorting prisms will be studied in greater detail in Ch. 4.
13 Oexle, "L'historicisation," 39–40. On the history of meaning(s), see Assmann, *Ägypten. Eine Sinngeschichte* and *Moses the Egyptian*. See also Thompson, "Reception Theory."

requires that we take the opposite approach, one that is replete with different hypotheses and doubts. This approach does offer the advantage of preserving a chronological thread; this firmly heuristic method is the only way to write a true history of meanings.

2.1.2 *Marwanid Writings and Rewritings*

During the Marwanid era, four major strata are identifiable; although these layers present various differences and internal evolutions, they nevertheless display a remarkable coherence with respect to Umayyad historiography.

2.1.2.1 Phase 1: Affirmation of Marwanid Authority (*c.*72–96/692–715)

Without making assumptions as to the nature of a historiography produced during the Sufyanid period, which predates the chronological framework of this inquiry but should by no means be excluded *a priori* with regard to Muʿāwiya's political stature and oft-noted interest in history – prevalent in the sources and mentioned in the preceding chapter – we must first turn our attention to the turmoil that characterised the beginning years of the period examined in this study. The conflict between Ibn al-Zubayr and the Umayyad caliphate poses several questions relevant to our purposes here, foremost among them: was this competition for power and caliphal legitimacy transferred into the written domain?[14]

Limited evidence exists to address this question, although it is clear that the opposition between these two parties had a polemic dimension which lent itself perfectly to lengthy historiographic discussions. The dominant figure of the period was ʿUrwa b. al-Zubayr, famous for the letters he exchanged with ʿAbd al-Malik.[15] An episode familiar to specialists in the period merits our attention, despite the fact that it slightly predates the period under examination here, concerning the attitude of the traditionist – the brother of the anti-caliph – during the battle of al-Ḥarra (64/683).[16] On the occasion of this Umayyad victory over the Medinese insurgents, ʿUrwa is said to have burned the works of *fiqh* in his possession out of caution, an act that he would later regret.[17] Scholarly opinion is divided over the question of whether ʿUrwa himself authored these texts or if they were merely texts belonging to him that

14 Like the image of Ibn Zubayr himself, this episode has undergone numerous significant revisions. See Campbell, *Telling Memories*; Madelung, "ʿAbd Allāh b. al-Zubayr," and Cook's remarks in "Eschatology and the Dating," 32–8.

15 For more on these letters, see de Prémare, *Les fondations*, 14–6.

16 See Kister, "The Battle."

17 Ibn Saʿd, *al-Ṭabaqāt*, vol. v, 179; see also Schoeler, *The Genesis*, 51 n. 19.

were composed by other authors.[18] Landau-Tasseron has questioned the veracity of the episode itself, suggesting that it is simply a literary artifice that should be situated within the context of the early Muslim debate over the permissibility of writing;[19] indeed, it is entirely possible that burning books figures into this *topos*, as various similar events are attested in the sources during this same period.[20] If ʿUrwa's destructive actions during this battle are taken at face value, however, another possible interpretation arises: fearing for his life, he burned his works (or those in his possession) because they were clearly written in the service of his brother and the Zubayrid claims to power. The sources show that Medinese scholars often found themselves in this ambiguous and uncomfortable position; al-Zuhrī, whose father fought alongside Ibn al-Zubayr, was one such figure. This conflict motivated ʿAbd al-Malik's decision to strike the names of the al-Zubayr family from the *dīwān*, which subsequently complicated ʿUrwa's integration in the caliphal entourage.[21] The second *fitna* quite possibly marked a turning point in the writing of history. Although Medinese intellectuals may have originally supported Ibn al-Zubayr, ʿAbd al-Malik's efforts allowed them to later take up their pens in service of the Umayyads; al-Zuhrī is an example of this situation, for although initially he was subjected to financial sanctions, he was later well compensated for his services.

Poetry offers a similar example to that of historiography during this period; the poet al-Akhṭal (d. c. 92/710) composed a panegyric dedicated to ʿAbd al-Malik in celebration of the restoration of Marwanid power.[22] Although the conditions surrounding this text's transmission merit greater attention,[23] Suzanne Stetkevych proposes that its composition dates to "the year [of the reestablishment of] the community" (*ʿām al-jamāʿa*) marking the end of the second *fitna* in 73/692.[24] This ode to Umayyad victory introduced a new link to the past, one that Stetkevych does not hesitate to call a "culture-defining moment:" by deliberately choosing the pre-Islamic *qaṣīda* form, al-Akhṭal and his colleagues established a "code [that] allows a community to consolidate its historical experiences, conferring sense on them." This "epic code" became "the medium through which society takes possession of its own past and gives

18 De Prémare, *Les fondations*, 387, and Schoeler, *The Genesis*, 42, support the first hypothesis, while the second is presented by Landau-Tasseron, "On the Reconstruction," 52–3.
19 Landau-Tasseron, "On the Reconstruction," 53.
20 Al-Iṣfahānī claims, for instance, that ʿAbd al-Malik burned the *Maṭālib al-ʿArab* of Ziyād b. Abīhi. See Elad, "Community of Believers," 269.
21 See Lecker, "Biographical Notes," 47, and Elad, "Community of Believers," 266–7.
22 The specific problems posed by Umayyad poetry are discussed in Ch. 3.
23 On the transmission of al-Akhṭal's *dīwān*, see Seidensticker, "Al-Akhṭal."
24 Stetkevych, "Umayyad Panegyric," 92.

that past the matrix value of a model."[25] It is also the formal means of transmitting an imperial ideology and a "rhetoric of the caliphate"[26] in the context of constructing a "vision of a legitimizing past."[27] Al-Akhṭal's panegyric attests to the Marwanids' pressing need to write themselves into history at the end of the greatest crisis the Umayyads had ever faced. By weaving new threads in the direction of the Arab past and the *jāhiliyya*, a period of Umayyad tribal dominance, ʿAbd al-Malik and his cohort initiated the process of reaffirming the authority of the first Islamic dynasty.

Caskel has shed light on the important genealogical work that took place during the Umayyad era both before and after the battle of Marj Rāhiṭ (64–65/684).[28] The second *fitna* contributed to the reconstruction of certain lines of tribal division. New alliances emerged, such as the incorporation of the tribe of Ṣāliḥ into Tanūkh in the confederation of Quḍāʿa; for now, however, it is interesting to note that these efforts at codification were also part of a larger project aimed at forging new links with the past.

The sweeping efforts at reasserting power initiated by ʿAbd al-Malik had a distinct written dimension. These initiatives first took place in the scriptural realm, judging from al-Ḥajjāj's sizable intervention on the Qurʾānic text,[29] the Qurʾānic inscriptions on the Dome of the Rock, and the institution of a strictly epigraphic currency. The caliph's ambitious reforms aimed at the Arabisation of the Umayyad state administration must also be noted. Saliba has highlighted the foundational character of this transformation, seeing it as the inaugural force behind the famous "translation movement" from Greek and Persian into Arabic[30] that created an atmosphere conducive to the development of translators and scholars: these functionaries of the *dīwān*, their descendants and successors would become the *kuttāb* of the late Umayyad and early Abbasid periods. Saliba also suggests that these translated *dīwān*s were more than simple registers used for administrative purposes; rather, they were a much larger group of texts, comprised in particular of scientific works.[31] A historiographic dimension may have accompanied these different projects, among other

25 Stetkevych, "Umayyad Panegyric," 91, citing Conte, *The Rhetoric of Imitation*, 142.
26 Stetkevych, "Umayyad Panegyric," 90.
27 Stetkevych, "Umayyad Panegyric," 90, citing Khalidi, *Arabic Historical Thought*, 29.
28 Caskel, *Jamharat*, vol. 1, 41–4. See also Kennedy, "From Oral Tradition to Written Record," 540 ff., and Orthmann's exhaustive study *Stamm und Macht*.
29 De Prémare, "ʿAbd al-Malik."
30 Saliba opposes the idea that this "translation movement" did not begin until the Abbasid era, an idea notably defended by Gutas, *Greek Thought*. Saliba bases his arguments in particular on the evidence provided by Ibn al-Nadīm's *Fihrist*; see *Islamic Science*, Ch. 2.
31 Saliba, *Islamic Science*, 55.

better-known developments, with powerful men the likes of Rajāʾ b. Ḥaywa, al-Ḥajjāj and al-Zuhrī. If this hypothesis is valid, it implies that this recomposition of the past began just before the turn of the second/eighth century. The undertaking was essential at this time in order to quash Zubayrid claims and silence other dissenting voices contesting the legitimacy of the Umayyads or the Marwanids, who had recently come to power; ʿAbd al-Malik's policies, from the construction of the Dome of the Rock to financial reform, all bear witness to this necessity.[32] This overhaul of writing practices conditioned later rewritings because of the processes of selection and omission that it set in motion; it also partially explains why we consider the Marwanids to have played such a decisive role in matters of administration, historiography and codification.[33]

The caliphate of al-Walīd (86–96/705–715) generally appears to be a continuation of ʿAbd al-Malik's policies. He cultivated his father's ambitious architectural program with the construction of the great mosque of Damascus.[34] The peace and prosperity that characterised his caliphate in the wake of ʿAbd al-Malik's tumultuous restoration of Marwanid power has led some scholars to see al-Walīd's reign as the apogee of the Umayyad era. This political continuity, accompanied by the constant presence of al-Ḥajjāj,[35] doubtless required little to no historiographic revision; rather, it is under Sulaymān or ʿUmar II that new impulses must be sought.

2.1.2.2 Phase 2: Attempts at Reform and Counter-Reform (*c.*96–105/715–724)

As Shaban notes, these two caliphates – despite their relative brevity – were highly politically charged, presenting very different projects than those undertaken by ʿAbd al-Malik and al-Walīd.[36] Sulaymān's accession following al-Walīd's efforts to convince him to renounce his caliphal rights in favour of ʿAbd al-ʿAzīz b. al-Walīd, the latter's son,[37] likely necessitated the production of

32 Among many works on this subject, see Johns, "Archaeology and the History of Early Islam;" Robinson, *ʿAbd al-Malik*; and Donner, "Umayyad Efforts and Legitimation."

33 These efforts to control the past initiated by ʿAbd al-Malik may help to explain the particular difficulties that the first seventy years of the *hijra* pose to historians, from the question of historical writing (see Donner, *Narratives*, 120–1) to more recent archaeological issues (see Johns, "Archaeology and the History of Early Islam"). See also Donner, *Muhammad and the Believers*, ch. 5.

34 On the Umayyad mosque of Damascus, see Flood, *The Great Mosque*; Grafman and Rosen-Ayalon, "The Two Great Syrian."

35 See Shaban, *Islamic History*, vol. I, 100 ff., and Cobb, "The Empire in Syria."

36 Shaban, *Islamic History*, vol. I, 127–37; see also below, Ch. 8, on the consequences of the regionalisation of Marwanid power.

37 Al-Ṭabarī, vol. II, 1274; trans. vol. XXIII, 222.

a discourse intended to assert the new caliph's legitimacy. No less problematic was the designation of ʿUmar b. ʿAbd al-ʿAzīz as successor,[38] complicated by the fact that his father, the brother of ʿAbd al-Malik, had been dispossessed of his right of succession in favour of al-Walīd b. ʿAbd al-Malik.[39] The internal power-struggles of the Umayyad family and the complications to the line of succession beginning with Sulaymān and continuing through ʿUmar II resulted in a political transformation that was likely accompanied by a historiographic one; below, we shall see that historical writing more or less contemporary with the reign of ʿUmar II is well-attested in the sources. Additionally, an important effort at collection and codification is associated with ʿUmar II, in the field of *ḥadīth* as well as the Prophetic *sunna*; these aspects are combined with a strong caliphal epistolary tradition reflected in the narrative sources, in which several letters attributed to ʿUmar II are preserved.[40]

The policies of these two caliphs must also be viewed within the context of the apocalyptic and messianic expectations occasioned by the approach of the year 100 of the *hijra*.[41] Although these apprehensions turned out to be unwarranted, they necessitated another phase of rewriting so as to give new meaning to a present no one had expected to arrive. Sulaymān's complex portrait may have emerged from these successive layers of interpretation centred around the figure of the caliph.[42] We have only to consider Sulaymān's sweeping and ambitious plan to seize Constantinople, resulting in Maslama b. ʿAbd al-Malik's long siege of the city,[43] or ʿUmar II's fiscal reforms:[44] these policies are sufficient to highlight the existence of political projects distinct from those of the preceding period, as well as an important proliferation of writing – widely attested during ʿUmar II's caliphate – in both the religious and administrative spheres. Narrowing our focus to the caliph ʿUmar II's exceptional image in the Islamic tradition indicates the early date – 730 at the latest – at which these elements were recorded in writing, an act that may constitute an effort at historical rewriting.[45]

---

38 See Becker, "Studien," 21 ff.; Barthold, "The Caliph ʿUmar II," 79–80; Bosworth, "Rajāʾ ibn Ḥaywa," 48 ff.; Eisner, *Zwischen Faktum und Fiktion*, 213 ff.; Mayer, "Neue Aspekte," 109–15; and Borrut, "Entre tradition et histoire," 333.

39 Zettersteen, "ʿAbd al-ʿAzīz;" Cobb, "The Empire in Syria," 227.

40 The majority of these letters have been compiled by Ṣafwat, *Jamharat*, vol. II, 310–93.

41 Borrut, "Entre tradition et histoire," 339–45.

42 Eisener, *Zwischen Faktum und Fiktion*.

43 For more on this episode, see Ch. 5.

44 See Gibb's classic article "The Fiscal Rescript;" Guessous, "Le rescrit fiscal;" and Borrut, "Entre tradition et histoire," 359 ff.

45 Borrut, "Entre tradition et histoire," 345 ff.; see also Chs. 3 and 6 below.

Yazīd b. ʿAbd al-Malik's accession marked the return to ʿAbd al-Malik's preferred form of strictly filial succession following the caliphate of ʿUmar b. ʿAbd al-ʿAzīz. Shaban considers this a moment of "counter-reform"[46] in reaction to the two preceding caliphates, as they had decidedly different goals than those envisioned by ʿAbd al-Malik or al-Walīd. Despite this apparent return to the norms established by ʿAbd al-Malik, the caliphate of Yazīd II was burdened with the question of images:[47] could this iconophobia persist without writings aimed at justifying it? Could the justifications for this political decision be sought in the early history of the Islamic community? Questions such as these could easily have provoked rewritings of history on a much larger scale; thus, we must place this caliphate within this phase marked by many competing political projects.

Despite the divergences and successive reorientations, the period as a whole is characterised by changing needs distinct from the ambitions of ʿAbd al-Malik or al-Walīd. The latter's abortive attempt to upend his father's established line of succession doubtless set off the reaction that was only prolonged by the murky conditions of ʿUmar II's accession and the political choices of Yazīd II. Nevertheless, it should be noted that the short duration of these three caliphates tends to highlight the notion of this period's volatility in comparison with the relative stability that defined the final years of ʿAbd al-Malik's and al-Walīd's caliphates.

2.1.2.3 Phase 3: Hishām and al-Zuhrī (*c.*105–125/724–743)

Hishām was the last of ʿAbd al-Malik's sons[48] to hold the caliphate, thus bringing his father's plans to fruition; al-Zuhrī, already active under ʿAbd al-Malik, remained so throughout most of the Marwanid period until his death in 124/742. This phase is most notable for its changes in scale: the Hishām/al-Zuhrī team defined this period of vast codification projects and the creation of a Marwanid historiographic filter. Al-Zuhrī was truly the memory of the Umayyad tradition; indeed, his contributions marked a turning point in historiographic production. The acceleration of the processes of historical recomposition, alongside the formation of this caliph/scholar duo, was likely occasioned by the transition of the caliphate to al-Ruṣāfa, a move that required explanation and justification; it was also beneficial to the foundation of a "Marwanid orthodoxy" in the face of growing Qadarite sympathies. This project was predicated on defining the field of authorised political and religious interpretations; to stray from

46 Shaban, *Islamic History*, vol. I, 127 ff.

47 On this subject, see Crone, "Islam, Judeo-Christianity" and Griffith, "Images, Islam."

48 On his caliphate, see Blankinship, *The End of the Jihād State*.

the path prescribed by the caliphal authority was to commit heresy, the requisite obverse of any orthodoxy.[49] Such is the case regarding the change in attitudes toward Ghaylān al-Dimashqī, who was executed at the end of Hishām's caliphate.[50]

However, nothing embodies these efforts at controlling the tradition and production of the past as much as these two emblematic figures of the Umayyad era. Even the length of Hishām's caliphate, associated with al-Zuhrī's growing notoriety, was favourable to their intentions. In the previous chapter, we described the ties linking the great Medinese scholar to the Umayyad caliphs and his particular influence in committing *ḥadīth*s to writing and educating the crown princes during the reign of Hishām. The majority of his projects were likely undertaken and completed at al-Ruṣāfa.[51] Al-Zuhrī's remarkable longevity as a member of the caliphal entourage had important implications for the field of historiography. As one of the most significant producers of the tradition and historical writing during the first half of the second/eighth century, al-Zuhrī established himself as an "obligatory step" for future generations of historians and traditionists. This may explain al-Awzāʿī's particular concern in demonstrating al-Zuhrī's integrity, despite this latter's frequent and otherwise blameworthy contact with the Umayyads: the indispensable nature of al-Zuhrī's works "imposed" this more nuanced presentation of al-Awzāʿī's famous predecessor.[52] Al-Manṣūr himself invoked the example of al-Zuhrī to complete the education of his son, the future caliph al-Mahdī.[53] These are essentially the same reasons that led modern scholars to see al-Zuhrī as one of the major figures in the transition from oral to written transmission.[54]

His preeminence in texts from the first decades of the second/eighth century signifies that al-Zuhrī himself constitutes a historiographic filter. He is an essential and unavoidable figure of transmission, be it in the domain of history, tradition, or *fiqh*. The relationships between masters and their disciples, forming a dense network among scholars, further reinforced this state of affairs: al-Zuhrī, himself the heir of ʿUrwa b. al-Zubayr, produced numerous disciples, among them Mālik b. Anas. His famous students were largely responsible for the diffusion of accounts attributed to al-Zuhrī, thereby subsequently solidifying the existence of a historiographic filter. Mālik cites several passages related

49 On the implications of this definition of orthodoxy, see Judd, *The Third Fitna*.

50 See Judd, "Ghaylān al-Dimashqī."

51 On al-Ruṣāfa, see Fowden, *The Barbarian Plain*; Sack, *Resafa IV*; and Ch. 3 below.

52 Lecker, "Biographical Notes," 37.

53 Al-Ṭabarī, vol. III, 404; trans. vol. XXIX, 107.

54 Abbott, *Studies*, vol. II, 53, 80 ff., 184, 196; Cook, "The Opponents," 439.

to the Umayyads in the *Muwaṭṭaʾ* on the authority of al-Zuhrī.[55] On a more political note, ʿAbd al-Malik's project of reclaiming elite scholars in the service of the Umayyads in order to counter Zubayrid pretensions here reached its apogee: networks were henceforth established, and a historiographic filter was in place. The success of this enterprise was definitive. The Abbasids and their historiographers subsequently could not make do without al-Zuhrī, nor could they dispense with the circle of scholars in the entourage of the last Umayyad caliphs.

The undeniable success of this historiographic production could not completely conceal the rivalries within the ruling family, nor could it assuage the petty jealousies and resentments that had accumulated; on the contrary, the codification projects may have exacerbated them. Hishām's reign ended with the implosion of the Umayyad caliphate after this one last shining moment, and the third *fitna* broke the caliphate's momentum as well as the continuity of certain policies designed to exercise control over the past.

2.1.2.4 Phase 4: The Third *fitna* and the Fall of the Umayyad Caliphate (*c.*125–132/743–750)

The final years of the Umayyad caliphate are seen as a period of turmoil during which numerous projects were initiated that could not be completed under the circumstances.[56] The rivalry between the different contenders for the throne and the powerful groups supporting them was not merely a military conflict: it also had historiographic dimensions connected to each claimant's desire to prove his legitimacy.

The remarkable diffusion of al-Zuhrī's works took place despite the efforts taken to prevent it. The contentious relations between the scholar and the heir apparent, al-Walīd b. al-Yazīd, could not have produced a favourable environment for the transmission of his writings following the caliphate of Hishām. Furthermore, after the assassination of al-Walīd II (125/743),[57] we are told that al-Zuhrī's works were removed from the caliphal library; the number of his

55 For example: Mālik b. Anas, *Muwaṭṭaʾ*, 13 n. 1 (ʿUmar II); 521 n. 1410 (ʿAbd al-Malik). This chain of transmission is not exclusive, however, and the information relating to the Umayyads in the *Muwaṭṭaʾ* originates with several other sources. For ʿUmar II, see Borrut, "Entre tradition et histoire," 359 ff.; ʿAbd al-Malik's role in the *Muwaṭṭaʾ* is noted by Ibn Khaldūn, *The Muqaddimah*, vol. I, 423.

56 For more on the general context of this period, see Cobb, "The Empire in Syria," and Judd, *The Third Fitna*.

57 On this episode, see Judd, *The Third Fitna*, 72 ff.; Hamilton, *Walid and his Friends*; and Kennedy, "Al-Walīd II." On al-Bakhrāʾ, the site of his assassination, see Genequand, "Al-Bakhrāʾ."

works must have been considerable, as their removal required the labor of several pack animals.[58] This episode shows that the classic judgment concerning the Abbasid destruction and suppression of historiography and the Umayyad archives must be revisited; the casualties produced by the final turbulent years of Umayyad rule must be considered as well. The Qadarite rise to power with the accession of Yazīd III (126/744) represents a period of adamant opposition to the codification projects of previous eras;[59] reversals in tribal alliances posed similar problems. And what of the supposedly "justifiable" assassination of the caliph al-Walīd II? Acts of rewriting and purposeful selection were indispensable during this period: imposing a new orthodoxy required a total reinterpretation of previous sources, although the unrest that characterised the final days of the Umayyad era likely did not provide the most auspicious environment for this undertaking.

In the wake of these brief but politically-charged caliphates, Marwān II's attempts to regain control mark the end of the Umayyad period. Here again, we find that alongside the obvious military aspects accompanying the caliph's efforts to assert his authority throughout the empire, a written dimension played a role in this reaffirmation of caliphal power as well. The caliphate also witnessed a new transition of the Umayyad empire's centre of gravity; after moving to al-Ruṣāfa under Hishām, the capital would now cross the Euphrates and settle in Ḥarrān, a city controlled by northern Arabian tribes, new allies of the caliph.[60] This shift likely required the production of a discourse to justify it. It is also probable that the Qaysite elites were favourably disposed toward a reinterpretation of certain unfortunate events in Umayyad history; furthermore, the reversal of tribal alliances, more durable than that outlined during the brief caliphate of al-Walīd II, had serious repercussions at the highest levels of governance. It should be noted here that Ḥarrān's specific impact as a cultural centre deserves greater scholarly attention. Although little evidence exists to document these questions, the significant epistolary production attributed to ʿAbd al-Ḥamīd, a *kātib* of Marwān II, nevertheless attests to the political importance of writing.[61] This importance may have extended to other

---

58 The oldest source mentioning this episode is Ibn Saʿd, *al-Ṭabaqāt*, vol. II, 389; other authors would later recycle this information. See Schoeler, *The Genesis*, 48.

59 On the efforts to establish a Marwanid religious orthodoxy, see Judd, *The Third Fitna*, particularly 132 ff.

60 On the power dynamics of the Umayyad period, see below, Ch. 8.

61 On ʿAbd al-Ḥamīd's letters, see ʿAbbās, *ʿAbd al-Ḥamīd*; Schönig, *Das Sendschreiben*; al-Qāḍī, "Early Islamic State Letters" and "The Religious Foundation;" and below, Ch. 3. For general context on the period, see the older studies of Dennett, *Marwan ibn Muhammad*.

types of writing as well, and history, reinterpreted in the service of new needs, was naturally employed in epistles produced at court.

In light of these considerations, the Marwanid period must be studied from a new angle: as an era that constructed both a history and one or rather multiple historiographies. Although the power struggles of the Umayyad period manifested in political, economic, and tribal competition, a historiographic competition was underway as well. The processes of selection and destruction were already at work during the first Islamic dynasty. Relation by blood no longer signified political continuity or lasting agreements on major projects. Umayyad historiographies were not *one* but *many*; despite the fragmentary nature of our knowledge of these layers of rewriting, studying them is essential for elucidating the caliphs' plans and goals and understanding the transformations that occurred in the written corpus that survives. The supposed shockwave of the "Abbasid Revolution" must be qualified in historiographic terms; the active mechanisms of this historiography were already present under the Umayyads, and its continuities are well-attested in the historical sources, especially those from the Syrian space. The implications of this statement are important for our comprehension of early Islamic historiography: the authors of the Abbasid era did not have an unlimited amount of untouched material at their disposal for writing history. Rather, their texts were the involuntary products of the historiographic filters inherited from the recent Islamic past. With respect to the narrative sources, the early Abbasids are not better-documented than the late Umayyads: the period stretching from 132/750 through to the composition of the great "classical" sources of the third/ninth and fourth/tenth centuries was also subject to successive reinterpretations that must be decoded in light of the strata of Marwanid historiography.

Thus far, we have demonstrated the existence of an early historiographic production in the Syrian space, both during the Umayyad and Abbasid eras. However, these texts suffered very different fates, and many have fallen into oblivion. Additionally, the Umayyad caliphs, concerned with mastery of the political uses of the past, initiated several phases of historical rewriting in order to adapt the past to the changing needs of the present. The new Abbasid authority would undertake similar historiographic projects in the face of challenges to their legitimacy, in particular those of the Alids. While the political need for historiography remained roughly the same, however, the location of authoritative historiographic production changed. "Caliphal historiography" left the Syrian space for Iraq, a move solidified by the foundation of Baghdad in 145/762; this momentous occasion itself necessitated historical rewriting on a grand scale. A new situation thus arose, in which the history of Syria was henceforth written in Iraq, despite the fact that historiographic production endured in the Syrian space. The classical Islamic historiography that survives is the product of these Iraqi recompositions; thus, we now turn our attention to these texts.

2.2 Toward a Historiographic Vulgate: The History of Syria Rewritten in Abbasid Iraq

To study the production of Syrian history from Iraq requires that we step outside of the strictly Syrian framework adopted up until this point in order to understand the processes that presided over these Abbasid rewritings. The dating of the preserved sources also demands that we not limit ourselves to the authors of the second/eighth century: rather, it is essential that we move beyond these chronological boundaries to illuminate the successive layers of historiographic sedimentation and identify the distorting prisms that influenced these recompositions throughout the third/ninth and fourth/tenth centuries.

We know the history of the first centuries of Islam through the great compilations composed during the Abbasid period, particularly al-Ṭabarī's incomparable *Taʾrīkh al-rusul wa-al-mulūk*, which appears to be a pre-interpreted, "ready-to-use" history. El-Hibri has recently argued that such narrative sources were not originally composed to convey facts and information, but to provide commentaries on various political, social, economic and cultural aspects related to certain controversies.[62] Furthermore, an intense project of reinterpretation and rewriting was indispensable and clearly took place at the turn of the third-fourth/ninth-tenth centuries. The vulgate that resulted therefrom completed the recomposition efforts underway since the days of the first Abbasid caliphs. The relative and progressive descent of Syrian historiography into oblivion – even though its production is well-attested under the late Umayyads as well as the early Abbasids – was above all connected to this vast project initiated elsewhere aimed at establishing an "official past" in the service of the new dynasty. In this sense, the project was clearly one of "creative forgetting."[63]

2.2.1 *Layers of Historical Rewriting under the Early Abbasids*

Attempting to identify the stages of historical rewriting that took place during the Abbasid era is a risky endeavor, as witnessed by the difficulties of Umayyad

62 El-Hibri, *Reinterpreting*, 13; see also Keaney, *Remembering Rebellion*, 2 ff.

63 Geary, "Oblivion," 111.

historiography mentioned above. The greater regularity of the rhythm of political history in the early years of the new dynasty allows us to shed light on the Abbasids efforts to affirm the legitimacy of their rule in the face of competing claims. The first decades of the Abbasid era, from the fall of the Umayyads to the civil war between al-Amīn and al-Maʾmūn, were essentially dedicated to this enterprise.[64]

2.2.1.1 Phase 5: Affirming Abbasid Legitimacy (*c.*132–193/750–809)

Although this chronological division defines a period often treated by modern historians as a relatively homogeneous whole, this homogeneity is less certain from a historiographic perspective. A few textual indications from al-Mahdī's caliphate (158–169/775–785) offer a point of departure for our attempts to decode this process. The anonymous author of the *Akhbār al-dawla al-ʿAbbāsiyya*, an openly apologetic work, indicates that the caliph had affirmed the legitimacy of the imamate of al-ʿAbbās b. ʿAbd al-Muṭṭalib, the eponymous ancestor of the Abbasids.[65] The stakes here were high: the pre-Islamic past, like the Prophetic period, were decisive stages in this process of legitimation. Manipulating these historical origins was aimed at claiming proximity to the Prophet, as well as the early conversion of certain key figures to Islam or their ties to Muḥammad.[66] In order to establish themselves exclusively as the *ahl al-bayt*, the Abbasids had to contest the similarly-constructed Umayyad claims to legitimacy[67] as well as the rival claims to power of the Alids and others. To combat the Alids, the Abbasids tried to establish the legitimacy of al-ʿAbbās b. ʿAbd al-Muṭṭalib over that of his brother, Abū Ṭālib (see fig. 0.4).

This project was an integral part of a broader plan initiated by al-Mahdī aimed at integrating the Abbasid family into both Islamic history and the architectural landscape, as witnessed by the substitution of his name for that of al-Walīd b. ʿAbd al-Malik on the walls of the mosque of Medina.[68] Despite their fragmentary nature, these elements attest to the Abbasid caliphate's serious preoccupation with establishing its legitimacy. These episodes are particularly significant in the context of the layers of historiographic recomposition:

---

64 For the history of this period, and in particular the political history, see Kennedy, *The Early Abbasid Caliphate*, and Sourdel, *L'état impérial*, 9–91.

65 "*fa-raddahum al-Mahdī ilā ithbāt al-imāma li-al-ʿAbbās b. ʿAbd al-Muṭṭalib*," *Akhbār*, 165. See also Sharon, "The Umayyads," 142, and Crone, *Medieval Islamic*, 92.

66 See Afsaruddin, *Excellence and Precedence*.

67 Sharon, "The Umayyads."

68 On the embattled Umayyad memory, see below, Ch. 4; the patronage of the early Abbasids has been studied by Robinson, *Islamic Historiography*, 26.

they clearly describe manipulations of existing texts and the fabrication of a new past in accordance with the needs of the present.

Prior to al-Mahdī's rule, the historiographic production of the first twenty-five years of the Abbasid caliphate is more difficult to judge. *The Anonymous History of the Abbasids* does not specify their predecessors' policies toward their illustrious ancestor, the half-brother of the Prophet's father. The Shiite author al-Yaʿqūbī reports, however, that al-Manṣūr was the first Hashimite to make a distinction between the sons of al-ʿAbbās b. ʿAbd al-Muṭṭalib and those of Abū Ṭālib b. ʿAbd al-Muṭṭalib: this distinction is the origin of the terms ʿAbbāsī and Ṭālibī.[69] These episodes reveal the need to assert the superiority of the descendants of al-ʿAbbās over any potential challengers. The argument rests on the fact that the Prophet did not designate ʿAlī or anyone else as his successor, and that his paternal uncle, al-ʿAbbās, was thus invested with his authority upon death, due to his status as a paternal kinsman and in accordance with the rules of tribal society. The revolt of Muḥammad al-Nafs al-Zakiyya in 145/762, the first major challenge to Abbasid authority, was undoubtedly one of the main triggers of this legitimising project.[70] Led by a powerful adversary and motivated by his strong claims to power, rooted in his Ḥassanid lineage[71] and messianic aspects,[72] this revolt quickly led to the new dynasty's loss of the Arabian holy sites. Al-Manṣūr found himself in a situation somewhat similar to that faced by ʿAbd al-Malik from Zubayrid claims:[73] both caliphs needed to mount strong military and discursive counterattacks to these oppositions in order to regain control of the holy cities and defeat enemy propaganda.

Al-Manṣūr's caliphate (136–158/754–775) likely produced a vast historiographic project, marked as it was by the fierce rivalries of these early years of the dynasty[74] and the foundation of Baghdad in 145/762. How could such significant events *not* have necessitated the production of a discourse to explain and justify them? This question, however, is particularly difficult to

69 Al-Yaʿqūbī, *Mushākalat*, 22–3; trans. 338. On the hypothesis of a rivalry between the two Hashimite branches from the Umayyad period on, see Elad's reservations, "The Rebellion," 158, as well as Omar, "Some Aspects."

70 For a detailed analysis of this episode, see Elad, "The Rebellion."

71 Muḥammad b. ʿAbd Allāh b. al-Ḥasan b. al-Ḥasan b. ʿAlī b. Abī Ṭālib, better known as Muḥammad al-Nafs al-Zakiyya or the "pure soul," was a descendant of al-Ḥasan, the son of ʿAlī.

72 See Elad, "The Rebellion," 148, 153 ff., and Zaman, "The Nature."

73 The Zubayrids offered support during the revolt of Muḥammad al-Nafs al-Zakiyya; see Elad, "The Rebellion," 182.

74 In addition to the rebellion of al-Nafs al-Zakiyya, see also the pretensions of ʿAbd Allāh b. ʿAlī surrounding the succession of al-Saffāḥ; for more on this episode, see below, Ch. 7.

answer, as the problem of the return to Baghdad after an interlude in Sāmarrā' (221–279/836–892) looms over the founding of Baghdad itself. For this reason, it is often difficult to know whether a text about the round city or its founder should be read in the context of the city's foundation or the caliphate's return to Baghdad.

Al-Manṣūr's patronage of historical writing is relatively well-attested.[75] The most obvious example is that of Ibn Isḥāq (d. c. 150/767), who took refuge at the caliph's court and composed (or reworked) several volumes (in particular one on the *maghāzī*)[76] for him; of these, only the *Sīra* survives in the recension of Ibn Hishām (d. 218/833).[77] The fact that writing was used for political purposes under al-Manṣūr requires no additional demonstration. Gutas has insisted on the importance of the "translation movement" that constituted part of a broader imperial project.[78] The considerable attention given to astrology during this period is also salient, particularly with respect to the use of astrologers to determine the most auspicious date for the founding of Baghdad. This interest resulted in the composition of astrological histories,[79] where planetary conjunctions were the driving force of history; among these works are those by Abū Sahl b. Nawbakht (d. 170/786) and Māshā'allāh (active from the reign of al-Manṣūr through al-Ma'mūn).[80]

---

75 It should be noted that this caliph was also interested in other literary genres, as attested by his request for the compilation of a volume of poems collected by al-Mufaḍḍal b. Muḥammad b. Ya'lā al-Ḍabbī (d. 164/780 or 170/786), who was also the tutor of the future al-Mahdī; this collection quickly became known as *al-Mufaḍḍaliyyāt*. On this text, see Jacobi, "Al-Mufaḍḍaliyyāt," and Schoeler, "Writing and Publishing," 428.

76 Abbott, *Studies*, vol. 1, 89, and Sellheim, "Prophet, Calif und Geschichte," 40.

77 The importance of al-Manṣūr's patronage in the composition of the *Sīra* has been discussed by Sellheim, "Prophet, Calif und Geschichte." See also Robinson, *Islamic Historiography*, 26.

78 Gutas, *Greek Thought*, 28–60.

79 These astrological histories have been relatively little-studied, despite important works such as those of Pingree and Kennedy. This deficit has been noted by Gutas, *Greek Thought*, 46 n. 34. More broadly, the role of these astrologers/astronomers and historians at the court, especially under the early Abbasids, merits a more detailed inquiry, one which I propose to undertake elsewhere.

80 The collection of titles attributed to Abū Sahl b. Nawbakht is unfortunately lost; only a few citations have been preserved, in particular by Ibn al-Nadīm in the *Fihrist*, 238–9. This passage was translated by Gutas, *Greek Thought*, 38–40, who also provides a bibliography on Abū Sahl (see in particular Pingree, "Abū Sahl b. Nawbakht"). Māshā'allāh's *Astrological History* also does not survive in its original form, although large extracts have been preserved by a Christian astrologer of the ninth century named Ibn Hibintā. See Kennedy and Pingree, *The Historical Astrology*, and Pingree, "Māshā'allāh."

The existence of even earlier historical writing under the caliphate of Abū al-ʿAbbās al-Saffāḥ[81] is yet another question. The recent dynastic change would almost certainly have required a judicious use of the past; however, due to the lack of available sources, this statement remains pure conjecture. Despite the dearth of narrative sources, epigraphic elements attest to the new Abbasid caliphate's concern with writing itself into the space and affirming its messianic dimension: the inscriptions at Baysān in Palestine or Ṣanaʿāʾ in Yemen representing the first Abbasid caliph as the *mahdī* bear witness to this fact.[82] A historiographic phase may well have been the corollary of these records in stone.

Al-Mahdī, heir to an authority firmly established by his father, attempted to continue this latter's legitimising efforts by establishing a historiographic dimension aimed at definitively confirming the validity of his family's rule. The messianic aspects of the Abbasid caliphate and al-Mahdī in particular were an important element of this process. Numismatic evidence supports a similar hypothesis,[83] and evokes the question of the effects these messianic expectations may have had on the field of historiography. Furthermore, Theophilus of Edessa (d. 169/785) attests to the continued presence of court astrologers also working as historians during this period; we shall return to him later on.[84]

The lack of sources indicating caliphal proclivities toward reinterpreting historical writing after the caliphate of al-Mahdī complicates the task at hand going forward. The two subsequent caliphates of al-Hādī and Hārūn al-Rashīd likely continued the policies of the former despite troubles surrounding the order of succession.[85] The stakes remained more or less the same: affirming the legitimacy of the Abbasids was still a necessary task, resulting in the production of a "historiography of combat."[86] Al-Muʾarrij b. ʿAmr al-Sadusī's (d. 195/811) *Kitāb al-ḥadhf min nasab Quraysh* likely falls within this genre, a

81 This *laqab* is provisionally preserved here for convenience. For a discussion of this title, see below, Ch. 7.

82 On these inscriptions, see Elad, "The Caliph," v–vi (English summary of a Hebrew article), and Sharon, *CIAP*, vol. II, 214 ff.

83 Bates, "Khurāsānī Revolutionaries."

84 See below, Ch. 3.

85 For example, al-Hādī sought to convince his brother Hārūn to renounce his right of succession and increased his bullying when the latter refused; this continued until al-Hādī's suspicious death in 170/786. This subject has produced numerous studies. See Abbott, *Two Queens of Baghdad*; Moscati, "Le califat;" Bonner, "Al-Khalīfa al-Marḍī," "The Mint," and *Aristocratic Violence*; Kennedy, *The Early*, 106 ff. and "Succession Disputes;" and Kimber, "The Succession."

86 Notably in the face of the Alid pretensions characteristic of the early Abbasid period; see Sourdel, *L'état impérial*, 59–62.

veritable piece of early Abbasid propaganda.[87] This text divides Quraysh into two camps, the virtuous Abbasids and the blameworthy Umayyads, "who are destined to be killed."[88] The *Kitāb al-kharāj* of Abū Yūsuf Yaʿqūb, reportedly composed at al-Rashīd's behest, is another work that bears witness to the need for writing during this era. The practice (*ʿamal*) of prior caliphs played an important role in these texts, giving them at least a partial historical dimension. In addition, Sayf b. ʿUmar (d. 180/796) and Abū Mikhnaf (d. 157/774) – two of the greatest transmitters of historical traditions during the first centuries of Islam – flourished during this period, although their portrayals in later sources were mixed; the previous chapter discusses the fate reserved for Sayf in modern historiography. These two authors represent a profound labor of historiographic production, both confirming the existence of different concurrent versions in circulation regarding certain events in Islamic history: the very differences extant in Sayf's works are those responsible for the subsequent scholarly stigma against him. Both scholars are themselves *historiographic filters* who played a large role in determining the possible means of accessing the past that would be available to future generations of historians.

In spite of these signs of continuity, the intense activity on the border with the Byzantine empire during the caliphate of al-Rashīd could also have provoked a marked interest in questions of *jihād*;[89] this topic became ubiquitous in later historiography, particularly in the works of al-Ṭabarī.[90] Moreover, al-Rashīd spent several years away from Baghdad in Raqqa, on the banks of the Euphrates.[91] Like the other earlier transitions of the caliphal residence mentioned above, this move may also have occasioned a specific written production. The famous disgrace of the Barmakids and the upheavals it caused at the highest levels of the caliphate must also have resulted in the production of a discourse.[92] However, these events do not seem to have provoked any intense rewritings; rather, they involved certain forms of inflection. The crisis of succession on the brink of eruption after al-Rashīd's death would eventually turn matters on their heads and demand a profound reappropriation of the past.

87 Khalidi, *Arabic Historical Thought*, 54–5.

88 Al-Sadusī, *Kitāb Ḥadhf*, 33 and 36. On the need to legitimise the massacre of the Umayyads, see below, Chs. 4 and 7.

89 On this question, see Bonner, *Aristocratic Violence* and *Le jihad*. See also Picard, "Regards croisés."

90 Kennedy has remarked on this point as well in "Caliphs and their Chroniclers."

91 Meinecke, "Al-Raqqa."

92 On this episode, see Dakhlia, *L'empire des passions*.

2.2.1.2 Phase 6: From the Civil War to the Foundation of Sāmarrā' (*c.*193–232/809–847)

The period encompassing the civil war between al-Amīn and al-Ma'mūn must inevitably have created new historiographic trends.[93] Although the military phase of the conflict was hardly an auspicious time for an in-depth historiographic recomposition, despite the polemic exchanges that took place, al-Ma'mūn must have needed to affirm his authority and justify his new and unprecedented political choices in the wake of this fratricidal war. Above all, al-Ma'mūn needed to justify a regicide that was particularly traumatic for the Muslim community.[94] Initially, the new caliph abandoned Iraq – the Abbasids' heartland of power – and spent several years in Merv, where he had settled earlier as governor of Khurāsān following the death of his father. Even more significant, al-Ma'mūn designated a successor from outside the ruling family, choosing the Alid-Husyanid ʿAlī al-Riḍā,[95] and simultaneously replaced the traditional Abbasid black with the colour green.[96] This deeply political act, accompanied by the marriage of his own daughter to his new heir apparent,[97] represented al-Ma'mūn's attempt to reconcile the two rival Hashimite branches. The upheavals brought about by this radical transformation, in addition to the establishment of an anti-caliphate in Baghdad, were such that the caliph was forced to revise his plans and swiftly relocate his capital back to Iraq. The return proved fatal to the vizier al-Faḍl b. Sahl, the caliph's most trusted political adviser, who was assassinated at Sarakhs;[98] ʿAlī al-Riḍā also perished in this relocation, dying – likely poisoned – at Ṭūs at the end of Ṣafar 203/818.[99] The return to Baghdad and the reinstatement of the colour black marked a turning

93 For an outline and substantial bibliography of the modern historiography on this period, see Yücesoy, "Between Nationalism."

94 On this particularly sensitive issue, see El-Hibri, "The Regicide," and *Reinterpreting*, ch. 3.

95 The eighth Imam of Twelver Shiism, son of the seventh Imam, Mūsā al-Kāẓim. See Lewis, "ʿAlī al-Riḍā."

96 On this event, see al-Ṭabarī, vol. III, 1012 ff.; trans. vol. XXXII, 60 ff. For modern approaches, see Gabrieli, *Al-Ma'mūn*; Sourdel, "La politique religieuse du calife;" Madelung, "New Documents;" Kimber and Vasquez, "Al-Ma'mūn and Baghdad;" Tor, "An Historiographical Re-examination;" Cooperson, *Al-Ma'mūn*, 57 ff.

97 Al-Ṭabarī, vol. III, 1029; trans. vol. XXXII, 82.

98 Al-Ṭabarī, vol. III, 1027; trans. vol. XXXII, 80. On this location, see Yāqūt, *Muʿjam*, vol. III, 208–9.

99 Khalīfa b. Khayyāṭ, *Ta'rīkh*, vol. II, 766. According to al-Ṭabarī, he was buried at Ṭūs next to the tomb of Hārūn al-Rashīd (vol. III, 1030; trans. vol. XXXII, 84; Yāqūt gives the same account, *Muʿjam*, vol. IV, 49). The Shiite author al-Yaʿqūbī states that ʿAlī b. Hishām had al-Riḍā eat a poisoned pomegranate (*aṭʿimahu rummānan fīha samm*), *Ta'rīkh*, vol. II, 453. On ʿAlī b. Hishām, an influential Khurāsānī and governor of Jibāl later assassinated by al-Ma'mūn in 217/832, see Kennedy, *The Early*, index. The rumors of poisoning are

point in al-Maʾmūn's policies toward the Alids: from this point forward, the caliph turned resolutely in the direction of the Muʿtazilites. At the end of his reign, while engaged in a campaign of expansion against the Byzantines at Raqqa in 218/833, the caliph inaugurated his infamous *miḥna*, an inquisition aimed at imposing the dogma of the created Qurʾān.[100] This initiative resulted in an important use of writing attested by the missives the caliph sent to his governors. The *miḥna* marked the crystallisation of the conflict between the caliph and the *ʿulamāʾ*; aimed at defining the supremacy of the caliphate in religious matters, it necessitated a profound rewriting. This enterprise was largely erased thereafter by the "adversaries of a legislative caliphate ... that soon denied any *active* religious authority to the caliphs," in order to establish yet another reconstruction "undertaken in elaborating what is called the 'prophetic tradition' and forming a stable environment for virtuosos, learned specialists in religious knowledge, and monopolising their capital."[101] Al-Maʾmūn's rapid demise near Ṭarsūs[102] in the months following the institution of the *miḥna* ultimately proved unfavourable to the success of his projects.

After sixty years of relative calm, in particular after al-Manṣūr's consolidation of power, and in light of the major crisis that followed, the Abbasid caliphate could not afford to dispense with rewriting projects. Al-Maʾmūn's difficult caliphate, marked by numerous revolts, required new explanations to legitimise the conditions surrounding his accession and his armed struggle against his own brother, who had been named successor to the throne by al-Rashīd. The changes in caliphal favour, shifting from the Alids to the Muʿtazilites, also needed to be inscribed in history, and the theological debates that raged at the time provided ample justification for reinterpretations. The strong messianic

---

repeated by another Shiite author, al-Masʿūdī, *Murūj*, vol. VII, 61; trans. Pellat vol. IV, 1122, who notes that it was instead a grape (*ʿinab*) that supposedly contained the poison.

100 For a detailed account of these measures, including the supposed letters from al-Maʾmūn to his governors to ensure that the *qāḍīs* and traditionists adhered to Muʿtazilī doctrine, see al-Ṭabarī, vol. III, 1112–34; trans. vol. XXXII, 199–223. The *miḥna* has been the subject of numerous studies since Patton's pioneering work *Ahmad Ibn Hanbal and the Mihna* in 1897; it is impossible here to account for all of the important works on this topic. For those aspects most pertinent to this inquiry, see Sourdel, "La politique religieuse du calife;" Lapidus, "The Separation;" Crone and Hinds, *God's Caliph*; Zaman, "The Caliphs, the ʿUlamāʾ, and the Law" and *Religion and Politics*; Yücesoy, "Between Nationalism;" Décobert, "L'autorité religieuse;" Cooperson, *Al-Maʾmūn*; and Melchert, *Ahmad Ibn Hanbal*.

101 Décobert, "L'autorité religieuse," 41–2.

102 He was also buried in this city; see al-Ṭabarī, vol. III, 1140; trans. vol. XXXII, 231; al-Masʿūdī, *Murūj*, vol. VII, 2; trans. Pellat vol. IV, 1099; Yāqūt, *Muʿjam*, vol. IV, 28–9; Cooperson, "The Grave of al-Maʾmūn."

context of the period was also an important element in the discourses that would then flourish.[103]

Alongside these political and religious events, al-Maʾmūn was closely associated with the *Bayt al-ḥikma*, an institution he sponsored in Baghdad to promote the transmission of ancient knowledge.[104] Very little information about this institution survives, despite its great fame; the works issued by the *Bayt al-ḥikma* were perhaps not limited to translations from Greek – often via Syriac – into Arabic, but rather represented a much greater undertaking aimed at selecting, archiving, recording and categorising the available materials. In its capacity as a library, the *Bayt al-ḥikma* obviously played a role in the historiographical domain via the simple choice of which works would be collected and preserved there. The preservation of private collections was problematic; this state of affairs is attested during al-Maʾmūn's caliphate by the fate of al-Wāqidī's massive library, which was reportedly sold off by his heirs and dispersed after his death.[105]

It is interesting to note that some of the scholars employed by the caliph in this institution were historians. The famous mathematician and astronomer al-Khwārizmī (*c.*184–232/800–847) is one example; he is equally known as the author of a *Kitāb al-taʾrīkh*, a work that Vernet claimed was lost without noting that it was largely used by Ibn Abī Ṭayfūr (d. 280/893) in his *Kitāb Baghdād* as well as by the "Nestorian" author Elias of Nisibis (d. 1046).[106] Although these citations in later works cannot compensate for the loss of the original, analysing this exceptional source in greater detail presents interesting new possibilities; the stakes here are significant, as these citations are potentially a means of accessing a *taʾrīkh* more or less contemporary with the oldest one preserved: the history of Khalīfa b. Khayyāṭ (d. 240/854). Nevertheless, al-Khwārizmī attests to the existence of historical writing during this sixth phase, likely occasioned by the new needs that arose during al-Maʾmūn's caliphate.

---

103 Yücesoy, "Between Nationalism" and *Messianic Beliefs*, has recently argued for historians of the period to give greater consideration to this messianic context.

104 On the *Bayt al-ḥikma*, see Balty-Guesdon, "Le *Bayt al-Ḥikma*;" Gutas, *Greek Thought*; Touati, *L'armoire à sagesse*; Saliba, *Islamic Science*; and, more generally, Lyons, *The House of Wisdom*.

105 The sale brought 2000 gold dinars; see Touati, *L'armoire à sagesse*, 47–8.

106 Elias of Nisibis, *Chronography*; Ibn Abī Ṭāhir Ṭayfūr, *Kitāb Baghdād*. Elsewhere, I have emphasised Elias of Nisibis's historiographic importance; his *Chronography* is the only great eastern Syriac chronicle that survives, and it is particularly significant for its preservation of many lost Arab-Muslim works. See Borrut, "La circulation de l'information historique." On Ibn Abī Ṭāhir Ṭayfūr, see Toorawa, *Ibn Abī Ṭāhir Ṭayfūr*. On the other domains of al-Khwārizmī's works, see Toomer, "Al-Khwārizmī;" Vernet, "Al-Khʷārazmī;" Hill, "Mathematics;" King, "Astronomy;" Hopkins, "Geographical," 304–6.

Al-Ma'mūn's successors would continue the *miḥna*, demonstrating – at least for a few decades – that although a certain amount of continuity with respect to religious policy remained, an important change would take place in the years immediately following his death: the transfer of the administrative capital to Sāmarrā' (221/836), which gave new weight to the growing power of the Turks at the time. While the move to Sāmarrā' represented a major change in political terms,[107] from the perspective of the layers of historical rewriting, the break is not nearly as clean for a number of reasons. First and foremost, unlike military and administrative activities, intellectual life remained firmly rooted in Baghdad, even despite al-Mu'taṣim's (r. 218–227/833–842) departure from this latter city for Sāmarrā'.[108] Furthermore, the salient characteristics of the beginning of the "Sāmarrā' period," in particular the Turks' growing influence and the continuation of the *miḥna*, were in reality part of an obvious continuity with al-Ma'mūn's era.[109] The foundation of Sāmarrā' itself was undeniably a worthy inspiration for rewritings. Three-quarters of a century after al-Manṣūr founded Baghdad, undertaking a similarly ambitious project was not a foregone conclusion, especially in light of Baghdad's growing importance. However, the historiographic projects composed during this period appear largely to be a continuation of those initiated after the end of the fourth civil war. Al-Ma'mūn himself had left Baghdad for Merv (198–203/813–818). Numerous other elements also invite a more detailed analysis in order to identify the passage to a new historiographic phase, without minimising the various transformations that occurred during this time. It is rather to the caliphate of al-Mutawakkil (r. 232–247/847–861), which represented numerous important reorientations from previous caliphal policies, including above all the cessation of the *miḥna*, that we now turn our attention. Although a detailed description of al-Mu'taṣim's motivations for leaving Baghdad is impossible here,[110] it is sufficient to note that the two main sources – al-Ṭabarī and al-Ya'qūbī – agreed that the violence between the Turks and the inhabitants of Baghdad provoked this

107 Archaeologists also recognise the Sāmarrā' period as a turning point in light of its material culture; it is worth noting that this interlude is also where Goitein located a turning point in the history of early Islam in a pioneering article on the limitations of dynastic periodisation. See Goitein, "A Plea for Periodization."

108 The ambiguous conditions surrounding al-Mu'taṣim's succession of al-Ma'mūn are worth noting here: Gordon rightly points out that this episode merits greater scholarly attention, and highlights the fact that al-Mu'taṣim must have imposed himself as successor after his brother's sudden demise, especially in the face of 'Abbās b. al-Ma'mūn's aspirations to the throne. See Gordon, *The Breaking*, 47–50.

109 On this point, see Gordon, *The Breaking*, 15–46.

110 On the history of Sāmarrā', see in particular Gordon, *The Breaking*, and Northedge, *The Historical Topography*.

decision;[111] it is also possible that the impacts of the *miḥna* had a role to play as well.[112] Following in his father's footsteps, al-Wāthiq (r. 227–232/842–847) kept the caliphate in Sāmarrā', to the great delight of the Turkish elite, who took this opportunity to strengthen their hold on power.[113] Despite the displacement of the caliphate, the continuation of al-Ma'mūn's policies largely prevailed.

Two other essential transmitters of early Islamic history are associated with this historiographic sequence: al-Wāqidī (d. 207/823) and al-Madā'inī (d. c. 235/850). While al-Wāqidī's work on the *maghāzī* has survived the perils of transmission,[114] the works of these two authors dealing with the second/eighth century are only known to us today through the inherently uncertain citations preserved by later compilers. The omnipresence of these two transmitters in the *isnād*s cited in the great works of the ninth and tenth centuries attests both to the credit given the two men and the importance of this phase for the transmission of historical material. Al-Wāqidī and al-Madā'inī were the two driving forces behind the heavily influential historiographic filters that were put in place during this period.

Fortunately, other works composed during this historiographic phase have been preserved. This is the case for Ibn Saʿd (d. 230/845), al-Wāqidī's secretary, whose collection of biographical notices, *al-Ṭabaqāt al-kubrā*, is an especially rich source for information concerning the great figures of the first centuries of Islam.[115] The question of an affiliation between this text and al-Wāqidī's now-lost work of the same title is debatable.[116] In the Egyptian space, Ibn ʿAbd al-Ḥakam (d. 214/829) dedicated a biography to ʿUmar b. ʿAbd al-ʿAzīz, a testament to the widespread fame enjoyed by the Umayyad caliph.[117]

Ibn Aʿtham al-Kūfī and his *Kitāb al-futūḥ* should also probably be situated within this historiographic layer. Ibn Aʿtham remains little-studied, and numerous aspects of his character and works are still shrouded in mystery. The

111 Al-Ṭabarī, vol. III, 1180–1; trans. vol. XXXIII, 27–8; al-Yaʿqūbī, *Buldān*, 256; trans. 46. On these works, see Gordon, *The Breaking*, 50–4.

112 This is the hypothesis defended by Töllner, *Die türkischen*, on which see Gordon, *The Breaking*, 53–4.

113 Gordon, *The Breaking*, 78–9.

114 Al-Wāqidī, *Kitāb al-maghāzī*.

115 Ibn Saʿd, *al-Ṭabaqāt*.

116 Leder, "Al-Wāqidī," 113, proposes that Ibn Saʿd "mainly used materials from a work of al-Wāqidī carrying this same title," while de Prémare insists that "even if both worked largely, if not entirely, from the same sources, the works that we know from each respective authors are very different from each other, and we find in the notices of Ibn Saʿd things that are contradictory to those reported by al-Wāqidī," *Les fondations*, 389–90.

117 Ibn ʿAbd al-Ḥakam, *Sīra*; on the image of ʿUmar II, see Borrut, "Entre tradition et histoire," and below, Ch. 6.

chronology of his life is uncertain, and the date given for his death varies widely in modern scholarship; the most frequently proposed date is 314/926–927.[118] This dating issue is an "old Orientalist error,"[119] one that Conrad has been able to trace back to the middle of the nineteenth century. The confusion originates with a passage from Yāqūt (d. 626/1229), who states in his notice on Ibn Aʿtham that this latter's chronicle extended through the caliphate of al-Muqtadir (r. 295–320/908–932).[120] However, Conrad has shown that this reference is actually to a continuation of Ibn Aʿtham's chronicle rather than the original chronicle itself;[121] thus, an earlier date is probable. Shaban is of this opinion as well, and estimates that the *Kitāb al-futūḥ* was composed in 204/819.[122] Conrad corroborates this chronology, determining that Ibn Aʿtham's father was in contact with Jaʿfar al-Ṣādiq (d. 148/765), the sixth Imam, and may even have been his student. A poet and preacher (*qāṣṣ*)[123] of Shiite obedience,[124] Ibn Aʿtham appears to have written an earlier version of his *Kitāb al-futūḥ* during the caliphate of al-Maʾmūn in 204/819, judging by the date indicated in a Persian translation completed by al-Mustawfī in 596/1169. Based on the text preserved in the Persian translation, Ibn Aʿtham's preliminary version of this work appears to have concluded with the battle of Karbalāʾ (61/680).[125] Conrad suggests that Ibn Aʿtham later extended his chronicle at least through the caliphate of Hārūn al-Rashīd before his Sunni successors took over in their respective continuations.[126] This explains the fact that the text in its current form continues through to the overthrow of al-Mustaʿīn in 252/856; due to this extension of the chronicle, Conrad originally believed that Ibn Aʿtham must have been active around 254/858.[127] Conrad intended to dedicate a study of much broader scope to Ibn Aʿtham; however, this work never came to fruition, leaving us unable to clarify the numerous ambiguities regarding this author

118 Notably in *GAL*, vol. I, 144, and *GAS*, vol. I, 329. See Conrad, "The Conquest of Arwād," 349 n. 90.

119 Conrad, "Ibn Aʿtham," 314.

120 Yāqūt, *Irshād*, ed. Margoliouth, vol. I, cited by Conrad, "The Conquest of Arwād," 349 n. 90.

121 Conrad, "The Conquest of Arwād," 349 n. 90.

122 Shaban, "Ibn Aʿtham."

123 See Pellat, "Ḳāṣṣ."

124 Togan contests this point ("Ibn Aʿtham," 250), suggesting that Ibn Aʿtham merely had sympathies for the descendants of the Prophet, which would have justified the fact that he sometimes took openly favourable stances toward the Umayyads.

125 Conrad, "Ibn Aʿtham," 314. See also Togan, "Ibn Aʿtham;" Robinson, "The Conquest of Khūzistān" and *Islamic Historiography*, 34 n. 21.

126 Conrad, "Ibn Aʿtham," 314.

127 Conrad, "The Conquest of Arwād," 349 n. 90, and "Ibn Aʿtham," 314.

and his remaining works. The quality of the information transmitted by Ibn Aʿtham is frequently problematic and should be considered with caution, as Conrad notes with respect to his dubious account of the conquest of the small Syrian island of Arwād.[128] However, Ibn Aʿtham was undeniably popular, in particular in the Persian-speaking world, as attested by the numerous extant manuscripts of the Persian translation of his works; he seems to have been a particularly important source for Balʿamī (d. between 382/992 and 387/997).[129]

Ibn Aʿtham was thus a contemporary of scholars such as al-Madāʾinī – whom he seems to have known personally[130] – and al-Wāqidī. These factual elements aside, the very content of Ibn Aʿtham's chronicle corroborates the hypothesis of an earlier dating: his history is a perfect example of these texts on the margins of the vulgate that developed in the first half of the ninth century, and a later date is less capable of explaining Ibn Aʿtham's unique place in Islamic historiography, as we will demonstrate further below.

2.2.1.3 Phase 7: Resistance and Anarchy (*c.*232–279/847–892)

Al-Mutawakkil's accession upset the status quo, for the new caliph wanted to move in new political directions, exemplified by his abandonment of the *miḥna* and concern with curtailing the Turkish military's growing power. He thus made two attempts to distance himself from Sāmarrāʾ: the first took place in 244/858, when he tried to relocate the capital to Damascus before eventually turning back due to discontent among his troops;[131] the second, following this forced return, occurred when he began construction of a new palace complex north of Sāmarrāʾ that, judging from the numismatic evidence, was to be named al-Mutawakkiliyya.[132] These two undertakings resulted in a series of failures and the tragic demise of the caliph, who was assassinated in 247/861 by Turkish officers.[133] The elimination of the caliph who had tried to oppose the Turkish challenges to caliphal authority marked the beginning of a period of anarchy in Sāmarrāʾ, and several other caliphs met the same fate as al-Mutawakkil.[134] The Turkish military elite made and remade the caliphate over a series of several years. Finally, the caliph al-Muʿtamid (r. 256–279/870–892), at the end of

128 Conrad, "The Conquest of Arwād," 348–64.

129 Peacock, *Medieval Islamic Historiography*, 43 and 94–7. On the uncertainties surrounding Balʿamī's death date, see Daniel, "Balʿamī's Account," 164 n. 4, and Peacock, *Medieval Islamic Historiography*, 31–5.

130 Togan, "Ibn Aʿtham," 250.

131 See Gordon, *The Breaking*, 87–8, and Cobb, "Al-Mutawakkil's Damascus."

132 Gordon, *The Breaking*, 88; Northedge, *The Historical Topography*.

133 On the lasting impression this assassination left in court poetry, see Ali, *Ardor for Memory*.

134 On this tumultuous period, see Gordon, *The Breaking*, 90 ff.

a troubled reign thirty years after his father's assassination, ordered the return of the caliphate to Baghdad.

The new political directions of al-Mutawakkil's caliphate undoubtedly required rewritings, and the marked return of traditionalism was almost certainly important in erecting the past as a model for the present.[135] However, the chaos that occurred in the wake of his assassination leaves many details unclear. Did this weakening of caliphal power provide certain authors in Baghdad, far from the political upheaval in Sāmarrā', greater leeway? Alongside the political desires reorienting historical writing, the profound social transformations also underway at the time equally demanded a new direction in the texts.

Although a number of different authors are connected with this phase, two among them are of particular importance both for Islamic historiography and the subject of Syria in the second/eighth century: Khalīfa b. Khayyāṭ (d. c. 240/854) and al-Balādhurī (d. 279/892). The *Ta'rīkh* of Khalīfa b. Khayyāṭ is the oldest known chronography that survives in its entirety,[136] and its author was clearly distinct from the historiographic vulgate that would be established several decades later. In addition to the somewhat different information and interpretations he proposed, Khalīfa b. Khayyāṭ is particularly interesting for his reliance on sources produced in the Syrian space, such as those of al-Balādhurī, who was active at the very end of the Sāmarrā' period. Khalīfa relied on many of the Syrian authors mentioned previously in this inquiry, among them: from the Umayyad period, Maymūn b. Mihrān (d. 117/735–736) and 'Ubāda b. Nusayy al-Kindī (d. 118/736–737); from Abbasid Syria, Thawr b. Yazīd al-Kalā'ī (d. between 150/767 and 155/772), al-Walīd b. Muslim al-Umawī al-Dimashqī (d. 194/810), and Muḥammad b. 'Ā'idh al-Dimashqī (d. 232/847).[137] Scholars have long noted al-Balādhurī's reliance on Syrian authors.[138] His *Futūḥ al-buldān* goes well beyond the objective presented in its title, and is a source of primary importance for the period. These two authors are equally illustrious in the prosopographic genre: Khalīfa with a work of *ṭabaqāt*, al-Balādhurī with his famous *Ansāb al-ashrāf*.[139] In this work, to which we shall return later, al-Balādhurī dedicates an exceptional place to the Umayyads.[140] Another well-known author from the period, Muḥammad b. Ṣāliḥ al-Naṭṭāḥ (d. 252/866)

135 As noted by Robinson, *Islamic Historiography*, 92; see also Sourdel, *L'état impérial*, 149–63.

136 See Donner, *Narratives*, 133–4; Zakkar, "Ibn Khayyāt;" Robinson, *Islamic Historiography*, 77–9.

137 See Khalīfa, *Ta'rīkh*, index.

138 Wellhausen, *Das arabische Reich*, xii; Donner, "The Problem," 2.

139 On this work, see Goitein's introduction, *Ansāb*, v; Hamidullah, "Le livre des généalogies;" Athamina, "The Sources;" Khalidi, *Arabic Historical Thought*, 58–61.

140 See Ch. 3.

composed a *Book of the Abbasid Dynasty* (*Kitāb al-dawla al-ʿAbbāsiyya*), that Duri has tentatively identified as the *Anonymous History of the Abbasids* (*Akhbār al-dawla al-ʿAbbāsiyya*).[141] Although his hypothesis is improbable, al-Masʿūdī did use Ibn al-Naṭṭāḥ as a source when composing his works.[142] The *Anonymous History of the Abbasids* itself is difficult to date with any precision. Nevertheless, it may be situated with respect to another anonymous text, the *Taʾrīkh al-khulafāʾ*, published by Gryaznevich in 1967,[143] that offers a condensed version of events and demonstrates that the *Akhbār al-dawla* was employed in its composition. The *Taʾrīkh al-khulafāʾ* likely dates to the beginning of the fifth/eleventh century; thus, the *Anonymous History* must have been written prior to this date. Duri's crucial discovery of this apologetic text in 1955 significantly increased the amount of available material with which to study the clandestine phase of the Abbasid Revolution.[144] Unfortunately, the beginning of this text is lost, and it concludes with the death of Ibrāhīm al-Imām and the flight of members of the Abbasid family, led by Abū al-ʿAbbās, toward Kūfa.[145] Al-Wāqidī and al-Balādhurī are among the sources consulted in the *Akhbār*, as evidenced by the *isnāds*. Al-Balādhurī even appears to have had contact with the author of the *Anonymous History*, and the form of his *Ansāb al-ashrāf* is similar to that of the *Akhbār*. Several other elements support situating this work during the same period as those of al-Balādhurī at the end of the third/ninth century.[146] Daniel, studying the sources used in the composition of the *Akhbār*, has proposed that certain passages represent cohesive units based on older texts that were reincorporated as needed. He estimates that certain elements may date to the period of al-Mahdī;[147] the *Anonymous History* attests to the fact that this latter played an important role in the layers of historical recomposition. This text is thus simultaneously the richest extant source on the *daʿwa* and an important means of refining our knowledge of Abbasid historiography.

141 Duri, "Ibn al-Naṭṭāḥ."

142 Al-Masʿūdī, *Murūj*, vol. 1, 12; trans. Pellat vol. 1, 5.

143 *Taʾrīkh al-khulafāʾ*.

144 He later edited the *Akhbār al-dawla* with the assistance of al-Muṭṭalibī in 1971. On this crucial source, see Duri, "Ḍawʾ jadīd;" Omar, *The ʿAbbāsid Caliphate*, 16–9; Sharon, "The Abbasid *Daʿwa* Reimagined;" Daniel, "The Anonymous History of the Abbasid Family." On the Abbasid Revolution, see below, Ch. 7.

145 The title of this edition is the arbitrary choice of the editors, who defended the idea that the terms *daʿwa* and *dawla* were interchangeable at this early era. See Duri and al-Muṭṭalibī, *Akhbār al-dawla*, 10–1, along with Daniel's reservations, "The Anonymous History of the Abbasid Family," 419–20.

146 Daniel, "The Anonymous History of the Abbasid Family," 422. The question of the identity of the author of this work is discussed in detail in this article, 423–4.

147 Daniel, "The Anonymous History of the Abbasid Family," 426.

The historian and geographer al-Yaʿqūbī is the most prominent figure of the transitional period between the previous phase and the current one. We know that his *Kitāb al-buldān* was completed in Egypt in 278/891, and that his historical work does not extend past the caliphate of al-Muʿtaṣim (d. 279/892). Only a shorter treatise, his *Mushākalat al-nās li-zamānihim*,[148] surpasses this chronological limit and stretches to the reign of al-Muʿtaḍid (d. 289/902). His *Taʾrīkh*, which is of primary importance for this study, attests to the Alid sympathies of its author, who affirms the superiority of ʿAlī, dedicates specific notices to the Alid imams, and frequently passes harsh judgments on the Umayyads. His attitude toward the Abbasid dynasty is more ambiguous, although it should be noted that, like their predecessors, the Abbasid sovereigns mentioned in this work were not accorded the expected title of *khilāfa* – reserved solely for ʿAlī – and al-Yaʿqūbī designates their reigns simply as *ayyām*.[149] In his treatise dedicated to the adaptation of people to their eras, al-Yaʿqūbī tries to demonstrate the extent to which people are influenced by the model of their ruling sovereign and strive to follow his example. In this capacity, his text is a veritable essay, aimed at elucidating certain laws that govern history.

With the exception of Sayf b. ʿUmar, whose sections on the Umayyads and Abbasids have unfortunately not been preserved, and the aforementioned al-Khwārizmī, this historiographic phase associated with the Sāmarrāʾ period is where we encounter the first preserved Islamic chronographies. This stage undoubtedly played a decisive role in the development and maturation of historiographic writing processes during the first centuries of Islam. Comparing these sources with those making up the historiographic vulgate that was established soon after proves to be an especially productive endeavour.

2.2.1.4 Phase 8: Post-Sāmarrāʾ (279/892 – Fourth/Tenth Century)

The return to Baghdad after the interlude in Sāmarrāʾ required justification. The emphasis in the sources on al-Manṣūr's selection of the site and foundation of Baghdad likely dates to this era; this moment is also when authors tried to highlight al-Manṣūr's caliphate and his image, associated above all with Baghdad. The true architect of the Abbasid state had chosen the site and ordered the construction of the round city; the reinstallation of the caliphate in Baghdad signified a return to this "original Abbasid," the quintessential founding hero, a prerequisite for the expected restoration of caliphal authority. It is striking that the vast majority of the preserved Islamic narrative sources emerged from this post-Sāmarrāʾ period, the works of al-Ṭabarī foremost among them, and that

148 Al-Yaʿqūbī, *Mushākalat*.

149 Al-Yaʿqūbī's Shiism has been questioned by Daniel, "Al-Yaʿqūbī and Shiʿism," who also suggested that the rubrics in the manuscripts (e.g., *ayyām*) might be later interpolations.

this collected corpus would produce a historiographic vulgate that recognised only limited variations. Yet, is this state of affairs really so surprising?

From the perspective of a history of meanings, the problem cannot be reduced to certain caliphs demanding that the past be rewritten. The process remains an eminently political one, aimed at harmonising the different versions of the past in circulation with imperial projects.[150] However, it resulted in much more, in particular the perception that the "producers of the past" – that is, the "chroniclers" – had of their own era; the "social logic"[151] of these texts is a significant element that must be accounted for in order to more fully understand these historical rewritings.

We shall pause for a moment at the year 286/900, slightly after the caliphate's abandonment of Sāmarrāʾ for Baghdad. Over the course of a century and a half of Abbasid rule, the world had transformed considerably: in the last decades of the third century *hijrī*, "the evidence of this continuity had become unintelligible," to borrow Geary's apt expression.[152] The subsequent upheavals caused by the "Abbasid Revolution," the civil war, the *miḥna*, the Sāmarrāʾ "moment" and the growing power of the new Turkish elite – to cite only the most obvious events – are sufficient evidence of the disturbances to this continuity. Times of crisis are always auspicious for developments centred around memory and its two main attributes: remembrance and oblivion. Before we return in detail to the content that attracted the attention of the authors and thus was memorised, it will be helpful to identify the conditions that gave rise to these unintelligible continuities and this new rewriting that would prove much more durable than similar efforts undertaken in previous periods.

In an important article, Humphreys provides a general outline of the issues, summarised here as follows: from the perspective of a Muslim living during the Abbasid period, Islamic history was extremely problematic. It was the history of a community who had signed a pact with God such as no other group had done before them. However, this community had not remained cohesive and was now divided by bloodshed and schisms, a clear and undeniable state of affairs that forced scholars to confront crucial questions, resulting in the creation of three shared myths: pact, betrayal, and redemption. For those concerned with Islamic history, determining the circumstances under which the Prophet's pact had been betrayed and the nature of this betrayal was essential: the guilty parties must be identified. The official interpretation produced by the Abbasid court blamed the corrupt Umayyads, the tyrannical usurper

150 Robinson, *Islamic Historiography*, 41.

151 I borrow this expression from Spiegel, "History, Historicism and the Social Logic."

152 Geary, *Phantoms of Remembrance*, 25.

Muʿāwiya in particular. The history of the original community only became an object of nostalgia when redemption no longer seemed possible in the present, now instead a goal for the distant future. Humphreys dates the beginning of this moment to the second half of the ninth century; with the dislocation of the Abbasid empire in the tenth century, these sentiments solidified.[153] David Cook has highlighted the decrease in apocalyptic traditions after 250/864 in the Sunni world and 350–400/960–1000 in Shiite circles; prior to these dates, apocalyptic Islamic literature attests to *imminent* messianic expectations.[154] Thus, after al-Ṭabarī, it was no longer necessary to rewrite the history of early Islam;[155] it should be noted, however, that al-Ṭabarī's works do contain messianic expectations, and were indeed perceived as such by his Persian translator/adaptor, Balʿamī.[156]

The end of the third century *hijrī* was truly "a period of important reorganisation of traditions of all sorts. Archives were established or restructured. Documents were collected and recopied, or as frequently destroyed or invented. Families rethought their ties to distant ancestors in light of new obligations. Ruling dynasties began to deal with the problem of tidying up the often messy memory of their rise to power."[157] People tried hard to place these elements "into new structures of meaning, transforming memories into legends and finally into myths – that is, into creatable, exemplary, and hence repeatable models of past, present, and future. These myths were comprehensible within the new cultural systems in the process of being born. At the same time, these myths gave meaning, legitimacy, and form to these new systems."[158] The chroniclers played a role in this process because they presented a vision of the past that was "capable of giving meaning to a transformed present." As those with "the right to speak the tradition," they performed a fundamental task in the service of the caliphate, for "those who could control the past could direct

153 Humphreys, "Qurʾānic Myth," 278–81. See also Assmann, *La mémoire culturelle*, 207–30.

154 Cook, *Studies*, 330. On the messianic expectations stemming from the approach of the year 100 *hijrī*, especially under the caliphate of ʿUmar b. ʿAbd al-ʿAzīz, see Borrut, "Entre tradition et histoire," 339–45. The year 200 *hijrī* was associated with the same beliefs. See Yücesoy, *Messianic Beliefs*, 50–8. The reasons for the decrease in the appearance of these traditions require further explanation in light of Schmitt's similar inquiry for the West; he notes that "the eschatological representation of *futura*" was questioned during the Renaissance with the progressive discovery of an "open notion of the future." See Schmitt, "Le Temps," 49, and more generally, "L'appropriation du futur."

155 Humphreys, "Qurʾānic Myth," 281. This point, more complex than it appears here, is discussed in greater detail below.

156 Daniel, "Balʿamī's Account," 182.

157 Geary, *Phantoms of Remembrance*, 27.

158 Geary, *Phantoms of Remembrance*, 25–6.

the future."[159] This rationale explains the fact that al-Ṭabarī, like al-Yaʿqūbī before him, saw Islamic history as the history of humanity since Creation; this view represents a dramatic change from that of Khalīfa b. Khayyāṭ, for whom history proper began with the advent of Islam.[160] Al-Ṭabarī's approach to historiography constituted an act of "appropriation," to borrow Cheddadi's term; "appropriation" accurately translates the need for Islamic history to insert itself within a much longer history, in which the message of Islam was the ultimate outcome. The shift from a strictly Islamic perspective to a universal one resulted in a new relationship to time and chronology, the past and history,[161] while the annalistic form adopted by numerous authors could in some ways be read as a countdown to the End of Days.[162]

Islamic historiography underwent another important transformation during this phase: its form changed. Kennedy recently came to this conclusion, detecting a change in al-Ṭabarī's writing style when discussing the events of the third century *hijrī* (approximately the ninth century, 815–912). This evolution materialises both in the literary form of the text and in an abrupt decrease in the use of poetry and chains of transmission (*isnād*s);[163] essentially, the annalistic framework of the text is the only aspect that remains unchanged. Alongside this quantitative change, El-Hibri also detects a qualitative one: he notes that, broadly speaking, for the Abbasid period, al-Ṭabarī presents accounts that are "extremely diverse and anecdotal" and only rarely based on the chains of transmission he relied so heavily on for preceding eras.[164] As this transformation occurred more or less contemporaneous with al-Ṭabarī's lifetime (224–310/839–923), it is probable that the information he provides concerning this period is based on his own personal observations – he visited Sāmarrāʾ,[165] as well as Syria and Egypt[166] – or on the accounts of eyewitnesses or people who themselves knew eyewitnesses. These new circumstances offer an explanation for the disappearance of *isnād*s. As previously stated, the widespread reliance on *isnād*s and other sources – poetry, for example – was, especially for older eras, directly linked to the affirmation of the truth. When other

159 Geary, *Phantoms of Remembrance*, 6.

160 The section on the Creation in al-Yaʿqūbī's *Taʾrīkh* is lost; in its current form, it begins with Adam.

161 This question merits analysis in greater depth, which is outside the scope of this inquiry. This theme has been richly developed in scholarship on the medieval West, in particular McKitterick, *Perceptions of the Past*.

162 Peacock, *Medieval Islamic Historiography*, 80.

163 Kennedy, "Caliphs and their Chroniclers," 18–9; see also Gordon, *The Breaking*, 12.

164 El-Hibri, *Reinterpreting*, 219.

165 Al-Ṭabarī, vol. III, 1511–2; trans. vol. XXXV, 11; Gordon, *The Breaking*, 11.

166 Rosenthal, "General Introduction," 21.

means of guaranteeing truthfulness emerged, these earlier tools lost their functionality.

Another important element should be noted here regarding Spiegel's discussion of one of the most important formal developments in medieval Western historiography: the shift from poetry to prose. While the context is obviously different, this comparison is fundamentally relevant to the current inquiry. Spiegel links this development in thirteenth-century French chronicles to the social upheavals within the aristocracy during the first decades of this century: social change doubled as literary change, and the new problems that arose were relegated to the past.[167] Social transformations may have literary counterparts, and "post-Sāmarrāʾ" Islamic historiography may have been at least partially affected by a similar phenomenon. The growing power of the Turks, the decrease in caliphal authority and the dislocation of the Abbasid empire provided the necessary conditions for such changes. The shift in form attested in the works of an author as significant as al-Ṭabarī supports a similar hypothesis; as we shall see in the following chapters, projecting the caliphate's current problems into the past – especially problems of legitimacy – is a well-attested phenomenon in the sources.

Beyond the profound changes reflected in this wide-scale recomposition of history and historiography, the results of these transformations evoke certain observations for historians eager to push beyond those rewritings. The vulgate had been established, and this event had a significant influence on medieval authors and modern scholars alike. The "historiographic skeleton" constructed in the post-Sāmarrāʾ period was now the quintessential framework for historiography, its content considered to be the basis of any serious approach to the knowledge of the first centuries of Islam. The "skeptics" have justifiably detected the presence of forgeries originating from this period, but they reject the very existence of any common base material. This study – along with many others – attempts to refute this rejection by demonstrating the undeniable existence of prior historiographic production. Furthermore, this earlier historiography was itself subject to multiple stages of reinterpretation according to the changing needs and successive selections that conditioned subsequent possible rewritings. The culmination of these recompositions of the past occurred during the major social and political crisis that shook the Abbasid caliphate at the turn of the ninth-tenth century. All of these elements in combination allowed for the creation of a decisive post-Sāmarrāʾ historiographic filter embodied above all in the figure of al-Ṭabarī.

167 See Spiegel, "Social Change," *Romancing the Past*, and "Theory into Practice."

This vulgate was marked by a distinct Iraqi tropism due to the space in which it was produced. The implications of this observation are important for the present inquiry: Syria is only mentioned in this vulgate when it is absolutely essential to the authors' discussion. The relative dearth of references to Abbasid Syria in the chronographies may be explained by the fact that Abbasid Syria could no longer claim the same essential significance as Umayyad Syria. Ultimately, the material produced imposed a framework for reading Islamic history. This collection of narratives seems to be based on a limited number of key events that are shared among all authors regardless of their political sympathies; in contrast, numerous other events of great interest to the modern historian were passed over in silence.[168] More than a canonical history, a canonical historical framework was put in place;[169] while this framework did not preclude new interpretations, it aimed to limit the number of new interpretations that were possible.

2.2.2 *Al-Ṭabarī: The End of History?*

Al-Ṭabarī's influence on Islamic historiographic production following his *magnum opus*, which ends at the year 302/915, has been the subject of myriad scholarly inquiries.[170] Keaney, challenging a widespread consensus in modern scholarship, contests the idea that, with several exceptions, later medieval authors were constrained to merely paraphrase and summarise al-Ṭabarī.[171] This hypothesis, supported by Rosenthal,[172] does not stand up to closer historiographic analyses, few though these may be, despite the existence of several significant contributions demonstrating the profit to be gained from such projects. This is especially the case for Keaney, who studied the successive

168 Humphreys, "Qur'ānic Myth," 275. Crone has also remarked on this state of affairs, *Slaves*, 11: "wherever one turns, one finds compilers of different dates, origin and doctrinal persuasions, presenting the same canon in different arrangements and selections."

169 The bibliography related to the process of canonisation and decanonisation is immense. Above all, see Van der Kooij and Van der Toorn, *Canonization and Decanonization*, which includes an extremely valuable annotated bibliography on these subjects, see also Snoek, "Canonization and Decanonization. An Annotated Bibliography." In the field of Islamic studies, the essential text on this topic is Brown, *The Canonization*.

170 On al-Ṭabarī's life and the approximately 7800 pages of his *Taʾrīkh al-rusul wa-al-mulūk*, see Rosenthal, "General Introduction;" Gilliot, "La formation intellectuelle" and *Exégèse, langue et théologie*; Shoshan, *Poetics of Islamic Historiography*; Rydving (ed.), *Al-Ṭabarī's History*; and Kennedy (ed.), *Al-Ṭabarī*.

171 Keaney, *Remembering Rebellion*, 13.

172 "The attitude of the early ʿAbbāsid historians became the standard for later historiography as late as the fifteenth century," Rosenthal, *A History*, 63, cited by Keaney, *Remembering Rebellion*, 14.

reinterpretations of the figure of ʿUthmān b. al-ʿAffān during the medieval period.[173] Another, more extreme example is that of Daniel and Peacock, who have suggested that Balʿamī was more of an adaptor than translator of al-Ṭabarī in Persian,[174] while Khalidi has given numerous examples of the richness and variation characteristic of medieval Islamic historiography.[175] Despite the imposition of a historiographic vulgate beginning in the third–fourth centuries *hijrī*, al-Ṭabarī is by no means "the end of history." Other major crises, such as the fall of Baghdad in 656/1258, would later influence historiography in a manner similar to the turmoil of the tenth century.[176]

Nevertheless, prior to these later medieval reinterpretations, al-Ṭabarī did impose a certain reading of Islamic history whose analytical framework struck against the concurrent interpretations of the day. Judd has recently cited a convincing example of this phenomenon by demonstrating the divergent opinions of al-Balādhurī and al-Ṭabarī on the causes of the Umayyad fall from power, despite the fact that the two authors primarily used a single common source: al-Madāʾinī.[177] Al-Ṭabarī highlighted tribal factors, particularly the conflict between Kalb and Qays, and emphasised the greed of the last Marwanid rulers; his predecessor, however, centred the debate around the moral corruption and religious deviance of the last Umayyad caliphs.[178] Both authors relied heavily on individual character traits to support their arguments. Al-Walīd II is thus portrayed by al-Balādhurī as an orthodox yet morally deviant caliph who was unjustly overthrown by the heretical Yazīd III; conversely, al-Ṭabarī minimised the caliph's moral failings and condemned his inability to assuage the tribal tensions that ultimately led to his downfall.[179] Similar divergences of opinion exist between al-Ṭabarī's interpretations and those of pro-Alid authors such as al-Yaʿqūbī and al-Masʿūdī.[180]

Islamic historiography composed at the turn of the third-fourth centuries must be comprehended in all its depth, and the efforts to impose a vulgate

173 With a stated objective: "my own research bridges the gap between al-Ṭabarī and Ibn Khaldūn," *Remembering Rebellion*, 45.

174 Daniel, "Balʿamī's Account;" Peacock, *Medieval Islamic Historiography*.

175 Khalidi, *Arabic Historical Thought*.

176 Keaney, *Remembering Rebellion*, 48. See also Peacock, *Medieval Islamic Historiography*, 14.

177 Judd, "Character Development" and "Medieval Explanations." For another example of the different approaches to the available material by these two authors, see Leder, "Features of the Novel."

178 Judd, "Character Development," 210.

179 Judd, "Character Development," 223–4. Judd has also recently argued for a reinterpretation of the figure of al-Walīd II, who is traditionally portrayed very negatively in the sources, "Reinterpreting." On the image of this caliph, see also Vogts, *Figures de califes*.

180 Humphreys, "Qurʾānic Myth," 278; Keaney, *Remembering Rebellion*.

underway at this time in no way prevented the persistence of different possible readings of Islamic history. Al-Ṭabarī himself was beholden to the debates that characterised the earlier historiographic filters mentioned previously in this chapter. Although al-Ṭabarī's great masterpiece was subject to the same vagaries of transmission and antecedent debates that would hold sway over subsequent historiographic reconstructions, the influence of his text was considerable. If Spiegel was able to affirm that the monks of Saint-Denis became the "historical voice of France"[181] through their famous chronicles, can the same be said for al-Ṭabarī with respect to Islamic history?

Recognition for al-Ṭabarī's work was immediate, and he was widely praised by his contemporaries, including the jurist Ibn al-Mughallis (d. 324/936),[182] as well as his peers, al-Masʿūdī (d. 345/956) among them.[183] His *History* must have occupied a place of honour in the caliphal libraries; the Fatimid caliph al-ʿAzīz (r. 365–386/975–996), for example, spent 100 dinars to obtain a copy, only to discover that his library already possessed more than twenty! Two centuries later, Ibn Abī Ṭayyiʾ reported that the Fatimid library possessed 1220 copies when Saladin captured the palace complex in 567/1171.[184] A similarly keen interest would later incite Maḥmūd of Ghazna to exclaim that the *Shahnameh* was to Persians what al-Ṭabarī's history was to Muslims![185] Al-Ṭabarī's popularity was immense, both among the later Arab historians as well as in the Persian-speaking world; the considerable success of the Samanid vizier Balʿamī's work – largely adapted from al-Ṭabarī's – bears witness to this fact.[186] As a consequence of the vast recognition his work received, al-Ṭabarī naturally found his way into the biographical dictionaries. Abū Saʿīd b. Yūnus (d. 347/958) composed a notice for al-Ṭabarī in his volume on "foreigners in Egypt," a work that unfortunately does not survive.[187] The oldest extant biography is that of al-Khaṭīb al-Baghdādī (d. 463/1071) in his *Taʾrīkh Baghdād*,[188]

181 Spiegel, "Political Unity," 314.

182 Rosenthal, "General Introduction," 135.

183 Al-Masʿūdī, *Murūj*, vol. I, 15–6; trans. Pellat vol. I, 6–7: "The chronicle of Abū Jaʿfar Muḥammad b. Jarīr al-Ṭabarī shines forth among all the [historical] compositions and is superior to them; the variety of information, traditions, [and] scientific documents that it comprises render it as useful as it is instructive; how could it be otherwise, since the author is the *faqīh* of his century, the most pious of his time, and to whom has arrived all of the knowledge of the *fuqahāʾ* of the great cities (*fuqahāʾ al-amṣār*) and the bearers of religious traditions tracing back to the Prophet (*sunna*) and his companions (*athar*)?"

184 Rosenthal, "General Introduction," 141.

185 Ibn al-Athīr, *Kāmil*, vol. IX, 371–2, cited by Peacock, *Medieval Islamic Historiography*, 13.

186 On this point, see Peacock, *Medieval Islamic Historiography*, especially Ch. 5.

187 Rosenthal, "General Introduction," 8.

188 Al-Khaṭīb al-Baghdādī, *Taʾrīkh Baghdād*, vol. II, 162–9.

while the most extensive entry is that of Yāqūt (d. 626/1229) in his *Irshād*.[189] In general, al-Ṭabarī is well-represented in the great medieval biographical dictionaries; more than simple notices, he also elicited full biographies, such as the Egyptian scholar al-Qifṭī's (d. 646/1248) now-lost volume entitled *Al-Taḥrīr fī akhbār Muḥammad b. Jarīr*.[190] Al-Ṭabarī became an essential source for later historians such as Ibn al-Athīr (d. 630/1233), whose works would subsequently serve as an indirect means of accessing al-Ṭabarī for late medieval authors.

Modern scholars, however, are perhaps even more susceptible than their medieval predecessors to al-Ṭabarī's influence, and Donner has justifiably noted that we are often the victims of the "Tabarization" of Islamic history.[191] Al-Ṭabarī has been known to the West since the seventeenth century, as attested by Barthélemi d'Herbelot's (1625–1695) notice dedicated to him in his *Bibliothèque orientale*, published posthumously in 1697; in composing this notice, d'Herbelot relied primarily on information drawn from his contemporary Ḥājjī Khalīfa (1609–1657).[192] Al-Ṭabarī's importance was later emphasised by the Orientalist Andreas David Mordtmann, who in 1848 called him the "*Vater der arabischen Geschichte*."[193] However, it is above all thanks to Michael Jan de Goeje's late-nineteenth century edition of the text that al-Ṭabarī's fame spread widely throughout early modern scholarship. The undeniable influence of Wellhausen's work proved then decisive, and it remains an especially influential source even today: the first great sweeping study dedicated to the Umayyads faithfully followed al-Ṭabarī's presentation of the dynasty.[194] The American complete translation of the *Taʾrīkh al-rusul wa-al-mulūk* undoubtedly contributed to this "Tabarization" in modern scholarship,[195] as does the continued confusion – inexplicably maintained in the new edition – between al-Ṭabarī and his Persian adaptor Balʿamī in Zottenberg's French translation.[196] Even the "skeptical" historians do not stray far from the vision of Umayyad history imparted by al-Ṭabarī, as Hawting's overview has shown.[197] More recent studies have highlighted the danger of relying exclusively on al-Ṭabarī, and demand that we reconsider the very foundations of what we think we know about Umayyad history: for example, the tribal aspect, so prevalent in modern

189 Yāqūt, *Irshād*, ed. Rifāʿī, vol. XVIII, 40–94.
190 Rosenthal, "General Introduction," 8.
191 In his review of Kennedy's *The Prophet*, in *Speculum* 65 (1990): 182–4.
192 On d'Herbelot, see Laurens, *La bibliothèque orientale*.
193 Mordtmann, "Nachrichten;" Rosenthal, "General Introduction," 139.
194 Wellhausen, *Das arabische Reich*, English trans. *The Arab Kingdom*.
195 *The History of al-Ṭabarī*.
196 Al-Ṭabarī, *La chronique*.
197 Hawting, *The First Dynasty*.

scholarship on the period, was not a major focus of medieval authors on the subject; this fact reminds us to be cautious, and relativises the importance of certain historical elements that scholars today often take for granted.[198]

Although al-Ṭabarī is by no means the last word in Islamic historical thought, his rapid notoriety, accompanied by the remarkable diffusion of his text, had a tremendous influence on a considerable number of later historical works. The *Taʾrīkh al-rusul wa-al-mulūk*, an essential reference work, left its mark on medieval historiography as much as modern. This state of affairs is the result of the fact that al-Ṭabarī's *magnum opus* arose from a very particular context. As Brown has recently noted, the fourth/tenth century was a "period of intense canonical process," during which works of note such as the *ṣaḥīḥayn* of Muslim and al-Bukhārī became canonical.[199] These remarks echo those of Gilliot, who emphasised the fact that al-Ṭabarī lived during a "pivotal era," "at the end of a process of fixing doctrines and theses," and that he participated "to a certain extent in the elaboration of an 'orthodoxy'."[200] In this sense, al-Ṭabarī's presentation of history and its great figures constitutes not only a major historiographic filter, but also a distorting prism. We have no choice here but to note the minuscule place accorded to Syria through this filter, especially with respect to the second/eighth century.

Up until the abandonment of Sāmarrāʾ, there were pasts and histories over which historians and rulers had attempted to exert dominance through selection and rewriting, but there had never yet been historiographic projects of the grand scale of those that would soon be underway. In the post-Sāmarrāʾ period, these historiographic efforts proved successful: the past and history tend to conjugate in the singular, despite the possibility of certain variants, due to the very mode of writing that juxtaposed the *riwāyas*.[201] A vulgate had been imposed, which in no way meant that further developments would prove impossible; rather, the contrary was true, as it was not so much a specific content but a framework that needed to be firmly established. This framework was that of the history of the first centuries of Islam, composed of a core of limited elements that modern scholars still use and rely on today.[202] Nearly

198 See Judd's precautions, "Character Development," 224.

199 Brown, *The Canonization*, especially Ch. 4.

200 Gilliot, *Exégèse*, 8, 207 and 277.

201 For example, al-Ṭabarī juxtaposes the *akhbār* borrowed from al-Wāqidī and Sayf b. ʿUmar concerning the caliph ʿUthmān b. ʿAffān. Al-Wāqidī, suspected of Shiite sympathies, presents a fairly negative portrait of the caliph, contrary to Sayf b. ʿUmar, whose description is more favourable. See Keaney, *Remembering Rebellion*, 39 ff.

202 El-Hibri's important work, *Reinterpreting*, is significant in this respect: the author, who proposes a reinterpretation of Islamic history, elucidates the fact that fundamentally it was the authors he discusses who engaged in this practice.

all of the subsequent developments offered numerous new interpretations, but the historiographic skeleton itself could no longer be altered. The stakes of this enterprise rested precisely on this immutable foundation: successive reinterpretations mattered little, because they could no longer expand the fixed borders of a now authoritative past. Other historiographic developments on the margins of this solidifying vulgate nevertheless remained possible; we shall now turn our attention toward these sources originating from different logical foundations.

CHAPTER 3

A Time of Writings and Rewritings: Sources on the Margins of the Historiographic Vulgate?

> This is not simply "a lot of information" but information provided by different types of sources that guarantee the greatest chance of transmission. It is this combination of different forms of transmission that gives the historian confidence that his task is not a futile one to begin with. Yet in this case as well, perception of the asymmetrical losses of transmission is an essential aid because it leads to the identification of possible distortions in cases where these distortions are barely perceptible and thus particularly pernicious: the medievalist in particular is doomed to try to use the difficulties of transmission to his methodological advantage.[1]

∴

The outline sketched in the previous chapter is primarily valid for the Islamic chronographies; henceforth, the vulgate would condition the possible histories of early Islam, despite the persistence of concurrent interpretations. The search for an Islamic historiography on the margins of this vulgate is largely a question of seeking out different types of narrative sources; sources produced in Syria itself or having a spatial focus that renders the *Bilād al-Shām* unavoidable are particularly important in this regard. Originating from different logical foundations and responding to different needs, these sources did not entirely fit in among the more mainstream efforts underway at the time, nor were they completely free of the dominant trends and influences of this historiography. These texts thus occupied different, often ambiguous, spaces. However, existing on the margins of the vulgate did not necessarily mean that these sources were in opposition to the historiographic canon of the Abbasid era. Some of these texts were much more hostile to the Umayyads than those produced under the aegis of the Abbasids, while others displayed more favourable attitudes toward the first Islamic dynasty, in some cases because they echoed the

1 Esch, "Chance et hasard de la transmission," 19.

 DOI:10.1163/9789004466326_005

sentiments of a lost Umayyad historiography. In this chapter, I will continue by analysing these other Islamic sources, which must be situated in relation to the chronographies discussed in the preceding chapter. I shall then address the question of non-Muslim sources in order to shed light on the common threads uniting the different historiographies of the medieval Near East.

3.1 Islamic Sources on the Margins of the Vulgate?

Several different types of sources could potentially be included in this category. Three major groups make up this typology: first, the various extant sources produced – or supposedly produced – in the Umayyad or early Abbasid period; second, sources with a spatial focus that dedicate a predominant place to Syria; and third, texts offering other perspectives, such as later works, works produced by non-Muslim authors, or works written in specific contexts. An exhaustive presentation of all of these sources is impossible here; however, it is essential that we focus on several representative examples in order to understand what can be expected from such texts.

3.1.1 *Second/Eighth Century Sources?*

The first question to address is whether any documents produced by the Umayyad or Abbasid states survive. We will then discuss the monumental heritage of the first Islamic dynasty in the Syrian space, undoubtedly the most obvious Umayyad legacy,[2] followed by a more general analysis of artistic and cultural productions, in particular the rich poetic tradition associated with the caliphs of Damascus.

3.1.1.1 Caliphal and Administrative Documentary Sources

For generations, scholars have lamented the near-total lack of "documentary sources" for early Islam, jealously looking on as their colleagues sift through the vast and rich medieval archives of Europe. This dearth is one of the most sensitive subjects for any specialist in early Islamic studies; moreover, the highly fragmentary nature of these documents was noted in the preceding chapters. The most important archive of the first centuries of Islam is unquestionably the mass of papyri inherited mainly from the Umayyad administration. Unfortunately, this corpus offers limited access to the Syrian space of the second/eighth century, as Egypt is best represented in these materials; the Palestinian papyri that survive primarily date either to the first/seventh

2 See Borrut and Cobb, "Introduction."

century[3] or to eras later than the one that is the focus of this inquiry,[4] and sadly, second/eighth century Syria was not endowed with its own Qurra b. Sharīk.[5] The Egyptian papyri nevertheless attest to an administrative and epistolary written production that must equally have existed in the Syrian space – the epicentre of Umayyad authority – but does not survive. The chronographies offer scant reference to this now-lost Syrian production, although some documents attest to continued administrative and archival activity in Abbasid Damascus; the caliph al-Mahdī would later transfer the *dīwān*s of this production to Medina in 168/784–785 as part of his administrative reforms.[6] The lack of information related to Syria in these papyri means that we must turn our attention elsewhere in search of these "documentary sources."[7]

If we go so far as to include epigraphic and numismatic evidence in this category, we encounter clearer and better-attested examples. With these sources, we have access to texts definitively produced by the Marwanids or early Abbasids: fragments of administrative practice, diverse policies, and ideological programs emerge after deeper analysis. These two types of sources offer material characterised by its dispersion, a fact that negates the possibility of constructing a more global vision from the evidence they provide, despite the important studies conducted or currently underway in the field.[8] However, the information gleaned from this corpus must be systematically confronted with the chronographies. The contemporaneity of these sources with the period

---

3 Kraemer, *Excavations at Nessana*.

4 In particular, the papyri of Khirbat al-Mird, studied by Grohmann, *Arabic Papyri*, or texts dating to the caliphate of al-Mutawakkil possibly originating in Syria; see Abbott, "Arabic Papyri."

5 This important Umayyad administrative figure from Egypt, of which he was the governor from 90–96/709–714, produced numerous letters on papyri that have survived; for more on him, see Abbott, *The Qurrah Papyri* and *Studies in Arabic Literary Papyri*; Ragheb, "Lettres nouvelles." See also Sijpesteijn, *Shaping a Muslim State*.

6 Al-Ṭabarī, vol. III, 522; trans. vol. XXIX, 241. On the continuities between Umayyad and Abbasid administrative practice, see Bligh-Abramski, *From Damascus to Baghdad*, and Biddle, *The Development*.

7 A good survey of the first dated Islamic texts is provided by Hoyland, *Seeing*, 687–703. See also Hoyland, "New Documentary Texts."

8 For epigraphy, despite a multitude of very specific inquiries, regional studies remain somewhat lacking, apart from that of Imbert, *Corpus*, dedicated to present-day northern Jordan. A more theoretical approach to epigraphy as a historical source for the early years of Islam has been proposed by Hoyland, "The Content and the Context." The principle epigraphic indices comprise copious material, see in particular Van Berchem, *Corpus inscriptorum*; RCEA; CIAP; Diem and Schöller, *The Living and the Dead*. With regard to numismatic evidence, in addition to the numerous catalogs and more targeted studies available, see above all the works of Bates and Foss (a detailed list is provided in the bibliography), and the studies of Bone, *The Administration*, and Bresc, *Monuments numismatiques*.

studied here – a status that cannot be claimed by any of the extant Islamic narrative sources – as well as their deep roots in the Syrian space are ample justification for this approach. The religious policies of the Umayyads are particularly well-represented in these sources through the Qurʾānic inscriptions on the Dome of the Rock or the epigraphic coinage produced after the reforms of ʿAbd al-Malik, to cite but two of the most obvious examples. The development of the Syrian space is equally illustrated by inscriptions in stone, in particular ʿAbd al-Malik's milestones or the inscriptions of his son Hishām.[9] The early Abbasids' policies in the province that had been the preferred space of their predecessors remain relatively little-known.[10]

Other sources that seem closely related to the aforementioned Egyptian administrative documents are available, in particular epistolary ones. We possess a sizable number of letters attributed to different sovereigns of the period or their secretaries.[11] The most famous example is the collection of letters linked to ʿAbd al-Ḥamīd al-Kātib, the secretary of the last Umayyad caliph, Marwān II; these letters have been studied in detail by Iḥsān ʿAbbās and Wadād al-Qāḍī.[12] The letters offer material concerning an Umayyad ideology that has largely disappeared. Yet, unlike their Egyptian counterparts, these documents have not survived in their original forms: we know them only as they were integrated into later literary sources, not as documentary archives. Here again we are faced with the problem of transmission outlined in the preceding chapters. Some of the letters preserved in later compilations are clearly total reconstructions;[13] the question of authenticity is thus ever-present.[14] These letters, however, are not merely inserted into narratives for simple reasons of form, and meticulous studies of diplomatics demonstrate that some of these letters incontrovertibly contain older elements. This subject remains to be studied in-depth, and future investigations aimed at narrowing this gap in our understanding should be undertaken following the model of those fruitful inquiries on ʿAbd al-Ḥamīd.

---

9 On these inscriptions, see Elad, "The Southern Golan;" Rihaoui, "Découverte;" Khamis, "Two Wall Mosaic." For more details on these inscriptions and the policies they reveal, see below, Ch. 8.

10 For example, see Bacharach, "Al-Mansur."

11 The major problems these letters pose were exposed by Noth and Conrad, *The Early Arabic*, 76–87. The main attempt to collect all of these letters – in reality far from an exhaustive one – was undertaken by Ṣafwat, *Jamharat*.

12 ʿAbbās, *ʿAbd al-Ḥamīd*; al-Qāḍī, "Early Islamic State Letters" and "The Religious Foundation." See also Schönig, *Das Sendschreiben*.

13 Noth and Conrad, *The Early Arabic*, 77.

14 The letters attributed to ʿAbd al-Ḥamīd are generally considered authentic by modern scholars. See al-Qāḍī, "Early Islamic State Letters," 232 ff.

Along with these letters, the narrative sources contain numerous other documents, in particular treaties of surrender[15] and lists of various natures, in addition to discourses that were supposedly recorded *verbatim*.[16] Although the form remains problematic and the means of transmission are uncertain, these elements should not be rejected out of hand, as they may still preserve older information. Robinson, using an idea advanced by Chamberlain, notes that one of the functions of historiography is to enable a literary archival of documentary sources.[17] This observation is important, as it warns of the dangers of reducing this documentation to the level of simple literary artifice; although the original *forms* of these documents remain ambiguous, they nevertheless often provide *information* found in earlier originals. Moreover, these documents inform us of the period in which they were integrated into the literary sources and the meaning the compiler hoped to bestow upon the past in the process.

3.1.1.2 Artistic and Architectural Programs

Taking a step back from the textual sources that have been the primary focus of this study until now, we turn our attention here to another aspect of caliphal production: the architectural and iconographic projects undertaken in the Syrian space in the second/eighth century. Although dating these types of evidence with certainty is often difficult, they nevertheless offer another means of access to elements that have the great advantage of contemporaneity with the period under investigation here. Monumental architecture in Syria in the second/eighth century presents a situation directly opposite the image portrayed in the narrative sources. Whereas we only possess narrative sources produced during the Abbasid period, the architectural evidence offers a very different picture at first glance: Umayyad art and structures cover the Syrian landscape, although the continued occupation of these sites by the early Abbasids remains little studied.[18]

Archaeology has for some time now been an important means of expanding our knowledge of the first centuries of Islam. The contribution of this archaeological evidence is remarkable, both for economic and social history as well as with respect to the exercise of caliphal power,[19] especially as attested by

15 On these documents, see Hill, *The Termination*; al-Qāḍī, "Madkhal;" Noth, "Die 'Ṣulḥ;'."

16 On these various insertions in literary sources, see Noth and Conrad, *The Early Arabic*, 62–108.

17 Robinson, *Islamic Historiography*, 147; Chamberlain, *Knowledge*, 2 ff.

18 See Genequand, "Formation et devenir."

19 On this question, see below, Ch. 7.

the "desert palaces;"[20] these sites, largely forgotten in the narrative sources, are significant because they have been recovered to history by archaeology. Moreover, in our quest for sources on the margins of the historiographic vulgate made up of the great Abbasid chronographies, the artistic and iconographic programs of the Umayyad era are a point of access to the first Islamic dynasty's ideology of power. This "presentation of self"[21] reveals the manner in which the Umayyads wished to inscribe themselves into a continuous history and confirm the universal calling of their caliphate.[22] By creating a "visual culture,"[23] the best examples of which are perhaps the frescoes of Quṣayr ʿAmra,[24] the caliphs of Damascus affirmed their legitimacy and their power. The famous fresco of the six kings, in which all the kings of the earth come to pledge allegiance to the new masters of the world, offers a particularly striking example.[25] Umayyad architectural programs also engaged in an appropriation of the Syrian space, while their construction of religious edifices etched the new faith into the landscape. These artistic proofs, much like the epigraphic inscriptions and coinage mentioned above, are authentic Umayyad sources; as such, they represent the veritable preservation of an Umayyad memory.

Archaeology, particularly at al-Ḥumayma, illuminates the traces of an Abbasid Syrian memory as well, traces that the second Islamic dynasty attempted to erase.[26] Archaeology also indicates that certain sites were in continuous use, at least until the beginning of the third/ninth century. This archaeological evidence gives another perspective on the dynastic change that occurred in 132/750, as well as on the future of the Syrian space following the relocation of the caliphate to Iraq:[27] the uneven tempo of political history here gives way to the more regular rhythm of land use and settlement patterns.

20 Many studies address this subject. See Lammens, "La 'Bādiya';" Sauvaget, "Châteaux omeyyades;" Gaube, "Die syrischen Wüstenschlösser;" Hillenbrand, "La Dolce Vita" and "'Anjar;" Genequand, "Umayyad Castles," "Châteaux omeyyades" and *Les élites omeyyades*.

21 To use Goffman's famous phrase, *The Presentation of Self*, to be read in light of Habermas's discussion, *Logique des sciences sociales*, 413 ff.

22 Ettinghausen, *La peinture arabe*, 20, 40.

23 Here I borrow Flood's expression, *The Great Mosque*.

24 On this famous site, see the recent contributions of Fowden, *Quṣayr ʿAmra*, and Cheddadi, *Les Arabes*, 26 ff.; however, a number of the interpretations proposed in these two works should be considered with caution. For a systematic survey of paintings, see the excellent work of Vibert-Guigue, *Les peintures de Quṣayr ʿAmra*.

25 See Musil, *Kusejr Amra*; Herzfeld, "Die Könige;" Grabar, "The Painting of the Six Kings" and *La formation*, 68–71; Creswell, *Early Muslim Architecture*, vol. 1, 390–415 and *A Short Account*, 84–99; Almagro et al., *Quṣayr ʿAmra*; Cheddadi, *Les Arabes*, 26 ff.; Fowden, *Empire to Commonwealth*, 143–9 and *Quṣayr ʿAmra*. This fresco is discussed more below, Ch. 8.

26 See below, Ch. 4.

27 This point is further developed in Ch. 7 and 8.

3.1.1.3 Umayyad Poetry: Questions and Issues

The thorny question of Umayyad poetry also needs to be addressed.[28] Historians have long maintained ambivalence toward this literary genre, which was either accepted or rejected *in toto*: poetry has often been depicted either as the source par excellence for Umayyad history or, conversely, as an inconsequential source of historical knowledge. This latter view is indisputably that adopted by Watt in 1962.[29] This argument has since been picked apart by modern scholars, and poetry's contributions as a source have been well-established.[30] The modern historian's interest in poetry echoes the sentiments shared by the early Muslim scholars themselves, who stated that poets "were the only organs of historical memory,"[31] and, more precisely, that "poetry is the mine of the knowledge of the ancient Arabs (*al-shiʿru maʿdinu ʿilmi al-ʿarabi*), the book of their wisdom (*sifru ḥikmatihā*), the archives of their history (*dīwānu akhbārihā*), the treasury of their great days ... and the ramparts that guard their memorable facts (*al-sūru al-maḍrūbu ʿalā maʾāthirihā*)," as attested by this famous passage from the *Akhbār ʿUbayd*.[32] Moreover, poetry fulfills an essential function of proof, which at least partially justifies its frequent inclusion in historical texts;[33]

28 For an overview of Arabic literary production during the Umayyad period, see Pellat, *Langue et littérature*; Beeston, *Arabic Literature*. For Umayyad poetry in particular, see Jayyusi, "Umayyad Poetry." On the use of poetry by historians, see Cheikh-Moussa, "L'historien et la littérature arabe."

29 Watt, "The Materials," 28: "Not much requires to be said about the poetry, even if it is all authentic, it adds little to our historical knowledge." See also Cahen's skeptical remarks on the use of poetry by historians, later echoed by Cheikh-Moussa, "L'historien et la littérature arabe," 152 ff.

30 For example, see the criticisms addressed by Beeston and Conrad to the proponents of the widely shared opinion that poetry is of little historical importance, "On some Umayyad Poetry," 191.

31 As cited by Goldziher, *Muslim Studies*, vol. 1, 169, and, more recently, by Elad, "Community of Believers," 272.

32 Arazi, "Al-shiʿru," 205, citing *Akhbār ʿUbayd*, 352. This passage is taken up again by Elad, "Community of Believers," 272. The dominant place accorded to poetry from the *Jāhiliyya* period is also mentioned by al-Yaʿqūbī, *Taʾrīkh*, vol. 1, 262.

33 On this point, see Cheddadi, *Les Arabes*, 49–52. There are certainly other reasons for inserting poetry into chronographies that should not be ignored, as Humphreys notes, *Islamic History*, 90: "The function of verse citations in the historical texts has never been properly studied, but I believe that they serve much the same purpose as the speeches and letters which are periodically introduced ... to allow the historian to convey an explicit interpretation or evaluation of persons and events without having to speak for himself. Poetry, in short, is editorial comment, safely attributed to others." Beeston and Conrad also lament the lack of studies related to the role and place of poetry cited in historical texts, "On some Umayyad Poetry," 191. See also the important work of Ali, *Ardor for*

certain scholars have even gone so far as to speak of "Arabic historical poetry."[34] It is well-attested that poetry was also a means of identity affirmation,[35] and it seems clear that the Umayyads used court poets to promote the idea of their legitimacy.[36] Furthermore, it is impossible to study the first Islamic dynasty without immediately thinking of some of the famous and rival poets of this period: among the most renowned were Jarīr (d. c. 110/728), al-Farazdaq (d. c. 112/730), and al-Akhṭal (d c. 92/710), the "champion" of the Umayyads, to use Henri Lammens's expression.[37]

But is Umayyad poetry really *the* quintessential source for approaching the first Islamic dynasty, as some scholars have stated? Agha and Khalidi have recently suggested that poetry is perhaps the most fundamental Arabic source because it is also the earliest.[38] By comparison, there is less of a case for this idealistic view with respect to scholarly affirmations concerning pre-Islamic poetry, the famous *Muʿallaqāt*, and other pre-Abbasid poetic fragments that have survived. Since Ṭaha Ḥusayn, it has been confirmed that the *Jāhiliyya*'s real or supposed poetic legacy was reworked during the Abbasid era, and in particular passed through the filter of monotheism;[39] this desacralisation has provoked and sustained scholarly polemics. Rina Drory situates this recomposition of pre-Islamic poetry more precisely in the mid-760s.[40] The question of the date of composition and authenticity of the *Muʿallaqāt* remains a perennial subject of debate; recent opinions call for the analysis of these textual manipulations[41] and highlight the existence of earlier layers of writing, some of which are attested as early as the beginning of the Umayyad period under the reign of Muʿāwiya.[42] This situation is similar to the one presented regarding the chronographies: the past itself, both pre- and post-Prophetic, was reworked during the Abbasid period, *in the wake of previous successive rewritings* and in accordance with strategies of *selection*. How is it possible, then, to

Memory, and Shoshan's remarks, *Poetics of Islamic Historiography*, 82–4, following from the earlier opinions of Athamina, "The Sources," 192.

34 Beeston and Conrad, "On some Umayyad Poetry," 192.

35 Agha and Khalidi, "Poetry and Identity."

36 See above all Stetkevych, *The Poetics of Islamic Legitimacy*.

37 Lammens, "Le chantre." On al-Akhṭal, see Stetkevych, "Umayyad Panegyric" and *The Poetics of Islamic Legitimacy*, chs. 3 and 4.

38 Agha and Khalidi, "Poetry and Identity," 55 n. 1.

39 Ḥusayn, *Fī al-shiʿr al-jāhilī*.

40 Drory, "The Abbasid Connection."

41 Arazi, "Périodisation, oralité et authenticité."

42 On this point, see Kister, "The Seven Odes," and Arazi, "Périodisation, oralité et authenticité," 408–9.

imagine that Umayyad poetry remained unaffected by these processes at work in other literary genres at the time?

Our knowledge of the conditions presiding over the transmission of poetry invites the same caution and strategic approach adopted with respect to Islamic historiography. Schoeler has demonstrated that it was current among poets for transmitters to correct and improve the poems they transmitted, including during the lifetimes of the poets themselves. The sources echo this state of affairs: we are told that "in the past, transmitters were wont to improve the poems of the ancients,"[43] and the *Kitāb al-Aghānī* notes that there were certain transmitters of al-Farazdaq who were "straightening out whatever was 'crooked' in his poetry." Jarīr was in a similar situation, as his transmitters subscribed to the same practices and even corrected an "impure rhyme (*sinād*)."[44] From these examples, Schoeler concludes that in general "there was not a great deal of concern at the time for exact textual preservation in the process of transmission, nor for fidelity to the original. What was important was the preservation and amelioration of the artistic and linguistic quality of the poetry to be transmitted. This conception of transmission was incompatible with the idea of a definitive recension enabling the literary publication of the texts."[45] As a result of these combined factors, Umayyad poetry was by no means an exception in the realm of Islamic sources. Without neglecting the contribution of these texts, in particular for historical topography[46] or information concerning life at court and Umayyad ceremonial,[47] they also emphasise the work that remains to be done to better understand how and why certain poetic compositions were preserved through these complex processes of transmission and the subsequent distortions they underwent over the course of successive rewritings.

This task is precisely the object of Kilpatrick's studies of the *Kitāb al-Aghānī*.[48] Al-Iṣfahānī's (d. 356/967) anthology, whose methodology we understand better thanks to Kilpatrick, is a significant source of information on the Umayyads and early Abbasids. The chapters al-Iṣfahānī dedicated to the different caliphs combine elements of historical narrative similar to those found in biographical

43 Cited by Schoeler, *The Genesis*, 20.

44 *Kitāb al-Aghānī*, vol. IV, 54; trans. Schoeler, *The Genesis*, 20.

45 Schoeler, *Écrire et transmettre*, 21.

46 As Sauvaget has shown, "Notes de topographie," 104–5.

47 See especially Stetkevych's exemplary study, "Umayyad Panegyric," and Marsham, *Rituals*, which makes abundant use of the resources presented by Umayyad poetry.

48 Al-Iṣfahānī, *Kitāb al-Aghānī*. See Kilpatrick, *Making the Great Book of Songs*. The lack of studies devoted to the problems of transmission related to the *Kitāb al-Aghānī* is noted by Zolondek, "An Approach."

dictionaries or chronographies with abundant poetic citations. These elements allow us to better comprehend the relationships within the Umayyad clan, a subject difficult to ascertain from other sources; in some ways, the Umayyads are erected as representative models of their age.[49] Other corpora of poetic production are provided with quality editions and valuable tools for navigating the vagaries of poetic composition. This is especially the case for Khārijī poetry, and more recently, Shiite poetry as well.[50] Nevertheless, a systematic investigation of these works is well outside the scope of the present inquiry.

The links between poetry and history, in particular the frequent integration of poetry into historical sources, forbids any attempt at marginalising poetry completely. It should be noted that the general framework for poetic transmission was no different than that outlined for the transmission of historical texts, and that more work on this subject remains to be done. However, the specificity of the genre assured the preservation of a proper Umayyad *memoria*, for, as Kilpatrick notes, no other period of Islamic history could boast of as many poets as the Umayyad era.[51]

3.1.2 *Space before Chronology*

Chronology was the organising principle of the chronographies, and this approach privileged the centres of caliphal power rather than the marginal areas; however, other types of sources adopted an opposite approach. Instead of chronology, space presided over the organisation of the text, and thus, in these texts, Syria was at least on an equal footing with the other provinces of the empire.

3.1.2.1 Syrian Biographical Dictionaries: *libri memoriales* in the Service of the Umayyads and Syria?

The very structure of these prosopographic works required to make room for each generations of Muslims, as well as for anyone having traversed or lived in the geographic space covered by a specific biographical dictionary.[52] Important personages and lesser-known figures alike from the second/eighth century Syrian space responded to these imperatives. Whereas the chronographies could produce a "creative oblivion," the *ṭabaqāt* and *maʿājim* required a more systematic presentation, or at least the appearance of one: they preserved a

49 Kilpatrick, "ʿUmar ibn ʿAbd al-ʿAzīz, al-Walīd ibn Yazīd and their kin."
50 ʿAbbās, *Shiʿr al-khawārij*; El-Acheche, *La poésie shiʿite*.
51 Kilpatrick, "ʿUmar ibn ʿAbd al-ʿAzīz, al-Walīd ibn Yazīd and their kin."
52 On this literary genre, see Abiad, "Origine et développement;" Young, "Arabic Biographical Writing;" Auchterlonie, *Arabic Biographical Dictionaries*; al-Qāḍī, "Biographical Dictionaries;" Robinson, "Al-Muʿāfā b. ʿImrān" and *Islamic Historiography*, 66–74.

formidable mass of information that often could not be found anywhere else. This fact has frequently led researchers to see these sources as "gold mines" and to peremptorily decide that prosopography was the only means of accessing the history of the first centuries of Islam.[53] However, it must not be forgotten that, as Esch has noted with respect to the Italian commune of Lucca, "[an] abundance of documents ... does not preclude considerable losses ... it is, after the fact, a redistribution of reality via transmission."[54] As a result, although these sources are not subject to the same conditions as the chronographies, they nevertheless pose their own specific problems. Is it sufficiently understood, for example, that these sources were produced by the elite sector of a certain social group for other elites, thus marginalising and neglecting entire swathes of society? These lists and compilations, perhaps more than any other literary genre, were used to preserve the social or cultural memory of different groups. Al-Balādhurī's *Ansāb al-ashrāf*, discussed in the previous chapter, is a good example of this fact: this text is the swansong of the *ashrāf*, in particular the Syrian *ashrāf*.[55] The commemoration of a vanishing social order is perhaps first and foremost what justifies the considerable attention al-Balādhurī gives to the Umayyad family. The sheer number of these collections, which also remain understudied in modern scholarship, often makes it difficult to achieve a broader comprehension of the projects intended by these different authors and the conditions that presided over the selection and compilation of this information. It is not a question here of describing these texts in detail, especially since all of the *maʿājim* could potentially offer elements pertinent to this inquiry. Because of their spatial boundaries, the two most valuable Syrian biographical dictionaries for the present study are those of Ibn ʿAsākir (d. 571/1176) and Ibn al-ʿAdīm (d. 660/1262).

Ibn ʿAsākir's *Taʾrīkh madīnat Dimashq* is undoubtedly the most important biographical dictionary for the Syrian space of the second/eighth century;[56] despite the late date at which it was composed, its interest for

53 Crone, *Slaves*, 16–7: "The obvious way to tackle early Islamic history is, in other words, prosopographical. To the extent that the pages of the Muslim chronicles are littered with names, prosopography is of course nothing but a fancy word for what every historian of that period finds himself to be doing. But early Islamic history has to be almost *exclusively* prosopographical."

54 Esch, "Chance et hasard de la transmission," 18–9.

55 On the crisis of the *ashrāf*, see Cobb, *White Banners*, especially 78 ff.

56 For an overview of the editorial enterprise of Ibn ʿAsākir's masterpiece, see Mourad, "Publication History."

the first centuries of Islam is obvious.[57] After presenting the topography of Damascus,[58] Ibn ʿAsākir attempts to provide an exhaustive report of the events that took place in the Syrian space and to include all the major figures of Islamic history.[59] The focus on Syria offers a response to the Iraqi tropisms of the Abbasid-era chronicles, and, as a local history, provides new material on the Syrian elite.[60] It also has the immense advantage of preserving sources that were otherwise lost, such as the *Tasmiyat umarāʾ Dimashq* of Abū al-Ḥusayn al-Rāzī (d. 347/958), mentions of which were previously only known via al-Ṣafadī (d. 766/1363).[61] In general, this text relies on Syrian sources that were neglected by the Abbasid chronographers, and offers abundant citations from Ibn Saʿd (d. 230/845), Khalīfa b. Khayyāṭ (d. 240/854), and above all Abū Zurʿa al-Dimashqī (d. 281/894).[62] Ibn ʿAsākir also relies heavily upon al-Khaṭīb al-Baghdādī (d. 463/1071), whom he acknowledges as the model for his own work; al-Ṭabarī (d. 310/923), however, is conspicuously absent. For all of these reasons, Ibn ʿAsākir is fully engaged in elaborating a "Syrian" *memoria*.[63] However, the *Taʾrīkh madīnat Dimashq* that has survived is incomplete: between 600 and 800 biographies are missing.[64] The biographies of the Umayyad caliphs Sulaymān b. ʿAbd al-Malik and his brother Hishām, for example, are lost, and survive only in Ibn Manẓūr's *Mukhtaṣar*, which was completed based on Ibn ʿAsākir's text;[65] Yazīd III, however, is absent from both works.[66]

The other essential Syrian biographical dictionary is that of Ibn al-ʿAdīm.[67] His *Bughyat al-ṭalab fī taʾrīkh Ḥalab*, although only partially preserved, also

57 In particular, see the contributions of Lindsay, *Ibn ʿAsākir* and "Damascene Scholars;" Cobb, *White Banners*; in French, see the works of Élisséeff, *La description*; Abiad, *Culture et éducation*; Bianquis, *Damas et la Syrie*; Guérin, "Les territoires;" and Jalabert, "Comment Damas" and *Hommes et lieux*.

58 This constitutes the first volume of the *Taʾrīkh madīnat Dimashq*, and has been translated by Élisséeff, *La description*.

59 Donner, "ʿUthmān and the Rāshidūn Caliphs," 59–60.

60 Cobb, "Community versus Contention," 106, 108.

61 In his *Kitāb umarāʾ Dimashq fī al-islām*; see Cobb, "Community versus Contention," 107, and the works of Conrad, "Zur Bedeutung" and *Abū ʾl-Ḥusayn al-Rāzī*, 23–51.

62 On the sources used by Ibn ʿAsākir, see Judd, "Ibn ʿAsākir's Sources."

63 See Cobb, "Virtual Sacrality."

64 Today, this text contains 10,226 biographies. Lindsay, *Ibn ʿAsākir*, 141–3.

65 Ibn Manẓūr, *Mukhtaṣar*.

66 Although it is unknown if this is a lacuna or whether his Qadarite tendencies resulted in his exclusion from Ibn ʿAsākir's *Tarʾīkh madīnat Dimashq*.

67 On whom see Morray, *An Ayyūbid Notable*, and Eddé, "Les sources de l'histoire omeyyade," which rounds out the list of studies dedicated primarily to the Hamdanid period. See Eddé, "Les sources d'Ibn al-ʿAdīm sur le règne de Sayf al-Dawla," and the classic works

contains information related to northern Syria in the second/eighth century.[68] Ibn ʿAsākir's work served as a reference for Ibn al-ʿAdīm, who sought to make his own text on Aleppo in the image of the former's *Taʾrīkh madīnat Dimashq*: the biographies in both works are identically structured, and Ibn ʿAsākir's sources were also employed by his successor. However, the *Bughyat* does not possess the same wealth of information, not least because an entire section of the work is missing. For example, none of the biographies of the Umayyad caliphs have survived, although notices are dedicated to a number of figures from this era. The major advantage of Ibn al-ʿAdīm's text is that he cites his sources; for the early Islamic period, he reproduces the predominant *isnād-khabar* transmission format of the time. Ibn al-ʿAdīm also used the works of several important authors: he had direct access to al-Balādhurī's *Ansāb* and *Futūḥ*, as well as al-Masʿūdī's *Meadows of Gold* and his *Kitāb al-Istidhkār li-mā jarā fī sālif al-aʿṣār*, which does not survive.[69]

Other works of local or regional provenance but of more modest dimensions round out the list, including al-Qushayrī's (d. 334/946) *Taʾrīkh al-Raqqa wa-man nazalahā min aṣḥāb rasūlillāh wa-al-tābiʿīn wa-al-fuqahāʾ wa-al-muḥaddithīn* and al-Khawlānī's (d. between 365/975 and 370/981) *Taʾrīkh Dārayyā*.[70] Other local histories dedicated to Homs and Palestine have not survived, with the exception of a few scattered citations.[71] Despite the difference in regional focus, certain other works on Iraq or the Jazīra may also be added to the list as complementary sources: Baḥshal's (al-Wāsiṭī, d. c. 292/905) *Taʾrīkh Wāsiṭ* and al-Azdī's (d. c. 334/945) *Taʾrīkh al-Mawṣil* are but two examples.[72]

Are these sources really completely *external* to the historiographic vulgate represented by the chronographies? The answer to this question depends entirely upon the sources used by these sources, as well as the global projects of their authors. In the context of this inquiry, the focus on Syria is a decisive factor: for example, Ibn ʿAsākir's broader goal of reintegrating Syria into Islamic history. The fact that Ibn ʿAsākir makes relatively little use of al-Ṭabarī and relies more heavily on Syrian authors such as Abū Zurʿa al-Dimashqī is

of Canard, *Histoire de la dynastie*, in particular 16–49. For Ibn al-ʿAdīm's sources on the twelfth and thirteenth centuries, see Eddé, "Sources arabes."

68 Ibn al-ʿAdīm's history of Aleppo, the *Zubdat al-Ḥalab min taʾrīkh Ḥalab*, offers only limited information on the period under examination here, which covers only a few pages of this volume.

69 Eddé, "Les sources de l'histoire omeyyade."

70 Al-Qushayrī, *Taʾrīkh al-Raqqa*; al-Khawlānī, *Taʾrīkh Dārayyā*.

71 *GAS*, vol. 1, 347.

72 Baḥshal, *Taʾrīkh Wāsiṭ*; al-Azdī, *Taʾrīkh al-Mawṣil*. This latter work was used extensively by Robinson, *Empires and Elites*. On the connections between al-Ṭabarī and al-Azdī, see Robinson, "A Local Historian's Debt."

significant; even more important, these local biographical dictionaries reference sources that are often neglected in other texts. Although we lack definitive knowledge of the parameters of these authors' compositional criteria and selection strategies, these sources, when used with proper discretion, offer promising inroads to the vast field of Islamic historiography. By providing access to sources forgotten by the majority of the chronographies, biographical dictionaries preserve other historiographies, or other *memorisations* of history; in this sense, they are *libri memoriales* in the service of a space and a dynasty that elsewhere fell victim to veritable strategies of oblivion. These sources allow us to escape one of the great paradoxes of Islamic historiography, noted by Cobb, who remarked that our sources fundamentally present a vision in which "ʿAbbāsid history begins in Syria while at the same time Syrian history ends with the ʿAbbāsids."[73] This same interest in space was shared by the Muslim geographers, to whom we shall now turn our attention.

3.1.2.2 The Geographers

A detailed presentation of the great figures of Islamic geography in the manner of Miquel's seminal study is impossible here;[74] all of these authors provide pertinent information on Syria. However, these sources present us with the same problems as the narrative Islamic sources: they are all later compositions, generally written after the second/eighth century. Using these sources for information on this particular period is thus a delicate matter, and these texts do not lend themselves to an analysis of historiographic sedimentation as readily as the chronographies. Although geographical literature does not provide comparable access to the history of the late Umayyads and early Abbasids, it is nevertheless a wellspring of abundant material. This state of affairs is not surprising, especially in the context of an inquiry centred on the particular spatial bounds of the Syrian space.

The main advantage of the geographical sources is the predominant place they dedicate to Syria: while the chronographies composed in Abbasid Iraq mention Syria only when strictly necessary, the geographic sources recognise Syria – one of the provinces of the empire – as a space of great significance. This distinction highlights the different objectives guiding different types of sources: the goal of "administrative geography," such as that found in the *al-masālik wa-al-mamālik* genre or later in the *riḥla* texts, was to describe the Islamic empire in its entirety. This production is thus most valuable for its topographic elements and focus on historical geography. However, due

73 Cobb, "Community versus Contention," 99.

74 Miquel, *La géographie humaine*; see also Hopkins' overview, "Geographical."

to their reliance on anecdotal narratives and information pulled from *adab* works, the geographic sources in reality offer much more: they present visions of the world, mythical and symbolic elements that help to preserve and diffuse a *memoria* inscribed in the Syrian space.[75] In this sense, these texts are especially valuable for a study of the history of memory.

The colourful pages of the geographies of al-Yaʿqūbī (d. 284/897), Ibn al-Faqīh (active c. 290/903) or Ibn Ḥawqal (d. c. 380/990) follow the example provided by their predecessor al-Iṣṭakhrī (d. c. 350/961), and are sufficient proof of the significance of these texts.[76] Syrian authors such as al-Muqaddasī (d. after 378/988), a native of Jerusalem, or the Aleppan Ibn Shaddād (d. 684/1285), are especially useful.[77] Ibn Shaddād provides important information on the military campaigns led by the Umayyads and Abbasids against the Byzantines in northern Syria and Anatolia, while his predecessor is unrivalled in boasting of the merits of his home province. The topographic dictionary of Yāqūt al-Ḥamawī (d. 626/1229), an author of Byzantine and slave origins who lived in Syria, is an inexhaustible reference.[78] Although most geographies contain sections dedicated to describing marvels, the specific genre of the *faḍāʾil* is also a useful source of information: the *Kitāb faḍāʾil al-Shām wa-Dimashq* of ʿAlī b. Muḥammad al-Rabaʿī (d. 443/1052) concerning the sacred status of the Syrian space is a good example.[79]

Geographers and specialists in the *faḍāʾil* genre provide access to a memory inscribed in a particular space, the centre of Umayyad activity and also – at al-Ḥumayma – the cradle of their rivals, the Abbasids.[80] This production gave rise to a discourse that represented a symbolic geography, linking Syrian cities and sites to the first Islamic dynasty and, less frequently, to their Abbasid successors.

3.1.3 *Other Perspectives*

3.1.3.1 Later and Andalusian Historians

The previous chapters have emphasised the extent to which the unfortunate lack of documentation for the first centuries of Islam requires a heavy reliance

75 See below, Ch. 4.

76 Al-Yaʿqūbī, *Kitāb al-buldān*; Ibn al-Faqīh, *Mukhtaṣar*; Ibn Ḥawqal, *Kitāb ṣūrat*; al-Iṣṭakhrī, *Kitāb al-masālik*.

77 Al-Muqaddasī, *Aḥsan*; Ibn Shaddād, *al-Aʿlāq*.

78 Yāqūt, *Muʿjam al-buldān*.

79 Al-Rabaʿī, *Kitāb faḍāʾil al-Shām*. On this valuable source of information regarding the Syrian space, see Cobb, "Virtual Sacrality."

80 On the question of these dynastic memories inscribed in their respective spaces, see below, Ch. 4.

on narrative sources. How, then, do we define chronological and geographic boundaries when using this prolific narrative corpus? Later sources or those composed outside of the Near East can offer information on the second/eighth century. This corpus of literary sources potentially contains many pertinent elements, especially from the perspective of a history of memory and a history of meanings. However, an exhaustive treatment of these sources is well beyond the abilities of any one researcher. The complex questions of how the different texts in this corpus were transmitted – a still insufficiently understood topic – do not always allow us to target the sources most capable of providing new material. The following examples are given with the sole objective of highlighting the countless possibilities offered by these sources.

Alongside the chronographies (*taʾrīkh*) and the prosopographies (*ṭabaqāt* and *maʿājim*), Robinson has recently identified another historiographic genre: the biography (*sīra*).[81] Although the Prophet is most frequently the subject of these works, biographies were also written about other important figures, especially if they were renowned for their piety. For the period under examination here, ʿUmar II is the most striking example.[82] A *Sīrat ʿUmar b. ʿAbd al-ʿAzīz* was written in Egypt by Ibn ʿAbd al-Ḥakam (d. 214/829) and later imitated by Ibn al-Jawzī (d. 597/1201).[83] Like the *maʿājim*, the very form of these volumes required a different writing style than that used in the chronographies. Although somewhat exceptional, the biographies dedicated to ʿUmar II attest to the mechanisms of informational circulation within different historiographies: the apologetic discourses on ʿUmar II did not contradict the historiographic vulgate's image of this caliph.[84] This classic example demands that we situate this literary genre within the vast processes of transmission at work during this period. Thus, the *Sīrat ʿUmar b. ʿAbd al-ʿAzīz* reveals a strong juridic and jurisprudential influence but should not be set in opposition to the historiographic canon. This is not to say, however, that such an example is representative and would necessarily apply in other as-yet unexamined contexts.

Among later historians, three in particular merit our attention here. First, Ibn Kathīr (d. 774/1373), for the simple reason that he was Syrian: he was a native of Buṣrā who lived most of his life in Damascus,[85] where he completed his education, an experience marked by his decisive encounters with al-Mizzī

81 Robinson, *Islamic Historiography*, 55. On the hypothetical origins of this genre, see Cheddadi, *Les Arabes*, 225–6.

82 For a detailed analysis of this question, see Borrut, "Entre tradition et histoire," and below, Ch. 6.

83 Ibn ʿAbd al-Ḥakam, *Sīra*; Ibn al-Jawzī, *Sīra* (or *manāqib*) *ʿUmar b. ʿAbd al-ʿAzīz*.

84 Borrut, "Entre tradition et histoire," especially 364 ff.

85 On whom see Laoust, "Ibn Kathīr" and "Ibn Kathīr historien."

(d. 742/1341) and al-Dhahabī (d. 748/1348).[86] Similar to the Syrian biographical dictionaries mentioned above, his works are apt to contain Syrian material that is otherwise lost; Ibn Kathīr also produced a discourse aimed at reintegrating Syria into Islamic history. The *Bidāya wa-al-nihāya*, his major historical work, proposes to "write a history of the world from Creation to his own epoch and end his narrative with the torments of the Last Judgment."[87] The section dedicated to Islamic history is arranged chronologically: for each year, Ibn Kathīr presents the major events followed by the biographies of the famous individuals who passed away during them (*wafayāt*). In keeping with the defense of Sunnism characteristic of his era, he presents firmly anti-Shiite views and paints a flattering portrait of the Umayyads, attempting to "rehabilitate [their] image."[88] Ibn Kathīr's sources for the section devoted to the beginnings of Islam have yet to be analysed in detail.[89] Laoust has highlighted the importance of Ibn ʿAsākir's text in the *Bidāya*, which Ibn Kathīr used to access older sources. Contrary to his predecessor, Ibn Kathīr referenced al-Ṭabarī and the other great chronographies of the time, including those of Ibn al-Athīr and Ibn al-Jawzī. He was also familiar with Ibn al-Jawzī's aforementioned *Sīrat ʿUmar b. ʿAbd al-ʿAzīz*. Ibn al-ʿAdīm, whom Ibn Kathīr praised, was relatively little cited in the *Bidāya*, while the Shiite sources appear to have been carefully avoided.[90]

The Egyptian al-Maqrīzī (d. 845/1442) did not have the same geographical interest. Other than his *magnum opus*, the *Khiṭaṭ*, he composed two short treatises that are worth noting here: the *Kitāb al-Nizāʿ wa-al-takhāṣum fīmā bayna Banī Umayya wa-Banī Hāshim* and the *Kitāb fī dhikr mā warada fī Banī Umayya wa-Banī al-ʿAbbās*.[91] These two works attempt to establish the legitimacy of the Abbasid caliphate and condemn the Umayyad usurpation of power. The *Kitāb al-Nizāʿ* has been published in several editions, including an English translation with an accompanying commentary by Bosworth;[92] the second text, however, is only preserved in a single manuscript in Vienna that is as yet unedited.[93] We know that the *Kitāb fī dhikr* was composed while al-Maqrīzī was in Mecca in 837/1433, and that it was written in response to a discussion that took place during a *majlis* concerning the relative merits of the Umayyads

86 Laoust, "Ibn Kathīr historien," 45–6.
87 Laoust, "Ibn Kathīr historien," 63.
88 Laoust, "Ibn Kathīr historien," 73.
89 As noted by Eddé, "Les sources de l'histoire omeyyade."
90 Laoust, "Ibn Kathīr historien," 77–83.
91 Al-Maqrīzī, *Kitāb al-nizāʿ* and *Kitāb fī dhikr*.
92 Bosworth, *Al-Maqrīzī*.
93 On this text, see Bosworth, "Al-Maqrīzī's Epistle," and Cobb, "Al-Maqrīzī."

and the Abbasids.[94] The *Kitāb al-Nizāʿ* is mentioned in this second work, so its composition must predate the *Kitāb fī dhikr*; this latter is, in some ways, a summary of the former. Both works heap blame upon the Umayyads, who are accused of *bidʿa*, persecuting the Prophet, attacking Medina and Mecca, and even setting fire to the Kaʿba; the Abbasids, on the other hand, are presented as ruling by divine appointment. Al-Maqrīzī's main argument in support of his theses is based on the notion of *qarāba*, or proximity to the Prophet: according to the author, this virtue is the exclusive domain of the Abbasids, having assured their place among the *ahl al-bayt*.[95] His virulent anti-Umayyad polemic echoes the similar tone of the great al-Jāḥiẓ's epistles: the first, known either as the *Risāla fī-al-Nābita* or the *Risāla fī Banī Umayya*,[96] and the second, his *Kitāb Faḍl Hāshim ʿalā ʿAbd Shams*.[97] In the second text, al-Jāḥiẓ attempts to establish the superiority of the Hashemites over the Banū ʿAbd Shams in pre-Islamic history, a strategy adopted in turn by al-Maqrīzī.[98] The *Risāla fī-al-Nābita* also strongly condemns the Umayyads and elucidates the contemporaneous debates surrounding the history of the first Islamic dynasty. These texts are no longer trying to reintegrate the Umayyads into history, but rather to exclude them from Islamic memory and portray them as the bearers of all the faults of the early *umma*. These examples, while in no way favourable to the caliphs of Damascus, are proof that the historiographic vulgate that solidified around al-Ṭabarī was not always responsible for producing the most virulent discourse concerning the Umayyads.

Finally, we come to the most famous name among the later authors whose works treat the second/eighth century: Ibn Khaldūn. His masterwork merits our attention here because of its author's brilliant theory and interpretation of the period; in a landmark work, Martinez-Gros lays out the keys to reading this quintessential text.[99] The idea is no longer to oppose the Umayyads and the Abbasids at all costs; rather, both dynasties have a place within the same temporality of the fulfilled Prophecy, and the passage from one to the other fits perfectly with Ibn Khaldūn's logic.[100] Nevertheless, the question of the Umayyads'

94 On the possible identities of the patron of this *majlis*, see Bosworth, "Al-Maqrīzī's Epistle," 45, and Cobb, "Al-Maqrīzī," 79–80.

95 Al-Maqrīzī's opinion on the Abbasids may be more complex than it seems at first glance. See Cobb, "Al-Maqrīzī," 70–1 and 76–7. The Umayyads also claimed their place among the *ahl al-bayt*; see Sharon, "The Umayyads."

96 See Pellat's analysis and translation, "Un document important."

97 Al-Jāḥiẓ, *Kitāb Faḍl*. See Pellat, *Le milieu*.

98 Al-Jāḥiẓ, *Kitāb Faḍl*, 12–3; al-Maqrīzī, *Kitāb al-nizāʿ*, 2, trans. 42.

99 Martinez-Gros, *Ibn Khaldūn*. By the same author, see also "Le califat omeyyade selon Ibn Khaldūn."

100 Martinez-Gros, *Ibn Khaldūn*, 169–70.

legitimacy remains. To address this issue, Ibn Khaldūn concedes that there is a wrench in his theory: the life of the Prophet was a miracle in itself, and this miracle disturbed the normal functions of the world until the assassination of ʿUthmān and the *fitna*, which marked the end of this holy period. The laws governing history here regained control, and the Umayyads' stronger *ʿaṣabiyya* triumphed over that of the Hashemites, who had been placed at the top of the hierarchy during the supratemporal period of the Prophecy.[101] Two central elements of Ibn Khaldūn's theory in particular explain the history of the period under examination here: the duration of an *ʿaṣabiyya*, or political and military support for a dynasty, and the relationship between the centre and the periphery, both of which operate in tandem. The weakening of an *ʿaṣabiyya* implies its imminent replacement with another, more vigorous one. This new energy generally arises from the peripheries and generates a centripetal force that seals the fate of the centre. When applied to the history of the Marwanids and the early Abbasids, this interpretive framework unfolds as follows: al-Ḥajjāj's time corresponded with the inauguration of a new *ʿaṣabiyya* that resulted in peace in Iraq. This peripheral space then supplanted Syria, and Wāsiṭ took precedence over Damascus. The end of al-Ḥajjāj's *ʿaṣabiyya* coincided with the rise of Maslama b. ʿAbd al-Malik's,[102] which "took root west of the Euphrates"[103] in the Byzantine borderlands. The return to Syria, followed by Marwān II's transfer of the capital to Ḥarrān, is indicative of this new upheaval. Maslama was then named governor of Iraq, Khurāsān and Transoxiana. These new and far-flung spaces were by definition the ideal site for the emergence of a new *ʿaṣabiyya* – that of the Abbasids – who would once and for all put an end to Syria's claims to dominance. Al-Ḥajjāj's legacy ultimately fell into the hands of the new Abbasid caliphs, who settled in the recently pacified Iraq as the veritable successors of its former Umayyad governor; this groundswell arising from the eastern edges of the empire and settling in its centre in itself encapsulates Ibn Khaldūn's theory. The obverse of this coin was that a confrontation with Khurāsān was now unavoidable, and would bring about the downfall of Abū Muslim and ultimately lead to the civil war that would tear the empire apart after the death of Hārūn al-Rashīd.[104] To insist on the divergence induced by this reading of history from that presented in the "classical" sources is pointless:

101 Martinez-Gros, *Ibn Khaldūn*, 161–2.
102 On Maslama, see below, Ch. 5.
103 Martinez-Gros, *Ibn Khaldūn*, 168.
104 Martinez-Gros, *Ibn Khaldūn*, 159 ff.

this new intelligibility of the past sheds light on power dynamics that went unrecognised by other historians.[105]

Finally, the case of historians active in arenas far from the Middle East, the cradle of Islam and the seat of its imperial power, remains to be discussed. Muslim Spain, where the second Umayyad caliphate flourished, is logically the space to which we should now turn our attention. This Umayyad rebirth prevented any stifled forgetting of their Eastern ancestors on the other side of the Mediterranean.[106] The Umayyads of al-Andalus – or, more precisely, their historians – tasked themselves with preserving the memory of their predecessors by founding their own legitimacy on these Syrian roots.[107] The western Umayyads' regard for their eastern cousins affirmed their shared legitimacy and emphasised the deep *continuum* between the two "Umayyad moments." This presentation of history was not unknown in the Abbasid East: this fact is attested by al-Masʿūdī, who consulted the aforementioned volume entitled *The Book of Proofs of the Umayyad Imamate* in Tiberias in 324/935–936. In this work, the dynasty was presented without interruption, tracing the downfall of the Syrian Umayyads to the rise of their Andalusian counterparts, with ʿUthmān considered to be the first Umayyad.[108] Although some texts sought to affirm the unrivalled superiority of the Abbasids over the impious Umayyads, apologetic discourses with the opposite goal existed as well.

These few examples are particularly significant, although undoubtedly many others could also be cited in this respect. They attest to the broad scope of possible reinterpretations presented by the history of the first centuries of Islam. Alongside the historiographic vulgate imposed following the interlude in Sāmarrāʾ, a vast range of other positions existed as well: both more subdued projects aimed at restoring the second/eighth century Syrian space's place in history, and, conversely, more antagonistic works staunchly in favour of one dynasty over the other. This constant debate that endured throughout the medieval period[109] attests to the high stakes of situating this foundational Muslim history within the Islamic consciousness and memory.

3.1.3.2 Muslim Apocalyptic Literature and Heresiographies

Apocalyptic and heresiographical literatures are radically different genres that offer different perspectives on the period under consideration in this study.

105 On the question of the spaces of power and their dynamics, see below, Ch. 8.

106 On this *translatio imperii*, see Martinez-Gros, "Le passage vers l'Ouest."

107 Martinez-Gros, *L'idéologie omeyyade* and *Identité andalouse*.

108 Al-Masʿūdī, *Tanbīh*, 336–7, trans. 433. See above, Ch. 1.

109 For our purposes, we will confine our analysis of this debate to the medieval period, although it obviously continued through subsequent eras. See Ende, *Arabische Nation und islamische Geschichte*.

Although Muslim apocalyptic writing – in particular that of the Sunnis – has long been neglected in modern scholarship, David Cook's recent work on the subject has made great progress toward filling this historiographic gap.[110] Cook highlights the critical place occupied by Syria, and especially the city of Homs, in this production;[111] the Syrian space as a whole witnessed the development of numerous apocalyptic traditions.[112] The abundant Christian and Jewish apocalyptic literature circulating in the region likely played a role in stimulating the growth of their Muslim counterpart.[113] The *Kitāb al-fitan* of Nuʿaym b. Ḥammād al-Marwazī (d. 229/844),[114] a native of Merv who was active in Syria, is arguably the most important source, despite its under-utilisation in modern scholarship. In addition to what this source reveals concerning the messianic context of the third/ninth century, it is also a repository for apocalyptic traditions from the Umayyad era.

The focal period of this inquiry was marked by several moments or episodes characteristic of messianic expectations. Many of these expectations were centred around the arrival of the year 100 of the *hijra*, a date with strong eschatological connotations in the Islamic tradition, which must have contributed to the rapid spread of these ideas. The period preceding this anticipated *eschaton* was supposedly characterised by a time of peace, harmony and justice (chiliasm):[115] the caliph during these years was ʿUmar b. ʿAbd al-ʿAzīz, who controlled the fate of the community. For this reason, ʿUmar b. ʿAbd al-ʿAzīz was presented as the *mahdī*, destined to "fill the world with justice (*yamlāʾ al-arḍ ʿadālan*),"[116] or as the *mujaddid*, the renewer of the faith. The occurrence of various natural phenomena, such as the passage of a comet or an earthquake, reassured the contemporaries of this period of the validity of their eschatological beliefs; other Islamic traditions related to the End of Days also

110 David Cook, *Studies*; see also Michael Cook, "An Early Islamic;" García-Arenal, *Mahdisme et millénarisme*; and Yücesoy, *Messianic Beliefs*.

111 Madelung, "Apocalyptic Prophecies."

112 David Cook, *Studies*, 1, 326.

113 On this non-Muslim apocalyptic literature, see below.

114 Nuʿaym b. Ḥammād, *Kitāb al-fitan*.

115 García-Arenal, "Introduction," 8.

116 Al-Ṭabarī, vol. II, 1362–3, trans. vol. XXIV, 92; al-Balādhurī, *Ansāb*, vol. VII, 66; al-Iṣfahānī, *Kitāb al-Aghānī*, vol. VIII, 151; Ibn Saʿd, *al-Ṭabaqāt*, vol. V, 243; *Kitāb al-ʿuyūn*, vol. I, 39; Abū Nuʿaym, *Ḥilyat*, vol. V, 254; Ibn Qutayba, *Kitāb al-maʿārif*, 362; Ibn al-Athīr, vol. V, 59; Nuʿaym b. Ḥammād, *Kitāb al-fitan*, 67, 222, trans. 51, 205–6; Abū Zurʿa al-Dimashqī, *Taʾrīkh*, 572 n. 1592; *TMD*, vol. 45, 155; Ibn Kathīr, *Bidāya*, vol. IX, 203; al-Suyūṭī, *Taʾrīkh al-khulafāʾ*, 174a, 270. ʿUmar II's sense of justice (*ʿadl*) is equally stressed by the thirteenth-century Christian author Buṭrus b. Rāhib, *Taʾrīkh* 57, trans. 63. ʿUmar II was not the only figure on whom such expectations were centred; the later hope for an Abbasid *mahdī* similarly charged with "filling the earth with justice" attests to the continued presence of these sentiments, see *Akhbār al-dawla*, 52.

coincided to portray the arrival of the year 100 as the ultimate achievement of the *umma*, and the concurrent siege of Constantinople was tinged with the same apocalyptic hue.[117]

The brutal downfall of the Umayyads perpetuated these beliefs, which solidified around the burgeoning myth of the Sufyānī's return.[118] This messianic cycle developed above all in Syria: similar elements are attested from Muqātil b. Sulaymān's (d. 150/762) time, and later echoed in the *Kitāb al-fitan*.[119] The Sufyānī "sleeps in a cave at the Wādī al-Yābis ...,[120] where he will be wakened by a mysterious caller calling him three times."[121] As soon as he leaves the grotto, he will be joined by his supporters and his arrival will be accompanied by a terrible earthquake that will engulf a village neighboring Damascus called Ḥarastā' (or Kharastā' or Jābiya); horsemen will join him as well, and he will soon lead an army of 50,000 men.[122] He will lead two major campaigns in Iraq and Persia, followed by another in the Hijaz. The first campaign will culminate in an attack on Baghdad, a veritable bloodbath, as obvious revenge for the Abbasids' massacres of the Umayyads.[123] The Sufyānī, the *mahdī*'s doppelgänger, will also oppose other messianic figures, one of whom is al-Aṣhab, also known as al-Marwānī, a descendant of Marwān II.[124] This latter did not achieve the fame of his Sufyanid rival in the apocalyptic literature; nevertheless, he attests to the rivalry and competition for remembrance characteristic of the only two branches of the Umayyad family to hold the caliphate.

The fall of the Umayyads by no means spelled the end for these messianic expectations; rather, during their rise to power, the Abbasids relied on the same apocalyptic register and continued to present themselves in this light even after their accession to the throne. The inscriptions at Baysān in Palestine or at Ṣana'ā' in Yemen, both of which present the first Abbasid caliph as the *mahdī*, bear witness to this fact.[125] The unequivocal *laqab* of the third Abbasid caliph – al-Mahdī – figured into the same image. Bates rejects the classic hypothesis that the caliph received this *laqab* at the same time that his father, al-Manṣūr, was given his, in the immediate aftermath of his victory

117 On this point, see Borrut, "Entre tradition et histoire," 339 ff., and below, Ch. 6.

118 Lammens, "Le Sofiânî;" Hartmann, "Der Sufyānī;" Madelung, "The Sufyānī;" Cobb, *White Banners*; David Cook, *Studies*, 122–36.

119 See Nu'aym b. Ḥammād, *Kitāb al-fitan*, 165 ff., trans. 150 ff.

120 Nu'aym b. Ḥammād, *Kitāb al-fitan*, 168, trans. 152; David Cook, *Studies*, 124.

121 David Cook, *Studies*, 124. These three calls are exactly identical to the prophetic call received by Muḥammad.

122 David Cook, *Studies*, 125.

123 David Cook, *Studies*, 127. On the massacre of the Umayyads, see below, Ch. 4.

124 David Cook, *Studies*, 125.

125 On these inscriptions, see Elad, "The Caliph," v–vi [English summary of an article in Hebrew], and Sharon, *CIAP*, vol. II, 214 ff.

against the Alids. Numismatic evidence shows that al-Mahdī's *laqab* is actually attested earlier on a coin struck at Bukhārā' in 143/760–761, a date several years prior to the appearance of his father's *laqab*.[126] Bates suggests that this is a case of expression of spontaneous beliefs that should be understood in the broader context of the "revolutionary enthusiasm"[127] of the region rather than as a deliberate manipulation. Another coin from Bukhārā', dated 151/768, mentions the *imām* al-Mahdī: this is the first mention of a Muslim given the title of *imām* on a coin, and even more striking, it occurred during the caliphate of al-Mahdī's father! The fact that the future caliph al-Mahdī also bore the same name as the Prophet – Muḥammad b. ʿAbd Allāh – served to reinforce the notion that he might be The *Mahdī*.[128] However, the messianic dimension was particularly charged in the post-revolution period, and endured well after. We know that the year 200 *hijrī* witnessed comparable eschatological expectations, in precisely the same manner as a century before. Successive texts, such as Ibn al-Munādī's (d. 336/947) *Kitāb al-malāḥim*, attest to the vitality of these expectations in fourth/tenth-century Baghdad.[129] This messianic context is especially important for the present study's reflections on the conditions in which history was written. As noted above, this complex environment produced not only specifically messianic texts but all of the Abbasid-era authors and textual genres, including the chronographies themselves, all of which are deeply marked by heavy messianic currents.[130]

Heresiographic literature also offers a glimpse into the history of the second/eighth century. Shiite works provide the best-documented examples of this genre; its major foundational figures had suffered Umayyad persecution before being deprived of the benefits of the Abbasid coup d'état (132/750). Shiite-Imamite perspectives on Umayyad history have been studied by Kohlberg.[131] Several imams lived under the first Islamic dynasty;[132] one, al-Ḥusayn b. ʿAlī, even died at the hands of the Umayyad army at Karbalā' in 61/680, in one of the most consequential events of early Islamic

126 Bates estimates that al-Saffāḥ was only an occasional epithet and not the regnal name of the first Abbasid caliph. Thus, al-Mahdī would have been the first *laqab* given to a member of this dynasty. See Bates, "Khurāsānī Revolutionaries," 281 ff.; the question of the *laqab* al-Saffāḥ is discussed in detail in Ch. 7.

127 Bates, "Khurāsānī Revolutionaries," 295.

128 Bates, "Khurāsānī Revolutionaries," 295 ff.

129 Ibn al-Munādī, *Kitāb al-malāḥim*. This work in particular contains a Muslim apocalypse of Daniel; see David Cook, "An Early Muslim."

130 As noted by Yücesoy, "Between Nationalism" and *Messianic Beliefs*.

131 Kohlberg, "Some Imāmī."

132 These are al-Ḥasan b. ʿAlī (d. c. 49/669), his brother al-Ḥusayn (d. 61/680), Zayn al-ʿĀbidīn (d. 94/710–711 or 95/712–713), Muḥammad al-Bāqir (d. 114/732 or 117/735), and Jaʿfar al-Ṣādiq (d. 148/765).

history. This fierce rivalry sustained the production and circulation of blatantly anti-Umayyad traditions. One eschatological tradition states that on the day of the *mahdī*'s arrival, the Umayyads took refuge among the Byzantines and embraced Christianity; they were then forced to return and executed for their crimes![133] More broadly, the religious superiority of the Shiite imams was confirmed by an episode featuring Hishām b. ʿAbd al-Malik during a pilgrimage to Mecca prior to his accession to the caliphate. The future caliph could not reach the black stone due to the crowd thronging around it; however, when the imam Zayn al-ʿĀbidīn appeared, the crowd parted respectfully to allow him to touch the stone.[134] It is interesting to note that this anecdote features in the poetry of al-Farazdaq, who was supposedly present at the scene:[135] an Umayyad court poet cited a narrative in his own *Dīwān* that would become an aspect of Shiite anti-Umayyad polemic! This example is by no means an isolated one, and it demonstrates that the boundaries between different literary genres were porous, and that certain texts should not be catalogued in their entireties as exclusively pro- or anti-Umayyad. Among these Shiite texts, in theory the sources most hostile to the caliphs of Damascus, we also find certain positive exceptions, in particular ʿAbd al-Malik and ʿUmar b. ʿAbd al-ʿAzīz.[136] The son of the former, Saʿīd b. ʿAbd al-Malik, was even completely accepted by the Imamites, who recognised him as one of their own;[137] he was equally praised for his conduct beyond Shiite literature, as attested by his surname, Saʿīd al-Khayr.[138]

Other texts composed by opponents of the Umayyad regime[139] are more harshly critical. This is certainly the case of the Kharijite[140] Abū Ḥamza's sermon, a text preserved by al-Balādhurī in the *Ansāb* and studied by Crone and Hinds.[141] In this virulent diatribe, probably given at Medina or Mecca in 129/746 or 130/747, Abū Ḥamza curses the first Islamic dynasty after listing his

133 Kohlberg, "Some Imāmī," 153.

134 Kohlberg, "Some Imāmī," 152.

135 Al-Farazdaq, *Dīwān*, vol. II, 178–81.

136 Kohlberg, "Some Imāmī," 153–4. On ʿUmar II's image in the different historiographic traditions of the medieval Near East, see Borrut, "Entre tradition et histoire," and below, Ch. 6.

137 Kohlberg, "Some Imāmī," 154.

138 He was notably called this by al-Ṭabarī, vol. II, 1174; trans. vol. XXIII, 118. Al-Ṭabarī also remarks on his conduct, "*wa-kāna ḥasan al-sīra*," vol. II, 1831; trans. vol. XXVI, 189.

139 The importance of these political and religious oppositions to the Umayyad caliphate was first discussed by Wellhausen in 1901, *Die religiös-politischen*.

140 The term "Kharijite" is highly problematic for the period under consideration here. The designation "al-Khārijī" could simply indicate a rebel, without any further details or specifications, and thus should be approached with caution. On questions of Kharijite "identity," see Robinson, *Empire and Elites*, 109–26, and Lewinstein, "The Azāriqa" and "Making and Unmaking."

141 Crone and Hinds, *God's Caliph*, 74, 129–32.

grievances against each Umayyad caliph. Even here, however, ʿUmar II is an exception in this gallery of vitriolic portraits: thus, even in the most severe anti-Umayyad propaganda, certain positive figures were preserved.[142]

These different examples demonstrate the richness of the corpus of Islamic sources and the wide range of available texts other than those making up the historiographic canon. The confrontation between all of these different textual genres conditions the renewal of our knowledge today. Thus, it is essential to situate these various types of sources in relation to each other so as to illuminate their interactions. The commonly-held idea of a historiographic vulgate hostile to the Umayyads (i.e. the chronographies) that could be avoided by focusing on sources exempt from these successive historiographic filters, here demonstrates its limitations; in reality, the situation is much more complex, and the "strong" discourses often live side-by-side with much gentler passages. Once again, we find ourselves faced with a paradoxical situation, a reminder of the extent to which multiple reconstructions of the past are characteristic of medieval texts.[143] To complete this portrait, we must now confront a final corpus: non-Muslim sources. How does this collection position itself toward the vulgate of Islamic historiography? Is this a parallel historiography, or are these various historiographies in constant interaction?

3.2 Non-Muslim Sources: "External" or "Eastern" Sources?

The role of these primarily Christian texts (Arabic, Syriac, Byzantine, Coptic or Armenian)[144] in the context of this inquiry[145] remains a subject of debate.

---

142 Crone and Hinds, *God's Caliph*, 130; Borrut, "Entre tradition et histoire," 358.

143 Robinson, *Islamic Historiography*, 79.

144 For an overview of these sources, see the fundamental works of Hoyland, *Seeing* and "Arabic, Syriac and Greek Historiography." See also the various contributions compiled by Cameron and Conrad (eds.), *The Byzantine and Early Islamic Near East*, vol. I. For the Syriac sources, see more specifically Conrad, "Syriac Perspectives" and "The Conquest of Arwād," as well as Palmer, *The Seventh Century*, xi–xxxv, and also Debié (ed.), *Historiographie syriaque* and Debié, *L'écriture de l'histoire en syriaque*. On the Byzantine chronicler Theophanes, see Conrad, "Theophanes," as well as the introduction to Mango and Scott's English translation of *The Chronicle of Theophanes*. A more general reflection on the image of the Umayyads in Byzantine sources is that of Jeffreys, "Notes Towards a Discussion." It is above all the Coptic apocalyptic literature that interests us here, see Van Lent, "Les apocalypses coptes." On Armenian historiography, see Mahé, "Entre Moïse et Mahomet;" Garsoïan, "Reality and Myth" and Thompson, "L'historiographie arménienne."

145 The only extant non-Muslim sources and chronicles for this period are Christian. The question of Jewish historiographic activity is more problematic (see Yerushalmi's

Today, Sauvaget's stated opinion that "the Syriac and Byzantine authors, poorly informed on the institutions and dependent on each other, are but a mediocre addition,"[146] is no longer current; Brock, Palmer, Conrad, and Hoyland have all demonstrated the critical importance of these texts,[147] even if they are insufficiently employed. Certain scholars using this corpus have frequently and paradoxically done so to the neglect of the Islamic sources.[148] The problem comes down to the position granted to these non-Muslim sources with respect to the Arabic-Muslim corpus. The scholarship deems these non-Muslim sources "external" to the Islamic tradition, while the Islamic texts are thereby supposed to present an "internal" perspective. This argument places the two groups in confrontation with each other, and judges the first group to be "more reliable" than the second, thus forming the basis of the majority of "skeptical" scholarly works, above all Crone and Cook's *Hagarism*; this work proposes to write the history of early Islam on the sole basis of testimonies *external* to the Islamic tradition.

However, this approach does not stand up to closer analysis. The chronological limits of this hypothesis can be invoked here as well as those that become evident as soon as the perspectives of the social groups producing these texts are established. We have seen that the preserved narrative Islamic sources cannot be traced back earlier than the middle of the ninth century – despite the fact that Arabic-Muslim sources did exist prior to this date – whereas we do possess non-Muslim sources, notably Syriac ones, from the seventh and eighth centuries. How can we *a priori* consider these sources more "external" than the Islamic sources when they give us the distinct advantage of contemporaneity? There is also a human element to this observation: the first centuries of Islam represented a Muslim political hegemony, but the vast majority of the population remained non-Muslim. In this respect, how can we say that texts produced by majority communities were marginal with respect to Islamic sources?[149]

Finally, and most importantly, this dichotomy opposing "internal" and "external" sources is simply false. In reality, the non-Muslim sources arose from the same historiographic dynamics at work in the medieval Middle East, and

fundamental work on the subject, *Zakhor*), but occasionally emerges in the form of Jewish or Judeo-Arabic apocalyptic literature. On these texts, see below.

146 Sauvaget, "Châteaux omeyyades," 18.

147 Brock, "Syriac sources;" Palmer, *The Seventh Century*; Conrad, "Syriac Perspectives;" Hoyland, *Seeing*.

148 See, for example, the recent debate between Benkheira and de Prémare. See Benkheira, "L'analyse du *ḥadīth*," and de Prémare's response to this article.

149 As Calder remarks, *Studies*, 244: "all of the communities of the Middle East participated in the political, social and intellectual consequences of Arab political hegemony."

the circulation of information was constant. For this reason, it cannot possibly be said that the majority of non-Muslim sources were exclusively "external" to the *Muslim tradition*; to the contrary, they were an integral part of it, in spite of the divergent interpretations they proposed and the independent testimonies they placed side-by-side with borrowed materials.[150] As Hoyland has emphasised, "in the cosmopolitan world of Early Islam, no one tradition was insulated from the influence of others."[151] Moreover, it is clear that texts circulated across religious boundaries, and since "common factors [shaped] the lives of the people of the seventh and eighth-century Middle East, there are also likely to have been common features in their literatures."[152] If the two sides present a false image of events, how do we explain the fact that both present the very *same* image?[153]

This shared information attests to the asynchronous rhythms of transmission at work in each corpus. The designation of "external" sources should be rejected in favour of "eastern" sources, a descriptor that better accounts for the permanent interactions between the different historiographies of the medieval Near East. We must now turn our attention to these transmission processes before presenting the pertinent non-Muslim sources in greater detail. Only sources *intended* as strictly historical (*sources à* intention *directement historiques*) will be considered here, although the apocalyptic works will be studied as well, as they offer an alternative reading of history. This strategy necessarily implies that theological works will be left out, including the famous polemic texts of John of Damascus, written around 730, the discussion between Timothy – *katholikos* between 780 and 823 – and the caliph al-Mahdī, and the martyrologies.[154] Although these texts contain minimal historical information for the period under consideration here, they nevertheless reveal permanent exchanges and points of contact characteristic of the relations between Christians and Muslims. The circulation of historical information between the two communities is an integral part of the shared framework of collective knowledge.

---

150 This is precisely the same point Hoyland emphasises, *Seeing*, 592: "And this is perhaps the most valuable aspect of the non-Muslim sources: not so much that they give us independent testimony – though they often do that too – but that they can sometimes tell us what they Muslims were saying long before this was written down by the Muslims themselves."

151 Hoyland, *Seeing*, 32.

152 Hoyland, *Seeing*, 34.

153 Hoyland, *Seeing*, 591. On the question of a core of information that was shared in common because it was true, see also Donner, *Narratives*, 287–90, and Ch. 1, above.

154 On these texts, see Hoyland, *Seeing*, 480–9, 472–5, 354 ff.

3.2.1 *Intercultural Transmission*

The basic outlines of the transmission of Greek science and knowledge from Syriac into Arabic, a process most famously embodied in al-Maʾmūn's *bayt al-ḥikma*, are common knowledge.[155] The processes of transmission of historical information among non-Muslim authors were equally complex: reliance on ancient and biblical knowledge remained a primary point of reference, while at the same time the historical discourse produced by Arab-Muslim authors on the Islamic period was also circulating within the neighboring communities, especially among Christians of the Arabic, Greek, Coptic, Armenian and Syriac-speaking populations. In other words, the means available to the Christian chroniclers for accessing the historical knowledge of the first centuries of Islam are what is at stake here.

These Christian chroniclers, stunned by the rapidity of the Islamic conquests, tried to make sense of these events that would irrevocably upend the status quo in a region accustomed to conflict between the Persians and the Byzantines.[156] After the initial shock, historians were forced to contend with Islamic history in their texts. To do so, they needed Arab informants, be they written sources or oral accounts. The polyglot nature of the intellectual centres of the Near East, and particularly the monasteries, played a decisive role in making these exchanges possible;[157] the Christian secretaries of the caliphal administration were also essential in this regard.[158] From this perspective, the reciprocal interest involved in studying these intercultural transmissions should be stressed: if non-Muslim literary sources are the oldest to provide information on Islam, the Muslim sources clarify specific elements of these texts, in particular regarding certain vocabulary or borrowed ideas that became problematic when translated into Greek, Syriac or Armenian.[159]

Studying these transmissions aims to shed light on the routes that guaranteed the circulation of Islamic historical information and its integration in the historical texts of other communities. This methodology has been successfully applied to the formative Islamic period as well as the conquests. Conrad, one

155 On the translation movement under al-Maʾmūn, see Gutas, *Greek Thought*, Ch. 4, and Cooperson, *Al-Maʾmūn*.

156 Muslim authors also tried to shed light on the presence and histories of the different communities in the conquered areas. See, for example, Troupeau, "La connaissance des chrétiens syriaques."

157 Conrad, "Theophanes," 31 ff.

158 For example, see the case of the "Nestorian" secretaries in Abbasid Baghdad, Cabrol, "Une étude."

159 A good example of these difficulties arising from translation and material borrowed from the Arabic is the Byzantine chronicle of Theophanes. See Conrad, "Theophanes," 28 ff.; for an identical problem in the Syriac sources, see below.

of the pioneers of this approach, defined or elucidated a number of obscure points in the Islamic sources: for example, his work revealed the confusion in the conquest narratives over the tiny Syrian island of Arwād and the island of Rhodes.[160] For the second/eighth century, long overlooked in modern scholarship, a great deal of work remains to be done.[161] However, as we have demonstrated in the preceding chapters, an Islamic historiography from this period is well-attested, and Conrad estimates that it was precisely during the course of the eighth century that "Arabic narratives from the Islamic literary tradition were incorporated into Syrian Christian historical writing."[162]

This circulation of information has generally been used to corroborate or refute certain elements from the Islamic tradition. However, these eighth-century Christian sources, reliant on Arab informants, are especially valuable as a means of accessing lost Islamic historiographies, in particular those produced in Syria. The relevant Christian sources from the period were primarily composed in Syriac in the Jazīra or northern Syria, and it is mainly through these authors that their diffusion throughout Byzantium and the Caucasus was assured.[163] The monasteries of Upper Mesopotamia, such as those at Ṭūr ʿAbdīn,[164] or in northern Syria, such as at Qenneshrē,[165] and major intellectual centres like Edessa[166] played a decisive role in this process. The goal here is to recover – the prefix here is important – elements originating in a historiography written under the Marwanids or the early Abbasids, particularly in the Syrian space. We do not have access to the *form* of this historiography, only the *information* it provided. Although it is impossible to recover the original appearance of these texts – or narratives, in the case of orally transmitted accounts – we can *date* this historical information, or, more precisely, fix a *terminus ante quem* for its circulation. Moreover, the date of a specific Christian chronography's composition can allow us to determine whether certain elements were circulating during the Umayyad era, for example. The trajectory of this information enables us to establish a more-or-less precise chronological timeline of their appearance and to connect them to specific historiographic

160 Conrad, "The Conquest of Arwād." On the subject of the Colossus of Rhodes, supposedly destroyed by the Arabs, see Conrad, "The Arabs and the Colossus."
161 See Conrad, "Syriac Perspectives;" Fiey, "The Umayyads;" Borrut, "Entre tradition et histoire."
162 Conrad, "Theophanes," 43.
163 On the modes of historical writing of the Syriac authors, see Fiey, "Les chroniqueurs syriaques."
164 On this region, see Palmer, *Monk and Mason*.
165 Or Qenneshrīn. Not to be confused with the city of Qinnasrīn near Aleppo, nor with the *jund* bearing the same name as this city.
166 On the key role of Edessa, see Conrad, "Varietas Syriaca," especially 104.

layers. The question of historiographic filters developed in the preceding chapters is critical for determining the *historiographic origin* of a given piece of information: the Christian sources, in addressing Muslim history and echoing lost Islamic historiographies, do not belong to different traditions, but rather to different *moments* of the sedimentation of memory. This approach allows us to exhume certain aspects of long-buried historiographic projects composed under the late Umayyads and early Abbasids.

This strategy falls under the rubric of comparative historiography, and opens up numerous avenues for fruitful analysis. Following Lorenz, "if we accept Marc Bloch's view that all history is comparative history – implicit or explicit – then it is easy to see why comparative historiography is even more needed than comparative history."[167] This labor is arduous, as we find ourselves confronted with a double difficulty: not only do we face comparative judgments of the historiographic reconstructions themselves, but also historiographic reconstructions of these historiographic reconstructions.[168] Nevertheless, to borrow Robinson's fitting expression, it is essential to "marry history and historiography".[169] Numerous precautions must be taken in this approach, and access to these fragments of a lost historiography remains precarious. This undertaking is complicated by the fact that we are unable to compare these fragments to their originals; due to the uncertainties of the various translations that occurred as this information circulated among different linguistic communities, as well as the unfortunate tendency of the Syriac authors not to cite their Arabic sources,[170] the distortion of historical information is also a permanent concern.[171] We shall now present the principal routes of the transmission of historical information among non-Muslim authors; as part of a comparative historiographic framework, our analysis of these sources requires a somewhat systematic approach that focuses in particular on the sources these authors used to gather information on Islamic history.

3.2.2 *Theophilus of Edessa, the Chronology of Qartamīn and the Syriac Common Source*

The first key point that clearly emerges from examining these texts is the existence of a single Syriac Common Source for an entire group of Christian

167 Lorenz, "Comparative Historiography," 28.

168 Lorenz, "Comparative Historiography," 29.

169 Robinson, *Empires and Elites*, viii.

170 Elias of Nisibis is a singular exception to this rule due to his near-constant concern with citing his sources. See Borrut, "La circulation de l'information historique," and below.

171 For the methodological problems posed by this delicate operation, see Conrad, "Recovering Lost Texts," and Landau-Tasseron, "On the Reconstruction."

authors. After much research and speculation, the identity of this shared informant was finally determined to be the Maronite historian Theophilus of Edessa (d. 169/785), whose mid-eighth-century chronicle is unfortunately lost. He was notably the chief astrologer in Baghdad during al-Mahdī's caliphate.[172] Although Brooks hesitates between Theophilus and John Bar Samuel as the identity of the author of this common source, Becker opts for the former, as does Conrad later, based on the information provided by Agapius of Manbij (active *c.*942).[173] Several studies have corroborated this identification in the meantime,[174] although Palmer leans toward Theophanes's (d. 818) Byzantine predecessor George Synkellos (d. after 810);[175] however, this latter appears to have played only an intermediary role in this transmission process. Without going into too much detail describing the stages that led to this identification, it should briefly be noted that this common source was preserved by Theophanes, Agapius of Manbij and Dionysius of Tel Maḥrē (d. 230/845), as he himself is preserved in Michael the Syrian's chronicle (d. 1199) and the anonymous *Chronicle of 1234*. Despite the significant gaps in this transmission, the integrity of this circuit has largely been proven, although it should be borne in mind that "shared source" is not synonymous with "exclusive source." The period spanning the caliphate of Abū Bakr to 746 (or 754, per some sources) incontrovertibly attests to the use of a common resource that was undoubtedly subjected to various interpolations by Theophilus's successor(s).[176] It is now essential to describe in some detail the sources of which this circuit is composed.

The Jacobite patriarch Dionysius of Tel Maḥrē, who studied at the monastery of Qenneshrē, is one of the principal relays on this circuit;[177] Palmer does not hesitate to call him the "greatest Syriac historian."[178] Unfortunately, only a few fragments of his works have survived;[179] we are only able to

172 On Theophilus of Edessa, see Hoyland, *Seeing*, 400–9; Breydy, "Das Chronikon;" Pingree, "From Alexandria to Baghdād to Byzantium;" Borrut, "La circulation de l'information historique;" Debié, *L'écriture de l'histoire en syriaque*, 27–31, 139–43, and passim.

173 Agapius of Manbij, 525. See the studies of Brooks, "The Sources;" Becker, "Eine Neue christliche Quelle;" Conrad, "Theophanes," 42–4; Hoyland, *Seeing*, 400–9.

174 Particularly Conrad, "The Conquest of Arwād;" Cobb, "A Note;" Borrut, "Entre tradition et histoire."

175 Palmer, *The Seventh*, 98.

176 For an attempt to reconstruct the content of Theophilus's chronicle as it is preserved by later historians, see Hoyland, *Seeing*, 631–71.

177 On this author, see Palmer's detailed presentation, *The Seventh*, 85–104.

178 Palmer, *The Seventh*, 85.

179 These fragments have been edited and translated by Abramowski, *Dionysius von Tell-mahre*, 130–44.

recover the information he provided therein through later works reliant on the texts of Dionysius, Michael the Syrian and the *Chronicle of 1234*. These two thirteenth-century sources were composed entirely independent of one and other; thus, it has been firmly established that their shared information derives from a common source, the lost chronicle of Dionysius of Tel Maḥrē, which is cited explicitly by Michael the Syrian for the period from 582 until 228/842.[180] He also specifies that Dionysius's text was written in two parts, an ecclesiastical history and a secular history, each divided into eight books which were themselves divided into chapters.[181] Although these later authors certainly reworked Dionysius's original,[182] they nevertheless provide access to information on the ninth century. In the course of a remarkable assessment of Syriac historiography in the preface to his work (as reproduced by Michael the Syrian), Dionysius indicates that he relied on Theophilus of Edessa. However, he judges this latter rather severely, and claims that he referenced Theophilus for "only those parts which are reliable and do not deviate from the truth;"[183] behind this peremptory judgment may lie Dionysius's reaction to the Maronite Theophilus's unfavourable views of the Jacobites in his chronicle.[184] Dionysius also employed other sources, in particular Byzantine ones, ostensibly including George Synkellos, in addition to other chronicles available in Syriac.[185]

Theophanes (d. 818), born to a wealthy family, renounced a brilliant career in the imperial administration to become a monk. As he himself reports, he continued the work begun by George Synkellos (d. after 810) in accordance with this latter's request, as his premature death prevented him from extending his narrative beyond the time of Diocletian.[186] Theophanes bridged this gap, lengthening his chronography to the year 813. For Islamic history, Theophanes was basically dependent on Theophilus of Edessa, but he does present elements of this history through the year 780,[187] despite the fact that Theophilus's chronicle seems to have ended in 750. Thus, Theophanes likely

---

180 Michael indicates in his preface that "Dionysius the patriarch wrote from Maurice until Theophilus, the emperor of the Greeks, and Hārūn, the prince of the Arabs" (this is the caliph Hārūn b. Abū Isḥāq al-Wāthiq, who reigned between 227–232/842–847), *Chronique*, French trans. 2. He mentions him again at the end of Book 12, *Chronique*, vol. III, 544, French trans. III. Hoyland, *Seeing*, 417–8; Conrad, "Syriac Perspectives," 28–32.

181 Cited in Palmer, *The Seventh*, 87, 89.

182 Palmer, *The Seventh*, 101.

183 See Hoyland, *Seeing*, 418, and Palmer, *The Seventh*, 92.

184 As Palmer suggests, *The Seventh*, 101–2.

185 Palmer, *The Seventh*, 95 ff.

186 Theophanes, *Chronicle*, ed. 3–4, trans. 1.

187 After this date, Islamic history completely disappears from Theophilus's chronicle, which limits itself to Byzantine history, ending in 813.

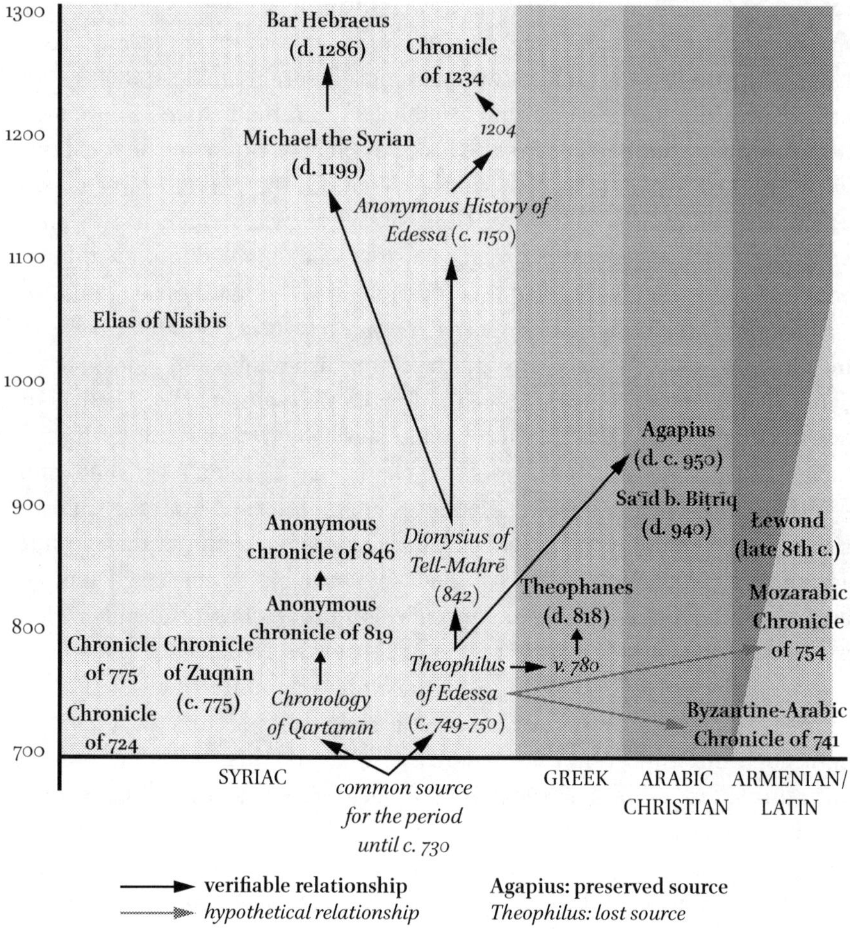

DIAGRAM 3.1 Circuits of Theophilus of Edessa and the chronology of Qartamīn

relied on a continuation of Theophilus; the abundance of elements related to Syria, and in particular the city of Homs, may indicate that his continuer was a native of the region.[188]

We have very little information concerning the life of the Melkite Agapius (or Maḥbūb) of Manbij; we know that he was the bishop of this city and wrote his works around 942.[189] His *Kitāb al-ʿunwān* begins with the Creation, and the Florence manuscript ends abruptly during the reign of Leo IV (775–780). The original must have been longer, as Agapius himself notes that 330 years had

188 Hoyland, *Seeing*, 431.

189 Graf, *Geschichte*, 39–41; Hoyland, *Seeing*, 440–2.

passed “from [the beginning] of the empire of the Arabs until the present,”[190] the year 330 of the *hijra* corresponding to 941–942. His works gained rapid renown after they were cited by al-Masʿūdī in his *Kitāb al-tanbīh wa-al-ishrāf*.[191] Agapius relied primarily on Theophilus of Edessa until the year 754, as he himself indicates: “and Theophilus the astronomer (*al-munajjim*), from whom we have taken this account (*al-akhbār*), reports: ‘I myself have not ceased to be an eyewitness to these wars, I have observed many things and nothing that concerns them has escaped me’.”[192] He must also have consulted a Muslim chronology to provide supplemental details when necessary.[193]

The Jacobite patriarch Michael I Qīndasī or Michael the Syrian (d. 1199), whose magistrate lasted from 561/1166 until 596/1199, is better known to modern scholars.[194] Born in 1126 in Malaṭya, he was Archimandrite of the monastery at Barṣaumā[195] starting in 1156, and was elected patriarch, thus replacing Athanasius VIII in 1166. Although he composed several ecclesiastical works, the chronicle *Maktbānūt zabnē* spanning the period from Creation until 1195 was his most famous.[196] The Syriac text comprises twenty-one books, each divided into chapters. The presentation of the chronicle, in parallel columns, follows the principle initiated by Eusebius of Caesarea (d. 339); most of the pages are divided into three columns, the first typically dedicated to ecclesiastical history, the second to secular history, and the third to various other topics, in particular miracles and natural disasters. Weltecke has highlighted the importance of this graphic and aesthetic arrangement,[197] although it was likely modified by later copyists and thus does not necessarily reflect Michael the Syrian’s autograph manuscript.[198] While other authors continued to treat ecclesiastical and secular histories as separate entities on the page, Michael invented a new system of presentation.[199] His concern with citing his sources is also relevant here; from the perspective of this inquiry, it is particularly important to note that Michael the Syrian relied heavily on the work of his predecessor, Dionysius of Tel Maḥrē. The fact that Michael’s work appears significantly later may invite

190 Agapius, *Kitāb al-ʿunwān*, 456.
191 Al-Masʿūdī, *Tanbīh*, 154.
192 Agapius, *Kitāb al-ʿunwān*, 525.
193 Hoyland, *Seeing*, 441; Conrad, “The Arabs and the Colossus,” 173.
194 See Weltecke, *Die “Beschreibung der Zeiten”* and “Les trois grandes chroniques.”
195 For an overview of the history of this monastery, see Kaufhold, “Notizen.”
196 Michael the Syrian, *Chronicle*. For the discovery of Michael the Syrian as a historian and the complete editorial undertaking of his chronicle, see Weltecke, “The World Chronicle.”
197 Weltecke, “The World Chronicle,” 27, and “Originality,” 182.
198 Weltecke, “Originality,” 183–88.
199 Weltecke, “The World Chronicle,” 27.

caution; however, while it is clear that he reworked the sources he employed, the *Chronicle of 1234*[200] provides important assurances.

The *Chronicle of 1234* was composed by an anonymous author at Edessa slightly after Michael the Syrian's own chronicle.[201] Both made significant use of Dionysius, but the *Chronicle of 1234* did not use Michael's text as an intermediary.[202] In other words, at the turn of the twelfth–thirteenth centuries, these two sources had recourse to a common source, to which they both had frequent and strikingly parallel access; the similarity of the information preserved in the chronicles of Michael the Syrian and the anonymous author of Edessa offers a gauge of the quality of the transmission of elements originating in the lost chronicle of Dionysius of Tel Maḥrē. The *Chronicle of 1234* also employs other sources, and it has been proposed that the use of the Armenian form of Armenian names – rather than their Syriac forms – implies the use of Armenian works.[203]

Bar ʿEbroyo (d. 685/1286), the Bar Hebraeus[204] of the Latin authors or the Abū al-Faraj b. al-ʿIbrī of the Arabs,[205] was unfamiliar with the *Chronicle of 1234*, and in contrast to the anonymous author of this latter, relied heavily on Michael the Syrian. Born in 1225–1226 in Malaṭya, he took the name Gregory on the occasion of his consecration as the bishop of Gūbbāsh, near his native city, in 1246, before being transferred to Laqabbīn. He was then named metropolitan of Aleppo in 1253, an appointment he was quickly forced to abandon due to a schism; he fled to the monastery of Barṣaumā, where he consulted Michael

200 *Chronicle of 1234*.

201 On the *Anonymous Chronicle of 1234*, see Hoyland, *Seeing*, index; Weltecke, "Les trois grandes chroniques;" Palmer, *The Seventh*, 85–222. Palmer develops the questions of the connections between this chronicle and that of Dionysius at length, and provides great detail concerning the editorial enterprise of the text, 103–4; he proposes an English translation of the section dealing with early Islam through the caliph ʿUmar II's recall of Maslama b. ʿAbd al-Malik's troops from the siege of Constantinople in 99/717, 111–221.

202 Although it is clear that the anonymous author of the *Chronicle of 1234* knew Michael the Syrian, if not personally then at least in reputation. In any case, he did know Michael's brother Athanasius, the metropolitan of Jerusalem, and his nephew Gregory, the *maphryānā* of the East.

203 Conrad, "Syriac Perspectives," 13.

204 On Bar Hebraeus, see Takahashi, *Barhebraeus*; Aigle (ed.), *Barhebraeus et la renaissance syriaque*; Weltecke, "Les trois grandes chroniques."

205 The *nisba* al-ʿIbrī does not indicate Jewish lineage, as has long been thought, but refers to the location of al-ʿIbr, ʿEbrō in Syriac, situated on the Euphrates near Malaṭya, where Bar Hebraeus was born. See Fathi-Chelhod, "L'origine du nom." However, Fathi-Chelhod incorrectly indicates (p. 25) that this toponymy is not mentioned by Yāqūt. The *Muʿjam al-buldān*, vol. IV, 78, dedicates an entry to al-ʿIbr, noting that the location derived its name from the Jewish community who had settled there.

the Syrian's autograph manuscript. In 1260, he witnessed the Mongol seizure of Aleppo, and in 1264 he was consecrated as *maphryānā*, or patriarch, of the Eastern Jacobite Church, a position that required frequent travel. He died in 1286 at the Mongol court of Marāgha in Azerbaijan, and was buried at the monastery of Mār Mattai in Mosul.[206] He was credited with thirty works, mainly in Syriac but in Arabic as well. He was also a prolific translator, both from Greek to Syriac or Arabic and from Arabic to Syriac. A scholar of many disciplines, Bar Hebraeus wrote two historical chronicles, one in Syriac (the *Maktbānūt zabnē*), which is divided into a universal history and an ecclesiastical chronicle, and the other in Arabic (the *Ta'rīkh mukhtaṣar al-duwal*).[207] These two chronicles are divided into eleven epochs[208] devoted to specific periods of governance, from the patriarchs of the Old Testament to the kings of the *Ṭayyoyē* to the Mongol rulers in 1258. His brother, Bar Ṣawmā Ṣāfī, continued his chronicle until the year 696/1297, or eleven years after Bar Hebraeus's death; he also revised his brother's text.[209] Although the *Mukhtaṣar* has long been viewed as a condensed version of his Syriac chronicle, both Conrad and, more recently, Aigle, have shown that this is not the case, and that the differences between the two texts are significant.[210] These variations are notably characterised by a change in sources: while Michael the Syrian was Bar Hebraeus's primary source for his Syrian chronicle, switching over to Arabic required a concomitant use of Muslim sources.[211]

It is tempting to associate the Latin *Byzantine-Arab Chronicle of 741* – albeit indirectly[212] – with this transmission circuit, as Hoyland notes.[213] This source, composed in Europe, clearly relied on an eastern source – perhaps the Greek translation of Theophilus of Edessa, also used by Theophanes – while frequently supplementing the information pulled from this source with more important developments.[214] It is probable that the *Mozarabic Chronicle of 754*[215]

206 Segal, "Ibn al-ʿIbrī."

207 For a study of Bar Hebraeus's projects undertaken throughout these chronicles composed in two different languages, see Conrad, "On the Arabic Chronicle," and Aigle, "Bar Hebraeus et son public."

208 The *Mukhtaṣar* actually only comprises ten epochs, combining the fifth and sixth parts of the Syriac chronicle. See Micheau, "Le *Kāmil* d'Ibn al-Athīr."

209 Conrad, "Syriac Perspectives," 14–7.

210 Conrad, "On the Arabic Chronicle;" Aigle, "Bar Hebraeus et son public."

211 See the example of Ibn al-Athīr as studied by Micheau, "Le *Kāmil* d'Ibn al-Athīr."

212 *Byzantine-Arab Chronicle of 741*, trans. Hoyland, *Seeing*, 611–30.

213 Hoyland, *Seeing*, 425.

214 Hoyland, *Seeing*, 425.

215 *Mozarabic Chronicle of 754*.

was based on the same source as the *Byzantine-Arab Chronicle of 741*.[216] The latter chronicle ends with the death of Yazīd II (105/724), but prior to this indicates that the Byzantine emperor Leo III ruled for twenty-four years (717–741); the *Mozarabic Chronicle of 754*'s narrative reaches the year 750 and the death of Marwān II in Egypt.[217] However, it is possible that the *Mozarabic Chronicle of 754* employs another source beginning with the year 105/724, as the narrative describing the end of the Marwanid period differs noticeably from the version proposed by the Syriac Common Source.[218] These two Latin chronicles both express decidedly favourable views of the Umayyads: ʿAlī's caliphate is passed over in silence, and several caliphs of the first Islamic dynasty are portrayed in a flattering light.[219]

Another, somewhat lesser-known and less well-documented circuit, one that is nevertheless directly linked to the circuit of Theophilus of Edessa for the early years of period under examination in this study, is the two anonymous Jacobite chronicles of *819* and *846*'s[220] reliance upon a chronology produced at the abbey of Qartamīn (or drafted by an author of this monastery). Once again, the use of a common source by the authors of these two texts was detected by scholars early on, and its identification has been the subject of several studies.

The *Chronicle of 819*, closely followed by the *Chronicle of 846*, was discovered by Barsaum in 1911. Dolabani, taking for granted that it originated in Qartamīn, went so far as to propose that Manṣūr, the abbot of Qartamīn and a renowned scribe, was the author of this chronicle.[221] Palmer does not agree with this attribution because of a lack of irrefutable proof, but he concludes that this chronicle was indeed composed at Qartamīn slightly later than 819, the last chronological entry mentioned in the text.[222] Conrad arrived at the same conclusions, and in addition suggests that the chronicle be divided into four

216 Hoyland, *Seeing*, 611. On these two sources, see Tolan, *Les Sarrasins*, 124 ff.

217 Hoyland, *Seeing*, 426, 627.

218 Hoyland, *Seeing*, 627, suggests that the existence of a single common source until the year 750 is most probable. However, the *Mozarabic Chronicle of 754* presents noticeable differences from the Syriac Common Source: the description of Hishām's caliphate is distinctly different; al-Walīd is given the surname "the handsome" or "the noble" (*pulcher*) but there is no mention of his assassination; and Yazīd III is said to have committed suicide. There is also confusion between Ṣāliḥ b. ʿAlī and his brother ʿAbd Allāh, although it is true that a certain fluidity with respect to different personages of the Abbasid period exists in the Christian sources.

219 On these two sources, see Tolan, *Les Sarrasins*, 124 ff., and Constable, "Perceptions of the Umayyads."

220 *819* and *846*. On these texts, see Palmer, "Les chroniques brèves."

221 Palmer, *Monk and Mason*, 13.

222 Palmer, *Monk and Mason*, 8–13.

successive sections: the first, which goes until 728 and was likely composed shortly after that date, is based on what he calls "the chronology of Qartamīn." Its focus is the history of the monastery, and it presents numerous elements of ecclesiastical, Byzantine and Islamic history;[223] this same chronology of Qartamīn was likely used by Theophilus of Edessa.[224] The second section, ending in 785, is primarily an ecclesiastical history with a few added elements of Islamic history, while the third consists of a list of Abbasid rulers up through 813, and the fourth and final part contains a list of Jacobite patriarchs through 819.[225] The *Chronicle of 846*, which survives in a single, heavily damaged manuscript, adds several significant developments to these elements, and also breaks off at the year 819, with the exception that the copyist specifies at the end of the text that John of the monastery of Zakai became patriarch in 846. Palmer has suggested that this chronicle was composed by David, the bishop of Ḥarrān, in this latter city rather than at Qartamīn like the chronicle of 819.[226] The reference to the plain of Dābiq, where Sulaymān gathered his troops before embarking on campaigns, is otherwise absent from the Syriac sources,[227] implying that once again, these chronicles were almost certainly based on an Islamic source.

These well-identified circuits of transmission are incontestably sound, despite the inevitable gaps imposed by lost sources. From the perspective of this study, it is a decisive point for our goal of *dating* the circulation of historical information. For their respective sections spanning until about 730, all of these texts are based on a common source. The circuits of Theophilus of Edessa and Qartamīn move in different directions subsequent to this date, while still preserving elements of dating and possibilities of verification (diagram 3.1 above clearly demonstrates a *vertical* transmission compared to weak *horizontal* connections, a fact which offers firm assurances) that are sufficiently significant to remain functional. Alongside these sequential sources, several other Christian chronicles help to refine our understanding of the early Islamic period in the Near East.

---

223 Conrad, "Syriac Perspectives," 6–7, 23–4; Brooks has already proposed a division of the chronicle of 846, whose first "layer," which ends at the year 728, is identical to the division identified by Conrad, see Brooks, "A Syriac," 570. More recently, Hoyland has also accepted this division, *Seeing*, 421.

224 As Brooks has also noted, "A Syriac," 570 (before identifying Theophilus of Edessa as the Syriac Common Source); see also Hoyland, who notes the similarity of certain notices for the period 728–733, *Seeing*, 421.

225 Conrad, "Syriac Perspectives," 23–4.

226 Palmer, *The Seventh*, 83.

227 Palmer, *The Seventh*, 84.

3.2.3 *Other Christian Sources*

This enrichment of our knowledge comes primarily from several short and extremely dry chronologies presenting lists of successive sovereigns. The use of these lists is well-attested in the Syriac sources, and their ties to Islamic historiography are evident. If we follow Robinson's hypothesis, this list-making tendency may well have preserved valuable information concerning the succession of the caliphs.[228] It is quite possible that the lists of caliphs contained in the anonymous Syriac chronicles of *705*, *724* and *775* were derived from Arabic originals.[229] More specifically, it may even be the case that these lists were composed from information emanating from or produced by the Syrian entourage of the Umayyad caliphate: these three sources effectively erase the name of ʿAlī b. Abī Ṭālib and indicate a power vacuum following the caliphate of ʿUthmān.[230] The vocabulary choices in these chronologies reveal the Arabic hiding behind the Syriac. The terms *rasūl/rasūlā* (*724*),[231] *fitna* (*724*),[232] and even an explicit mention to the battle of Ṣiffīn (*Ṣefē, 705*)[233] attest to this fact; elsewhere, describing the downfall of the Umayyads, the chronology of *775* mentions the *msawwedē* (Arabic: *musawwada*), or those who wore black, using the well-known Arabic periphrasis to designate the Abbasids.[234] These chro-

228 Robinson, *Islamic Historiography*, 23; see also Hoyland, *Seeing*, 396. For the problems associated with the chronology of the successive caliphs presented by these lists, almost certainly connected to a confusion between solar and lunar calendars, see Palmer, *The Seventh*, 257.

229 *705*; *724*; *775*. On these brief chronologies, see Hoyland, *Seeing*, 393–9, who offers English translations of the lists of caliphs; Palmer, *The Seventh*, 43–4, 49–52, and "Les chroniques brèves."

230 *705*, 11; trans. Hoyland, *Seeing*, 394; *724*, 155; Latin trans., 119, trans. Hoyland, *Seeing*, 395–6; *775*, 348; Latin trans. 274, trans. Hoyland, *Seeing*, 397.

231 *724*, 155; Latin trans. 119, trans. Hoyland, *Seeing*, 395. See also the chronicle of *Zuqnīn*, 149–50; trans. Hoyland, *Seeing*, 413, on which, see below.

232 *724*, 155; Latin trans. 119, trans. Hoyland, *Seeing*, 395.

233 *705*, 11; trans. Hoyland, 394, trans. Palmer, *The Seventh*, 43; the battle of Ṣiffīn/Ṣefē is also mentioned in the Syriac inscription at Ehnesh, which borrows the Arabic title "commander of the faithful" (*amīrā da-mhaymnē*) for al-Mahdī, whereas the typical Syriac formula is "king of the Arabs." See Hoyland, *Seeing*, 415; Palmer, "The Messiah and the Mahdi" and *The Seventh Century*, 71–4. The same battle and toponymy are also mentioned in the *Chronicle of Zuqnīn* (vol. II, 153, trans. Harrak, 146, trans. Palmer, 59, with identical spelling, with the exception of two points indicating a plural) and in the *Chronicle of 1234* (vol. I, 278; Latin trans. 217, trans. Palmer 184, with the spelling *ṣepīn*). See Palmer, "The Messiah and the Mahdi," 65.

234 *775*, 349, Latin trans. 275, trans. Hoyland, *Seeing*, 397. On the problems this term posed for Syriac authors, see the gloss proposed by the *Chronicle of Zuqnīn*, vol. II, 194, trans. Harrak 179, that suggests rendering the Arabic *musawwada* as the Syriac *ūkāmē*, which signifies "being or making black" (a good translation of the Arabic verb *aswadda*), or, in

nologies are almost certainly old: the chronicle of *724* is found in a manuscript from the eighth century, following the *Chronicle* of Thomas the Presbyter,[235] and it is generally agreed that the list of caliphs was composed just after the death of Yazīd II.[236] This example is not limited to Syriac sources; another short chronology in Greek ending in *818* attests to this fact: it also does not mention ʿAlī, describes the anarchy and war that followed the caliphates of ʿUthmān and Hārūn al-Rashīd, and does not neglect to include Yazīd III's pejorative surname, "the deficient" (Arabic: *al-nāqiṣ*).[237]

Among these shorter chronicles, another Syriac text dated *716* providing a list of the natural disasters that occurred between 712 and 716 (earthquakes, epidemics, etc.),[238] also merits our attention. This text was integrated into a manuscript dating to 874, following an account of the encounter between the Syrian Orthodox patriarch John I, who held the position between 632 and 648, and an anonymous Arab emir. Despite its brevity and information on natural disasters, this text preserves certain important elements related to the caliphate of Sulaymān b. ʿAbd al-Malik. A slightly more developed treatise, the *Anonymous Syriac Chronicle of 813* only survives in a single, heavily damaged manuscript that is unfortunately incomplete; all that remains is the section spanning 137/755 to 199/813. Conrad, however, deems the content of this chronicle important: although it primarily deals with ecclesiastical matters, it nevertheless contains several useful pieces of information, among them some concerning al-Manṣūr's construction of al-Rāfiqa near al-Raqqa (Kallinikos).[239]

Alongside these texts, which are often limited to only a few folios, the much longer *Chronicle of Zuqnīn* stands out. Composed in Syriac by a monk of the eponymous monastery near Amida (Diyarbakir), this chronicle is also frequently referred to as the *Chronicle of Pseudo-Dionysius* due to the fact that it was at first wrongly attributed to the Jacobite patriarch Dionysius of Tel Maḥrē.[240] In reality, this chronicle predates Dionysius, having been composed in 775/776,

---

its plural form, "black garments" rather than "wearers of black clothing," as the original Arabic term indicates. See Conrad's discussion, "Syriac Perspectives," 26. The Byzantine authors adopted the term *maurophoroi*; see Theophanes, *Chronicle*, 424, trans. 587.

235 On this author, who composed his text around 640, see Hoyland, *Seeing*, 118–20, and de Prémare, *Les fondations*, 385–6.

236 Hoyland, *Seeing*, 396. The *Asnān al-khulafāʾ* of al-Zuhrī was also composed around this time, attesting to a clear need to define the chronology of caliphal succession. See above, Ch. 1.

237 *818*, 97, English trans. Hoyland, *Seeing*, 436.

238 *716*; Palmer, *The Seventh*, 45–8; Reinink, "The Beginnings."

239 See Conrad, "Syriac Perspectives," 5, which notes the erroneous manner in which the chronicle describes al-Manṣūr's construction of al-Raqqa near Kallinikos.

240 *Chronicle of Zuqnīn*.

and thus it is a highly important source for information on the eighth century, as Cahen noted in a pioneering 1954 article;[241] since then, this chronicle has sustained scholarly interest, although it remains insufficiently used.[242] For the Islamic period, which comprises the fourth section of the chronicle, the author laments the fact that he was unable to find sources of suitable quality, and attempts to overcome this difficulty by basing his text on the oldest available oral testimonies as well as his own personal observations.[243] As Hoyland notes, although the period between 587 and 717 offers limited developments, the text devoted to the six subsequent decades provides a wealth of material: the *Chronicle of Zuqnīn* contains precious information, especially concerning Mesopotamia, most of which cannot be found in any other extant source.[244] It also preserves a particularly interesting account of Maslama's siege of Constantinople, to which we shall return below.[245]

In addition to these valuable indications, this chronicle plays an important role in Syriac historiography: it introduces a new means of interpreting historical events concerning the Arabs and Islam. Harrak has presented a remarkable analysis of this phenomenon, highlighting the fact that in the seventh and early eighth centuries, Syriac authors sought to give historic and religious meaning to the events that occurred in the wake of the Islamic conquests.[246] Two opposing interpretations thus arise: either that the end of the world is imminent, or that it is divine retribution punishing the Christians for their sins. The shift in these views occurred during the eighth century, when chroniclers stopped relying on the Book of Daniel, which imposed a strictly apocalyptic reading,[247] and turned instead to the Book of Isaiah, which proclaimed

241 Which nevertheless takes for granted the chronicle's attribution to the patriarch Dionysius of Tel Maḥrē; however, despite this confusion, he was one of the first to call the attention of the Islamic scholars to this important text. See Cahen, "Fiscalité, propriété, antagonismes sociaux."

242 See above all Witakowski, *The Syriac Chronicle*; Hoyland, *Seeing*, 409–14; Palmer, *The Seventh*, 53–70; Ishaq, "The Significance;" Harrak, "La victoire arabo-musulmane." In spite of these important contributions, Harrak has recently and rightly emphasised the clear deficit of studies using the *Chronicle of Zuqnīn*, "Ah! The Assyrian," 45.

243 *Chronicle of Zuqnīn*, 146–7, trans. Harrak 139, and Hoyland, *Seeing*, 409–10.

244 Hoyland, *Seeing*, 414. It should be noted that the division of the chronicle in historiographic layers attributed to different "hands," proposed by Conrad, "Syriac Perspectives," 24–6, has been contested by Hoyland, *Seeing*, 410–1. On the contrary, Hoyland suggests that the chronicle was composed by a single author relying on different sources.

245 *Chronicle of Zuqnīn*, 156–60, trans. Harrak 150–53, and Palmer, *The Seventh*, 62–5. See below, Ch. 5.

246 The following development relies on the work of Harrak, "Ah! The Assyrian," 46 ff.

247 The genre of Daniel's apocalyptics was very popular, both in the Christian (see below) and Muslim spheres.

divine omnipotence over history and can be read as a theology of history. It should be noted that the object of the Book of Isaiah was to announce the fall of Israel and Judah and the punishment of the people's sins. The Assyrian king Tiglath-Pileser III (745–727 BCE) was to be the instrument of this divine retribution, "the rod of [God's] anger,"[248] consecrating Assyrian control of the kingdom of Judah; however, the Assyrian, forgetting that he was merely an instrument of God, grew intoxicated by his military success, and in his arrogance, scorned the God of Israel and thus brought divine wrath down upon his own head. The *Chronicle of Zuqnīn* equates the Arabs with the Assyrians of the Bible; more specifically, the Abbasid defeat of the Umayyads led the chronicler to identify the Assyrians with the Abbasids, and the colour black reinforced this interpretation.[249] While the Assyrians were not a new motif in Syriac literature, in this chronicle the theme became associated with the second Islamic dynasty, who were thus seen as "the Assyrians of the Old Testament resurrected."[250] Taking this framework for reading into account is essential to a better understanding of the meaning the chronicler of Zuqnīn imparted to Islamic history.

The Armenian chronicler and man of the Church Łewond[251] is the author of a would-be universal history relating events from 632 to 789, entitled: *The History of Łewond, the eminent vardapet of the Armenians, on the subject of the appearance of Muḥammad and his followers: how and in what manner they conquered the universe and in particular our Armenian nation.*[252] Łewond's precise dates are unknown, and often debated; from the indication provided by a colophon stating that his chronicle was composed at the request of Shapuh Bagratuni (d. 824), it is probable that he lived either during the eighth or the first half of the ninth century.[253] Łewond was above all famous for preserving the pseudo-correspondence between the caliph ʿUmar II and his Byzantine counterpart Leo III. This text is the subject of numerous studies:[254] in its current form, it appears to date from the third/ninth century, having preserved notable elements from the Islamic-Christian polemic from the second century

248 Isaiah 10:5.
249 According to Nahum 2:10.
250 Harrak, "Ah! The Assyrian," 64.
251 Łewond, *Lewond erets' patmut'iwn.*
252 Mahé, "Entre Moïse et Mahomet," 136–7.
253 Mahé, "Entre Moïse et Mahomet," 136.
254 Primarily those of Jeffrey, "Ghevond's Text," 269–332; Gaudeul, "The Correspondence;" Hoyland, "The Correspondence." As complements to Gaudeul's work, see Sourdel, "Un pamphlet," and Cardaillac, *La polémique.*

hijrī, as Hoyland has shown.[255] This correspondence was perhaps later integrated into the chronicle.[256] As for the remainder of the information he provides concerning Islamic history, Łewond specifies that he gathered some of it "from the enemy himself,"[257] attesting here as well to the intercultural transmission processes at work in the medieval Near East and the Caucasus.

Saʿīd b. Biṭrīq (263–328/877–940), who adopted the name Eutyches when he was elected patriarch of Alexandria (935–940), is the author of a universal history composed in Arabic that is known to us today from a single manuscript, in addition to the numerous copies of his continuer Yaḥyā b. Saʿīd al-Anṭākī, who wrote around the year 1030.[258] His history is a synthesis, integrating many well-known elements of Islamic historiography while also providing some original information, particularly concerning the relations between Christians and Muslims.

As we know it today, the *History of the Patriarchs of Alexandria*[259] is the product of complex processes of transmission and translation. Primitively written in Coptic, the text is organised around the biographies of the Coptic patriarchs of Egypt. These notices, which may have existed independently, were collected and translated into Arabic by Mawhūb b. Manṣūr al-Mufarrij (d. c. 1100); once again, it must be added that this rewriting is lost, and that we only have access to later recensions from the thirteenth and fourteenth centuries.[260] Although this source is primarily concerned with aspects directly related to Egypt, it nonetheless presents many elements relevant to Islamic history as well. The *History of the Patriarchs* is especially valuable for the second/eighth century, as the passages related to the period were composed by contemporaries. For the beginning of the century, the section ending with the caliphate of Sulaymān b. ʿAbd al-Malik (96–99/715–717) was written by Abba George, archdeacon and secretary (*kātib*) of Abba Simon (692–700), the patriarch of Alexandria;[261] John, the bishop of Wasīm, continued the work until the time of the patriarch Michael I (743–767).[262] This latter provides a very detailed account of the "Abbasid Revolution," stating that he was an eyewitness

255 Hoyland, "The Correspondence" and *Seeing*, 490–501.

256 Mahé, "Entre Moïse et Mahomet," 136.

257 Łewond, XXXIV, trans. Arzoumanian, 137, cited in Hoyland, *Seeing*, 439.

258 Saʿīd b. Biṭrīq, *Annals*. On this author, see Graf, *Geschichte*, 32–8; Breydy, *Études sur Saʿīd b. Biṭrīq*; and Hoyland, *Seeing*, 442–3. Yaḥyā b. Saʿīd al-Anṭākī, *The History of Yaḥyā b. Saʿīd of Antioch*.

259 *History of the Patriarchs*. On this essential source, see Den Heijer, *Mawhūb ibn Manṣūr*, and Trombley, "The Documentary Background."

260 Hoyland, *Seeing*, 446; Den Heijer, *Mawhūb ibn Manṣūr*.

261 *History of the Patriarchs*, PO, vol. V, 90–1. See also Hoyland, *Seeing*, 447.

262 *History of the Patriarchs*, PO, vol. X, 360. See Hoyland, *Seeing*, 447.

to the events he reports, in particular the execution of Marwān II.[263] An anonymous author then took up the pen in continuation at the behest of the patriarch Abba Shanūda,[264] at which point the chronicle shifts its focus to ecclesiastical history.

The *Continuatio of the Samaritan Chronicle* offers an important description of the beginning of the Islamic era through the caliphate of al-Rāḍī (d. 332/934); it is mainly focused on Palestine, but also touches on the rest of Syria and Egypt.[265] This text, preserved in its entirety in a single copy, is found at the end of the *Kitāb al-taʾrīkh* of Abū al-Fatḥ b. Abī al-Ḥasan al-Sāmirī al-Danafī in 1355; however, the first section, ending with the death of al-Rashīd, exists in an incomplete form in various other manuscripts.[266] It is written in Samaritan Arabic, a dialect of Middle Arabic.[267] This source has the dual advantage of presenting a *dhimmī* perspective and centring its discourse on Palestine, as this province is often marginalised in the larger historical compilations. As Levy-Rubin notes, this Palestinian tropism gives the chronicle an exceptional character among the works of Near Eastern historiography.[268] In addition, it seems that the *Continuatio* made use of a contemporary source from the first third of the ninth century: several passages written in the first person in the manner of testimonials concerning episodes from the caliphates of al-Rashīd and al-Maʾmūn support this hypothesis.[269] It is certain that the *Continuatio* employed sources, in particular Samaritan sources, that do not survive.[270] These elements converge with those concerning Palestine, most of which cannot be found elsewhere. The chronicle presents a positive image of the situation in Palestine under the Umayyads, and judges this dynasty in a similarly favourable manner; according to the author, the Umayyads governed "according to what he [Muḥammad] had enjoined upon them; they did no more or less, and did not harm anyone." Even more surprising, the Umayyads are depicted as the direct successors of the Prophet, the Rāshidūn being

263 *History of the Patriarchs*, PO, vol. V, 171 ff.; Hoyland, *Seeing*, 448. See also Amélineau, "Les derniers jours," who contests John's affirmation.

264 *History of the Patriarchs*, PO, vol. X, 360. See Den Heijer, *Mawhūb ibn Manṣūr*.

265 On this source, see Levy-Rubin's introduction, *The Continuatio*, 1–45.

266 Levy-Rubin, *The Continuatio*, 1; this is the only version that preserves a detailed description of the siege of Caesarea; see Levy-Rubin, *The Continuatio*, 10.

267 Levy-Rubin, *The Continuatio*, 19; on Middle Arabic and its dialects, see Blau, "The Importance" and *A Grammar*.

268 Levy-Rubin, *The Continuatio*, 2.

269 Levy-Rubin, *The Continuatio*, 11.

270 Levy-Rubin, *The Continuatio*, 23–7.

considered members of the first Islamic dynasty;[271] these sympathetic views of the Umayyads are corroborated by the fact that ʿAlī's caliphate is passed over in silence. After this period, the *Continuatio* may be based on a pro-Zubayrid source, as ʿAbd Allāh b. al-Zubayr is presented as the legitimate successor of Marwān b. al-Ḥakam; ʿAbd al-Malik's caliphate is consequently reduced to a period of thirteen years and six months.[272] The format adopted from this point on – simple notices indicating the names of the caliphs and the length of their reigns, from Muʿāwiya until Marwān II, interspersed with more important developments – appears to signal that for this section, the author relied on a basic list of sovereigns, identical to certain examples we possess from the Syriac tradition. Moreover, the fact that the chronicle designates the caliph Hishām with the name Hāshim could also indicate the use of a Syriac source, where this spelling is common as well; however, this could also be merely an error on the part of the copyist.[273] The *Continuatio*, like the short and anonymous Greek *Chronicle of 818*, also does not ignore Yazīd III's pejorative surname *al-nāqiṣ*. Numerous elements suggest that this passage reproduces an identical or near-identical source to the lists noted above. The rise of the Abbasids is portrayed as a significant upheaval in the lives of the *dhimmī*s in the region, in particular as a result of the financial pressure placed upon them;[274] the *Continuatio* ultimately provides significant information on the tribal conflicts in Palestine under the early Abbasids.

The chronicle of Elias bar Shēnāyā[275] (975–1046),[276] appointed metropolitan of Nisibis in 1008 – better known as Elias of Nisibis – is the only great

271 *The Continuatio*, 207 (following the pagination given on the facsimile of the manuscript rather than the pagination of the volume), trans. 53. It is clear that the Umayyads tried to present themselves as the *ahl al-bayt*, aiming to affirm their proximity (*qarāba*) to the Prophet. This affirmation was imposed in Syria, as attested by a passage from al-Balādhurī, for example, in which the Syrian *ashrāf* state before the new Abbasid caliphs that they were unaware of the existence of any *ahl al-bayt* other than the Umayyads. See *Ansāb*, vol. III, 159–60, and more generally, Sharon, "The Umayyads." Similar traditions were perhaps at work in the composition of this passage of the *Continuatio*.

272 *The Continuatio*, 207–8, trans. 54–5. On the question of the length of ʿAbd al-Malik's caliphate, see Robinson, ʿAbd al-Malik, 4 ff.

273 For example, see the *Chronicle of 846*, 235, ed. Brooks 575; the *Chronicle of 819* offers a spelling without the long vowel, 16.

274 *The Continuatio*, 209–10, trans. 57–8.

275 Here I am following Witakowski's reading of "Elias," 220. He estimates that the name derives from his native city of Elias, Shēnā, situated at the confluence of the Tigris and the Great Zāb, and rejects the common vocalisation of Shīnāyā.

276 There is some confusion surrounding Elias' death date in modern scholarship. Per Assemanus, the most commonly proposed date is that of 1049, which Samir shows to be erroneous, "Date de la mort d'Élie de Nisibe." Elias actually died on 18 July 1046. Elias of

Nestorian chronicle that survives. It is preserved in a single copy composed in 1019, and offers a chronology of the principal events that took place up through the year 1018. The manuscript follows the Seleucid epoch but is unfortunately incomplete, especially between 1096 and 1189 (169/785–264/878). The text, which is subdivided into a chronicle followed by chronological tables that are accompanied by a treatise on date calculation, is interesting in that it is bilingual: the text of the chronicle is presented as a table,[277] with one column in Syriac and the other in Arabic, while the other columns specify the date of the event and, in a remarkably systematic fashion, the source or sources from which Elias acquired his information! Although several different hands can be identified for the Arabic part of the chronicle, the Syriac text was composed by single author – perhaps Elias himself.[278] Elias's list of sources is impressive: he employed about sixty sources in total, including authors from antiquity as well as Syriac and Arabic-Muslim sources.[279] Elias also appears to have taken great care to rely as often as possible on sources contemporary with the facts and events they record. For Arabic sources concerning the period under investigation here, Elias depends heavily on the famous Muslim mathematician and astronomer of al-Maʾmūn's *bayt al-ḥikma*, al-Khwārizmī (*c.*184–232/800–847). Al-Khwārizmī was also known as the author of a *Kitāb al-taʾrīkh*, widely employed by Elias – that is, if it is indeed the same work Elias designates as the *Yūbāl zabnē* in Syriac.[280] I have attempted elsewhere to demonstrate the value of the information Elias transmits, both as a source for al-Khwārizmī's lost chronography as well as for elucidating the mechanisms of the Abbasid fabrication of history, in particular by *dating* the circulation of historical information.[281] Thus, the stakes here are high, given that this text could potentially provide access to a lost *taʾrīkh* more or less contemporary with the oldest surviving history we possess: the history of Khalīfa b. Khayyāṭ (d. c. 240/854). Elias cites seven sources in addition to al-Khwārizmī, including al-Ṭabarī and the Shiite scholar al-Ṣūlī (d. 335/947),[282] as well as other texts, both anonymous and of known authorship, that do not survive. A variety of Syriac sources were

Nisibis has not sustained the interest of modern scholars, despite the pioneering work of Delaporte, *Chronographie*. See Hoyland, *Seeing*, 421–2; Pinggera, "Nestorianische Weltchronistik;" Witakowski, "Elias;" Borrut, "La circulation de l'information historique."

277 On this format, see Aigle, "L'histoire sous forme graphique."

278 Hoyland, *Seeing*, 422.

279 The collection of sources used by Elias of Nisibis is presented by Delaporte, *Chronographie*, vii–xiv. See also Witakowski, "Elias," and Borrut, "La circulation de l'information historique," 144–5.

280 Vernet, "Al-Khʷārazmī."

281 Borrut, "La circulation de l'information historique," especially 148–55.

282 Leder, "Al-Ṣūlī."

also consulted, among them the aforementioned chronicle of Dionysius of Tel Maḥrē, cited several times between 138/755 and 153/770; this source is consistently presented in red ink in the manuscript.

In addition to these chronicles, historical apocalypses provide another valuable source of information. This form of writing, perhaps more than any other, facilitated explanations of Islam's astonishing ascendancy as well as the early failures of the caliphate, the culmination of which was the fall of the Umayyads, who enjoyed great success in apocalyptic literature. The oldest extant texts may preserve materials from the second/eighth century, and, like similar older texts, they provide valuable insight into the meanings authors tried to bestow on history.

3.2.4 *Historical Apocalypses*

The swift rise of Islam lent itself easily to the profusion of apocalyptic literature. Christians and Jews tried to present this phenomenon in eschatological terms, which explains the abundance of historical apocalypses from the first/seventh century. The long-lasting caliphal political hegemony provoked numerous reinterpretations over the following centuries. The very nature of apocalyptic literature enabled subsequent rewritings: the apocalyptic structure of a text was often preserved in order to enhance the significance of the events of one's own time.[283] This tendency offers a precise explanation of the specific problems posed by this genre: it is frequently difficult to identify the figures alluded to in the texts, as they have often undergone numerous reconfigurations from a common narrative base, ultimately designating different successive protagonists. The myriad extant versions of Daniel's apocalyptics, composed in Arabic, Coptic, Greek, Hebrew and Judeo-Persian offer a perfect example of this proliferation.

As previously stated with respect to the Muslim apocalyptic literature, there were certain subjects that sustained authorial interest, in particular the Abbasid overthrow of the Umayyads. The Christian apocalypse of Baḥīra, preserved in Arabic and Syriac, is one example of this phenomenon. The main part of the text dates to the era of al-Ma'mūn and was subsequently reworked, although it contains elements that are plausibly older, dating to the time of the Abbasid Revolution.[284] The Coptic apocalypse of Daniel divides modern scholars. The text begins with the classic vision of four beasts, the last with nineteen horns instead of the usual ten, corresponding to nineteen Muslim

283 Lewis, "An Apocalyptic Vision," 308.

284 Hoyland, *Seeing*, 276, 273.

rulers. Macler argued early on that this number should be identified with the Fatimids, whereas Becker preferred an Umayyad interpretation;[285] Meinardus, followed by Suermann, suggested that this apocalyptic originally implied the Umayyads, but was later reinterpreted near the end of the Fatimid era.[286] Hoyland, faced with these uncertainties and the vast complexity of the text, has expressed doubts concerning the historicity of the figures mentioned in this apocalypse.[287] The recent edition of a new source confirms the existence of an older core of information as well as the early use of the motif of nineteen Muslim kings in the Coptic tradition. Van Lent has meticulously compared this new document, an apocalypse of Shenute[288] written in Middle Arabic from a Coptic original,[289] with Daniel's fourteenth vision and the apocalypse of Samuel of Qalamūn. The textual analysis reveals that the document was rewritten under al-Amīn, during the civil war, a context that lent itself easily to this literary genre; however, the text was still based on an older version dating to the beginning of the Abbasid period.[290] The last sovereign – in theory, the nineteenth, although some texts mention a greater number of kings despite their initial indications of a list of nineteen – may originally have represented Marwān II (r. 127–132/744–750), later changed to al-Amīn (r. 193–198/809–813), and subsequently to other rulers as needed, in particular the last Fatimid caliph al-ʿĀḍid (r. 555–567/1160–1171).[291]

Another salient episode with eschatological connotations occurred when Sulaymān b. ʿAbd al-Malik's armies laid siege to Constantinople, an event that occupies an equally significant place in apocalyptic literature. The most important text on this subject is the Greek apocalyptic of pseudo-Daniel, due to the precise information it provides about the siege itself: the routes taken by the Arab generals, the construction of a boat bridge by the assailants, and the flight of Byzantine notables. This detailed information concerning the siege

285 Becker, "Das Reich;" Macler, "Les apocalypses apocryphes."

286 Meinardus, "A Commentary;" Suermann, "Notes." However, the former later revised this hypothesis, stating that the text was composed in its entirety at the end of the Fatimid period. See Meinardus, "New Evidence."

287 Hoyland, *Seeing*, 289–90.

288 Abbot of the White Monastery near Akhmīm (*c.*350–465), Van Lent, "The Nineteen," 646.

289 This text is preserved in two different manuscripts, one in Paris and the other in Cairo. For a detailed presentation of these two manuscripts, see Van Lent, "The Nineteen," 673–80, as well as the edition and English translation of these texts, 681–93. Shenute's apocalyptic is contained in the Paris manuscript, and has been presented by Troupeau, "De quelques apocalypses."

290 Van Lent, "The Nineteen," 661 ff.

291 Van Lent, "The Nineteen," 666.

may indicate that the author himself was an eyewitness to these events.[292] Other texts also describe the siege of the Byzantine capital, among them the vision of Enoch the Just, which only survives in Armenian.[293] Outside of these limited contexts, apocalyptic literature also provides descriptions of the different caliphs and their policies. For example, the Coptic apocalypse of pseudo-Athanasius – a reference to the patriarch Athanasius of Alexandria (d. 373) – dating to approximately 96/715 mentions the administrative monetary reforms of ʿAbd al-Malik, as well as a census or the establishment of a cadastre.[294]

With respect to Jewish apocalyptic, Simon ben Yōḥai, a rabbi of the second Christian century, is also credited with visions that are known to us today through several texts composed at different periods, all centred around a common core: *the prayer*, *the secrets*, and *the Midrash of the ten kings*. Lewis performed a detailed analysis of these texts and convincingly demonstrated that this apocalypse was composed in several successive stages.[295] The section describing the Umayyads and their tragic end was written under the early Abbasids, most likely under al-Manṣūr.[296] It offers certain significant indications concerning the perception of the caliphs as well as a number of measures or acts attributed to them; for example, it discusses the efforts to develop the Syrian space undertaken by Hishām or al-Walīd II. The abundant rivalries of the Abbasid Revolution and the decade that followed are also well-documented. More broadly, these texts provide important testimony for the profoundly messianic context characteristic of the early Abbasid period. Another Jewish apocalypse, much shorter and more fragmentary, also presents a list of caliphs, beginning with the death of ʿUthmān and passing over ʿAlī's caliphate in silence before being cut off abruptly in the middle of a description of ʿUmar II.[297]

The continuous production of this literary genre attests to the importance of apocalyptic expectations during the period examined here and beyond. The major political crises of the history of the first centuries of the caliphate often served as pretexts for rewriting, relying on a core of older information that could easily be molded to conform with present needs. Alongside the factual

292 Hoyland, *Seeing*, 297–9; Berger, *Die griechische Daniel*.
293 Hoyland, *Seeing*, 299–302.
294 Hoyland, *Seeing*, 282–5.
295 Lewis, "An Apocalyptic Vision." See also Hoyland, *Seeing*, 308–12.
296 Lewis, "An Apocalyptic Vision," 309–11.
297 Lévi, "Une apocalypse judéo-arabe;" Hoyland, *Seeing* 316–7.

information they contain, these texts are particularly valuable for providing insight into the atmosphere in which they were composed.

Many other sources should be mentioned as well, including Greek[298] and Syriac inscriptions,[299] mosaics,[300] etc., and consideration should be given to the important diffusion of this history of the first centuries of Islam – well-attested within the confines of the Islamic empire – to the Christian authors of Spain[301] or Chinese sources.[302] This presentation of sources on the margins (or supposedly on the margins) of the historiographic vulgate established in the post-Sāmarrā' period does not claim to be exhaustive. The idea here was to situate these different corpora with respect to a dominant presentation of the history of the Syrian space in the second/eighth century. This reflection offers some surprising results, and also invites caution. Certain sources that appear to be external to the vulgate by nature, such as Umayyad poetry, in reality pose similar problems to those presented by the historiographic canon; others that are frequently placed in opposition to the Islamic tradition, such as non-Muslim narrative sources, actually depended heavily upon this very tradition. Alongside these two examples, sources of various natures preserve elements that the chronographies chose to forget, due to the different objectives of their respective genres. To reiterate Esch's expression cited as a preamble to this chapter, these are truly "different types of sources guaranteeing the greatest chance of transmission."[303] The vast dispersion of historical information and the specific problems posed by each individual genre of sources serve to highlight the many difficulties faced in trying to approach the history of the second/eighth century Syrian space.

Nevertheless, an appropriate methodology opens new horizons for comparative historiography. The intercultural transmission between the different communities of the Near East offers additional proof of the existence of an older Islamic historiography. As a result of the asynchronous rhythms of transmission, accessing different *moments* of historiographic sedimentation is possible. This is undoubtedly the best means of renewing our understanding:

298 Gatier, "Les inscriptions grecques."

299 See Briquel-Chatonnet, Debié and Desreumaux, *Les inscriptions syriaques*, including in particular a focus on the famous inscriptions on the quarry stones of Kāmid al-Lūz, left by the workers who built ʿAnjar.

300 See Duval, *Les églises de Jordanie*.

301 Besides the *Byzantine-Arab Chronicle* and the *Mozarabic Chronicle of 754*, see for example the thirteenth-century authors studied by Constable, "Perceptions of the Umayyads."

302 Hoyland, *Seeing*, 243–54.

303 Esch, "Chance et hasard de la transmission," 19.

seeking different pasts or different meanings given to certain eras. However, this strategy operates on the assumption that it is possible to illuminate the specific elements the editors of the Islamic historiographic vulgate wanted *to remember* from the history of Syria in the second/eighth century, thus deciding what deserved to become memory and what was better left to oblivion. Only when this stage of our study has been completed may we attempt to listen to the murmurs of these alternative pasts.

CHAPTER 4

The Second/Eight-Century Syrian Space: Between Memory and Oblivion

> No indeed, surely it [the Qur'ān] is a Reminder: whoever wills shall remember it. And they will not remember, except that God wills.[1]

•••

> Any story about the past is told because of its present-day relevance.[2]

∴

The caliphate's return to Baghdad following the Sāmarrāʾ interlude inaugurated a period of intense historical rewriting.[3] In this recomposition effort, historians were primarily engaged in committing information to memory. These historians were perfectly aware of the choices they were making based on the material available for reporting the past, although, as noted in the previous chapters, this material was equally subject to the influence and selective transformations of earlier generations. The later rewritings demand to be examined through the lens of a history of memory; such an undertaking has not been employed previously, yet is essential for renewing our perspective on the period. In fact, a history of memory approach is equally valid for all of the narrative sources on the history of early Islam, as the state in which these sources have been preserved for us today means that the Umayyads and the early Abbasids constantly walk a fine line between remembrance and oblivion. As Geary notes:

> This competition for power over the past needs to be explored for two reasons. First and most obviously, by examining the creation of a past, we can understand better the modes of perception and structures of

1 *Qur'ān* 74: 54–56, trans. Arberry.
2 Van Houts, "Introduction: Medieval Memories," 10.
3 A portion of this chapter served as the basis for my article "La *memoria* omeyyade."

 | DOI:10.1163/9789004466326_006

> understanding of the people … and how people used these mental categories to construct their world and to order their lives. But as important, this creation determined not only contemporaries' understanding of the past but ours as well.[4]

We must reflect further on "the use of memories in different social groups"[5] in order to reveal "the problem of the relation between memory and history in the medieval sources themselves;"[6] once written down, these memories reflect the "social logic of the text."[7] In addition to social memory, the competition between memories also takes place in the political sphere: "all memory, whether 'individual,' 'collective' or 'historical,' is a memory *for* something, and this political (in a broad sense) purpose cannot be ignored."[8] Memorialisation thus must be integrated into, and largely harmonised with, the imperial project.[9] Control over what should be remembered and what was more convenient to forget was a necessary prerequisite for the construction of a caliphal history. After determining the various forms and frameworks that structure these rewritings, we must then study their content in order to understand why new interpretations were essential.

4.1 *Memoria* as an Object of Study

Before addressing what the Muslim authors of the third–fourth/ninth–tenth centuries themselves wanted to transmit from the early years of Islam, it is helpful to briefly consider the most notable advancements in modern scholarship on *memoria*, first and foremost the links between Islam and memory. If Judaism[10] and Christianity became religions of memory – Christianity thanks in large part to the Eucharistic injunction to "do this in remembrance of me" – why not Islam as well?

4 Geary, *Phantoms of Remembrance*, 7.
5 Borgolte, "Memoria," 68.
6 Monnet, "Conclusions," 627.
7 Spiegel, "History, Historicism and the Social Logic."
8 Geary, *Phantoms of Remembrance*, 12.
9 Robinson, *Islamic Historiography*, 41.
10 See Yerushalmi, *Zakhor*.

4.1.1 *Islam and Memory*

There is a general lack of modern research focusing on the role of memory in Islam, particularly for the medieval period,[11] despite its deeply pervasive "memorial culture"[12] that notably grew out of a "robust culture of memorization."[13] Memory and memorisation were at the heart of medieval Muslim scholarship: the *ḥāfiẓ* was one who memorised the Qur'ān, and transmission – at least during the first centuries of Islam – was based on the *isnād* system intended to memorialise chains of authorities. *Ḥadīth* and *sunna* were similarly aimed at preserving the memory of the Prophet or the Companions, and genealogy, *ṭabaqāt*, poetry, and many other genres are all founded on the basis of perserving social and cultural memory as well. Together, all of these practices were engaged in the commemoration of the original community and the formation of an Islamic identity and memory.[14] Medieval authors, like Ibn al-Jawzī in his *Al-Ḥathth ʿalā ḥifẓ al-ʿilm wa-dhikr kibār al-ḥuffāẓ*, insisted on the importance of memorising the Tradition.[15] Thus, it is surprising that this dual theme of memory and memorisation is not more central to modern research on medieval Islam, despite certain important studies and projects that are currently underway.[16]

Among the most significant modern works are Dakhlia's pioneering studies,[17] which emphasise the rich complexity of the phenomena to be understood in these texts. By highlighting the different degrees of the mobilisation

11 This observation is actually valid well beyond the medieval period, as Hartmann notes, "Rethinking Memory and Remaking History."

12 This is an essential characteristic of all medieval culture, as Carruthers notes, *The Book of Memory*, 9: "It is my contention that medieval culture was fundamentally memorial, to the same profound degree that modern culture in the West is documentary." Geary agrees, affirming that "*memoria* was a key organizing principle, not only in medieval theology but in every aspect of medieval life," *Phantoms of Remembrance*, 18. It should also be noted that memory was held in high regard in the pre-modern period: "The difference is that whereas now geniuses are said to have creative imagination which they express in intricate reasoning and original discovery, in earlier times they were said to have richly retentive memories, which they expressed in intricate reasoning and original discovery," Carruthers, *The Book of Memory*, 4. See also Assmann, *Cultural Memory and Early Civilizations* and *Moses the Egyptian*, 8 ff.

13 Robinson, *Islamic Historiography*, 172.

14 Marzolph has notably emphasised the relations between Islamic memory and the foundational period in "Islamische Kultur als Gedächtniskultur," 316.

15 Ibn al-Jawzī, *al-Ḥathth ʿalā ḥifẓ al-ʿilm wa-dhikr kibār al-ḥuffāẓ*. See Michael Cook, "The Opponents," 437 ff.

16 I will not address the Ṣūfī practice of *dhikr* here; on this topic, see Gardet, "Dhikr."

17 Dakhlia, "Des prophètes à la nation;" *L'oubli de la cité*; "Collective Memory and the Story of History;" "New Approaches in the History of Memory." See also Valensi, *Fables de le mémoire*.

of memory and the strategies of oblivion working in tandem, Dakhlia has shed light on the stakes associated with the memory of lineage that developed in the context of these memorial competitions. This point is particularly interesting for the period under investigation here, especially considering the efforts the Abbasids expended to present themselves as *ahl al-bayt*, basing their legitimacy on their proximity (*qarāba*) to the Prophet.[18]

The question of an Islamic memory that predates the development of Islamic historiography has been examined from different perspectives with respect to the early Islamic period by Cheddadi,[19] while Décobert concentrated on the Prophet's recovery of a monotheistic memory.[20] In the chronological context of the present inquiry, a long-neglected Umayyad memory has recently provoked scholarly interest.[21] Lassner's study on the Abbasid Revolution is undoubtedly the other most significant analysis on this subject. In *Islamic Revolution and Historical Memory*, Lassner proposed a different approach, suggesting that the extant texts from the period were subject to successive reinterpretations during the Revolutionary propaganda phase and especially in the aftermath of the coup d'état as a consequence of the new dynasty's changing needs for legitimation. At the time of its publication, this work provoked a lively polemic.[22] Other still-unpublished studies, such as Campbell's on the future of the Zubayrid memory, help complete this picture.[23]

The different projects initiated by German scholars are also a valuable resource. Inspired by their colleagues in the field of Western medieval studies and other disciplines, to whom we shall return later, scholars of medieval Islam have undertaken various projects centred on *memoria* and *Erinnerungspraxis*. Marzolph, focusing on Iran, advanced the idea that Islamic culture was a culture of memory (*Gedächtniskultur*).[24] The important works of Neuwirth and Pflitsch,[25] as well as those of Hartmann and her team,[26] should also be

18 See above, Ch. 2.

19 Cheddadi, "À l'aube de l'historiographie."

20 Décobert, "La mémoire monothéiste."

21 See El-Hibri, "The Redemption," and the studies in Borrut and Cobb (eds.), *Umayyad Legacies*.

22 Lassner, *Islamic Revolution*. By the same author, see also *The Middle East Remembered*. On the Abbasid Revolution, see Ch. 7.

23 Campbell, *Telling Memories*. See also Ali, *Ardor for Memory*, and Keaney, *Remembering Rebellion*.

24 Marzolph, "Islamische Kultur als Gedächtniskultur."

25 Neuwirth and Pflitsch, *Crisis and Memory*.

26 In particular for the *Sonderforschungsbereich 434* of the University of Giessen, directed by Hartmann: "Der 'wahre' Islam: Exegesehorizont und Erinnerungspraxis religiöspolitischer Bewegungen der zeitgenössischen muslimischen Ökumene." Several studies

noted here. Hartmann, lamenting the absence of a "Pierre Nora of the Near and Middle East,"[27] studied the relevance of using the concept of "realms of memory" (*lieux de mémoire*) in Islamic societies.

The textual realm has also been approached in relation to the processes of committing information to memory. The typology established by Schoeler presented in Chapter 1 distinguishes between *syngramma* and *hypomnēma*: the second term indicates notes that were intended to serve as memory aids.[28] The lists presented in various forms in many of the sources, perhaps foremost among them the *isnād*s and the biographical enumerations, were similarly "techniques and uses of memory, and the formation or attempted formation of cultural memory,"[29] in particular near the end of the third/ninth century. The maps produced by the Balkhī school, such as those of al-Iṣṭakhrī, were part of the same logic. Although these maps have at times been harshly criticised for their inaccuracies or their tendency to oversimplify,[30] Savage-Smith has shown that they actually functioned as memory aids,[31] which justified their straightforward format, since geographic precision was not their intended goal. Maps and lists were thus included among the Islamic "arts of memory," which remain largely unstudied.[32]

Despite the growing interest in these topics, the second/eighth century has never been considered from this perspective, with the possible exception of the studies of El-Hibri and Lassner, and, to a lesser degree, those of Campbell as well.[33] For the specific period examined in this inquiry, however, the dual question of memory and memorisation is a crucial one. As part of the period of "the foundations of Islam" – to echo de Prémare's recent study[34] – where does

have already been published: Hartmann, Damir-Geilsdorf and Hendrich, *Mental Maps – Raum – Erinnerung*; Hartmann, *Geschichte und Erinnerung in Islam* and "Rethinking Memory and Remaking History." These projects were produced following a symposium held in Berlin in 1994 by Neuwirth entitled *Memoria. Kulturelle Erinnerung und Formen ihrer Bewahrung im Islam und seinem Umfeld.*

27 Hartmann, "Rethinking Memory and Remaking History," 53.

28 Schoeler, *The Genesis of Literature in Islam*, 54. See above, Ch. 1.

29 Bray, "Lists and Memory," 210.

30 Savage-Smith, "Memory and Maps," 109–10.

31 Savage-Smith, "Memory and Maps," 109, 120.

32 We should no longer lament the lack of a "Pierre Nora of the Near and Middle East," but rather the lack of a "Mary Carruthers of the Islamic Middle Ages"! See her foundational works: *The Book of Memory* and *Machina Memorialis*, in addition to Yates' classic *The Art of Memory*.

33 El-Hibri, "The Redemption;" Lassner, *Islamic Revolution*; Campbell, *Telling Memories*. To this list should be added the contributions gathered in Borrut and Cobb (eds.), *Umayyad Legacies*.

34 De Prémare, *Les fondations*.

the second/eighth century fit in the recording or memorisation of the recent Islamic past, Prophetic memory, scriptural development, etc.? It is essentially a question of the Umayyads' role in these processes of the memorialisation of Islamic knowledge; however, the answer to this question falls well outside the scope of the present study.[35] Since our knowledge of the period is largely dependent – at least where the narrative Islamic sources are concerned – on what the later authors, in particular during the Abbasid era in the third-fourth centuries of the *hijra*, wanted to know and hand down from this past, we must attempt to understand the motivations and value systems that presided over the decision as to which *memorabilia* were "*memoranda* – that is, those worth remembering,"[36] and "the transformations these sources underwent in the process of placing them within a new written context."[37]

This second series of questions is central to this study. The problem is complex, as we are confronted with different successive layers of memorisation which in turn gave rise to the various historiographic strata discussed in the preceding chapters. How did the late Umayyads and early Abbasids wish to portray themselves, and which achievements did they want recorded for posterity? How would future generations manipulate this image and these achievements in accordance with the constantly changing needs of the present? These competitive historiographies convey competing memories, and it is these memories that we must try to understand in all their rich depth. Before clarifying certain aspects thereof, it is useful to briefly outline the modern scholarship on memory outside the field of Islamic studies in order to identify its major theories and dominant paradigms.

4.1.2 Memoria *outside the Field of Islamic Studies: A Historiographic Overview*

Although memory remains a little-studied theme in the context of Islamic studies, specialists in other fields and disciplines have produced many valuable contributions on the subject. The bibliography on this topic is immense, and it is helpful here to give a brief synthetic but by no means exhaustive sketch

---

35 On this point, see Donner, "Umayyad Efforts at Legitimation" and *Muhammad and the Believers*; de Prémare, *Aux Origines du Coran* and "'Abd al-Malik." On the larger question of the legacy of the first Islamic dynasty, see Borrut and Cobb (eds.), *Umayyad Legacies*.

36 Geary, *Phantoms of Remembrance*, 9. On the question of how *memoranda* were selected, see Given-Wilson, *Chronicles*, 57 ff.

37 Geary, *Phantoms of Remembrance*, 9.

of this production in order to shed light on the aspects most important to the present inquiry.[38]

Halbwachs's foundational studies on "collective memory" continue to dominate the field.[39] His theories, however, are not unproblematic, as Geary notes:

> Although Halbwachs's analysis of memory remains the touchstone of all of understandings of social memory, one aspect of his analysis has led to a false dichotomy – that is, the difference not only between individual and collective memory but between collective memory and history. ... This dichotomization of memory and history also ignores the political or intentional dimensions of both collective memory and history ... Similarly, if historical memory is essentially political, so too is collective memory.[40]

Fentress and Wickham have also proposed the term "social memory" rather than "collective memory," arguing that: "[social memory] does more than provide a set of categories through which, in an unselfconscious way, a group experiences its surroundings; it also provides the group with material for conscious reflection."[41] These initial remarks take into account the political dimension characteristic of any attempt to control the past. Thus, "rather than an unreflected sharing of lived or transmitted experience, [collective memory] too has been orchestrated no less than the historical memory as a strategy for group solidarity and mobilization through the constant processes of suppression and selection;"[42] "remembering was an act of legitimation"[43] and *memoria*, the basis of the "social connection,"[44] is the foundation of "social domination."[45] It should be noted from the outset that the word *memoria*, in medieval terminology, was not strictly reserved to the liturgical domain, but was defined as a

38 The most complete recent reflection on the theme of memory, its relation to history and its counterpart – oblivion – is that of Ricœur, *La mémoire, l'histoire, l'oubli*. See also Cubitt, *History and Memory*.

39 Halbwachs, *Les cadres sociaux de la mémoire* and *La mémoire collective*.

40 Geary, *Phantoms of Remembrance*, 10–2.

41 Fentress and Wickham, *Social Memory*, 26, cited in Geary, *Phantoms of Remembrance*, 12.

42 Geary, *Phantoms of Remembrance*, 12. Ricœur has emphasised the manipulation of memory as characteristic of all ideological processes. See Ricœur, *La mémoire, l'histoire, l'oubli*, 97 ff.

43 Innes, "Keeping it in the Family," 31.

44 Lauwers, "*Memoria*," 111.

45 Oexle, *Memoria als Kultur*, 38.

"complete social phenomenon,"[46] a *culture*[47] that "infiltrated every register of transmission."[48] This cultural dimension of memory was not inconsequential: "if 'we are what we remember,' *the truth of memory lies in the identity that it shapes* … In this way, *memories can themselves becomes historical actors*."[49]

The opposition between history and memory arising from Halbwachs's theses has become widespread in French scholarship,[50] much like the distinction between collective memory and historical memory popularised in Pierre Nora's quintessential *Lieux de mémoire*. Geary, however, has emphasised that "such distinctions are deceptive, particularly for understanding history and memory in the Middle Ages," and that "postulating a dichotomy between collective memory and history ignores the social and cultural context of the historian."[51] This false dichotomy between collective memory and history presents yet another obstacle, opposing literate societies with oral ones; oral societies are thus seen as societies of memory, whereas writing made forgetting possible. The classic example in medieval Western scholarship is presented by Clanchy and Stock, for whom the eleventh century marked the passage from orality to literacy.[52] Geary has contested this theory, arguing that even if "the nature and quantity of writing changed" during this period, there is no proof that "it was a development from an oral culture."[53] McKitterick has demonstrated that literacy was much more widespread than previously imagined in medieval Europe; relationships to texts were a powerful social marker that defined the identity and the memory of elite groups.[54]

This debate is reminiscent of certain recurring discussions on Islamic historiography, which was allegedly the product of the late crystallisation of an oral tradition.[55] However, it should be noted that the rarity of older written documents – the disappearance of Umayyad-era historiography being the most obvious example – does not in any way signify that these traditions were

46 Oexle, *Memoria als Kultur*, 39.
47 Oexle, *Memoria als Kultur*.
48 Borgolte, "*Memoria*," 62. See also Lauwers' contribution in the same volume, "*Memoria*," 105–26.
49 Assmann, *Moïse l'Égyptien*, 37 (italics mine, translated from the French).
50 As recently noted by Schmitt, "Le Temps," 48. See also Guenée, "Temps de l'histoire."
51 Geary, *Phantoms of Remembrance*, 11.
52 Clanchy, *From Memory to Written Record*; Stock, *The Implications of Literacy*.
53 Geary, *Phantoms of Remembrance*, 13.
54 See McKitterick, *History and Memory*, 7, as well as his classic works *The Carolingian and the Written Word*, *The Uses of Literacy in Early Medieval Europe* and *Perceptions of the Past*.
55 For a presentation of the major trends in modern research on this subject, see Donner, *Narratives*, 5 ff.

oral, but rather that written documentation fell victim to selection processes.[56] In addition, these oppositions (oral vs. literate, memorisation vs. written recording allowing for oblivion) have been largely exaggerated in modern scholarship, while in reality, these seemingly opposing aspects were intrinsically interconnected;[57] in the field of Islamic studies, recent works by Günther, Schoeler and Robinson have highlighted this fact.[58] The narrative Islamic sources, interspersed with fragments of orality (*qāla, akhbarna, ḥaddathana,* etc.) offer many convincing examples to a familiar reader. The texts themselves were meant to be read in public, as attested by the certificates of audition (*samāʿāt*) and transmission (*ijāza*) in the manuscripts, and here again we see that literacy and orality worked in tandem rather than in opposition to each other. Geary notes this factor as well, insisting on the idea that "even heavily text-oriented societies communicate values (and, one should add, the interpretative structures within which to understand these written memories) orally."[59] Writing and committing to memory were not antithetical, for, as Carruthers notes, "*memoria*, as these writers understood and practiced it, was a part of *litteratura*: indeed, it was what literature, in a fundamental sense, was for … merely running one's eyes over the written pages is not reading at all, for the writing must be transferred into memory, from graphemes on parchment or papyrus to images written in one's brain by emotion and sense."[60]

Alongside the important and aforementioned concept of "social memory" is that of "cultural memory," developed in particular by Jan Assmann.[61] The great German Egyptologist recalls the ancient Greek tradition, wherein memory was the foundation of culture, while "culture [was] not only based on memory but [was] a form of memory in itself."[62] The German medievalists reflected at length on the concept of *memoria*.[63] For the medieval period, Oexle also spoke

56 Compare with Geary, *Phantoms of Remembrance*, 15.

57 See Innes, "Memory, Orality and Literacy;" Geary, "Land, Language and Memory," 173.

58 Günther, "Due Results," 5–6; Schoeler, *The Genesis*, in particular 16–27 and 36–7; Robinson, *Islamic Historiography*, 8–13.

59 Geary, *Phantoms of Remembrance*, 15, based on the remarks of Fentress and Wickham, *Social Memory*, 96–8.

60 Carruthers, *The Book of Memory*, 11.

61 Assmann, *Cultural Memory* and "What is Cultural Memory?". See also his other works, in particular *Stein und Zeit* and *Moses the Egyptian*.

62 Assmann, *Moses the Egyptian*, 15.

63 Oexle, "Memoria und Memorialüberlieferung;" Schmid and Wollasch, *Memoria*; Haverkamp and Lachmann, *Memoria. Vergessen und Erinnern*; Geuenich and Oexle, *Memoria in der Gesellschaft*; Tellenbach, "Erinnern und Vergessen." A good outline of this production has been presented by Borgolte, "Memoria," and Lauwers, "*Memoria*."

of *Memoria als Kultur*,[64] which "consequently implied forms specific to each individual and group, constantly transformed over time, of memory in thought and action, in philosophy and liturgy, the writing of history and art."[65] Memory thus was not confined to a corpus of texts, but was also rooted in space; the architectural landscape is particularly significant in this respect. As Paul Veyne has noted regarding the Roman empire, public monuments and inscriptions allowed a "confiscation of collective memory;"[66] by inscribing their power in space, the Umayyad caliphs engaged in similar actions. The new Abbasid authority could not have remained indifferent to this monumental legacy: control of the cultural landscape was critical.[67] While utility in the present secured the chances that certain memories would survive, other, more contentious remembrances were destined to be confronted. Wherever the choice to preserve memory presented itself, the option to forget was available as well. Social memory, monopolised by those in power, became a double-edged sword after their death or overthrow. Those who had been subjugated previously could then take their revenge, seizing power and, by extension, control over memory. It was easy for them to efface or substitute names of caliphs or family members on monumental inscriptions[68] or in the *dīwān*s, in the context of a *damnatio memoriae*: "the power to destroy memory is a counterweight to power achieved through the production of memory."[69]

Assmann has rightly noted that "memories may be false, distorted, invented or implanted. … But for the historian of memory, the "truth" of a given memory lies not so much in its "factuality" as in its "actuality." Events tend to be forgotten unless they live on in collective memory."[70] It is precisely this "actuality" of memory that we must trace in the sources for the late Umayyads and the early Abbasids, in order to sketch out a history of memory for the first two Islamic dynasties, even if it is difficult to treat them equally in the context of the Syrian space. Abbasid Syria is much less represented in the sources that survive than

64 Oexle, *Memoria als Kultur*.
65 Oexle, *Memoria als Kultur*, 9, cited in Borgolte, "Memoria," 67.
66 Cited in Le Goff, *History and Memory*, 67.
67 I will not address here the question of antique monuments and the theft and defacement thereof practiced at the time. For more on this vast subject, see the recent thought-provoking works of Ward-Perkins, "Re-Using the Architectural Legacy of the Past," Esch, "Chance et hasard de la transmission," in particular 22–3, and Effros, "Monuments and Memory," which mentions other useful titles as well.
68 Especially in the case of the inscriptions on the Dome of the Rock and the mosque of Medina, discussed below.
69 Le Goff, *History and Memory*, 68.
70 Assmann, *Moses the Egyptian*, 9.

Syria under the caliphs of Damascus. This inquiry undertakes a close analysis of what the Abbasids wanted preserved from the past and the Umayyad Other after leaving Sāmarrāʾ; this alterity recalls Borgolte's studies of "*memoria* and the other."[71] The manner in which the authors of the third-fourth century *hijrī* wanted to present the Abbasid rise to power and the progressive affirmation of the imperial power that abandoned Syria for Iraq requires investigation as well. We are constantly looking through the lens of the history of meanings, as the history of memory "analyzes the importance which a present ascribes to the past."[72]

"Social memory," "cultural memory," and "memory and otherness" are all productive concepts that enrich our understanding of the place granted the late Umayyads and early Abbasids in the narrative Islamic sources. As Le Goff notes: "To make themselves the master of memory and forgetfulness is one of the great preoccupations of the classes, groups and individuals who have dominated and continue to dominate historical societies. The things forgotten or not mentioned by history reveal these mechanisms for the manipulation of collective memory."[73] Choosing the vectors that assured the diffusion of this controlled memory was a decisive act. Similar to the medieval West as studied by Geary,[74] but contrary to Judaism,[75] "classical" Islam tried to cement its memory in history; the chronographers were the principal actors in this process. Thus, we must dedicate "special attention to the processes of memory sedimentation themselves, the layering of memorial strata and the influence that these exerted on chroniclers, the chroniclers' attitudes toward the instruments of memory, the presence of memorial *topoi* and the creative faculties of this historical memory, which was governed by these *topoi* and incessantly combined oblivion and invention."[76] For this reason, we must address the "past as it is remembered" before turning our attention to "the past as such."[77]

71 Borgolte, "*Memoria*," 68.

72 Assmann, *Moses the Egyptian*, 10.

73 Le Goff, *History and Memory*, 54.

74 Geary, *Phantoms of Remembrance*.

75 This is especially the case for the medieval period, as Yerushalmi has shown in his classic work *Zakhor*, 55: "Historiography was never the primary vehicle for Jewish memory in the Middle Ages."

76 Fried, "Le passé à la merci de l'oralité et du souvenir," 72.

77 Assmann, *Moses the Egyptian*, 9.

4.2 Umayyad Memoria

Strictly with respect to the Islamic (narrative) sources, we cannot escape the distorting prism of the Abbasid chronographies in our quest for knowledge of the first Islamic dynasty. Most of these sources postdate the early Abbasid era; the majority date to the second half of the third/ninth century, particularly the turn of the third–fourth/ninth–tenth centuries. Thus, it is essential that we try to understand the meaning the Abbasids wished to give the Umayyad period in the historiographic vulgate that emerged following the caliphate's return to Baghdad. How Umayyad history was recorded and how the Abbasids made use of the past are the main questions here; rather than the *memoria* developed by the Umayyads themselves, we must first examine the memory constructed for them by the Abbasid historians.[78]

In the chronological context of this study, our primary interest is how Umayyad memory was received by the early Abbasids. However, most of the textual indications that survive were composed at a later date. Thus, comprehending the history of this Umayyad memory under the early Abbasids is a particularly complicated task, as demonstrated in the following table:

TABLE 4.1 Umayyad *memoria* under the early Abbasids

	Political History	Sources
Moment 1	The Umayyads (661–750)	No preserved narrative Islamic sources
Moment 2	The early Abbasids (v. 750–809)	No preserved narrative Islamic sources
	From the civil war to Sāmarrā' (c.809–892)	*Earliest preserved narrative Islamic sources*
Moment 3	Abbasid post-Sāmarrā' period (after 279/892)	"Classical" narrative Islamic sources and the imposition of a historiographic vulgate

In essence, we are confronted with three distinct moments: moment 1 (the Umayyad period), remembered in moment 3 (the Abbasid post-Sāmarrā' period after 279/892), using the memories and discursive elements situated in moment 2 (the early Abbasids). Thus, it is essential to understand why

78 See Borrut, "La *memoria* omeyyade."

moment 1 was important during moment 3, and what the intended goal of insisting on the role – real or imagined – of this moment 1 during the course of moment 2 might have been. The interactions between these three temporalities and the stakes – particularly political – underlying the rewriting processes of this remembered history must be elucidated here. We shall start by shedding light on the Umayyad "realms of memory" that populate the Islamic narrative sources.

4.2.1 *Umayyad "Realms of Memory"*

The most enduring legacy of these recompositions of the past is the foundation of a "historiographic skeleton," common to nearly all of the sources, that reduces Umayyad history to its simplest expression. This "historiographic skeleton" is organised around a certain number of Umayyad "realms of memory," primarily in the Syrian space, that emerge from these rewritings and are easily distinguishable. Like Pierre Nora, we must first insist on the fact that "the realms of memory are not *that* which one remembers, but *there* where memory is at work; it is not the tradition itself, but its laboratory."[79] In this sense, these sites offer an authoritative context in which each new narrative from the past henceforth participated.

Schematically, one could draw up the list of events, reforms, monuments and *topoi* that emerged out of what subsequent generations wanted to preserve from the recent Islamic past:

- A linear sequence of events beginning with the assassination of ʿUthmān and ending with the Umayyads' decisive defeat at the battle of the Great Zāb, including: the *fitna* between rivals Muʿāwiya and ʿAlī, the high point of which was the battle of Ṣiffīn, when Syrian troops brandished pages of the Qurʾān on the points of their lances; the murder of al-Ḥusayn by Yazīd I's soldiers at Karbalāʾ; the battle of Marj Rāhiṭ; the attack on the Kaʿba carried out on the order of al-Ḥajjāj; the siege of Constantinople by Maslama b. ʿAbd al-Malik; the assassination of al-Walīd II; the massacres at Nahr Abī Fuṭrus.
- In the administrative domain: the coinage reform and the policy of Arabisation undertaken by ʿAbd al-Malik; al-Ḥajjāj b. Yūsuf's iron fist; ʿUmar II's "fiscal rescript" and his attempts to improve the situation of converts; Hishām's prowess at governance and administration.
- The images of certain caliphs or princes, such as Maslama b. ʿAbd al Malik's military valor, ʿUmar II's piety, Hishām's greed or al-Walīd II's frivolity.[80]

79 Nora, *Les lieux de mémoire*, vol. I, 17–8.

80 Maslama, ʿUmar II and, to a lesser extent, Hishām are discussed in detail below. On al-Walīd II's image, see Vogts, *Figure de califes* and Judd, "Reinterpreting."

- Other aspects, including the opposition between Kalb and Qays, which de Prémare has recently and rightly deemed an "element of symbolic organisation,"[81] etc.

In addition to these historical elements, numerous other influences also participated in the construction of this Umayyad *memoria*. Some of the most obvious examples include:

- The monumental legacy of the Umayyad dynasty, including most notably the Dome of the Rock and the great mosque of Damascus.
- The city of Damascus itself, the quintessential repository of Umayyad memory, which is inscribed into its architectural landscape, as al-Yaʿqūbī notes in his *Kitāb al-buldān*: "[the] palaces [of the Banū Umayya] make up most of the residences. There is also the Green (Dome) of Muʿāwiya, which is the Governor's Residence, and its mosque. None more beautiful than it exists in Islam in terms of its marble and gilded decoration. Al-Walīd b. ʿAbd al-Malik b. Marwān built it during his caliphate."[82]
- Other locations were also associated with the Umayyads in later geographical sources: Ibn Ḥawqal (d. c. 380/990), using information provided by al-Iṣṭakhrī (d. c. 350/961), remarks that Maʿān was inhabited by the Umayyads, and emphasises that the inhabitants of Raqqa had strong connections to the first Islamic dynasty.[83]
- More broadly, the cults of worship that developed around certain Umayyad caliphs and persisted throughout the Abbasid era are worth noting as well, the most obvious examples being Muʿāwiya and ʿUmar b. ʿAbd al-ʿAzīz.[84] These practices clearly figure into a commemoration of the Umayyads, guaranteeing the survival of their memory.
- Finally, the Sufyānī (discussed in the previous chapter) merits our attention as an element of an Umayyad memory projected into an eschatological future. Wellhausen has noted that, in the wake of the Abbasid Revolution, Syrian revolutionaries looked to the Sufyanids rather than the newly deposed Marwanids,[85] thus returning to the memory of the early Umayyads. Although Cobb's recent studies[86] have shown that the revolts that took place

81 De Prémare, *Les fondations*, 63.

82 Al-Yaʿqūbī, *Kitāb al-buldān*, 326; trans. vol. 1, 162.

83 Ibn Ḥawqal, 185, 226; trans. 183, 220; al-Iṣṭakhrī, 65. In the passage dedicated to Raqqa, al-Iṣṭakhrī says nothing of these connections, 75.

84 Pellat, "Le culte de Muʿāwiya;" Borrut, "Entre tradition et histoire," 352 and below, Ch. 6. On the pro-Umayyad elements circulating during the Abbasid era, see Bellamy, "Pro-Umayyad Propaganda."

85 Wellhausen, *Das arabische Reich*, 346.

86 Cobb, *White Banners*. See also Madelung, "The Sufyānī."

in Abbasid Syria were not universally pro-Umayyad in nature, the "myth" of the Sufyānī and the messianic expectations surrounding him were nonetheless a commemoration of the first Umayyad caliphs, Muʿāwiya foremost among them. Al-Aṣhab or al-Marwānī, the Marwanid messianic figure, on the contrary sank into oblivion, a fact that invites an investigation into the existence of a "memorial competition" between the two caliphal branches of the Umayyad family.

One obvious initial observation is how deeply rooted this heritage is in the Syrian space; this fact in turn invites us to consider the idea – to which we shall return later – of a Syrian-Umayyad *memoria*, or the relationship between a dynasty and a space of privileged power. No less important are the other realms of memory, most of which are largely absent from the narrative sources but have been recovered to Umayyad history, primarily by archaeology:[87] the "Umayyad palaces," the frescoes of Quṣayr ʿAmra, the stucco murals of Qaṣr al-Ḥayr al-Gharbī, the mosaics of Khirbat al-Mafjar. To these examples could be added many others: the sites significant today as essential sources of information on the first Islamic dynasty are but poorly documented in the texts. Thus, modern research creates new "realms of memory," locations which were passed over by the medieval authors, demonstrating that Umayyad memory has retained its vitality despite the passage of centuries and the vagaries of transmission; the *memoria* of the first Islamic dynasty is not fixed, but rather is the object of constant renewal. This implies that, while the narrative Islamic sources condition our perception of Umayyad memory through choices made during the third–fourth/ninth–tenth centuries, in other areas our point of view is much different than that of the scholars of Abbasid Baghdad. We are still insufficiently aware of this gap in perception in modern research.

In order to better understand the conditions that presided over which aspects of Umayyad memory were recorded, we must first account for the critical role played by the early Abbasids' control over this caliphal past as a means of asserting their own legitimacy. The first layers of memory sedimentation produced by this process can be unearthed with difficulty from the many anecdotes preserved in the narrative sources, which feature a certain Abbasid caliph or dignitary confronted with the memory of the previous dynasty.

87 Archaeology, interested in sites that have been buried and then excavated, is a discipline situated by its very nature in a dialectic between oblivion and memory. On this theme, see Esch, "Chance et hasard de la transmission," 22–3.

4.2.2 *The Early Abbasids and Umayyad Memory*

The evocation of the Marwanid past in the Abbasid sources poses two main problems: first, the question of the motivations behind inserting these anecdotes into the narrative sources; and second, that of their interpretation and comprehension in terms of the changing attitudes toward the survival of an Umayyad memory. We must insist here on the difficulty of a global approach to these anecdotes and the need for more in-depth studies in this material before presuming to set forth any sort of precise typology. Thus, we shall limit ourselves to several examples that offer good demonstrations of the major trends and tendencies behind these narratives.

4.2.2.1 The Massacre of the Umayyads: An Impossible Oblivion

The Abbasid massacre of many members of the Umayyad family following the coup d'état that brought this second Islamic dynasty to power is an episode as infamous as it is complex. In 1950, Moscati tried to collate all of the pertinent texts and organise the various traditions they contained.[88] While certain texts suppressed the butchery, some merely mentioning its occurrence without offering any further information, others provided lengthy accounts, scrupulously reporting the gruesome details of the carnage and its aftermath. Moscati concluded his analysis by affirming that the wide variety and diffusion of narratives on this subject were contrary to a historiography based on an "official doctrine" favourable to the Abbasids and hostile to the Umayyads.[89] Rather, Moscati took a "source-critical approach," to use Donner's expression,[90] and attempted to untangle the reliable material in the texts from the unreliable in order to reconstruct the facts. Although he took the later nature of the sources narrating this bloody event into account, he did not consider the motivations that presided over their composition. However, if we reconsider these texts, adding to them a number of others – in particular those written by Christian authors – that Moscati failed to take into account, we find a radically different interpretation: certain authors tried in vain to relegate the grisly memory of this massacre to oblivion.

It is only right that we begin with al-Ṭabarī. He modestly draws a curtain over this violent scene, merely noting that ʿAbd Allāh b. ʿAlī killed 72[91] Banū

88 Moscati, "Le massacre."

89 Moscati, "Le massacre," 106.

90 Donner, *Narratives*, 9.

91 This number – which varies slightly from one source to another – mirrors the infamous episode at Karbalāʾ: the number of Umayyad victims is precisely identical to the number of martyrs killed alongside al-Ḥusayn, a fact that effectively confirms the perfection of the Abbasid vengeance enacted on the banks of the Nahr Abī Fuṭrus. Elad estimates

Umayya at Nahr Abī Fuṭrus.[92] Compared with the detailed accounts provided elsewhere and to which we shall return below, this succinct narrative is problematic.[93] Al-Ṭabarī's silence regarding these events demonstrates the great anxiety they caused historians at the time: at a moment when authors were trying to rewrite the history of the dynasty and present the Abbasid rise to power in a more civilised manner, this brutal massacre created disorder. In effect, this episode seemed like a vendetta uncharacteristic of the Abbasids, the supposed protectors of lofty Islamic principles. As Robinson has noted, al-Ṭabarī's apparent amnesia regarding these events was an attempt to suppress concurrent versions[94] as part of a strategy of oblivion. Al-Ṭabarī, however, was not the only author to pass over this episode in silence; many others also dedicate little more than a few words to the massacre. In these terse summaries, only the number of victims varies, mounting to more than 80 in the accounts of Khalīfa b. Khayyāṭ,[95] Ibn Qutayba[96] and al-Masʿūdī; this latter even specifies the date: 15 Dhū al-Qaʿda 132/25 June 750.[97] In his *Muʿjam al-buldān*, the geographer Yāqūt also identifies the Nahr Abī Fuṭrus – which he situates some 12 miles north of al-Ramla – as the site of the massacre perpetrated by ʿAbd Allāh b. ʿAlī.[98]

In order to succeed, any attempt to bury the past is dependent on the spread of a given piece of information. A widespread and early transmission effectively prohibits complete erasure, as we shall see frequently in the following chapters. This state of affairs is essentially what ensured the preservation of

that the total death count for the massacre was likely closer to 81 individuals, "Aspects of the Transition," 92. More generally, the different totals proposed by the medieval authors should be treated with caution. They arise from a numeric symbolism, more often signifying "many" rather than a quantifiable reality. In particular, the number 7 and its derivatives, including 72, are highly significant, as Conrad has noted, "Seven and the tasbīʿ," especially 51 for the example in al-Ṭabarī presented here.

92 Al-Ṭabarī, vol. III, 51; trans. vol. XXVII, 175.

93 As Williams, the translator of this volume of al-Ṭabarī's *Taʾrīkh*, has noted, 172, note 411 and 175, note 419.

94 Robinson, *Islamic Historiography*, 41: "Unpleasant and controversial history was occasionally suppressed, an early example being the revolutionary excesses of the Abbasids: of the horrific slaughter of the Umayyad family undertaken by the Abbasids, al-Ṭabarī, writing as he was in Abbasid Baghdad, says not a single word, while an anonymous eleventh-century history written in Spain, which lay outside of Abbasid control, describes the violence in some detail." Here, Robinson alludes to the *Akhbār Majmūʿa*, to which we shall return below.

95 Khalīfa b. Khayyāṭ, *Taʾrīkh*, vol. II, 612.

96 Ibn Qutayba, *Kitāb al-maʿārif*, 372.

97 Al-Masʿūdī, *Murūj*, vol. IV, 75–6; trans. Pellat vol. IV, 931. See also *Tanbīh*, 329; trans. 425.

98 Yāqūt, *Muʿjam al-buldān*, vol. V, 315.

descriptions of the massacre, a vulgate of which seems to have preceded the silence of al-Ṭabarī and his colleagues. A "standard" version of the carnage and its aftermath is preserved in the works of two very different authors of the same period: al-Balādhurī and al-Yaʿqūbī.[99] Numerous elements of their accounts figure in the narratives presented by later sources. Let us thus attempt to recount the story – or rather, how it was recorded.

The massacre at Nahr Abī Fuṭrus (known as Antipatris to the Byzantine authors), the occasion of the Abbasid extermination of the Umayyads and any other potential competitors, properly belongs to the Umayyad memory as the martyrdom of many members of the Umayyad family under the blows of the Abbasid soldiers' clubs.[100] The episode is followed by other murders and brutal acts. However, the richly detailed accounts of this event given in certain sources show that it is centred around the memory of other significant episodes in Umayyad history; it is this memory that justified the right of the Abbasids – newly in possession of a Weberian monopoly on legitimate violence – to proceed with the assassination of the former rulers of Damascus in the name of a duty to Islamic memory. We shall briefly recount how the event itself unfolded before returning to this last point.[101]

A large number – the sources vary between 70 and 90, some preferring to fix the total at 80[102] – of members of the Umayyad family were guests of ʿAbd Allāh b. ʿAlī, uncle of the first Abbasid caliph, who promised them safety. During their stay, Abū Muḥammad al-ʿAbdī, a poet, recited several verses against the first Islamic dynasty, condemning them to hell.[103] ʿAbd Allāh b.

99 Al-Balādhurī, *Ansāb*, vol. III, 103–4; al-Yaʿqūbī, *Taʾrīkh*, vol. II, 355 ff.

100 On the question of the weapons used and the eventual symbolism attached to them, see Elad, "The Ethnic Composition," 286–9, in response to Crone, "The Significance of Wooden Weapons," 181–2. Crone defended the idea that the Umayyads were massacred with *kāfir kūbāt*, weapons made of wood used during the revolt of al-Mukhtār in 66/685 that were characteristic of the Iranian *mawālī* and were one of the symbols of the troops who overthrew the Umayyads in 132/750. Elad contests this theory, rightly emphasising that most of the sources agree that clubs made of iron (*ʿumūd al-ḥadīd*) were used and more generally challenging Crone's interpretation of the symbolic representations of these weapons.

101 See Moscati, "Le massacre des Umayyades."

102 The anonymous Spanish chronicle, the *Akhbār Majmūʿa* (46 ff., trans. 74ff.), takes care to specify that ʿAbd al-Raḥmān b. Muʿāwiya b. Hishām, the future founder of the Andalusian branch of the Umayyads, escaped the massacre and was thus able to undertake his journey west. On this episode, see Martinez-Gros, "Le passage vers l'Ouest."

103 Only al-Yaʿqūbī mentions the presence of this poet, whose verses he cites (*Taʾrīkh*, vol. II, 355). Although al-Balādhurī does not include these details, they were later taken up and developed by Ibn ʿAbd Rabbih (*al-ʿIqd*, vol. IV, 452–3). Ibn al-Athīr (*Kāmil*, vol. V, 329–31) notes that it was the poet Shibl b. ʿAbd Allāh who was in attendance, and links to him the

ʿAlī then interrupted him, and remembered (*dhakara*) the death of al-Ḥusayn and the other Alids.[104] With a gesture, he ordered his soldiers to massacre his guests,[105] despite the desperate attempts of these latter to gain his pardon. He then threw carpets over the still-moving bodies of his victims, ordered his dinner to be served, and ate, accompanied by the music of their death-rattles.[106]

The massacre of Nahr Abī Fuṭrus is followed in the narrative sources by another slaughter of the Umayyads at Damascus,[107] as well as by the infamous violation of the tombs of the caliphs[108] – with the exception of ʿUmar II's according to some[109] – whose remains were smashed and burned, their ashes scattered by the wind. The legendary nature of these events is relatively unimportant from the perspective of a history of memory. The destruction of tombs, quintessential spaces of commemoration that, as Chiffoleau has shown for the medieval West, allow the dead to maintain a place among the "society of the living,"[110] is a clear sign: more than just the Umayyads themselves, their memory was under attack, per the logic of *damnatio memoriae*. In the narrative dimension of these two episodes, we find ourselves in the cadre of Bourdieu's

verses al-Balādhurī attributes to Sudayf b. Maymūn on the occasion of the execution of Sulaymān b. Hishām by the caliph al-Saffāḥ himself. Ibn al-Athīr was well aware of the confusion surrounding the identity of the poet and the location of his performance. On the murder of Sulaymān b. Hishām, see below.

104 Al-Yaʿqūbī, *Taʾrīkh*, vol. II, 355; Ibn ʿAbd Rabbih, *al-ʿIqd*, vol. IV, 453.

105 Only al-Maqrīzī, *Kitāb al-nizāʿ*, 53, trans. 91–2 indicates that ʿAbd Allāh played an active role in the carnage, killing a large number of people by himself.

106 Al-Yaʿqūbī, *Taʾrīkh*, vol. II, 355; Ibn al-Athīr, *Kāmil*, vol. V, 329–31; Moscati, "Le massacre des Umayyades," 91–2. Al-Iṣfahānī, *Kitāb al-Aghānī*, vol. IV, 92 ff., offers a similar account that takes place in this instance at al-Ḥīra in the presence of the caliph.

107 Al-Yaʿqūbī, *Taʾrīkh*, vol. II, 356. Al-Masʿūdī (*Murūj*, vol. VI, 75–6, trans. Pellat vol. IV, 931) places the Damascus massacre *before* the carnage at Nahr Abī Fuṭrus, which seems more logical considering ʿAbd Allāh's north-south itinerary in Syria while pursuing Marwān II. Moscati made note of this as well, although the incriminating paragraph in his article is clearly erroneous, reversing the statements of the two authors, "Le massacre," 101. Al-Maqrīzī (*Kitāb al-nizāʿ*, 53, trans. 91) also adopts this order of events, placing the slaughter at Damascus before that of Nahr Abī Fuṭrus.

108 Al-Yaʿqūbī, *Taʾrīkh*, vol. II, 356–7; al-Balādhurī, *Ansāb*, vol. III, 103–4; al-Maqrīzī, *Kitāb al-nizāʿ*, 53–4, trans. 92. Other authors record this episode as distinct from the massacre at Nahr Abī Fuṭrus, placing it after the martyrdom of Zayd b. ʿAlī at the hands of Hishām b. ʿAbd al-Malik: al-Masʿūdī, *Murūj*, vol. V, 470 ff., trans. Pellat vol. IV, 891–2.

109 Al-Balādhurī, *Ansāb*, vol. III, 103–4; al-Masʿūdī, *Murūj*, vol. V, 416, trans. Pellat vol. IV, 867: "His tomb ... was otherwise respected, while the sepulchres of the other Umayyads were profaned [by the Abbasids]." Al-Maqrīzī, *Kitāb al-nizāʿ*, 54, trans. 92.

110 See his magisterial work: Chiffoleau, *La compatabilité de l'au-delà*, which should be read in light of his later remarks, "Pour une histoire de la religion." More recently, see the fine work of Lauwers, *La mémoire des ancêtres*.

"symbolic violence,"[111] in the broader context of the construction of Abbasid legitimacy.

The sources are clear once again that these tombs were violated in the name of memory. Hishām inflicted a similar fate upon Zayd b. ʿAlī:[112] this latter's body, supposedly hidden, was exhumed and hung from a gibbet before being burned and the ashes scattered.[113] In retaliation, ʿAbd Allāh b. ʿAlī systematically destroyed the tombs of the caliphs, taking great care to inflict on Hishām's well-preserved corpse a similar fate to that visited upon Zayd: "ʿAbd Allāh gave him eighty lashes with the whip, then gave him over to the flames."[114]

Sulaymān b. Hishām, one of the most serious Umayyad claimants to caliphal power, was not present at the massacre of Nahr Abī Fuṭrus, but also fell victim to a gruesome fate during an interview with the new caliph, Abū al-ʿAbbās. Once again, the catalyst for the ensuing violence was a poet, Sudayf b. Maymūn, who was also an Abbasid *mawlā*; he recited the following verses:[115]

> Distance yourself from them, o Caliph, with the sword sever the root of ignominy!
> And remember (*wa-adhkurū*) the massacre of al-Ḥusayn, of Zayd [b. ʿAlī, ...]
> And of the imām,[116] for whom the promise of a tomb resided in Ḥarrān, in exile and oblivion (*tanāsīy*).[117]

The evocation of these deaths provoked the caliph's ire and precipitated Sulaymān's execution.[118] Here again, the Umayyads were massacred in the name of memory and a duty of remembrance. However, there was some confusion over the details of these two events – namely, the murder of Sulaymān

111 Bourdieu, *Esquisse*.

112 See Madelung, "Zayd b. ʿAlī."

113 Al-Masʿūdī, *Murūj*, vol. V, 470–1; trans. Pellat vol. IV, 891.

114 Al-Masʿūdī, *Murūj*, vol. V, 471; trans. Pellat vol. IV, 891.

115 It should be noted again here that poetry was typically used as proof in the narrative historical sources. This function perhaps explains the recurring role of the poet in these events, as he serves as an incontrovertible means of justification for the decisions behind the massacres.

116 Ibrāhīm b. Muḥammad (al-Imām), brother of the caliph al-Saffāḥ, who died in Marwān II's prisons in Ḥarrān in 132/749. See Omar, "Ibrāhīm b. Muḥammad."

117 Moscati, "Le massacre des Umayyades," 107, 112. See also Ibn ʿAbd Rabbih, *al-ʿIqd*, vol. 5, 81.

118 According to the *Akhbār Majmūʿa*, 47, trans. 74, the caliph decided to execute Sulaymān b. Hishām after seeing the heads of the Umayyads massacred by ʿAbd Allāh at Nahr Abī Fuṭrus.

and the massacre at Nahr Abī Fuṭrus – as evidenced by Ibn al-Athīr[119] and later echoed by Ibn ʿAbd Rabbih, who juxtaposed the two episodes by merely indicating one as *wa-fī riwāya ukhrā*.[120] Thus, the verses previously attributed to Abū Muḥammad al-ʿAbdī became those cited by Sudayf b. Maymūn before the caliph, etc.

This confusion stems from an earlier debate. Judging from the *isnād*s in the *Kitāb al-Aghānī*, which offers two concurrent versions of events on the authority of the same Zubayr b. Bakkār (d. 256/870), the variability of the details in these accounts may be due to the fact that the location and instigator of the Umayyad massacre were uncertain, while the scene of death-by-clubs and the feast served over the twitching bodies of the victims dominated the different narratives. It is likely that many members of the Umayyad family were also hunted down and murdered in Syria, Iraq, Egypt and the Hijaz.[121] During the historicisation of these events, authors could not always clearly distinguish between the different versions, hence the ambiguity present in the sources. In addition, the longstanding confusion over these episodes can also almost certainly be linked to the use of the epithet *al-Saffāḥ*. Although modern scholars generally agree that this epithet was a *laqab* of Abū al-ʿAbbās, the first Abbasid caliph, it is not certain that this is indeed the case (although I have chosen to preserve its use up until this point out of convenience); in fact, some texts even use this *laqab* for ʿAbd Allāh b. ʿAlī![122] This confusion may have served the Abbasids' purposes to some extent, since they could not avoid recording these unflattering events: it was preferable for the Abbasids to attribute the massacre to ʿAbd Allāh, who revolted during al-Manṣūr's accession to the caliphate. He who had threatened the integrity of the now-Abbasid caliphate deserved to be portrayed as a bloodthirsty brute; this had the dual effect of sullying his memory while removing any blame from the memory of Abū al-ʿAbbās. The competition of memory that raged among members of the Abbasid family also conditioned the dynasty's relationship to Umayyad *memoria*.

The stakes of recording and presenting these facts were understandably high, as what began as a simple vendetta could now play an active role in legitimising the Abbasid dynasty. Vows of revenge were now necessary in

119 Ibn al-Athīr, *Kāmil*, vol. V, 329–31; Moscati, "Le massacre," 93.

120 Ibn ʿAbd Rabbih, *al-ʿIqd*, vol. 4, 453.

121 Elad has enumerated seven different locations where the Umayyads were put to death: al-Ḥīra and al-Baṣra in Iraq; Damascus, Nahr Abī Fuṭrus and Qalansuwa in Palestine; the Hijaz; and Egypt. Elad, "Aspects of the Transition," 92–3.

122 This is notably the case in the *Akhbār Majmūʿa* (46, trans. 73–74), a fact which struck Moscati as an "egregious error" ("Le massacre," 94). This question is discussed in detail below, Ch. 7.

the name of a duty to Islamic memory. This attitude is especially clear among Shiite authors such as al-Yaʿqūbī; unfortunately, the surviving documents do not offer enough information to ascertain whether this position was indicative of an Alid interpretation of events or whether it was a discourse produced by the Abbasid caliphal entourage to justify the massacres while simultaneously attempting to reconcile with the Shiites. This latter hypothesis is corroborated by another episode reported by al-Masʿūdī, although here again we have an account that is impossible to date. If we believe al-Masʿūdī, when the head of Marwān II was brought before the caliph Abū al-ʿAbbās, he claimed to have thus avenged al-Ḥusayn and the descendants of ʿAlī b. Abī Ṭālib with the blood of the Umayyads.[123] The Shiites may have subsequently preserved accounts similar to this one to remind the Abbasids of the original ideals of the movement that overthrew the Umayyads and deprived the Alids of the fruits of power, as the Abbasids were the ones to ultimately seize control of the caliphate. Although these episodes occurred chronologically during the early years of the Abbasid period, the literary form in which we know them today was produced much later. These narratives attest to a need to present the Abbasid rise to power in a new, less polemic light; in other words, Abbasid legitimacy remained a subject of debate. Portraying the massacre of the Umayyads as a tribute to the memory of the great Alid figures was likely intended first and foremost for the Shiites.

Several Christian sources have also preserved accounts of this bloody episode. The oldest of these is the *Chronography* of Theophanes; however, the information in this source has obviously been distorted, as it describes the traitorous massacre of Christians on the banks of the Antipatris.[124] Agapius of Manbij's narrative also contains several surprises, although for the most part it closely follows the Muslim tradition. In his account, it is not ʿAbd Allāh who orders the massacre but rather his brother, Ṣāliḥ b. ʿAlī, who the Muslim sources generally agree was hunting down Marwān II at the time. Agapius also describes the Umayyads as appearing spontaneously before their host, reciting the Quran and hoping to obtain clemency, in response to which he grants them *amān* for their persons and their goods. Ṣāliḥ then invites them into his palace (*qaṣr*), where the scene becomes familiar: the Umayyads are butchered by the clubs of the *Abnāʾ Khurāsān*, and the victims' heads are sent to the caliph.[125] As soon as we arrive at these well-known details in Agapius's account,

123 Al-Masʿūdī, *Murūj*, vol. VI, 101–2; trans. Pellat vol. IV, 942.

124 Theophanes, *Chronicle*, 427; trans. 590.

125 Agapius, *Kitāb al-ʿunwān*, 529.

the similarity of his text to al-Yaʿqūbī's becomes striking.[126] Agapius writes: "*aqāma ʿinda ra's kull wāḥid minhum rajulayn min abnā' Khurāsān bi-aydayhim al-ʿumūd al-ḥadīd*,"[127] whereas al-Yaʿqūbī has "*aqāma ʿalā ra's kull rajul minhum rajulayn bi-al-ʿumūd*."[128] The *Anonymous Syriac Chronicle of 1234* also presents a description that agrees with the Islamic sources, in which 70 Umayyads are killed by ʿAbd Allāh, who sends his victims' heads to Abū al-ʿAbbās.[129] The thirteenth-century Christian Arab author Buṭrus b. Rāhib most faithfully follows the vulgate's sequence of events with respect to the massacres, including the episode at Damascus and the violation of the caliphal tombs. Although the location of the first massacre is not specified, and seemingly takes place in the presence of the caliph and of ʿAbd Allāh, the depiction is eloquent: the textual similarity with al-Yaʿqūbī here is even more striking, down to the description of the carpets thrown over the dying victims for the morbid feast and the repetition of the same poetic fragments![130]

There is no evidence that Agapius of Manbij had direct access to al-Yaʿqūbī's *Ta'rīkh*; thus, we must assume a common source rather than a direct lineage, especially since the notable differences between the two would be much more difficult to explain were Agapius's account based directly on al-Yaʿqūbī's. With the exception of Buṭrus b. Rāhib, who is more difficult to situate and whose textual similarities with al-Yaʿqūbī are particularly troubling, the other Christian authors noted above belonged to the circuit of Theophilus of Edessa, as discussed in the previous chapter. It is thus tempting to think that any shared information was derived from this well-attested common source.[131] This hypothesis implies the prior existence of a shared kernel of information and its near-contemporaneity with the events themselves, as Theophilus's chronicle was supposedly written in the years immediately following the Abbasid Revolution. If this is the case, we find ourselves faced with elements produced at the beginning of what we have designated *phase 5*, or the historiographic period ranging from approximately 132/750 to 192/809.

In sum: there was a push to hunt down and exterminate the Umayyads in the wake of the Abbasid coup d'état. Elad has proposed that these murders were selective, aimed in particular at the descendants of Marwān b. ʿAbd

126 This lineage is also noted by Hoyland, *Seeing*, 669, note 230.
127 Agapius, *Kitāb al-ʿunwān*, 529.
128 Al-Yaʿqūbī, *Ta'rīkh*, vol. II, 355.
129 *Chronicle of 1234*, 233; trans. 260.
130 Buṭrus b. Rāhib, *Ta'rīkh*, 60–1; trans. 66–7.
131 See Hoyland's compilation of the material from the Syriac Common Source, *Seeing*, 668–9, including these elements related to the massacre of the Umayyads.

al-Ḥakam and more marginally at those of ʿUthmān b. ʿAffān:[132] in other words, it was of the utmost necessity to dispose of those with any claim to the caliphate. The most spectacular episode was the mass slaughter of the Umayyads, during which many members of the family were brutally clubbed to death. However, this carnage subsequently became a cause for embarrassment, an episode out of sync with the precepts established during the *daʿwa*, the period of anti-Umayyad propaganda antecedent to the fall of the first Islamic dynasty. Thus, reinterpretations in the service of the specific interests of different groups (Abbasids, Alids, etc.) were necessary.[133]

This bloody massacre was recorded by the chroniclers at an early date, thus forming a base of material that could be reworked. For partisans of memory, the advantage of this common kernel of information was that it allowed for any number of desired interpretations. For the apostles of silence, the disadvantage was that this information was in circulation early on, making it almost impossible to obviate entirely: that which is already infamous cannot be erased. However, it was possible to create confusion, as evidenced by the uncertainty surrounding the identity of the massacre's instigator – ʿAbd Allāh b. ʿAlī or the caliph himself – although ultimately, the latter appears to have been more of a silent partner than the active party in these events.[134]

While certain authors preferred silence, a reading of these events centring the duty of remembering Shiite martyrs emerges in the Islamic sources. In particular, Hishām b. ʿAbd al-Malik, who executed Zayd b. ʿAlī, is singled out: the fact that his body was recovered nearly intact allowed his enemies to exact a brutal revenge that would not have been possible had only his skeleton remained It is impossible to know whether it was the Alids themselves who promoted this version of events, or whether the Abbasids, hoping to placate their former allies, initiated this approach. In any case, perhaps because al-Manṣūr deprived both ʿAbd Allāh b. ʿAlī[135] and the Alids of the benefits of the coup, this latter group found some common ground with the former. The "official" version of this episode elaborated in the Shiite sources conveys a sense of belonging to a single initial revolutionary movement. Although the

132 Elad, "Aspects of the Transition," 92.

133 For another example of how the massacres that followed the Abbasid Revolution were rewritten, see Robinson, *Empire and Elites*, 127–46.

134 Al-Masʿūdī attributes the orders to the caliph, who boasts of having killed 200 Umayyads and burning Hishām's corpse, but this description may be better understood as indicating that the caliph sanctioned these actions. See his *Murūj*, vol. VI, 100–1; trans. Pellat vol. IV, 942.

135 On the intense conflict surrounding the succession of the first Abbasid caliph, see below, Ch. 7.

Alids and ʿAbd Allāh were denied the caliphate, they spearheaded the *daʿwa* and the *dawla* that ultimately led to the Umayyads' downfall. In this sense, the Alids came close to claiming ʿAbd Allāh as one of their own. He could only have massacred the Umayyads because of their scandalous conduct toward ʿAlī and his descendants, al-Ḥusayn foremost among them. Their texts convey the memory of the exiled: the Alids, ʿAbd Allāh, and ultimately, the Umayyads themselves.

Other concurrent interpretations undoubtedly existed, but were suppressed as a result of the ever-more-selective vagaries of transmission. For example, it is possible that an Umayyad account of this event once existed, of which only vague echoes remain in the sources extant today. The theme of the Qurʾān, preserved in Agapius's account, obviously recalls the famous episode when Muʿāwiya's troops placed pages of the Qurʾān on the tips of their spears at a perilous moment during the battle of Ṣiffīn against ʿAlī's forces. Moreover, it also echoes the murders of ʿUthmān and al-Walīd II, who were killed while reading the holy book; it is said that the sacred text was stained with their blood. In other words, the Qurʾān is a *topos* of Umayyad death: it served both to affirm the family's legitimacy and to define the illegitimacy of their demise.

In the Islamic memory under construction at the time, a project spurred on by the many crises that plagued the unstable Abbasid caliphate at the turn of the third–fourth/ninth–tenth centuries, several strategies were possible, ranging from pure oblivion to the creation of selective memories intended to give meaning to a particularly troubling episode. Although strategies of silence were often successful, forcing us to trace murmurs in the sources, the early circulation of certain historical information overcame this intentional amnesia and assured the preservation of this material through numerous channels of transmission. Thus, Abbasid cruelty escaped oblivion.[136]

In other instances, however, Umayyad memory proved useful: after the bloodshed, we may now turn our attention to politics and the judgments passed by the Abbasids on the works of their predecessors in Damascus.

4.2.2.2 Al-Manṣūr and the Caliphs of Damascus: A Necessary Remembrance

Al-Masʿūdī, a champion of *adab*, provides the most abundant material on the attitudes of the first Abbasid caliphs toward the memory of the first Islamic dynasty. The best-documented examples occurred during the caliphate of

136 Ibn ʿAbd Rabbih (*al-ʿIqd*, vol. IV, 456) and al-Maqrīzī (*Kitāb al-nizāʿ*, 53, trans. 91) both emphasise the extreme cruelty of ʿAbd Allāh.

al-Manṣūr, founder of the Abbasid state, who gave the following overview of his predecessors:

> Al-Manṣūr said: ʿAbd al-Malik was an arrogant tyrant who acted without concern for the consequences. Sulaymān was driven only by gluttony and lust. ʿUmar b. ʿAbd al-ʿAzīz was like a one-eyed man among the blind. Hishām was the only great man in the dynasty. The Umayyads ruled over their empire with a firm hand; they knew how to control, protect, and defend the gifts granted them by God, as they were careful to remain above the fray and avoid any vulgar acts. Their sons, however, surrounded by luxury, had no other thought than to satisfy their desires; they violated divine laws and gave themselves over to base pleasures when they took power. Ignorant of the knowledge that God's vengeance is slow to come and unafraid of His retribution, they neglected to protect the caliphate, trampled the rights of God and crown underfoot, and became incapable of governing. Thus, God stripped them of their power, covered them in shame, and denied them His beneficence.[137]

Although his opinion of the Umayyads was harsh, it is interesting to note that al-Manṣūr emphasises the Umayyads' weakness rather than their illegitimacy. In other words, if God was responsible for revoking divine power from the Umayyads, He was equally responsible for then granting it to the Abbasids. The "blessed dynasty" presents itself as specially and divinely selected for rule, thereby seeking to establish the legitimacy of its seizure of caliphal power. The Abbasid portrayal of the Umayyads is nuanced, and leaves room for certain positive exceptions. An Umayyad typology emerged: ʿUmar II's and Hishām's images were rehabilitated by the caliph, the first thanks to his piety and the second for his "greatness" in political, fiscal, and administrative matters. In the following chapters, we shall see how these qualities became *topoi* of medieval Islamic literary production.

Al-Manṣūr then calls upon a lengthy succession of interlocutors, seemingly in an attempt to put the dynasty on trial. The first of these is a son of Marwān II, ʿAbd Allāh b. Marwān, a prisoner of the caliph, who is forced to recount his desperate flight from the advancing Abbasid armies, ultimately seeking refuge with the king of Nubia. The king offers him hospitality; however, concerned by

137 Al-Masʿūdī, *Murūj*, vol. VI, 161–2; trans. Pellat vol. IV, 963. Ibn Khaldūn repeats this passage from al-Masʿūdī, *The Muqaddimah*, vol. I, 424. See also al-Maqrīzī, *Kitāb al-nizāʿ*, 6, trans. 46, who indicates that ʿUmar II, because of his sense of justice, should not have accepted the caliphate from an illegitimate ruler.

the many rumours swirling around the Umayyads at the time, he interrogates ʿAbd Allāh b. Marwān on the deviance attributed to his family members. ʿAbd Allāh tries to defend himself and his family by shifting these faults – among them, consuming alcohol and other acts forbidden by the Qurʾān – onto others:

> The king bowed his head, fidgeting his hands, and murmured: "Our slaves, our subjects, foreigners who have embraced our religion!" Then, lifting his head, he cried: "It is not as you said; no, your people have allowed themselves to do what God has forbidden. They have violated his prohibitions and abused their power; that is why God has stripped you of your authority and covered you in shame, to punish you for your crimes. God's vengeance knows no limits; I fear that his retribution will arrive while you are in my lands and that I will share in your fate. The rights of hospitality last for three days: take what you need and leave my kingdom." – "I will obey this command." Al-Manṣūr was struck by this tale; he gave himself over to reflection and, moved by the trials his prisoner had endured, considered setting him free; however, ʿĪṣā b. ʿAlī reminded him that the man had received the oath of allegiance (*bayʿa*),[138]and he had him led back to prison.[139]

The unequivocal criticism of Umayyad power in this passage is granted even more legitimacy because it is issued by a foreign ruler: it is the condemnation of a fallen power by an existing power. This judgment served primarily to corroborate the judgment passed previously by the Abbasids themselves. The risk of being "infected" with this impiety unsettled the Nubian king, who sent ʿAbd Allāh b. Marwān away from his court and back to the Abbasids, his asylum with the Nubians no longer practical. The lack of protest or argument on ʿAbd Allāh's part is a tacit acceptance of these criticisms by an Umayyad heir who did not attain the caliphate; it is an implicit avowal of failure, in a sense his testimony at the trial underway against his forebears. Nevertheless, the Umayyads were reintegrated into the "great family of rulers;" ʿAbd Allāh is treated as a distinguished guest by the Nubian king, and his plight moves al-Manṣūr.[140]

---

138 As Marwān II's presumed heir.

139 Al-Masʿūdī, *Murūj*, vol. VI, 166–8; trans. Pellat vol. IV, 963–4. This account is also found, with some minor variations, in Ibn ʿAbd Rabbih, *al-ʿIqd*, vol. IV, 444–5, and in Ibn Khaldūn, *The Muqaddimah*, vol. I, 425.

140 Al-Masʿūdī also reports that ʿAbd Allāh b. Marwān, imprisoned under al-Saffāḥ, was freed as a blind old man by al-Rashīd; he died during the reign of al-Rashīd or al-Amīn. Al-Masʿūdī, *Tanbīh*, 330; trans. 426.

Other anecdotes also attest to the merits attributed to these rival but nonetheless appreciated rulers by the founder of Baghdad. For example, in a meeting between a former companion (*ṣāḥib*) of Hishām b. ʿAbd al-Malik and al-Manṣūr, reported both by al-Masʿūdī and al-Ṭabarī, the caliph summons this *ṣāḥib*, who lived at al-Ruṣāfa, to his court to ask him about Umayyad military strategy. When brought before al-Manṣūr, the officer responds as follows:

> "He did this or that, may God be pleased with him! He acted in such and such a way, may God have mercy on him!" These phrases angered al-Manṣūr: "Get out!" he cried, "and may God punish you! Here you tread my carpets while praising my enemy!" The *shaykh* backed away, muttering: "Your enemy placed around my neck a chain of gratitude that will only be removed by he who washes my corpse!" Al-Manṣūr demanded he be brought back and asked what he had said. The elderly man responded: "Hishām protected me from want and spared me the shame of begging; in all the time that I knew him, I never once needed to knock on any door. Is it not thus my duty to praise him and favourably invoke his memory (*adhkaruhu*)?"[141]

The story continues and al-Manṣūr, impressed by the man's loyalty, offers him compensation, even going so far as to express his hope that he might find men such as the *ṣāḥib* among the members of his own army. Memory and loyalty are central to this anecdote. Commemoration of a member of the fallen dynasty in the caliph's presence is an act that initially provokes his ire, as it places Hishām among the "society of the living" at a moment when the early Abbasids were justifiably trying their best to exclude the majority of the Umayyads from this circle. However, al-Manṣūr admires the officer's loyalty to Hishām, and perhaps even more so his ability to remain loyal despite the circumstances. This anecdote is thus inherently ambiguous. Hishām is admired for his skillful military strategy – the reason behind this meeting in the first place – and his ability to inspire unwavering loyalty. The destruction of such a man's tomb was thus all the more reason to boast.[142] Al-Masʿūdī also notes that, "most of the time in political and administrative matters, al-Manṣūr followed the precedents established by Hishām, whose history and governance he had studied in depth."[143]

---

141 Al-Masʿūdī, *Murūj*, vol. VI, 166–8; trans. Pellat vol. IV, 965–6 (with minor modifications); al-Ṭabarī, vol. III, 412–3; trans. vol. XXIX, 115–6.

142 As with some of Hishām's other works, which were destroyed by Dāwūd b. ʿAlī following the Abbasid Revolution, per al-Masʿūdī, *Murūj*, vol. V, 466; trans. Pellat vol. IV, 879.

143 Al-Masʿūdī, *Murūj*, vol. V, 479–80; trans. Pellat vol. IV, 894. Al-Masʿūdī adds that Muʿāwiya and ʿAbd al-Malik were also recognised as great rulers by al-Manṣūr. Al-Ṭabarī recounts

As Goitein noted concerning the space dedicated to the first Islamic dynasty in the *Ansāb al-ashrāf*,[144] the Abbasids indeed saw the Umayyads as providing precedent in the art of governance. Following al-Madāʾinī (d. c. 235/850), al-Balādhurī also notes al-Manṣūr's admiration for his Umayyad predecessor.[145]

4.2.2.3 From Adversity to Alterity

The various anecdotes concerning the Umayyads in al-Masʿūdī's text (the original order of which has been preserved above) convey a clear trend: the Umayyads passed from adversity to alterity. A redemption of their memory is thus not only possible, but necessary.[146] After the initial shock of the Abbasid coup d'état and the ensuing violence, perception of the Umayyad caliphs gradually shifted from mortal enemies to mere predecessors as the *memoria* of the other became increasingly more widespread. Control over the past was the primary reason for this transformation. This shift was not in itself surprising: the Umayyads did precisely the same thing after taking control of Sasanian lands and subsequently studying their history.[147] While the basic outlines of this change are relatively easy to trace, understanding the tempo of this transition is more problematic. First, because this new gaze directed toward an Other and the qualities the new rulers shared with the former rulers could not but give rise to some outbursts of anti-Umayyad sentiments; and second, because, relying on the sources available to us, we must contend with the fact that this vision of history is the one that ultimately became dominant in the post-Sāmarrāʾ period.

We thus return to the observation presented above in Table 4.1: the Umayyad moment (moment 1) was remembered in the post-Sāmarrāʾ moment (moment 3), and the elements of this memory were put in place under the early Abbasids (moment 2). This strategy remains somewhat problematic. In order to present the Abbasid rise to power in a less polemic light, it was essential for the new rulers to emphasise their connection to the Umayyad past. Above all, establishing approval for Abbasid rule *as early as possible* was the goal. Someone must be blamed to justify the coup, and the Umayyads themselves filled this role; however, it was also essential that the Umayyads' reputation remain somewhat

another anecdote in which al-Ḥajjāj is the figure admired by the Abbasid caliph, who saw him as a loyal and efficient servant. See al-Ṭabarī, vol. III, 400–1; trans. vol. XXIX, 102–3.

144 *Ansāb*, vol. V, 15.

145 Athamina has noted the favourable portrayal of Hishām in the *akhbār* attributed to al-Madāʾinī, "The Sources," 249 ff.

146 As El-Hibri notes, "The Redemption," as well as Khalidi, *Arabic Historical Thought*, 111.

147 Hishām in particular was known for his interest in Sasanian administrative practices, see Gibb, *Studies*, 63.

intact in order to affirm the political continuity of the caliphate and Islamic history in general. Every legitimate authority was enlisted to aid in this endeavour: poets, scholars, "external" rulers, and of course, the chroniclers.

Al-Manṣūr's caliphate was *the* quintessential moment for establishing the Abbasid position with respect to the Umayyads following the violence of 132/750. With the succession of Abū al-ʿAbbās, the Revolution *became* an Abbasid one, to the vast disappointment of the Alids. The new caliphs desperately needed their Umayyad predecessors, with whom they shared an enforced dynastic system of succession; in a sense, Umayyad precedent justified the Abbasid seizure of power. The caliphate's return to Baghdad in 279/892 was equally *the* moment to emphasise the importance of the caliph who founded the city in order to justify this new *translatio imperii*. Al-Manṣūr is thus critical for a variety of reasons, and the narratives crystallise around this foundational historical figure as rewritings aimed to give the past new meaning. Following the caliphal transition to Baghdad, al-Masʿūdī became an important part of this movement. Born in Baghdad around 280/893, al-Masʿūdī was a product of the reinstallation of the caliphate in the city founded by al-Manṣūr.

The manner in which the Abbasids situated themselves with respect to the memory of their recently-deposed rivals is more ambiguous. Although the Christian sources – inasmuch as they provide access to an Islamic historiography that no longer exists – record the massacres perpetrated in 132/750, they convey nothing of how the early Abbasids understood their predecessors. Ibn al-Muqaffaʿ, an "adviser" of al-Manṣūr (to borrow Pellat's terminology), while not directly interested in the Umayyads, does devote a section of his epistle to Syria. Concerning the *ahl al-Shām*, he notes that "if they are treated justly – as has not been done – they are indeed free from any violence or immoderation."[148] The same transition from adversity to alterity is at work here with respect to the Syrians. Ibn al-Muqaffaʿ adds: "[it must not be forgotten that] sovereignty is not taken from a people (*qawm*)[149] without leaving behind a resentment that pushes them to act." Ibn al-Muqaffaʿ died in 140/757; thus, this precocious statement highlights the need to transition to politics following periods of rancor and warfare. Does it also apply to attitudes toward the memory of the first Islamic dynasty?

---

148 Ibn al-Muqaffaʿ, *Risāla*, 49; trans. 48.

149 Pellat translated *qawm* as family, which would imply that Ibn al-Muqaffaʿ was only referring to the Umayyads, who would then be associated with Syria. However, the term has a broader sense and the passage refers to the *ahl al-Shām* without any further clarification. See Ibn al-Muqaffaʿ, *Risāla*, 48.

4.2.3 *Umayyad Memory and Culture*

To borrow François Furet's idea that the memory of the French Revolution was invoked for three different purposes during the nineteenth century, the memory of the Umayyad era throughout the subsequent decades and centuries was enlisted by those hoping to varyingly efface, continue or renew it (for example, the early Abbasids, the Andalusian Umayyads and the rebellious Sufyanids); there were also scholars who worked to preserve it by reintegrating it into *adab* and history. The link between the Syrian space and the Umayyads was important for those who wished to preserve an Umayyad memory, as shown by its prevalence in the *faḍāʾil* genre[150] and the regional biographical dictionaries, all of which were veritable *libri memoriales*.

This *memoria* must have been at least somewhat embattled. It emanated from long-established traditions affirming the greatness of the Umayyad dynasty; thus, reaction against this memory was necessary in order to clear the way for the legitimation of the Abbasids, especially in the face of widespread competition for this legitimacy from the Alids and others. As we have seen, the force of this initial reaction would eventually and inevitably be diluted by the requirements of *Realpolitik*, a force that transformed distasteful memories into useful precedent. This transition was not necessarily a smooth one: periods of turmoil call for scapegoats, and the Umayyads filled this role perfectly. It was no coincidence that periods of trouble for the Abbasid caliphate translated to bouts of hostility toward Muʿāwiya, the quintessential Umayyad. Al-Ṭabarī reports that in 211/826–827, the caliph al-Maʾmūn proclaimed that anyone who favourably mentioned Muʿāwiya's name would be severely punished, just as would those who declared the Umayyad caliph's superiority over any other Companion of the Prophet.[151] Al-Masʿūdī further added that anyone who used a pious expression in conjunction with Muʿāwiya's name would be excommunicated and cast out of the *umma*.[152] Al-Maʾmūn wanted this proclamation spread throughout the empire, and he issued missives directing his governors to apply these new measures, stipulating that the Sufyanid caliph must be systematically cursed in the *khuṭba*. However, al-Maʾmūn was ultimately dissuaded from these projects by his advisers, who feared that the initiative would stir up discontent among the populace. In 284/897, al-Muʿtaḍid attempted a similar project based on the document originally issued by al-Maʾmūn, but was

---

150 Cobb, "Virtual Sacrality."

151 Al-Ṭabarī, vol. III, 1098; trans. vol. XXXII, 175.

152 Al-Masʿūdī, *Murūj*, vol. VII, 90–3; trans. Pellat vol. IV, 1132–3.

also forced to give it up.[153] Problems related to *memoria* clearly lurk behind these abortive initiatives. As Lauwers notes, "naming had strong implications. More than a sign of recognition, the name constituted the person … by reciting the names of the dead, their 'memory' was perpetuated and they became once more present among the living."[154] If the act of naming "*was* essentially the memory of the dead," the act of cursing "also had the power to destroy it."[155] This tactic was one of the primary means of combatting the "presence of the dead."[156]

These unsuccessful projects nevertheless bear witness to the fact that Umayyad memory remained a force that required confrontation. It was one thing to contest the memory of Umayyad caliphs and rulers; confronting Umayyad culture was quite another. If we are to believe al-Masʿūdī, al-Manṣūr experienced this difficulty firsthand during an encounter with a blind poet whom he had met previously in Syria during the reign of Marwān II. The poet, not knowing whom he addressed, recited the same verses favourable to the Umayyads that he had declaimed at their first meeting:

> The Umayyads' wives are now widows; death has orphaned their daughters.
> This dynasty's fortune now slumbers and their star has fallen, for stars turn and fortune grows weary.
> Their pulpits and thrones sit empty: yet they will receive my blessing til the hour of my death!

After revealing his identity and frightening the poet, al-Manṣūr decided not to punish him for the verses.[157] The Abbasids were firmly in control of the caliphate, yet the Umayyads remained strong in the memories of the poets and the people thanks also to the architectural and cultural landscape that best symbolised the majesty and endurance of the first Islamic dynasty.

The initiatives undertaken by al-Mahdī and al-Maʾmūn to replace the names of al-Walīd and ʿAbd al-Malik with their own on the walls of the mosque of Medina and the Dome of the Rock, respectively, must be understood in this

153 Al-Ṭabarī, vol. III, 2165 ff; on these episodes, see Zaman, "The Caliphs, the ʿUlamāʾ, and the Law," 33–4, and Sourdel, "Appels et programmes" and *L'état impérial*, 111, 135.
154 Lauwers, *La mémoire des ancêtres*, 106.
155 Lauwers, *La mémoire des ancêtres*, 108.
156 This echoes the concept developed by Oexle, "Die Gegenwart der Toten." Although the theme of death in Islam has been relatively little studied, see the massive work of Diem and Schöller, *The Living and the Dead*, as well as Halevi, *Muhammad's Grave*.
157 Al-Masʿūdī, *Murūj*, vol. IV, 159–60; trans. Pellat vol. IV, 962–3.

context. Which monuments were most representative of the glory of the Umayyads and best perpetuated their memory?[158] Here once again, ambiguity is an important factor. The desire to reappropriate Umayyad patrimony did not preclude admiration for their achievements. In his *Kitāb faḍāʾil al-Shām wa-Dimashq*, ʿAlī b. Muḥammad al-Rabaʿī records that the caliph al-Mahdī, during a journey to Syria accompanied by his vizier Abū ʿUbayd Allāh al-ʿAsharī, a native of the province,[159] visited Damascus and Jerusalem in 163/780. During these visits, the caliph listed four areas in which the Umayyads surpassed the Abbasids, including the construction of mosque of Damascus and the Dome of the Rock.[160] Despite the fact that al-Maʾmūn's name had replaced that of ʿAbd al-Malik, the Dome of the Rock remained Umayyad in the social memory. This ambivalence in the face of the Umayyad architectural landscape, similar to the caliphs' attitudes when faced with the *memoria* of the first Islamic dynasty, marks the process of defining a new Abbasid identity undertaken in the post-Sāmarrāʾ period; for this reason, it was essential to construct a perception of Umayyad alterity.

Despite the best efforts of several Abbasid caliphs, even the most intense political machinations sometimes failed to overcome the memory of the Umayyads or their cultural landscape. The nature of Umayyad history, however, offered latitude to historians tasked with giving voice to the past. While it was not always possible to remain silent on certain issues or events, it was relatively easy to bestow new meaning on the past in accordance with the needs of the present, or even to produce a sort of "creative oblivion."

The premise of this inquiry is that most of what we think we know about the Umayyads is largely dependent on what the men and authors of the Abbasid period – particularly at the turn of the third–fourth century – themselves wanted to know and bequest from their Islamic past. For this reason, studying the various layers of memory sedimentation is essential to understanding the first centuries of Islam, as this third–fourth-century filter was fundamental in determining how future generations could access these "alternative pasts."[161]

Abbasid legitimacy was constantly contested, in particular by the Alids, who felt that they had been deprived of the benefits of the Umayyads' downfall. As a result, the Abbasids were deeply concerned with self-presentation, and they

158 On this subject, see Assmann, *Stein und Zeit*.

159 On this native of Tiberias, see Sourdel, *Le vizirat*, vol. 1, 94–103.

160 The two other areas mentioned were the nobility of the Umayyad *mawālī* and the piety of the caliph ʿUmar II. See ʿAlī b. Muḥammad al-Rabaʿī, *Kitāb faḍāʾil al-Shām*, 42. This anecdote is also found in al-Suyūṭī, *Itḥāf al-akhiṣṣā*, 160–1. See also Cobb, "Virtual Sacrality," 50; El-Hibri, "The Redemption," 243; Borrut, "Entre tradition et histoire," 334.

161 To borrow Geary's expression, *Phantoms of Remembrance*, 177.

attempted to efface their most shameful episodes, including the massacres that followed the Revolution of 132/750. Historiography played an important role in this process, as Gueneé has noted in his studies of the medieval West:

> the life and security of States depends less on their institutions and more on the ideas, sentiments and beliefs of the governed. Yet, aren't these political mentalities themselves largely shaped by the past in which every individual believes? A social group, a political society, a civilisation defines itself first and foremost by its memory, or, in other words, its history – not the history that actually occurred, but the history that the historians created.[162]

At the turn of the third-fourth century *hijrī*, the formation of a sense of collective past that the Abbasids belonged to and had inherited was underway. The narrative forged an identity through the creation of a common memory; history books, combining texts old and new, reflected a particular manipulation of the potential of written culture in the Abbasid world.[163] In this sense, control over memory and the Umayyad past was a central preoccupation for the Abbasids.

The Umayyad "realms of memory" were part of a larger cultural memory, or of an Umayyad culture, that posed the question of the existence and persistence of an Umayyad identity and, more specifically, of an Umayyad identity that could be assimilated (or not) to a Syrian identity. We shall now turn our attention to the division of dynastic memories and their association with different distinct spaces.

4.3 Spaces of Memory

The fall of the Umayyads in 132/750 marked the transition of power from Syria to Iraq. If we pursue the memory of the second/eighth century from a dynastic perspective, we are consequently led outside the spatial scope of our inquiry. This is not to say that a history of the memory of the early Abbasids would be in vain; rather, as emphasised above and contrary to what one may initially presume, the early Abbasids found themselves in a situation similar to that of the Umayyads, at least on a historiographic level. The early Abbasids were also documented by much later sources, and thus pose very similar difficulties for historians of the period. El-Hibri has sketched out the broad strokes on

162 Guenée, *Histoire et culture historique*, 16.
163 To loosely paraphrase McKitterick, *History and Memory*, 8 and 22.

this subject, although a more comprehensive study remains to be done. These points are crucial, not only in determining what we think we know about the beginnings of the second Islamic dynasty, but also more generally because they condition all of this rewritten Islamic history. In other words, the history of the first Abbasid century is also, and perhaps above all, a remembered – or rather, forgotten – history in the Syrian context that is the focus of this study; as Cobb has noted, the Abbasids' arrival seems to set the seal on the Islamic history of the Syrian space.[164] However, it is useful to note the salient traits of this Abbasid "ego history" before moving on to investigate the spaces of memory that characterise the first two Islamic dynasties.

4.3.1 *The Distorting Prisms of Post-Sāmarrā' Historiography*

Our knowledge of the history of the first centuries of Islam is shaped by a number of distorting prisms, as the major events of the Abbasid period defined the interpretations proposed by the chronographers, and the first Abbasid century is no exception. El-Hibri offers a detailed analysis of this period, with elaborate reading grids of the classical narrative sources. He notes how difficult it is to define how the Muslims remembered the history of the first *fitna*s following the death of al-Rashīd, as the narratives of these episodes are deeply marked by the chroniclers' concerns regarding the causes and consequences of the civil war between al-Amīn and al-Ma'mūn and the latter's subsequent institution of the *miḥna*.[165] The shockwaves of the civil war that shook the caliphate after Hārūn al-Rashīd's death are one of the most defining features of classical Islamic historiography. The significance given to this tragic episode shaped the interpretation of Islamic history in its entirety; in order to comprehend such a massive catastrophe, one that signalled the end of a united *umma*, it was necessary to weave new threads toward the Islamic past and the Holy Texts. The first three *fitna*s were thus reread in the light of the fourth.

The outcome of the civil war and the murder of al-Amīn were especially problematic, both from political and historiographic standpoints, as it was necessary to justify and "legitimise" a regicide. Presentations of the two brothers from early youth on were thus reworked by the chronographers and partially constructed on the basis of the Old Testament rivalry between Cain and Abel.[166] Similar adaptations were popular in historiographic production

164 Cobb, "Community versus Contention," 100.

165 El-Hibri, *Reinterpreting*, 105.

166 With certain notable differences, however, since Cain (identified with al-Ma'mūn) claimed a more noble lineage than his brother, which was rather the case for al-Amīn (the Arab) over al-Ma'mūn (the Persian). See El-Hibri, *Reinterpreting*, 172.

because of their easily transposable nature. The events recorded in these preconceived narrative structures were not fictitious; rather, alongside its factual existence, a given event also had a literary or topological existence of its own.

The period spanning the end of the third and beginning of the fourth centuries *hijrī* also marked the start of the progressive disintegration of the Abbasid empire. This critical moment produced a discourse centred around memory and its two main attributes, remembrance and oblivion; at the same time, new interpretations of bygone eras of Islamic history emerged. We must consider the fact that, after a century and a half of Abbasid dominance between 750 and 900, "the evidence of this continuity had become unintelligible."[167] The Abbasid Revolution, the civil war between al-Rashīd's sons, the *miḥna*, the caliphate's shift to Sāmarrāʾ, the rise of the Turkish military, the assassination of al-Mutawakkil and the loss of real caliphal power, etc., were ample reason to explain breaches in continuity. From this point on, reinterpretation was essential and rewriting was indispensable: it was necessary to present "recollections of the past that could give meaning to the transformed present."[168] All of Islamic history was revisited: as with Umayyad history, controlling the uses of the Abbasid past was crucial, and this effort notably included rewriting the history of the dynasty's origins. This is a classic strategy employed by all powers when they attain a certain level of maturity, in this instance tinged with messianic connotations, as discussed in the previous chapter. In this context, as illustrated above all in the *Anonymous History of the Abbasids*, recomposition was not only an integral part of the writing process – it was its motivation.

In this vast reconstructive enterprise, Syria's fate was tied to that of the two successive Islamic dynasties' preferred spaces of power. The oblivion into which Abbasid Syria fell is profound in the chronographies: the vulgate effaced the links between the new dynasty and the province.[169] However, these links certainly did exist; thus, we shall now focus on the processes that governed the inscription of dynastic memory into distinct and bounded spaces.

4.3.2 *Syrian-Umayyad* Memoria *versus Iraqi-Abbasid* Memoria: *A False Dichotomy?*

This inquiry has emphasised the strong connection between the Syrian space and the heritage of the first Islamic dynasty; this connection gives rise to the

167 Geary, *Phantoms of Remembrance*, 25.

168 Geary, *Phantoms of Remembrance*, 6.

169 The sources' disinterest in Abbasid Syria has long been accompanied by an equivalent disinterest among modern scholars, as Sourdel notes, "La Syrie." This historiographic void has been partially filled by Cobb, *White Banners*. See below, Ch. 7.

notion of a *memoria* that is not merely Umayyad, but Syrian-Umayyad in nature.[170] Similarly, Abbasid memory is seemingly rooted in Iraq, and Baghdad in particular. The Euphrates's two banks are thus each identified with the Umayyads or the Abbasids respectively, echoing the symbolic opposition between Muʿāwiya and ʿAlī during the battle of Ṣiffīn.[171]

4.3.2.1 The Euphrates as Mirror?

An architectural example reveals the importance of this geographic boundary, especially considering that whether an archaeologist uncovers Umayyad or Abbasid artifacts depends on which side of the river he digs. Moreover, a site such as Qaṣr al-Ḥayr al-Sharqī, an Umayyad construction, was until recently seen as an *exclusively* Umayyad site, despite the fact that it witnessed two decades of Umayyad use compared to two centuries under the Abbasids – to say nothing of later medieval occupations.[172] Oleg Grabar has drawn attention to this fact in a statement that sheds light on the state of modern scholarship in the field:

> even our preliminary and limited work appears to have established the fact that the small enclosure was considerably redone in the 9th century. This, of course, poses a central problem for the archaeological history of Syria since the 9th century is usually assumed to have been a period of impoverishment in Syria proper and either this hypothesis may have to be revised or one would have to conclude that the development of Qaṣr al-Ḥayr at that time *was somehow connected with the Jazīra much more than with traditional Syria*.[173]

In other words, construction work in Syria during the Abbasid period – seemingly impossible at the time – must have been connected with the "good" side of the Euphrates! This presumed dichotomy creates a rigidly divided presentation of the two dynasties, whereby political rivalries are transposed onto the geographic terrain.

Damascus was to the Umayyads what Baghdad was to the Abbasids; Syria flew the white flag, Iraq adopted the black. This is history oversimplified: black

---

170 On the construction of a discourse extolling the virtues of the province, see Cobb, "Virtual Sacrality." This Syrian-Umayyad *memoria* was widely used by the Andalusian Umayyads, on whom see Martinez-Gros, *L'idéologie omeyyade*.

171 It should be noted that Assmann emphasised the fact that a phenomenon of spatialisation is inherent to all forms of memory, *La mémoire culturelle*, in particular 54–5.

172 On Qaṣr al-Ḥayr al-Sharqī, see Genequand, *Les élites omeyyades*.

173 Grabar, "Qasr al-Hayr al-Sharqi, Preliminary Report," 120 (italics mine).

versus white, West versus East and, ultimately, Syria versus Iraq. This dualistic vision has numerous weaknesses, in particular because it tends to *centralise* Umayyad and Abbasid histories around Damascus and Baghdad, despite the fact the use of the term "capital" was unstable during these periods.[174] By "Syrianising" Umayyad history and "Iraqicising" Abbasid history, we deny ourselves the possibility of a broader understanding of the projects these two dynasties conceived throughout the Islamic empire as a whole.[175] Umayyad Iraq, or the "Abbasid Syrians" before 132/750 remain little-known entities. Alternative Umayyad and Abbasid memories were "forgotten" via the processes of redaction at work during the classical period; the authors of these classical texts attest to the existence of a "creative oblivion." This "new past ... is an enduring creation: its central outlines, accepted and elaborated upon by subsequent medieval generations, have been largely accepted by modern historians."[176]

However, was this redistribution of reality after the fact undertaken in accord with Umayyad projects in Iraq, or with the tenuous links between the Abbasids and Syria prior to 132/750? The answer to this question lies partially outside the scope of the present study, as a detailed investigation of Umayyad Iraq is beyond our means here.[177] It should be noted, however, that despite Ibn Khaldūn's apt emphasis on the importance of the foundation of Wāsiṭ[178] and the subsequent new direction characteristic of Umayyad policy in Iraq,[179] Umayyad Iraq in general remains a *terra incognita* in modern scholarship. Unfortunately, archaeology at present has not overcome this deficit.[180] Nevertheless, it is possible that a certain number of sites traditionally attributed to the Sasanians were actually later or at least still in use during the Umayyad era, a hypothesis that may allow us to better understand Umayyad activity in

174 See Brühl, "Remarques sur les notions de 'capitale' et de 'résidence'." The spatial dimensions of late-Umayyad and early-Abbasid power are further discussed below in Ch. 8.

175 Grabar also noted this point in 1960, highlighting the tendency of modern scholars to "identify Umayyad architecture with Syria" and neglect the existence of Umayyad architecture in Iraq. See Grabar, "Al-Mushatta, Baghdād, and Wāsiṭ," 103.

176 Geary, *Phantoms of Remembrance*, 23.

177 See Morony, *Iraq after the Muslim Conquest*; on the subject of Upper Mesopotamia, see Robinson, *Empire and Elites*.

178 On Wāsiṭ, see Sakly, "Wāsiṭ" and Elad, "The Siege."

179 On Ibn Khaldūn's analysis, see Martinez-Gros, *Ibn Khaldūn*, 164 ff.; for an account of the foundation of Wāsiṭ, see al-Ṭabarī, vol. II, 1125 ff; trans. vol. XXIII, 70 ff.

180 Among the most significant contributions on the subject, see Creswell, *Early Muslim Architecture*; Rousset, *L'archéologie islamique en Iraq*; Morony, *Iraq after the Muslim Conquest* and "Land Use and Settlement Patterns;" Northedge, "Archaeology and New Urban Settlement," *Entre Amman et Samarra*, 54–6, and *The Historical Topography*.

the future heart of Abbasid power; however, systematic research must be done before this can be determined with any certainty. Even the site of Ukhaydir has not been accurately dated, and could be Umayyad;[181] the textual sources mention various projects undertaken by the Umayyads in the province. These efforts contributed to Iraq's economic vitality, and Wāsiṭ was an active and important mint.[182]

This state of affairs cannot but strengthen our perception of a fundamentally Syrian caliphate, an image popularised in the writings of the Belgian Jesuit Henri Lammens.[183] Modern research's lack of interest in the subject, with the notable exception of several already-dated works on al-Ḥajjāj,[184] stems from this simultaneously real and exaggerated Syrian identity attributed to the rulers of Damascus. We shall return later to the Umayyads' role in this process. Without denying the existence of special links connecting the two dynasties to two distinct spaces of power, it should be noted that these ties are preferential rather than exclusive, and the opposition between the two was further reinforced by an Iraq-centric Abbasid historiography. In reality, the two spaces successively filled the same roles: one was the seat of the caliphate, while the other was the province of rebellion. Umayyad Iraq and Abbasid Syria shared a similar taste for insurrection against a "central" caliphal authority, and this fact is one aspect of this history viewed through the mirror of the Euphrates.

4.3.2.2 The Abbasid Syrians: al-Ḥumayma and Strategies of Oblivion

The dearth of available information on Abbasid Syria in the classical Islamic sources is somewhat surprising. Prior to their accession to the caliphate, the future rulers of Baghdad had strong ties to al-Ḥumayma, a site located in southern Syria.

During the conflict between ʿAbd al-Malik b. Marwān and Ibn al-Zubayr, ʿAbd Allāh b. ʿAbbās, then on his death bed, advised his son ʿAlī to settle in Syria, as the Banū Umayya were more favourable to him than the Zubayrids.[185] In accordance with his father's dying wishes, ʿAlī b. ʿAbd Allāh visited ʿAbd al-Malik, who proposed that he settle in Damascus in the residence of his choice. ʿAlī asserted that he preferred not to live in Damascus, so the caliph suggested he settle in the Balqāʾ, a location with the strategic advantage of being halfway between Damascus and the Hijaz;[186] following this advice, ʿAlī

181 Northedge, "Ukhaydir;" Grabar, "Al-Mushatta, Baghdād, and Wāsiṭ," 107–8.

182 Darley-Doran, "Wāsiṭ;" DeShazo and Bates, "The Umayyad Governors."

183 See Lammens, *La Syrie*, 46 ff.

184 See notably Périer, *Vie d'al-Ḥadjdjādj* and Darkazally, *Al-Ḥajjāj*.

185 *Akhbār al-dawla*, 130.

186 *Akhbār al-dawla*, 154.

went to the region of al-Sharāt, "where he bought a village (*qariyya*) called al-Ḥumayma and settled there."[187] The anonymous author of the *History of the Abbasids*, who took great care in insisting on the messianic dimension of his Abbasid subjects, added that before he died, ʿAbd Allāh b. ʿAbbās had advised his son to consider the mountains of al-Sharāt. This region, he claimed, would harbor the man who would be called upon to wield divine power after the Umayyads' downfall.[188] Al-Ḥumayma thus became the Abbasid residence from 68/687–688 until 132/749. Although al-Ṭabarī makes no mention of the Abbasid presence in al-Ḥumayma, he does note that ʿAlī b. ʿAbd Allāh died there in 118/736–737.[189] It was also the birthplace of the first three Abbasid caliphs: Abū al-ʿAbbās, al-Manṣūr and al-Mahdī.[190]

Al-Ḥumayma was an important site in the decades after ʿAlī settled there, as it was the nerve centre of the machinations that would lead the Abbasid family to the caliphate.[191] The initiation of the *daʿwa* occurred here[192] in the year 100 *hijrī* in the context of well-documented apocalyptic expectations.[193] This unrest did not attract Umayyad attention until much later; a letter intercepted under Marwān II[194] led this latter to order the governor of the Balqāʾ to go to al-Ḥumayma and arrest Ibrāhīm al-Imām.[195] Ibrāhīm was captured in the village mosque and sent before the caliph;[196] he would later die in the jails of Ḥarrān[197] after having bequeathed his authority to his brother Abū al-ʿAbbās.[198] Al-Ṭabarī reports a different version of these events, once again emphasising

187 *Akhbār al-dawla*, 108. Sharon, *Black Banners*, 120. See also Ibn Saʿd, *al-Ṭabaqāt*, vol. V, 314.

188 *Akhbār al-dawla*, 131.

189 Al-Ṭabarī, vol. II, 1592; trans. vol. XXV, 129. Al-Yaʿqūbī, *Taʾrīkh*, vol. II, 321, states that his death took place in al-Ijhīr (*sic*, the vocalisation is uncertain), a village between al-Ḥumayma and Adhruḥ. This location was apparently unknown to the Arab geographers.

190 Abū al-ʿAbbās: see Khalīfa b. Khayyāṭ, *Taʾrīkh*, vol. II, 629. Al-Manṣūr: see Khalīfa b. Khayyāṭ, *Taʾrīkh*, vol. II, 667; al-Ṭabarī, vol. III, 391, trans. vol. XXIX, 93. Al-Mahdī: see Khalīfa b. Khayyāṭ, *Taʾrīkh*, vol. II, 693; Ibn ʿAbd Rabbih, *al-ʿIqd*, vol. V, 103.

191 On al-Ḥumayma's key role in this clandestine period, see Agha, *The Revolution*, index.

192 Al-Dīnawarī, *Akhbār*, 332. Ibn Kathīr, *Bidāya*, vol. IX, 196–7; Ibn al-Athīr, *Kāmil*, vol. V, 53. Al-Ṭabarī, vol. II, 1358, trans. vol. XXIV, 87, does not mention al-Ḥumayma, only the surrounding area, *arḍ al-Sharāt*.

193 See above, Ch. 2.

194 Al-Ṭabarī, vol. III, 25; trans. vol. XXVII, 148.

195 This complicated episode was subject to important historiographic reconstructions aimed at affirming Abbasid legitimacy, as it was critical that Abū al-ʿAbbās be designated as Ibrāhīm's successor. On this question, see Blankinship, "The Tribal Factor," especially 601–3. This point is discussed in detail below, Ch. 7.

196 Al-Ṭabarī, vol. II, 1974–5, trans. vol. XXVII, 84; al-Dīnawarī, *Akhbār*, 357 ff.

197 Al-Ṭabarī, vol. III, 42–4; trans. vol. XXVII, 166–8.

198 Al-Masʿūdī, *Murūj*, vol. VI, 90; trans. Pellat vol. IV, 938.

the messianic aspect of the Abbasids. Rather than a letter informing the caliph of the threat represented by this secretive movement, it was a mysterious text (*kitāb*) that provided the description of a man who would bring about the end of the Umayyads. This work physically described Abū al-ʿAbbās, who would become the first Abbasid caliph, and Marwān II reproached his men for not having already apprehended him. Thanks to this error, Abū al-ʿAbbās was able to escape to Iraq before being captured.[199] In a final *riwāya*, the confusion over the identity of the person being sought – Ibrāhīm b. Muḥammad – and his appearance – Abū al-ʿAbbās – is even more obvious. Marwān's emissary, on the basis of the second criterion, arrested the future caliph, only to release him when Ibrāhīm presented himself.[200] These two versions attest to a dominant and recurring trend in Abbasid historiography: the Umayyads' primary role was to enable the Abbasids to accede to the caliphate.[201] The abortive capture of Abū al-ʿAbbās is a perfect example of this theme.

This episode signalled the end of the Abbasid presence in al-Ḥumayma and their exodus from Syria. The escape to Kūfa was as unavoidable as it was necessary.[202] In the beginning, al-Sharāt was an area of contact between the caliphs of Damascus and those who would later overthrow them. Abbasid relations with ʿAbd al-Malik were excellent,[203] but al-Walīd's accession changed the tone: unlike his father, his attitude was hostile.[204] Al-Walīd travelled to al-Ḥumayma in person[205] to interrogate ʿAlī b. ʿAbd Allāh, who was accused of murdering his supposed half-brother by Umm Salīṭ.[206] The body had already been buried in the garden (*bustān*) of ʿAlī's home (*manzil*),[207] and ʿAlī categorically denied the accusations against him. The garden was searched, and the disinterred corpse was brought before the caliph, who declared ʿAlī guilty and

199 Al-Ṭabarī, vol. III, 25; trans. vol. XXVII, 149.

200 Al-Ṭabarī, vol. III, 25–6; vol. XXVII, 149.

201 This point has been noted by El-Hibri, "The Redemption," 251. See also Borrut, "Entre tradition et histoire," 366.

202 Al-Ṭabarī, vol. III, 34; trans. vol. XXVII, 158.

203 As attested, for example, by ʿAlī b. ʿAbd Allāh's role in the marriage of ʿAbd al-Malik to Shaqrāʾ bt. Shabīb. See *Akhbār al-dawla*, 156–7.

204 *Akhbār al-dawla*, 155. The relations between ʿAlī b. ʿAbd Allāh and al-Walīd were not always bad, however; see *Akhbār al-dawla*, 151–2.

205 Per al-Yaʿqūbī, *Taʾrīkh*, vol. II, 290. In another version, the caliph does not seem to have travelled there in person, see *Akhbār al-dawla*, 149.

206 Umm Salīṭ was a slave of ʿAbd Allāh b. al-ʿAbbās, ʿAlī's father. Upon the father's death, she claimed to have had a son by him named Salīṭ, after her; this would seem to indicate that ʿAlī did not recognise the child.

207 *Akhbār al-dawla*, 149; al-Yaʿqūbī, *Taʾrīkh*, vol. II, 290.

ordered that he stand out in the hot sun as punishment;[208] following this incident, ʿAlī was sent back to al-Ḥumayma and never left the village again.[209] It should also be noted that, despite essentially being under house arrest, ʿAlī b. ʿAbd Allāh was in a highly strategic position in al-Ḥumayma.[210] A man from the tribe of Kināna reported that his grandfather, while travelling back to the Hijaz following a meeting with the caliph Sulaymān b. ʿAbd al-Malik in Damascus, stopped several days with ʿAlī b. ʿAbd Allāh. "Every day, groups (*nafar*) from the Hijaz and the *ahl al-Shām* stopped at his home and were his guests. He lodged them, gave them provisions and inquired about the inhabitants of the Hijaz from the travellers of the Hijaz, and the inhabitants of Syria from the *ahl al-Shām*."[211] When these visitors left, others came and took their place, and when one guest remarked on the high cost of his generosity, ʿAlī replied that the information he gathered from these visits was priceless.[212] The knowledge he gained from this hospitality doubtless played a determining role in the Abbasids' success.[213]

The Abbasid family's residence in Syria was well-known to their contemporaries; during the conflict with Hishām b. ʿAbd al-Malik, Khālid al-Qasrī (d. 126/743–744)[214] supposedly threatened to join one who was "Iraqi in passion, Syrian in residence (*shāmī al-dār*)[215] and Hijazi in origin," meaning Muḥammad b. ʿAlī b. ʿAbd Allāh b. al-ʿAbbās.[216] Later, the association between the Abbasids and al-Ḥumayma seems less certain; al-Masʿūdī expresses some confusion in the *Tanbīh* over the two towns of al-Ḥumayma and Kirār,[217] despite the fact that he had previously noted in the *Meadows of Gold* that the

208 The text of the *Anonymous History of the Abbasids* is incomplete, but may be pieced together from the information provided by al-Balādhurī, *Ansāb*, vol. III, 322.

209 *Akhbār al-dawla*, 149–50; al-Yaʿqūbī, *Taʾrīkh*, vol. II, 290.

210 Sharon, *Revolt*, 19.

211 *Akhbār al-dawla*, 142.

212 *Akhbār al-dawla*, 142. The verses ʿAlī gives in reply are also presented in al-Balādhurī, *Ansāb*, vol. III, 318, as well as in the *Aghānī*, vol. XIII, 66.

213 See another example of ʿAlī's requests for information on the Umayyads, *Akhbār al-dawla*, 150. The weakness of the Umayyads' intelligence operations has been proposed by a number of authors as the reason for their downfall, see below, Ch. 7.

214 A famous figure who was notably the governor of Mecca and Iraq. See Hawting, "Khālid b. ʿAbd Allāh al-Ḳasrī" and Leder, "Features of the Novel."

215 Hillenbrand proposes a translation of "Syrian in family," al-Ṭabarī, trans. vol. XXVI, 170.

216 Al-Ṭabarī, vol. II, 1816, trans. vol. XXVI, 170–1. Al-Dīnawarī, *Akhbār*, 345, suggests that it is Ibrāhīm b. Muḥammad b. ʿAlī b. ʿAbd Allāh b. al-ʿAbbās, better known as Ibrāhīm al-Imām, who is designated here.

217 Al-Masʿūdī, *Tanbīh*, 338, trans. 435, 436.

town was known as Kirār al-Ḥumayma (the wells of al-Ḥumayma),[218] a name also occasionally used by al-Ṭabarī.[219]

The confusion only grows as time passes, judging from Samhūdī's (d. 911/1505) later affirmation in the final geographic section of his history of Medina that ʿAlī b. ʿAbd Allāh and his children lived at Badā (or Badan), near Wādī al-Qurā.[220] Based on an obscure passage from the *Lisān al-ʿarab*, Lecker sees this claim as an alternative to the tradition situating the Abbasids in al-Ḥumayma during the Marwanid period.[221] Using the name Shaghb, in reference to the aforementioned village of Shaghb wa-Badā[222] situated between Medina and Syria, Ibn Manẓūr reports a *ḥadīth* attributed to al-Zuhrī stating that he owned "properties at Shaghb and Badā, the two [sites] being locations in Syria, and it was there …[223] that ʿAlī b. ʿAbd Allāh and his children resided until they acceded to the caliphate."[224] The blank space left in the manuscript may indicate that the name of the location of ʿAlī's residence remained to be specified; Lecker suggests that "*wa-bihi*" "likely" designated a site near Shaghb wa-Badā,[225] although it could also be a reference to al-Shām. It is also possible that the gap in Ibn Manẓūr's text was subsequently forgotten by later authors like Samhūdī, who named Badā – and not Shaghb wa-Badā, the two toponyms clearly understood as designating two distinct locations[226] – as ʿAlī b. ʿAbd Allāh's place of residence. Nearly a century before Ibn Manẓūr (d. 711/1311–1312), Yāqūt's (d. 626/1229) *Muʿjam al-buldān* also expresses uncertainty: it situates al-Zuhrī's tomb at Shaghb wa-Badā, located in this instance between Medina and Ayla, *and* at Shaghb, near Wādī al-Qurā.[227] Badā is given a proper entry in the dictionary, stating that the name designates a coastal valley near Ayla, a place near Wādī al-Qurā, or a location in the Wādī ʿUdhra

218 Al-Masʿūdī, *Murūj*, vol. VI, 70, trans. Pellat vol. IV, 929.

219 Al-Ṭabarī, vol. II, 1975, trans. vol. XXVII, 84.

220 "*Badā: mawḍiʿ qurb Wādī al-Qurā kāna bihi manzil ʿAlī b. ʿAbd Allāh b. ʿAbbās wa-awlādihi*," cited in Lecker, "Biographical Notes," 56–7. On Wādī al-Qurā, situated between Medina and Syria, see Yāqūt, *Muʿjam*, vol. V, 345.

221 Lecker, "Biographical Notes," 57.

222 Al-Zuhrī had a residence there. See above, Ch. 1.

223 There is a blank space in the manuscript.

224 Ibn Manẓūr, *Lisān*, vol. VIII, 97: "*wa-fī ḥadīth al-Zuhrī annahu kāna lahu māl bi-Shaghb wa-Badā humā mawḍiʿāni bi-al-Shām wa-bihi* […] *kāna muqāmu ʿAlī b. ʿAbd Allāh b. ʿAbbās wa-awlādihi ilā waṣalat ilayhim al-khilāfa*."

225 Lecker, "Biographical Notes," 57.

226 This is indicated by the dual "*humā*" in the above-cited passage from the *Lisān*.

227 Yāqūt, *Muʿjam*, vol. III, 351 and 352.

near Syria.[228] This confusion arises from the fact that this area on the border between Syria and the Hijaz is especially difficult to define.[229] However, Yāqūt does not once mention the Abbasids in association with any of these locations, as the geographer is quite certain that al-Ḥumayma was the residence of the Banū ʿAbbās.[230] Beyond the obvious toponymic confusion, a different aspect may also explain this uncertainty. The *Anonymous History of the Abbasids* reports that Muḥammad b. al-Ḥanafiyya, not wanting to choose sides in the conflict between Ibn al-Zubayr and ʿAbd al-Malik, left Mecca for Ayla, where he remained until Ibn al-Zubayr's death;[231] he then settled his family in al-Ṭāʾif with ʿAbd Allāh b. ʿAbbās and his kin.[232] As mentioned above, Ibn ʿAbbās advised his family to settle in Syria just before his death, and they ultimately chose to reside in al-Ḥumayma under the leadership of ʿAlī b. ʿAbd Allāh.[233] The ambiguity of the location would ultimately be combined with an erroneous attribution arising from the subsequent peregrinations of the Alids and the Abbasids, who were closely related at the time.[234]

Al-Ḥumayma seems to be the sole "Syrian" survivor of an Abbasid *memoria* that was definitively reoriented toward Iraq in the historiography. Although this Syrian past was not completely erased, this period of Abbasid history was largely buried, thus generally masking its future prospects. The Abbasid Revolution began in Syria so that it could later return there after having garnered support from the eastern regions of the empire. Moreover, after the coup of 132/750, other Abbasids, in particular ʿAbd Allāh b. ʿAlī and his brother Ṣāliḥ, appropriated both the Umayyad and Abbasid Syrian space. The caliphs themselves, like al-Manṣūr at al-Rāfiqa or al-Rashīd at Raqqa, maintained relationships with the province, to say nothing of al-Mutawakkil's later abortive attempt to reinstall the caliphate in Damascus.[235] We shall return in greater detail below to these Abbasid power dynamics.[236]

Robinson has recently remarked that, paradoxically – but unsurprisingly – studying al-Ḥumayma has revealed nothing of the Abbasid Revolution, despite

228 Yāqūt, *Muʿjam*, vol. I, 356–7. These three definitions can be traced to a single location, see Lecker, "Biographical Notes," 59, note 161.

229 Lecker, "Biographical Notes," 58–61; Lammens, "L'ancienne frontière."

230 Yāqūt, *Muʿjam*, vol. II, 307: "*kāna manzil banī al-ʿAbbās*." See also Abū al-Fidāʾ, *Taqwīm*, 228.

231 This point is unclear. Ibn Saʿd, *al-Ṭabaqāt*, vol. V, 107–9, indicates that Muḥammad b. al-Ḥanafiyya went to Ayla, but that he was at al-Ṭāʾif at the time of Ibn al-Zubayr's death.

232 *Akhbār al-dawla*, 107–8.

233 Ibn Saʿd reports that they went to Ayla first, *al-Ṭabaqāt*, vol. V, 108.

234 ʿAbd Allāh, a son of Muḥammad b. al-Ḥanafiyya, died at al-Ḥumayma under the caliphate of Sulaymān b. ʿAbd al-Malik. See Ibn Saʿd, *al-Ṭabaqāt*, vol. V, 328.

235 On this point, see Cobb, "Al-Mutawakkil's Damascus."

236 See below, Ch. 8.

archaeological digs at the site where the insurrection began.[237] While it is not surprising that material culture and land use provide little information on the subject, these excavations are nevertheless helpful in uncovering the Syrian roots of the Abbasid family under the late Umayyads: archaeology thus reveals a Syrian-Abbasid historical *memoria*. Without denying the existence of certain select spaces of power, opposing a Syrian-Umayyad memory with an Iraqi-Abbasid memory is largely a later Abbasid historiographic construction that emerged in the context of the new identities taking shape at the turn of the ninth–tenth centuries. In its quest for legitimacy, the new Abbasid dynasty tried to minimise – or suppress – its Syrian lineage by emphasising its links to Iraq instead, imposing a strong dichotomy in the sources. An additional factor has intensified this oppositional tendency in modern scholarship: the anti-Umayyad policies of the early Abbasids were often conflated with their Syrian policies. Syria thus become an outlet for the new caliphate's hatred of their old political rivals.[238]

While the Abbasid family's ties to the Syrian space were subject to strategies of oblivion, as we shall see below, this relationship was on the contrary the basis for the construction of Umayyad legitimacy.

4.3.3 *The Syrian Space in Umayyad Ideology: Appropriation of Solomonic Precedent*

The Abbasid chronographers indirectly reinforced the connection between the Umayyads and Syria by insisting on their own Iraqi roots. This does not mean that the Umayyads themselves did not stress their attachment to the province where they had held power; rather, it seems that this link was used by the Umayyads in constructing the ideology of their dynasty. To these ends, different authorities were invoked as models of inspiration and wisdom. One figure rose above the others in the Syrian pantheon of the Arab authors: King

237 Robinson, *Islamic Historiography*, 53. For the excavations at al-Ḥumayma, see the works of Oleson and his team listed in the bibliography. See also a substantial presentation of the archaeological mission supplemented by a vast bibliography at this address: http://web.uvic.ca/~jpoleson/Humayma/HumaymaDesc.html (consulted 11 October 2022). On the Abbasid Revolution, see below, Ch. 7.

238 This is the portrait painted by Lammens; discussing Abbasid Syria, he notes that "trembling under a power it considered foreign, from which it continually experienced hostility, it was systematically excluded from participation in any affairs." See Lammens, *La Syrie*, 89.

Solomon.[239] Contrary to the Christian tradition,[240] the Arab authors' image of Sulaymān b. Dāwūd was unambiguous both in the sources and the Qur'ān: it was extremely positive, and conferred prestige and legitimacy.

The Arab geographers associate a large number of sites with this mythic figure, from Jerusalem to Palmyra, Baalbek to Hebron.[241] Beauty or monumental aspects are frequently cited as justification for this affiliation. Aided by djinns, Solomon was capable of achieving architectural wonders impossible for normal mortals. However, the sources go even further. While the architectural landscape of Syria owed much to this ancient king of Israel, several Umayyad caliphs were also associated with Solomon. This connection poses the question of an apologetic Umayyad discourse using Solomon as an ideal model and claiming direct descent from his line.[242] If this is not the case, then how do we explain the persistence of this theme in the Abbasid sources? Did the authors of the second Islamic dynasty preserve earlier discourses because it was unavoidable, or did they produce these discourses themselves? The first hypothesis is much more likely, and we shall see below that there is significant evidence for the Umayyad production of these narratives.

4.3.3.1 Solomon: An Architect, Wise and Just

One of Solomon's most obvious attributes is that he was a builder, and a number of legendary constructions are linked to his name.[243] His architectural prowess is the reason for his association in several Arab sources with al-Walīd b. ʿAbd al-Malik, who built the mosque of Damascus and thus was known as an architect in his own right. Another direct and "palpable" link was established between these two rulers during the initial work on the construction of the mosque of Damascus. The anecdote, related by the Damascene Ibn ʿAsākir, states that during work on the mosque's southern wall, a mysterious and indecipherable tablet was discovered; the Byzantines and the Hebrews were unable to offer any assistance, and only Wahb b. Munabbih[244] was able to provide a translation. The text, which began with the *basmala* and was addressed

239 See Borrut, "La Syrie de Salomon." On the use of these mythic figures in the Muslim world, see Aigle, *Figures mythiques*, and Neuwirth et al., *Myths, Historical Archetypes and Symbolic Figures in Arabic Literature*.

240 Le Goff, *Saint Louis*, 389; Langlamet, "Pour ou contre Salomon."

241 On this point, see Borrut, "La Syrie de Salomon," 108–13. The role of archetypal figures in the *awāʾil* genre has been discussed by Al-Azmeh, "Chronophagous Discourse," 165.

242 Soucek, "Solomon's Throne/Solomon's Bath," 114.

243 Soucek, "The Temple of Solomon."

244 On whom see de Prémare, "Wahb b. Munabbih." On this episode, see Khoury, *Wahb b. Munabbih*, 195–6.

to Adam's son, advised concern for the afterlife and acting properly in order to prepare as best one could. It ended with the following statement: "this was written during the time of Solomon son of David, peace be upon them both."[245] This curious passage attests to the desire to affirm continuity between the son of David and the great caliph and architect al-Walīd by emphasising the affiliation between the two men. Moreover, both sovereigns' architectural achievements were emblematic of their piety; Solomon and al-Walīd oversaw the construction of the most famous religious edifices of their respective eras. The connection between the construction of the Temple and that of the mosque of Damascus is significant. Descriptions of the two undertakings in the sources are very similar, and read as *topoi* of these monumental constructions:[246] massive sums invested in the projects, importance assigned to the length of time taken to build them, the magnificence of their interiors and exteriors, etc. Ibn Khaldūn identifies Jerusalem as the site of religious continuity between Solomon's day and the Islamic period due to the successive monuments erected in this sacred space.[247] And alongside this geographic continuum, Solomon is the unifying link between all the *ahl al-kitāb*, or people of the Book, adherents of the three major monotheistic religions.

Solomon is the quintessential wise king of the Old Testament[248] and the Qurʾān. Logically, then, disagreeing parties should refer themselves to him; for this reason, he takes on the role of definitive reference or infallible model.[249] Ibn al-Faqīh offers a good example of how this model was used in an epistolary exchange between al-Walīd and the Byzantine emperor during the construction of the great mosque of Damascus:

245 *TMD*, vol. I, 9–10, trans. 14. See also al-Rabaʿī, *Kitāb faḍāʾil al-Shām*, 35.

246 For example, Ibn al-Faqīh, *Mukhtaṣar*, 98 ff., 106 ff., trans. 121 ff., 131 ff.

247 Ibn Khaldūn, *The Muqaddimah*, vol. II, 258–63. However, the passage is obscure, since Ibn Khaldūn, after mentioning the works of ʿUmar b. al-Khaṭṭāb near the Rock, notes: "Al-Walīd b. ʿAbd al-Malik later on devoted himself to constructing the Mosque of (the Rock) in the style of the Muslim mosques, as grandly as God wanted him to do it. He had done the same with the Mosque in Mecca and the Mosque of the Prophet in Medina, as well as the Mosque of Damascus." If Ibn Khaldūn is still describing the Dome of the Rock, he is almost certainly confusing al Walīd with his father ʿAbd al-Malik, even if the date at which construction was completed remains a subject of debate. See Raby and Johns, *Bayt al-Maqdis*; Elad, "Why did ʿAbd al-Malik" and *Medieval Jerusalem*; Grafman and Rosen-Ayalon, "The Two Great Syrian Umayyad Mosques;" Johns, *Bayt al-Maqdis*; Robinson, *ʿAbd al-Malik*, 1–9.

248 Le Goff, *Saint Louis*, 394 and 592–4.

249 For another example of his justice, see Dakhlia, "Sous le vocable de Salomon."

> after he [al-Walīd] had demolished the church, the Byzantine emperor wrote to him thus: "You have demolished the church that your father saw fit to leave [standing]. If what you have done was just, then your father was at fault; if it was needless, then you have contradicted your father." Al-Walīd, not knowing how to respond, asked among his people … Al-Farazdaq replied: Tell him, O Commander of the Faithful, by the word of Allāh:[250] "David and Solomon, when they gave judgment concerning the tillage, when the sheep of the people strayed there, etc." through the words "judgment[251] and knowledge;" al-Walīd wrote to the emperor using these words, and the emperor did not reply.[252]

Citing this Qurʾānic passage gave al-Walīd the best possible justification: Solomonic precedent. This anecdote, reported in a very similar manner by Ibn ʿAsākir,[253] demonstrates direct use of the Solomonic model by the Umayyads and perhaps, more specifically, by authors concerned with conferring legitimacy on the Umayyads.

The Solomonic model of the just ruler may also be at work in the portrayals of ʿUmar b. ʿAbd al-ʿAzīz and Hishām b. ʿAbd al-Malik as righteous caliphs,[254] following in the footsteps of Muʿāwiya. Although the illustrious king of Israel was not explicitly referenced in these depictions, making a comparison – conscious or not – between the sovereigns was a likely eventuality. This conjecture, however, is a delicate one, as the medieval Arab authors' imagination passed through the filter of *adab* is a question well outside the scope of this investigation.

4.3.3.2 Umayyad Ideology and Solomonic Legitimacy

More conclusive links between Solomon and the Umayyads can be found at a later date in the works of Ibn Khaldūn. Although the elements described above aided in legitimating certain caliphs, royal power and governing prowess were at the heart of these associations between Solomon and the Umayyad rulers.

For Ibn Khaldūn, political virtues were the domain of Muʿāwiya, the quintessential Syrian ruler, and he transferred these skills to his Sufyanid and Marwanid "descendants." Ibn Khaldūn attempts to rehabilitate the Umayyads, portraying the best of them as Solomon's "direct" heirs. Solomon's name is

250 *Qurʾān* 21:78–9, trans. Arberry.

251 Blachère translates this as "illumination," *Qurʾān* 21:79, trans. Arberry.

252 Ibn al-Faqīh, *Mukhtaṣar*, 106–7, trans. 130.

253 *TMD*, ed. by the Arab Academy in Damascus, vol. II, 26–7, trans. Élisséeff, 40–1.

254 For ʿUmar II, see Borrut, "Entre tradition et histoire," 359–64. On Hishām, see for example the episode reported by al-Ṭabarī, vol. II, 1731, trans. vol. XXVI, 73.

invoked not only to legitimise the choice of a successor, but also to justify Muʿāwiya's establishment of the dynastic principle that would be perpetuated thereafter:

> When royal authority is obtained and we assume that one person has it all for himself, no objection can be raised if he uses it for the various ways and aspects of the truth. Solomon and his father David had the royal authority of the Israelites for themselves, as the nature of royal authority requires, and it is well known how great a share in prophecy and truth they possessed. Likewise, Muʿāwiyah appointed Yazīd as his successor, because he was afraid of the dissolution of the whole thing, in as much as the Umayyads did not like to see the power handed over to any outsider. Had Muʿāwiyah appointed anyone else his successor, the Umayyads would have been against him. Moreover, they had a good opinion of (Yazīd). ... The same applies to Marwān b. al-Ḥakam and his son(s). Even though they were kings, their royal ways were not those of worthless men and oppressors. They complied with the intentions of the truth with all their energy, except when necessity caused them to do something (that was worthless). Such (a necessity existed) when there was fear that the whole thing might face dissolution. (To avoid that) was more important to them than any (other) intention. That this was (their attitude) is attested by the fact that they followed and imitated (the early Muslims). It is further attested by the information that the ancients had about their conditions. Mālik used the precedent of ʿAbd al-Malik (b. Marwān) as argument in the *Muwaṭṭa'*. Marwān belong to the first class of the men of the second generation, and his excellence is well known. The sons of ʿAbd al-Malik, then, came into power one after the other. Their outstanding religious attitude is well known. ʿUmar b. ʿAbd al-ʿAzīz reigned in between them. He eagerly and relentlessly aspired to (follow) the ways of the first four caliphs and the men around Muḥammad.[255]

The comparison is unequivocal: if these acts were legitimate, it was because of Solomonic precedent.[256] The valor and integrity of these men were thus beyond suspicion, and the superior interests of the state and the community justified their respective conducts, which conformed to the very nature of

255 Ibn Khaldūn, *The Muqaddimah*, vol. I, 422–3. On the initiation of the dynastic principal by the Umayyads, see Crone, *Medieval Islamic Political Thought*, 36–40.

256 Ibn Khaldūn established the same parallel for Muʿāwiya's accession of the throne thanks to Solomonic precedent. See *The Muqaddimah*, vol. II, 53.

politics. Besides power, Solomon embodied justice and the law: in other words, he was the ideal caliph. Muʿāwiya, presented as his most direct "successor," and the Marwanids thus reestablished a political system that had been weakened by the Christians and the Jews. The parallels with David and Solomon conferred perfect legitimacy on the beneficiaries of this comparison, which also allowed them to inscribe themselves into a line of political continuity. Al-Ṭabarī notes: "Hishām [b. ʿAbd al-Malik]'s rule (*mulk*) and authority (*sulṭān*) have lasted a long time. It is nearly twenty years. People say that Solomon asked his lord to bestow on him sovereignty such as should not belong to any after him. They do claim that that period was twenty years."[257]

What, then, is the origin of these elements affirming Umayyad legitimacy through Solomon, found in the works of Ibn Khaldūn as well as numerous other Abbasid-era authors, in particular the geographers? Several points demonstrate that this phenomenon can be traced back to the Umayyad period itself:

- The famous Umayyad poet al-Farazdaq stated unequivocally that al-Walīd b. ʿAbd al-Malik inherited governance from his father just as Solomon did from David, and that it was a bequest from God (*niḥlan min Allāh*).[258] Jarīr echoed this statement:[259] this comparison is well-attested in Umayyad poetry.[260]
- The apocalypses dedicated to the Umayyads also reflect this view. A Judeo-Arabic apocalyptic offers a striking example: Muʿāwiya is presented as one who "will restore the walls of the temple;" ʿAbd al-Malik as one who "will rebuild the temple of the Everlasting," referring to the Dome of the Rock; and Sulaymān as a "valiant warrior, bearing the name of a king of Israel."[261]
- Although they do not explicitly mention Solomon by name, the extant letters attributed to certain caliphs – in conditions too complex to examine here – in particular al-Walīd b. Yazīd, attest to the same concern with rooting Umayyad legitimacy in the precedent of the prophets.[262]

257 Al-Ṭabarī, vol. II, 1739–40, trans. vol. XXVI, 82–3; see Shoshan, *Poetics*, 95. The length of Solomon's reign is generally estimated at forty years (1 Kings 11:42), see notably al-Masʿūdī, *Murūj*, vol. I, 112, trans. Pellat vol. I, 46. On the symbolism of the number 40, see Conrad, "Abraha and Muḥammad."

258 Al-Farazdaq, cited in Rubin, "Prophet and Caliphs," 99.

259 Jarīr, cited in Crone and Hinds, *God's Caliph*, 44.

260 Rubin, "Prophets and Caliphs," 93–9; Crone and Hinds, *God's Caliph*, 44.

261 Lévi, "Une apocalypse judéo-arabe," 179.

262 See Crone and Hinds, *God's Caliph*, 117–26, and Rubin, "Prophets and Caliphs," 88–93.

- The letters of ʿAbd al-Ḥamīd Kātib, the secretary of the last Umayyad caliph Marwān II, express similar sentiments, as Wadād al-Qāḍī has shown.[263]
- Alongside these texts, there is also the evidence provided by Marwanid architecture. Did not ʿAbd al-Malik build the Dome of the Rock on the same land where Solomon's temple once stood in an effort to present himself as the prophet's rightful successor? And if we acknowledge the fact that ʿAbd al-Malik went so far as to name one of his sons after Solomon, is it not also reasonable to assume that his policies were essentially Solomonic in nature?[264]
- Umayyad art, preserved in particular in the civil architecture of the caliphs, like the famous "desert palaces," confirms the Umayyad caliphs' constant concern with situating themselves within a continuity of prophets and great figures from the Qurʾān and the Old Testament. The Umayyad baths of Quṣayr ʿAmra in present-day Jordan are evidence of this tendency, especially with their emphasis on the figure of Adam.[265]
- The site of Khirbat al-Mafjar was likely "a symbolic edifice created to evoke the memory of both the throne and bath of Solomon."[266] Following Soucek's conclusions, the caliph's statue overlooking the entry to the bath was placed on a pedestal of lions symbolising Solomon's throne, which was protected by the same ferocious beasts (fig. 4.1). The site's patron was presented in the manner of the great king of Israel, whose heir he claimed to be.[267] The identity of Khirbat al-Mafjar's founder is a subject of debate. Hamilton proposes al-Walīd b. Yazīd, but this is only a guess, as some verses attributed to the future al-Walīd II in which he presents himself as the "son of David" have been used to support this theory.[268] These verses attest once more to the tenuous links connecting the Umayyad rulers and Solomon.

A wide range of evidence indicates that Solomon's recurring association with various Umayyad caliphs in the sources emerged during the first Islamic dynasty.[269] It was an important aspect of the political ideology developed by the Umayyads to affirm their caliphal legitimacy and establish their

263 Al-Qāḍī, "The Religious Foundation," especially 244–8.

264 On this point, see Robinson, *ʿAbd al-Malik*, 7. See also Flood, *The Great Mosque*, 239.

265 If we follow Fowden's conclusions, *Quṣayr ʿAmra*, 138 ff.

266 Soucek, "Solomon's Throne/Solomon's Bath," 124. On Khirbat al-Mafjar, see Hamilton, *Khirbat al-Mafjar*.

267 Soucek, "Solomon's Throne/Solomon's Bath," 122.

268 See Hamilton, *Walid and His Friends*, 148, and Soucek, "Solomon's Throne/Solomon's Bath," 123.

269 See Crone and Hinds, *God's Caliph*, 115.

authority. While the Abbasids would later present themselves as the heirs of the prophets,[270] Solomon included,[271] the Umayyads had a distinct advantage: they shared his space of power.

4.3.3.3 Solomon and the Syrian Pact

Establishing continuity between the Solomonic period and the Islamic era legitimised Arab control of the spaces they shared with their illustrious predecessor. Wielding power in the spaces once governed by these ancient heroes brought the new rulers in proximity to the old, even more so when the sacred functions of these sites were preserved between the mythic days of Solomon and the Islamic period. However, it should be noted that these frequent allusions to the forebears of Antiquity belonged to the discourse of *adab*.[272] That Solomon, Nebuchadnezzar or even Alexander were mentioned in conjunction with the geographical domain of the Muslim world attests to this fact. Syria is particularly fertile ground for the study of these Solomonic sites or monuments because it was the geographic centre of his power. The various implied parallels between Solomon and certain Umayyad caliphs read primarily as apologetic discourse. Beyond the personal qualities mentioned above, the Syrian space was the main aspect linking Solomon to the caliphs of Damascus. Be that as it may, the literary elements established during the Umayyad era resisted the destructive influences of the vagaries of transmission and subsequent historiographic projects, including those aimed at effacing Umayyad legitimacy. Solomon's image in the Islamic sources provides access to an Umayyad political program that is otherwise lost, or largely forgotten. It is also interesting to note that some of the most recent studies on ancient Israel have shown that Solomon's importance and notoriety were relative, and should be put into perspective.[273] Solomon is both a historical figure and a symbol of memory, and the Umayyad use of his image heavily exploited this latter role.

270 Al-Ṭabarī, vol. III, 1112, trans. vol. XXXII, 199–200, cites a letter of al-Ma'mūn affirming that the caliphs were the heirs of the prophets.

271 For example, see Ibn ʿAbd Rabbih, *al-ʿIqd*, vol. II, 130, where al-Manṣūr is explicitly designated as the heir (*ʿalā irth min …*) of Solomon, Job and Joseph. See Crone and Hinds, *God's Caliph*, 81, note 146.

272 See Dakhlia, *Le divan des rois*, 21 ff.

273 See Finkelstein and Silberman, *Les rois sacrés de la Bible*, and their now-classic study, *La Bible dévoilée*, especially 194 ff.

FIGURE 4.1 Khirbat al-Mafjar: Statue of the caliph on a pedestal of lions

Behind these strong ties lay a reciprocity based on respect for sites connected with Solomon's memory and control over shared spaces. When this pact was ultimately broken by Marwān II, the last Umayyad caliph of the East, the dynasty's fate was sealed:

> it is said that [when] Marwān ... demolished the mural of Tadmur [Palmyra], he arrived at a plastered room closed by a lock, which he opened: there was a woman inside, resting her head, and on one of her tresses lay a piece of copper bearing this inscription: "In your name, O Allāh! I am Tadmur, daughter of Ḥassān. May God curse anyone who approaches me and enters my chamber." [The narrator adds:] By Allāh! Marwān then reigned for but a few days; ʿAbd Allāh b. ʿAlī, having set off on campaign, soon killed him, dispersed his cavalry and destroyed his army. It is also said that he had fulfilled the woman's invocation. It is said that the city of Tadmur was built by Solomon.[274]

The parallel here is pushed to its limit. The construction of a Syrian-Umayyad *memoria* by appropriating Solomon's image is clearly obvious in this anecdote. However, while his image was a source of legitimacy, it also carried certain limitations. This affiliation rests on the exercise of power in a shared space: Syria. Marwān II's transition of the "capital" to Ḥarrān in Upper Mesopotamia, shifting the locus of power away from Damascus and Syria, should perhaps be seen as the beginning of the end for this Syrian compact. Crossing the Euphrates signalled the breaking of this Syrian-Solomonic pact; certain authors used this fact to justify the downfall of the Umayyads, who claimed Solomonic descent and affiliation but were no longer entirely Syrian.

Second/eighth-century Syria's position among the memories that make up Islamic historiography was ambiguous; it was either memorialised at any cost or plunged into oblivion. The chronographers' processes of selection in the period following the caliphate's return to Baghdad could not completely surmount the difficulties presented by elements that were too firmly entrenched. The unavoidable Umayyad "realms of memory" justified the construction of a "historiographic skeleton" that reduced Umayyad history to a common kernel in nearly all the sources. The Abbasid caliphs could not ignore this Umayyad past that was simultaneously abhorrent and a source of useful precedent. Affirming the political continuity of the caliphate demanded that this memory of Islamic power be rehabilitated: the Umayyads thus passed gradually from adversity to alterity. In truth, their memory was too firmly rooted to be completely erased.

274 Ibn al-Faqīh, *Mukhtaṣar*, 110, trans. 134.

The cultural landscape built by the Umayyads inscribed the dynasty permanently into time and space. Unable to attack the Umayyads' temporal continuity, the Abbasid historians focused their efforts on the spatial traces of their predecessors. The monumental legacy of the Damascus caliphs formed an inseparable bond between Syria and the first Islamic dynasty, between their power and the space in which it was exercised and which it had ultimately helped to shape; the Umayyads themselves had granted Solomon a privileged place in their ideological program, thus affirming their deep connection to Syria. The solution was that from this moment on, memories were confined in distinct spaces: Umayyad Syria, Abbasid Iraq. The *memoria* of the other occupied a space that was presented as hostile; the border between these two regions was clearly marked by the Euphrates. This deliberate choice resulted in a double oblivion – that of Umayyad Iraq, despite the continued interest of the caliphs in the area, and Abbasid Syria, despite the fact that the Abbasids lived there for more than sixty years and formulated their plans to seize power in the region. However, these strategies of oblivion were not equally successful, largely due to processes of transmission. For this reason, we shall continue our quest in search of these fragments of pasts that refuse to remain buried by tracing not the silences, but the "murmurs." We shall seek out these "alternative pasts"[275] in order to untangle the threads of this historicised memory, torn between an oblivion that was not always possible and a remembrance that was frequently necessary.

275 Geary, *Phantoms of Remembrance*, 21, 177.

CHAPTER 5

The Creation of Umayyad Heroes: Maslama b. ʿAbd al-Malik, Combat Hero

> A prince, therefore, must not have any other object nor any other thought, nor must he adopt anything as his art but war … because that is the only art befitting one who commands. This discipline is of such efficacy that not only does it maintain those who were born princes, but it enables men of private station on many occasions to rise to that position. On the other hand, it is evident that when princes have given more thought to delicate refinements than to military concerns, they have lost their state.[1]

•••

> During every military campaign, he was surrounded by historiographers …, painters and engravers …, in command of his own glory, Louis XIV created the foundations of this representation of "absolute power" that war, and only war, allowed him to embody.[2]

∴

Two elements discussed in the previous chapter determine the continued course of this inquiry. First, we saw that Abbasid historiography, despite its reputation for hostility to the first Islamic dynasty, preserved certain "positive exceptions" among the Marwanids, ensuring the redemption of their memory; and second, we know that the Umayyads invoked mythic figures like Solomon to construct their ideology. The combination of these two elements invites an examination of the modalities that presided over the genesis of these Umayyad figures who would later be rehabilitated by Abbasid historiographers, and the

1 Machiavelli, *The Prince*, 50.
2 Cornette, *Le roi de guerre*, 249.

DOI:10.1163/9789004466326_007

role of the Umayyad caliphs in creating these heroic personae.[3] Two major Marwanid figures stand out in this regard: Maslama b. ʿAbd al-Malik, the war hero, and ʿUmar b. ʿAbd al-ʿAzīz, the "pious" caliph. Although their personal relationship was complicated, these two protagonists both figure prominently in the sources. Moreover, it is possible to show that certain elements of their respective images were developed earlier, during the Umayyad era, and that these elements can be traced through the Christian sources that bear the imprint of a now-lost Islamic historiography. We must thus examine the motivations behind these historiographic constructions and the reasons for their dissemination throughout the different historiographic corpora of the medieval Near East; we may then shed some light on the conditions in which these heroic Umayyad figures were created, in a constant tug-of-war between history and tradition. We shall return to ʿUmar II in the following chapter; here, we shall focus on Maslama, whose courage, power, and bravery exemplified the quintessential hero.

Carl Von Clausewitz stated that "war is … a strange trinity, composed of the original violence of its essence …, of the play of probabilities and chance … and of the subordinate character of a political tool."[4] The third term of this equation is especially pertinent with respect to the Umayyad "century of war,"[5] which was marked by the tremendous territorial expansion of the *dār al-islām* initiated by the caliphs of Damascus; if we follow Blankinship's conclusions, the end of this expansion precipitated the Umayyads' downfall.[6] Maslama b. ʿAbd al-Malik was one of the most prominent figures of this period: perhaps more than any other, he embodied the ideal of the Muslim war hero. The sources credit him with an astonishing number of military campaigns, whose geographical scope ranged from Asia Minor to the Caucasus to Iraq. During this lengthy period of activity, his revered military prowess brought death to the enemies of the caliphate, both those who posed external threats – the Byzantines, the Turks and the Khazars – and internal ones – the rebel Yazīd b. al-Muhallab. His career spanned nearly thirty years; he first appears in the textual sources during an expedition in Byzantine territory in 86/705, the final year of his father's reign, and exits the stage after his last battles in the Caucasus in 112–113/730–732. It was only in the final years of his life, from 114/732 until his

3 On the mechanisms at work in these constructions, see Fabre's stimulating contributions, "L'atelier des héros."
4 Von Clausewitz, *On War*, 18.
5 I borrow this expression (*siècle de guerre*), used in the context of the seventeenth century in Europe, from Cornette, *Le roi de guerre*, 23.
6 Blankinship, *The End of the Jihād State*.

death in 120/738, that he took his leave of the battlefield for a more peaceful life at his residence in northern Syria.[7]

In the Islamic cultural memory, Maslama remains best-known for his campaigns against the Byzantines, the pinnacle being his expedition against Constantinople in 97–99/715–717. Our inquiry must thus begin here; his Caucasian campaigns against the Turks and the Khazars, to which we shall return, received less attention in the sources, a fact that may explain the relative disinterest of modern scholars in this subject. To follow Maslama, we must similarly tread the soldier's path, a route that will inevitably lead us outside the geographic bounds of the Syrian space. The general embodied Syria, which projected itself outward in the context of the expansionist policies imposed – or retracted – by the caliphate. The deeper object of our inquiry here is not the military theatres themselves, but the processes by which they were historicised. Maslama's example is an informative and valuable one: his is one of the best-documented cases in the sources, a fact that aids our understanding of how these foundational Umayyad historical figures were constructed in the Syrian space.

5.1 The Siege of Constantinople: Military Failure, Narrative Success

Maslama owes most of his fame to the expedition he led against the Byzantine capital that resulted in a lengthy siege of the city;[8] it is somewhat paradoxical that his greatest military feat ended in resounding failure.[9] However, this episode has attracted a great deal of attention in modern scholarship. Studies dedicated to the expedition of 97–99/715–717, many of which are already

7 For an overview of Maslama's career, see Rotter, "Maslama b. ʿAbd al-Malik." The Umayyad prince owned numerous domains between Raqqa and Ḥarrān, as well as in the region of Antioch and Alexandretta. See al-Balādhurī, *Futūḥ*, 149, 151, trans. 228–9, 232–3, echoed in Ibn Shaddād, *al-Aʿlāq*, 305, 366–7, 398–9, trans. 263, 99, 6–7. The most important site associated with his name is Ḥiṣn Maslama, near Balīkh, which provoked the geographers' admiration, in particular for its irrigation systems. See Yāqūt, *Muʿjam*, vol. II, 265. The site has generally been identified as Madīnat al-Fār, and was excavated under the direction of Haase. See his publications: "Is Madinat al-Far," "Madīnat al-Fār," "Une ville des débuts de l'islam" and "The Excavations." See also Bartl and Hauser (eds.), *Continuity and Change in Northern Mesopotamia*, and Bonner, *Aristocratic Violence*, 141.

8 On the Muslim perception of Constantinople and the Byzantine Empire, see El-Cheikh, *Byzantium*.

9 On the "utility" of this defeat, see below.

outdated,[10] have been aimed at organising the profusion of information in the sources in order to distinguish historical fact from the "legendary" aspects of Maslama's persona; Canard has identified and collated most of the pertinent information.[11] The scattered nature of the information related to Maslama in the historical sources complicates any attempt at a more global approach. However, he is most often portrayed as the ideal hero fighting on the frontiers, the *ghāzī*, champion of *jihād*.[12] Despite certain medieval authors' harsh judgment of his inability to take Constantinople,[13] this defeat did not ultimately diminish his notoriety. Anthropologists have demonstrated that a hero's individual victories or defeats are secondary, as each part is weighed against the whole of his achievements; in other words, "heroism is not linked to the result of the enterprise, but to the acceptance of risk and suffering, and ultimately, death."[14]

5.1.1 *Epic Tradition and Monumental Legacy*

The great Umayyad warriors of the Byzantine front, foremost among them Maslama and his epigone al-Baṭṭāl, have long been subjects of widespread interest and numerous epic cycles. While we cannot analyse in detail here their place or that of the broader myth surrounding the seizure of Constantinople in the popular literature of the medieval Islamic period,[15] it is nevertheless impossible to mention these figures without evoking certain tales from the *Thousand and One Nights*[16] and in particular from the *Hundred and One Nights*.[17] The Arabic epic poem *Dhāt al-Himma* and the Turkish *Sayyid Baṭṭāl*[18] also extol the legendary exploits of Maslama and his heirs. In the sections most

10 Brooks, "The Arabs in Asia Minor" and "The Campaign of 716–718;" Wellhausen, "Die Kämpfe der Araber mit den Romäern;" Canard, "Les expéditions;" Guilland, "L'expédition;" Lilie, *Die Byzantinische Reaktion*.

11 Canard, "Les expéditions," especially 94–102 and 112–121. See also Gabrieli, "L'eroe omayyade."

12 The bibliography on this subject is vast. In the context of the Byzantine borders, discussed further in the following pages, see Bonner, *Aristocratic Violence*. On the broader theme of *jihād*, see Donner, "The Sources of Islamic Conceptions of War," Morabia, *Le ǧihâd*, in addition to Bonner, *Le jihad* and Cook, *Understanding Jihad*.

13 In particular, see *Kitāb al-ʿuyūn*, 27–8.

14 Albert, "Du martyr à la star," 18.

15 For an overview of this question, see Lyons, *The Arabian Epic*.

16 The tale of ʿUmar al-Nuʿmān and his sons is primarily about an expedition against Constantinople. Canard, "Les expéditions," 114 ff.

17 In particular, see the stories of Sulaymān b. ʿAbd al-Malik and Maslama. Canard, "Les expéditions," 115.

18 On this Turkish romance, see Mélikoff, "Al-Baṭṭāl."

relevant to this study,[19] the Arabic epic describes a figure named al-Ṣaḥṣāḥ, the eldest son of the heroine Dhāt al-Himma and hero of the expedition against Constantinople, which he led alongside Maslama at the behest of the caliph ʿAbd al-Malik. The narrative recounts the Byzantine use of Greek fire to destroy the Muslim navy, whose men were only saved from this catastrophe by the courage of al-Ṣaḥṣāḥ. This event was followed by the siege of Constantinople, which dragged on so long that Maslama built a new city facing the Byzantine capital where his men lived off of agriculture and trade awaiting their enemies' capitulation. Leo, the Byzantine emperor, under the looming threat of famine, negotiated with Maslama, who agreed to the retreat of his troops, thus ending the blockade of the city. The Marwanid general made the construction of a mosque in Constantinople a condition of the treaty, and demanded that he be allowed to enter the city and even the Hagia Sophia itself on horseback. Leo accepted his terms, and once the treaty had been signed, the Muslims entered the city, prayed at the mosque, and sullied the walls of the basilica with their horses' excrement. They then returned to Syria.

The majority of the episodes included in these texts are constructed on a core of information well-attested in certain sources. These epic poems, however, pose a number of difficulties with respect to their dates of composition, authorship, and manuscript traditions; their emergence may be traceable to the time of the Byzantine Reconquest and the Crusades, two tumultuous periods for the Muslims. In a series of studies on *Dhāt al-Himma*, Canard concluded that the poem was composed in two distinct phases: the first focused on Maslama, while the second concerned al-Baṭṭāl, who had been largely ignored during the Abbasid period.[20] These two sections of the poem arose out of different eras and origins, and the foundations of the first may have been elaborated under the Umayyads. In any case, the poem as a whole was reworked during the Crusades. These elements were known in northern Syria around 390/1000, as they served as the basis for the Byzantine epic poem of Digenes Akritas.[21] In the context of the present study, *Dhāt al-Himma* represents the "final version" of the Maslama myth, and thus it is important that we examine the genesis of these traditions.

Alongside Maslama's central role in heroic literature, certain sites of memory remained attached to his name in Byzantine territory, even in the heart of

---

19 The brief summary that follows is based on Canard's various studies on the subject. See Canard, "Les expéditions," 117 ff; "Dhū al-Himma;" "Del-hemma;" "Les principaux personnages."

20 See Grégoire, "Comment Sayyid Baṭṭâl."

21 Canard, "Dhū al-Himma."

Constantinople itself. Ibn Khurradādhbih mentions an Arabic inscription in the mosque of Ephesus that commemorates Maslama's entry into the *Bilād al-Rūm*.[22] A well, the *ʿAyn Maslama*, at Abydos is associated with the Arab general;[23] according to al-Masʿūdī, it was there that he joined the Muslim fleet while preparing to besiege the capital.[24] Another author even tried to situate the tomb of Abū ʿUbayda b. al-Jarrāḥ, a famous companion of the Prophet, beneath the city's ramparts, affirming that he was killed there while fighting alongside Maslama![25] Although this account is pure legend, given that Abū ʿUbayda died in the plague of ʿAmwās in 18/639, its goal was to associate the great figures of early Islam with the Marwanid general's siege of Constantinople and the myth of the city's capture.[26]

Maslama's memory also remains attached to the mosque he built in the Byzantine capital, mentioned in the epic of *Dhāt al-Himma*. This fact is well-attested in the later Islamic sources, and the maintenance of this mosque was a longstanding topic of discussion between the Byzantines and Muslims in the centuries that followed;[27] during the Turkish capture of the city in 857/1453, the assailants were quick to visit Maslama's mosque.[28] Older texts also mention this place of Muslim worship. Ibn al-Faqīh (writing *c.*290/903) was almost certainly the first geographer to mention the mosque, albeit in a somewhat confusing passage.[29] The *De administrando imperio* by the Byzantine emperor Constantine VII Porphyrogenitus (913–959) offers more detail, and explicitly records the construction of a mosque at the request of the Umayyad prince in the *Praetorium*, a palace that also served as a prison for Arab captives.[30] This account more or less agrees with al-Muqaddasī's slightly later version of events,[31] which specifies that the general demanded Leo III build a house for

22 Ibn Khurradādhbih, *Kitāb al-masālik*, 106, trans. 78.

23 Ibn Khurradādhbih, *Kitāb al-masālik*, 104, trans. 75.

24 Al-Masʿūdī, *Murūj*, vol. II, 317, trans. Pellat vol. II, 277.

25 Al-Zuhrī, *Kitāb al-jughrāfiyā*, section 117; El-Cheikh, *Byzantium*, 211.

26 El-Cheikh, *Byzantium*, 211.

27 See the traditions collected by Canard, "Les expéditions," 94–8, and El-Cheikh, *Byzantium*, 210–1. On the restorations of the mosque, in addition to the sources mentioned by these two authors, see Ibn Shaddād, *al-Aʿlāq*, 325, trans. 206, which indicates work carried out in 441/1049–1050.

28 Canard, "Les expéditions," 97.

29 Ibn al-Faqīh, *Mukhtaṣar*, 145, trans. 174. On the Arab geographers' perception of Constantinople, see Marín, "Constantinopla en los geografos arabes."

30 Constantine Porphyrogenitus, *De administrando imperio*, 92, trans. 93. The use of the praetorium as a prison is noted by the same author in *Le livre des cérémonies*, ed. Reiske, vol. II, 592. See Canard, "Les expéditions," 97.

31 As Canard notes, "Les expéditions," 98.

prisoners of war, which led to the construction of a *dār al-balāṭ* near the *dār al-mulk*, on the other side of the hippodrome (*maydān*).[32] The geographer does not mention the foundation of a mosque at this time, and it should be assumed that, in light of the information provided by Constantine Porphyrogenitus, there was at the very least a prayer room in the *dār al-balāṭ*.

This epic literature affirms Maslama's triumph, and the elements inscribed in the topography of the Byzantine capital attest to the Muslims' "symbolic possession"[33] of Constantinople. We shall now turn our attention to the narratives of Maslama's siege in order to seek out the older elements that presided over their development.

5.1.2 *The Expedition against Constantinople in the Islamic Chronographies*

First, a note about context: this massive operation against the Byzantine capital was another in a continuing series of *ṣawā'if* led by Maslama in Asia Minor over the course of a decade. During these campaigns, the Marwanid military leader achieved several important victories, capturing the strategic cities of Tyana (Ṭawāna) and Amorium ('Ammūriyya). Spurred on by these successes, the Marwanid caliphs – like their Sufyanid predecessors – wanted to launch a direct attack on Constantinople. Plans for the offensive were apparently already in the works during al-Walīd's time, as Anastasios II (713–715) sent a supposedly diplomatic delegation to the caliph with the goal of gathering information on Muslim military strategy and preparations. The spies returned with distressing news regarding the size and might of the enemy's forces, and the emperor ordered that food and supplies be stocked in reserve, resumed construction of a naval fleet, restored the city's fortifications and reinforced its defenses with catapults and other siege weapons.[34] Al-Walīd's death derailed these plans for a time, but his successor Sulaymān eventually restarted the momentum, assembling his troops at Dābiq[35] and launching attacks on the city from land and sea. The offensive seemingly began at an opportune moment, as the Eastern Roman Empire was in a state of political turmoil and anarchy that resulted in Anastasios II's overthrow and replacement with Theodosius III (715–717). The Anatolic *Strategos* and future Leo III (717–741) did not recognise

32 Al-Muqaddasī, *Aḥsan*, 147. Blankinship, *The End of the Jihād State*, 3, sees it as an "Abbasid diplomatic mosque."

33 El-Cheikh, *Byzantium*, 211.

34 Theophanes, *Chronographia*, 383–4, trans. 534.

35 Dābiq was the traditional place for assembling troops before departing on campaigns into Byzantine territory. See Sourdel, "Dābiq."

Theodosius III's authority, and used the Muslim assault on the city as an opportunity to seize power and establish the Isaurian dynasty.

There are multiple accounts of the Muslim siege of the Byzantine capital in the Islamic and Christian sources,[36] and the episode is presented as the most important operation ever undertaken by the caliphate.[37] The caliphs of the first Islamic century seemingly aspired to take Constantinople as their own capital, a decidedly lofty ambition.[38] Umayyad poetry also widely attests to this desire.[39] Before we evaluate the information provided in the various sources, in particular the possible dates for when this historical information entered into circulation, we must identify what the Muslim authors wanted to pass down to future generations concerning these military feats. Two main versions of events live side-by-side in the sources, each with a number of variations. While these two major accounts agree on certain facts and details, their endings are radically different. One states that the operation ended in disastrous defeat, and roundly criticises the general who led his troops into this debacle (*version 1*); the other describes Maslama as a triumphant hero, leader of a symbolic victory over Constantinople (*version 2*).

Al-Ṭabarī recorded *version 1*. However, the account as a whole is somewhat confused, as three different *riwāyas* are presented one after the other, despite several obvious and mutually incompatible discrepancies. The initial narrative (*version 1.1*), related on the authority of al-Wāqidī, begins with a description of Maslama and his troops beneath the ramparts of Constantinople on an order from the caliph Sulaymān. This account is limited to logistics: Maslama orders his men to stock as much food as possible and then forbids them to touch it. He advises that they feed themselves with whatever they can gather on their raids, it being the time of year when the fields were yielding their first harvests.[40] In preparation for the approaching winter, wooden houses (*buyūtan min khashab*) were built. This first account then ends, without a single mention of

36 Despite the profusion of accounts in these sources, Kennedy has rightfully highlighted the relative lack of information on the composition of the Muslim army who undertook the expedition in 98–99/716–717, *The Armies of the Caliphs*, 47.

37 Blankinship, *The End of the Jihād State*, 31.

38 See El-Cheikh, *Byzantium*, 62. Umayyad Damascus was arranged in a layout similar to that of Constantinople; see Flood, *The Great Mosque*, 163–72. The Byzantine capital's port was also much admired, and likely inspired the development of port infrastructure along the Syrian coast, in particular at Tyre and Acre. See Borrut, "Architecture des espaces portuaires," "L'espace maritime syrien."

39 El-Cheikh, *Byzantium*, 34. See also the verses collected by Agha and Khalidi, "Poetry and Identity."

40 Other sources also report that the Muslims sustained themselves through agriculture. See al-Yaʿqūbī, *Taʾrīkh*, vol. II, 299; *Kitāb al-ʿuyūn*, 26–7.

combat, by noting that Maslama left the *Bilād al-Rūm* following the announcement of Sulaymān b. ʿAbd al-Malik's death.[41]

A second narrative then begins (*version 1.2*), this time on the authority of al-Madāʾinī. Sulaymān once again sends his brother off on campaign after assembling his troops at Dābiq. The Byzantines are nervous due to Maslama's reputation, and Leo proposes that they negotiate;[42] ʿUmar b. Hubayra[43] is chosen to lead the talks. Ibn Hubayra meets with the *Strategos*, who insults the Muslim emissary's leader, accusing him of thinking only of food, thus revealing his lack of intelligence,[44] and proposes that they pay tribute in exchange for peace. Ibn Hubayra relays the Byzantine offer to Maslama, who rejects it. In a second meeting with Leo, Ibn Hubayra informs him of this refusal while also criticising Maslama's conduct, claiming his judgment had been obscured by overeating at a sumptuous meal. It must then be inferred that the Muslim armies besieged Constantinople, as the patricians (*al-baṭāriqa*) promised Leo that they would make him emperor if he could rid them of Maslama. Leo, pretending that the Byzantines are ready to hand over control of the city, tells Maslama to burn his provisions: he convinces him to do so by claiming that the Byzantines are prepared for a siege but not an immediate attack, which would be signalled by the destruction of their reserves. Deceived by this ruse, Maslama executes this strange request and the Byzantines immediately profit from the starvation that soon overtakes their enemies. This second account

41 Al-Ṭabarī, vol. II, 1314–5, trans. vol. XXIV, 39–40. This account is reproduced almost identically in Balʿamī, 194. See also Ibn Qutayba, *Kitāb al-maʿārif*, 360.

42 Leo is described as fluent in Greek and Arabic, *Kitāb al-ʿuyūn*, 257. See Canard, "Les expéditions," 92, and El-Cheikh, "Byzantine Leaders."

43 Commander of the Muslim navy during the expedition, see Khalīfa b. Khayyāṭ, *Taʾrīkh*, vol. I, 425; al-Yaʿqūbī, *Taʾrīkh*, vol. II, 299. On this figure, see Crone, *Slaves*, 107.

44 Leo's allusion could be to either Sulaymān or Maslama; al-Ṭabarī's account is unclear. Powers, in his translation of the *Taʾrīkh al-rusul wa-al-mulūk* (vol. XXIV, 40, note 149), estimates that this is an allusion to the caliph. Balʿamī is also of this opinion; his reproduction of this same paragraph includes an explicit note that Sulaymān is the person intended (Balʿamī, 194–5). However, several lines below this passage, Ibn Hubayra addresses the exact same reproach to Maslama; elsewhere, the caliph ʿUmar II is the one criticising the Marwanid prince's gluttony (see Balʿamī, 212–3). It is possible that the two figures were criticised for similar reasons, hence the confusion in the sources. Sulaymān had the reputation of an insatiable eater, as al-Masʿūdī notes, *Murūj*, vol. V, 400–2, trans. Pellat vol. IV, pp. 858–9: "Sulaymān was a great eater … It is said that Sulaymān left his bath one day with a keen appetite; he ordered that preparations for his meal be hastened, and while waiting for it to be ready, he had every available morsel brought before him. He was served twenty lambs whose insides he devoured with forty rolls. When his dinner arrived, he ate with his guests as though he had not consumed a thing beforehand. It is also said that he left baskets filled with sweets at his bedside. When he awoke, his hand naturally fell into one of these baskets."

ends by stating that terrible famine ravaged the Muslim camp until the death of Sulaymān.[45]

The third *riwāya* (*version 1.3*), given without *isnād*, is similar to the preceding narrative, except that here Leo himself goes directly to Dābiq to meet with the caliph following the death of the Byzantine emperor, promising to hand him the Empire; Sulaymān then sends Maslama and his troops, accompanied by the *Strategos*, to lay siege to Constantinople. While the Muslim general gathered as many provisions as possible in preparation for the hostilities, Leo entered the city and proclaimed himself emperor. He then wrote to Maslama that he hoped to resolve the situation peacefully, and ordered that he give his supplies over to the city, claiming that this act would cause the inhabitants to view the Muslims as equals, thus allowing them to circulate freely in the capital. As in the previous narrative, Maslama is deceived and transports all of his army's provisions into Constantinople. The Muslims then suffer a terrible famine that forces them to eat "[domesticated] animals, skins (*al-julūd*),[46] tree roots, leaves – indeed, everything except dirt"![47] This drastic situation again supposedly drags on until the death of the caliph.[48] Later, al-Ṭabarī adds three other familiar details: the capture of the *madīnat al-Ṣaqāliba*, the city of Slavs, generally attributed to Maslama;[49] the attack on the Muslim troops, most likely during the siege, by the *Burjān*, the most important Bulghār group;[50] and finally ʿUmar II's recall of the troops besieging Constantinople, sending horses and provisions to the front to facilitate their retreat.[51]

45 Al-Ṭabarī, vol. II, 1315–6, trans. vol. XXIV, 40–1; Balʿamī, 194–5.

46 This could equally indicate the skins of animals or human beings; this remark may be the origin of the accusations of cannibalism found in several Christian sources. *Zuqnīn*, 158, trans. Harrak 151, trans. Palmer 63; Theophanes, *Chronographia*, 397, trans. 546; Łewond, trans. 108.

47 Al-Ṭabarī, vol. II, 1317, trans. vol. XXIV, 41; See also Balʿamī, 196; Ibn al-Athīr, vol. V, 12; Ibn Shaddād, *al-Aʿlāq*, 353, trans. 134.

48 Al-Ṭabarī, vol. II, 1316–7, trans. vol. XXIV, 41; Balʿamī, 195–6. See also the very similar account offered by al-Masʿūdī, *Tanbīh*, 165–6, trans. 226–7.

49 Al-Ṭabarī, vol. II, 1317, trans. XXIV, 42; al-Yaʿqūbī, *Taʾrīkh*, vol. II, 299; Ibn Shaddād, *al-Aʿlāq*, 353, trans. 134.

50 Al-Ṭabarī, vol. II, 1317, trans. XXIV, 42; Khalīfa b. Khayyāṭ, *Taʾrīkh*, vol. I, 425. On the *Burjān*, see Hrbek, "Bulghār." After the Bulghārs' devastating attacks, the caliph Sulaymān sent reinforcements to Maslama, but they were dispersed by the Slavs; see al-Ṭabarī, vol. II, 1317, trans. XXIV, 42. On the Bulghārs' important role during the siege in harassing Maslama's troops, see Gjuzelev, "La participation des Bulgares."

51 See al-Ṭabarī, vol. II, 1346, trans. vol. XXIV, 74; Khalīfa b. Khayyāṭ, *Taʾrīkh*, vol. I, 432; al-Yaʿqūbī, *Taʾrīkh*, vol. II, 302; Balʿamī, 208; al-Masʿūdī, *Tanbīh*, 319, trans. 413.

The *Kitāb al-ʿuyūn*, composed in the second half of the fifth/eleventh century, offers one of the longest extant accounts of the expedition.[52] It is essentially a more developed rendition of *version 1.2*, characterised by the Muslim army burning their supplies.[53] However, the narrative is much more detailed, and provides a number of additional elements, including several secondary figures who are not mentioned in the other Muslim sources (Sulaymān b. Muʿādh; "the forty-cubit man"); this fact led Canard to propose that the *Kitāb al-ʿuyūn*'s author had access to different sources.[54] First, a man named Sulaymān b. Muʿādh al-Anṭakī, who appears to have held a high-ranking position in the ground forces,[55] plays the role of Leo's interlocutor. His position is delicate, and when the Byzantine strategy is revealed to be a trick, Sulaymān b. Muʿādh cries: "you have killed me … for the emir will hold me responsible for all this."[56] Indeed, Maslama suspects Sulaymān b. Muʿādh of having willfully deceived him, or at least of having known Leo's true intentions. Anticipating his inevitable punishment, Sulaymān b. Muʿādh takes his own life by swallowing a dose of poison hidden in the stone of his ring; this desperate act confirms Maslama's suspicions, and he hangs the supposed traitor's corpse from a gibbet. The mysterious "forty-cubit man"[57] next arrives on the scene, a patrician who presents himself to ʿUmar b. Hubayra – Maslama having refused to receive him – as an envoy of the inhabitants of Constantinople rather than the emperor, perhaps an indication of the active political rivalries in the city as Leo III tried to secure his grasp on power. This man offers to pay tribute of up to a dinar per man of age to bear arms in exchange for the Muslim army's retreat. Despite ʿUmar b. Hubayra's insistence, Maslama stubbornly rejects the offer, arguing that he is under orders to persevere until either the city is taken or the caliph

52 *Kitāb al-ʿuyūn*, 24–33. On this text, see Brooks, "The Campaign of 716–718," which offers a translation of the relevant passage; Canard, "Les expéditions," 84 ff., and El-Cheikh, *Byzantium*, 63–4.

53 The destruction of the Muslims' provisions is augmented by the promise Leo extracts from his rivals to help resupply Constantinople with several ships laden with foodstuffs. This account is perhaps an attempt to fuse *versions 1.2 and 1.3*.

54 Canard, "Les expéditions," 89–90.

55 This figure is not mentioned in the other Muslim sources, where it is generally ʿAmr b. Qays who leads the ground troops; for example, see al-Yaʿqūbī, *Taʾrīkh*, vol. II, 299. However, he is well-represented in the Christian sources. See Theophanes, *Chronographia*, 386, trans. 538; Agapius, *Kitāb al-ʿunwān*, 501; Michael the Syrian (who confuses him with the caliph Sulaymān b. ʿAbd al-Malik), vol. II, 453, French trans. 484; *1234*, 301, trans. 234–5.

56 *Kitāb al-ʿuyūn*, 29, trans. Canard, "Les expéditions," 87.

57 Tessarakontapechys. See Brooks, "The Campaign of 716–718," 26, note 2, who states that a Jewish individual of the same name – supposedly an adviser to the Umayyad caliph Yazīd II – is mentioned in the Acts of the seventh council.

recalls him. It is then that the order to return reaches him, issued by ʿUmar b. ʿAbd al-ʿAzīz in place of the recently deceased Sulaymān, who had proven incapable of sending aid to his doomed soldiers at the walls of Constantinople. One final element from the *Kitāb al-ʿuyūn*'s version of events is the presence of ʿAbd Allāh al-Baṭṭāl, a famous Umayyad war hero, in Maslama's entourage. This epic figure, who traditionally only appears during Hishām's caliphate in most of the other Muslim sources,[58] is one of the most important protagonists of the second main version of the expedition against Constantinople in the chronographies, to which we shall now shift our focus.

Version 2 is much less widespread in the sources, and offers a completely different narrative of these events. This more flattering portrayal of the expedition against the Byzantine capital is preserved by Ibn Aʿtham al-Kūfī (who wrote his text *c.*204/819)[59] and Balʿamī (d. between 382/992 and 387/997), among others; Balʿamī juxtaposes this second account with *version 1*, which he recounts for the reader, faithfully following al-Ṭabarī's narrative.[60] The Persian historian is careful to specify that he found this account in works other than al-Ṭabarī's,[61] and it is clear that he relied heavily on Ibn Aʿtham's *Kitāb al-futūḥ*;[62] this latter is known to have been one of his sources, and he uses it here to give a more synthetic version of the story. The two texts are essentially in perfect accord, even if the Samanid vizier's version is incomplete, omitting an entire section of his predecessor's account. For his part, Ibn Aʿtham describes the context of Maslama's departure for Byzantine lands in detail.

The chronology in this narrative is quite different from that presented in *version 1*, notably because Maslama is said to have set off on campaign on the orders of his father, ʿAbd al-Malik. In a series of virulent speeches given in Damascus, the caliph calls for *jihād* and presents his son as a weaponised extension of himself, "his sword, his lance and his arrow" (*wa-hadhā*

58 Canard, "Al-Baṭṭāl."

59 On the complicated question of Ibn Aʿtham's chronology, see above, Ch. 2.

60 Balʿamī's marked interest in Maslama's expeditions may perhaps be explained by his family ties to this figure. Al-Samʿānī (d. 506/1113), the famous author of the *Kitāb al-ansāb*, relates a tradition stating that one of Balʿamī's ancestors was an Arab of the Tamīm tribe who accompanied Maslama on his expeditions; however, al-Samʿānī notes that, per al-Madāʾinī, this forebear actually participated in the campaigns of Qutayba b. Muslim. See Dunlop, "Balʿamī," and Sellheim, "Al-Samʿānī."

61 Balʿamī, 208. This is one of many examples where Balʿamī deviates from his main source, which supports Daniel's conclusions that the Samanid vizier was an adaptor rather than a translator of al-Ṭabarī. See Daniel, "Balʿamī's Account." See also Peacock, *Medieval Islamic Historiography*, in particular chapters 3 and 4.

62 As Dunlop has also noted, "Balʿamī."

ibnī Maslama wa-huwwa sayfī wa-rumḥī wa-sahmī).[63] The troops are then assembled at Marj Dābiq, where pious Muslims, hoping to participate in the *jihād*, arrive from all corners of the empire and swell their ranks.[64] The army thus complete, they set off and march on Constantinople, conquering numerous cities along the way, among them Tyana (Ṭawāna) and Amorium (ʿAmmūriyya); al-Baṭṭāl is also among Maslama's soldiers.[65] The Muslims reach the straits of the Bosphorus (*khalīj al-baḥr*),[66] and the Marwanid general orders the Byzantines among his ranks (perhaps captives) to organise the crossing by boat. After three months of preparation and naval construction, the troops take to the sea, carrying all their equipment with them, and disembark on the peninsula (*al-jazīra*) of Constantinople.[67] At the walls of the city, Ibn Aʿtham's account concurs with Balʿamī's,[68] both indicating that Maslama ordered the construction of a city facing Constantinople, which he fortified, endowed with gates and named *madīnat al-Qahr*,[69] doubtless in reference to his anticipated victory. Al-Masʿūdī supports this theory, citing a tradition that states: "Maslama b. ʿAbd al-Malik, after having built a city in the straits of Constantinople (*khalīj al-Qusṭanṭīniyya*) dubbed *madīnat al-Qahr*, was named conqueror with the aid of Allāh Most High (*al-qāhir bi-ʿawn Allāh taʿāla*)."[70] These events took place during ʿAbd al-Malik's caliphate, and the siege continued throughout al-Walīd's reign;[71] Ibn Aʿtham notes that Maslama spent forty years outside the *dār al-islām*.[72] The general then receives a letter from the new caliph, Sulaymān, asking him to return in order to quash the violent rebellion of Yazīd b. al-Muhallab, then governor of Khurāsān. Forced to renounce his most cherished dream, Maslama attempts to make a gallant last stand, and the two armies, Byzantine and Muslim, meet on the battlefield; the bloody

63 Ibn Aʿtham al-Kūfī, vol. VII, 123–4.

64 Ibn Aʿtham al-Kūfī, vol. VII, 125.

65 Ibn Aʿtham al-Kūfī, vol. VII, 135 ff.

66 The Arab geographers generally considered the Dardanelles, the Sea of Marmara and the Bosphorus to be a single strait or canal (*khalīj*) connecting the Mediterranean with the Black Sea. See Mordtmann, "Al-Qusṭanṭīniyya." Ibn Ḥawqal's map of the Mediterranean gives a clear idea of this perception, *Kitā ṣūrat al-arḍ*, 193, trans. 188.

67 Ibn Aʿtham al-Kūfī, vol. VII, 143–4.

68 Balʿamī begins his account by simply noting that Maslama had been on campaign in Byzantine territory since his father's reign, 208.

69 Ibn Aʿtham al-Kūfī, vol. VII, 144. Balʿamī, 208, calls it *madīnat al-Fahr*; this is undoubtedly an understandable scribal error, since the word *fahr* has no meaning and a single diacritical point distinguishes the letter "q" from "f" in Arabic.

70 Al-Masʿūdī, *Tanbīh*, 336, trans. 432 (with minor changes).

71 Ibn Aʿtham al-Kūfī, vol. VII, 144 ff. (ʿAbd al-Malik's death, 148; al-Walīd's death, 186); Balʿamī, 208.

72 Ibn Aʿtham al-Kūfī, vol. VII, 222.

combat turns in the Muslims' favour, and they inflict heavy losses upon their enemies before returning to *madīnat al-Qahr*. Leo then wrote to his adversary stating that the war had gone on long enough and requesting that they make peace, on the condition that the Muslims leave the peninsula and retreat to al-Masīḥiyya;[73] in addition, the Byzantines agreed to pay tribute.

Maslama replied that he could not accept these terms because he was bound by an oath: he had sworn not to leave the region without having entered Constantinople! Having sent his response, Maslama put his words into action and once more directed his troops to march on the gates of the capital, but the Byzantine emperor requested a meeting with him before any fighting began. Leo offered to respect his oath: Maslama could enter the city,[74] on the condition that he did so alone. The general accepted, but demanded that the city gates remain open so that al-Baṭṭāl and the rest of his troops could stand at the ready to invade the city if anything should happen to him. Finally, the negotiations were concluded. The Byzantines lined the streets from the city gates to the Hagia Sophia, and Maslama, having given his instructions to al-Baṭṭāl, cried the *takbīr* and entered Constantinople alone on horseback. He was dressed and turbaned in white, proudly bearing his sword and lance, openly displaying the Umayyad colour before the inhabitants of *Rūm*, who admired his courage. Leo was waiting for Maslama at the palace (*qaṣr*) gate, and demonstrated his submission by kissing the conquering hero's hand; he then accompanied him on foot to the basilica, while Maslama remained astride his steed. Without setting foot on the ground, the Marwanid hero entered the Hagia Sophia and grabbed hold of a golden cross encrusted with precious stones, despite Leo's entreaties not to do so, fearing that this provocative gesture would spark a riot. Maslama, ignoring his pleas, left the church and crossed the city once more with the "inverted cross on the point of his lance" (*al-ṣalīb munakkasan ʿalā ra's rumḥihi*),[75] an unequivocal symbol of Islam's triumph over Christianity. As agreed, Maslama reached the city gates at the hour of *ʿaṣr* prayers, while al-Baṭṭāl remained at attention, ready to attack. The Muslims rejoiced at the sound of his *takbīr* and celebrated their victory as they returned to the aptly-named *madīnat al-Qahr*. Leo paid tribute, as promised, in addition to allowing this orchestrated victory in the streets of the capital. Maslama

73 Ibn Aʿtham al-Kūfī, vol. VII, 223; Balʿamī, 209, speaks of al-Masjana instead. In both cases, these toponyms are seemingly unknown to the Muslim authors, although the site indicated was situated in Asia Minor rather than the European side of the Bosphorus. Could the mysterious toponym "al-Masīḥiyya" echo the messianic expectations characteristic of the period?

74 Al-Muqaddasī, *Aḥsan*, 147, also explicitly mentions Maslama's entry into the city.

75 Ibn Aʿtham al-Kūfī, vol. VII, 225. See also Balʿamī, 210.

gathered his troops and informed them of Sulaymān's letter, thus retracing more than a decade of Islamic history, from the death of ʿAbd al-Malik through the caliphate of his brother[76] and the reign of al-Walīd. After demanding that the crowd swear allegiance to Sulaymān, Maslama ordered his troops to depart, and the Muslims crossed the straits of the Bosphorus once more.[77] Having reached the other side, Maslama wrote a final missive to his rival asking that he leave the mosque at *madīnat al-Qahr* standing. Accordingly, Leo demolished the city but preserved this holy site.[78] On route to al-Masīḥiyya, an epidemic (*wabāʾ*) decimated the Muslims; the city's inhabitants formed plans to attack the weakened forces, but Maslama, apprised of their intentions, put them to the sword and destroyed the city.[79] Further along, he received a letter from ʿUmar b. ʿAbd al-ʿAzīz informing him that he had been granted the *bayʿa* on Sulaymān's death; the new caliph invited him to pledge his allegiance and not rebel, and Maslama consented,[80] in recognition of ʿUmar II's piety.[81] Ibn Aʿtham states that the Umayyad general returned to Damascus with 30,000 men from the original 80,000 with whom he had departed.[82] Thus concludes the second version of the siege of Constantinople.[83]

The Islamic tradition has preserved two radically different accounts of Maslama's expedition to the Byzantine capital. Certain interpolations occur between these two versions: for example, the construction of wooden houses noted by al-Ṭabarī (*version 1.1*) may echo the erection of *madīnat al-Qahr* in *version 2*.[84] Uncertainty over the location of Maslama's mosque is perhaps due

---

76 Who had then reigned, as Maslama notes, for 23 months.

77 Ibn Aʿtham al-Kūfī, vol. VII, 226.

78 Ibn Aʿtham al-Kūfī, vol. VII, 226–7. Leo, in his response to Maslama where he promises to preserve his rivals' mosque, even goes so far as to describe himself as the general's servant (*ʿabd*).

79 Ibn Aʿtham al-Kūfī, vol. VII, 228; Balʿamī, 211.

80 Certain traditions recognise Maslama's despair at seeing "the transfer of power from the hands of his father's sons to those of the children of his paternal uncle." See Ibn Abī al-Ḥadīd, *Sharḥ*, vol. VII, 137–8; Sharon, *Revolt*, 237.

81 Ibn Aʿtham al-Kūfī, vol. VII, 229–30; Balʿamī, 211.

82 Ibn Aʿtham al-Kūfī, vol. VII, 230; Balʿamī, 211–2, claims the original number of troops to be 180,000.

83 For later reprisals of this version of events, see Canard, "Les expéditions," 99 ff.

84 It should be added that among the Byzantine authors, the patriarch Nikephoros indicates that the Muslim army erected a fence (*charax*) around the city, if we follow Mango's proposed translation, *Short History*, § 54. The passage is difficult to interpret, as *charax* could also signify an "entrenched encampment," unless it is meant to indicate that the Muslims built a fence around their own camp and not around Constantinople itself. Theophanes, using the same source as Nikephoros, also conveys the idea that the Muslims built an enclosure of the space surrounding the Byzantine capital; in this version of events, the

to certain authors equating the mosque of *madīnat al-Qahr* preserved by Leo with the mosque built in the *Praetorium* of Constantinople. Confusion over the length of the siege may stem from conflicting reports given by the short and long versions, from one year in the former to more than twelve years in the latter.

In general, determining the dates at which these different narratives entered circulation is problematic. *Version 1* occurs in al-Ṭabarī (d. 310/923), and only scattered fragments of the narrative figure in the works of older chronographers such as al-Yaʿqūbī (d. after 295/908) or Khalīfa b. Khayyāṭ (d. c. 240/854). If we trust al-Ṭabarī's *isnāds*, given for two of the three variants he presents, these traditions trace back to al-Wāqidī (d. 207/823) and al-Madāʾinī (d. c. 235/850). These narratives are then generally taken up again by later authors. *Version 2*, however, poses more difficult problems. Uncertainty over Balʿamī's death date, probably between 382/992 and 387/997, is relatively unimportant here, as he relied on al-Ṭabarī for *version 1* and Ibn Aʿtham for *version 2*. Although the available information on this latter is problematic, his *Kitāb al-futūḥ* seems to have been written around 204/819. If this is true, then this version would be contemporary with that attributed to al-Wāqidī, which makes sense in that it would have been composed prior to the installation of the major post-Sāmarrāʾ historiographic filter. Taking only the Muslim sources into account, this narrative, including Maslama's entry into Constantinople, which Canard had once regarded as mere legend,[85] may potentially have been in circulation *at the same time* as the "standard version" describing a short siege ending in total defeat. As archaeology has not yet offered any assistance in determining how these events may have unfolded, we must delve deeper into the Christian sources to try to clarify certain elements of these accounts.

5.1.3 *The Christian Sources and the Construction of Heroes*

In accordance with the methodological principles outlined in the previous chapters, we have seen that the Christian sources are helpful when we try to *date* the circulation of certain historical information, in part because they provide access to an Islamic historiography that no longer survives.[86] The goal here is not to oppose these different textual traditions[87] but, more broadly, to

Muslims supposedly dug a trench to do so, which included a parapet of dry stones, *Chronographia*, 395, trans. 545. Michael the Syrian states that two trenches were dug, one facing Constantinople, the other behind the Muslims' camp to protect them from the Bulghārs' attacks. See Michael the Syrian, vol. II, 455, French trans. 485.

85 Canard, "Les expéditions," 99 ff.

86 See above, Ch. 3.

87 For example, as done by Guilland, "L'expédition de Maslama," 96.

comprehend their role in the intercultural processes of transmission at work at the time; moreover, these processes were not restricted to non-Muslim sources.

Perhaps because he threatened Constantinople, one of the most important Christian sites, Maslama and his military assault on the city received a great deal of attention from the Christian chroniclers, who often described the event at length. Canard's pioneering works in the 1920s demonstrated the appeal of the Byzantine chronographer Theophanes's account; in general, the Christian sources provide a wealth of information, especially in the richly detailed descriptions of the anonymous Syriac chronicles of *Zuqnīn* or *1234*. The patriarch Germanus I's (715–730) homily for the assumption of the Virgin offers a somewhat peculiar contemporaneous eyewitness account of the event authored by one of the prominent political actors of the period.[88] Without listing all of the numerous extant Christian accounts of the siege, some of which are quite colourful, it should be noted that the majority follow the same narrative framework outlined in *version 1*. The Muslims' siege is unsuccessful, and takes a tragic turn when famine decimates their army and forces them to beat an ignominious retreat on the orders of ʿUmar II; conversely, Leo's clever ruses and deception of his adversaries are the high points of the narrative.[89]

The Christian texts sometimes offer surprising information. Sulaymān b. Muʿādh, who only appears in the Islamic sources in the *Kitāb al-ʿuyūn*, is much better documented in the Christian texts; in these sources, he is accompanied by a figure named Bakhtarī b. al-Ḥasan, who does not appear in the Muslim works. These two men lead the ground troops, while ʿUmar b. Hubayra is in charge of the naval fleet.[90] These protagonists play important roles in the Christian narratives, as it is now Sulaymān b. Muʿādh who negotiates with Leo, still the Anatolic *Strategos* at the time. As in the *Kitāb al-ʿuyūn*, Sulaymān is tricked by Leo and precipitates the Muslim army's defeat by introducing him to Maslama. However, unlike the anonymous fifth/eleventh century source, these texts make no mention of betrayal or Sulaymān's lack of integrity, much less his suicide. Many other details related to the Muslims' means, strategies,

88 Grumel, "Homélie de Saint Germain."

89 A convenient overview of the elements offered by these sources is proposed by Hoyland in his presentation of information originating with the Syriac Common Source, *Seeing*, 653.

90 Theophanes, *Chronographia*, 386, trans. 538 (Bakcharos); Agapius, *Kitāb al-ʿunwān*, 501; Michael the Syrian, vol. II, 453, French trans. 484 (ʿUmar b. Hubayra is the only general mentioned, the leader of the entire expedition); *1234*, 301, Latin trans. 235, trans. Palmer, 212.

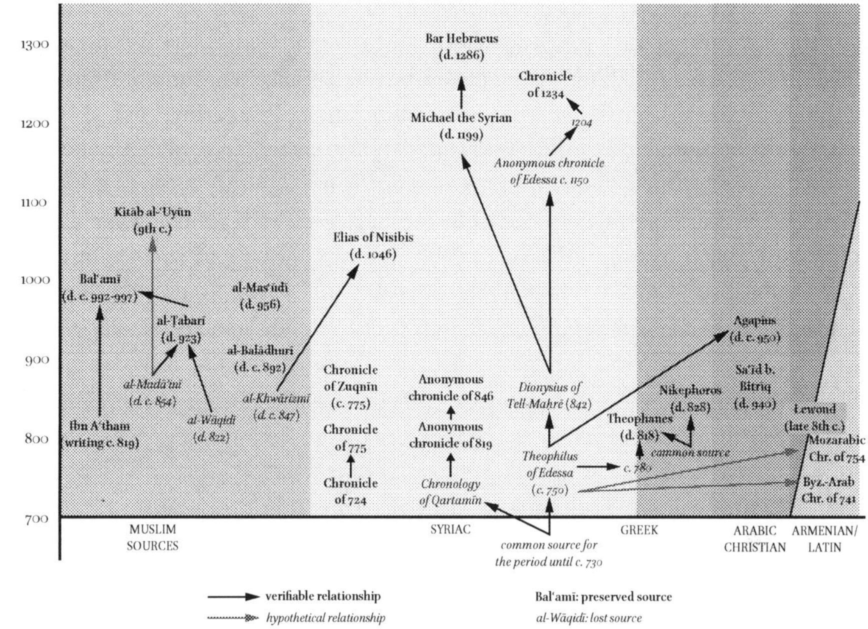

DIAGRAM 5.1 Transmission of elements related to Maslama

and itineraries, or even the rivalry between Theodosius III and Leo,[91] could also be mentioned here; however, this would force us to deviate from our goal of understanding the creation of Maslama's image. The main points relevant to our inquiry have been catalogued in table 5.1 below. By examining these well-known circuits of transmission, we can determine the chronological order of the circulation of information related to Maslama and his siege of Constantinople (diagram 5.1 above).

In a brief and relatively dry narrative of only a few lines, the two anonymous Syriac chronologies of *819* and *846*, both in the transmission circuit of Qartamīn, present a paradoxical image. Prior to the campaign against the Byzantine capital, these texts insist that Maslama was nominated as governor of the Jazīra (*amīrā d-kullāh Gāzartā*), where he carried out a cadastre and a census with a view to enacting tax levies.[92] However, the Marwanid general's name is conspicuously absent from the brief account of the expedition against

91 For example, see *1234*, 300 ff., Latin trans. 234 ff., trans. Palmer 211 ff.; for the military aspects of the operation, see Daniel's Greek apocalyptic, Berger, *Die griechische Daniel.*

92 *819*, 15, trans. 10; *846*, 233, Latin trans. 177, trans. Brooks 582; *1234*, 299, trans. 233, trans. Palmer 209. See also the *Chronicle of Zuqnīn*, 155, trans. Harrak 149, trans. Palmer 61, who mentions a second *taʿdīl* without indicating that Maslama was the author. On the administration of the Marwanid Jazīra, see Robinson, *Empire and Elites*, 33–62.

Constantinople! Despite this omission, several elements characteristic of later and more developed narratives are already established in these earlier sources: the attack of the Bulghārs, Leo's deception (*ṣnīʿā*) and the terrible famine endured by the Muslim assailants, who were reduced to eating flesh (*besrā*) and the excrement (*zeblā*) of their livestock (*qenyānē*).[93]

We know that these facts are part of a historiographic layer current until about 728,[94] thus making them the oldest we possess on the subject. Even more important, this information dates to the Umayyad period and corresponds to our *phases 2* or *3*: at the latest, a narrative existed only a decade after the siege of Constantinople – composed under ʿUmar II, Yazīd II or Hishām – recounting the undeniable military failure and suffering endured by the Muslims. Maslama the war hero is almost completely absent from these accounts: although he is mentioned prior to narratives of the siege as the governor of the Jazīra, he is not associated with the military operation ordered by his brother, Sulaymān. The Marwanid general is presented slightly earlier, invading Byzantine territory and capturing various cities and fortresses. Perhaps these authors simply forgot to mention his name, an obvious mistake, or deemed his presence incompatible with that of ʿUbayda[95] as general.

The transmission circuit originating with Theophilus of Edessa relied on the same basic core of information, but presented more elaborate narratives. Maslama's campaigns in Asia Minor prior to his expedition against Constantinople are also described in greater detail, in particular the aforementioned capture of Amorium, to which we shall return below. In these accounts, Maslama takes centre stage as the leader of the forces that lay siege to the Byzantine capital. He is accompanied by Sulaymān b. Muʿādh, who plays a key role in the negotiations with Leo. Emphasis is placed on Leo's clever stratagems, by which he tricks his enemies while pretending to be their ally. Military details are also prominent, from the Byzantines' use of Greek fire to partially destroy the Muslim fleet[96] to descriptions of Maslama's army caught between Leo's troops and the Bulghārs during the siege. Even the caliph's reinforcements are described, and the famine endured by Maslama's troops is portrayed in familiar detail: per Theophanes, the Muslims were forced to eat domestic

93 *819*, 15, Latin trans. 10–1, trans. Palmer 80; *846*, 234, Latin trans. 177, trans. Brooks 583, trans. Palmer 80.

94 See above, Ch. 3.

95 Apparently an erroneous transcription of Hubayra, in reference to ʿUmar b. Hubayra.

96 The homily of Germanus I may also reference this destruction by fire, to which we shall return below: "[The Virgin] destroyed our enemies in the sea with fire in their ships." Grumel, "Homélie de Saint Germain," ed. and trans. section 18.

TABLE 5.1 Main information related to Maslama in the Christian sources

Information \ Sources	Circuit of Theophilus of Edessa							Circuit of Qartamīn				
	Theophanes	Agapius	1234	Michael the Syrian	716	Zuqnīn	Łewond	819	846	Nikephoros	Constantine Porphyrogenitus	Elias of Nisibis
Maslama as governor of the Jazīra (cadastre and census)			X					X	X			
Earthquake (under al-Walīd I)	X	X	X	X	X			X	X			X
Campaign ending with the seizure of Amorium	X	X	X	X								X
Various campaigns in Asia Minor	X	X	X	X				X	X			X
Siege of Constantinople	X	X	X	X		X		X	X	X	X	X
Sulaymān b. Muʿādh meets Leo	X	X	X	X								
Leo deceives Maslama	X	X	X	X		X		X	X[a]			
Epistolary exchange between Maslama and Leo			X				X					

a The text of the two chronicles of *819* and *846* merely describes Leo as cunning (*ṣnīʿā*).

TABLE 5.1 Main information related to Maslama in the Christian sources (*cont.*)

Information / Sources	Circuit of Theophilus of Edessa							Circuit of Qartamīn				
	Theophanes	Agapius	1234	Michael the Syrian	716	Zuqnīn	Łewond	819	846	Nikephoros	Constantine Porphyrogenitus	Elias of Nisibis
Bulghārs attack the Muslims	X		X	X				X	X			
Trench and/or parapet constructed by the assailants	X			X						X		
Muslims grow and harvest crops						X						X
Famine strikes the Muslims	X		X	X		X	X	X	X			
Treachery of Coptic sailors	X									X		
Maslama conceals the situation from ʿUmar II			X	X								
ʿUmar II calls for Maslama's return	X	X[b]	X	X		X						
Maslama enters Constantinople on horseback						X						
Maslama has a mosque built											X	

b The passage is fragmentary and unreliable, Agapius, *Kitāb al-ʿunwān*, 502.

TABLE 5.1 Main information related to Maslama in the Christian sources (*cont.*)

Information / Sources	Circuit of Theophilus of Edessa							Circuit of Qartamīn				
	Theophanes	**Agapius**	**1234**	**Michael the Syrian**	**716**	**Zuqnīn**	**Łewond**	**819**	**846**	**Nikephoros**	**Constantine Porphyrogenitus**	**Elias of Nisibis**
Muslim navy decimated	X		X	X								
Muslims vanquish the Byzantines						X						
Earthquake (under ʿUmar II)	X	X		X		X			X			X
Campaign against Yazīd b. Muhallab	X	X	X	X								X
Campaign of 107/725, seizure of Caesarea	X	X	X	X		X		X	X			X
Campaign against the Khazars	X	X	X	X		X		X	X			X
Maslama is afraid and/or flees	X	X	X	X			X	X	X			
Second victorious campaign against the Khazars				X			X	X	X			X
Maslama undertakes construction projects						X	X	X	X			
Maslama reaches the "Gate"	X	X				X	X					

animals, manure, and even human cadavers![97] ʿUmar II then calls the troops back from the front, despite Maslama's repeated futile attempts to convince the caliph that the city was on the brink of collapse. Caliphal order eventually forces the general to concede, and the Byzantines profit from the Muslim army's retreat by destroying the remainder of their defeated enemies' naval fleet; some authors claim that an act of divine justice sent a tempest to demolish the Muslim ships as they headed back toward Syria.[98] As mentioned previously, certain factors support the hypothesis that the Spanish Latin chronicles of 741 and 754 may have relied on this circuit as well. These two texts also describe the caliph Sulaymān – portrayed as the "scourge of Byzantium" – sending his brother Maslama to lay siege to Constantinople. On the orders of ʿUmar II, the Umayyad general returned to Syria, defeated, leading an army decimated by famine.[99]

It is clear that part of Theophanes's account is not based on the Syriac Common Source, but on another Byzantine text also undeniably echoed in the work of the patriarch Nikephoros (d. 828).[100] The two Greek authors place particular emphasis on naval operations, noting that a fleet arrived from Egypt in order to resupply the Muslim army with men, weapons and provisions. Coptic sailors saw the docking of the Muslim fleet as an opportunity to flee and take refuge with the Byzantines; the emperor, thus informed of his rivals' naval position, seized their precious cargo and was simultaneously able to supply Constantinople while undermining the Muslim forces.[101] The rest of Theophanes's account can be traced back to Theophilus of Edessa's mid-eighth-century chronicle. Again, most of this information likely dates to the Umayyad period: if Theophilus composed his chronicle at the beginning of our *phase 5* (*c.*132–193/750–809), his own sources for the facts concerned here must have been produced in one or more of the previous phases, although it is impossible to date them with any certainty.

The account provided in *version 2* is not attested in any of the sources in these two circuits, the oldest available to modern scholars. However, two other texts do provide certain details characteristic of the second narrative: the *Chronicle*

---

97 Theophanes, *Chronographia*, 397, trans. 546. See also *Zuqnīn*, 158, trans. Harrak 151, trans. Palmer 63; Łewond, trans. 108.

98 Theophanes, *Chronographia*, 386–99, trans. 538–50; Agapius, *Kitāb al-ʿunwān*, 501–2; Michael the Syrian, vol. II, 454, French trans. 486; *1234*, 300–6, Latin trans. 234–8, trans. Palmer, 211–9.

99 *Byzantine-Arabic Chronicle of 741*, § 38; *Mozarabic Chronicle of 754*, § 50; trans. Hoyland, *Seeing*, 624–5.

100 As Hoyland notes, *Seeing* 653, note 139. On this author and his *Breviarium*, see Mango, *Nikephoros*, 1 ff.

101 Theophanes, *Chronographia*, 397, trans. 546; Nikephoros, *Short History*, § 54.

of Zuqnīn, written in 775/776, and that of the Armenian historian Łewond, which almost certainly dates to the eighth or early ninth century. These two accounts are noticeably different from those presented in the other Christian sources and thus merit our attention. Unlike Ibn Aʿtham al-Kūfī's narrative, these texts make no mention of Maslama founding a city, nor of his triumphant entry into the Byzantine capital. The allusions are more subtle because they are part of a very different historiographic project. These two sources reflect the creation of a panegyric for the new emperor, Leo the Isaurian, and this aim sets them apart from other Christian sources, many of which denounce Leo's low birth and his opportunism in seizing power.[102] This fact has led Palmer to hypothesise that the author of the *Chronicle of Zuqnīn* was Leo's contemporary and, like the emperor, a native of Marʿash (Germanicia) or the vicinity.[103] On another level, however, these accounts attest to a competition over the heroisation of Leo and Maslama.[104] While these two Christian sources are firmly pro-Leo, they nevertheless reveal the origins of a historiographic competition later taken up by Ibn Aʿtham in a properly Muslim version of events.

The *Chronicle of Zuqnīn* begins its narrative of the expedition against Constantinople with Maslama's troops marching across the Anatolian plateau; the inhabitants flee at his approach, perhaps a testament to the famous general's fearsome reputation. The chronicler notes that these regions, once prosperous, are now deserted. The Syriac source then highlights the pact the Anatolic *Strategos* negotiated with the Muslims, provoking Theodosius III's abdication. This treaty marks Leo's deception of Maslama, and relieves the Byzantines from the looming threat of looting and pillaging by the Muslim army. Leo is described as valiant (*lbībā*) and strong (*ḥayltānā*), the quintessential warrior (*qrābtānā*). Thanks to these noble qualities, Leo is crowned emperor upon his arrival in Constantinople, and the anonymous chronicler of Zuqnīn insists above all on his heroism (*gabrūtā*) and might. Leo then reinforces the city's defenses and destroys the boat bridge spanning the Bosphorus, trapping the Arabs on the peninsula; their roles reversed, the besiegers become the besieged, and Maslama orders that a vine (*kārmā*) be planted, an act that should doubtless be understood more generally as an order to cultivate the land in order to provide sustenance for the troops. This initiative, however, proves insufficient, and once more we encounter scenes of terrible famine, the

102 For example, see Theophanes, *Chronographia*, 391–5, trans. 542–5. The post-iconoclasm Byzantine sources are noticeably hostile to Leo III, who initiated the first iconoclasm.

103 Palmer, *The Seventh Century*, 65–6.

104 Lammens has rightly stated that in Leo, Maslama found "a worthy adversary," *La Syrie*, 62.

Muslim soldiers first reduced to eating their pack animals (*bʿīrā*) and horses (*rakshē*), then their sandals (*sūnāyhōn*)[105] and finally human cadavers (*besrā d-mītē*)! Leo continues to deceive Maslama, claiming he needs more time to obtain agreement from the city's notables; ʿUmar II then orders the retreat of the Muslim army. Upon receiving this injunction, Maslama asks Leo to grant him entry into Constantinople for a meeting. Accompanied by thirty horsemen, Maslama enters the city and spends three days admiring the emperors' monuments. The Muslims then finally return home, defeated. On their journey back, the Byzantines attempt to attack the retreating army, but their plans are stymied by al-ʿAbbās b. al-Walīd,[106] who ambushes them and puts them to the sword.[107]

Despite some chronological confusion over whether the siege of Constantinople occurred under the caliphate of Yazīd II or Hishām, Łewond's account is no less interesting than the anonymous chronicler of Zuqnīn's. It seems clear that the Armenian chronicler relied on older narratives; although the two texts differ in nature and perspective, Łewond's version incontestably shares certain elements with the patriarch Germanus I's (715–730) homily, likely given around 728 in the Church of Saint Mary of Blachernae.[108] Łewond first mentions a campaign Maslama led against the Byzantines in Asia Minor following Leo's refusal to pay tribute to the Muslims. The Muslim army then sets up camp directly facing their enemies' encampment; as this approach yields few results, Maslama decides that his army should move on and ravage the region. Ignoring the emperor's injunction, the Byzantine forces set off in pursuit of Maslama, who ambushes and massacres them during a disorderly and imprudent advance. The descriptions of combat unequivocally recall those depicting the attack on the retreating Muslim army in the *Chronicle of Zuqnīn*.[109] Here,

105 Per the suggested correction in the manuscript edition, 158.

106 The caliph al-Walīd I's son.

107 *Zuqnīn*, 156–60, trans. Harrak 150–2, trans. Palmer 62–5. This episode may echo the aforementioned events at al-Masīḥiyya, see Ibn Aʿtham al-Kūfī, vol. VII, 228; Balʿamī, 211.

108 Following the conclusions of Grumel, "Homélie de Saint Germain," 187–8. Contrary to Łewond's text, in which Leo III plays a key role in protecting the city, the emperor is not mentioned in the homily, which attributes the city's salvation entirely to the Virgin, as "the event took place … on the very same blessed day that we customarily celebrate the holy Mother of God's journey to heaven," i.e. the Assumption. This account, which passes over the emperor's role in silence, may be indicative of Leo's conflict with the patriarch over the worship of images between 723 and 726. See Grumel, "Homélie de Saint Germain," ed. and trans. section 19, 188. However, twelve years earlier, Germanus I did play an important role in the negotiations that brought Leo to power, see Theophanes, *Chronographia*, 390, trans. 540.

109 See Łewond, trans. 102–5 and *Zuqnīn*, 159–60, trans. Harrak 152, trans. Palmer 64–5.

however, the episode takes place *before* the siege of Constantinople. The operation is a success, celebrated by the caliph upon the army's return; Maslama is awarded numerous titles of distinction, and becomes the caliphate's military enforcer, the hero of the dynasty.[110]

Strengthened by this victory, the Muslims assemble "a formidable army," and Maslama swears an *oath* to his brother[111] never to return home again without having destroyed the Byzantine Empire and Constantinople. The Marwanid general reaches the Sea of Marmara, where he sends a threatening missive to Leo III. He reminds him that Islam is a universal calling, and urges him to submit, warning that he is under *oath* not to return to his homeland without having achieved his aims. In the face of this looming threat, Leo III asks his people to pray for three consecutive days, and replies to Maslama that God will not allow him to accomplish his goal, for divine omnipotence will destroy the ships of the impious, just as the Red Sea once swallowed Pharaoh. This motif was already in use in Byzantine rhetoric describing the siege of Constantinople, judging from the homily of Saint Germanus.[112] Irritated by this response, Maslama sets sail against Constantinople. Leo organises processions through the city ending at the shore: the emperor then uses the True Cross to trace the sign of the cross on the surface of the sea, and God immediately unleashes a tempest that decimates the enemy fleet. In Germanus I's homily, the Virgin guarantees the safety of the city.[113] The survivors seek refuge on land, unable to attack the city,[114] and Leo imposes a blockade that results in the now-familiar famine; Łewond indicates that the men were forced to butcher and eat their horses, their servants and even their concubines! After this catastrophe, Maslama begs Leo to pardon him and his remaining troops;

110 Łewond, trans. 101–3.

111 This detail, however, does not elucidate the caliph's identity, since all of ʿAbd al-Malik's sons held this position.

112 See Grumel, "Homélie de Saint Germain," ed. and trans. section 14, 17.

113 See Grumel, "Homélie de Saint Germain," ed. and trans. section 20: "The Egyptians, pursuing the sons of Israel, sank like a stone to the bottom of the sea, and the Lord caused great waves to overtake them and they vanished into the abyss. The Saracens, fleeing before us, fell victim to the same disaster. A strange tempest and typhoon, a whirlwind, fell upon the sea and destroyed nearly the entire famous fleet of a thousand ships, such that all the islands, headlands, mouths of the ports and bays were filled with piles of enemy corpses, and scripture, without changing a single word, verified for us: 'And Israel saw its enemies dead on the shore.'"

114 See Grumel, "Homélie de Saint Germain," ed. and trans. section 18: "She did not allow our enemies to launch a single war machine against the city, and, just as her conception was immaculate, her protection of the city during this great war repelled every attack and preserved the city's crown from harm."

the emperor meets with the general and reproaches him for his attitude and his arrogance. Maslama recognises his failings, and asks that he be allowed to return home; Leo grants his request, and he arrives back in Muslim territory covered in shame, never again to wield a sword.[115]

While the *Chronicle of Zuqnīn* emphasises the heroism and military valor of the Anatolic *Strategos*, Łewond's account conversely attributes these praiseworthy qualities to Maslama, who appears unstoppable but for divine intervention, invoked by Leo's prayers and foreshadowed in his missive. It is the tempestuous waves of God's wrath, not Byzantine soldiers, that stop the Muslim army in its tracks. Leo is no longer a model warrior but a pious emperor whose request for a miracle is answered; Maslama becomes the vanquished hero, yet his defeat comes only at the hands of the divine, a fact he himself acknowledges following his return to Syria: "it was impossible for him to wage war on God."[116] Where the anonymous *Chronicle of Zuqnīn* describes the military preparations for the upcoming siege, Łewond addresses the moral and religious preparations instead. The battle to be fought was one of faith; Maslama's letter makes quite clear that Islam will defeat Christianity. Łewond's account presents a version of events diametrically opposed to that in Ibn Aʿtham's text: the inverted cross representing Muslim victory is replaced with a cross that punishes the besiegers, equating Maslama's fate with that of Pharaoh.

115 Łewond, trans. 103–10. This version of events seems to have been taken up in particular by Armenian historiography, judging from the very similar narrative presented by the chronicler Stepʿanos Tarōnecʿi in the eleventh century: "And when the emperor Leo saw the tumultuous mass which had become a forest over the sea, he gave the order to set up the fortifications made of iron bars and to shut the chained door of the fortress and he forbade anyone to engage with the enemy. Rather, trusting in God, he waited for an intervention from on high. And the king himself took the invincible symbol upon his back, and the patriarch and the whole mass of the community, with candles and with the perfume of incense, lifted up blessings. And going out through the gate of the city, the king struck the water of the sea with the symbol of the Cross, saying: 'Help us, Christ, Saviour of the world.' And at the same time, the depths of the sea shook and submerged the forces of Ismael. And half, beaten by the surging sea were carried to the country of the Thracians, and the rest [were carried] to distant islands, because they were more than 50,000 men. And they seized Maslama and brought him to the king. And the king said, 'The Lord has rendered justice in my favour. I shall not lay my hands on you. Go to your land and report the miracles of God.' And he went in shame to his own land and he never again sought to lift his sword against anyone." Greenwood, *The* Universal History *of Stepʿanos Tarōnecʿi*, 191–92, also cited in Guilland, "L'expédition," 109–10.

116 Łewond, trans. 110. See Grumel, "Homélie de Saint Germain," ed. and trans. section 19: "and it was only understandable that they cried out as the Egyptians once did: "Flee before the face of Israel, for God fights alongside them."

Nevertheless, certain elements of *version 2* are discernible in Łewond's otherwise contradictory account. The most obvious detail is Maslama's entry into Constantinople. The *Chronicle of Zuqnīn* is the oldest narrative of this episode extant today,[117] and in this account, the general does not enter the city as a conqueror, but rather is accompanied by thirty horsemen and allowed to ride freely through the city for three straight days. Rather than a symbolic victory, this version suggests a symbolic appropriation of Constantinople and its monumental patrimony. While Łewond does not explicitly mention the Marwanid general's entrance into the Byzantine capital, it is implicit in the Emperor's invitation to Maslama to humble himself before him and plead for the salvation of his men. Where could this scene have taken place, if not behind the walls of the impregnable city, in the imperial palace, a testament to the glory of the Byzantines? Łewond twice references another important aspect of *version 2*: Maslama's oath, sworn to the caliph, to never again return to Syria without having conquered Constantinople. Maslama highlights this promise in his letter to Leo to emphasise his determination; in *version 2*, this oath is the key to Maslama's entry into the city. Finally, the Armenian chronicler portrays the Marwanid prince as a hero from the first, describing his victory on the Anatolian battlefields and how his triumph was celebrated in style at the caliph's insistence upon his return to Syria.[118] Maslama is still, it is true, a vanquished hero, but only because of divine intervention in response to Leo's prayers, the *Strategos* here portrayed as a paragon of virtue; during their meeting, the defeated hero acknowledges Leo's piety with reverence. Łewond's depiction of Maslama's unsuccessful retreat underscores the hero's failure; having finally learned his lesson, he lays down his weapons once and for all.

It seems clear that these texts share a common core of information with Ibn Aʿtham, among others; nevertheless, this information was used to develop very different narratives of historiographic competition, in which each of the opposing leaders were ultimately vaunted as conquering heros. The drive to heroise was in full effect, and both the caliphate and the Byzantine Empire were competing to promote their own models and legitimacy; in other words, both sides were attempting to establish and spread their respective authoritative readings of history. In both cases, these historiographic developments took place early on; for example, consider certain elements in the Greek homily of

117 As Canard has noted, "Les expéditions," 100.

118 Łewond, trans. 103: "[The Muslims] returned in triumph to their country. The caliph, on the occasion of this great victory, ordered solemn feasts be given and took part in them himself, along with his main dignitiaries; he showered his brother in honours, blessed the victory, distributed the spoils among his troops, kept the captive slaves for himself, and spent the remainder of the year at rest."

Germanus I, composed approximately a decade after the events it described, or the Syriac chronicles based on Islamic originals, practically contemporaneous with their subject matter. The Muslims and the Byzantines both laid claim to Maslama, and the expedition against Constantinople was an equally important event in Byzantine and Islamic history. The capital of the eastern Roman Empire was indeed conquered, but by Leo the Isaurian rather than Maslama the Umayyad. However, we cannot base our profile of Maslama entirely on the accounts of the siege of Constantinople. In order to complete our portrait, we must also examine the extant narratives of his other military campaigns.

5.2 From Hero of the Byzantine Frontier to Islamic Hero?

While Maslama is associated with numerous military operations beyond his expedition against Constantinople, two of these campaigns merit deeper analysis: one in Iraq against the rebel Yazīd b. al-Muhallab, an internal enemy of the caliphate, the other in the Caucasus against the Turks and the Khazars. These two military actions were critically important for the caliphate, and offered Maslama the opportunity to face new adversaries, having already honed his skills in battle against the Byzantines.[119]

ʿUmar II's accession to the throne and the recall of the troops besieging Constantinople meant that Maslama had failed, which was a serious blow to the general's military career; the reigns of Yazīd II and Hishām would provide new opportunities for Maslama to display his talents as a strategist and refine his image as a conquering hero. The general is thus a sort of unifying link between these caliphates with opposing political aims. However, the hero's transition to new battlefields was not without consequence: by entering arenas heretofore occupied by other Umayyad generals, Maslama was forced to compete with them. These unavoidable rivalries were in the great Marwanid soldier's interest, however, as the significant increase in the range of his military activities allowed him to surpass the level of a localised glory – expert in the Byzantine front – to achieve the status of a true Islamic hero. New challenges, this time posed by other great Umayyad military figures, were now added to those presented by the competition for heroisation with Leo the Isaurian.

119 Maslama had previously led a campaign in the Caucasus in 97/710.

5.2.1 *The Competition for Heroisation*

Maslama's march toward other adversaries led him first to Iraq, where he was sent to quash the rebellion of Yazīd b. al-Muhallab.[120] Yazīd, formerly the Umayyad governor of Iraq and Khurāsān, had been stripped of his functions by ʿUmar II and then thrown in prison. Just before the caliph's death, the prisoner had escaped his cell and fled to Iraq where, after a futile attempt to reconcile with the new caliph Yazīd b. ʿAbd al-Malik, he revolted against his former masters.[121] The conditions of the rebellion and Yazīd b. al-Muhallab's own aspirations for its outcome remain uncertain.[122] Al-Balādhurī, for example, states that the rebel claimed *al-riḍā min banī Hāshim*,[123] presaging certain slogans adopted by the Abbasid *daʿwa* several decades later; others say that he justified his claim to the caliphate by invoking the Qurʾān and the *sunna* of the Prophet.[124] If we believe al-Ṭabarī's account, notably relying on Abū Mikhnaf, Yazīd b. al-Muhallab's discourse took a decidedly hostile tone toward Syria, stating without hesitation that *jihād* against the *ahl al-Shām* was preferable to waging war on the Turks and Daylamites![125] In any case, the threat posed by Yazīd b. al-Muhallab was significant enough to justify sending in Maslama, who was charged with destroying the rebel and his supporters.

Maslama's first direct confrontation with a Muslim rebel marked a shift from his previous campaigns against infidels, and it is this shift that allows us to gauge the Marwanid general's image within the Islamic empire. Here as well, his reputation as a war hero preceded him, and Yazīd's troops are described as nervously awaiting the arrival of this famous soldier.[126] Yazīd b. al-Muhallab, sensing the fear beginning to overtake his men, tried to rouse them by affirming that Maslama was nothing but a "yellow locust" (*jarāda ṣafrāʾ*)![127] The colour is almost certainly a reference to the *Banū al-aṣfar*, the Byzantines, with whom Maslama had been at war for most of his life; Ibn Aʿtham al-Kūfī's text leaves no room for doubt on this point, reporting that Yazīd b. al-Muhallab called Maslama *Qusṭanṭīn b. Qusṭanṭīn* in his diatribe.[128] Yazīd's intentions in

120 Recall that, per *version 2* of the expedition against Constantinople, Maslama was called back by his brother Sulaymān, fearing Yazīd b. al-Muhallab's looming revolt.

121 On this complicated episode, see Gabrieli, "La rivolta," and Crone, "Muhallabids."

122 See Bonner, *Aristocratic Violence*, 4–9.

123 Gabrieli, "La rivolta," 215.

124 Al-Ṭabarī, vol. II, 1398, trans. vol. XXIV, 131; *Aghānī*, vol. X, 43; Crone and Hinds, *God's Caliph*, 61, 64–5; Crone, "Muhallabids."

125 Al-Ṭabarī, vol. II, 1391, trans. vol. XXIV, 123.

126 Ibn Aʿtham, vol. VII, 250; Balʿamī, 225.

127 Ibn Aʿtham, vol. VII, 250; Balʿamī, 225; al-Ṭabarī, vol. II, 1398, trans. vol. XXIV, 130; al-Masʿūdī, *Murūj*, vol. V, 454, trans. Pellat vol. IV, 883.

128 Ibn Aʿtham, vol. VII, 250.

this insult are clear: he was trying to enclose his rival in a bounded space – a space in which he was defeated – in order to reduce him to a mere local celebrity at a time when Maslama was on the verge of becoming a true Islamic hero.

The first battle finally arrived. The confrontation took place near Karbalāʾ, in the region of al-ʿAqr,[129] in 102/720. Without dwelling on the details of the fighting, in which Maslama's forces were vastly superior,[130] the sources agree that Yazīd was deeply shocked by the death of his brother, Ḥabīb. Despite his advisers' recommendations that he retreat toward Wāsiṭ, he launched a desperate counterattack against Maslama's troops and died in the ensuing battle.[131] Ibn Aʿtham adds that prior to his demise, Yazīd b. al-Muhallab challenged Maslama to single combat. Not wanting to lose face, the Marwanid general considered agreeing to the duel, in spite of his advisers' cautions against it, arguing that he had no choice between shame (*al-ʿār*) and death; Yazīd, described as the greatest hero of Iraq (*fāris al-ʿIrāq qāṭibatan*), was ultimately killed by Maslama's soldiers, thus avoiding an uncertain result in single combat.[132] Finding this account in Ibn Aʿtham's text is somewhat surprising, as he typically has nothing but high praise for the Marwanid general: Maslama displays a certain cowardice, or perhaps a coldly calculating side, in this narrative, traits otherwise unsuited to the image of his heroic persona. Ibn Aʿtham's account betrays a certain ambiguity surrounding the Umayyad prince, perhaps a result of the historiographic competition constructed in contemporaneous traditions on the relative merits of Yazīd b. al-Muhallab and Maslama. Nevertheless, the victorious Maslama is granted the position once held by his deceased rival, becoming governor of Baṣra, Kūfa and Khurāsān; however, his tenure in this post was brief, cut short by his failure to send the proceeds from the *kharāj* to Damascus.[133]

The accession of Hishām, Maslama's fourth and final brother to hold the caliphate, marked the general's return to favour. Maslama was put in charge of Armenia and Azerbaijan in place of Saʿīd al-Ḥarashī. The transition of power was not without difficulty, judging from Ibn Aʿtham's account: upon his arrival in the Caucasus, Maslama met with his predecessor and roundly criticised him for not having obeyed his orders, as Maslama had previously sent him a letter commanding him to suspend military operations against the Khazars until after his arrival. Saʿīd defended himself, claiming he had not received the

129 Or al-ʿAqr Bābil. See Yāqūt, *Muʿjam*, vol. IV, 136, who also locates the episode there.
130 Gabrieli, "La rivolta," 225.
131 For example, see al-Ṭabarī, vol. II, 1404–5, trans. vol. XXIV, 136–7.
132 Ibn Aʿtham, vol. VII, 252; Balʿamī, 228.
133 Al-Ṭabarī, vol. II, 1416–7, 1432 ff., trans. vol. XXIV, 148, 162 ff.; this speedy removal from power is discussed more below, Ch. 8.

letter until after his stunning victory over these latter.[134] Maslama, however, was not satisfied by this argument, and accused him of lying and rashly seeking personal glory instead of prudently waiting for reinforcements and ensuring the safety of his Muslim forces. Consequently, Maslama subjected him to various corporal punishments and threw him behind bars. The caliph, furious at Maslama's treatment of Saʿīd, personally intervened, resulting in his immediate release and apologies from Maslama, whom Hishām reproached for having acted purely out of jealousy.[135]

Yazīd b. al-Muhallab's attitude toward Maslama, or Maslama's attitude toward Saʿīd, translate into power struggles, particularly those that existed between the various Umayyad generals and governors. Like the opposition between Maslama and Leo III, these antagonistic encounters are also indicative of a competition for heroisation. In this anecdote, Maslama's machinations to preserve his power and dominance against the ambitions of his many rivals are easily detectable. These accounts, appearing in sources that are otherwise quite favourable to Maslama, provide a much more negative picture of the Marwanid general.[136]

It is clear that Maslama's position within the patrilineal structure of Umayyad power gave him a theoretical superiority over most of his political and military adversaries. His family ties proved to be a double-edged sword, however, as the Marwanid general's prestige was liable to incite caliphal disfavour, especially since Maslama was a potential candidate for the ruling position, although in principle he had no real claim to the throne because his mother was a concubine slave. Nevertheless, his control over the army represented a palpable threat to the caliphate; in recognition of this fact, ʿUmar b. ʿAbd al-ʿAzīz wrote Maslama a letter intended to guarantee his allegiance and prevent any possibility of his rebelling.[137] In fact, Maslama played a significant role in discussions of caliphal succession, in particular under Yazīd II, where he sided with

134 The Armenian chronicler Łewond reports a completely different version of events, stating that Maslama gave up on any military plan as soon as he joined Saʿīd, since the Khazars had recently trounced Saʿīd's army, massacring a large number of his troops and causing the rest to flee. This devastating defeat was the result of not waiting for reinforcements to arrive, and this imprudence was the cause of Maslama's anger. Łewond, trans. 101.

135 Al-Yaʿqūbī, *Taʾrīkh*, vol. II, 317; Ibn Aʿtham, vol. VII, 280–1; Balʿamī, 244–5.

136 The hostility of Balʿamī, who relied on Ibn Aʿtham's text in this account of the conflict between Maslama and Saʿīd, has been previously noted by Gabrieli, "Il califfato di Hisham," 79, note 4.

137 Ibn Aʿtham, vol. VII, 229–30; Balʿamī, 211.

Hishām over the son of the caliph, al-Walīd.[138] An "almost-caliph"[139] in some regards, Maslama nonetheless respected the prescribed rules of succession and did not attempt to seize power by force, despite any latent temptation to do so. Ibn Aʿtham presents another letter, this time from Maslama to Leo III, which begins: "*min Maslama b. ʿAbd al-Malik amīr al-mūʾminīn ilā Ilyūn ṣāḥib al-Rūm*."[140] Unless it is a scribal error, perhaps reflexively substituting *mūʾminīn* for *muslimīn*, this letter reveals Maslama's unrealised ambitions. In any case, the general did not become caliph, unlike Marwān b. Muḥammad, Maslama's heir in more than one respect in the Caucasus and the Jazīra, who succeeded in establishing a military chokehold on political power several years later.[141]

Despite never reaching the highest office, Maslama tried hard to defend his "heroic monopoly," as shown in the two anecdotes discussed above. There was no room for competition, and his rivals were either eliminated or imprisoned. In this context, the Caucasus, where he was sent by Hishām, offered Maslama fertile ground for solidifying this monopoly; like Constantinople, this region was replete with eschatological references and mythic figures. We shall thus complete our portrait of Maslama by examining a number of episodes from this Caucasian phase of his career.

5.2.2 *Maslama and the Borders of the World: A New Alexander?*

Maslama's Caucasian expeditions allow us to refine our understanding of how his image developed. Indeed, the region suited Maslama well: following his defeat at Constantinople, the Turks and the Khazars were prime targets and fighting them rehabilitated his heroic aura, especially given that these enemies' bloody raids in the area had been extremely detrimental to the caliphate. Although the Marwanid general had already been given ample opportunity to demonstrate his military prowess between the Black Sea and the Caspian in 91/710, this time he would return, nearly twenty years later, to make his mark on this memory-laden region by following in the footsteps of the mythical Dhū al-Qarnayn.

Focusing his efforts on the two "gates of the Caucasus," Bāb al-Lān and Bāb al-Abwāb (this latter typically referred to only as al-Bāb), Maslama identified strategic locations for defeating the Khazars. During this initial phase, in 110/728–729, he reached the gate of the Alans,[142] and after nearly a month

138 Rotter, "Maslama b. ʿAbd al-Malik."

139 Similar to the status of "almost-king" that scholars of the medieval West associate with Charles Martel. See Riché, *Les Carolingiens*, 48–66; Lebecq, *Les origines franques*, 191.

140 Ibn Aʿtham, vol. VII, 226.

141 On this point, see Crone, *Slaves*, 40–1.

142 The Darial Pass (or Darial Gorge).

of brutal combat, the *Khāqān* was defeated.[143] Al-Ṭabarī notes that Maslama, returning from this campaign, took the route that led by the mosque (*masjid*) of Dhū al-Qarnayn.[144] If, as Blankinship suggests, this location was near Bāb al-Lān,[145] it is a different site than another locale typically associated with Dhū al-Qarnayn located near the source of the Tigris, not far from Mayyāfāriqīn, which al-Muqaddasī calls a *ribāṭ* and Ibn Ḥawqal terms a *ḥiṣn*.[146] Dhū al-Qarnayn's identity is uncertain, although this name is generally assumed to be a sobriquet of Alexander the Great. However, this hypothesis is not universally accepted; the "two-horned" figure in the Qur'ān had a "quasi-prophetic, or at least eschatological mission … whereas [Alexander] belongs to the history of the great world conquerors."[147] Other traditions suggest he was a Yemenite king, a successor of the queen of Sheba; this theory has led certain authors to conclude through a process of assimilation that Alexander himself was of Yemenite extraction, a descendant of Qaḥṭān![148] Some authors, such as Qudāma b. Jaʿfar (d. 326/938), unquestioningly accepted the identification of the Macedonian ruler with the Qur'ānic Dhū al-Qarnayn.[149] In any case, it is clear from the familiar topography of the medieval Muslim authors that the region east of the Anatolian plateau to the foothills of the Caucasus preserved the memory of the "two-horned" one.

Before examining this figure in greater detail, we must briefly consider Maslama's second grand offensive against Bāb al-Abwāb, which al-Ṭabarī dates to 114/732–733,[150] following several lesser campaigns carried out in previous years.[151] In this new assault, Maslama passed right by the citadel (*qalʿa*) of

143 Khalīfa b. Khayyāṭ, *Ta'rīkh*, vol. II, 497; al-Ṭabarī, vol. II, 1507, trans. vol. XXV, 45. Other authors date this campaign to 109/727–728, particularly al-Yaʿqūbī, vol. II, 329; Elias of Nisibis, relying on al-Khwārizmī, describes two successive campaigns in the years 109 and 110 respectively, 164–5, Latin trans. 78–9, trans. Delaporte 101–2.

144 Al-Ṭabarī, vol. II, 1507, trans. vol. XXV, 45.

145 Al-Ṭabarī, vol. II, 1507, trans. vol. XXV, 45, note 207.

146 Al-Muqaddasī, *Aḥsan*, 20, trans. 55; Ibn Ḥawqal, *Kitāb ṣūrat*, 196, trans. vol. I, 191.

147 Bacqué-Grammont, De Polignac, Bohas, "Monstres et murailles," 120. See al-Masʿūdī's discussion on the subject, *Murūj*, vol. II, 248–9, trans. Pellat vol. II, 251–2.

148 Al-Masʿūdī, *Murūj*, vol. II, 249, trans. Pellat vol. II, 252; Bacqué-Grammont, De Polignac, Bohas, "Monstres et murailles," 120–1. There are other identifications as well, including ʿAlī b. Abī Ṭālib in a passage of the *Muqaddima* where Ibn Khaldūn cites these words of the Prophet: "'You are the possessor of its two periods (*qarn*)' – meaning (the two periods of) the nation (the beginning and the end). That is, you (ʿAlī) are the caliph at its beginning and your descendants will be caliphs at its end," *The Muqaddimah*, vol. II, 192.

149 Qudāma, *Kitāb al-kharāj*, 265. On this author, see Heck, *The Construction of Knowledge*.

150 Al-Ṭabarī, vol. II, 1562, trans. vol. XXV, 98. Al-Ṭabarī also notes that Maslama had reached al-Bāb once before, in 112/730–731, vol. II, 1531–2, trans. vol. XXV, 70.

151 See Khalīfa b. Khayyāṭ, *Ta'rīkh*, vol. II, 500–6.

al-Bāb and marched directly against the *Khāqān*'s troops, routing them and wounding the Khazar ruler.[152] Returning from battle, Maslama captured the supposedly impregnable fortress at al-Bāb by poisoning its primary water source. After this victory, Maslama handed the governorate of Armenia and Azerbaijan over to Marwān b. Muḥammad and returned to Syria for good.[153] Prior to his departure, the Marwanid general appointed a governor for the city of al-Bāb and ordered the construction of new fortifications for the city, including the installation of iron gates (*abwāban min al-ḥadīd*).[154]

The specific reference to iron clearly echoes the Cave Sura (*al-Kahf*), in which Dhū al-Qarnayn builds a rampart out of "ingots of iron" (*zubar al-ḥadīd*) to keep out Gog and Magog.[155] Alongside the problems posed by this "two-horned" figure, the medieval authors also faced the issue of trying to identify Gog and Magog, who spread "corruption in the earth."[156] Various locations have been proposed as the site of this rampart, from China to the Iberian Peninsula; however, the mountainous regions of the Caucasus were those most frequently suggested by medieval Muslim authors. The Khazars and the Turks were thus often identified with the people of Gog and Magog in the Islamic tradition. Ibn al-Faqīh, following Muqātil b. Sulaymān's explanation, goes so far as to suggest that the name "Turks" is derived from the fact that they were the people left (*turikū*) behind Dhū al-Qarnayn's wall![157] This mythical construction was a subject of keen interest among Muslim scholars, and became a *topos* of any literature that touched on the fantastic. Several geographers report that the Abbasid caliph al-Wāthiq (227–232/842–847) saw in a dream that the gate (*sudda*) protecting the *dār al-islām* from Gog and Magog had been opened; this vision prompted the caliph to send men to ensure that the gate remained firm and closed. The sources varyingly report that the expedition

152 Ibn Aʿtham, vol. VII, 282–6; Balʿamī, 246–7. Al-Ṭabarī mentions that the *Khāqān*'s son had been killed the year before, vol. II, 1560, trans. vol. XXV, 95–6. According to Ibn Qutayba, *Kitāb al-maʿārif*, 365, it was not the *Khāqān*'s son but the *Khāqān* himself who was killed. The importance of Ibn Aʿtham's text for the Muslims' various operations in the Caucasus has been discussed by Kurat, "Abū Muḥammad Aḥmad b. Aʿtham al-Kūfī's."

153 Ibn Aʿtham, vol. VII, 288; Balʿamī, 248. Per al-Yaʿqūbī, *Taʾrīkh*, vol. II, 318, it was Hishām who ousted Maslama and replaced him with Marwān. This hypothesis is discussed below, Ch. 8.

154 Ibn Aʿtham, vol. VII, 287–8; Balʿamī, 247–8. These projects are also mentioned by al-Ṭabarī, vol. II, 1562, trans. vol. XXV, 98, and Ibn Qutayba, *Kitāb al-maʿārif*, 365.

155 *Qurʾān* 18:96, trans. Arberry. This was an important and popular theme in medieval Islamic literature. On the Syriac sources of this Qurʾānic motif, see van Bladel, "The Alexander Legend."

156 *Qurʾān* 18:94, trans. Arberry.

157 Ibn al-Faqīh, *Mukhtaṣar*, 299, trans. 355.

was entrusted either to Sallām the Interpreter, due to his skill with languages, or to the astronomer al-Khwārizmī.[158] Questions of leadership aside, the explorers travelled to the court of the Khazar king, who provided them with guides for the remainder of their journey; after a long trek, they arrived at the rampart of Dhū al-Qarnayn and verified its solidity. This anecdote irrefutably demonstrates the ties linking the people of the Caucasus to Dhū al-Qarnayn's wall, despite the fact that this particular narrative seems to locate the rampart in a remote region far from al-Bāb.[159]

Some confusion likely arose between this legendary edifice and the wall erected by Khusraw Anūshirvān "between the slopes of the Caucasus and the Caspian Sea to protect Iran from nomadic raids" in the pass of Bāb al-Abwāb.[160] Al-Masʿūdī notes that the Sasanian ruler's wall still existed in 332/943, and he provides a detailed description:

> the ... sovereign constructed this famous wall that, in one section, rose above the Caucasus, following its peaks, valleys and gorges, at a length of forty parasangs, until it reached a fortress known as Ṭabarsarān. Approximately every three miles, according to the importance of the route onto which it opened, he built an iron gate, beside which he installed, inside the enclosure, a group of people tasked with keeping watch over the gate and that section of the contiguous wall. This rampart was an impenetrable barrier against attacks from the neighboring peoples of this mountain range: Khazars, Alans, various Turks, Avars, and other infidel tribes.[161]

158 Sallām: Ibn Khurradādhbih, *Kitāb al-masālik*, 162 ff.; Ibn al-Faqīh, *Mukhtaṣar*, 301, trans. 357 (the passage is incomplete). Al-Khwārizmī: al-Muqaddasī, *Aḥsan*, 362; this information is later reported by the erudite Ottoman scholar Ḥajjī Khalīfa (1609–1657, also known by the name Kātib Çelebī), in his *Cihān nümā*, see Bacqué-Grammont, De Polignac, Bohas, "Monstres et murailles," 118, 121. Earlier in this study, I stated that al-Khwārizmī's *Kitāb al-taʾrīkh* is lost, but that certain elements from the text were preserved by the Nestorian chronicler Elias of Nisibis. However, Elias's manuscript is unfortunately fragmentary, and the passage concerning the period in which this expedition took place is missing.

159 The expedition dispatched by al-Wāthiq did not return through the Caucasus, but rather through Central Asia and Khurāsān. See Ibn Khurradādhbih, *Kitāb al-masālik*, 169.

160 Bacqué-Grammont, De Polignac, Bohas, "Monstres et murailles," 122. The site known as the "Door of Doors" in Arabic is called Derbend in Persian, meaning "gorge," and Demür Qapu in Turkish, meaning "iron gate." See Bacqué-Grammont, De Polignac, Bohas, "Monstres et murailles," 112.

161 Al-Masʿūdī, *Murūj*, vol. II, 2–3, 196–7, trans. Pellat vol. I, 159, 231–2.

Maslama's fortifications at al-Bāb were perhaps part of an effort to restore Khusraw Anūshirvān's defensive rampart. The Muslim sources are not alone in recording this initiative. Two short and anonymous Syriac chronicles dated *819* and *846* also mention that the Umayyad general undertook projects of a grand scale, gathering stonemasons (*pāsūlē*) and carpenters (*nagārē*) to build citadels (*ḥeṣnē*) and cities (*mdīnātā*).[162] It is important to note that in both texts, this information concludes the rewriting phase that ended in 728, and both works situate these events in this year, although this dating is somewhat problematic with respect to the chronology established in the Islamic sources. The inclusion of this information in this particular historiographic layer is nonetheless extremely significant: we are presented with an account that is practically contemporaneous with the events it describes, corresponding to *phase 3*, or the era of Hishām, Maslama's brother, under whom these projects were carried out! The authors reliant on Theophilus of Edessa are unfortunately more reserved on this subject, while Theophanes and Agapius merely mention that Maslama arrived at "the Gate."[163]

Contrary to the Muslim authors, their Christian colleagues offer mixed reviews of Maslama's campaigns in the Caucasus. They emphasise the Umayyad hero's fear during his expeditions in the region, in particular during a confrontation with the Khazars, where he and his men were ultimately forced to flee.[164] Only Łewond mentions projects at Derbend/al-Bāb, but initially of demolition rather than construction; he notes that the Muslims set about destroying the fortifications after their capture of the city, before they were stopped by the discovery of an inscription proclaiming that: "in a later era, the children of Ishmael will demolish it and rebuild it at their own expense." This warning was scrupulously heeded, and the workers were ordered to rebuild the fortress.[165]

The *Chronicle of Zuqnīn* offers the most complete picture of Maslama's campaign. The general arrived at the gate (*tarʿā*) of the Turks, who were responsible for widespread unrest in the region; he swiftly killed a large number of them, and inspired so much fear that they begged him for mercy.[166] In this account, terror strikes the opposite camp, shaking the infidels rather than the

162 *819*, 17, trans. 12; *846*, ed. Brooks 235, Latin trans. 178, trans. Brooks 585.

163 Theophanes, *Chronographia*, 409, trans. 567; Agapius, *Kitāb al-ʿunwān*, 507.

164 Theophanes, *Chronographia*, 407, trans. 563; Agapius, *Kitāb al-ʿunwān*, 507; *1234*, 311, trans. vol. I, 241; Michael the Syrian, vol. II, 463, French trans. 501; Bar Hebraeus, 119, trans. 110. The two anonymous chronicles of *819* and *846* also report an earlier defeat for Maslama: *819*, 17, trans. 12; *846*, 235, Latin trans. 178, trans. Brooks 585.

165 Łewond, trans. 38.

166 *Zuqnīn*, 168, trans. Harrak 159.

courageous general. Maslama, however, concerned that the discord among the Turks behind the gate would spread into the *dār al-islām*, continued his offensive by ordering the destruction of this gate constructed by Alexander the Macedonian. In so doing, the Muslims crossed the borders of the world established by the son of Philip II. The following year, Maslama gathered artisans (*ūmānē*), carpenters (*nagārē*) and workers (*qlāgrē*) and rebuilt the gate of the Turks. A treaty was signed, stipulating that the wall could no longer be crossed; however, this pact was swiftly broken by the Barbarians, who easily recouped their losses after the Marwanid's retreat. Al-Jarrāḥ b. ʿAbd Allāh al-Ḥakamī's army counterattacked, but their forces were decimated and their commander killed. Maslama, apprised of the situation, hurried to the Muslim army's aid, but arrived too late. His only return to the region nevertheless inspired terror (*zawʿā*) among the Turks, "who feared his reputation more than his person."[167] While the portrait presented in the anonymous chronicle is more flattering to the Umayyad general, it should be noted that, from 775 on, the sources established a definitive link between Maslama and Alexander the Great.

Scholars consider that "the legend according to which Alexander built a monumental wall to repress the invasions of Barbarian nomads seems to have taken shape in the first century of our era. The identification between these people and those of Magog … is already recorded by Flavius Josephus" and subsequently spread, in particular thanks to Syriac Christianity.[168] This Syriac vector perhaps explains the "contamination" in the *Chronicle of Zuqnīn*, which implies a direct connection between the two war heroes; however, it is equally possible that this is a panegyric for Maslama, who is presented as a new Alexander in keeping with an Umayyad ideology that laid claim to mythic figures, Solomon among them (as discussed in the previous chapter). Maslama's avowed interest in Alexander and his campaigns[169] gives credence to this theory, in a similar manner to the tenuous links established between the Marwanid and the sites of memory associated with Dhū al-Qarnayn in the Islamic sources, despite the persistent ambiguity surrounding this figure's identity.

Endowed both with an eschatological dimension and with the characteristics of a world conqueror, Maslama seems to have fostered the creation of a connection between Dhū al-Qarnayn and Alexander the Great in the sources.

167 *Zuqnīn*, 168–70, trans. Harrak 159–60.

168 Bacqué-Grammont, De Polignac, Bohas, "Monstres et murailles," 120. On the circulation of information related to Alexander, see van Bladel, "The Syriac Sources" and "The Alexander Legend."

169 See Abbott, *Studies*, vol. I, 16–8. This point has also been noted by Cheddadi, *Les Arabes*, 44.

If this is indeed the case, Maslama founded a genre that would become immensely popular in later eras, in particular during the Mamluk period.[170] This is not an incongruous proposition, especially if we consider that Maslama and Alexander shared essentially the same function: they were the "master[s] of boundaries and artisan[s] of the closing of the world" (*figure de maître des seuils et de grand ouvrier de la clôture du monde*).[171] Alexander's rampart, constructed to keep out Gog and Magog, was later destroyed and rebuilt by Maslama. Thus, the Macedonian's wall became the Umayyad's; the borders of the world were no longer defined by the son of Philip II, but by the son of ʿAbd al-Malik. Maslama's stature then changes: no longer merely a regional hero of the Byzantine frontier, he achieves the status of a universal Islamic hero.

The numerous accounts dedicated to Maslama in the Islamic and Christian sources reveal the creation of a Muslim combat hero. The context of the period, including the general's supposed ambitions, fully participates in the construction of a messianic dimension that largely explains this critical need for heroes.

5.3 Eschatology and the Creation of Heroes

The two main "cycles" of Maslama's expeditions – Constantinople and the Caucasus – reveal essentially the same basic fact: Maslama is the warrior trying to fulfill the necessary conditions to bring about the End of Days, or more precisely, to delay their onset. The fall of Constantinople is supposed to presage the apocalypse,[172] as is the invasion of the peoples of Gog and Magog. By failing to conquer the Byzantine capital and resealing Alexander's gates,

170 This presentation of the major figures of Islamic history associated with Alexander the Great is well-attested, without even accounting for the Iranian aspects of how these traditions spread. See the works of De Polignac, "L'image d'Alexandre," "Cosmocrator," "Alexandre maître des seuils et des passages," and "Un 'nouvel Alexandre' mamelouk." See also Aigle, "Les inscriptions dans Baybars."

171 Bacqué-Grammont, De Polignac, Bohas, "Monstres et murailles," 122. See also De Polignac, "Alexandre maître des seuils et des passages."

172 On the eschatological traditions associated with the capture of Constantinople, see El-Cheikh, *Byzantium*, 60–71. Ibn Khaldūn clearly indicates that "He who will destroy the Byzantine emperor and will spend his treasures in God's behalf will be the expected (Mahdī) when he conquers Constantinople. The ruler of Constantinople will be an excellent one, and the army (that will conquer Constantinople) will be an excellent one," *The Muqaddimah*, vol. II, 193. For later examples concerning the fall of Constantinople, see Lellouch and Yérasimos, *Les traditions apocalyptiques*.

Maslama pushes the *eschaton* into the distant future: Islamic space – if not Islamic time – has been defined.

Beginning in the Umayyad era, an entire genre of apocalyptic literature developed around these episodes to justify the Muslims' inability to accomplish their monumental task: to conquer the world completely before the imminent arrival of the End of Days.[173] It should be noted here that, in addition to its eschatological dimensions, the campaign against Constantinople took place in the years leading up to the year 100 *hijrī*, the expected end of the world; this point may well have been a key factor in Sulaymān's decision to attack the city.[174] The sources are filled with messianic elements prior to this presumed expiration date,[175] and the occurrence of certain natural phenomena, such as the earthquakes that occurred frequently during this period, undoubtedly strengthened these beliefs.[176]

Among the apocalyptic cycles that developed, the apocalypse of al-Aʿmāq is perhaps the most important in the context of the present inquiry; its name derives from the northern Syrian plain stretching from Antioch to the foothills of the Taurus mountains between the Amanus mountains and the Kurd Dagh, a territory the Byzantines and Muslims disputed.[177] These accounts are notably preserved in the *Kitāb al-fitān*, where the Rūm are described as the adversaries of the End of Days (*ākhir al-dahr*).[178] During this final battle between the Byzantines and the Muslims, these latter, after many setbacks, gain the upper hand thanks to divine intervention and begin their march on Constantinople, arriving first at Amorium (*ʿAmmūriyya*). The Islamic troops then reach the straits (*khalīj*) of the Bosphorus, whose strong currents prevent their crossing. With the elements working in their favour, the Byzantines rejoice, believing divine aid to be on their side once again. Alas, this illusion passes swiftly, as the straits dry up and the sea retreats, allowing the enemy troops to surround "the city of unbelief" (*madīnat al-kufr*) on a Friday evening, passing the night praising Allah and reciting the *takbīr* and the *tahlīl*. At dawn, a final *takbīr*[179]

173 Cook, "Muslim Apocalyptic and *Jihād*," 103 and note 134; Bashear, "Apocalyptic and Other Materials;" Vasiliev, "Medieval Ideas of the End of the World," 472 ff.

174 Crone, *Medieval Islamic Political Thought*, 76.

175 On the year 100 *hijrī* and its associated expectations, see below, Ch. 6.

176 Two earthquakes, one under al-Walīd I, the other under ʿUmar II, are frequently mentioned in the Christian sources, as shown in table 5.1.

177 On this toponym, see Yāqūt's entry, *Muʿjam*, vol. 1, 222. It is also more frequently referred to as al-ʿAmq, see Sourdel, "Al-ʿAmq." On this apocalyptic cycle, see David Cook's works, "Muslim Apocalyptic and *Jihād*," 83 ff., and *Studies*, 49–54.

178 Nuʿaym b. Ḥammād, *Kitāb al-fitān*, 292, trans. 292.

179 On the *takbīr* as a *topos* in the Islamic sources, especially as a signal of attack, see Noth and Conrad, *The Early Arabic*, 143–5.

rose up over the walls of the city.[180] The traditionist al-Ṭabarānī (d. 360/971) reports that, upon hearing this narrative, Maslama resolved to wage immediate war on Constantinople![181] This tale implies that the tradition existed prior to the general's expedition, although the inverse seems much more likely. Here again, these apocalyptic texts function in a similar manner to those mentioned previously: they express frustration in the face of defeat, and situate these failures against an eschatological backdrop, pushing the Muslim conquest of Constantinople into the distant future.[182]

The similarities between this apocalyptic version of events and the itineraries presented in the Islamic and Christian chronographies, including the well-attested capture of Amorium, are worth noting. The raging waters of the Bosphorus and the Sea of Marmara echo the tempest that strikes the Muslim fleet during the siege, a phenomenon that Łewond attributes to divine intervention. David Cook has rightly pointed out that certain naval and maritime details of the story have been carefully erased from the Muslim apocalypse, in which the Bosphorus dries up, allowing the army to cross it on foot; mentioning the naval attacks would have required recognition of the use of Copts in the Islamic navy, and Christians had no place in this sort of literature.[183] Finally, the *topos* of the *takbīr* that precedes the capture of Constantinople is also found in the symbolic conquest presented in *version 2*. The parallels between the versions in the chronicles and the apocalypses are clear, and invite speculation as to the date at which these traditions from the second corpus were produced. David Cook estimates that these accounts date to the era of ʿAbd al-Malik and his successors, a period in which Muslims were confident in their ability to conquer the world before the End of Days.[184] In other words, it is quite possible that, like the historical accounts, the broad strokes of this apocalyptic cycle were composed in the last decades of the Umayyad period. These narratives were produced to try to account for the fact that certain expected events did not take place; apocalyptic literature offered a convenient means of deferring explanation by situating these events in a distant messianic future.

180 Nuʿaym b. Ḥammād, *Kitāb al-fitān*, 260–1, trans. 248–9, and Cook, "Muslim Apocalyptic and *Jihād*," 86–8.

181 Al-Ṭabarānī, *al-Muʿjam al-kabīr*, vol. 11, 38, nº 1216, cited in Cook, "Muslim Apocalyptic and *Jihād*," 88, note 82. Maslama would then have cried: *la-niʿma al-amīr wa-la-niʿma al-jaysh*.

182 This is the conclusion Cook arrives at, "Muslim Apocalyptic and *Jihād*," 103, note 134, adding that this conclusion corroborates Blankinship's analysis, *The End of the Jihād State*, 223–36.

183 Cook, "Muslim Apocalyptic and *Jihād*," 90.

184 Cook, "Muslim Apocalyptic and *Jihād*," 103. However, it should be noted that Madelung has on several occasions proposed much older dating, which Cook rejects. See Madelung, "Apocalyptic Prophecies."

The development of *ḥadīth*s related to the conquest of Constantinople was part of the same process. The anonymous author of the *Kitāb al-ʿuyūn* states that a *ḥadīth* announcing that the city would be defeated by a caliph bearing the same name as a prophet mentioned in the Qur'ān spurred Sulaymān b. ʿAbd al-Malik's decision to launch an attack on the Byzantine capital, believing himself to be the intended caliph.[185] Following the expedition's failure, new traditions were circulated. Henceforth, there would be three campaigns against Constantinople: the first destined to end in utter defeat, the second concluding in a peace treaty (*ṣulḥ*) and the construction of mosques (*masājid*), and the final assault resulting in success, thanks to divine intervention.[186] While the first is undoubtedly a reference to Muʿāwiya's campaign, the second is almost certainly an allusion to Maslama, whose aforementioned expedition ended with the construction of a mosque within the city walls.

Furthermore, to demonstrate that Constantinople could not have fallen during Maslama's siege, certain traditions even claimed that the city was protected by the Prophet Muḥammad himself![187] During his lifetime, the Prophet supposedly sent letters to a number of rulers – among them the Byzantine emperor, the Sasanian sovereign and the Negus of Abyssinia – urging them to convert to Islam and recognise the new religion.[188] The authenticity of these missives, accepted by the medieval authors as fact, has divided modern scholars.[189] Be that as it may, our sources confirm that upon receiving the courier, Heraclius immediately saw that the letter was marked with the seal of prophecy; he replied by recognising Muḥammad as the messenger of God, as foretold by Jesus, and said that he had ordered his subjects to convert, but that they had unfortunately refused.[190] Here we encounter the recurring myth of Heraclius's conversion. Based on the evidence provided by the *isnād*s, this theme was developed early on, as a tradition reported on the authority of al-Zuhrī states that the Byzantine emperor sent the letter to Rome for authentication and received an unambiguous response: "there is no doubt about it.

185 *Kitāb al-ʿuyūn*, 24. See Canard, "Les expéditions," 107; El-Cheikh, *Byzantium*, 65.

186 Nuʿaym b. Ḥammād, *Kitāb al-fitān*, 288, trans. 286. On this well-known *ḥadīth*, see Canard, "Les expéditions," 111; Cook, *Studies*, 53; El-Cheikh, *Byzantium*, 68.

187 El-Cheikh discusses this point in detail, *Byzantium*, 43 ff.

188 Ibn Saʿd, *al-Ṭabaqāt*, vol. I, 258 ff. This motif clearly reflects the famous fresco of the six kings in the Umayyad baths at Quṣayr ʿAmra, discussed further below, Ch. 8.

189 See the opposite opinions of Hamidullah ("La lettre du Prophète" and *Six originaux*, 149–72) and Serjeant ("Early Arabic Prose"). See also Conrad, "Heraclius in Early Islamic Kerygma," and El-Cheikh, *Byzantium*, 43–4.

190 Yaʿqūbī, *Ta'rīkh*, vol. II, 77–8.

Follow him and believe him."[191] From the Umayyad era on, narratives placed great emphasis on Heraclius's conversion to Islam. Justification for the impenetrability of the Byzantine capital was thus established: the emperor's favourable response to this missive guaranteed the city's protection. Al-Yaʿqūbī goes even further, stating that the Prophet, upon receiving Heraclius's reply, stipulated: "their kingdom will endure as long as my letter remains with them."[192] Thus, it was the Prophet himself who guarded the walls of Constantinople, provided that his letter remained in the Byzantines' possession. The divine protection of the city, attested by Christian authors like Łewond, whose account describes Maslama stating that he cannot fight against God, is here turned on its head: the omnipotence of the Christian God is replaced by the omnipotence of the Prophet of Islam, preventing military triumph.

On the Caucasian front, messianic elements dating to the Umayyad period are rare, as the Turkish threat is most frequently associated with the Abbasids, who were considered guilty of allowing this danger to spread.[193] Broadly speaking, the apocalyptic traditions present less favourable outcomes when describing the Muslim battles against the Turks than when treating their conflicts with the Byzantines.[194] Two Turkish invasions were feared, one in Azerbaijan, the other near the Euphrates;[195] this cycle was reworked after Nuʿaym b. Ḥammād's (d. 229/844) era, as it was necessary at the time to explain how the Turks became integrated into the caliphate. It is possible that Maslama's campaigns in the Caucasus were linked to fears of this expected Turkish incursion into Azerbaijan: in general, conflating the Turks and Khazars with the Yājūj and Mājūj confirmed their eschatological dimensions.[196]

Certain synchronisms characterised these various apocalyptic cycles. One of these is particularly important for the present study, as it attests to the link between the capture of the Byzantine capital and the mountainous region near the Caspian Sea, later echoed by al-Suyūṭī (d. 911/1505): "if the world only had a single day left to live, God would lengthen it to allow a man from my family (*rajul min ahl baytī*) to conquer the mountains of Daylam and Constantinople."[197]

191 Al-Ṭabarī, vol. I, 1566, trans. vol. VIII, 105. This passage also occurs in the *Sīra* of Ibn Hishām, 972, trans. Guillaume 656.

192 Al-Yaʿqūbī, *Taʾrīkh*, vol. II, 78.

193 On the historical apocalypses linked to the Turkish invasions, see David Cook, *Studies*, 84–91.

194 Cook, "Muslim Apocalyptic and *Jihād*," 97.

195 Nuʿaym b. Ḥammād, *Kitāb al-fitān*, 128, trans. 115.

196 Nuʿaym b. Ḥammād, *Kitāb al-fitān*, 412ff., trans. 419ff. On the traditions related to Gog and Magog, see David Cook, *Studies*, 182–8.

197 Al-Suyūṭī, cited in Canard, "Les expéditions," 107. On the current association between these two geographical areas, see Cook, *Studies*, 169. While the Turks are usually associated

The gloss proposed by the Egyptian scholar specifies that the designated man was none other than the *mahdī*, and Canard suggests that he may be identified with Hārūn al-Rashīd, who forced Daylam into submission;[198] perhaps an earlier stratum existed, tracing back to Maslama – who was active on both fronts – that was subsequently reworked in the service of the Abbasid caliphate. In any case, the Marwanid general, champion of Umayyad *jihād*, was destined to become a messianic figure; as David Cook has shown, there were strong ties connecting *jihād* and apocalyptic.[199] Maslama's closing of the Islamic world provides a good illustration of this relationship: the end of the "*Jihād State*" pushed the apocalypse into the distant future.

In sum, the narrative accounts of Maslama's expeditions reveal that great efforts were made to portray the Marwanid general as a combat hero who achieved symbolic victory over Constantinople and presented himself as a new Alexander in the Caucasus. All of these elements were fixed by 775 at the latest, as attested by the *Chronicle of Zuqnīn*, which provides the most complete rendition in the Christian corpus. If these traditions were then recorded in writing, they *must* have existed beforehand, and thus they could easily date to the Umayyad period as part of the first Islamic dynasty's ideological program. The privileged place reserved for Maslama in this anonymous Syriac text may indicate that the author relied on a pro-Umayyad source, perhaps even a panegyric dedicated to the heroic warrior. The anonymous chronicles of *819* and *846*, while presenting less-detailed portraits of Maslama, also indicate an earlier recomposition of a specific core of facts related to the general's expeditions. The pertinent historiographic stratum concerning his expeditions was thus written around 730, or nearly simultaneous with the exploits and military failures of the Umayyad hero himself! The sources in Theophilus of Edessa's circuit establish a *terminus ante quem* as well, proving that the texts were compiled using information circulating during the Umayyad period.

The Christian corpus also – and most importantly – demonstrates that these elements were composed in the Bilād al-Shām in a profoundly Syrian context: Maslama fights for his own glory and that of the Umayyad dynasty on the borders of the Islamic empire – the Byzantine and Caucasian frontiers being relatively close to Syria and particularly strategic for the security of the

---

with the people of Gog, those of Magog are generally associated with Daylam, see Cook, *Studies*, 183.

198 Canard, "Les expéditions," 107. On the allegiance of the provinces of Daylam and the Caspian to Hārūn al-Rashīd, see al-Ṭabarī, vol. III, 705–6, trans. vol. XXX, 254–6.

199 See Cook, "Muslim Apocalyptic and *Jihād*," especially 72–3.

region as a whole[200] – but it is in the Syrian space that his image develops. The history and legend of Maslama are both inscribed in the Syrian landscape as a result of his military campaigns, themselves the outcome of political decisions made in Damascus. Stepping briefly outside the Syrian context of this inquiry in order to follow Maslama's trajectory has allowed us to better understand the scope of the Umayyad ideological project, written and developed in Syria, but conceived at the level of the caliphate. This information confirms al-Ṭabarī's statement: scholars and traditionists participated in Maslama's military operations. On the authority of Sulaymān b. Mūsā he affirms that Khālid b. Maʿdān al-Kalāʿī al-Ḥimṣī[201] took part in the siege of Constantinople.[202] Just like Louis XIV traversing the battlefields with his historiographers in tow,[203] Maslama led his campaigns escorted by those charged with ensuring and preserving his glory. Figures such as Sulaymān or Khālid played an undeniable role in the circulation and spread of traditions related to these highly significant episodes. The raw material, collected *in situ*, spread freely in the Syrian space and became the foundation of a historiography that promoted the merits of the rulers in whose names it was written.

In creating this heroic image, certain of Maslama's other attributes were neglected. His administrative talents seem largely forgotten, which has led certain scholars to promptly declare that ʿAbd al-Malik's son was little more than an unskilled functionary.[204] However, the Marwanid general frequently combined his governing tasks with his military actions. He was consecutively in charge of the *jund* of Qinnasrīn,[205] the vast region of the Jazīra, Armenia and Azerbaijan multiple times, as well as Iraq and Khurāsān. Although this last experience ended in failure, it must not be forgotten that Maslama actively contributed to submitting the Jazīra – a Marwanid fiscal invention – to strong

200 As Décobert has noted ("Notule sur le patrimonialisme omeyyade," 236): "The Syria of the late Umayyads and of the first Abbasid century was almost entirely a region of *ʿawāṣim* and of caliphal land." Additionally, numismatic evidence has demonstrated the strong unity between the mints in this "Umayyad North" – from Syria to Armenia to Azerbaijan, including the Jazīra – indicating that these zones were understood as a collective whole. See Bates, "History, Geography and Numismatics;" Spellberg, "The Umayyad North;" Bonner, "The Mint."

201 These two Syrian traditionists, both of whom worked for the Umayyads, were introduced in Ch. 1.

202 Al-Ṭabarī, vol. II, 1315, trans. vol. XXIV, 39–40. See also Donner, "The Problem," 4–5, 7–9; Elad, "Community of Believers," 263; Van Ess, *Theologie*, 111–4; Bonner, *Aristocratic Violence*, 107.

203 See the epigraph to this chapter, Cornette, *Le roi de guerre*, 249.

204 Blankinship, *The End of the Jihād State*, 87–8.

205 Michael the Syrian, vol. II, 449, French trans. 474; Crone, *Slaves*, 125.

financial and political regulation, implementing a cadastre and a census, then imposing the wearing of the lead seal around the necks of tributaries to ensure payment of the *kharāj*.[206] A dual motive lay behind this partial effacement of Maslama's administrative functions: the narratives were trying to create the image of an exclusively military hero, which required certain processes of selection. Moreover, the role of model administrator was unavailable for Maslama to fill, as it belonged to another great figure from the Umayyad pantheon and the general's own brother, the caliph Hishām.[207] Maslama was thus limited to the role of warrior, the quintessential hero. He is presented in the sources as the "greatest captain of the Umayyad century,"[208] an analysis that Ibn Khaldūn himself likely would have supported,[209] and took "to his grave the fortunes of the Marwanids, which steadily declined after his death."[210]

Although he never became the "war caliph"[211] he undoubtedly would have been had he attained this highest office, Maslama was a warrior prince, the military arm of the Umayyad dynasty. His glory, acquired weapon in hand, caused the poet Abū Nukhayla to exclaim: "Maslama, o son of all the caliphs, hero [on the field] of battle (*fāris al-hayjā*), pride of the world (*jabal al-arḍ*)!".[212] The poet, however, was severely reprimanded by the first Abbasid caliph for his audacity in having once praised the great Umayyad soldier. Once again, we find ourselves faced with the problem of the Abbasids in confrontation with the memory of their predecessors. Even if we give precedence to the narratives emphasising Maslama's failures rather than his triumphs, the general's heroic image was already too widespread and too well-known to efface completely. Furthermore, Maslama's disappointment at Constantinople served Abbasid interests: it preserved the potential for the new Islamic dynasty to take the Byzantine capital themselves, thus fulfilling the conditions for the End of Days.

206 *819*, 15, trans. 10; *846*, 233, Latin trans. 177, trans. Brooks 582; *1234*, 299, trans. 233, trans. Palmer 209. On the Marwanid creation of the Jazīra as an administrative and fiscal entity, see Robinson, *Empire and Elites*, 33–62. The question of *dhimmī*s wearing the seal was not limited to the unique function of tax payment, as Fattal claims, *Le statut légal*, 289, but was also a discriminatory practice, as Robinson has shown, "Neck-Sealing."

207 On Hishām's administrative skill, see below, Ch. 8.

208 Gabrieli, "La rivolta," 222.

209 On Ibn Khaldūn's interpretation of Maslama's role, see Martinez-Gros, *Ibn Khaldûn*, 168.

210 Lammens, "Maslama b. ʿAbd al-Malik," 448.

211 In a liberal adaptation of the title of Cornette's foundational work, *Le roi de guerre*.

212 I am following Pellat's literary translation here. *Jabal* can also be translated in a sense closer to the original text to mean "leader" or "master." The *Kitāb al-Aghānī* reproduces these verses, but replaces *jabal* with *qamar*, thus making Maslama the "luminary" of the world. See al-Masʿūdī, *Murūj*, vol. VI, 119, trans. Pellat (slightly modified) vol. IV, 947; *Aghānī*, vol. I, 243.

From an eschatological perspective, it goes without saying that Maslama's fiasco was indispensable to the Abbasid rise to power, as the End of Days had thus been delayed.

The Marwanids seem to have developed a triumphant narrative: they wanted to construct the image of a conquering hero, necessary for the Umayyads and particularly in the context of the end of the "*Jihād State*." In the face of defeat, they sought victors. In this sense, Maslama as a figure of failure makes him more of an Abbasid hero than an Umayyad one: praise of his deficiencies justified the political rise of the second Islamic dynasty. An exemplar of failure was thus born, a noble hero faced with inevitable defeat. The old Arab virtues (*murūʾa*) Maslama embodied were emphasised: he was first and foremost an Arab, an Umayyad second. It was likely in the context of Hārūn al-Rashīd's planned expedition against the Byzantine capital[213] prior to his accession to the caliphate that the image of Maslama was heavily reworked by the Abbasid chroniclers. This campaign ended on the banks of the Bosphorus, where Hārūn signed a peace treaty with the Byzantines,[214] but the change in attitude toward Maslama, the Muslim who had come closest to capturing Constantinople, is palpable thereafter.

The following anecdote is revealing in this respect. When leaving on campaign, Hārūn was accompanied by his father, the caliph al-Mahdī. Hārūn was headed for Anatolia, al-Mahdī for Syria. Riding alongside one another, the two men reached Qaṣr Maslama,[215] between Ḥarrān and Raqqa, in 163/779–780. Al-ʿAbbās b. Muḥammad was with them, and took advantage of the occasion to recall the Abbasid family's debt to the Marwanid prince, who had been particularly generous to their forebear Muḥammad b. ʿAlī.[216] Maslama had given this latter a substantial recompense of 4000 dinars, adding that he could request even more if necessary. Informed of this commendable act, the caliph showed the same generosity to Maslama's descendants in the area as well as their *mawālī*, affirming that he had "repaid and rendered justice" to the one-time master of the region.[217] This episode is presented as a pilgrimage in the footsteps of the Umayyad hero, Hārūn in a sense trying to become his successor by marching on the legendary Byzantine city that had obsessed

213 Or, more precisely, in the narrative that was subsequently developed. Similarly, al-Balādhurī's silence on the siege of Constantinople in his *Ansāb al-ashrāf* is also problematic.

214 See, for example, al-Ṭabarī, vol. III, 504–5, trans. vol. XXIX, 220–2.

215 Al-Ṭabarī, vol. III, 495, trans. vol. XXIX, 210. The site is more generally known by the name Ḥiṣn Maslama.

216 The father of the first two Abbasid caliphs.

217 Al-Ṭabarī, vol. III, 495, trans. vol. XXIX, 210.

generations of Muslim conquerors. Redeeming the memory of one who had failed to capture Constantinople was not only possible, but necessary.

This chapter provides an outline of Maslama's passage from adversity to alterity;[218] however, the complexity of these historiographic creations was not limited to the domain of tensions between the first two Islamic dynasties. Within the Umayyad family, colourful personalities were constantly in competition. Maslama, the military arm of the caliphate, relied on the political goodwill of his kin, as witnessed by ʿUmar b. ʿAbd al-ʿAzīz's recall of the general during the siege of Constantinople. Upon his return to Damascus, Maslama presented himself at the palace along with his troops, and the caliph refused to see him. This refusal persisted over the course of several days, or as long as Maslama arrived accompanied by a military escort. Finally, Maslama presented himself more humbly before the caliph, and this time he was granted an audience: ʿUmar II stated that he hoped that the valiant soldier had undertaken all his expeditions and conquests in the service of God rather than for his own personal glory. Ibn Aʿtham notes that following this meeting, Maslama went regularly to pay homage to the caliph, whose moral lessons he appreciated and whose fervent admirer he became.[219] A final anecdote reports that ʿUmar II heard tell of Maslama's extravagant spending on his feasts. Shocked by this imprudence, the caliph – the pinnacle of asceticism – conceived a strategy with his cooks and invited Maslama to dinner. He had his cooks prepare great quantities of the most delectable dishes, alongside a simple plate of lentils with onion and olive oil (*al-ʿadas wa-al-baṣal wa-al-zayt*). The scheme consisted in first serving Maslama the lentils, which he devoured until he was sated, and then presenting the other dishes, of which he was unable to take even a single bite! ʿUmar then pointed out that it was unnecessary to spend a thousand dirhams a day on nourishment, and that this sum would be better spent feeding the hungry (*jāʾiʿa*); thereafter, Maslama tried to change his behaviour and follow this generous advice.[220] The images of the two great Umayyads clash here: the pious ʿUmar educates the careless and gluttonous warrior, and faith overtakes military valor.

The many complex developments that led to the general's failure did not occur by chance, but arose from a logic proper to the evolution of the Marwanid policies of the "*Jihād State*." Maslama, both at the walls of Constantinople as

218 The general's tomb was vandalised, like those of most of the Umayyad caliphs, after the Abbasid Revolution. Maslama's skull was unearthed and used as an archery target until it was completely destroyed. See al-Maqrīzī, *Kitāb al-nizāʿ*, 54, trans. 92.

219 Ibn Aʿtham, vol. VII, 231; Balʿamī, trans. 212.

220 Ibn Aʿtham, vol. VII, 231; Balʿamī, trans. 212–3.

well as in the Caucasus, was the man who "closed" the Muslim world; in so doing, he affirmed a certain relationship between the Umayyads and space, with Syria as their centre of power. Naturally, he was aided, or perhaps incited, to take up this function by ʿUmar II, the caliph who brought the expansion of the empire to a halt[221] and subsequently tried to teach the soldier the superior merits of piety over military valor. We must now turn our attention to this other quintessential figure of Umayyad history, the unanimously praised and virtuous "holy" caliph.

221 Blankinship estimates that it was precisely this disastrous defeat at Constantinople that motivated ʿUmar II's initial attempts to pause the empire's expansion, *The End of the Jihād State*, 33–4.

CHAPTER 6

The Creation of Umayyad Heroes: ʿUmar b. ʿAbd al-ʿAzīz, the "Holy" Caliph

> One of the main properties of heroicity rests in the propitious or, at least, retrospective reading of a contemporary event. The present-day hero is nearly always presaged by older figures whose memory he now reawakens. National history derives its most palpable teleological spirit from its heroes.[1]

•••

> In the Islamic context, all sovereigns, sultans and caliphs – albeit in various literary registers – appear as "commonplace kings," as the topoi of good and bad governance who populate the sources, which repeat the same examples, invoking the same figures and the same metaphors.[2]

∴

Prior to Maslama's attempts to model his conduct after that of the virtuous ʿUmar II, the short-lived rivalry between the general and the caliph may also have had a historiographic dimension.[3] The available sources have much less to say about ʿUmar b. ʿAbd al-ʿAzīz than the son of ʿAbd al-Malik; his brief caliphate (99–101/717–720) could not compete with Maslama's long and storied career in the chronicles. Unlike the general's military expeditions, the caliph's deeds did not lend themselves so easily to historiographic development. While the details of his reign are less concrete, they nevertheless attest to a similar process aimed at the creation of an Islamic hero: alongside the warrior, the quintessential combat hero, we find the figure of the "holy" caliph,

1 Centlivres, Fabre, Zonabend, "Introduction," 6.
2 Dakhlia, *Le divan des rois*, 12.
3 An earlier version of this chapter was published previously, see Borrut, "Entre tradition et histoire."

 | DOI:10.1163/9789004466326_008

the quintessential Muslim hero. Anthropologists have established that being a "savior, … a foretold actor, a redeemer or messianic prophet"[4] was essentially the quality that *made* the hero what he was. Whereas Maslama b. ʿAbd al-Malik was a divisive figure in medieval texts, the caliph ʿUmar II held a place of privilege across different historiographic traditions, Islamic as well as Christian. The sources unanimously praise ʿUmar II as a paragon of virtue best known for his ascetic lifestyle.[5]

This widespread consensus over the merits of an Umayyad caliph in Abbasid historiography is somewhat surprising. The general agreement that ʿUmar II exemplified the traits of a good ruler perhaps suggests that, in this instance, we are not faced with what Assmann deems a "counter-memory," or a memory that privileges elements suppressed by the official memory in the creation of a counter-history.[6] In order to verify this hypothesis, we must seek out the caliph's earliest image, bearing in mind that the hero is never simply presented as-is in history, but rather is constructed on cultural, social, and political levels. Modern scholarship has long taken an interest in ʿUmar II's portrayal in the sources and, to a lesser extent, the unique conditions surrounding his caliphate. However, the modalities that dictated the genesis of these *topoi* that created the image of a just and pious caliph and the means of their diffusion remain little understood. Similar to the methodology used in the previous chapter, it is important that we try to date the circulation of these elements in order to understand *when* and *where* this image of the "holy" caliph emerged; we must also try to identify *who* worked to promote this image and *how* its transmission was assured. Although all of the available sources on the early Islamic period mention ʿUmar II, conducting an exhaustive survey of these texts is unnecessary here. Rather, we must construct a rough outline of the caliph's image in the Islamic tradition, followed by an analysis of the conditions in which the creation of an archetypal figure arose and evolved.

6.1 ʿUmar II in the Islamic Tradition

Three main characteristics dominate the list of qualities attributed to ʿUmar b. ʿAbd al-ʿAzīz in the Islamic sources: his piety and virtue, which made him the fifth of the *Rāshidūn* caliphs; his indelible links to his predecessor and model,

---

4 Albert, "Du martyr à la star," 16.
5 Dakhlia, *Le divan des rois*, 246.
6 Assmann, *Moses the Egyptian*, 12.

ʿUmar b. al-Khaṭṭāb; and his dual status as *mahdī* and *mujaddid*, which gave him an undeniable soteriological dimension.

6.1.1 *The Fifth Orthodox Caliph*

Medieval authors – Sunni and Shiite alike – were unanimously favourable to ʿUmar II; these chroniclers consistently emphasised his praiseworthy qualities, ultimately earning him the distinction of being the fifth orthodox caliph.[7] His merits reflected in particular on his immediate predecessor, Sulaymān b. ʿAbd al-Malik, and to a certain extent on the Umayyad dynasty as a whole, since it had "produced" this virtuous caliph. Sulaymān was praised for having chosen ʿUmar as his successor, although the conditions of this selection remain obscure.[8] Sulaymān earned his nickname "key to goodness" (*miftāḥ al-khayr*)[9] due to the fact that his reign opened and closed with blessed events: the liberation of al-Ḥajjāj's prisoners and the designation of ʿUmar II as his successor,[10] although it is important to note that this designation challenged the direct line of succession envisioned by ʿAbd al-Malik. While Sulaymān's caliphate marked the point at which ʿAbd al-Malik's regionalisation of Marwanid power began to bear fruit,[11] ʿUmar II's accession brought a temporary end to any further progress in this direction. ʿUmar b. ʿAbd al-ʿAzīz nevertheless maintained very good relations with his father-in-law: in the *Kitāb al-Aghānī*, Abū al-Faraj al-Iṣfahānī remarked that ʿAbd al-Malik held his son-in-law in higher regard than any of his own sons, with the exception of al-Walīd.[12] Barthold suggests that ʿUmar II rose to even greater prominence under al-Walīd's caliphate.[13] Based on al-Ṭabarī's citation of some verses by Jarīr, prior to al-Walīd's death, Sulaymān was posited as his successor, at which suggestion ʿAbd al-ʿAzīz presented himself as a serious competitor for the throne;[14] if we trust this account, a rivalry between ʿAbd al-Malik's sons and his brother ʿAbd al-ʿAzīz's branch of the family predated the accession of

7 For example, see Ibn al-Athīr, vol. V, 65; Ibn Kathīr, vol. IX, 207; al-Suyūṭī, *Taʾrīkh al-khulafāʾ*, 270 (who also calls him *al-khalīfa al-ṣāliḥ*). For modern inquiries on the subject, see Becker, "Studien;" Barthold, "The Caliph ʿUmar II;" Murad, "ʿUmar II's View;" Cobb, "ʿUmar (II)."

8 See Becker, "Studien," 21 ff.; Barthold, "The Caliph ʿUmar II," 79–80; Bosworth, "Rajāʾ ibn Ḥaywa;" Eisener, *Zwischen Faktum und Fiktion*, 213 ff.; Mayer, "Neue Aspekte," 109–15.

9 Al-Ṭabarī, vol. II, 1337, trans. vol. XXIV, 62; see also Ibn Qutayba, *Kitāb al-maʿārif*, 360.

10 See al-Māwardī's opinions on the subject, *al-Aḥkām*, 48, trans. 13–14.

11 On this point, see Bacharach, "Marwanid Umayyad Building Activities," 28 ff., and below, Ch. 8.

12 *Kitāb al-Aghānī*, vol. VIII, 151.

13 Barthold, "The Caliph ʿUmar II," 73.

14 Al-Ṭabarī, vol. II, 1283–4, trans. vol. XXIV, 5–6.

ʿUmar II.[15] These connections perhaps played a decisive role in ʿUmar's nomination, while simultaneously provoking the hostility of ʿAbd al-Malik's sons, especially Hishām.[16]

Beyond the reflection of ʿUmar II's prestige on his predecessor, a few examples will sufficiently demonstrate the caliph's great renown in the Muslim sources. He was even admired by his Abbasid successors, who were typically unenthusiastic toward the Umayyads. During a visit to Jerusalem and Damascus in 780, the caliph al-Mahdī described the four domains in which the Umayyads outshone the Abbasids, among them the caliphate of the pious ʿUmar II, cited as evidence of their ability to produce such a ruler.[17] The narrative sources have preserved a wealth of sayings and letters attributed to ʿUmar II – so many, in fact, that it is questionable how many of these are authentic or apocryphal[18] – all of which offer the occasion to highlight the caliph's moral virtues. These qualities are clear in the sermon – said to have been his very last – that ʿUmar II gave before the people of Khunāṣira,[19] and more generally in the Sunni tradition.

ʿUmar II enjoyed the same high stature among the Shiite authors. Al-Masʿūdī depicted ʿUmar II as the only just Umayyad caliph, although he also credited Muʿāwiya, ʿAbd al-Malik and Hishām with political and administrative talents.[20] Al-Yaʿqūbī reports that:

> ʿUmar b. ʿAbd al-ʿAzīz ruled with humility (*tawāḍuʿ*), devotion (*nask*), asceticism (*tazahhud*) and faith (*dīn*), and he surrounded himself with people of merit (*ahl al-faḍl*). He removed al-Walīd's governors and appointed those more qualified for the task. His governors acted in conformity with his conduct and put an end to the injustice and oppression to which the people had been accustomed. He abandoned [the practice of] cursing ʿAlī b. Abī Ṭālib – peace be upon him – in the pulpits and substituted [the phrase]: "Our Lord, forgive us and our brothers, who preceded us in belief, and put Thou not into our hearts any rancour

15 Barthold, "The Caliph ʿUmar II," 77.

16 On this point, see Hishām's reaction in Ibn al-Athīr, vol. V, 40–1 and *TMD*, 45, 159 ff.; Cobb, "ʿUmar (II)," 886. See also al-Masʿūdī, *Murūj*, vol. VI, 106, trans. Pellat vol. IV, 944.

17 Al-Rabaʿī, *Kitāb faḍāʾil al-Shām*, 42; al-Suyūṭī, *Itḥāf al-akhiṣṣā*, 160–1. See Cobb, "Virtual Sacrality," 50; El-Hibri, "The Redemption," 243.

18 Crone and Hinds, *God's Caliph*, 77; see also al-Qāḍī, "Early Islamic State Letters," 215–75; Noth and Conrad, *The Early Arabic*, 76–87.

19 Al-Ṭabarī, vol. II, 1368–9, trans. vol. XXIV, 98–9. See also Ibn ʿAbd al-Ḥakam, *Sīra*, 37 ff.

20 Al-Masʿūdī, *Murūj*, vol. VI, 161–2, trans. Pellat vol. IV, 963, on which see Khalidi, *Islamic Historiography*, 128 ff.; see also al-Maqrīzī, *Kitāb al-nizāʿ*, 6, trans. 46; Ibn Khaldūn, *The Muqaddimah*, vol. I, 424. This text is cited above, Ch. 4.

> towards those who believe, Our Lord, surely Thou art the all-gentle, the all-compassionate,"[21] and the people still use this expression in the *khuṭba* even today.[22]

This attitude toward ʿAlī obviously met with the approval of the Shiite authors,[23] but it is also mentioned by the Sunni and Christian authors.[24] The image of this pious caliph was undeniably popular throughout Islamic literature.[25] The great Ibn Khaldūn describes ʿUmar II's piety as follows: "The sons of ʿAbd al-Malik, then, came into power one after the other. Their outstanding religious attitude is well known. ʿUmar b. ʿAbd al-ʿAzīz reigned in between them. He eagerly and relentlessly aspired to (follow) the ways of the first four caliphs and the men around Muḥammad."[26] These direct links between ʿUmar II and the *Rāshidūn* caliphs have long interested scholars,[27] with the special connection between the caliph and his predecessor ʿUmar b. al-Khaṭṭāb receiving much of this attention.

6.1.2 *A New ʿUmar b. al-Khaṭṭāb*

These two caliphs are connected by more than just a name. First, they share a familial connection: ʿUmar II's mother was ʿUmar b. al-Khaṭṭāb's granddaughter. The sources place a great deal of emphasis on this genealogical link, which also helps to establish ʿUmar II's legitimacy: blood relations partially explain ʿUmar II's praiseworthy qualities and his identification as a new ʿUmar I.[28]

---

21 *Qurʾān* 59:10, trans. Arberry.

22 Al-Yaʿqūbī, *Mushākalat*, 19–20, trans. 337 (with minor changes).

23 See the verses by the Shiite poet Kuthayyir cited by al-Yaʿqūbī, *Taʾrīkh*, vol. II, 305; *Kitāb al-ʿuyūn*, vol. I, 62; Abū Nuʿaym, *Ḥilyat*, vol. V, 322; these verses also appear in the more developed accounts of Ibn Saʿd, ed. Sachau, *al-Ṭabaqāt*, vol. V, 291, and particularly Ibn al-Jawzī, *Sīra*, 290 ff.; al-Masʿūdī, *Murūj*, vol. V, 419, trans. Pellat vol. IV, 868, notes that according to other opinions, the formula: "Surely God bids to justice and good-doing and giving to kinsmen, and He forbids indecency, dishonour, and insolence, admonishing you, so that haply you will remember" (*Qurʾān* 16:90, trans. Arberry) was substituted for the cursing of ʿAlī, or that both expressions were recited simultaneously, and that this practice remained current in his day. This information is corroborated by al-Suyūṭī, 285. See Murad, "ʿUmar II's View," 40–2.

24 See al-Ṭabarī, vol. II, 1483, trans. vol. XXV, 19–20; Ibn al-Athīr, vol. V, 42; and the Christian Arab author Saʿīd b. Biṭrīq, 43.

25 ʿUmar II was also famous for his generosity to the needy and the ill, whom he granted pensions and inscribed in the *dīwān*. Al-Ṭabarī, vol. II, 1367, trans. vol. XXIV, 97; Ibn al-Jawzī, *Sīra*, 154 ff.; see Crone, *Medieval Islamic Political Thought*, 307, 309.

26 Ibn Khaldūn, *The Muqaddimah*, vol. I, 423.

27 See notably Murad, "ʿUmar II's View."

28 Cobb, "ʿUmar (II)," 887; Murad, "ʿUmar II's View," 31.

Beyond their shared lineage, ʿUmar I was also an avowed model for ʿUmar II. Poetry accentuated his similarity to his illustrious predecessor,[29] and several sources mention that ʿUmar II decided to follow the *sīra* of ʿUmar b. al-Khaṭṭāb. To do so, he wrote to this latter's grandson, requesting letters and decisions handed down by the caliph concerning Muslims and *dhimmīs* alike.[30] Crone and Hinds have noted that this demand indicates that information on ʿUmar I's administrative practice must not have been readily available.[31] In any case, this account attests to ʿUmar II's real desire to follow the example of his predecessor, or at the very least, to use him as a source of inspiration.[32]

The medieval authors were not unaware of the similarities between the two ʿUmars, nor the fact that the first served as a role model for the second. A passage related by both Abū Nuʿaym al-Iṣfahānī (d. 430/1038)[33] and Ibn al-Jawzī (d. 597/1201)[34] attests to this awareness, as it unexpectedly describes ʿUmar II passing an unfavourable judgment on his predecessor; unsurprisingly, this posed numerous difficulties for these authors. In this narrative, ʿUmar II explained that the Prophet had left an accessible river (*nahr mawrūd*) for mankind, and that his successor had not drawn anything from this river (*lam yastanqiṣ minhu shay'an*); on the contrary, his successor had dug a canal (*sāqiyya*)[35] diverging from this source. Did ʿUmar II here claim that ʿUmar b. al-Khaṭṭāb was the first to have deviated from the path laid out by the Prophet?[36] The second caliph's notoriety and the relations linking the two caliphs led Ibn al-Jawzī to try to explain this passage. He states that while ʿUmar I was indeed the intended subject of this allusion, a mistake was made, as in actuality ʿUmar II was talking about ʿUthmān. To corroborate his hypothesis, Ibn al-Jawzī presents a second version of this narrative, nearly identical to the one preserved by Abū

29 Crone and Hinds, *God's Caliph*, 79.

30 Ibn ʿAbd al-Ḥakam, *Sīra*, 103; Abū Nuʿaym, *Ḥilyat*, vol. V, 284, 286; Ibn Saʿd, ed. Sachau, *al-Ṭabaqāt*, vol. V, 292. Elsewhere, ʿUmar II simply claims the *sīra* of his predecessor: al-Balādhurī, *Ansāb*, vol. VII, 109; *TMD*, 45, 175; Ibn al-Jawzī, *Sīra*, 127–33 (letter reproduced with slight differences in Ṣafwat, *Jamharat*, vol. II, 375); Ibn Kathīr, *al-Bidāya*, vol. IX, 199 ff.; al-Suyūṭī, *Ta'rīkh al-khulafā'*, 273; Crone and Hinds, *God's Caliph*, 79; Murad, "ʿUmar II's View," 38.

31 Crone and Hinds, *God's Caliph*, 79.

32 See Wellhausen, *Das arabische Reich*, 166 ff., trans. *The Arab Kingdom*, 267 ff.

33 On ʿUmar II's place in Abū Nuʿaym's work, see Donner, *Narratives*, 94–7.

34 Abū Nuʿaym's influence on Ibn al-Jawzī is well-known, see Laoust, "Ibn al-D̲jawzī," 774–5; other than his *manāqib* dedicated to ʿUmar II, Ibn al-Jawzī, a specialist in the genre, also devoted an entire volume to ʿUmar I, *Manāqib amīr al-mu'minīn ʿUmar b. al-Khaṭṭāb*.

35 Abū Nuʿaym, *Ḥilyat*, vol. V, 273–4; Ibn al-Jawzī, *Sīra*, 115–7. See Murad, "ʿUmar II's View," 34–8.

36 For a condemnation of such deviation, see *Qur'ān* 4: 115.

Nuʿaym, having merely changed the name of one of the transmitters: between the first two successors of the Prophet described in the initial version, he inserts a phrase mentioning "another man who did not seek to take from it anything at all" (*rajul ākhar fa-lam yastanqiṣ minhu shayʾan*),[37] thus removing any blame from ʿUmar b. al-Khaṭṭāb. As Murad has rightly noted, this change was clearly a manipulation of information by inserting a (false) variant in the chain of transmission.[38] A slightly different version of this famous anecdote appears in Ibn al-Athīr, Ibn ʿAsākir and the *Kitāb al-Aghānī*:[39] to avoid any confusion, these three sources present essentially the same text, designating the Prophet's successors by name and specifying that neither Abū Bakr nor ʿUmar b. al-Khaṭṭāb deviated from the Prophet's path, while Abū al-Faraj al-Iṣfahānī even goes so far as to assert that the third caliph, ʿUthmān, was the party at fault. Murad has highlighted the implications of these passages that contradict the idea that ʿUmar I served as a role model for ʿUmar II.[40] However, they all attest to the desire of later authors to confirm these parallels, even if it meant distorting historical information.[41]

The two caliphs may also share a messianic dimension;[42] while ʿUmar II's eschatological aspects are well-attested, ʿUmar b. al-Khaṭṭāb's have long been subject to debate. In *Hagarism*, Crone and Cook proposed that ʿUmar I was identified with the messiah announced by the Prophet himself. The surname *al-Fārūq*,[43] given to ʿUmar I in the Islamic tradition, served as proof; these messianic elements were later suppressed in the sources.[44] Donner has challenged this claim, refuting the notion of a primitive Islamic messianism, but he does admit that the messianic idea would later become extremely important. He adds that Crone and Cook's argument is based largely on Christian and Jewish

37 Ibn al-Jawzī, *Sīra*, 116.

38 Murad, "ʿUmar II's View," 36–7.

39 *Kitāb al-Aghānī*, vol. VIII, 152; Ibn al-Athīr, vol. V, 64; *TMD*, 45, 180.

40 Murad, "ʿUmar II's View," 37.

41 The other possibility is that the medieval commentators incorrectly interpreted this passage: the term *sāqiyya* is problematic, as it can designate a canal (a meaning retained by the authors of the Middle Ages to indicate practices that led one astray from the path traced by the Prophet), but also a well, cistern, or reservoir that served as a source of drinking water or was used for irrigation. If we use this latter sense of the word, the *ḥadīth* could be interpreted in a radically different manner as a text intended to legitimise ʿUmar I, who had multiplied the resources bequeathed him by the Prophet for the benefit of his subjects. A more methodical investigation of the entries in the medieval dictionaries would be necessary in order to shed further light on this issue. I thank Paul Cobb for the suggestion.

42 On the use of this term as applied to Islam, see García-Arenal, "Introduction," 7.

43 On the meaning of this term, see Bashear, "The Title 'Fārūq'," 48 ff.

44 Crone and Cook, *Hagarism*, 3–6.

texts, whose authors perceived the rise of Islam in highly apocalyptic terms, and that the existence of this apocalyptic sentiment among non-Muslims did not presuppose the existence of a similar feeling among the early Muslims themselves.[45] Bashear has also shown that the qualifier *fārūq* was primarily given to ʿUmar I by the Jews of Jerusalem, whom the caliph had allowed to resettle in the city.[46]

Even if ʿUmar I's messianic dimension is somewhat uncertain, ʿUmar II's is incontestable.[47] This aspect played a decisive role in determining the qualities attributed to this caliph in the Islamic sources.

6.1.3 Mahdī *and* Mujaddid*: The Caliph of the Year 100 Hijrī*

The functions of *mahdī* and *mujaddid* (renewer) are frequently associated with the caliph ʿUmar II.[48] Some evidence suggests that he may even have considered himself as such.[49] The date of his caliphate – the year 100 *hijrī*, with all of its associated eschatological connotations – certainly played a major role in the spread of these ideas. The period leading up to this highly anticipated *eschaton* was supposed to be an era of peace, harmony and justice (chiliasm),[50] ushered in and largely orchestrated by ʿUmar II himself.

The sources contain an abundance of elements announcing the arrival of an Umayyad caliph, descended from ʿUmar I and bearing a mark on his face, who was destined to "fill the world with justice" (*yamlāʾ al-arḍ ʿadālan*).[51]

45 Donner, "La question du messianisme," 18–9, 24.

46 Bashear, "The Title 'Fārūq'," 69; Donner, "La question du messianisme," 23. On the related issue of ʿUmar I's ties to Jerusalem, see the works of Busse, "ʿOmar b. al-Khaṭṭāb" and "ʿOmar's Image;" Cobb, "A Note on ʿUmar's;" Elad, *Medieval Jerusalem*, especially 29–33.

47 Alongside ʿUmar II, another Umayyad figure also has strong messianic connotations: the Sufyānī. On this subject, see Lammens's classic study "Le Sofiânî;" Madelung, "The Sufyānī;" Cobb, *White Banners*; and David Cook, *Studies*.

48 See Madelung's important contribution, "Al-Mahdī," 1221–2 and David Cook, *Studies*. More broadly, Umayyad poetry attests to the strong messianic currents associated with the caliphs of the first Islamic dynasty. See Crone, *Medieval Islamic Political Thought*, 41, 75–7.

49 Crone and Hinds, *God's Caliph*, 114.

50 García-Arenal, "Introduction," 8.

51 Al-Ṭabarī, vol. II, 1362–3, trans. vol. XXIV, 92; al-Balādhurī, *Ansāb*, vol. VII, 66; *Aghānī*, vol. VIII, 151; Ibn Saʿd, ed. Sachau, *al-Ṭabaqāt*, vol. V, 243; *Kitāb al-ʿuyūn*, vol. I, 39; Abū Nuʿaym, *Ḥilyat*, vol. V, 254; Ibn Qutayba, *Kitāb al-maʿārif*, 362; Ibn al-Athīr, vol. V, 59; Nuʿaym b. Ḥammād, *Kitāb al-fitan*, 67, 222, trans. 51, 205–6; Abū Zurʿa, *Taʾrīkh*, 572, note 1592; TMD 45, 155; Ibn Kathīr, *al-Bidāya*, vol. IX, 203; al-Suyūṭī, *Taʾrīkh al-khulafāʾ*, 270; *Taʾrīkh al-khulafāʾ*, 174a. The significance of ʿUmar II's justice (*ʿadl*) is also highlighted by the thirteenth-century Christian Arab author Buṭrus b. Rāhib, *Taʾrīkh*, 57, Latin trans. 63. ʿUmar II was not the only figure to have sustained such expectations; the Abbasids

This caliph was none other than ʿUmar II, whose ties to his predecessor were now newly reinforced. As a child, ʿUmar b. ʿAbd al-ʿAzīz's face had been injured by one of his father's animals. While his mother, Umm ʿĀṣim, comforted the child and tended to his wound, his father entered and was roundly scolded by his wife, who reproached him for having left the boy unattended. ʿAbd al-ʿAzīz, however, far from being upset by the news of his son's injury, rejoiced in the realisation that his son was destined to be "the Umayyad with a scar on his forehead."[52] This theme of predestination was widespread in Arabic-Muslim literature. Many sources designate the future ʿUmar II as "Ashajj Quraysh," "Ashajj banī Umayya," or "Ashajj banī Marwān."[53] ʿUmar b. ʿAbd al-ʿAzīz's brother, al-Aṣbagh, who was said to be able to predict the future, supposedly recognised him immediately as the foretold Umayyad,[54] and Ibn Qutayba suggests that the roots of this prophecy trace back to the book of Daniel.[55] ʿUmar II's calling to the caliphate is echoed in the *Anonymous History of the Abbasids*: while in the mosque of Damascus, a man informs the future caliph that Ayyūb will not outlive his father Sulaymān, and that ʿUmar II will accede to the caliphate upon the death of this latter. This revelation provokes ʿUmar II's anger.[56]

In the sources, these elements constitute ʿUmar II's presentation as the *mahdī*,[57] *mahdī al-khayr* or *mahdī al-ḥaqqan*.[58] He is said to have been recognised as such by Saʿīd b. Musayyab (d. 93 or 94/712–713) at Medina, where he served as governor prior to his accession to the caliphate.[59] Muḥammad b.

also eagerly anticipated the arrival of a *mahdī* who would fill the world with justice, see *Akhbār al-dawla*, 52.

52 Al-Ṭabarī, vol. II, 1362–3, trans. vol. XXIV, 92.

53 Also in the *Aghānī*, vol. VIII, 151; *Kitāb al-ʿuyūn*, vol. I, 39 (in which the incident where ʿUmar II is wounded takes place in Egypt rather than Damascus, as in al-Ṭabarī); al-Ṭabarī, vol. II, 1362–3, trans. vol. XXIV, 92; Ibn al-Athīr, vol. V, 59; Ibn ʿAbd al-Ḥakam, *Sīra*, 21; Ibn Saʿd, ed. Sachau, *al-Ṭabaqāt*, vol. V, 243; al-Balādhurī, *Ansāb*, vol. VII, 66; Abū Nuʿaym, *Ḥilyat*, vol. V, 256; Ibn Kathīr, *al-Bidāya*, vol. IX, 207; *TMD* 45, 134; al-Suyūṭī, *Taʾrīkh al-khulafāʾ*, 270; al-Masʿūdī, *Tanbīh*, 319, 413; *Taʾrīkh al-khulafāʾ*, 174a; see also the Christian author Saʿīd b. Biṭrīq, who similarly mentions the scar on the caliph's forehead ([*wa-*]*fī jabhatihi uthr*), 44.

54 Ibn Qutayba, *Kitāb al-maʿārif*, 362.

55 Ibn Qutayba, *Kitāb al-maʿārif*, 362; Barthold, "The Caliph ʿUmar II," 73.

56 *Akhbār al-dawla*, 168.

57 For example, Abū Nuʿaym, *Ḥilyat*, vol. V, 254.

58 Nuʿaym b. Ḥammād, *Kitāb al-fitan*, 222, 230, trans. 206, 213; Crone and Hinds, *God's Caliph*, 114.

59 Ibn Saʿd, ed. Sachau, *al-Ṭabaqāt*, vol. V, 245; Ibn Kathīr, *al-Bidāya*, vol. IX, 207; Barthold, "The Caliph ʿUmar II," 74–5; Madelung, "Al-Mahdī," 1222.

ʿAlī al-Baqīr, the fifth Shiite Imam,[60] was also said to have called ʿUmar II the *mahdī*: "the Prophet belongs to our people, and the *mahdī* belongs to the Banū ʿAbd Shams. We do not know who he could be, if not ʿUmar b. ʿAbd al-ʿAzīz."[61] He was not, however, unanimously identified as the *mahdī*, particularly in the Meccan tradition.[62]

As mentioned above, the date of ʿUmar II's caliphate was clearly a decisive factor in his association with these roles. The same might also be said of Sulaymān, who could potentially have been the caliph of the year 100 *hijrī* and seemingly sought to portray himself as the *mahdī* as well.[63] The end of the first century of the *hijra* holds an important place in the Islamic tradition, where the year 100 is often presented as the foretold date of the Last Judgment.[64] The belief that the Islamic Empire would not last more than one hundred years was so widespread that it even reached the prince of Samarqand, who wrote of this prophecy in a letter to the Emperor of China and suggested that this would be the perfect moment to launch an attack against the caliphate.[65] In a *ḥadīth* directly attributed to him, the Prophet himself supposedly announced that no soul would survive on earth beyond a period of one hundred years. As Bashear has clearly demonstrated, commentators writing after the year 100 *hijrī* changed this *ḥadīth* so that it would make sense, explaining that the Prophet had meant that none of the Companions who accompanied him during his final days would still be alive a century later.[66] This tradition offers a classic example of an instance where the past, here represented by a Prophetic *ḥadīth*, was preserved because later authors could easily make it conform to the needs of the present. When nothing happened in the year 100 AH, numerous traditions and prophecies needed to be reinterpreted, since the future

60 See Kohlberg, "Muḥammad b. ʿAlī, dit al-Bāqir."

61 Ibn Saʿd, ed. Sachau, *al-Ṭabaqāt*, vol. V, 245; Madelung, "Al-Mahdī," 1222; Kohlberg, "Muḥammad b. ʿAlī, dit al-Bāqir," 399; Becker, "Studien," 29.

62 See Madelung's discussion, "Al-Mahdī," 1222.

63 The poet al-Farazdaq clearly designates Sulaymān as the *mahdī*, announced by "the preachers and the rabbis," *Dīwān*, 327 ff.; Madelung, "Al-Mahdī," 1221; Eisener, *Zwischen Faktum und Fiktion*, 147 ff.; Crone, *Medieval Islamic Political Thought*, 75–6. Additionally, king Solomon, the caliph's homonym, is also presented as the *mahdī* in the sources; see for example *TMD*, vol. 2/1, ed. al-Munajjid, 27, trans. Élisséeff, 43.

64 On this point, see Bashear, "Muslim Apocalypses and the Hour." For older studies, see Vasiliev, "Medieval Ideas of the End of the World," especially 471–3, and Abel, "Changements politiques et littérature eschatologique."

65 Barthold, "The Caliph ʿUmar II," 80; Vasiliev, "Medieval Ideas of the End of the World," 473; Hoyland, *Seeing*, 331, note 227.

66 Bashear, "Muslim Apocalypses and the Hour," 90.

events they described had not come to pass: the image of ʿUmar II figured into these rewriting processes.

The traditions stating that the year 100 would mark the end of the world are widely echoed in both the Islamic and Christian sources, and were supported by the occurrence of various natural phenomena that confirmed the eschatological beliefs of their contemporaries. The passage of a comet is noted on 8 December 100/718,[67] and David Cook estimates that its appearance must have been significant for the messianic dimension of ʿUmar II's caliphate.[68] The Christian sources also record several events with eschatological connotations, the largest of which was a violent earthquake,[69] to which we shall return in greater detail below. In the memory preserved in the Islamic[70] and Christian sources alike, the end of the first century of the *hijra* was rich in messianic traditions. This general atmosphere played an important role in establishing ʿUmar II's soteriological dimension.

The belief that twelve caliphs would succeed the Prophet before the End of Days was another element of the Islamic tradition that may have helped affirm ʿUmar II's status as the *mahdī*: "this religion will endure until you have been governed by twelve caliphs, on each of whom the *umma* has agreed."[71] The majority of those who transmitted this *ḥadīth* specify that all of these caliphs will be from the tribe of Quraysh. Ibn Ḥanbal adds that these caliphs will be twelve in number, much "like the number of leaders (*nuqabāʾ*) of the children of Israel," thus establishing the Biblical and Qurʾānic roots of this tradition.[72] It is possible to claim that ʿUmar II was the twelfth caliph,[73] thus reinforcing his messianic dimension. However, this narrative poses certain difficulties. First, one must ignore either the caliphate of al-Ḥasan b. ʿAlī or that of Muʿāwiya II, as do most of the medieval authors. Ibn al-Zubayr's claims to the throne must also be overlooked. Second, it presupposes the existence of two problematic conditions: 1) that the concept of the four *Rāshidūn* caliphs – including ʿAlī – was already well-established during the Umayyad period,

67 Cook, "Messianism and Astronomical Events" and "A Survey;" Rada and Stephenson, "A Catalogue of Meteor Showers."

68 Cook, "Messianism and Astronomical Events," 38.

69 The eschatological dimension of which is obvious, see *Sūra al-Zalzala, Qurʾān* 99.

70 As Nuʿaym b. Ḥammād's *Kitāb al-fitan* attests; on this subject, see Madelung, "The Sufyānī" and "Apocalyptic Prophecies in Ḥimṣ," and above all, Cook, *Studies*.

71 Abū Dāwūd, *Sunan*, vol. IV, 106, no. 4279; Muslim, *Ṣaḥīḥ*, vol. XII, 202–4; Aḥmad b. Ḥanbal, *Musnad*, vol. V, 294, no. 3781. See Donner, *Narratives*, 42, note 24.

72 *Qurʾān* 2:130, 134; 3:78; 4:161; *Genesis*, 49, 1–28.

73 This idea is defended by Rubin, "Apocalypse and Authority," 12.

which seems highly unlikely, and 2) that all of ʿUmar II's Umayyad predecessors were recognised as legitimate caliphs, which seems doubtful from the Abbasid point of view. Since the earliest attestations of this *ḥadīth* about the twelve caliphs do not predate the third/ninth century,[74] it is quite possible that these traditions initially designated a different caliph instead;[75] later reinterpretations would then eventually assign the twelfth caliphal status to ʿUmar II.

In any case, the *ḥadīth*s concerning the twelve caliphs are particularly widespread in the sources, and have been the subject of various important studies in modern scholarship.[76] Moreover, these *ḥadīth*s required later commentaries that excluded several caliphs from this enumeration because the End of Days did not take place on ʿUmar II's death. Ibn Khaldūn relates:

> It has been mentioned in (the sound tradition of) the *Ṣaḥīḥ* that Muḥammad said: "This (Muslim) state will not cease to be until the Hour arises," or: "… until the (Muslims) have been ruled by twelve caliphs" – that is, from the Quraysh. The facts suggest that some of them were at the beginning of Islam, and that some of them will be at its end. Muḥammad said: "The caliphate after me will last for thirty, or thirty-one, or thirty-six (years)." It ends with the caliphate of al-Ḥasan and the beginning of the caliphate of Muʿāwiya. The beginning of the rule of Muʿāwiya is a caliphate only according to the original meaning of the word. He is the sixth of the caliphs. The seventh caliph is ʿUmar b. ʿAbd al-ʿAzīz. The remaining five (of the twelve caliphs mentioned in the tradition) are five of ʿAlī's descendants, members of Muḥammad's family.[77]

---

74 The oldest mention catalogued by Rubin is in Nuʿaym b. Ḥammād's (d. 229/844) *Kitāb al-fitan*; see "Apocalypse and Authority," 11.

75 In particular al-Maʾmūn, who also lived through a period of strong messianic currents, who could have been considered the twelfth caliph during the first decades of the third/ninth century by retaining the first four *Rāshidūn* and ʿUmar II as the only legitimate Umayyad caliph, and then adding the successive Abbasid caliphs to the list. I am grateful to Christopher Melchert for having drawn my attention to the problems associated with identifying ʿUmar II as the famous "twelfth" caliph, and for having shared his reflections on the subject.

76 See Rubin, "Apocalypse and Authority;" Donner, *Narratives*, 42–3. For the Syriac tradition, see Drijvers, "The Gospel of the Twelve Apostles" and "Christians, Jews and Muslims in Northern Mesopotamia in Early Islamic Times."

77 Ibn Khaldūn, *The Muqaddimah*, vol. II, 192.

These *a posteriori* explanations, however, still reserve a place of privilege for 'Umar II.[78] The siege of Constantinople, discussed in detail in the previous chapter, is the final element of the caliph's messianic dimension. In stark contrast to the policies of his predecessor Sulaymān, 'Umar II chose to defer Islam's universal calling. Per al-Ṭabarī, 'Umar II was staunchly opposed to further conquest, and believed that the Muslims should be satisfied with the territories already granted them by God.[79] In 100/718, he asked his new governor of al-Andalus for a description of "al-Andalus and its rivers," as he hoped to evacuate the Muslims from this dangerous region.[80] 'Umar II is presented as the caliph who condensed the empire, although his apparent reservations toward expansion do not seem to have led to a decrease in military activity.[81] Michael the Syrian, however, attributes the caliph's increasing mistreatment of Christians to the widespread Muslim disappointment following their defeat at Constantinople.[82]

The end of this large-scale military operation in no way signalled the end of Muslim projects in the Byzantine world, particularly with respect to Constantinople. The famous pseudo-correspondence between 'Umar II and Leo III (717–741) merely transferred the stakes of converting the Byzantine emperor and his subjects to Islam onto the epistolary plane; these supposed letters are widely attested in the Christian sources,[83] in particular in the works of the Armenian chronicler Łewond,[84] who claimed to have preserved this exchange. This correspondence has been the subject of numerous studies:[85] it is currently thought that the letters date to the third/ninth century,

78 The Mu'tazilites similarly consider 'Umar II as one of the imams who succeeded 'Alī. See Crone, *Medieval Islamic Political Thought*, 69, note 10.

79 Al-Ṭabarī, vol. II, 1365, trans. vol. XXIV, 95; Barthold, "The Caliph 'Umar II," 82; Wellhausen, *Das arabische Reich*, 167.

80 Hopkins, "Geographical," 301.

81 Cobb, "'Umar (II)," 886.

82 Michael the Syrian, vol. II, 456, French trans. 488–9; Bar Hebraeus, 117, trans. 108–9; see Schick, *The Christian Communities of Palestine*, 167.

83 This pseudo-correspondence is mentioned by Agapius, *Kitāb al-'unwān*, 502–3, and by Theophanes, *Chronographia*, 399, trans. 550.

84 Łewond, trans. 40–98. See also Jeffery, "Ghevond's Text of the Correspondence," which offers an English translation, 277–330.

85 Foremost among them Jeffery, "Ghevond's Text of the Correspondence," 269–332; Gaudeul, "The Correspondence Between Leo and 'Umar;" Hoyland, "The Correspondence." As a complement, see the works of Gaudeul and Sourdel, "Un pamphlet musulman" and Cardaillac, *La polémique anti-chrétienne*.

although, as Hoyland notes, they do preserve certain notable elements of the Islamic-Christian polemic of the second/eighth century.[86]

Such are the most significant characteristics attributed to the pious – almost saintly – caliph ʿUmar II in the Islamic tradition. However, a few minor details from his youth and life prior to becoming caliph contrast this idealised portrait. These narratives, which depict ʿUmar II as an Umayyad prince like any other, perhaps figure into the construction of a hagiographic discourse around the caliph, aimed at using this contrast in behaviour to reinforce his worthy conduct as a model of caliphal piety.[87] Despite the existence of a vast number of resources on the subject, however, two basic questions remain: how did these narratives spread outside the Muslim community, and how were they received? What were the stages and conditions under which this image of the pious caliph developed? The first question allows us to establish a chronological timeline for the circulation of these *topoi*; this timeline will then enable us to refine our analysis in order to address the second question.

6.2 ʿUmar II in the Christian Sources

As expected, the Christian texts, like their Muslim counterparts, do not have nearly as much information to offer on ʿUmar II as they did on Maslama (see table 6.1 and diagram 6.1).

6.2.1 *Muslim Apocalyptic and Christian Tradition*

The strong eschatological currents that marked the period leading up to the year 100 *hijrī* and the campaign against Constantinople are widely attested in the Syriac sources, the corpus most directly attuned to Muslim expectations. The short Syriac chronicle of *716* provides an impressive list of catastrophes said to have taken place between 712 and 716; its author explains that this series of disasters was divine punishment for the sins of mankind. The evidence was clear: troubling signs in the sky, earthquakes,[88] various epidemics, droughts and plagues of locusts that destroyed harvests, thunderstorms and hail that decimated crops. So many misfortunes in so short a period certainly contributed to the creation of an apocalyptic atmosphere.[89] Michael the Syrian

86 Hoyland, "The Correspondence," 177.

87 See Cobb, "ʿUmar (II)," 887.

88 This was the earthquake of 28 February 713, under the reign of al-Walīd. See Sbeitani, Darawcheh and Mouty, "The Historical Earthquakes of Syria," 361–2. I must thank Mustapha Meghraoui for having drawn my attention to this article.

89 *716*; Palmer, *The Seventh*, 45–8; Reinink, "The Beginnings."

TABLE 6.1 Main information related to ʿUmar II in the Christian sources

	Circuit of Theophilus of Edessa								Circuit of Qartamīn				
Information / Sources	Theophanes	Agapius	1234	Michael the Syrian	Bar Hebraeus	724/775	Zuqnīn	Łewond	819	846	Saʿīd b. Biṭrīq	Patriarchs of Alexandria	Elias of Nisibis
Beginning of caliphate	X	X	X	X	X		X	X	X	X	X	X	X
Call for Maslama's return	X		X	X	X		X						
Maslama visits Constantinople							X						
Muslims forced to retreat (by the Byzantines or a storm)	X			X	X								
Muslims vanquish the Byzantines							X						
Earthquake	X	X		X			X			X			X
Caliph's virtue and piety		X	X	X				X	X	X			
Mistreatment of Christians	X		X	X	X							X	
Expulsion of corrupt people		X											
Fiscal exemption for converts	X			X								X	

TABLE 6.1 Main information related to ʿUmar II in the Christian sources (*cont.*)

	Circuit of Theophilus of Edessa								Circuit of Qartamīn				
Information / **Sources**	**Theophanes**	**Agapius**	**1234**	**Michael the Syrian**	**Bar Hebraeus**	**724/775**	**Zuqnīn**	**Łewond**	**819**	**846**	**Saʿīd b. Biṭrīq**	**Patriarchs of Alexandria**	**Elias of Nisibis**
Christian testimony against Muslims invalid	X												
Penalty for Muslim murder of a Christian			X	X									
Prohibition of alcohol	X	X		X									
End of cursing ʿAlī											X		
ʿUmar bears a mark on his forehead											X		
Letter to Leo III	X	X						X					
Leo III's reply		X						X					
Death of ʿUmar II	X	X	X	X	X		X		X	X	X	X	X
Place of death or location of tomb									X	X	X		
Length of caliphate		X				X	X	X	X	X			

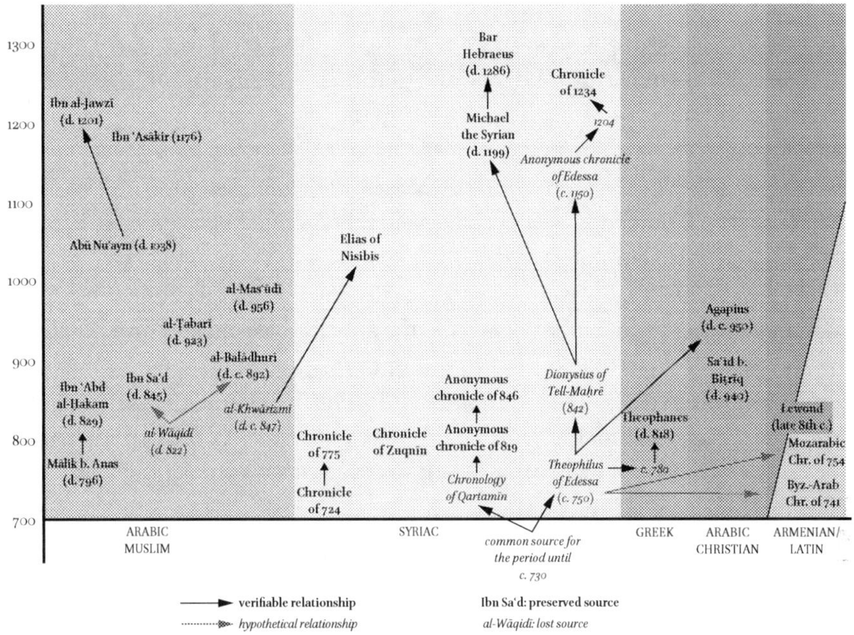

DIAGRAM 6.1 Transmission of elements related to the Caliph ʿUmar II

presents an identical version of events, albeit with the timeframe shifted slightly later:[90]

> In the year 1031 [720 CE], a great plague of locusts arrived during the harvests; they devoured the vines, fig trees, olive trees, to the point that their trunks withered and their fruits were completely destroyed. Wine was scarce everywhere. During this period, a Syrian named Severus from the Mardē district mocked the Jews, saying to them: "I am the Messiah;" to others, (he said): "I am the messenger of the Messiah." He received gold and silver in great quantities. The prince seized him and he confessed his fraud … In the year 1032 [721], the wells dried up and the rivers shrank due to the lack of rain and snow. In many places, men were in great distress, to the extent that they had to travel seven miles or more to draw water. Many places lost all of their inhabitants; in this year, there was a shortage of grains and all types of legumes. This occurred in the months of Āb and

90 Michael the Syrian frequently dates certain events at least a year later than most other sources. The chronological errors may be the result of incorrect conversions between the different calendars in use in the medieval Near East.

> Īlūl (August through September). In the month of Nīsān (April) of the following year, there were even more locusts that destroyed the crops, and misfortunes grew further due to the lack of any sort of food for men and animals.[91]

Here again, the description of events is unequivocal. In addition, all of these hardships were preceded by an earthquake that caused heavy damage in Syria; the date of this temblor is varyingly given as 98/716–717,[92] 99/717–718[93] or 100/718–719.[94] In reality, this was the earthquake of 24 December 717;[95] the fact that the medieval authors describe the shockwaves of this natural disaster spanning a period from 40 days to 6 months may explain the chronological confusion in the texts.[96] The *Chronicle of Zuqnīn*, so eloquent with respect to Maslama yet so disappointing on the subject of ʿUmar II, offers an interesting description of this event, stating that the earthquake was interpreted as divine retribution:

> The year one thousand and twenty-nine [717–718]: A powerful and dreadful earthquake took place and destroyed many places, shrines, churches and great buildings, particularly in (Bēth) Maʿdē,[97] as well as the Old Church of Edessa. Large and high buildings collapsed on their inhabitants. The earthquake left marks on even the ones that remained standing, so that their inhabitants might tremble before the Lord, whenever they would see the earthquake's marks.[98]

6.2.2 *The Caliph's Image*

Despite the brevity of his reign, ʿUmar II's caliphate was frequently the subject of detailed notices in the sources. The elements related to caliph himself are of varying quantitative and qualitative importance. Before addressing the sources from the circuits of Qartamīn and Theophilus of Edessa, we shall briefly cover the information provided by other authors on the subject.

---

91 Michael the Syrian, vol. II, 455–6, French trans. 490–1.

92 Agapuis, *Kitāb al-ʿunwān*, ed. and trans. 502.

93 *Zuqnīn*, 170, trans. Harrak 160 (the earthquake that damaged or destroyed the church of Edessa); Theophanes, *Chronographia*, 399, trans. 550; Elias of Nisibis, 161–2, trans. 100 (the earthquake dated 15 Jumāda II 99/23 January 718).

94 Michael the Syrian, vol. II, 455–6, French trans. 490.

95 Specialists estimate that it reached a VI/VII on the European macroseismic scale (EMS 1992).

96 Sbeitani, Darawcheh and Mouty, "The Historical Earthquakes of Syria," 362.

97 A village in Ṭūr ʿAbdīn in the region of Amida (Diyarbakir).

98 *Zuqnīn*, 170, trans. Harrak 160.

The terse chronologies of *724* and *775* merely give the regnal dates for each caliphate, and they differ by two months over the length of ʿUmar's reign;[99] a similarly concise account fixing the duration of his caliphate at two years and six months is provided by the *Continuatio of the Samaritan Chronicle*, which was likely based in part on lists such as those found in the aforementioned chronologies.[100] Łewond presents a very positive image of ʿUmar II, praising his leniency and generosity over that of his Armenian compatriots. Łewond's chapter on the caliph is almost exclusively dedicated to the pseudo-correspondence between ʿUmar II and the Byzantine emperor Leo III, as noted above. Saʿīd b. Biṭrīq's short notice on the caliph is mainly valuable for the information it provides on the restitution of churches to the Christians of Damascus and the Ghūṭa. He also mentions the end of the practice of cursing ʿAlī b. Abī Ṭālib in the pulpits and the scar on the caliph's forehead, which symbolised fulfillment of the prophecy that a descendant of ʿUmar I would bring justice to the world.[101] The *History of the Patriarchs of Alexandria* offers some interesting information on ʿUmar II, likely due to the fact that his father, ʿAbd al-ʿAzīz, had previously served as governor of Egypt. Although this text focuses primarily on Egypt, it also paints a portrait of ʿUmar II in two diametrically opposed phases. In the first, the caliph is presented as a just ruler who is favourable to Christians, guaranteeing them safety and peace (*amān wa-hudūʾ*); in the second phase, his image is abruptly transformed, and he is depicted as the Christians' sworn enemy[102] and the Antichrist (*al-dajjāl*).[103] This radical change may be explained as a function of the caliph's messianic dimension, here used to portray him in a decidedly negative light.

Compared to other Christian sources, the authors in the circuit of Theophilus of Edessa offer by far the most information on ʿUmar II. These authors were primarily interested in his juridic rulings and decrees, doubtless because they had significant impacts on the *dhimmī* population. The Christians were mistreated,[104] forced conversion became common practice and, per

99 Two years and five months according to the chronicle of *724*, 156, trans. 119; two years and seven months in the chronicle of *775*, 348, trans. 274.

100 *The Continuatio*, 208, trans. 55. See also the anonymous Greek chronology of *818*, which indicates a reign of two years, 97, trans. Hoyland 436.

101 Saʿīd b. Biṭrīq, 43–4.

102 Michael the Syrian gives two reasons explaining the caliph's hostility toward the Christians: his desire to establish "Muslim laws" and the residual trauma of his defeat at Constantinople, vol. II, 456, French trans. 488.

103 *History of the Patriarchs*, 152–3.

104 Theophanes, *Chronographia*, 399, trans. 550; Michael the Syrian, vol. II, 455–6, French trans. 488–9; *1234*, 307–8, Latin trans. 239–40; Bar Hebraeus, 117, trans. 108–9.

Theophanes, led numerous individuals to martyrdom.[105] Various incentives were offered to convert to Islam[106] foremost among them tax exemption.[107] The superiority of the new religion was confirmed by the fact that a Christian could no longer provide valid testimony against a Muslim,[108] and that the only penalty for a Muslim who murdered a Christian was payment of a simple fine![109] To round out this new legal arsenal, corrupt individuals (*ahl al-fasād*) were driven out of the empire,[110] and alcohol was prohibited.[111]

These elements are essential for understanding the conditions that governed the genesis and diffusion of *topoi* associated with the caliph in the Christian sources, in particular his role as legislator. Michael the Syrian provides the most detailed description of the measures enacted by the caliph whose major fault, in the eyes of the Christian authors, was the oppression of his co-religionists:

> it is said that he was fanatical about their laws (*nāmūsē*), he had the reputation of being pious and distancing himself from sin, and he decreed the oppression of the Christians in any manner possible in order to force them to become Muslims. He ordained that any Christian who became Muslim would not have to pay the tax, and many apostatised. He also decreed that Christians would not be allowed to testify against Muslims, that Christians could not hold government positions (*shūlṭānā*), that they could not raise their voices in prayer, nor play the simandron,[112] nor wear the *qabiya*,[113] nor ride in a saddle. If one of the Ṭayyāyē killed a Christian, he was not put to death, but only paid the sum of 5000 *zūzē*.[114] He prohibited and abolished levies on homes, inheritances and portions of

105 Theophanes, *Chronographia*, 399, trans. 550.

106 On the Islamisation of the Syrian space, see Jalabert, *Hommes et lieux*.

107 Theophanes, *Chronographia*, 399, trans. 550; Michael the Syrian, vol. II, 456, French trans. 488–9. This exemption is also mentioned in the *History of the Patriarchs of Alexandria*, 152–3.

108 Theophanes, *Chronographia*, 399, trans. 550.

109 Michael the Syrian, vol. II, 456, French trans. 488–9; *1234*, 307–8, Latin trans. 239–40.

110 Agapius, *Kitāb al-ʿunwān*, 502.

111 Theophanes, *Chronographia*, 399, trans. 550; Agapius, *Kitāb al-ʿunwān*, 502; Michael the Syrian, vol. II, 456, French trans. 488–9.

112 Wooden planks that were used as a substitute for bells.

113 From the Arabic *qabāʾ*: a masculine garment with narrow sleeves, see Dozy, *Dictionnaire détaillé des noms de vêtements*, 352–62. This prohibition is corroborated in Abū Yūsuf Yaʿqūb, *Kitāb al-kharāj*, 152, trans. 196.

114 *Zūzō*, pl. *zūzē*, meaning money, without any further clarification.

> harvests for the benefit of churches, convents and the poor. He forbade the Ṭayyāyē from drinking wine or must.[115]

The caliph's imposition of restrictive legislation on the Christian community did not prevent historians from highlighting his virtue and piety, as attested by the above passage from Michael the Syrian; Agapius also mentions the caliph's devotion (*nask*)[116] and godliness (*waraʿ*).[117] This description is certainly an older one, as it is also found in the two anonymous chronicles of *819* and *846*. Although the sections of these two texts devoted to ʿUmar II are unfortunately incomplete, they nevertheless emphasise the caliph's positive attributes: "[a good man] and a merciful king (*meraḥamnā*), more so than [any of the kings] who preceded him."[118] This passage is very similar to that in the chronicle of *1234*,[119] and the Latin *Byzantine-Arab Chronicle of 741* employs the same adjectives – good and merciful – to describe ʿUmar II, whom even strangers admired.[120]

The chronicles of *819* and *846* also provide details that are absent from the rest of the Christian sources. An example is the name of the site associated with ʿUmar II's tomb: while the Islamic sources mostly agree that he was buried in Dayr Simʿān,[121] the anonymous chronicles of *819* and *846* propose a different location whose name is varyingly spelled Dayr Ānqirōntā and Dayr Īqrōntā.[122] These two spellings corroborate the hypothesis of Janine and Dominique Sourdel, who argued that several different toponyms were used to designate a single site that marked the location of the caliph's tomb: Dayr al-Naqīra, the Arabic equivalent of the locations mentioned in the two anonymous Syriac

115 Michael the Syrian, vol. II, 456, French trans. 489 (with minor changes); for a similar if slightly abridged version of this account, see also *1234*, 307, Latin trans. 239; Bar Hebraeus, 117, trans. 109. See Schick's remarks, *The Christian Communities of Palestine*, 88–9, 167.

116 See al-Yaʿqūbī, *Mushākalat*, 19, trans. 337, cited above.

117 Agapius, *Kitāb al-ʿunwān*, 502. See also *1234*, 306, Latin trans. 238.

118 *819*, 15, Latin trans. 11; *846*, 234, Latin trans. 177, trans. Brooks 583. See also Hoyland, *Seeing*, 654.

119 *1234*, 307, Latin trans. 238.

120 *Byzantine-Arab Chronicle of 741*, 14, trans. Hoyland 625.

121 See Khalīfa b. Khayyāṭ, *Taʾrīkh*, 321–2; Ibn Saʿd, ed. Sachau, *al-Ṭabaqāt*, vol. V, 301; al-Masʿūdī, *Tanbīh*, 319 and *Murūj*, vol. V, 416, trans. Pellat vol. IV, 867; *Kitāb al-ʿuyūn*, vol. I, 63; al-Ṭabarī, vol. II, 1362, trans. vol. XXIV, 92; Ibn al-Athīr, vol. V, 58; *Taʾrīkh al-khulafāʾ*, 187b; the Arabic-language Christian author Saʿīd b. Biṭrīq also locates his tomb there, 44. Al-Balādhurī, *Ansāb*, vol. VII, 66, merely indicates that he died at Dayr Simʿān, without mentioning his tomb; see also Ibn Qutayba, *Kitāb al-maʿārif*, 363; TMD, vol. 45, 128, 131, 132; al-Suyūṭī, *Taʾrīkh al-khulafāʾ*, 288.

122 Following the readings proposed by the editors of these two texts. The vocalisation remains uncertain: *819* offers the spelling *ʾynqyrwntʾ* while *846* has *ʾyqrwntʾ*.

chronicles,[123] Dayr Simʿān, and Dayr Murrān.[124] As al-Masʿūdī attests, ʿUmar II's tomb later became a place of pilgrimage.[125]

6.2.3 *A Chronology of these* topoi *in the Syrian Space: Propositions and Hypotheses*

Having briefly summarised the information on ʿUmar II in the Christian sources, we must now establish the chronology of when these elements first appeared and spread throughout the corpus. The sources, however, do not consistently cite their own respective sources for the information they provide.

Based on the textual evidence, it is clear that ʿUmar b. ʿAbd al-ʿAzīz's virtuous image was firmly established around 730, the date more or less corresponding to the historiographic stratum of the chronicles of *819* and *846*. Although both the original form and substance in which this historical information first appeared remain uncertain, the date at which this information circulated is here a sort of *terminus ante quem*; its appearance in the Christian sources does not mark the date of its creation, but rather its integration in Syriac historiography. This point is extremely important in the context of the present inquiry. As previously noted with respect to Maslama, here again we have an example of a history written in "real time" tracing back to either *phase 2* or *3*. The first option here seems more plausible, as it is unlikely that Hishām's hostility toward ʿUmar following this latter's nomination as Sulaymān's successor gave rise to narratives praising the man who had obstructed his path to the caliphate. If this hypothesis holds true, it implies that ʿUmar II himself may have played an important role in constructing his own image and place in history.

Alongside the chronological context, it is essential to note that the details provided in the Christian sources originated in the Syrian space. Once again, the Christian texts preserved traditions that emerged from the heart of

123 The Greek *Nikertai* is behind this toponym, see Théodoret de Cyr, *Histoire des moines de Syrie*, vol. I, 252, trans. 253; Becker, "Studien," 35.

124 Janine and Dominique Sourdel, "Notes d'épigraphie et de topographie," 83–8. On this point, see also Dickie's appendix to Bosworth's article "Rajāʾ ibn Ḥaywa," 80 and plate I, in addition to the corresponding notices in Yāqūt, *Muʿjam*, vol. II, 517, 533–4 and 539.

125 Al-Masʿūdī, *Murūj*, vol. V, 416, trans. Pellat vol. IV, 867: "His tomb still stands in the same place; it is venerated and attracts many pilgrims from the city and desert alike; it was also treated with respect when the tombs of the other Umayyads were vandalised [by the Abbasids]." The oldest recorded visitor to ʿUmar II's tomb was Makḥūl (d. between 112/730 and 119/737), mentioned by the famous Damascene *muḥaddith* Hishām b. al-Ghāz (d. between 153/770 and 159/776). See Donner, "The Problem," 19. This is not the only example of posthumous veneration of an Umayyad caliph; see Pellat, "Le culte de Muʿāwiya." On these Umayyad "realms of memory," see above, Ch. 4.

Umayyad Syria,[126] although the role played by the Umayyads in the elaboration of these elements remains to be seen. It is tempting to follow this hypothesis: that the construction of the caliphal ideal embodied by ʿUmar II can be read as an apologetic discourse intended to promote the Umayyad caliphate and its legitimacy. However, a final question must be addressed before we conclude our inquiry: where and how was this image created? Since these elements trace back to the Umayyad period, we must turn our attention to the sources used in the composition of the first great biographies of the caliph, in particular that of Ibn Saʿd and the *Sīra* of Ibn ʿAbd al-Ḥakam. In other words, a detailed investigation of the spread of this motif in the Christian sources invites us to pursue the inquiry in Islamic historiography to shed light on its genesis and the stages of its development.

6.3 Constructing the Image of the Holy Caliph: Stages and Conditions

This examination of the stages of the construction of ʿUmar II's image is by no means exhaustive. The sources offering information on the caliph are abundant, and thus it is more beneficial to trace the broad strokes of the process that resulted in the crystallisation of the primary attributes of this important early Islamic historical figure.

6.3.1 Sunna *and* Sīra*: The Traditionists' Caliph*

The development of a literature focused on ʿUmar II's conduct and virtues should be understood in the broader context of the development of the Prophet's *sunna*. This question has been addressed in detail in numerous studies, and remains a subject of scholarly debate.[127] ʿUmar II's promotion of the Prophet's *sunna* likely made him an exceptional figure among the rest of the Umayyad caliphs; he made great efforts to conform to the Prophet's example[128] and advised others to do the same, among them his governor of Iraq, whom he ordered to follow the tenets of the *Kitāb Allāh wa-sunna nabiyyihi*.[129] Crone and Hinds have suggested that his attempts to apply the Prophet's *sunna*

126 See Conrad, "Theophanes," 43–4.

127 See Goldziher, *Muslim Studies*, vol. II, 25–88; Schacht, *The Origins*, 58–81 and "Sur l'expression 'Sunna du Prophète';" Abbott, *Studies in Arabic Literary Papyri*, vol. II, 22 ff.; Juynboll, *Muslim Tradition*, 30–9; Crone and Hinds, *God's Caliph*, 58–80; Dutton, "ʿAmal v. Ḥadīth in Islamic Law;" Décobert, "L'autorité religieuse," 30 ff.

128 Crone and Hinds, *God's Caliph*, 73.

129 Crone and Hinds, *God's Caliph*, 62; al-Ṭabarī, vol. II, 1347, trans. vol. XXIV, 76; Ibn Saʿd, ed. Sachau, *al-Ṭabaqāt*, vol. V, 358; Ibn ʿAbd al-Ḥakam, *Sīra*, 63 ff.

ended in failure;[130] however, anthropologists remind us that success was not necessarily an essential factor in the creation of a heroic image, as individual events and their results were weighed against their cumulative outcome in the long-term.[131]

ʿUmar II is considered the first "theorist" of the *sunna*,[132] although his activities in this regard garnered some opposition,[133] in particular from the Qadarites.[134] As Juynboll has noted, the caliph's interest was not limited to the *sunna* of the Prophet, but extended to his successors as well.[135] In addition, ʿUmar II supposedly played an important role in recording traditions and knowledge (*ḥadīth* and *ʿilm*) by soliciting scholars to put their respective fields of expertise in writing;[136] in any case, these elements should be approached with caution, even if the caliph may have had a hand – however limited – in the composition process.[137] A *musnad* attributed to ʿUmar II survives,[138] although *isnād* criticism, based on the *maʿrifat al-rijāl*, deems it generally "weak."[139] While this text merits more detailed analysis, at minimum it attests to an ulterior motive to corroborate the caliph's role as a traditionist. Nevertheless, ʿUmar II's attitude toward this prophetic memory influenced later Muslim authors' interest in the caliph. His concern for the Prophet's *sunna* would ultimately contribute to the development of a *sunna* of the caliph himself in later apologetic literature. ʿUmar b. ʿAbd al-ʿAzīz's just and proper modes of conduct resulted in the creation of his own well-attested caliphal *sunna*. This *sunna* should be contextualised with the important and previously mentioned concept of *ʿadāla*, as well as the caliph's messianic dimension. Al-Ṭabarī preserves a valuable example of the existence of *sunna*s linked to figures other than the Prophet, including ʿUmar II and his predecessor ʿUmar b. al-Khaṭṭāb: despite his hostility to the Umayyads, Yazīd b. al-Muhallab invoked the Qurʾān,

---

130 Crone and Hinds, *God's Caliph*, 80.

131 Albert, "Du martyr à la star," 18.

132 Juynboll, *Muslim Tradition*, 35, and Van Ess, "ʿUmar II and his Epistle," 19.

133 A letter sent by the caliph to ʿAdī b. Arṭāt (d. 102/720), his governor of Baṣra, attests to this; see Ibn al-Jawzī, *Sīra*, 88.

134 On this important subject, see the works of Van Ess, "ʿUmar II and his Epistle," 19–26; *Anfänge muslimischer Theologie*; *Theologie und Gesellschaft*, vol. I, 134–5. Additionally, see Michael Cook, *Early Muslim Dogma*, 124–36, and Zimmermann, "The Particle Ḥattā."

135 Juynboll, *Muslim Tradition*, 34.

136 Juynboll, *Muslim Tradition*, 34; Goldziher, *Muslim Studies*, vol. II, 210 ff.; Abbott, *Studies in Arabic Literary Papyri*, vol. II, 22 ff.; GAS, vol. I, 56 ff.

137 Crone and Hinds, *God's Caliph*, 74, 80; Juynboll, *Muslim Tradition*, 37–8.

138 (Attributed to) ʿUmar b. ʿAbd al-ʿAzīz, *Musnad*.

139 Juynboll, *Muslim Tradition*, 37.

the *sunna* of the Prophet and also the *sunnas* of both ʿUmar I and ʿUmar II[140] before heading into battle with Maslama b. ʿAbd al-Malik and his army.

In addition to the *sunna*, ʿUmar II's interest in the *sīra* of ʿUmar I also contributed to the early development of a literature dedicated to the caliph; this interest in his predecessor's *sīra* likely led to the creation of his own. As Crone and Hinds have noted, ʿUmar's many roles and predominant position in the sources immediately gave him a place of privilege among the caliphs of his dynasty: hardly twenty years after his death, the virulently anti-Umayyad rebel Abū Ḥamza al-Khārijī spared ʿUmar II in his vicious attacks on the dynasty.[141] The Abbasids even refrained from vandalising his tomb,[142] and his sons and grandsons were spared, eventually taking up positions in the entourage of the first three Abbasid caliphs.[143] In order to proceed further in our investigation of the origins of the earliest apologetic texts dedicated to ʿUmar II, among them Ibn ʿAbd al-Ḥakam's valuable *Sīrat ʿUmar b. ʿAbd al-ʿAzīz*, we must conduct a more detailed study of the caliph's legislative function. The fact that Ibn ʿAbd al-Ḥakam, himself a noted Malikite scholar, begins his *sīra* with an *isnād* tracing back to some of the greatest transmitters in Islamic history – including Mālik b. Anas, the celebrated jurist of the eponymous *madhhab* – is reason enough to adopt this analytical framework.

6.3.2 *The Caliph and the Law: ʿUmar II and Mālik b. Anas*

ʿUmar II is associated with jurisprudence in the Christian and Muslim sources alike. Numerous examples of his juristic activities exist, among them the caliph's famous "fiscal rescript," which was the subject of a pioneering study by H. A. R. Gibb.[144] His justice and piety were equally important and mutually beneficial attributes, and as his legislative function exceeded the typical bounds of the position, it will be helpful to examine its origins.

In order to shed light on his affiliation with the traditionists of Medina, we must look to the period prior to ʿUmar b. ʿAbd al-ʿAzīz's accession to the caliphate.[145] At his father's behest, as a youth he was sent to study in the

140 Al-Ṭabarī, vol. II, 1392, trans. vol. XXIV, 124; Crone and Hinds, *God's Caliph*, 66. On Yazīd b. al-Muhallab's rebellion, see above, Ch. 5.

141 Crone and Hinds, *God's Caliph*, 74, 129–32.

142 Moscati, "Le massacre," 89 ff.; see above, Ch. 4.

143 Crone and Hinds, *God's Caliph*, 74, n. 103; Kilpatrick, *Making the Great Book of Songs*, 156 ff., 325.

144 Gibb, "The Fiscal Rescript;" Guessous, "Le rescrit fiscal."

145 On the emergence and role of the "*ḥadīth* party" (*aṣḥāb al-ḥadīth*) at the end of the Umayyad period, see Crone, *Medieval Islamic Political Thought*, 125–9.

Prophet's city.[146] He eventually settled there in the residence of his forefather Marwān following his nomination as governor of the city in 87/706.[147] He gathered ten Medinese jurists (*fuqahā'*) and exhorted them to respect the law and to inform him of any transgressions or injustices that occurred, affirming that he would frequently seek their advice before making his decisions.[148] ʿUmar was ultimately relieved of the position at al-Ḥajjāj's (93/712) insistence, leaving Abū Bakr b. Muḥammad b. ʿAmr b. Ḥazm as the *qāḍī* of Medina.[149] This *qāḍī* was renowned for his wisdom and piety, and it was said that he was descended from the *anṣār*. As Barthold has noted, this nomination demonstrated that ʿUmar b. ʿAbd al-ʿAzīz had created solid ties to religious circles during his governorate.[150] Several authors also report that he maintained relations with Anas b. Mālik Abū Ḥamza, a former servant of the Prophet and a prolific traditionist[151] who taught him the Prophet's sermons and sayings.[152] His presence among the *ʿulamā'* of Medina is incontrovertible, and this group likely played a decisive role in establishing ʿUmar II's role in the legislative corpora. As Dutton notes, the Mālikī *madhhab* was the oldest and most conservative form of Medinese Islamic law during the first two centuries of the *hijra*.[153] Thus, alongside Ibn ʿAbd al-Ḥakam's *Sīra*, Mālik b. Anas's seminal work, the *Muwaṭṭa'*, is an essential source for elucidating the oldest elements of the Islamic tradition associated with the caliph.

Before we progress further in our inquiry, two critical points must be addressed: the date of the *Muwaṭṭa'*'s composition and Mālik's methodology. The first question has been the subject of several important debates following

146 *Kitāb al-ʿuyūn*, vol. I, 40; al-Suyūṭī, *Ta'rīkh al-khulafā'*, 271; Barthold, "The Caliph ʿUmar II," 73, n. 9. Wellhausen noted in 1902 that the young ʿUmar b. ʿAbd al-ʿAzīz "was brought up upon the tradition of the city of the prophet" (*"Er nährte sich an der Tradition der Stadt des Propheten"*), *Das arabische Reich*, 166, trans. *The Arab Kingdom*, 267.

147 Barthold, "The Caliph ʿUmar II," 74; Khalīfa b. Khayyāṭ, *Ta'rīkh*, 301, 311; al-Ṭabarī, vol. II, 1182, trans. vol. XXIII, 131; al-Yaʿqūbī, *Ta'rīkh*, vol. II, 283.

148 Al-Ṭabarī, vol. II, 1183, trans. vol. XXIII, 132. The ten jurists were: ʿUrwa b. al-Zubayr, ʿUbayd Allāh b. ʿAbd Allāh b. ʿUtba, Abū Bakr b. ʿAbd al-Raḥmān, Abū Bakr b. Sulaymān b. Abī Ḥathma, Sulaymān b. Yasār, al-Qāsim b. Muḥammad, Sālim b. ʿAbd Allāh b. ʿUmar, ʿAbd Allāh b. ʿAbd Allāh b. ʿUmar, ʿAbd Allāh b. ʿĀmir b. Rabīʿa and Khārija b. Zayd. See also Ibn Kathīr, *al-Bidāya*, vol. IX, 201. ʿUmar II's connections to the traditionists and other pious figures in Medina has long attracted scholarly attention: see Goldziher, *Muslim Studies*, vol. II, 39, 43; Wellhausen, *Das arabische Reich*, 167; Cobb, "ʿUmar (II)," 886.

149 Al-Ṭabarī, vol. II, 1255, trans. vol. XXIII, 203; Juynboll, *Muslim Tradition*, 34, 37.

150 Barthold, "The Caliph ʿUmar II," 76; Wellhausen, *Das arabische Reich*, 167.

151 Robson [Wensinck], "Anas b. Mālik Abū Ḥamza."

152 See Ibn Saʿd, ed. Sachau, *al-Ṭabaqāt*, vol. V, 244; Ibn al-Jawzī, *Sīra*, 12; Becker, "Studien," 15–6.

153 Dutton, "ʿAmal v. Ḥadīth in Islamic Law," 14.

the publication of Calder's work. Calder has suggested that the *Muwaṭṭaʾ* was written much later than generally assumed, proposing that the Malikite text was composed in Cordoba near the end of the third century *hijrī*, between 250/864 and 270/883.[154] This hypothesis has been criticised by Dutton[155] and Motzki,[156] who argue in favour of an earlier date of composition. Dutton estimates that "the *Muwaṭṭaʾ* is not only a product of Mālik in Madina before his death in 179 AH [795–796], but was also substantially in place before the year 150 AH [767–768]."[157] As for Mālik's methodology, precedent and custom were the main principles of authority: "legitimacy was that which was already practiced."[158] For obvious reasons, Medinese custom took precedence. Thus, the "Medinese period" of ʿUmar b. ʿAbd al-ʿAzīz is crucial for the present study.

Per Décobert, Mālik relied on two types of authorities: "the actor and the reporter," or, to use a different dichotomy, "the Companions-eyewitnesses and people of knowledge."[159] Mālik systematically depended on transmitters when reporting the words and actions of the Prophet or one of "those who in one way or another played a determining role in the history of this primitive community."[160] For these reasons, ʿUmar II's role in the *Muwaṭṭaʾ* is problematic, as he occupies neither of these two categories. In order to resolve this issue, we must follow Dutton's important conclusions suggesting that the *Muwaṭṭaʾ* was not merely a work on *ḥadīth*, but rather was a text on practice (*ʿamal*), or more precisely, a work on *ḥadīth* in the context of *ʿamal*.[161] From this perspective, ʿUmar II's practice linked him to the actors in the context of his own personal *sunna*.

We must now examine how and when ʿUmar II's name is invoked by Mālik in order to identify the major themes associated with the caliph. The following table offers an overview:

154 Calder, *Studies*, 38, 146.

155 Dutton, review of "Studies in Early Muslim Jurisprudence by N. Calder" and "ʿAmal v. Ḥadīth in Islamic Law," 28–33.

156 Motzki, "The Prophet and the Cat."

157 Dutton, "ʿAmal v. Ḥadīth in Islamic Law," 28, based notably on the papyrus studied by Abbott, *Studies in Arabic Literary Papyri*, vol. II, 114–28.

158 Décobert, "L'autorité religieuse," 33. See also Assier-Andrieu's suggestive remarks, "Penser le temps culturel du droit."

159 Décobert, "L'autorité religieuse," 35–6.

160 Décobert, "L'autorité religieuse," 35.

161 Dutton, "ʿAmal v. Ḥadīth in Islamic Law," 33, and also *The Origins of Islamic Law*; see also Décobert, "L'autorité religieuse," 37.

TABLE 6.2 Themes associated with ʿUmar II in the *Muwaṭṭaʾ*

***Muwaṭṭaʾ* chapter**		**References**	**Comments**
Wuqūt al-ṣalāt		p. 13–14, n. 1	
Al-ʿAmal fī ṣalāt al-jimāʿa		p. 97, n. 300	
Zakāt		p. 123, n. 579; p. 169, n. 594; p. 170, n. 596; p. 180, n. 609; p. 187, n. 615	
	Jizya ahl al-kitāb wa-al-majūs	p. 189, n. 621	Tax exemption for converts to Islam. *Cf.* Theophanes (p. 399, trans. p. 550); Michael the Syrian (p. 486, trans. p. 488–9); *History of the Patriarchs*, p. 152–3.
Ḥajj		p. 231, n. 755; p. 260, n. 847	
Jihād		p. 297, n. 974; p. 303, n. 984	
K. al-Farāʾiḍ		p. 352, n. 1096	
K. al-Nakāḥ		p. 358, n. 1110	
K. al-Ṭilāq		p. 374, n. 1159	
K. al-Buyūʿ		p. 427, n. 1306	
K. al-Aqḍiya		p. 511, n. 1404; p. 514, n. 1405	
K. al-Mudabbar		p. 586, n. 1491	
K. al-Ḥudūd		p. 595, n. 1509; p. 596, n. 1510; p. 599, n. 1520; p. 601, n. 1525	
K. al-ʿUqūl		p. 622, n. 1574	The blood price of a *dhimmī* was half that of a Muslim. *Cf. 1234*, p. 308, trans. p. 239–40; Michael the Syrian, p. 486, trans. p. 488–9
K. al-Jāmiʿ		p. 641–2, n. 1061	A *ḥadīth* in which ʿUmar II fears that, by leaving Medina, he will be grouped with those who were cast out of the city. This *ḥadīth* is recorded by Ibn ʿAbd al-Ḥakam (p. 27) and Ibn Kathīr (IX, p. 202)
		p. 643, n. 1608	

TABLE 6.2 Themes associated with ʿUmar II in the *Muwaṭṭaʾ* (*cont.*)

Muwaṭṭaʾ chapter	References	Comments
Al-Nahy ʿan al-qawl bi-al-qadar	p. 649, n. 1622	Persuading the Qadarites to renounce their beliefs or fight. *Cf.* ʿUmar II's famous letter to the Qadarites.
Mā jāʾa fī ʿadhāb al-ʿāmma bi-ʿamli al-khāṣa	p. 701, n. 1820	

The *Muwaṭṭaʾ* mentions ʿUmar II twenty-eight separate times in seventeen of its sixty-one chapters. Some passages (nº 1010, nº 1520) clearly refer to ʿUmar's time as governor of Medina; the space granted ʿUmar in the *Muwaṭṭaʾ* seems to be largely determined by his ties to this city.

ʿUmar b. ʿAbd al-ʿAzīz appears in the *Muwaṭṭaʾ* in connection with a wide variety of questions, be they related to religious life or civil litigation. Several themes associated with the caliph in Mālik's text echo elements of the Islamic tradition, including that recorded by the Christian authors, such as tax exemption following conversion to Islam[162] or the blood price of a *dhimmī*. Schacht has used this latter example as part of a project aimed at demonstrating the fictional nature of these frequent references to ʿUmar II: he estimates that many of these accounts claiming that the caliph initiated new practices were based on weak criteria from an *isnād*-criticism perspective.[163] Schacht is aware that the institution of this *wergeld* is reflected in the Syriac sources;[164] however, by espousing the verification methods of the Muslim traditionists, he maintains that the transmitters of these elements are far from authoritative. Another approach is possible, however: investigating the reasons for the attribution – real or assumed – of these elements to ʿUmar II. In the context of the present inquiry, aimed at illuminating the conditions under which the caliph's image developed, the following question then arises: regardless of the historical veracity of any of these episodes, do these references in the *Muwaṭṭaʾ* not constitute a new addition to the dossier attesting to the strong ties between the creation and diffusion of ʿUmar II's image and the emerging *fiqh* discipline? The caliph occupies an important place in the *Muwaṭṭaʾ*, granting him an aura

162 On this measure, see Abū Yūsuf Yaʿqūb, *Kitāb al-kharāj*, 157, trans. 202–3.
163 Schacht, *The Origins*, 205–6.
164 Michael the Syrian, vol. II, 456, French trans. 489; *1234*, 308, Latin trans. 239–40.

of Malikite legitimacy.[165] The overarching themes developed by Mālik can also be found in historiographic works that share no direct ties with the *Muwaṭṭa'*: these links between *fiqh* and *ta'rīkh* now require our attention.

The *Muwaṭṭa'*'s references to ʿUmar II and the famous relations between Ibn ʿAbd al-Ḥakam and Mālik invite a deeper analysis of this transmission circuit. Ibn ʿAbd al-Ḥakam's role in spreading Mālikī doctrine throughout Egypt is well-known.[166] It would seem that ʿUmar II's place in the *Muwaṭṭa'* was a determining factor in Ibn ʿAbd al-Ḥakam's portrayal of the caliph as a virtuous role model in his *Sīra*. There was another reason for Ibn ʿAbd al-Ḥakam's interest in the caliph: the Banū ʿAbd al-Ḥakam were clients (*mawālī*) of the Umayyads. They originally resided at Ayla, whence Ibn ʿAbd al-Ḥakam's father, ʿAbd al-Ḥakam b. Aʿyan b. al-Layth al-Aylī (d. 171/787–788) left to settle in Alexandria, where he established himself as an important Mālikī jurist; his son later followed in his footsteps.[167] Gil has suggested that the Banū ʿAbd al-Ḥakam, as *mawālī* of the Umayyads, decided to flee Abbasid persecution and take refuge in Egypt.[168] ʿUmar b. ʿAbd al-ʿAzīz's Egyptian dimension must also be considered; he may have been born in Egypt,[169] and he spent part of his youth there while his father served as governor of the region (65–86/686–705). Ibn ʿAbd al-Ḥakam's reasons for writing a *Sīra* of ʿUmar II were thus several: Mālikī tradition, Umayyad *memoria*, Egyptian roots. The combination of the caliph's intrinsic qualities, in addition to the contemporaneous messianic expectations surrounding his reign and his insertion in traditionist circles – primarily at Medina – in a sense predestined the emergence of an apologetic literature dedicated to ʿUmar II.

6.3.3 *The Circulation of Elements Related to ʿUmar II: Propositions and Hypotheses*

These elements from the Islamic tradition complement the information provided in the Christian corpus, and they allow us to identify two main geographic centres in the genesis of ʿUmar II's image: Medina and the Syrian space. These two locales are doubled in the context of the diffusion of this image: this first toward Egypt, the second toward the Jazīra. Medina and Syria are the two main spaces that produced traditions about this pious and virtuous caliph; Ibn ʿAbd

165 Which does not preclude differences of opinion between Mālik and ʿUmar II: for example, see al-Māwardī, *al-Aḥkām*, 125, trans. 68.
166 Rosenthal, "Ibn ʿAbd al-Ḥakam," 696.
167 Cobb, "Scholars and Society," 426.
168 Gil, "*A History of Palestine*", 126; Cobb, "Scholars and Society," 426–7.
169 It is more likely that ʿUmar II was born in Medina, although the sources are divided on the subject.

al-Ḥakam's Egypt and the Syriac authors' Upper Mesopotamia were the most important (but not exclusive) locations for the writing of these traditions and the new impetus they generated. Interaction between these two epicentres seems obvious; however, it is also significant that each space corresponds with a distinct phase in ʿUmar II's life.

ʿUmar b. ʿAbd al-ʿAzīz was educated in Medina, and he would later gain his first political experience as governor of the city. During these periods, he formed strong ties to the traditionists, who were instrumental in his integration into the Islamic tradition. Aided by Mālik b. Anas's legitimation, the *sunna* of the governor and then of the caliph spread rapidly in the sources via the same channels that ensured the diffusion of Mālikī doctrine, particularly in the case of Ibn ʿAbd al-Ḥakam. ʿUmar II then rose to the caliphate in Syria; the messianic and eschatological expectations linked to him in the sources would crystallise there in the period preceding the arrival of the year 100 *hijrī*. Historiography produced in the Syrian space developed rapidly in the Marwanid era and spread throughout the Upper Mesopotamian Christian sources, primarily in Syriac.

This analysis of ʿUmar II's image and its development in the sources may be summed up by paraphrasing Jacques Le Goff's question about Saint Louis: did ʿUmar II exist?[170] Was the ʿUmar II of the Islamic tradition merely the archetypal figure of the "holy" caliph? The answer to these questions must be sought in the successive layers of reinterpretation to which his image was subject. The unrealised eschatological expectations linked to the year 100 AH in particular required new explanations and recompositions. The following outline thus emerges: during his lifetime, ʿUmar II was widely believed to be the *mahdī*, and the caliph may even have seen himself in this light. Since the world did not end as foretold, various reinterpretations necessarily arose after his death. In the first decades of the third/ninth century,[171] ʿUmar II entered another category, that of the "renewer" or *mujaddid*, a variant conception of the *mahdī* in Sunni Islam: this figure was linked to "ideas of cyclical reform … and also to the

170 Le Goff, *Saint Louis*, 311–522.

171 If we follow Landau-Tasseron's conclusions, which suggest that the idea of the *mujaddid* actually arose around the figure of al-Shāfiʿī (d. 204/820). This latter was supposed to be the first true *mujaddid*, although it was necessary to identify his predecessor to corroborate the tradition stating that Allāh was supposed to send the *umma* a reviver of religion (a *mujaddid*) once every century. ʿUmar b. ʿAbd al-ʿAzīz naturally filled all the necessary conditions, both from a chronological perspective as the caliph of the year 100 *hijrī*, as well as with respect to his virtue and piety. The fact that certain circles believed him to be the *mahdī* confirmed his suitability for this role. On this question, see Landau-Tasseron's detailed study, "The Cyclical Reform," especially 112–3.

notion of *tajdīd al-dīn*, the renewal of religion … he could bring about a return to the golden era in the midst of Time, a "revitaliser" (*mahdi du milieu*) who is formally analogous to the concept of the *mujaddid*."[172] ʿUmar II's ties to the concept of the *sunna* and his role as a legislator – which surpassed the typical level of caliphal legislative involvement and was thus subject to challenges[173] – are also two quintessential aspects of the *mahdī*:

> Mahdism is a bridge between the past and the present, politics and religion. It implies a charismatic authority, prepared to rigorously break with norms if needed, but generally *in the name of the Tradition* [*sunna*], *thus reviving a lost mythic past* [*the era of the earliest caliphs, in particular the days of ʿUmar b. al-Khaṭṭāb*];[174] a charismatic movement could lead to the radicalisation and transformation of the tradition itself. The mahdi is infallible and the highest legal authority – his is the ultimate say in making and repealing the Law. *The mahdi's reform efforts are necessarily tied to jurisprudence*.[175]

The caliph naturally and inevitably had to engage in legislative activities; thus, it is logical that he played a significant role in the jurisprudential corpus under development at the time. The *mahdī*'s intrinsic ties to legislative roles makes ʿUmar II's inclusion in the *Muwaṭṭaʾ* relatively unsurprising, even if Mālik b. Anas's connections to the late Umayyads require further analysis.

The fact that the material in the Christian sources – much of which was produced during the Umayyad era – is quite similar to that of the Abbasid sources invites several remarks. First, it implies that we should rethink certain ideas regarding the place granted to the Umayyads in the successive strata of Abbasid historiography, in particular ʿUmar II's portrayal in this production. Understanding the Abbasid historiographers' view of the Umayyads' essential function in these texts is crucial: the Umayyads ensured the future possibility of the Abbasids' accession to the throne.[176] ʿUmar II played a key role in this process: for example, he reinstated the practice of granting pensions to the Hashimites during his caliphate after years of pleading in vain with his predecessors, al-Walīd and Sulaymān, to do the same.[177] More importantly, in the *Anonymous History of the Abbasids*, ʿUmar II is described as allowing the union

172 García-Arenal, "Introduction," 10.
173 See Décobert, "L'autorité religieuse."
174 Emphasis and additions mine.
175 García-Arenal, "Introduction," 14.
176 El-Hibri, "The Redemption," 251. See above, Ch. 4.
177 Ibn Saʿd, ed. Sachau, *al-Ṭabaqāt*, vol. V, 289.

of Muḥammad b. ʿAlī and Rayṭa bint ʿUbayd Allāh b. ʿAbd Allāh b. ʿAbd al-Midān al-Ḥārithī, despite the fact that ʿAbd al-Malik had strictly prohibited marriages between the Banū Hāshim and the Banū al-Ḥārith; the future Abbasid caliph Abū al-ʿAbbās was born of this union.[178] The Abbasid historiographers' interest in promoting the image of the caliph who essentially permitted the birth of the second Islamic dynasty is thus quite understandable.

Finally, most sources situate the institution of the Abbasid *daʿwa* during ʿUmar II's caliphate, in the year 100 *hijrī*.[179] ʿUmar II played significant roles in both ensuring the possibility of Abbasid rule and initiating the process itself. It is unsurprising that the Umayyad caliph found such favour among the Abbasid historiographers, nor is it surprising that he was later held up as a model by the caliph al-Muhtadī (255–256/869–870), for example.[180] ʿUmar II's favourable attitude toward the Hashimites – which Barthold deems suspect[181] – perhaps contributed to the spread of the "rumors" that the caliph died after being poisoned.[182] By treating his own family members in a manner similar to how he treated his subjects in general – that is, more harshly – he endured hostility from a certain segment of his entourage, to the extent that he was "warned of the likely unhappy consequences of such a policy to himself." The caliph simply responded: "May I never be spared the suffering I fear on any day other than the Day of Judgement."[183] Alongside the uncertain circumstances of the caliph's death, his piety is praised in the texts through anecdotes recounting voices heard by his widow Fāṭima and Maslama b. ʿAbd al-Malik near his remains, or even describing a text that fell from the heavens announcing an *amān* for ʿUmar II.[184]

Although a large portion of the history of the Umayyad dynasty and the Syrian space was based on the successive historiographic reconstructions produced in the third/ninth and fourth/tenth centuries – in other words, during the Abbasid era – the chronology of the appearance and development of *topoi* related to the caliph demonstrate that older elements, in some cases tracing back to the first half of the second/eighth century, survived later recompositions. This past

178 *Akhbār al-dawla*, 200–1.

179 Al-Ṭabarī, vol. II, 1358, trans. vol. XXIV, 87; Ibn Kathīr, *al-Bidāya*, vol. IX, 196–7; Ibn al-Athīr, vol. V, 53; see also Sharon's classic study, *Black Banners*, and El-Hibri, *Reinterpreting*, 3.

180 Muʿaffa b. Zakariyya al-Jarīrī, *Jalīs al-ṣāliḥ*, vol. II, 384–6; Zetterstéen [Bosworth], "Al-Muhtadī," 476–7; Cook, "Messianism and Astronomical Events," 42.

181 Barthold, "The Caliph ʿUmar II," 90.

182 Cobb, "ʿUmar (II)," 887.

183 Al-Māwardī, *al-Aḥkām*, 150, trans. 88.

184 Ibn Saʿd, ed. Sachau, *al-Ṭabaqāt*, vol. V, 301; *Aghānī*, vol. VIII, 158; *Kitāb al-ʿuyūn*, vol. I, 61; al-Suyūṭī, *Taʾrīkh al-khulafāʾ*, 287; Barthold, "The Caliph ʿUmar II," 95.

refused to remain buried, and "it was not to be forgotten altogether but rather transformed, both memorialized and commemorated."[185] Simultaneously embodying a Medinese and a Syrian-Umayyad memory, and moreover, occupying a crucial role in preserving the possibility for the Abbasids' accession to the caliphate, ʿUmar II was a figure who fulfilled the necessary conditions to ensure the survival of his own memory, despite the vagaries of transmission. More than any other, ʿUmar II personified the qualities of the sovereign as defined by Umayyad ideology: he was the best of men on earth (*khayr al-nās*), the possessor of unrivalled merit (*al-afḍal*).[186]

These Umayyad historiographic constructions proved particularly solid. Among others, the holy caliph and the combat hero shape our perception of Marwanid history. The historiographic competition that flourished among these various protagonists, however, complicates the situation to a certain degree. Hishām b. ʿAbd al-Malik is sometimes held up as a foil for ʿUmar II: the ruler who oversaw further expansion of the empire was opposed with the caliph who contracted it.[187] While ʿUmar II was the apostle of stasis in the face of the looming End of Days, Hishām was the caliph who sought to delay this *eschaton* at any cost. Maslama, the weaponised arm of these contrasting policies, was thus successively recalled from Constantinople, then charged with reclosing the gates of Gog and Magog in the Caucasus. Maslama is a unifying link between these two caliphs, as well as between these two antithetical conceptions of Islamic power and time. The caliph who "renounced the world" acts as a complement to the "world conqueror,"[188] and naturally to the caliph who advocated expansion as well.

These models produced by the texts were not the only ones, as the first caliphs and, of course, the Prophet – the quintessential founding hero – also fall into this category. Although the fact that the Umayyads are emphasised here seems surprising initially, it should not be forgotten that these figures were raised aloft from the "Marwanid pantheon" for very specific reasons: to preserve the potential for the Abbasids to one day seize power, for apocalyptic purposes, and as models of governance. Moreover, there was essentially an *Umayyad interregnum*. The first Islamic dynasty served as a link between the Prophet and the Abbasids, thus guaranteeing an Islamic *continuum*. The prodigious efforts at creating models did not prevent the Umayyads' tragic downfall.

185 Geary, *Phantoms of Remembrance*, 8.
186 On this Umayyad presentation of the caliph, see Crone, *Medieval Islamic Political Thought*, 34.
187 The consequences of this political choice are detailed below, Ch. 8.
188 See al-Azmeh's remarks, *Muslim Kingship*, 39, and those of Goldziher, *Le dogme et la loi*, 111 ff.

The famous statement – "unhappy is the land that needs a hero" – here takes on its fullest sense, when worship is transformed into nostalgia: "woe ... unto those whose present is so precarious that they seek exemplary representatives of their threatened identity in the past."[189]

These compositions, and the manipulations of varying importance that accompany them, were not the sole purview of the first Islamic dynasty. Their Abbasid successors were also largely preoccupied with their own historicisation, a fact that by its very nature conditions our access to these alternative pasts. These reconstructions were sometimes so monumental that they became nearly invisible, forcing us to try to trace their "murmurs." One of these reconstructions, approached through a Syrian lens, allows us to pursue our investigation further.

189 Albert, "Du martyr à la star," 16. The quote is often wrongly attributed to Hegel when, in fact, it comes from Brecht's *Life of Galileo*.

CHAPTER 7

Interpreting the Abbasid Revolution in the Syrian Space

> What sets the French Revolution apart is that it was not a transition but a beginning and a haunting vision of that beginning.[1]

•••

> The ʿAbbāsid Revolution represents, above all, a problem of medieval historiography.[2]

∴

The Abbasid Revolution was *the* defining event[3] of the first centuries of Islam. The history of the Syrian space in the second/eighth century cannot be approached without an understanding of this episode and how it came to represent the irreversible decline of the province and the growing importance of Iraq. In addressing this fundamental precursor to the history of meanings outlined in the next chapter, we must "exploit the event," while bearing in mind Duby's remarks:

> Events are like the foam of history, bubbles large or small that burst at the surface and whose rupture triggers waves that travel varying distances. This one has left very enduring traces that are not yet completely erased today. It is those traces that bestow existence upon it. Outside of them, the event is nothing, and it is thus with them that this book is essentially concerned.[4]

1 Furet, *Interpreting the French Revolution*, 79.
2 Lassner, *Islamic Revolution and Historical Memory*, ix.
3 The Andalusian descendants of the first Islamic dynasty used this understated term to describe the tragic memory of this episode. See *Akhbār majmūʿa*, 51, trans. 75–6; Martinez-Gros, *L'idéologie omayyade*, 54.
4 Duby, *The Legend of the Bouvines*, 1–2. In the French original preface, not included in the English translation, Duby explained that one of his main goals was to "exploit the event" (*exploiter l'événement*), see *Le dimanche de Bouvines*, 8.

 | DOI:10.1163/9789004466326_009

These traces are above all narratives of the event that brought about the fall of the Umayyads in 132/750: the Abbasid Revolution. The expression befits this bloody moment in the history of Islam, marking the overthrow of the first Islamic dynasty, the Umayyads (661–750), and the instauration of Abbasid line (750–1258). Medieval and modern authors alike declare this event to be a major historical turning point. However, we are first faced with an origin myth, and then with a uniquely historiographical problem. From the perspective of the present study, it is important to analyse the vulgate imposed via these chronographies in order to show how this narrative was constructed, and the stakes involved in such a project are sizable, both with respect to a history of meanings and as a way of approaching the history of the Syrian space.

In both the medieval Islamic sources and modern scholarly works, Syria almost entirely "disappears" from the year 132/750 on. Descriptions of the foundation of the second Islamic dynasty are particularly significant in this regard: the Syrian space largely falls into oblivion in the successive layers of historiographic recomposition, in which the geographic centre of interest shifts abruptly to the east. The Abbasids, concerned with affirming their still-tenuous legitimacy, undertook to rewrite the fundamental moment that established their origins. In so doing, they emphasised the importance of Khurāsān, the insurrectionary hotbed of the movement that would lead to the Umayyads' defeat, while diminishing the family's Syrian roots, which would ultimately fall victim to the strategies of oblivion discussed previously in Chapter 4. The Abbasid vulgate of the revolution reduced Syria to a mere transitional space: the decisive battles took place in Iraq, on the Great Zāb or beneath the walls of Wāsiṭ, and the end occurred in Egypt with the execution of Marwān II at Būṣīr.[5] Syria's role in the conflict was limited to a small number of episodes: the arrest of Ibrāhīm al-Imām, leader of the movement, captured at al-Ḥumayma and held captive at Ḥarrān; ʿAbd Allāh b. ʿAlī's frantic pursuit of the retreating Umayyad army, followed by his brother Ṣāliḥ's hunt for Marwān II as he fled to Egypt; and then the sack of Damascus and the massacre of the Umayyads, detailed above, in order to strengthen the link between the extinction of the family and the effacement of the province. Finally, several years later, in 136/754, the Syrian space would be the epicentre of ʿAbd Allāh b. ʿAlī's rebellion after the death of the first Abbasid caliph, putting an end once and for all to any plans to keep the caliphate on Syrian soil.

This acknowledgment of the events sanctioning Syria's disappearance should be accompanied by the following remark: the Abbasid Revolution

5 On the problems associated with locating this site, see Wiet, "Būṣīr."

represents a fundamental caesura in Islamic history. Here we return to an important conclusion from Chapter 2, which sheds light on the fact that the chronographers were trying above all to build the framework for an authorised reading of the first centuries of the *hijra*. The year 132/750 thus became indicative of a rupture *in and of itself*, and the strategies employed to this end insisted in particular on the sequestration of dynastic memories in distinct geographic spaces. This obsessive spatialisation created necessary oppositions between the regions one wished to portray as antagonistic.[6] As a consequence, this presentation of history has led a number of modern scholars to the conclusion that Syria's decline was inevitable following the overthrow of the dynasty that had given the province its badge of honour; the classic works of Hitti or the Belgian Jesuit Lammens are good examples of this approach.[7] It was not until Sourdel's 1980 article or, more recently, the works of Cobb, that Abbasid Syria truly attracted and retained scholarly attention in modern research.[8] The Abbasid Revolution itself has been the subject of a vast number of studies, to which we shall return below. Beyond its historical importance, it also generated massive historiographic shockwaves: as emphasised in the previous chapters, the new dynasty, which had taken power by force, initiated sweeping rewriting projects, and these efforts become especially palpable in descriptions of the precise moment marking the Umayyads' downfall and the Abbasids' seizure of the caliphate. The reconstructions undertaken were so significant that they became almost invisible. How, then, should we approach an edifice that was entirely reinterpreted, the product of a targeted ideological project, aimed at

6 On this point, see above, Ch. 4.

7 See Lammens's firm assessment in *La Syrie*, 89–90: "The Umayyad century forms a unique chapter in the history of Syria. With their disappearance, Syria ceased to be the center of a vast empire. Trembling under a power that it considered foreign, from whom it never ceased to experience hostility, it was systematically marginalized from participating in any affairs [...] In *Syrie moderne* [... J.] David states that 'once Abbasid revenge had been achieved, peace and calm once again reigned in Syria [...] Henceforth, what would it matter to the fickle Syrians if the caliph ruled from Baghdad? [...] The plains of the Tigris and Euphrates had dethroned the prairies of the Orontes; but the latter had gained in security, rendering them greener, richer, and more appealing than ever.' Our rapid exposé will show what must be thought of this poetry, bearing witness to a complete misapprehension of the historical situation. Two centuries would pass before Syria resigned itself to its humiliation and political abdication" (Lammens's critique is directed at the work of Yanoski and David, *Syrie ancienne et moderne*, 172 ff). Hitti's analysis (*History of Syria*, 534) is even more laconic and unambiguous: "With the Umayyad fall the hegemony of Syria in the world of Islam ended and the glory of the country passed away."

8 Sourdel, "La Syrie au temps des premiers califes abbasides;" Cobb, "Al-Mutawakkil's Damascus" and above all *White Banners*. For the situation on the coast, see Borrut, "L'espace maritime syrien" and "Architecture des espaces portuaires."

asserting the caliphal legitimacy of the Abbasids? It is this question that invites us to examine the Syrian elements of this production, as they reveal a period more complex than that described in the classical Islamic sources.

7.1 The Abbasid Revolution: Medieval and Modern Vulgates

Like any origin story, the narrative that came to define the early Abbasids and their violent rise to power reads as the result of intense rewriting efforts. A vulgate was produced, a "revolutionary catechism,"[9] that dictated the authoritative reading of this heavily significant episode while also aiming to limit the field of concurrent interpretations.

7.1.1 *The Revolutionary Canon*

More than any other source, the *Anonymous History of the Abbasids* (*Akhbār al-dawla al-ʿAbbāsiyya*) establishes the "official version" of the revolutionary movement;[10] moreover, it was perhaps with the express purpose of solidifying this "official version" of events that the work itself was composed.[11] It can be summarised as follows: the overthrow of the first Islamic dynasty was the result of a lengthy process that began with an initial clandestine period lasting at least thirty years, during which efforts were aimed at organising the movement and rallying support. During this stage, the Abbasids were based at al-Ḥumayma, in the southern Syrian space, and sent emissaries to plead their case in Kūfa and especially in the eastern Iranian plateau, in Khurāsān. Muḥammad b. ʿAlī presided over the fate of the *Hāshimiyya* at the time: he had inherited this role in 98/716–717 from the "testament" of the Alid Abū Hāshim, son of Muḥammad b. al-Ḥanafiyya, thus establishing the ties that united the Abbasids and the proto-Shiites. After Muḥammad b. ʿAlī's death in 125/743, his son Ibrāhīm al-Imām took over and named one of his *mawālī*, Abū Muslim, as chief propagandist in Khurāsān. Upon hearing of this sedition,[12] the caliph Marwān II ordered the arrest of Ibrāhīm al-Imām at al-Ḥumayma, then imprisoned him in Ḥarrān, where he would later die in 132/749. Before his

9 I have borrowed this expression from Furet, *Interpreting the French Revolution*, 81 ff.

10 The most recent discussion of this "official version" is that of Cobb, "The Empire in Syria."

11 Daniel, "The Anonymous History of the Abbasid Family," 425.

12 Several sources, however, explain the fall of the Umayyads as a result of the loss of their intelligence networks. See al-Ṭabarī (vol. III, 414, trans. vol. XXIX, 118), al-Masʿūdī (*Murūj*, vol. VI, 36, trans. Pellat vol. IV, 911), and finally, the text of *Siyāsat al-mulūk*, studied by Silverstein, "A New Source" and *Postal Systems*, 87.

death, Ibrāhīm transferred the rights to the imamate to Abū al-ʿAbbās; from this moment on, the processes set in motion were impossible to stop.

The narrative recounted in the *Akhbār al-dawla al-ʿAbbāsiyya* ends there, its account limited to this secretive evolution. Successive events, presented following the same logic, must be sought in other sources, al-Ṭabarī in particular. The story continues: Abū Muslim's energetic recruitment of supporters was an unqualified success.[13] Having reached a critical mass of followers, Abū Muslim launched the military operation, marked by his troops' triumphant march westward and crowned by their resounding victory in the battle of the Great Zāb, heralding the defeat of the final Umayyad caliph.[14] Marwān II fled and was pursued throughout Syria first by ʿAbd Allāh b. ʿAlī and his men, then by his brother Ṣāliḥ and his forces, before being captured and put to death in Egypt.[15] Abū al-ʿAbbās, however, had not even bothered to wait for the victory at Great Zāb to proclaim himself caliph at Kūfa, thus becoming the first Abbasid ruler.[16] Without dwelling on the details of this latter's caliphate, the conditions of his succession in 136/754 should be mentioned, as they are particularly important with respect to the Syrian space. Abū Jaʿfar, brother of the deceased and the future caliph al-Manṣūr, set out to suppress the rival pretensions of his uncles, ʿAbd Allāh b. ʿAlī foremost among them.[17] This latter, then governor of the Shām and on the verge of launching an offensive against the Byzantines, received the *bayʿa* from his troops. Abū Jaʿfar, who was on pilgrimage in Mecca, dispatched Abū Muslim against ʿAbd Allāh b. ʿAlī, who was defeated near Nisibis after several months of brutal combat. ʿAbd Allāh b. ʿAlī was nevertheless able to flee to Baṣra, taking refuge with his brother Sulaymān.[18] He died in 147/764, crushed by the collapsing walls of the house in which he had been residing, under conditions that remain obscure.[19]

It is clear that this brief summary poses numerous problems for historians of the period. In many ways, it reads as an *ex post facto* reconstruction of events, presenting them in a light favourable to the second Islamic dynasty. This presentation of the Abbasid Revolution has nevertheless had lasting effects on scholarly interpretations, which we shall outline briefly below.

13 See notably al-Ṭabarī, vol. II, 1949 ff., trans. vol. XXVII, 61 ff; on the strategies implemented by Abū Muslim, see Karev, "La politique d'Abū Muslim dans le Māwarāʾannahr."

14 Al-Ṭabarī, vol. III, 38–42, trans. vol. XXVII, 162–6.

15 Al-Ṭabarī, vol. III, 45–51, trans. vol. XXVII, 168–75.

16 Al-Ṭabarī, vol. III, 23 ff., trans. vol. XXVII, 145 ff.

17 For a detailed presentation of the troubled beginnings of al-Manṣūr's caliphate, see Kennedy, *The Early Abbasid Caliphate*, 57 ff.

18 Al-Ṭabarī, vol. III, 92–9, trans. vol. XXVIII, 8–18.

19 Al-Ṭabarī, vol. III, 330, trans. vol. XXIX, 17. This point is discussed in further detail below.

7.1.2 *A Century of Interpretations of the Abbasid Revolution*

The subject has produced an abundant bibliography, although an exhaustive presentation of these studies is impossible here. However, the most significant works and the dominant interpretative paradigms merit further attention in order to shed light on successive scholarly approaches to the Abbasid Revolution. Humphreys offers the most comprehensive discussion of the modern historiographic production on the topic, noting that historians have made much use of the "art of interpretation."[20]

Chronologically, modern scholarship on this subject began with the works of Van Vloten in the final decade of the nineteenth century.[21] His pioneering studies aimed to define the history of the *Hāshimiyya*, the long-secretive movement that would precipitate the downfall of the Umayyads at the hands of Abū Muslim and his forces. In his second study, dating to 1894, Van Vloten was interested primarily in the expected arrival of a liberator or a messiah, touching on the messianic ideology characteristic of the uprising, to which we shall return in greater detail below. Contrary to what had long been thought, he analysed the phenomenon more in sociopolitical and economic terms than in ethnic ones. Thus, it was the conquered peoples, primarily Iranian given that the movement arose in Khurāsān, who opposed the elite Arab Muslims, who had imposed their authority on them by force. In 1902, Wellhausen's classic work then offered an extremely valuable presentation of the environment in which the rebellion developed based on al-Ṭabarī's version of events.[22] Without denying the role played by the Arab populations of Khurāsān, he portrays the Revolution as a fundamentally Iranian uprising. For these two founding fathers of the discipline, there was no doubt that the Abbasid Revolution was an exceptional phenomenon accompanied by major transformations.

The subject would not attract significant scholarly interest again until the 1940s, a fact that only underscores the importance of Van Vloten and Wellhausen's initial analyses. In 1947, Frye was the first to defend an Arab-centric interpretation of the revolution.[23] This idea was then taken up and supported by Omar and Shaban, two proponents of a movement organised and led by Arabs.[24] Shaban in particular was interested in studying the role of Arab tribes in Khurāsān from the middle of the first/seventh century to the Abbasid Revolution. In the meantime, Cahen, building on Van Vloten and

20 Humphreys, *Islamic History*, 104–27. Another useful presentation of this question is offered by Marín-Guzmán, "The Abbasid Revolution in Central Asia and Khurāsān."

21 Van Vloten, *De Opkomst* and "Recherches sur la domination arabe."

22 Wellhausen, *Das arabische Reich*, 247 ff.

23 Frye, "The Role of Abu Muslim."

24 Omar, *The ʿAbbāsid Caliphate*; Shaban, *The ʿAbbāsid Revolution*.

Wellhausen's idea that revolutionary propaganda was linked to Shiism, suggested reading the *daʿwa* as an authentically Shiite movement. At the time, Shiism was only a general trend representing a small number of consensual views, rather than an organised current of thought.[25] Fifteen years later, Daniel interpreted the uprising in socioeconomic terms, arguing that it arose as a form of resistance from rural communities against the new elite populations in Khurāsān.[26] Sharon then produced the most comprehensive study on this subject in two volumes.[27] Per Sharon, during the rebellion's clandestine phase, the Abbasid propagandists recruited supporters indiscriminately, from cities and the countryside, Arabs and Iranian *mawālī*, Muḍarīs and Yemenīs alike. However, in order to form an army capable of bringing the Abbasids to power, Abū Muslim needed to enlist soldiers, and for this purpose he turned to the Yemenite tribal confederation; his army was thus entirely composed of Arabs, both its commanders and its infantry. Blankinship later emphasised the connections between the Abbasid Revolution and the Yemenite tribes, rather than the Muḍarīs, thus reinforcing the Arab-centric approaches to the topic.[28]

Crone demonstrated that the primitive appeal of the revolutionaries, who called for *al-riḍā min āl Muḥammad*, never once specified an individual who was supposed to take power in the aftermath of the expected military victory. Rather, this call was indicative of the fact that the uprising was waiting for or anticipated the appearance of someone on whom the general consensus would fall, meaning that their objective was not specifically to put an Abbasid in power, but simply someone of merit. The Abbasids would later reconstruct the elements related to this period to make it seem as though the revolution was taken up fully in their name.[29] Agha has recently reaffirmed that the Revolution was not Arab, but "Iranian," returning to and further developing Wellhausen's conclusions; furthermore, nor was the uprising an Abbasid one, because it was not originally undertaken in their name.[30] Agha essentially studied the question from a demographic point of view, for which he employed modern resources and tools, even if it meant relying on extremely fragmentary information of highly questionable reliability. However, before this work – a development of his dissertation research carried out a decade

25 Cahen, "Points de vue."

26 Daniel, *The Political and Social History of Khurasan*.

27 Sharon, *Black Banners* and *Revolt*. However, see also Crone's reservations, "Review of M. Sharon, *Black Banners*," as well as those of Daniel, "Review of M. Sharon, *Black Banners*." Sharon's second volume, *Revolt*, is notably discussed by Daniel, "Arabs, Persians."

28 Blankinship, "The Tribal Factor."

29 Crone, "On the Meaning of the ʿAbbāsid Call."

30 Agha, *The Revolution which Toppled the Umayyads*.

earlier in Toronto – was published in 2003, Elad critiqued numerous aspects of his argument, including both his perspectives on the ethnic aspects of the phenomenon as well as his methodological approach.[31] More broadly, Elad criticised these "new revisionists" who returned to the thesis of a revolutionary Iranian population while ignoring important scholarly advances demonstrating that the Arab element was, in fact, significant.[32] This very same notion of a profoundly Iranian phenomenon underlies Arjomand's analysis. Developing the concept of an "integrative revolution," he espoused the idea that the *mawālī*, primarily Iranians and recent converts, were reclaiming a space on the political chessboard; the *kuttāb* in particular fell into this category, as despite their substantial role in the Umayyad administration, they remained victims of their status as clients.[33]

Lassner took a radically different approach, suggesting that the Abbasid Revolution should be studied from a historiographic angle, based on the fact that the accounts that have survived are aimed less at providing historical information than at affirming Abbasid legitimacy.[34] This material is thus a narrative construct, fabricated by propagandists in the service of the second Islamic dynasty, and it should be understood as such. Despite this innovative methodology, his study sustained a number of critiques, especially with respect to the "case studies" that formed the basis of his argument.[35] Nevertheless, his work made several important advances in this historiographic construction, among them his demonstration of the key role played by al-Manṣūr and his entourage. Certain of Lassner's conclusions agree with those reached by Shacklady who, despite relying solely on al-Ṭabarī, challenged the very existence of the *daʿwa*: even if the Abbasids undoubtedly had networks in place in Khurāsān, they could not have developed the idea of this phase of clandestine propaganda until after the coup as a response to their need to confirm their legitimacy.[36]

While these numerous studies have considerably expanded our knowledge of the Abbasid Revolution, it is clear that the Syrian aspect of the episode has attracted much less scholarly attention than its eastern dimensions.

31 Elad, "The Ethnic Composition."

32 Other than the works already mentioned here, Elad also criticised Daniel, "The 'Ahl al-Taqādum'" and "Arabs, Persians;" Crone, "The ʿAbbāsid Abnāʾ" and "The Significance of Wooden Weapons;" Zakeri, *Sāsānid Soldiers in Early Muslim Society*; Agha, "The Arab Population in Ḫurāsān."

33 Arjomand, "ʿAbd Allāh Ibn al-Muqaffaʿ."

34 Lassner, *Islamic Revolution and Historical Memory*. From the same author, see also *The Shaping*.

35 For example, see Daniel's remarks in "Review of M. Sharon, *Black Banners*."

36 Shacklady, "The ʿAbbasid Movement."

Cobb's recent work should be mentioned here, as it lays the groundwork for further reflection on the Revolution's extent in the specific context of the Bilād al-Shām. Like other scholars, Cobb challenges the active role of the Abbasids during the clandestine phase of the revolt, suggesting rather that they reaped the rewards of an Alid uprising in which they had played only a minor part. He also insists on the idea that in Syria, the Abbasid Revolution was the final blow to the Umayyad regime in the context of the third *fitna*, the civil war that raged in the province at the time. However, he correctly highlights the fact that "from a Syrian point of view, the battle for the caliphate was far from over even in 750,"[37] and that struggles would continue throughout Abū al-ʿAbbās's caliphate and his succession, as attested in particular by the uprising of ʿAbd Allāh b. ʿAlī.[38]

7.1.3 *The "Abbasid Revolution" and Modern Scholarship: Questions and Debates*

Two lines of questioning have dominated the debates: first, that of the uprising's identity, in which supporters of an "Iranian" movement generally oppose those of an "Arab" Revolution; and second, arising from the first, is that of the very nature of the event, which was long exclusively presented as an incontestable rutpure. Behind these two problems, which are in reality closely intertwined, lie both the deep influences of some of the major ideologies of the twentieth century through whose lenses the episode has been interpreted, but also, more fundamentally, obstacles related to a terminology that is difficult to define.

7.1.3.1 The Identity of the Uprising

Until the end of the 1960s, the Abbasid Revolution was presented as an Iranian national revolution, despite the inherent anachronism of this characterisation.[39] As a result, the entire beginning of the Abbasid period has been analysed in light of these supposed Iranian influences. However, this argument has been challenged by concurrent and contrary theories insisting on the Arab element of the revolutionary movement, and these controversies surrounding the identity of the episode have shaped modern historiography on the topic. Goitein, in 1968, and Elad more recently, have emphasised that the second Islamic dynasty was fundamentally marked by Arabness, and that the transition from the Umayyads to the Abbasids corresponded to

37 Cobb, "The Empire in Syria," 266. From the same author, see also *White Banners*, 75 ff.

38 Cobb, "The Empire in Syria," 266–7 and *White Banners*, 23–6.

39 As highlighted notably by Elad, "The Ethnic Composition," 246.

nothing more or less than the shift from one Arab dynasty to another.[40] Elad and Bligh-Abramski before him remarked that the importance of the Iranian *mawālī* in the early Abbasid state needs to be put in greater perspective.[41]

The central problem is actually related to the terminology used by the medieval authors to designate the various players in the Abbasid Revolution. It is above all a question of understanding what is encompassed by the term *ahl Khurāsān* in the texts. Elad has shown that this phrase was used primarily to designate military units, principally of Arab origin.[42] This expression is also attested among the eastern Umayyad armies – in particular those of Naṣr b. Sayyār, the last Marwanid governor of Khurāsān – which, if we follow the conclusions of the "new revisionists" (Crone, Daniel, Agha) who see this denomination as employed exclusively for Iranian elements, would amount to an assertion that the Umayyad army itself was largely composed of soldiers of Iranian origin! In concentrating on the ethnic dimension of the Revolution, modern scholarship has developed a "classic" framework opposing Persians and Arabs. Agha's recent work does not deviate from this tradition; by relying on Van Vloten and Wellhausen, the "founding fathers" of studies on this subject, the research comes full circle, and after a century of debates and disagreements, we return once more to the theory of a popular Revolution led by the Iranian element.[43] Thus, we must once again focus on the vocabulary.

The most recent proponents of this interpretation have relied primarily on a letter written by ʿAbd al-Ḥamīd al-Kātib addressed to Naṣr b. Sayyār,[44] in which Marwān II's secretary details an uprising in Khurāsān orchestrated by an individual of unspecified identity who was spreading propaganda, calling for support for a descendant of the Prophet's family and taking advantage of the partisan divides in the province. It is tempting to subscribe to the hypothesis that this letter describes Abū Muslim's activities in the region. However, this interpretation poses numerous problems, particularly from a chronological perspective, as al-Qāḍī notes.[45] This issue led Elad to conclude that the letter

40 Elad, "The Ethnic Composition," 247.

41 Elad, "Aspects of the transition;" Bligh-Abramski, *From Damascus to Baghdad* and "Evolution Versus Revolution."

42 Elad, "The Ethnic Composition," 249–55, 274–5; see also Sharon, *Revolt*, 188.

43 Agha, *The Revolution which Toppled the Umayyads*.

44 This is letter n. 8, edited by ʿAbbās in *ʿAbd al-Ḥamīd*, 198–201.

45 This opinion is upheld by the editor of ʿAbd al-Ḥamīd's letters, ʿAbbās, *ʿAbd al-Ḥamīd*, 87–92; Agha, *The Revolution which Toppled the Umayyads*, 200–6. See also al-Qāḍī, "The Earliest Nābita," 32–7, which nevertheless proposes other possible identifications, 37, note 32.

is referring to the revolt of al-Ḥārith b. Surayj al-Tamīmī (128/745–746) rather than the one that brought about the downfall of the Umayyad regime.[46]

Another epistle by ʿAbd al-Ḥamīd also calls for not abandoning the Arab *dawla* to a group of non-Arabs (*wa-lā tumkinū nāṣiyat al-dawla al-ʿarabiyya min yad al-fiʾa al-ʿajamiyya*).[47] It goes without saying that the supporters of an Iranian revolution see this letter as solid proof confirming that these *ʿajam* are undoubtedly Iranians.[48] However, this interpretation seems far from assured in light of the fact that the term *ʿajam*, the equivalent of *barbaroi* for the Greeks, was applied to non-Arabs generally without further specification.[49] While *ʿajam* in medieval texts can designate Persians, it must not be forgotten that the term had much broader applications. The *Lisān al-ʿarab* also notes the terminological opposition between *ʿarab* and *ʿajam*, implying that the word was in no way limited solely to Iranians.[50]

This problem lies at the heart of determining what was encompassed by the terms *ʿarab* and *ʿajam* in the early period in the context of defining the new identities at play within the caliphate. While this question, which must also include the inevitable variations in usage that occurred throughout the empire, is well beyond the scope of the present inquiry,[51] it is nonetheless important to note that this dichotomy cannot be translated exclusively in ethnic terms, signifying Iranians with certainty. In reality, this is a circular argument: is there not something paradoxical in trying to demonstrate the "Iranian-ness" of an event that originated in the eastern Iranian plateau? Is this not an interrogation that runs the risk of a systematically affirmative reply? When understood in sociocultural terms, the question of "Iranisation" is not a self-evident one. Goitein concluded to the contrary that "the first hundred years of the ʿAbbāsids did not see the eclipse of the Arabs, but were the very apogee and consummation of Arabism,"[52] while Grabar emphasised, following Sauvaget, "that ʿAbbāsid art (and civilization) did not start with a break from Umayyad art

46 Elad, "The Ethnic Composition," 289–92. On this rebellion, during the course of which al-Ḥārith called upon his supporters to adopt the colour black, see al-Ṭabarī's detailed narrative, vol. II, 1917–37, trans. vol. XXVII, 28–48; Crone, "On the Meaning of the ʿAbbāsid Call," 97–8.

47 See letter n. 38, edited by ʿAbbās, *ʿAbd al-Ḥamīd*, 289. This brief missive was translated into English by Agha, *The Revolution which Toppled the Umayyads*, 201.

48 See Agha, *The Revolution which Toppled the Umayyads*, 201; Agha and Khalidi, "Poetry and Identity," 89; Fowden, *Quṣayr ʿAmra*, 315.

49 Gabrieli, "ʿAdjam;" Retsö, *The Arabs in Antiquity*, 26.

50 Ibn Manẓūr, *Lisān*, vol. X, 49 ff.; this question is discussed by Retsö, *The Arabs in Antiquity*, 24 ff., who gives several other pieces of evidence to confirm this assertion.

51 See the works of Retsö, *The Arabs in Antiquity*, and Hoyland, *Arabia and the Arabs*.

52 Goitein, "A Plea," 226.

and civilization, but was rather its continuation."[53] Elad later adopted these conclusions, supporting them with new examples and notably insisting on the vitality of Arabic poetry – and thus, Arab culture – at the Abbasid court.[54]

The Abbasid Revolution has largely been interpreted as an integrative revolution[55] that enabled the assimilation of entire swathes of society that had been abandoned by the Umayyads, above all the Iranian elements. This supposed social promotion implied a depiction of the Revolution as a fundamental rupture that provoked major transformations. Naturally, it is to this presentation of the facts, a corollary of these questions concerning identity, to which we must now turn our attention.

7.1.3.2 Revolution or Evolution?

In the wake of Van Vloten and Wellhausen's pioneering works, scholars have acknowledged that the events of 132/750 produced upheavals of a magnitude rivalled only by the meteoric rise and spread of Islam. In 1950, Lewis did not hesitate to affirm that:

> the replacement of the Umayyads by the ʿAbbāsids in the headship of the Islamic community was more than a change of dynasty. It was a revolution in the history of Islam, as important a turning point as the French and Russian revolutions in the history of the West.[56]

This statement reveals a classic risk associated with comparatism: ethnocentrism. The Abbasid Revolution was supposed to have been for medieval Islam equivalent to the French Revolution in *Ancien Régime* France or the Bolshevik Revolution in 1917 Russia: namely, a major historical turning point with immediate and irreversible effects.

This frequent overinterpretation is undoubtedly due in part to the very terminology used to describe the episode. The word 'revolution' imposes itself on the scholarly tradition as a faithful translation of the Arabic term *dawla*, which designates above all a period, a revolution of time and, by extension, a change, a power, an empire or a dynasty. It is in its accepted sense of change – inherently understood to be both brutal and profound – that scholars have adopted this term in a privileged manner;[57] certain ideological implications, in particular Marxist ones, have contributed to the proliferation of this reading. In the

53 Grabar, "Al-Mushatta, Baghdād, and Wāsiṭ," 108.

54 Elad, "Aspects of the Transition," 118–28.

55 Arjomand, "ʿAbd Allāh Ibn al-Muqaffaʿ," 11.

56 Lewis, *The Arabs in History*, 84.

57 The term *thawra*, used in modern Arabic to designate a revolution or an insurrection, is rarely used or attested in the medieval sources. The polysemous word *dawla* is used

medieval vulgate and modern scholarship alike, this semantic choice in discussions of the episode allows us to clearly distinguish the successful revolt of 132/750 from the innumerable uprisings against the caliphate under the late Umayyads and early Abbasids.[58] It is obvious that this qualification suited the Abbasids' objectives quite well, as they thus were the embodiment of a salutary change for the Islamic empire. The violence of the Umayyads' overthrow gave rise to a new order, superior to the previous situation; the *dawla* was thus in stark opposition to the *fitna*, source of chaos and disorder. However, this choice is not an innocent one, considering that, at least from the Syrian perspective, the coup d'état of 132/750 was merely one episode among many others – characteristic of the final years of the Umayyad era – that took place during the third *fitna*, starting from the death of Hishām: did the coup truly take precedence over, for example, the assassination of al-Walīd II in the minds of the contemporaries of these events? Was the installation of Abū al-ʿAbbās at Anbār more significant than that of Marwān II at Ḥarrān? It should be added, again in the context of Syria, that Marwān II's ouster was far from the end of the battle for the caliphate, or even the cessation of the troubles that would continue to shake the province for more than a decade.

These remarks reveal the limitations of the clear-cut dynastic divisions imposed through the periodisation of Islamic history,[59] in particular by the Abbasids. This framework, developed by historiographers of the second Islamic dynasty, was generally adopted without question, thus reinforcing the caesura of 132/750. Wellhausen's classic study, or perhaps, more accurately, the use that

---

instead, as attested for the late Umayyad period by the letters of ʿAbd al-Ḥamīd al-Kātib. See especially letter n. 8, edited by ʿAbbās, *ʿAbd al-Ḥamīd*, 198–201.

58 On this point see Lewis, "On Revolutions in Early Islam" and "Islamic Concepts of Revolution;" Lassner, "The ʿAbbāsid *Dawla*" and *Islamic Revolution and Historical Memory*.

59 This question is immense and largely beyond the scope of our inquiry here. Consider, for example, the problems posed by the term "medieval" Islam borrowed from Western periodisation (see Varisco, "Making "Medieval" Islam Meaningful," elaborating on Hodgson's reflections that coined the curious terms "Islamdom" and "Islamicate" to create distance between this borrowed terminology, see *The Venture of Islam*, vol. I, especially 56 ff.). Even more important is the question of including the rise of Islam in Late Antiquity, as does Brown in *The World of Late Antiquity*. Although this approach became fairly common thereafter (see, for example, an article simply titled "Islam" edited by Kennedy in Bowersock, Brown and Grabar (eds.), *Late Antiquity*; the most complete study on this subject is that of Fowden, *Empire to Commonwealth*), it did not receive more in-depth discussion until relatively recently, both from specialists in the Late Antique period as well as scholars of Islam. See Cameron, "Ideologies and Agendas;" Robinson, "Reconstructing Early Islam;" and Rousseau (ed.), *A Companion to Late Antiquity*, in particular the contributions of Rebenich, "Late Antiquity in Modern Eyes" and Marsham, "The Early Caliphate and the Inheritance of Late Antiquity." For a staunchly comparatist approach to the period from 400–800, see Wickham, *Framing* and *The Inheritance of Rome*.

was made thereof, contributed to this opposition of an Umayyad "Arab kingdom" with an Abbasid "Islamic empire."[60] In the 1960s, Goitein pointed out the inherent dangers of this fragmented approach and called for the implementation of a different analytical framework that would treat the period from around 500 until 850 – or more precisely, the foundation of Sāmarrā' in 221/836 – as a whole.[61] He was thus firmly opposed to Lewis's above statement. Similarly, Morony also attempted to distance himself from the narrow confines of this political history, and proposed "a non-dynastic approach to the history of western Asia."[62]

These suggestions have not received the attention that they deserve in the field of Islamic history, although the idea of the Abbasid Revolution as a caesura has been called into question by Bligh-Abramski and Elad.[63] These two scholars have challenged the notion of a brutal rupture between the two dynasties and highlighted the many continuities linking the Umayyad and Abbasid periods. These extensions are notably illustrated by the continuation of the political, administrative and military careers of a number of individuals who took up their positions under the Marwanids and continued to hold them under the Abbasids.[64] Some Umayyad functionaries served the Abbasids, and a few of them were even promoted to positions of power. One of the most striking examples is that of Abū Ayyūb Sulaymān b. Makhlad[65] al-Mūryānī al-Khūzī, a minor functionary for an Umayyad governor who became a vizier under al-Manṣūr and was placed in charge of several *dīwān*s.[66] Abū ʿUbayd Allāh Muʿāwiya b. ʿUbayd Allāh b. Yassār,[67] al-Mahdī's vizier, came from a family of Umayyad secretaries from al-Urdunn;[68] numerous other examples could also be cited. This reintegration of former elites with experience in the caliphal

60 Wellhausen, *Das arabische Reich*. It should be noted that the German title evokes an Arab *empire* (*Reich*) rather than a kingdom (which would instead be *Königreich*), despite the English translation that popularised the work under the title *The Arab Kingdom*.

61 Goitein, "A Plea."

62 Morony, "Bayn al-Fitnatayn," 249.

63 Bligh-Abramski, *From Damascus to Baghdad* and "Evolution vs. Revolution;" Elad, "Aspects of the Transition."

64 These continuities, products of different elite strategies, are not surprising. This is a classic process, similar in certain respects to that which occurred during the Islamic conquests. On this point, see Robinson, *Empire and Elites* and Haldon and Conrad (eds.), *Elites Old and New*.

65 His name is also given as Sulaymān b. Ayyūb or b. Dāwūd.

66 Al-Jahshiyārī, 97–8; Bligh-Abramski, "Evolution vs. Revolution," 233–4; Elad, "Aspects of the Transition," 113. On Abū Ayyūb, a controversial figure suspected of embezzlement and nepotism, see Sourdel, *Le vizirat*, vol. 1, 78–87.

67 See Sourdel, *Le vizirat*, vol. 1, 94–103.

68 Al-Jahshiyārī, 126, 141; Bligh-Abramski, "Evolution vs. Revolution," 233–4; Elad, "Aspects of the Transition," 113.

administration previously in the service of the Umayyads was undoubtedly necessary for putting the affairs of the young Abbasid empire in order,[69] while these families used their own strategies to maintain their ranks.[70] The situation among the *qāḍīs* was the same,[71] as was that of the military,[72] including for some soldiers and officials who had fought directly against the Abbasids alongside Marwān II!

Such was the case for Isḥāq b. Muslim al-ʿUqaylī, a former commander under Hishām, who alongside his brother Bakkār led the rebellion against the Abbasids in the Jazīra in 133/750–751. However, they were both treated well by Abū al-ʿAbbās, and Isḥāq is portrayed as a confidant of al-Manṣūr.[73] Their privileged status among the Qaysite tribes of the Jazīra may be one explanation for this treatment. The Abbasid regime could not risk alienating itself from the Qaysīs or, for that matter, from any other powerful group:[74] the integration and influence of the military in the Syrian tribal system was essential for the new caliphal authority to try to preserve a fragile equilibrium. However, one should not conclude from the previous examples that all those who served under the Umayyads continued to do so under the Abbasids. Executions are well-attested, among them that of ʿAbd al-Ḥamīd al-Kātib, and logically only those who could serve the interests of the new dynasty were spared so as to provide favourable conditions for the recomposition of power structures that would guarantee that the caliphate operated smoothly.

These individual trajectories, like the sociocultural elements noted above, invite us to inscribe the Abbasid Revolution into a continuity. However, as Geary notes:

> arguments about continuity and change, apart from forcing scholars to reexamine their premises, seldom add much that is positive to historical debate. All too often they degenerate into a kind of sterile semantic argument about the difference between revolution, mutation, transformation and evolution. What is most interesting however is not primarily the rate

69 This is the hypothesis defended by Bligh-Abramski, *From Damascus to Baghdad*. See also Biddle, *The Development of the Bureaucracy*.

70 We are ignoring here the debate related to the collective ambitions of this group of elite bureaucrats who, according to Kennedy, tried to reconstruct the powerful administration of the late Sasanian period. These objectives reached their peak under the Barmakids. See Kennedy, *The Early Abbasid Caliphate*, 101 ff., and Elad's reservations, "Aspects of the Transition," 115–7.

71 Bligh-Abramski, "Evolution vs. Revolution," 236 ff.; see also Tillier, *Les cadis d'Iraq*, 96 ff.

72 Bligh-Abramski, "Evolution vs. Revolution," 230–2; Elad, "Aspects of the Transition," 97–111.

73 Bligh-Abramski, "Evolution vs. Revolution," 231–2.

74 As expressly emphasised by al-Balādhurī, *Ansāb*, vol. III, 158.

> of change itself or how such change should be quantified or classified, but why and how generations perceived discontinuity, and how these perceptions continued to influence the patterns of thought for a thousand years.[75]

Thus, it is precisely this perception of rupture – or its absence – by contemporaries in the context of the Syrian space that should be the focus of our attention here, alongside the "traces that bestow existence upon"[76] the event, to remain faithful to the perspective of a history of memory and meanings adopted in this study.

To conduct this inquiry, it is essential that we not limit ourselves to Abbasid sources, as they present a canonical version of the episode. Instead, we must use the Christian corpus, as it offers access to an Abbasid historiography still in-progress at the time as well as to alternative perspectives, detached from the imperative need to mark the break between the two dynasties. This approach is essential here, as these texts have as yet been relatively little-studied with respect to their accounts of the Abbasid Revolution.

7.2 Syrian Memories of the Abbasid Revolution

The Christian sources provide important elements that have the advantage of giving us access to layers of historiographic sedimentation that predate the crystallisation of an Abbasid vulgate (see table 7.1). Thus, they allow us to investigate the perceptions of this crucial episode in Islamic history before the canonical version had taken shape.

The events that shook the Umayyad caliphate, beginning with the death of Hishām b. ʿAbd al-Malik, received a great deal of attention from the Christian authors, who had much to say on the subject. They also present material of primary importance, sometimes contemporary to the events themselves, as discussed in detail in Chapter 3. The rich description preserved in the *History of the Patriarchs of Alexandria* is a notable example; the author of the pertinent passage, John, bishop of Wasīm, was a privileged observer of Marwān II's final days in Egypt.[77] In the Syrian context, the sources relying on Theophilus of Edessa are especially fertile, as they also have the great advantage of being based on first-hand accounts.

75 Geary, *Phantoms of Remembrance*, 25.
76 Duby, *The Legend of Bouvines*, 2.
77 *History of the Patriarchs*, PO, vol. V, 171 ff.; Hoyland, *Seeing*, 448. See also Amélineau, "Les derniers jours," who contests John's statement.

TABLE 7.1 Main information related to the "Abbasid Revolution" in the Christian sources

Information \ Sources	Circuit of Theophilus of Edessa							Circuit of Qartamīn				
	Theophanes	Agapius	1234	Michael the Syrian	775	Zuqnīn	Łewond	819	846	Continuatio	Patriarchs of Alexandria	Elias of Nisibis
Abū Muslim's rebellion in Khurāsān	X	X	X				X					
Rebels' allegiance to Ibrāhīm al-Imām	X	X	X									
Ibrāhīm captured and imprisoned at Ḥarrān		X	X									
Ibrāhīm names Abū al-ʿAbbās his successor		X	X									
Earthquake (747–749)	X	X	X	X		X				X		X
Abū al-ʿAbbās's proclamation at Kūfa		X	X				X					
Marwān's defeat at the battle of Great Zāb	X	X	X	X		X	X			X		
ʿAbd Allāh b. ʿAlī destroys Marwān's palace at Ḥarrān		X	X	X								
Power passes from the Banū Umayya to the Banū Hāshim		X	X									
ʿAbd Allāh b. ʿAlī takes Damascus		X	X									

TABLE 7.1 Main information related to the "Abbasid Revolution" in the Christian sources (*cont.*)

Information / Sources	Circuit of Theophilus of Edessa							Circuit of Qartamīn				
	Theophanes	Agapius	1234	Michael the Syrian	775	Zuqnīn	Łewond	819	846	Continuatio	Patriarchs of Alexandria	Elias of Nisibis
ʿAbd Allāh b. ʿAlī massacres the Umayyads in Palestine		X	X									
ʿAbd Allāh b. ʿAlī named governor of Syria		X	X									
ʿAbd Allāh b. ʿAlī and Abū Jaʿfar claim the caliphate	X	X	X	X		X						
ʿAbd Allāh b. ʿAlī in Dābiq; Abū Jaʿfar in Mecca	X	X	X	X								
Abū Muslim defeats ʿAbd Allāh at Nisibis	X	X	X	X								
Abū al-ʿAbbās succeeds Marwān II								X	X			
Abū al-ʿAbbās razes the walls of the cities of Syria								X	X			
Abū al-ʿAbbas succeeded by his brother, ʿAbd Allāh								X	X			
War between Persians and Arabs						X		X	X			

Theophilus himself confirms this, as reported by Agapius of Manbij, who used Theophilus as his primary source for the period: "myself, I have not ceased to be an eyewitness to these wars, I have recorded many things and nothing concerning them has escaped my attention."[78] Still other sources, composed following the fall of the first Islamic dynasty, contain convincing evidence.

The Christian corpus may be divided into two main categories: texts that offer unique access to Abbasid history in the making and the construction of an origin myth; and texts that provide noticeably different versions of events than that offered by the vulgate. Confronting these distinct presentations allows us to try to define the rhythms and modalities of successive rewritings in addition to the manipulations to which they were subject.

7.2.1 *In the Workshop of Abbasid History*

Unsurprisingly, Theophilus of Edessa, who wrote at the Abbasid court, and the sources derived from his works present an Abbasid history under construction. Agapius of Manbij and the anonymous Syriac chronicle of 1234 are the best-documented sources on the subject. Theophanes, who undoubtedly relied primarily on Theophilus's continuer, also offers important information.

The general outline provided in the sources from this circuit largely intersects with the narrative given in the Islamic chronographies. The dissensions characteristic of the Umayyad caliphate beginning in the reigns of al-Walīd II and Yazīd III are well-documented. It was in reaction to the assassination of the former that Marwān b. Muḥammad marched on Damascus and usurped caliphal authority.[79] In attempting to solidify his hold on power and reestablish order, the new ruler was faced with battles on numerous fronts from different pockets of resistance. Notably, he was forced to destroy the ramparts of several villages in Syria.[80] Abū Muslim's arrival on the scene is described in the context of these troubles; he is portrayed as calling for revolt and instigating the uprising of the *maurophoroi*[81] – who were loyal Ibrāhīm al-Imām[82] – in

78 Agapius, *Kitāb al-ʿunwān*, 525.

79 Theophanes, *Chronography*, 418–9, trans. 580; Agapius, *Kitāb al-ʿunwān*, 512–4; Michael the Syrian, vol. II, 464, French trans. 505; *1234*, 316–8, Latin trans. 246–8.

80 Theophanes, *Chronography*, 422, trans. 584 (Baalbek, Damascus and Jerusalem); Agapius, *Kitāb al-ʿunwān*, 520 (Homs and Baalbek); Michael the Syrian, vol. II, 464, French trans. 505.

81 Theophanes retains the Greek term to designate the "wearers of black" (Arabic: *musawwada*). The Syriac authors used either the term *msawwedē*, simply transliterating the Arabic word into Syriac, or *ūkāmē*. See further discussion of this point above, Ch. 3.

82 Theophanes, *Chronography*, 424–5, trans. 587; Agapius, *Kitāb al-ʿunwān*, 521–2 (who places Abū Muslim's activities in Kūfā); *1234*, 323–4, Latin trans. 252–3; Elias of Nisibis, 171, Latin trans., vol. I, 81, trans. Delaporte, 105.

Khurāsān. Theophanes gives an especially detailed account of this episode:[83] he states that the sons of Echim (Hāshim) and Alim (ʿAlī) were responsible for this movement, and that they rallied around Chaktaban (Qaḥṭaba b. Shabīb). The Byzantine chronicler also mentions the tribal divisions between the rebels, split between the *Kasinoi* (Qays[84]) and the *Imanites* (Yemenites[85]), and describes the dichotomy between the Northern and Southern Arabs that spanned the entire Umayyad period. Judging the Yemenites to be superior, Abū Muslim incites them to eliminate the Muḍarites.[86] In response to these worrisome threats, Marwān II orders the arrest of Ibrāhīm al-Imām, who dies in prison at Ḥarrān,[87] although only after having named his brother Abū al-ʿAbbās as his successor.[88] Then came the battle at the Zāb where the Marwanid forces were routed, forcing the caliph to flee to Ḥarrān. Accompanied by his entourage and having taken care to bring his riches with him, he fled across Syria to Egypt, where he was ultimately captured and killed.[89] Shortly after his military defeat on the Tigris, Agapius notes: "that day, power (*al-mulk*) was transferred from the Banū Umayya to the Banū Hāshim."[90] In Iraq, Wāsiṭ was taken at the end of a siege led by Abū Jaʿfar, while Abū al-ʿAbbās oversaw the construction of al-Anbār on the Euphrates, where he would take up residence.[91] Revolts broke

83 As Hoyland notes, *Seeing*, 665, note 215.

84 Sometimes also designated as Mudarites or Nizarites.

85 The most preeminent group during the first Islamic dynasty being Kalb.

86 Theophanes, *Chronography*, 424–5, trans. 587. Modern scholars have long defended the idea that the Abbasid Revolution neutralised the rivalries between these two antagonistic tribal groups. The information provided by Theophanes, related to the tribal strategies of the rebels, corroborates the hypotheses of Blankinship ("The Tribal Factor"), who suggests that the Abbasids were deeply hostile to the Mudarites.

87 Agapius, *Kitāb al-ʿunwān*, 523; *1234*, 324–5, Latin trans. 253.

88 Agapius, *Kitāb al-ʿunwān*, 523; *1234*, 324–5, Latin trans. 253. Theophanes indicates that it was only after the death of Marwān II that the *maurophoroi*, who had not helped pursue the caliph in Egypt but had rather remained in Samaria and Jordan, agreed to the following order of succession: Abū al-ʿAbbās, then his brother ʿAbd Allāh (Abū Jaʿfar, the future al-Manṣūr), and then ʿĪsā b. Mūsā. See *Chronography*, 425, trans. 588.

89 Theophanes, *Chronography*, 425, trans. 587; Agapius, *Kitāb al-ʿunwān*, 524 ff.; Michael the Syrian, vol. II, 465, French trans. 505–6; *1234*, 328 ff. See also *The Continuatio of the Samaritan Chronicle*, which mentions the "War of the Blacks" (*ḥarb al-kūshīyīn*; this last word comes from Samaritan Aramaic and means "black," see Levy-Rubin, *The Continuatio*, 57, note 80) before reporting the Umayyads' defeat and Marwān II's murder in Egypt by Abū Muslim himself. Abū Muslim then returned to Iraq "and passed the rule to the Banū l-ʿAbbās, who were of Banū Hāshim." *The Continuatio*, 209, trans. 56–7.

90 Agapius, *Kitāb al-ʿunwān*, 526. The anonymous chronicle of 1234 offers an identical account, *1234*, 330, Latin trans. 257.

91 Agapius, *Kitāb al-ʿunwān*, 527–8; *1234*, 332, Latin trans. 259.

out in Syria in response to the new Abbasid rule,[92] while ʿAbd Allāh b. ʿAlī was named governor of the Shām and Abū Jaʿfar was placed in charge of the Jazīra and Armenia.[93] In 754, Abū Jaʿfar's brother tasked him with leading the *ḥajj*, while ʿAbd Allāh b. ʿAlī was charged with conducting an expedition against the Byzantines.[94] Then came the death of the caliph, sharpening the two claimants' ambitions: ʿAbd Allāh b. ʿAlī and Abū Jaʿfar both proclaimed themselves caliph, one in Syria, the other in Kūfā. On these events, Theophanes notes that ʿAbd Allāh b. ʿAlī was favourable to the Syrians, who supported him, and hostile to the Persians. The inevitable confrontation between the two aspiring caliphs resulted in the latter's defeat near Nisibis at the hands of Abū Muslim's troops, who had been dispatched by Abū Jaʿfar.[95] ʿAbd Allāh b. ʿAlī was able to escape and took refuge in Baṣra with his brother Sulaymān.[96] The new caliph then imprisoned him in a dilapidated house whose foundations had been purposely undermined, causing ʿAbd Allāh's death when the structure collapsed.[97] To solidify his authority, Abū Jaʿfar set out to eliminate any potential rivals, assassinating Abū Muslim[98] and passing over ʿĪsā b. Mūsā for succession in favour of his son, the future al-Mahdī.[99]

The *Mozarabic Chronicle of 754* offers a shorter account, although it notes that Marwān was pursued by Zali (Ṣāliḥ b. ʿAlī), paternal uncle of the caliph

92 Theophanes, *Chronography*, 427, trans. 590; Agapius, *Kitāb al-ʿunwān*, 529 ff.; *1234*, 333 ff., Latin trans. 260 ff.

93 Agapius, *Kitāb al-ʿunwān*, 532 (which omits ʿAbd Allāh b. ʿAlī's governorate); *1234*, 338, Latin trans. 264.

94 Agapius, *Kitāb al-ʿunwān*, 532–3; *1234*, 339, Latin trans. 264–5 (which specifies that ʿAbd Allāh b. ʿAlī went to Dābiq). Theophanes, *Chronography*, 428, trans. 592, also mentions Abū Jaʿfar's presence in Mecca.

95 Theophanes, *Chronography*, 428–9, trans. 592–3; Agapius, *Kitāb al-ʿunwān*, 533 ff.; Michael the Syrian, vol. II, 472–3, French trans. 518; *1234*, 339, Latin trans. 265.

96 Agapius, *Kitāb al-ʿunwān*, 536.

97 Theophanes, *Chronography*, 428–9, trans. 592–3, 607.

98 Theophanes, *Chronography*, 429, trans. 593; Agapius, *Kitāb al-ʿunwān*, 537; Michael the Syrian, vol. II, 473, French trans. 518; *1234*, 340, Latin trans. 265. Theophanes reports that Abū Muslim, exasperated by the Syrians, planned to attack them, but al-Manṣūr dissuaded him from doing so, thus provoking the general's ire. Anxious on account of his rival's growing power, the caliph invited him to his court under false pretenses and used the occasion to assassinate Abū Muslim with his own hands. Al-Manṣūr then paid the general's troops a handsome wage to ensure their loyalty.

99 Theophanes, *Chronography*, 435–6, trans. 602–3. Abū al-ʿAbbās had bequeathed the caliphate to his brother Abū Jaʿfar, and then to ʿĪsā b. Mūsā. On the pretext of wanting to help treat his migraines, al-Manṣūr persuaded ʿĪsā b. Mūsā to inhale a preparation concocted by his personal physician. This poisonous mixture caused ʿĪsā to lose his mental faculties as well as his speech, and the court then agreed with the caliph that he should be removed from the line of succession.

Abdella Alescemi (ʿAbd Allāh al-Hāshimī, i.e. Abū al-ʿAbbās), whom the majority of Muslims had chosen as sovereign; after crossing the Nile, Marwān II was captured and decapitated.[100] These sources, relying to various degrees on Theophilus of Edessa or his continuator, and thus composed in the immediate entourage of the first Abbasid caliphs, offer unique access to an Abbasid history that was still in the process of being written. The vulgate was in production: from this point on, the new rulers were also those in charge of writing history. While Theophilus was able to transmit a number of elements originating from Umayyad-era sources that the later Abbasid chronographers would more or less try to efface, the coup in 132/750 logically altered the situation. After this moment, the composition of chronographies was undertaken for a different purpose. It is not surprising, then, that we find in these sources an account similar to that given in the Islamic narratives. This corpus, however, provides valuable elements allowing us to date when this official history was developed. Here again, the conclusion is the same as for the Umayyad period: history was written in real time.

Without addressing fully the wealth of information in this circuit, other sources fall into the same category, similarly making note of the dynastic change. The brief anonymous Syriac chronicle of *775* also mentions the uprising of the *msawwedē* in addition to Marwān II's flight to Egypt, where he was killed. It also specifies that his successor, Abū al-ʿAbbās, was a Hashimite (*hashmāyā*).[101]

This "Abbasid version" of history was widely diffused, as witnessed by its proliferation in the Chinese sources, most notably the *Old Tang History*, which dedicates a chapter to the Arabs. Since the events it records do not postdate the caliphate of al-Rashīd, it has been suggested that the entire work dates to this period, despite some later retouching.[102] The description of the Revolution clearly presents the Abbasids in a favourable light, and passes in silence over the rivalries that exploded in the wake of Abū al-ʿAbbās's death. From this fact, we may conclude that the passage transmitted was based on a pro-Abbasid source, which may be explained by the geographic proximity of China to Khurāsān. However, other readings of the period exist throughout Christian historiography on the margins of the Abbasid history under construction at the time. The perception of the event in these texts is therefore very different.

100 *754*, § 74, 76, trans. Hoyland, 630.

101 *775*, 349, trans. 275.

102 Hoyland, *Seeing*, 249–53.

7.2.2 *History Continues?*

Several chronicles do not detect a rupture in 132/750, merely noting that Abū al-ʿAbbās succeeded Marwān II. There is no question of a coup d'état, nor of dynastic change, nor even of any element that would distinguish this caliphal transition of power from any other succession. Such is the case in the chronicles of *819* and *846*, as well as in the Greek chronicle of *818*.[103] In his *De administrando imperio*, Constantine Porphyrogenitus mentions no caesura and even omits the reign of Abū al-ʿAbbās entirely: he indicates that Abdelas (ʿAbd Allāh) succeeded Marouam (Marwān) and ruled for twenty-one years.[104]

The two anonymous Syriac chronicles nevertheless provide other important elements: while they say nothing of the transition from the Umayyads to the Abbasids, they record echoes of the conflicts that shook the caliphate following the death of Abū al-ʿAbbās. These texts note that a war broke out among the Persians and the Arabs; the *Chronicle of 819* adds that the rebellion originated in Syria.[105] It should be kept in mind that the events with which we are concerned here are part of a different historiographic layer in these chronographies than the one we have primarily dealt with until now. As frequently stated, these two sources have the invaluable benefit of providing access to information recorded in writing around 730, the end of an initial historiographic phase. After this chronological limit, the author employs a different source, one that privileges ecclesiastical history while integrating various aspects of the political history of the caliphate. It has been demonstrated that this layer ends around the year 785,[106] shortly after which date it was doubtless composed: it is this second phase that we must now examine. The terrain here is less certain, as this layer offers different elements than those in the tributary sources of Theophilus of Edessa, thus limiting the possibilities for comparison.

After specifying that Abū al-ʿAbbās began his caliphate by razing the walls of Syrian cities, the *Chronicles of 819* and *846* mention that on his death, his brother Abū Jaʿfar took power and that a violent war (*qrābā*) erupted between

---

103 *819*, 19, Latin trans. 12; *846*, 236, Latin trans. 179, trans. Brooks, 586; *818*, 97, trans. Hoyland, 436.

104 Constantine Porphyrogenitus, *De administrando imperio*, 96, trans. 97. The period of twenty-one years corresponds to the caliphate of Abū Jaʿfar al-Manṣūr (136–158/754–775). The omission of Abū al-ʿAbbās's caliphate may be explained by a certain confusion in the sources related to the homonymy of the first two Abbasid caliphs, as both brothers were called by the name ʿAbd Allāh. However, Constantine Porphyrogenitus omits several caliphs with brief reigns, both under the Umayyads and the Abbasids, among them those of al-Walīd II, Yazīd III, Ibrāhīm and al-Hādī.

105 *819*, 18, Latin trans. 12–3; *846*, 236, Latin trans. 179, trans. Brooks, 586.

106 Conrad, "Syriac Perspectives," 24.

the Persians (*Fōrsāyē*) and the Arabs (*Ṭayyāyē*).[107] The *Chronicle of Zuqnīn*, written around 775, offers the same account.[108] These texts reference the triangular power struggle between ʿĪsā b. Mūsā, ʿAbd Allāh b. ʿAlī and Abū Jaʿfar that raged following the death of Abū al-ʿAbbās,[109] attesting to the bitter rivalries at the heart of the Abbasid family. Before we return to the fact that the dynastic change was overlooked and the emphasis placed on the events of 136/754, we should pause for a moment to consider the manner in which the main actors in this account were perceived. The use of the terms "Persians" and "Arabs" is worth noting, since, as we have seen previously, they have played a central role in modern historiographic treatments of the Abbasid Revolution. We have already discussed the problems posed by the words *ʿajam* and *ʿarab* in the Arab sources, and now we must extend that question to the Syriac texts as well. This is an important step since, given their date of composition, these Syriac sources offer access to a contemporary understanding of the main actors in these events. However, it seems here as well that, despite the temptation to read these terms in a strictly ethnic sense, the words refer to different realities, and there are at least three reasons that may be advanced to support this claim.

Opposing the *Ṭayyāyē* and the *Fōrsāyē* is first and foremost the result of a reading imposed by the events themselves. The most convincing illustration is found in the *Chronicle of Zuqnīn*, which presents a vision of history indebted to the Book of Isaiah. Seen through this distorting prism, the actors' roles are predetermined. The chronicler reports that

> the year one thousand and sixty [748–749]: the Persian people invaded the land of Syria, subdued the Arabs and ruled over the land in their place. Isaiah too formerly prophesied about these ones, saying: *Ah the Assyrian is the rod of my anger, and the stick of my punishment in their hand, against an idolatrous nation I will send him, and against a wrathful people I will command him* [...] Indeed, the Persians were "the rod of anger and the stick of punishment in their hand," as the prophet said.[110]

The use of this motif is well-attested even much earlier in Syriac literature: the Persians are similarly depicted in an anonymous chronicle of Edessa from the sixth century. However, the *Chronicle of Zuqnīn* is the first to make

107 *819*, 18, Latin trans. 12–3; *846*, 236, Latin trans. 179, trans. Brooks, 586.

108 The *Chronicle of Zuqnīn*, however, mentions the Umayyads' downfall beforehand, also by opposing the Persians and the Arabs. *Zuqnīn*, 192, 215, trans. Harrak, 178, 196.

109 Arjomand, "ʿAbd Allāh Ibn al-Muqaffaʿ," 26–7.

110 *Zuqnīn*, 192, trans. Harrak, 178.

the distinction using these terms in Syriac literature between the first two Islamic dynasties.[111] The assimilation is even more coherent in the Book of Isaiah, when the Assyrian king Tiglath-Pileser III succeeded in conquering the Aramean kingdom of Damascus: "See, Damascus will cease to be a city, and will become a heap of ruins," and "the kingdom from Damascus" will disappear.[112] Thus, it is not a question of ethnicity in this theology of history, but rather a choice in a very narrow presentation of history that *imposes* this identification of the Abbasids with the Assyrians, who themselves would later be associated with the Persians. In the eyes of the Christian chroniclers, this also solved the problem of the victory of the unrighteous: the Assyrian was merely an instrument of God.

Since the designation of the actors stems from an interpretative framework, it is conceivable that it could have varied based on changing interpretations of history. A concrete example of these fluctuations is found in the *Passion of Michael the Sabaite*, a monk at the monastery of Mar Sabas in Palestine. Per Griffith, the Georgian version of this text derives from an Arabic original dating to the ninth century.[113] Michael the Sabaite was allegedly martyred by ʿAbd al-Malik b. Marwān at the conclusion of a theological sparring match from which the monk had emerged victorious. However, the text presents the caliph as arriving "from Babylon" – ostensibly Baghdad – and the later Greek version calls the him "the king of the Persians"![114] The relatively late date of this text may justify this confusion surrounding the identity of the Umayyads. However, it is also possible that the events related in this document were artificially implanted in the Marwanid era simply by mentioning ʿAbd al-Malik's name. Another point deserves some attention here: before turning to Isaiah, the Christian authors made frequent use of the apocalypse of Daniel to explain the upheavals taking place at the time. In this context, the Arabs, and consequently the Umayyads as well, were referred to as "Persians." In Christian eschatological literature, these latter represented one of the four kingdoms that would disappear to give way to God's reign, and the Christian authors often presented Islam as a temporary resurgence of this doomed power.[115] In other words, polemical usage sometimes required this assimilation.

111 Harrak, "Ah! The Assyrian," 52.

112 Isaiah 17:1–3; see also 2 Kings 16:9.

113 See Griffith, "Michael, the Martyr and Monk," especially 121, 132–3.

114 Griffith, "Michael, the Martyr and Monk," 132. The *History of the Patriarchs of Alexandria* also curiously states that Marwān II's supporters were Persian! *History of the Patriarchs*, PO, vol. V, 153.

115 Griffith, "Michael, the Martyr and Monk," in particular 133.

Finally, if we take a step back from these imposed readings, another distinction made by the Syriac authors becomes pertinent in clarifying the debate: the opposition of the "people of the West" with the "people of the East." The labels *Ṭayyāyē* and *Fōrsāyē* seem frequently interchangeable with these terms. The Occident, understood here as Syria, was the chosen land of the former, and the Euphrates marked the clear border between this region and the Persian Empire in antiquity.[116] The secular framework of the Byzantine-Persian wars served as an interpretative model. In the context of the Abbasid Revolution, these geographic dynamics presided over the designation of the principle actors: the rebels originating to the east of this river are necessarily and understandably associated with the Persians, while the Umayyads represent the Arabs on the other side of the Euphrates. Although identities remain difficult to determine during this period, the texts echo the risks exacerbated by this symbolic division of the world. Michael the Syrian reports that when the caliph Marwān II decided to make Ḥarrān his "capital" – thus becoming the first Umayyad ruler to abandon the eastern bank of the river – "the Westerners (*maʿrbāyē*) began to become discontent with him, as he no longer resided with them."[117] This classic opposition was thus in current usage in the Syriac sources *prior to* the Abbasid Revolution. John Bar Penkāyē, who composed his *Rish Mellē* before 693/694, also described the conflict between ʿAlī and Muʿāwiya as well as Ibn al-Zubayr's uprising against the "people of the West" in these terms.[118]

It is thus clear that, despite the problematic terminology, aspects of identity did not determine how these events were presented. Rather, it was a distinctly theological approach to history combined with the specific perspective of the Syriac chroniclers that contributed to these choices. The proposed spatialisation was unambiguous: Syria was interpreted as an Arab space. The Euphrates was a natural symbolic point of organisation central to two worlds whose occupants had identities distinct from one another. The qualification "Persian" indicated above all that one came from the eastern side of river, without signifying any specific identity or ethnicity, even if the two elements were clearly confused in certain instances.

Alongside these terminological considerations, the other essential element in the two anonymous Syriac chronicles of *819* and *846* is, of course, the absence of any mention to the events of 132/750. It is possible to see this lack as a choice made by the individual chronographers who, as noted above,

116 The religious caesura of Syriac Christianity must be considered here as well.

117 Michael the Syrian, 464, French trans. 505.

118 John Bar Penkāyē, book XV, 146, trans. Brock, 61. This same statement is found in the chronicle of *Zuqnīn*, 152, trans. Harrak, 145.

were more concerned with ecclesiastical history than anything else in this section. However, even if this hypothesis is plausible, omitting such events would reveal the minimal importance accorded to them by a Christian author in the second half of the eighth century. Here, comparison with the much more detailed *Chronicle of Zuqnīn* proves fruitful. The author, who was a contemporary of these events, offers a very colourful narrative that nevertheless differs in numerous ways from the Abbasid vulgate under construction at the time. The Abbasids' victory is thus described at length, although the passage itself is somewhat confusing, perhaps because the chronographer was relying on several sources.[119]

A number of different accounts were thus in circulation, and an official version was soon to impose itself at the end of this historiographic competition. These divergent presentations provide valuable access to different ways of giving voice to the past. They also reveal the various manipulations effectuated by the Abbasid historiographers, who strove to present 132/750 as a definitive break. To echo Furet's quote from the beginning of this chapter: following the logic of the new dynasty, the Revolution did not mark a transition, but an origin. From this point on, the foundational moment would be highlighted and adorned with a suitable discourse that would quickly transform it into a myth of origin. A second factor rendered this need more pressing still: this project would also be aimed at covering up the rivalries that troubled the caliphate in the wake of Abū al-ʿAbbās's death. The narrative construction of the Abbasid Revolution essentially was intended to mask the true revolution, which had not been so much Abbasid as "Mansurid." To this end, the chronographers performed a slight chronologic shift: the difficulties of 136/754 were projected onto the past, to the year 132/750. This attempt to assimilate the two episodes meant that any faults would be attributed to the Umayyads, which then made it possible to affirm a legitimacy that was both Abbasid and Islamic at the same time. This effort was part of the active process of legitimating the new dynasty that was particularly palpable under the caliphates of al-Manṣūr and his son, al-Mahdī.[120]

Alongside questions of identity, the other major problematic of modern historiography looms, one related to the complex nature of the event, something between a revolution and an evolution. Two very different perceptions

119 Here we are following Hoyland's demonstration that the fourth part of the chronicle of *Zuqnīn* was composed by a single author relying on a number of sources, rather than Conrad's hypothesis that different authors produced this section of the chronicle. See Hoyland, *Seeing*, 409–14.

120 As mentioned above, Ch. 2.

are opposed here. In constructing its legitimacy, the Abbasid dynasty imposed its own reading of the episode, thus spreading an authorised presentation that would have a lasting influence on both medieval and modern historians. As emphasised abundantly above, this effort was concentrated primarily on the institution of a historical framework that would portray the Abbasid Revolution as a glaring exception among the various other rebellions that occurred during the first centuries of Islam. This strict delineation would later be taken up in modern scholarship: from the conflict between ʿAlī and Muʿāwiya to the civil war between al-Rashīd's sons that would later tear the caliphate asunder – including the battle of Marj Rāhiṭ or the murder of al-Walīd II – four *fitna*s frame a Revolution. The fact that the events of 132/750 received fundamentally different treatment in the sources offers further proof that it was, in fact, a narrative construction. The distinction between a violence that creates order and one that creates disorder was noted above; the Abbasid historiographers worked to inscribe the movement that brought their dynasty to power in the first of these two categories. However, at least from a Syrian perspective, the perception is necessarily different. The period presents itself as a *continuum*, an era of revolts that shook the Umayyad caliphate from the death of Hishām on. Leaving the construction of an Abbasid creation myth to one side, Marwān II's defeat was but another episode in the continuous progression of troubles that had ravaged the empire for a number of years. This period of rebellions extends beyond 132/750, at the very least until al-Manṣūr's victory over the pretentions of ʿAbd Allāh b. ʿAlī.

This periodisation and spatialisation of Islamic history must thus be called into question. Why not evoke a third *fitna* between the years 126/743 and 136/754 – or even until 145/762[121] – rather than a third *fitna* followed by the Abbasid Revolution?[122] The oldest texts on the subject demonstrate at once that the dynastic caesura was not perceived as such in all places at the same time while the "revolutionary" rhetoric was still under construction; the nascent Abbasid century would soon refine this rhetoric. We must now shift our attention to the strategies employed to this effect, focusing on a fundamental example related to Ibrāhīm al-Imām's transfer of authority.

121 Date of Muḥammad al-Nafs al-Zakiyya's rebellion. See Elad, "The Rebellion" and El-Hibri, *Reinterpreting*, 2.

122 On this point, see Cameron and Conrad, "Introduction," 8–9 and Hawting, *The First Dynasty*, 104. For an analysis of the third *fitna*, see Judd, *The Third Fitna*.

7.2.3 *Ibrāhīm al-Imām*

In the movement to overthrow the Marwanids, the Shām was undoubtedly the insurgents' main objective. However, before becoming a theater of military operations, the province was an ambivalent space for the Abbasids, at once an adopted residence and dangerous territory by virtue of its proximity to the seat of Umayyad power. This ambiguity defined Ibrāhīm al-Imām's bitter experience following his arrest on the orders of Marwān II. His detention was indicative of the troubles that characterised this period for the Abbasid family. The capture and assassination of the movement's leader posed a crucial problem in terms of the designation of his successor, one who would guarantee the continuation of the movement and possess a sure legitimacy in order to reap the rewards of the moment when it arrived.

Ibrāhīm al-Imām's arrest at al-Ḥumayma[123] and death in Marwān II's prisons at Ḥarrān offer concrete examples of the historiographic manipulations undertaken by Abbasid historiographers aiming to legitimate the authority of their patrons. Blankinship has treated this question in detail, demonstrating that the chronographers attempted to situate these two events as late as possible in order to reduce to the maximum extent the *interregnum* between Ibrāhīm and the future Abbasid caliph Abū al-ʿAbbās, who had ostensibly been designated as his successor. Thus, traditions were put into circulation dating his arrest to Muḥarram 132/August-September 749, despite it being clear that the incident had earlier been dated to 130/747–748.[124] The initial interval between the Imam's detention and the proclamation of Abū al-ʿAbbās as caliph allowed for doubt to spread as to the veracity of latter's designation as successor by Ibrāhīm. By shortening the delay, this uncertainty was quashed and the continuity of the Abbasid imamate was confirmed: this affirmation was critical for the new Abbasid regime, whose legitimacy was still far from assured.[125]

To overcome the difficulty posed by the transfer of authority made by an imam who, having been arrested and imprisoned, would theoretically have been unable to communicate with his family members, historians came up with a number of imaginative solutions. An early version linking these events to the pilgrimage of 129/747[126] is presented in the *Kitāb al-ʿuyūn*. In this

123 On the possible confusion between Ibrāhīm and Abū al-ʿAbbās during the arrest, see above, Ch. 4.

124 Blankinship, "The Tribal Factor," 601–3. Sharon suggests that Ibrāhīm was never actually imprisoned, *Revolt*, 230.

125 Blankinship, "The Tribal Factor," 602.

126 Certain sources explicitly state that Ibrāhīm's machinations came to light during the *ḥajj* and were judged suspect enough to be reported to the caliph, who then ordered his arrest. However, these texts date the pilgrimage to the year 131/749, likely as a result of

account, it was Qaḥṭaba b. Shabīb al-Ṭāʾī[127] who, incognito, was able to infiltrate the prison where Ibrāhīm was being held in order to relay instructions regarding his succession.[128] The choice of messenger to transmit this important information was very judicious, despite his authority being in principle inferior to that of the Abbasids themselves, designated in other traditions as the direct recipients of this transfer of power. Qaḥṭaba was dead by 132/749: the only witness and guarantor of this designation had conveniently taken his secret to the grave, making it henceforth unverifiable. Others claimed that various members of the family or of Ibrāhīm's entourage accompanied him to Ḥarrān[129] alongside those who had come to seize him, and that he himself had transferred his authority to his brother. Ibrāhīm entreated his family and friends to leave al-Ḥumayma immediately and take refuge in Kūfā, where they should obey Abū al-ʿAbbās from that moment on as leader of the clan.[130] According to other reports, Ibrāhīm wrote his will in his cell, conveying identical instructions to those described in the previous narrative. Aware that he would be unable to save himself from Marwān II's wrath, he entrusted his will to his *mawlā*, Sābiq al-Khwārizmī, and tasked him with delivering it to Abū al-ʿAbbās upon his death. On hearing news of his master's decease, Sābiq did as instructed and completed his mission by travelling to al-Ḥumayma. Abū al-ʿAbbās announced the death of his brother, but kept the will's existence secret, and then left for Kūfā.[131]

These concrete examples of authorial interventions in historical narrative were, all told, relatively effective. The transfer of power was reduced from several years to several months by shifting the timeline of Ibrāhīm's capture and death from 130/747–748 to 132/749. Additionally, these efforts reworked the transfer of authority in various phases, giving it an air of indisputable legitimacy. However, in all of these cases it is important to note that the testament

manipulations intended to bring the dates of Ibrāhīm al-Imām's death and Abū al-ʿAbbās's proclamation as close together as possible. See Blankinship, "The Tribal Factor," 601. The *ḥajj* brought many different groups together, offering an auspicious occasion to foment revolution and form bonds among those who opposed power. This question has not garnered a great deal of attention among medievalists but has been recently studied in the context of the colonial era, in Chiffoleau's "Le pèlerinage à La Mecque à l'époque coloniale." For a thoughtful discussion of the bibliography on the *ḥajj*, see Mayeur-Jaouen, "Lieux sacrés, lieux de culte, sanctuaires en islam," 159 ff.

127 On this preeminent figure of the *daʿwa*, see Sharon, "Qaḥṭaba b. Šabīb."

128 *Kitāb al-ʿuyūn*, 190–1.

129 This seems highly unlikely, as Blankinship has noted ("The Tribal Factor," 602), particularly in light of information provided by al-Dīnawārī, *Akhbār*, 357–8.

130 *Akhbār al-dawla*, 401–2; al-Ṭabarī, vol. III, 26–7, trans. vol. XXVII, 149–50.

131 Al-Masʿūdī, *Murūj*, vol. VI, 89–90, trans. Pellat vol. IV, 937–8.

and its communication both took place in Syria, once again playing the role of an arena for the preservation of the Abbasid potential to ascend to the caliphate, represented above all by the family's years of residence at al-Ḥumayma.

Indeed, the Shām would soon become a region of rebellion where the new authority would find itself in danger. The magnitude of the crisis that shook the caliphate after Abū al-ʿAbbās's death attests to this upheaval. Syria's space on the new political chessboard is also discernible behind ʿAbd Allāh b. ʿAlī's ambitions. These elements invite us to push further ahead in our search for this "Syrian Abbasid" and the various Abbasid projects underway in 136/754.

7.3 ʿAbd Allāh b. ʿAlī and the Allure of a Syrian Abbasid Caliphate?

ʿAbd Allāh b. ʿAlī was not an unproblematic figure for medieval historians, who had to work around the multiple facets of his personality. The great architect of the victory over the Umayyads and then governor of Syria, ʿAbd Allāh b. ʿAlī would later come into direct confrontation with the future al-Manṣūr when attempting to assert his own rights to the caliphate following the death of Abū al-ʿAbbās. From the Mansurid perspective that would eventually prevail, the hero slowly transformed into a rebel, putting the still-fragile political stability of the young Abbasid caliphate in danger.[132] Such was the dilemma facing the authorities charged with giving voice to the past in the classical period.

7.3.1 *Strategies of Isolation*

At the heart of the conflict between Abū Jaʿfar and two of his uncles after his brother's death lay the hopes nurtured by these three protagonists, each believing he possessed valid rights to the throne. Thus, the arguments presented by ʿAbd Allāh b. ʿAlī and his supporters merit our attention here.

7.3.1.1 ʿAbd Allāh b. ʿAlī's Pretentions

On 13 Dhū al-Ḥijja 136 (9 June 754), the first post-Umayyad caliph, Abū al-ʿAbbās, succumbed to smallpox (*jadarā*) at al-Anbār.[133] By naming a second caliph from the same family as his successor, the Revolution became a firmly

132 On this episode, see Lassner, *The Shaping*, 19–38; Kennedy, *The Early Abbasid*, 57–61; Tuqan, "Abdallāh Ibn ʿAlī;" Sharon, *Revolt*, 234–42; Bonner, *Aristocratic Violence*, 53–5; Cobb, *White Banners*, 23–6.

133 Al-Ṭabarī, vol. III, 88, trans. vol. XXVII, 212. The sources vary between the dates 12 and 13 Dhū al-Ḥijja, but it is the latter date that fell on a Sunday in 136. Besides al-Ṭabarī, who offers both versions, see, for example, al-Masʿūdī, *Murūj*, vol. VI, 88, trans. Pellat vol. IV, 937 and *Tanbīh*, 339, trans. 436.

Abbasid one. However, the identity of this successor was contested. Although the Abbasid historiographic vulgate states that Abū al-ʿAbbās recognised Abū Jaʿfar as his heir prior to his death,[134] other claimants did not agree. Thus, a triangular power struggle broke out between Abū Jaʿfar, the deceased's brother, and two of his uncles, ʿAbd Allāh b. ʿAlī and ʿĪsā b. ʿAlī (see fig. 4).[135] Without any military assistance, the latter's ambitions fizzled out, leaving the conflict to come to a head between Abū Jaʿfar and ʿAbd Allāh.

At the moment of Abū al-ʿAbbās's death, his brother was in Mecca performing the *ḥajj*, while ʿAbd Allāh was preparing to undertake a campaign against the Byzantines with his troops in northern Syria. Their geographic distance from each other only postponed the inevitable confrontation while also leaving the field open for someone quicker and more vigilant to seize the opportunity. In the race against the clock that ensued, each tried to cover his bases. Abū Jaʿfar's nephew, ʿĪsā b. Mūsā[136] – who had left Kūfā for al-Anbār – received the *bayʿa* in his uncle's name and stood guard over the prize; informed of the situation, his uncle set off for al-Anbār, calling Abū Muslim to his side.[137] Upon his arrival in the city, ʿĪsā b. Mūsā handed power over to him and Abū Jaʿfar received the oath.[138] At this point, ʿAbd Allāh b. ʿAlī was in Dulūk, just north of Aleppo. Some time before this, he had visited al-Anbār and the caliph himself had charged him with leading a *ṣāʾifa*, putting him in command of an army made up of *ahl Khurāsān* as well as *ahl al-Shām wa-al-Jazīra wa-al-Mawṣil*.[139] As he was preparing to launch the operation, a message arrived announcing the caliph's death. ʿAbd Allāh immediately gathered his men and shared the news, enjoining them to support his own pretentions.[140] He justified his claim by citing the will of Abū al-ʿAbbās: the caliph had affirmed that he who defeated Marwān II

134 In accordance with these arrangements, ʿĪsā b. Mūsā should then have succeeded his uncle Abū Jaʿfar. See al-Ṭabarī, vol. III, 87, trans. vol. XXVII, 212.

135 Al-Dīnawārī, *Akhbār*, 378.

136 This passage is problematic. It is possible that there is some confusion here, or else a deliberate manipulation by which ʿĪsā b. Mūsā's name was substituted for that of ʿIsa b. ʿAlī. Indeed, it was this latter who gave Abū al-ʿAbbās's eulogy and led his funeral procession. It would seem, then, that ʿĪsā b. ʿAlī was the true master of al-Anbār. This point is discussed further below.

137 Abū Jaʿfar had formed a rudimentary plan to eliminate Abū Muslim just before completing the pilgrimage; see al-Ṭabarī, vol. III, 85–6, trans. vol. XXVII, 209–10.

138 Al-Ṭabarī, vol. III, 88, 92, trans. vol. XXVIII, 2, 8.

139 Al-Ṭabarī, vol. III, 91, trans. vol. XXVIII, 5. On Dulūk, see Yāqūt, *Muʿjam*, vol. II, 461.

140 Al-Ṭabarī, vol. III, 92, trans. vol. XXVIII, 8; *Kitāb al-ʿuyūn*, vol. I, 216–7; al-Dīnawārī, *Akhbār*, 378; al-Yaʿqūbī, *Taʾrīkh*, vol. II, 364–5; al-Azdī, *Taʾrīkh*, 159, 163.

would be his successor (*walī ʿahdī*).[141] Several of his generals – among them certain influential figures in the movement that had brought the Abbasids to power – confirmed this statement, which led his troops to decide en masse to give him the *bayʿa*. ʿAbd Allāh then travelled to Ḥarrān, which he seized despite the resistance of Abū Jaʿfar's representative in town, Muqātil al-ʿAkkī. Abū Muslim was then sent to confront ʿAbd Allāh b. ʿAlī.[142]

The argument invoked by ʿAbd Allāh to legitimise his aspirations was based on a promise made by Abū al-ʿAbbās, while Abū Jaʿfar based his ambitions on his designation as successor, which supposedly took place during his brother's reign.[143] Ibn Abī al-Ḥadīd reports a discussion in which Abū al-ʿAbbās mentioned the promise he had made offering succession to he who vanquished Marwān II. The caliph also specified that his uncle, ʿAbd Allāh b. ʿAlī, was the one who accomplished this task. However, in confidence, Abū al-ʿAbbās appeared to want to go back on this oath in favour of his brother, Abū Jaʿfar, who seemed to him the best candidate to inherit the throne. His interlocutor, Saʿīd b. ʿUmar b. Jaʿda b. Ḥubayra al-Makhzūmī, then describes to Abū al-ʿAbbās an anecdote taking place during the siege of Constantinople alongside Maslama b. ʿAbd al-Malik. This latter received a letter informing him of the death of the caliph Sulaymān and the nomination of ʿUmar b. ʿAbd al-ʿAzīz as the new ruler. Maslama began to weep, and explained that he was not mourning the death of his brother, but rather that he was upset "because the power had been transferred from the hands of [his] father's children to the children of [his] paternal uncle." Abū al-ʿAbbās interrupted Saʿīd's narration, stating that he understood what needed to be done.[144] Here, the Umayyads serve as a source of useful precedent, while this anecdote credited ʿAbd Allāh b. ʿAlī's affirmations that he had fallen victim to the caliph's machinations in the interests of another claimant.

Alongside Abū al-ʿAbbās's possible commitment to letting his successor be chosen through bloodshed, other elements also argue in favour of ʿAbd Allāh b. ʿAlī. Abbasid legitimacy, still under construction, was centred primarily on the transfer of power from the Prophet to al-ʿAbbās instead of Abū Ṭālib. As an agnatic parent, Muḥammad's paternal uncle is presented as worthier of receiving the imamate.[145] Such an argument could easily be used to serve ʿAbd Allāh's purposes, as he was one of Abū al-ʿAbbās's paternal uncles,

141 Al-Ṭabarī, vol. III, 92–3, trans. vol. XXVIII, 8–9; al-Yaʿqūbī, *Taʾrīkh*, vol. II, 365; al-Balādhurī, *Ansāb*, vol. III, 179.

142 Al-Ṭabarī, vol. III, 93, trans. vol. XXVIII, 9–10.

143 On these questions, see Kennedy, "Succession Disputes."

144 Ibn Abī al-Ḥadīd, *Sharḥ*, vol. VII, 137–8; Sharon, *Revolt*, 237.

145 This perspective of the Abbasids' supporters is notably presented by al-Masʿūdī, *Murūj*, vol. VI, 54 ff., trans. Pellat vol. IV, 923 ff.

especially considering that this latter's succession also wasn't as clearly defined – or accepted – as the sources would have us believe. Sharon has hypothesised a secret arrangement, established during Ibrāhīm al-Imām's lifetime, envisaging a line of succession starting with Abū al-ʿAbbās, followed by ʿAbd Allāh b. ʿAlī and finally ʿĪsā b. Mūsā.[146] ʿAbd Allāh's rebellion thus arose from not respecting this accord and Abū al-ʿAbbās's decision to modify Ibrāhīm al-Imām's wishes to the benefit of his brother.[147] ʿAbd Allāh's uprising was in a sense a result of the conflicting wishes of the first two leaders of the movement. Lassner has criticised this analysis, rejecting the idea of a secret agreement between the movement's protagonists and preferring to think that, from a military and political perspective, "ʿAbd Allāh b. ʿAlī was the most logical choice as a successor to Abū al-ʿAbbās."[148] This remark is also pertinent if we consider that ʿAbd Allāh almost certainly shared military power in the empire with Abū Muslim.

In addition, ʿAbd Allāh b. ʿAlī was not alone; he could count on the support of his brothers, who held key positions: ʿĪsā b. ʿAlī was notably close to Abū al-ʿAbbās, while Ṣāliḥ governed Egypt and Sulaymān was the governor of Baṣra. This fact has led Arjomand to suggest the existence of an "uncles' faction."[149] This party could rely on important connections and pens sharpened in their service. Al-Balādhurī reports that Ibn al-Muqaffaʿ entered the employ of the Banū ʿAlī b. ʿAbd Allāh when the Abbasid *dawla* came into existence. He wrote their letters and was especially close to ʿĪsā b. ʿAlī.[150] Arjomand suggests that Ibn al-Muqaffaʿ's downfall was a consequence of the *amān* that he composed for ʿAbd Allāh b. ʿAlī.[151] His famous *Risāla fī al-ṣaḥāba* was written in this context, not at al-Manṣūr's behest as generally believed, but as a "revolutionary program" for the "uncles' faction," specifically during the months of deep uncertainty that followed the death of Abū al-ʿAbbās:[152] the "caliph's advisor"[153] would have been the "rebel's advisor."

In any case, ʿĪsā b. ʿAlī appears to have been in control of the situation at al-Anbār in the immediate aftermath of the caliph's death. He led the prayer

146 Sharon, *Revolt*, 234 ff.
147 Sharon, *Revolt*, 236.
148 Lassner, *The Shaping*, 31–3. See also Cobb, *White Banners*, 24.
149 Arjomand, "ʿAbd Allāh ibn al-Muqaffaʿ," 24 ff.
150 Al-Balādhurī, *Ansāb*, vol. III, 218; Arjomand, "ʿAbd Allāh ibn al-Muqaffaʿ," 24–5.
151 Arjomand, "ʿAbd Allāh ibn al-Muqaffaʿ," 25.
152 Arjomand, "ʿAbd Allāh ibn al-Muqaffaʿ," 25–6. On Ibn al-Muqaffaʿ, see Gabrieli, "L'Opera;" Sourdel, "La biographie;" Pellat's introductory remarks, *Ibn al-Muqaffaʿ*, 1–15; and Cooperson, "Ibn al-Muqaffaʿ."
153 To borrow Pellat's famous expression (*le conseilleur du calife*), *Ibn al-Muqaffaʿ*.

over Abū al-ʿAbbās's mortal remains and interred his body in the palace at al-Anbār.[154] It was also ostensibly he, rather than ʿĪsā b. Mūsā, who took charge of the government and the treasury.[155] ʿĪsā b. ʿAlī was then sworn in by the crowd and stripped Abū Jaʿfar of his rights of succession. Abū Muslim's arrival, however, changed the stakes, as the population turned away from ʿĪsā b. ʿAlī.[156] Perhaps wanting to back a candidate who appeared more docile than Abū Jaʿfar, Abū Muslim tried in vain to persuade ʿĪsā b. Mūsā to take the oath.[157]

This hypothetical support, perhaps thought to be beneficial to ʿAbd Allāh b. ʿAlī, could not have succeeded in these circumstances: the personal ambitions of his brother ʿĪsā prevented a unified front among the uncles. Al-Yaʿqūbī also expressly signals that upon the caliph's death, ʿĪsā b. ʿAlī and the *abnāʾ* at his sides were loathe (*kariha*) to write to ʿAbd Allāh, instead contenting themselves with warning Ṣāliḥ in Egypt.[158] Nevertheless, informed of the situation, ʿAbd Allāh declared himself caliph and wrote immediately to his brother ʿĪsā to notify him that he had received the *bayʿa* from his generals and the *ahl al-Shām* as Abū al-ʿAbbās's successor.[159] ʿAbd Allāh then travelled to Ḥarrān, more as Marwān II's symbolic heir than Abū al-ʿAbbās's actual heir, where he named his brother ʿAbd al-Ṣamad as governor of the Jazīra and successor to the throne.[160] One of his advisors warned ʿAbd Allāh against the *fitna* that would ensue if he was unable to come to an agreement with the people of al-Anbār.[161] These fraternal rivalries allowed Abū Jaʿfar to take up his initiative anew by instigating conflict between the two figures who most directly threatened his own ambitions. He thus pitted Abū Muslim against ʿAbd Allāh b. ʿAlī. The battle, bitterly fought at Nisibis over the course of long weeks, resulted in the latter's defeat; he then sought refuge with his brother Sulaymān in Baṣra. After this conflict, Abū Jaʿfar rid himself of Abū Muslim, whom he perceived as too dangerous a rival.

If we believe al-Balādhurī's account, ʿAbd Allāh's fate was far from sealed at this point, as he could still depend on a sizable amount of military support.

---

154 Al-Ṭabarī, vol. III, 88, trans. vol. XXVII, 212; al-Balādhurī, *Ansāb*, vol. III, 178; al-Azdī, *Taʾrīkh*, 160.

155 Arjomand, "ʿAbd Allāh ibn al-Muqaffaʿ," 27, offers several examples of the confusion between these two figures. Al-Ṭabarī mentions ʿĪsā b. Mūsā, vol. III, 92, trans. vol. XXVIII, 8.

156 Al-Dīnawārī, *Akhbār*, 378.

157 Al-Ṭabarī, vol. III, 100, trans. vol. XXVIII, 21. Al-Manṣūr knew how to exploit the ties between ʿĪsā b. Mūsā and Abū Muslim to convince this latter to come to his court in order to assassinate him. See al-Ṭabarī, vol. III, 105, 116, trans. vol. XXVIII, 27, 40.

158 Al-Yaʿqūbī, vol. II, 364.

159 Al-Yaʿqūbī, vol. II, 365.

160 Al-Balādhurī, *Ansāb*, vol. III, 106.

161 Al-Balādhurī, *Ansāb*, vol. III, 105; Arjomand, "ʿAbd Allāh ibn al-Muqaffaʿ," 28.

It also seems that his followers flocked to swear oaths of allegiance to him, although Sulaymān was able to dissuade them from doing so. This latter preferred to compromise with Abū Jaʿfar and ordered that his brother ʿĪsā lead the negotiations.[162] Ibn al-Muqaffaʿ wrote the *amān* guaranteeing ʿAbd Allāh b. ʿAlī's security during this period. However, the text left open the possibility that the new ruler could be revoked if the conditions of the pact were violated.[163] Arjomand suggests that the uncles, who still had serious claims to argue, thus profited from their position to obtain an accord that had profoundly negative consequences for al-Manṣūr.[164] Al-Yaʿqūbī states that ʿAbd Allāh b. ʿAlī appeared before the caliph on 17 Dhū al-Ḥijja 137/3 June 755 to ratify this treaty.[165] Such an early date could signify that, nearly one year to the day after Abū al-ʿAbbās's death, al-Manṣūr had prevailed. The "uncles' faction" fell victim to its own divisions. Fraternal rivalries prevented Abū Jaʿfar's uncles from fully taking advantage of a seemingly favourable situation.

As a final illustration of the shifting power relations between the different claimants to the throne, ʿAbd Allāh b. ʿAlī was arrested on the very same day that he met with the caliph to endorse the *amān*, or, according to several other sources, several months after this document was signed.[166] The *amān* guaranteed his safety, but not his freedom. He spent the rest of his days in prison, where he died in 147/764–765.[167] However, this lengthy incarceration did not appease al-Manṣūr's anger. When he decided to embark on the *ḥajj* in 147, the caliph met with ʿĪsā b. Mūsā to instruct him to use the opportunity of his absence to assassinate ʿAbd Allāh. Sensing a trap at a moment when al-Manṣūr was plotting to name his son al-Mahdī as his heir over ʿĪsā b. Mūsā,

162 Al-Balādhurī, *Ansāb*, vol. III, 111.

163 Al-Azdī is the only source to have preserved the text of this *amān*, *Taʾrīkh*, 167–70. Marsham and Robinson's recent study dedicated to this exceptional document ("The Safe-Conduct") concluded that the text was authentic and would have been composed in 137/754–755 or at the beginning of the year 138/755. On the conditions in which this safe-conduct was composed, see Jahshiyārī, 103–7. This passage is translated and discussed by Sourdel, "La biographie" and Marsham and Robinson, "The Safe-Conduct."

164 Arjomand, "ʿAbd Allāh ibn al-Muqaffaʿ," 29.

165 Al-Yaʿqūbī, *Taʾrīkh*, vol. II, 368; al-Ṭabarī also dates this episode to 17 Dhū al-Ḥijja, but in 139 (12 May 757), vol. III, 126, trans. vol. XXVIII, 56.

166 While the date of this *amān* divided medieval authors, that of ʿAbd Allāh's arrest also varies between 138/755–756 and 140/757–758. Al-Ṭabarī and al-Azdī agreed that ʿAbd Allāh was captured at the time of his encounter with Abū Jaʿfar (although they do differ with regard to the date of this meeting), when the former presented himself to receive the *amān*. Al-Azdī, *Taʾrīkh*, 170 (trans. Marsham and Robinson, "The Safe-Conduct," 257); al-Ṭabarī, vol. III, 126–7, trans. vol. XXVIII, 56–7.

167 Here again, other dates are proposed as well. For example, see al-Masʿūdī, who places ʿAbd Allāh's death in 149/766–767, *Murūj*, vol. VI, 214, trans. Pellat vol. IV, 985.

this latter hid the prisoner away. The caliph continued to scheme by declaring to his paternal uncles that he was ready to pardon their brother and release him. The caliph then met with ʿĪsā b. Mūsā and commanded that he bring ʿAbd Allāh to him. ʿĪsā expressed his surprise, reminding the ruler that he had previously ordered him to silence the rebel. Abū Jaʿfar vehemently denied this accusation and ordered that ʿĪsā be executed on the grounds that he was guilty of having his uncle killed. Before the execution came to pass, however, ʿĪsā b. Mūsā revealed his plot and had ʿAbd Allāh brought before the caliph to corroborate his story.[168] Al-Manṣūr's ploy to rid himself of both his despised uncle and the meddlesome nephew who had interfered with his plans for succession at once thus failed. The goals of the founder of Baghdad, never short of resources, would nevertheless come to fruition in the months following this confrontation.

Al-Ṭabarī reports that the caliph imprisoned ʿAbd Allāh in a house whose foundations had been purposely undermined,[169] leading to his captive's demise under the convenient guise of a tragic accident.[170] Lassner has rightly noted that the goal of this covert operation was to conceal the assassin's hand.[171] However, the story may be more complex than meets the eye, especially considering that a similar plot was employed by Marwān II to do away with Ibrāhīm al-Imām: the caliph orchestrated the collapse of a room's walls atop the spiritual leader of the *daʿwa*.[172] These machinations seem to indicate either that the two rulers tried to conceal their crimes, or that historians – for reasons unclear – wanted to create an indelible link between Ibrāhīm and ʿAbd Allāh, both victims of a selfsame crime. Al-Masʿūdī's narrative, however, points a finger at a single guilty party: Abū al-Azhar al-Muhallab b. Abī ʿĪsā. Abū al-Azhar, finding ʿAbd Allāh in the company of one of his slaves, strangled (*khanaqa*) the lovers and posed their corpses in an embrace. He then had the house demolished, its ruins becoming a sort of temporary tomb, until witnesses came to identify the bodies.[173] ʿAbd Allāh's remains were then

168 Al-Ṭabarī, vol. III, 329–30, trans. vol. XXIX, 15–17; al-Masʿūdī, *Murūj*, vol. VI, 214–6, trans. Pellat vol. IV, 985.

169 The foundations were filled with salt and then injected with water to cause the collapse of the load-bearing walls.

170 Al-Ṭabarī, vol. III, 330, trans. vol. XXIX, 17; *Kitāb al-ʿuyūn*, 258–9.

171 Lassner, "Did the Caliph," 87–8.

172 Al-Ṭabarī, vol. III, 43, trans. vol. XXVII, 167.

173 Al-Masʿūdī, *Murūj*, vol. VI, 215–7, trans. Pellat vol. IV, 985–6.

transferred to the cemetery of Bāb al-Shām, inaugurated for the occasion,[174] where he would rest, Syrian even in death.

ʿAbd Allāh b. ʿAlī's demise gave al-Manṣūr free rein to complete his plans. His cursed uncle's assassination set in motion the events which were to follow: that same year, the caliph named his son al-Mahdī as his successor over his nephew ʿĪsā b. Mūsā.[175] In a sense, the Mansurid Revolution came to an end when ʿAbd Allāh breathed his last. The chronographers then entered the picture, ready to address this somber episode in the history of the young Abbasid caliphate. Erasure of the figure who had triumphed over the Marwanid armies and then hunted down and exterminated the remaining members of the defeated family was impossible: a protagonist of the foundational movement that brought the Abbasids to power could not be obliviated completely.[176] Since silence could not be the weapon of choice here, historians would employ other tactics in the face of this troubling but necessary memory. ʿAbd Allāh b. ʿAlī thus fell victim to strategies of isolation aimed at portraying him as a rebel.

7.3.1.2 The Creation of a Syrian Rebel

The most significant episodes that occurred during ʿAbd Allāh's revolt against al-Manṣūr took place in Iraq: the battle with Abū Muslim's troops, his imprisonment in the caliph's jails and the rival uncle's murder. However, his was fundamentally a Syrian rebellion, the uprising of a Syrian. The Shām exported its propensity for disorder, taken for granted in the post-revolutionary period. To present ʿAbd Allāh as a renegade trying to thwart Abū al-ʿAbbās's intended line of succession and not as the legitimate heir to the throne, traditions were fabricated presaging his treachery so as to better dismiss his claims.[177] The legitimacy of his uprising itself was under attack.

We shall begin with an anecdote recounted by al-Masʿūdī bringing us back to the moment of Ibrāhīm al-Imām's death, when his last will and testament was supposed to have been conveyed to Abū al-ʿAbbās at al-Ḥumayma. Abū al-ʿAbbās decided at this point to announce his brother's death, but conceal the existence of the will bequeathing his authority to him. He then set off for Kūfā, accompanied by Abū Jaʿfar as well as ʿAbd Allāh b. ʿAlī. When stopping at

174 Al-Ṭabarī, vol. III, 300, trans. vol. XXIX, 17. Al-Masʿūdī mentions the "Abū Suwayd cemetery," noting that it was located near the Bāb al-Shām, *Murūj*, vol. VI, 217, trans. Pellat vol. IV, 986.

175 Al-Ṭabarī, vol. III, 331, trans. vol. XXIX, 17.

176 In many ways, these were the same conditions that presided over the possible rewritings of Abū Muslim, the quintessential heroic figure of the movement that overthrew the Umayyads, in the wake of his assassination at the hands of al-Manṣūr.

177 As Arjomand notes, "ʿAbd Allāh ibn al-Muqaffaʿ," 26.

a well along the route, they meet a Bedouin woman (*ʿarābiyya*) who exclaims: "By God, I have never seen men with faces such as yours! Here is a caliph, a second caliph and a rebel (*khārijī*). – Servant of God, Abū Jaʿfar al-Manṣūr asked her, what do you mean? – In truth, she replied, this man will rule, and she pointed to al-Saffāḥ; you shall succeed him, and this is the man who will revolt against you, indicating ʿAbd Allāh b. ʿAlī."[178] And if the testimony of a simple Bedouin was insufficient, higher authorities were invoked as well, including the Prophet himself.[179] First, the Alid Abū Hāshim b. Muḥammad b. al-Ḥanafiyya – the very same person who had transmitted his authority to the Abbasids in his testament – found the strength on his deathbed to prophesise the downfall of the Umayyads and the reigns of Abū al-ʿAbbās and his elder brother Abū Jaʿfar.[180] This latter would then have a vision of his own when residing in al-Ḥumayma: he saw himself in Mecca, accompanied by Abū al-ʿAbbās and ʿAbd Allāh b. ʿAlī. The Prophet was present in the Kaʿba, and a herald (*munādī*) cried out: "where is ʿAbd Allāh?" Abū al-ʿAbbās presented himself first and was given a black flag, symbol of the Abbasid Revolution. The herald called out once more; ʿAbd Allāh and Abū Jaʿfar replied, and the latter was led into the sanctuary, where Muḥammad entrusted him with his community (*umma*), placed a turban on his head and named him "father of the caliphs."[181] The message is free from ambiguity, as this dream is intended to exclude both ʿAbd Allāh b. ʿAlī and ʿĪsā b. Mūsā at once from succession, because al-Manṣūr was destined to be the progenitor of his own successors.[182]

To complete this picture, al-Manṣūr is presented as a legitimate sovereign, while ʿAbd Allāh b. ʿAlī is relegated to the category of tyrant. In a conversation, the caliph asked:

> Do you know a tyrant (*jabbār*) whose name begins with the letter *ʿayn*, who killed three other despots whose names also begin with *ʿayn*? Yes, Commander of the Faithful, […] ʿAbd al-Malik b. Marwān, who murdered ʿAmr b. Saʿīd b. al-ʿĀṣ, then ʿAbd Allāh b. al-Zubayr, and finally ʿAbd al-Raḥmān b. Muḥammad b. al-Ashʿath. The caliph replied: do you know a caliph (*khalīfa*) whose name begins with the letter *ʿayn*, who killed three other tyrants whose names also begin with the same letter? You, yourself, O Commander of the Faithful, […] as you killed ʿAbd al-Raḥmān

178 Al-Masʿūdī, *Murūj*, vol. VI, 90–1, trans. Pellat vol. IV, 938.
179 Lassner, "Did the Caliph," 78.
180 Al-Yaʿqūbī, *Taʾrīkh*, vol. II, 297.
181 *Kitāb al-ʿuyūn*, 216; al-Azdī, *Taʾrīkh*, 162.
182 As Lassner notes, "Did the Caliph," 79, note 19.

> b. Muslim and ʿAbd al-Jabbār b. ʿAbd al-Raḥmān; in addition, your uncle ʿAbd Allāh b. ʿAlī died beneath the ruins of his house (*bayt*). His house collapsed on top of him, replied the caliph, therefore I am not at fault. No, you are not [...]. Al-Manṣūr smiled.[183]

Al-Manṣūr is thus in a sense "responsible but not guilty" of killing his uncle. By presenting himself as the only caliph, he rose above both the Umayyads, reduced to the rank of despots, and ʿAbd Allāh b. ʿAlī, who got what he deserved.

One of the arguments presented to further portray a rebel was based on ʿAbd Allāh's Syrian dimension. This spatial connection associated him with the Umayyads and facilitated the claim that he was a natural troublemaker thanks to the Abbasids' general perception of the province as a cradle of revolutionary activity.[184] However, this Syrianisation also ensured the preservation of ʿAbd Allāh b. ʿAlī's memory in the works of an author like Ibn ʿAsākir. In his biographical notice, the Damascene scholar highlights ʿAbd Allāh's ties to the region. The initial antagonism that characterises the beginning of the notice written for the man who provoked the fall of the caliphs of Damascus slowly dissipates: ʿAbd Allāh is above all a Syrian whom the *ahl al-Shām* readily gave the *bayʿa* after Abū al-ʿAbbās's death. In his account, Ibn ʿAsākir includes an anecdote in which ʿAbd Allāh pays a visit to Hishām's court. One of Hishām's sons is playing with a bow and arrows, which fall in such a way that Maslama b. Hishām predicts that his father's guest will destroy the dynasty. Thus, the die is cast: ʿAbd Allāh is fundamentally Syrian – as attested by his visit to the court during Hishām's reign – and his role in the Marwanids' downfall is inevitable, as prophesied by the arrows of fate.[185] While the Umayyads passed quietly from adversity to alterity beneath the pens of the Abbasid chronographers, the figure of ʿAbd Allāh took an opposite course in the works of the Syrian authors. His burial in the cemetery of Bāb al-Shām in Baghdad reinforced the Syrian roots of one who had aspired to an Abbasid caliphate while maintaining his ties to the province and its inhabitants.

Thus, it was above all the Syrian sources that tried to restore some semblance of order to these conflicting traditions. Ibn ʿAsākir is the most vocal

---

183 Al-Masʿūdī, *Murūj*, vol. VI, 217–8, trans. Pellat vol. IV, 986. A slightly different version of this tradition is proposed by al-Ṭabarī, vol. III, 331, trans. vol. XXIX, 17: al-Manṣūr asks if he is to blame for the collapse of ʿAbd Allāh's residence, to which his interlocutor responds in the negative.

184 On this subject, see Ibn al-Muqaffaʿ's biting remarks on the Syrians' propensity for chaos, *Risāla*, 46–7. For a classification of the uprisings in Syria during the Abbasid period, see Cobb, *White Banners*.

185 TMD, 31, 54–69; Judd, "Medieval Explanations."

concerning ʿAbd Allāh reception of the *bayʿa*,[186] while Abū Zurʿa al-Dimashqī sows doubt on al-Manṣūr's legitimacy: where he uses the term *istakhlafa* to designate the accessions of Abū al-ʿAbbās and al-Mahdī, he settles for *aqāma* when discussing Abū Jaʿfar's rise to power.[187] The emphasis placed on ʿAbd Allāh's Syrian dimension is ultimately indicative of his own political project, to which we shall now turn our attention.

7.3.1.3 The Meaning of the Revolt

We do not know where ʿAbd Allāh b. ʿAlī intended to install the seat of his power if his rebellion had succeeded. However, it is likely that his reign would have been destined to take root west of the Euphrates, judging by his support base. As noted above, perhaps more so than anyone else, ʿAbd Allāh (alongside Abū Muslim) embodied the figure of the general. He was first and foremost the leader of an army. While it is impossible to accurately determine the size of his forces, the sources agree that they comprised the *ahl Khurāsān* as well as the *ahl al-Shām wa-al-Jazīra*. ʿAbd Allāh had limited confidence in the former, as he feared that they would abandon him at the first opportunity to join the ranks of Abū Muslim's armies: in them, he saw a potential "fifth column,"[188] and the facts supported this suspicion.[189] Logically, then, ʿAbd Allāh's preference fell upon the latter. In reality, the interests of the two camps converged, considering that the Syrians hoped that the caliphate would remain in their lands. This idea, notably defended by Crone, has been questioned by Iḥsān ʿAbbās and more recently by Cobb. Where the former saw a "Syrian attempt" to regain the upper hand, the two latter hypothesised a strictly military revolt.[190] Thus, it was only the soldiers who supported ʿAbd Allāh's claims to the throne and not the majority of the province's population.[191] In this sense, ʿAbd Allāh undeniably appears as a successor of Marwān II: a "war caliph" should succeed another so that the army – here, the *ahl al-Shām* and perhaps even the *ahl al-Jazīra* – maintains its dominant position. This episode is particularly indicative of the

186 TMD, 31, 54–69.

187 Abū Zurʿa, *Taʾrīkh*, vol. I, 196–7.

188 Cobb, *White Banners*, 26. ʿAbd Allāh's defiance toward the *ahl Khurāsān* is also mentioned by the Christian authors, following the accounts of Theophanes (*Chronography*, 428, trans. 592) or Agapius (*Kitāb al-ʿunwān*, 534).

189 During the confrontation in Nisibis, Abū Muslim called the *ahl Khurāsān* to join his ranks, and many did. In response to this sedition, ʿAbd Allāh had those who remained among his troops executed. For example, see al-Ṭabarī, vol. III, 94, trans. vol. XXVIII, 12, who reports the massacre of 17,000 soldiers, and Lassner, *The Shaping*, 258, note 30.

190 Crone, *Slaves*, 71; ʿAbbās, *Taʾrīkh Bilād al-Shām fī al-ʿaṣr al-ʿAbbāsī*, 23; Cobb, *White Banners*, 24.

191 Cobb, *White Banners*, 24.

continuity of the methods adopted by the last Umayyad caliph in Syria and he who aspired to be the first Abbasid caliph in the province. Confronted by the same figures as his predecessor, whose downfall he had caused, ʿAbd Allāh and his entourage worked to rebuild the networks of power in Syria and Upper Mesopotamia. The local *ashrāf* chose to unite themselves behind him, as he "offered a future, whereas al-Manṣūr offered only uncertainty."[192]

These policies were limited by ʿAbd Allāh's mediocre credit among the Syrian-Mesopotamian army that made up the bulk of his support base. An officer summarised it for him in these terms: "your reputation with the Syrian army is not good, so nothing will be of use to you except someone like me who has a good reputation and supporting hands, or else a dissenting leader who hopes to attain honor in it [revolt]."[193] The Christian chronicler Agapuis of Manbij gives the same analysis, suggesting that ʿAbd Allāh "undertook to lead all the Arabs of the *Jazīra* and the *Shāmāt* after they had despaired and lost the will the to live."[194] Abū Muslim's ruse, before engaging ʿAbd Allāh in combat, was to affirm that he had not come to defy him, but only to take over as governor of the *Shām*, a position bequeathed to him by Abū Jaʿfar; this ploy no doubt contributed to the Syrians' anxiety. Some soldiers defected to protect their families in the face of this new danger, whereas others must have seen this as an additional reason to fight alongside ʿAbd Allāh.[195]

Even more than the appeal of a potential Syrian caliphate, ʿAbd Allāh offered an Abbasid caliphate relying primarily on the support of the Syrian army. While certain other caliphs had sometimes flirted with the Syrian space, such as Hārūn al-Rashīd (to whom we shall return in the next chapter), the only other Abbasid ruler who could boast similar ambitions was undoubtedly al-Mutawakkil, who briefly tried to make Damascus his new capital in 244/858.[196] After this initiative, the caliph suffered a similarly tragic fate as ʿAbd Allāh b. ʿAlī. This goal of a Syrian Abbasid caliphate, or more precisely an Abbasid caliphate for the Syrians, would eventually fall into oblivion. The Christian sources bear witness to this fact, not only because oblivion was possible, but because the homonymy of the two main protagonists – who both responded to the name ʿAbd Allāh – lent itself marvelously to the occasion.

192 Cobb, *White Banners*, 26. This opinion is shared by Shaban, *Islamic History*, vol. II, 6.

193 Al-Balādhurī, *Ansāb*, vol. III, 105: *"innu bulāʾuka ʿindu ahl al-Shām ghayr jamīl fa-lan yanfaʿaka illā mithlī mimman ʿindahu balāʾ ḥasan wa-ayādī mutaẓāhira aw rajul ṣāḥib fitna yaltamis an yudrik fīha sharafan,"* cited by Cobb, *White Banners*, 25.

194 Agapius, *Kitāb al-ʿunwān*, 536 (translation modified).

195 On Abū Muslim's strategy, see al-Ṭabarī, vol. III, 95–6, trans. vol. XXVIII, 13–4; al-Balādhurī, *Ansāb*, vol. III, 107–8.

196 On this point, see Cobb, "Al-Mutawakkil's Damascus."

Beyond systematic strategies of silence, it is possible to see a sort of accidental oblivion here as well, resulting from a failure to clearly identify the various figures of the period.

The presentation of the uprising in the *History of the Patriarchs of Alexandria* is illustrative of this situation, although the account is relatively confusing and much different than that encountered in the majority of the sources. A young Bedouin from the steppe named ʿAbd Allāh, presented as a son of Abū Muslim, receives a vision in a dream, a treble call for him to fight Marwān II, with victory guaranteed.[197] His father has the same vision, and embroiders the appeal on his tent. Impressed by this miracle, the Muslims flock en masse to assist the two men; armed with palm branches fitted with spearheads, they set off to confront the caliph. Marwān marks the beginning of combat by speaking of David and Goliath: "Am I a dog, that you come to me with sticks?"[198] The result of the confrontation is henceforth sealed; like the hero of the Philistines, the caliph is destined to fall, as his adversary is fighting in the name of God and for the salvation of his people. Marwān then takes flight, while his enemies clothe themselves in black and set off in pursuit.[199] ʿAbd Allāh arrives in Damascus, where he initiates massacres and captures the caliph's daughter.[200] This scene is followed by a lengthy description of Marwān's tribulations in Egypt, to which the author of this section was an eyewitness, followed by the inevitable execution of the sovereign.[201] ʿAbd Allāh then ruled the empire and issued his first edicts.[202] After comes the era of ʿAbd Allāh Abū Jaʿfar, "who belonged to the family of the first princes;" Abū Muslim is presented as his uncle.[203] ʿAbd Allāh is a son of the *ahl Ḥarrān*,[204] and he takes a wife from this city before installing himself in Damascus following his accession to the caliphate![205]

These confusions undoubtedly stem from the homonymy of the various protagonists: ʿAbd Allāh is a name shared by Abū al-ʿAbbās, Abū Jaʿfar and ʿAbd Allāh b. ʿAlī. In addition, it is a characteristic element of the titulary of the first Abbasid caliphs, continuing an Umayyad practice.[206] While Abū Muslim's supposed familial ties are more difficult to define, it is nevertheless possible to

197 This treble call echoes the identical one received by the Prophet.
198 1 Samuel 17:43.
199 *History of the Patriarchs*, PO, vol. V 150–3.
200 *History of the Patriarchs*, PO, vol. V, 158.
201 *History of the Patriarchs*, PO, vol. V, 170–86.
202 *History of the Patriarchs*, PO, vol. V, 189.
203 *History of the Patriarchs*, PO, vol. V, 206.
204 *History of the Patriarchs*, PO, vol. V, 207.
205 *History of the Patriarchs*, PO, vol. V, 364.
206 Sharon, CIAP, vol. II, 215.

determine ʿAbd Allāh's identity from the implications given in each individual event of this narrative. ʿAbd Allāh b. ʿAlī is clearly the central figure, both in vanquishing Marwān II and in perpetrating massacres in Damascus. He is also without a doubt the personage associated with the *ahl Ḥarrān* and Damascus.

In the Islamic sources, similar uncertainties surrounding the identity of the actors in this uprising served the purposes of the Abbasid historiographers as they undertook to rewrite the dynasty's origins. The most successful example of the strategies of isolation developed at this time is perhaps what we think we know about the titulature of the early Abbasids: modern historiography nearly unanimously associates the *laqab* al-Saffāḥ with the first Abbasid ruler, despite the evidence indicating that this epithet should rather be applied to ʿAbd Allāh b. ʿAlī.

7.3.2 *Confiscation for and by Messianism*

Analysis of this question allows us to shed light more broadly on the strategies developed by the new dynasty aimed at asserting their authority in the face of several different concurrent competing claims. The messianic dimension of the first caliphs was emphasised in order to give absolute legitimacy to the family. The example of ʿAbd Allāh b. ʿAlī presents a concentrated case study of the tactics adopted to these ends by the chronographers.

7.3.2.1 From Bloodthirsty to Generous?

The title "al-Saffāḥ" associated with Abū al-ʿAbbās only appears in the texts at a relatively late date. The first incontestable mention is found in al-Balādhurī,[207] whereas an author as important as al-Ṭabarī never uses the *laqab* in conjunction with this caliph.[208] The only time this term is employed for Abū al-ʿAbbās is in the context of the very first discourse he issued on the occasion of his accession. After announcing an increase in pay for his troops, he defines himself as follows: "*anā al-saffāḥ al-mubīḥ wa-al-thāʾir al-mubīr*."[209] "Saffāḥ" indicates someone who pours or spreads, be it blood or wealth.[210] The passage is thus ambiguous in that the increase in wages suggests an interpretation privileging the caliph's generosity, while describing himself as an "avenger [who spreads] desolation" invites the idea of bloodthirstiness.[211] In addition,

207 Al-Balādhurī, *Futūḥ*, 209.

208 Bates, "Khurāsānī Revolutionaries," 281.

209 Al-Ṭabarī, vol. III, 30, trans. vol. XXVII, 154.

210 Kazimirski, *Dictionnaire*, I, 1097.

211 Bates suggests that the first option is the better one, "Khurāsānī Revolutionaries," 281, note 4, whereas Williams, translator of the relevant volume of al-Ṭabarī, refrains from choosing between the two (vol. XXVII, 154, note 379), while noting that during his lifetime,

al-Masʿūdī reports that Abū al-ʿAbbās initially used the *laqab* al-Mahdī,[212] and this assertion is corroborated by the only two known inscriptions extant today from the first caliph of the new dynasty, in which he is presented with the titulary *al-mahdī ʿabd Allāh ʿAbd Allāh amīr al-muʾminīn* ("the *mahdī*, servant of God, ʿAbd Allāh Commander of the Faithful").[213] The second epigraph, dated to 136/754, ordering the restoration of mosques, was discovered at Ṣanaʿāʾ, while the first offers the advantage of being located in Syria. The inscription, uncovered at Baysān, is dated to Dhū al-Qaʿda 135/9 May–7 June 753 and describes works ordered in the city by the caliph and confided to the care of ʿAbd Allāh b. ʿAlī!

The various elements to which we have access reveal the doubts surrounding Abū al-ʿAbbās's titulature and invite us to reject the *laqab* al-Saffāḥ as being solely his prerogative. Moreover, earlier allusions offer ample topic for discussion, and other sources identify ʿAbd Allāh b. ʿAlī as the original bearer of this title. A poet at the Umayyad court in the entourage of ʿAbd Allāh b. ʿAlī, al-Ḥafṣ b. Nuʿmān al-Umawī, identifies the latter as such in one of his verses;[214] the *Akhbār Majmūʿa*, which relates that the head of Marwān II was sent first to al-Saffāḥ and *then* to Abū al-ʿAbbās, falls in the same category.[215] The title is elsewhere deformed by al-Balādhurī, who calls him *al-Shammākh*, or the vainglorious.

The problem becomes clearer when we read Ibn Saʿd's biography of ʿAlī b. ʿAbd Allāh. In the list of the numerous children presented by the biographer, two ʿAbd Allāhs appear, the elder (*al-akbar*) and the younger (*al-aṣghar*). On the subject of the latter, Ibn Saʿd notes: "*wa-ʿAbd Allāh al-aṣghar al-Saffāḥ alladhī kharaja bi-al-Shām*."[216] This identical turn of phrase is also found in the *Anonymous History of the Abbasids*![217] One of the oldest texts (Ibn Saʿd, d. 230/845) and the most openly apologetic work dedicated to the Abbasids (the *Anonymous History*) both proclaim that the epithet al-Saffāḥ was the title of ʿAbd Allāh b. ʿAlī.

---

the caliph seemed to have been designated exclusively by his *kunya*, Abū al-ʿAbbās. The sense of "generosity" is also mentioned by Elad, "The Caliph."

212 Al-Masʿūdī, *Tanbīh*, 338, trans. 434–5. Al-Masʿūdī nevertheless uses the *laqab* al-Saffāḥ for the caliph.

213 On these inscriptions, see Elad, "The Caliph," v–vi [English summary but article in Hebrew] and Sharon, *CIAP*, vol. II, 214 ff.

214 Ibn Manẓūr, *Mukhtaṣar*, vol. VII, 212–3.

215 *Akhbār Majmūʿa*, 46, trans. 73. See also al-Maqdisī, *Kitāb al-badʾ*, vol. VI, 74, the evidence provided by Lewis, "The Regnal Titles," Duri, "Al-Fikra al-mahdiyya" and Crone and Hinds, *God's Caliph*, 81, note 142.

216 Ibn Saʿd, *al-Ṭabaqāt*, vol. V, 312–3.

217 *Akhbār al-dawla*, 148.

Most of the evidence corroborates the hypotheses of those who refuse to consider al-Saffāḥ the *laqab* of the first Abbasid caliph, but they also lend credence to the idea that the epithet migrated from ʿAbd Allāh b. ʿAlī to Abū al-ʿAbbās.[218] This transfer was the result of a historiographic manipulation undertaken at a moment difficult to ascertain.[219] The change in ownership of the *laqab* was accompanied by a semantic shift that served the interests of the Abbasid caliphate. Recuperating the *laqab* allowed not only for the erasure of the burdensome traces of the rebel uncle, but in shifting from bloodthirsty to generous, also promoted Abū al-ʿAbbās's image at a time when the violence characteristic of the Abbasid empire was in the process of being concealed.[220]

In addition, the epithet was given a messianic connotation that had previously been absent:[221] thus, it perfectly suited the caliph's original surname, *al-Mahdī*. Abū al-ʿAbbās was al-Saffāḥ's figure of memory, while ʿAbd Allāh undoubtedly represented that of history.[222] The creation of an eschatological meaning for a *laqab* that *had* to be associated with the dynasty's founder[223] was inscribed within the broader context of the Abbasids' confiscation of messianism to silence any competing claims to power at the time.

7.3.2.2 Revolution and Messianism

The previous chapters have emphasised the predominance of eschatological expectations during the second century of the *hijra* and their importance in understanding and interpreting events. An episode as significant as a coup d'état resulting in a dynastic change was no exception to this rule.[224] Commentators embellished it with strong messianic connotations that spread like a trail of breadcrumbs through nearly all of the sources covering this period. As had occurred leading up to the year 100 of the *hijra*, various natural disasters gave credence to these apocalyptic interpretations, echoed in the Christian sources

218 See Lewis, "The Regnal Titles;" Crone and Hinds, *God's Caliph*, 81, note 142; Elad, "The Caliph;" Arjomand, "ʿAbd Allāh ibn al-Muqaffaʿ," 28.

219 For example, it should be noted that al-Masʿūdī, who used the *laqab* al-Saffāḥ for Abū al-ʿAbbās, presents this latter in no uncertain terms as being both generous (*samḥan bi-al-amwāl*) and bloodthirsty (*bi-safk dimāʾ*)! See *Tanbīh*, 339, trans. 436.

220 See above, Ch. 4.

221 Bates, "Khurāsānī Revolutionaries," 311, note 4.

222 I borrow this distinction from Assmann comparing Moses and Akhenaten, *Moses the Egyptian*, 2.

223 See Sharon, *Revolt*, 232–4.

224 For an overview of the messianic context under the early Abbasids, see Duri, "Al-Fikra al-mahdiyya."

in particular. The terrible earthquakes that shook Syria between 747 and 749,[225] in addition to the troubles rampant in the province after the death of Hishām, were seen as harbingers of an imminent *eschaton*.[226] Coastal regions suffered these temblors twice; at least one was accompanied by a tsunami.[227] Other seemingly supernatural elements corroborate this analysis: sightings of comets and other celestial phenomena,[228] epidemics, famines, plagues of insects and various other calamities.[229] The succession of catastrophes was such that, in Michael the Syrian's account, Marwān II sent missives throughout the empire demanding that the people show penitence in order to escape these divine punishments.[230]

The messianic context is illustrated by a bourgeoning apocalyptic literature during this period: for example, the apocalypse of Baḥīrā[231] or the one written in Coptic that served as the basis for the apocalypses of Shenute, Daniel and Samuel of Qalamūn,[232] all of which date to the era of the Abbasid Revolution. The ancient core of the visions of Rabbi Shimon bar Yoḥaī was composed under the early Abbasids, presumably during the reign of al-Manṣūr.[233] The text of *secrets*, including both older and more detailed elements, clearly describes the

225 Identifying one or more earthquakes in the period leading up to the Abbasid Revolution is a subject of continuous debate among specialists. Those who support the hypothesis of a single earthquake (accompanied by the inevitable shockwaves) date the event to 18 January 749, on the basis of archaeological evidence uncovered at Baysān. A coin dated to 131/748–749 was discovered in this village under the debris created by this temblor (see Tsafrir and Foerster, "The Dating"). However, some recent studies question the idea of a single high-magnitude earthquake and propose instead that several smaller earthquakes with different epicentres occurred, located primarily in Palestine and Northern Syria. See Karcz, "Implications," in particular 778–787. See also Sbeitani, Darawcheh and Mouty, "The Historical Earthquakes," 362–4, who present various different dates and accounts of these earthquakes.

226 Theophanes, *Chronography*, 422, 426, 430, trans. 585, 589, 594; Agapius, *Kitāb al-ʿunwān*, 521; Michael the Syrian, 464, 466–7, French trans. 507, 509–11; *1234*, I, 326, Latin trans. 254–5; *Zuqnīn*, 191–2, trans. Harrak 177–8; Nikephoros, *Short History*, 69; *The Continuatio*, 209, trans. 56; Elias of Nisibis, 171–2, Latin trans. 82, trans. Delaporte 105.

227 Michael the Syrian, 466, French trans. 509.

228 Theophanes, *Chronography*, 431, trans. 597; Agapius, *Kitāb al-ʿunwān*, 513, 515, 520; Michael the Syrian, 465, French trans. 507–8; *Zuqnīn*, 195, trans. Harrak 180; Nikephoros, *Short History*, 71.

229 For example, see Michael the Syrian, 465–6, French trans. 507–8; *1234*, I, 319, 326–8, Latin trans. 248–9, 254–6; *Zuqnīn*, 200 ff., trans. Harrak 184 ff.

230 Michael the Syrian, vol. II, 466, French trans. 508.

231 Hoyland, *Seeing*, 276, 273.

232 On the debates surrounding these apocalypses, see above, Ch. 3. The connections between these texts have been discussed in Van Lent, "The Nineteen."

233 See above, Ch. 3.

fall of the Umayyads in an apocalyptic light: the collapse of Bāb Jayrūn, one of the gates of the mosque of Damascus, presaged the dynasty's ruin.[234] Marwān II's defeat had been prophesised[235] by Isaiah, according to the author of the text, who suggests that the last Marwanid ruler is intended in the following verse: "the Lord has broken the staff of the wicked."[236] The messianic elements associated with the early Abbasids are also confirmed in Jewish apocalypses: a Geniza fragment mentions al-Manṣūr as the sovereign of the Ishmaelites in the end days,[237] and a passage from the *Pirqē* (chapters) of the Rabbi Eliezer specifies that the messiah will arrive after the reign of two brothers.[238] Several interpretations of this passage have been proposed, identifying the two brothers as al-Amīn and al-Maʾmūn, ʿAbd al-Malik and ʿAbd al-ʿAzīz, or even Muʿāwiya and Ziyād b. Abīhī. Lewis, however, rightly preferred Abū al-ʿAbbās and Abū Jaʿfar for these roles, given the prevalence of evidence bearing witness to the importance of messianism under the early Abbasids.[239]

In Muslim apocalypses, similar expectations were connected with the Abbasids. It is also probable that the first caliphs were the subjects of eschatological conjectures even during their lifetimes. We have already mentioned the case of Abū al-ʿAbbās being presented as *al-Mahdī* in two inscriptions. If we continue our inquiry, the epithet al-Manṣūr was also linked to strong messianic connotations, taking on the usage well-attested in Southern Arabic in the pre-Islamic period.[240] Al-Balādhurī reports that the caliph in a dream received a flag from the Prophet to fight the Antichrist.[241] Perhaps due to this dimension, the most extreme partisans of the movement that brought the Abbasids

234 Lewis, "An Apocalyptic Vision," 326. See also the text of *the prayer of rabbi Simon b. Yōḥay*, 313. This announcement of Bāb Jayrūn's collapse may be read as an allusion to the destruction caused by the earthquakes that struck Damascus. Al-Suyūṭī (d. 911/1505) also reports that the roof of the mosque was damaged in 131/748–749, *Kashf al-ṣalṣala*.

235 Opposing traditions were also in circulation, as attested by Michael the Syrian, who echoes the forgery of an *Apocalypse of Enoch*, written by a bishop named Cyriacus, who added elements announcing Marwān II's caliphate and affirming that his son would succeed him. This text would have pleased Marwān II, who commissioned Cyriacus to write a commentary on it. The bishop tried to profit from his new position of power by requesting the then-vacant seat of Ṭūr ʿAbdīn. Michael the Syrian, II, 465, French trans. 507.

236 Isaiah 14:5. Lewis, "An Apocalyptic Vision," 326; see also the text of the *prayer of the rabbi Simon b. Yōḥay*, 313.

237 Marmorstein, "Les signes du Messie."

238 On this text, see Hoyland, *Seeing*, 313–6.

239 Lewis, "An Apocalyptic Vision," 331.

240 Lewis, "The Regnal Titles," 16–7; Omar, "A Note on the *laqab*s," 142–4; Madelung, "Apocalyptic Prophecies," 157–8; Cook, *Studies*, index; Bates, "Khurāsānī Revolutionaries," 284.

241 Al-Balādhurī, *Ansāb*, vol. III, 198; Cook, *Studies*, 144–5.

to power, the Rāwandiyya,[242] considered al-Manṣūr their God (*rabb*), provider of their subsistence. While the caliph was undoubtedly inclined to such excessive displays, he was finally forced to take action against the Rāwandiyya in 141/758–759.[243] Despite these elements, the caliph did not immediately adopt this *laqab*, which was only chosen in late 145/762–763, following the caliph's victory over the rebellious Alids Muḥammad b. ʿAbd Allāh (al-Nafs al-Zakiyya) – who called himself *al-Mahdī* – and his brother Ibrāhīm.[244]

However, these expectations would culminate around al-Manṣūr's son, al-Mahdī: nearly a decade after the death of Abū al-ʿAbbās, the title would be used once more as the *laqab* of the future third caliph of the dynasty.[245] The essential question rests in the chronology of this *laqab*'s adoption, as it is clear that the decision was made prior to his accession to the throne. On the basis of numismatic evidence, some dirhams struck at Rayy in 145/762–763 bearing the phrase *mimmā amara bihi al-Mahdī Muḥammad b. Amīr al-Muʾminīn*, Bacharach suggested that this title was adopted at al-Manṣūr's insistence as a reaction to Alid pretentions.[246] The two *laqab*s thus appeared concomitantly. It has been demonstrated to the contrary, however, that this was not the case, and that the title al-Mahdī was in use from 143/760–761 onwards, based on a coin struck at Bukhārā.[247] This discovery is significant, as it implies that the *laqab* al-Mahdī was used *before* that of his father and prior to his being named heir-apparent to the throne![248] Bates has proposed that this is a mark of

242 See Kohlberg, "Al-Rāwandiyya" and Laoust, *Les schismes*, especially 62.

243 Al-Ṭabarī, vol. III, 129, trans. vol. XXVIII, 63.

244 As al-Masʿūdī reports, *Tanbīh*, 341, trans. 439. This assertion was confirmed by other elements, in particular the caliph's titulary in his correspondences, such as they have been preserved in al-Ṭabarī, vol. III, 208–9, trans. vol. XXVIII, 166–7 (an exchange of letters between the caliph and Muḥammad b. ʿAbd Allāh at the beginning of this latter's uprising; the *laqab* 'al-Manṣūr' does not appear among these titles) and vol. III, 338–41, trans. vol. XXIX, 24–8 (a letter addressed by the caliph to ʿĪsā b. Mūsā aimed at convincing him to renounce his rights of succession in favour of al-Mahdī; in this missive dated 147/764–765, the caliph used the *laqab* 'al-Manṣūr.') See Bates, "Khurāsānī Revolutionaries," 283–5. Among the other pieces of evidence to be added to the dossier, it should be noted that, during the foundation of Baghdad, slightly earlier in the same year of 145/762, the city was designated Madīnat Abū Jaʿfar rather than Madīnat al-Manṣūr. See al-Yaʿqūbī, vol. II, 373; al-Ṭabarī, vol. III, 906, trans. vol. XXXI, 176; Northedge, "Archaeology and New Urban Settlement," 245–6. On the rebellion of al-Nafs al-Zakiyya, see Elad, "The Rebellion."

245 On al-Mahdī's caliphate, see Moscati's foundational studies, "Studi" and "Nuovi studi," and also Kennedy, *The Early Abbasid*, 96 ff.

246 Bacharach, "*Laqab* for a Future Caliph."

247 Bates, "Khurāsānī Revolutionaries," 292 ff.

248 According to al-Ṭabarī, this nomination took place in 147/764–765, vol. III, 331, trans. vol. XXIX, 17. See Kennedy, *The Early Abbasid*, 91–3.

"revolutionary enthusiasm" and an expression of spontaneous belief that led supporters of the movement to consider the young prince bearing the name of the Prophet (Muḥammad b. ʿAbd Allāh) as destined to be the long-awaited *mahdī*.[249] If ideas such as this were in circulation in Khurāsān, the province governed by the future caliph starting in 141/758–759,[250] Bates suggests that they were echoed by troops native to the province who had emigrated to Iraq.[251] This hypothesis is especially meaningful in the Syrian space, if we are to believe the Byzantine chronicler Theophanes, who notes that in 759–760 the *ahl Khurāsān* (*Maurophoroi*) rose up in Dābiq – a traditional gathering-place for troops setting off on campaigns against the Byzantines since the reign of Sulaymān b. ʿAbd al-Malik – while affirming that the son of al-Manṣūr was a God and their "nurturer" (*tropheus*).[252] With respect to the Shām, it should also be mentioned that the name al-Mahdī is found in an inscription at Ascalon dated to 155/771–772 ordering the construction of a mosque and a minaret.[253] While Sharon defends the argument that al-Manṣūr himself used this title at the time,[254] the chronology of the use of his son's *laqab*, attested by Bates's numismatic evidence, further supports the hypothesis of works ordained by the future caliph.

It is clear that the situation under al-Manṣūr's reign served the interests of a caliph[255] who hoped to upend the established order of succession by removing ʿĪsā b. Mūsā as heir in favour of his own offspring. The designation of Abū Jaʿfar's son as the awaited *mahdī* offered a weighty argument in this regard. This belief is also corroborated by an inscription with apocalyptic connotations at Ehnesh dated to the end of the second/eighth century that expressly mentions al-Mahdī.[256] It is also preserved by later authors, including Ibn Ḥajar al-ʿAsqalānī (d. 852/1449) who reports that, when al-Mahdī received the *bayʿa*, the poet Mutīʿ b. Iyās stated that he was the *mahdī*, that he bore the birthmark (*shāma*) and that he was destined to fill the world with justice.[257]

249 Bates, "Khurāsānī Revolutionaries," 295–8.
250 Al-Ṭabarī, vol. III, 134, 138, trans. vol. XXVIII, 69, 75–6.
251 Bates, "Khurāsānī Revolutionaries," 298.
252 Theophanes, *Chronography*, 431, trans. 597. However, it should be noted that this may amount to a confusion with the beliefs of the Rāwandiyya who took al-Manṣūr to be their God (*rabb*), as mentioned above. The Rāwandiyya were also closely associated with al-Mahdī. See Kohlberg, "Al-Rāwandiyya."
253 *RCEA*, vol. I, n. 42; Sharon, *CIAP*, vol. I, 144–6.
254 Sharon, *CIAP*, vol. II, 217.
255 Cahen, "Points de vue," 156.
256 Palmer, "The Messiah and the Mahdi;" Hoyland, *Seeing*, 415–6.
257 Ibn Ḥajar al-ʿAsqalānī, *Lisān*, vol. VI, 61, cited by Cook, *Studies*, 145, note 35.

Al-Hādī and al-Rashīd also had *laqab*s with strong messianic connotations. Al-Ṭabarī notes that this latter was assigned the epithet in 166/782–783,[258] and this qualifier can be found on coins dating to 170/786–787.[259] Due to the difficult conditions surrounding Hārūn's accession, given that al-Hādī died under mysterious circumstances after attempting to thwart the order of succession in favour of his son Jaʿfar,[260] it seems that the new caliph temporarily used the *laqab* al-Marḍī in an appeal for harmony and reconciliation. After restoring unity, the surname was replaced with that of al-Rashīd, which had been in use prior to the accession of Hārūn.[261]

To complete their strategies of distinction, the Abbasids circulated various traditions in which they were presented as destined to supplant the Umayyads.[262] Divination rounded out these soteriological functions to legitimate the new caliphs in advance. Premonitions announced their triumph, like that reported by al-Masʿūdī, in which al-Manṣūr's mother, Sallāma, saw a lion birthed from her loins in a dream vision during her pregnancy: "then, lions emerged from all sides and moved towards her, each one approaching and prostrating itself before her."[263] The symbolism is unequivocal: Sallāma's son was destined to rule the world. This recognition by a member of the Hashimite family was nonetheless insufficient in the face of concurrent pretentions to power. Thus, there was no hesitation in invoking incontrovertible authorities: the Alids and the Umayyads themselves, that is, the two main rivals of the Abbasids, were called upon to recognise either implicitly or explicitly the legitimacy of Abbasid rule!

Al-Ṭabarī, for example, tells of the vision of a descendant of Jaʿfar, ʿAlī b. Abī Ṭālib's own brother, named Muḥammad b. ʿAbd Allāh b. Muḥammad b. ʿAlī b. ʿAbd Allāh b. Jaʿfar b. Abī Ṭālib. In a dream, he walked in his sleep to the Prophet's mosque in Medina, where he saw the inscription mentioning the name al-Walīd b. ʿAbd al-Malik, who had undertaken some projects there. A voice then pierced the silence and ordered him to erase this name and replace it with that of a member of the Banū Hāshim named Muḥammad. The visitor responded that this was his given name, and that he was also a Hashimite. He asked the voice to describe in detail the genealogy of the person destined to be named in the inscription, and believed himself to be the chosen one until al-ʿAbbās was cited as the recipient's grandfather. The epilogue of this vision,

258 Al-Ṭabarī, vol. III, 506, trans. vol. XXIX, 223.
259 Bonner, "The Mint" and "Al-Khalīfa al-Marḍī."
260 See Moscati, "Le califat d'al-Hādī" and Bonner, "Al-Khalīfa al-Marḍī," 84–7.
261 Bonner, "Al-Khalīfa al-Marḍī," in particular 90–1.
262 See Sharon, *Black Banners*, 82 ff.
263 Al-Masʿūdī, *Murūj*, vol. VI, 157–8, trans. Pellat vol. IV, 961.

which occurred toward the end of the Umayyad caliphate, would come several years later, when al-Mahdī took offense at the epigraph in Medina mentioning the name of an Umayyad caliph and effaced it, substituting his own name in its place.[264] Indeed, the caliph's name was Muḥammad b. ʿAbd Allāh b. Muḥammad b. ʿAlī b. ʿAbd Allāh b. al-ʿAbbās, thus nearly homonymous with Jaʿfar's progeniture. This edifying anecdote gives precedence to the sons of al-ʿAbbās over those of Abū Ṭālib; even better, it was one of the latter who proclaimed it thus. Traditions such as these may have been circulated under al-Manṣūr or al-Mahdī, both of whom were trying to assert the superiority of their own ancestor over Abū Ṭālib.[265]

The *Anonymous History of the Abbasids* reports that ʿAlī b. ʿAbd Allāh, originator of the plan to install the family in Syria, affirmed in the presence Sulaymān b. ʿAbd al-Malik – or, in another version, Hishām – in al-Ḥumayma that his two grandsons, the future Abū al-ʿAbbās and Abū Jaʿfar, had both been called to rule.[266] Hishām is presented as especially reverential toward ʿAlī b. ʿAbd Allāh, for whom he had even recited a panegyric poem, while several decades earlier, ʿAbd al-Malik had also shown him a warm welcome.[267] Marwān II is sometimes portrayed as omniscient in order to better herald the Abbasids' future victory. Al-Iṣfahānī also notes that Marwān II was not at all concerned with the pretentions of Muḥammad b. ʿAbd Allāh b. al-Ḥasan (al-Nafs al-Zakiyya), who claimed to be the *mahdī* despite many warnings from his advisors. The caliph knew that power would not fall to him, but rather would return to "the son of a slave" (*umm walad*), an indication that undoubtedly references al-Manṣūr.[268] These visions, while not always as openly messianic as other traditions, nevertheless were aimed at preserving the potential for the Abbasids to fulfill the conditions necessary for the End of Days, in the same way that Maslama did so after failing to succeed in his conquests.

This profusion of elements with strong eschatological connotations is explained by the competition for messianism that raged throughout the early Abbasid period. Similar to the accent placed on the soteriological dimension of the new masters of the caliphate, concurrent claims to power culminated around the figure of the Sufyānī, who presaged the return of the first Umayyad or, on the Alid side, the rise of Muḥammad al-Nafs al-Zakiyya. After the assassination of Abū Muslim, some of his supporters claimed that their

264 Al-Ṭabarī, vol. III, 535, trans. vol. XXIX, 254–5.

265 On this point, see above, Ch. 2.

266 *Akhbār al-dawla*, 139–40.

267 *Akhbār al-dawla*, 141, 154–6.

268 Al-Iṣfahānī, *Maqātil*, 247, 258, cited by Elad, "The Rebellion," 163.

hero would return to spread justice throughout the world, and that he would be the awaited redeemer.[269] Messianic aspects also played a crucial role in the context of the civil war that would tear the empire asunder following the death of Hārūn al-Rashīd.[270] In other words, the Abbasids had an even greater need to develop their messianic dimension because they did not possess a monopoly on power. Syria, then, emerged as a strategic space, especially the northern part of the province, perhaps echoing the expectations stirred by the battles with Byzantines and the hope of one day taking Constantinople. Both in the Muslim historical apocalypses, above all that of Nuʿaym b. Ḥammād (d. 229/844), and in Christian eschatology, the Shām proved fertile territory for such connotations.

The weight of these expectations is not surprising. Messianic beliefs were indissociable from the Abbasid *dawla*. The awaited radical upheaval was an integral part of the context of "affirming a very specific idea of collective human time."[271] For this reason, the Revolutionary vulgate was destined to be replete with messianic elements, while an entire apocalyptic literary corpus developed around the episode itself. A prime example is the insistence on the fact that the *daʿwa* was launched in the year 100 of the *hijra*, an era also marked by strong eschatological speculation. Messianism was thus a target of confiscation while also becoming a means of maintaining dominance at the same time. The sought-after eschatological monopoly was intended to stifle any concurrent Alid or Sufyanid pretentions to the throne.

The Abbasid Revolution is presented above all as a myth of origin. This narrative construction resulted in the foundation of a medieval vulgate for the episode. The ensuing historiographic shockwaves had profound consequences: because the movement arose in Khurāsān, the decisive battle took place on the Great Zāb, and the final Umayyad caliph was killed in Egypt, the Bilād al-Shām was largely forgotten after 132/750. Moreover, the Khurāsānī and Iraqi tropism in the sources discussing the downfall of the Marwanids has largely been echoed in modern historiography as well. In the Syrian context, events related to the coup d'état that removed the Umayyads from power were at the heart of the various rewriting processes. The search for long-buried fragments of Syrian history invites us both to define the conditions and the rhythms according to which the revolutionary canon was composed, and also to shed light on alternative pasts that reveal the choices made by medieval historians. The example of ʿAbd Allāh b. ʿAlī, the first major threat to the new dynasty, is illustrative

269 Al-Masʿūdī, *Murūj*, vol. VI, 186–7, trans. Pellat vol. IV, 973.
270 Yücesoy, "Between Nationalism" and *Messianic Beliefs*, 59 ff.
271 Benoist and Merlini, "Révolution et messianité," 9.

of the strategies of isolation enacted to fabricate the figure of a Syrian rebel. His defeat at the hands of Abū Muslim's troops sealed his fate, both historically and historiographically, as "the rebel did not produce the sources, but rather the state authority that repressed it."[272] The various tactics employed were part of a messianic current that offered a broader perspective on Abbasid ambitions. This logic cost ʿAbd Allāh nearly everything, including his epithet, stripped from him and reapplied to Abū al-ʿAbbās: al-Mahdī became al-Saffāḥ at the same time that the bloodthirsty became the generous. In the face of Alid pretentions, embodied foremost by Muḥammad al-Nafs al-Zakiyya, and the hoped-for return of the Sufyānī, the Abbasids strove to confiscate messianism for themselves. This eschatological monopoly would prove particularly useful in affirming their contested legitimacy.

From a historiographic perspective, the project is clear: the event was fabricated. To do so, the various episodes spanning the period surrounding the year 132/750 were compressed in order to reduce the period of uncertainty to the greatest extent possible. The solution adopted resulted in a manipulation of *revolutionary time*. This statement is valid for every narrative account of the Abbasid Revolution, and is especially pertinent in the Syrian context. In this coveted space, more so than anywhere else, time was reduced: that of the interregnum following the death of Ibrāhīm al-Imām, that of the violence, that of the Syrians rallying around ʿAbd Allāh b. ʿAlī and the threat he posed to al-Manṣūr, and finally that of the Revolution itself. By concentrating the troubles around the year 132/750, rather than extending them for a longer duration, a brief and unique event was created. Any faults could be easily projected upon the recently overthrown Umayyads. In this sense, the Abbasid Revolution was more of a Mansurid Revolution. Al-Manṣūr used force to eliminate any potential rivals: as Cahen notes regarding his success, "the caliph was such as his army made him."[273] The military victory of 136/754 marked the end of the Syrian army's pretentions, which had until that point tried to reassert its supremacy: after the defeat at the Great Zāb under Marwān II's command, that at Nisibis under ʿAbd Allāh b. ʿAlī spelled the double failure of the *ahl al-Shām wa-al-Jazīra*. However, this debacle was not the end of the influence of ʿAlī b. ʿAbd Allāh's descendants in Syria for, as we shall see, Ṣāliḥ b. ʿAlī would later assert his grasp on power shortly after his brother's failed attempt to do so.

In constructing the event, its meaning was also created. ʿAbd Allāh b. ʿAlī's claims are presented as simply another revolt in a period full of such activity. Attempts were made to try to justify al-Manṣūr's brutal elimination of all

272 Esch, "Chance et hasard," 17.
273 Cahen, "Points de vue," 153.

his potential rivals, including the murder of Abū Muslim, the soul and military leader of the uprising that led to the Umayyads' downfall. Similarly, the development of the concept of *dawla* allowed the coup d'état overthrowing the Umayyad dynasty to be excluded from the general category of revolts and rebellions that proliferated during this period, almost as if the Abbasids possessed in advance a Weberian monopoly on legitimate violence. Fabricating a myth of origin popularised the idea of a rupture that brought about an irreparable change in Syria's situation. The elements analysed in this chapter now invite us to reconsider the question in order to try to propose a different history of meanings in the Syrian space throughout the long eighth century.

CHAPTER 8

Exercising Power in the Syrian Space in the Second/Eighth Century: A History of Meanings

> When kings journey around the countryside, making appearances, attending fetes, conferring honors, exchanging gifts, or defying rivals, they mark it, like some wolf or tiger spreading his scent through his territory, as almost physically part of them.[1]

•••

> The real objective of Islamic architecture is space itself.[2]

∴

The men and events discussed in the preceding pages serve both to validate a methodology and to shed light on the successive significations given to one episode or another. This chapter will conclude the present study by demonstrating that these are the protagonists or key moments needed to reconstitute a history of meanings. Analysing ideological constructions and historiographies has shown that what we thought we knew about the history of the Shām in the second/eighth century was in fact the product of a canonisation of history contextualised by two contrasting dynastic frameworks. The infamous Abbasid Revolution in particular received longstanding historiographic attention, as it was the crux of the second Islamic dynasty's attempts to fabricate an origin myth. It imposed itself as a critical turning point announcing Syria's irreversible decline, henceforth dethroned by Iraq. However, we have also tried to show that access to alternative pasts was still possible, and that concurrent projects existed as well.

This final chapter, in a more exploratory vein, will sketch out another reading of the history of the Syrian space in the second/eighth century, that of a history of meanings. We labor under no delusions here: without doubt, the pages

1 Geertz, "Centers, Kings and Charisma," 153.

2 Burckhardt, *Art of Islam*, 23–4.

 | DOI:10.1163/9789004466326_010

that follow merely offer one out of many meanings that could be ascribed to the period. The approach, however, demonstrates the value of illuminating the deep coherence in the history of the Shām, connecting the period of the foundation of the Dome of the Rock by ʿAbd al-Malik (72/692) to the abandonment of Raqqa as a caliphal residence after the death of Hārūn al-Rashīd (193/809). This is an attempt to establish a history of meanings for the Syrian space within these two chronological limits, one that reveals the spatial practices of power; it is also an effort to retrace the "Syrian policies" of the late Umayyads and early Abbasids in order to better shed light on the changing spaces of caliphal power.

However, this approach is not without difficulties. We have seen that the spaces of memory for the first two Islamic dynasties were formed in part by a historiographic construction aimed at creating an opposition between two regions that were supposed to be mutually antagonistic.[3] By limiting our analysis to Syria, the danger that arises is that of reinforcing this deceptive image with respect to the Umayyads. This is not because the Shām *was not* the privileged space of Marwanid power – this chapter will offer abundant evidence to the contrary – but rather because the scope of their policies was obviously not limited to Syria. At the very heart of the Syrian space, we risk perpetuating another imbalance, for reasons mentioned previously that we shall briefly recall here. First, there is asymmetry in the sources, given that Umayyad Syria is better-documented in the Islamic chronographies than its Abbasid counterpart. This statement also applies to the Christian sources, albeit for different, strictly chronological reasons: the chronicle of Theophilus of Edessa – the Syriac Common Source so useful for the present study – does not continue beyond the 750s, and the *Chronicle of Zuqnīn* ends in the 770s. Furthermore, the archaeological record does not compensate for the limitations of this textual corpus. While this inquiry has shown that more and more evidence points to continuous land use between the Umayyad and Abbasid eras, there are almost no known sites founded by the Abbasids in the Syrian space, with the most notable exceptions being al-Manṣūr and al-Rashīd's projects around al-Rāfiqa and al-Raqqa. Al-Ḥumayma, the most important Abbasid Syrian site, clearly dates to the Umayyad period. Nothing comparable to the vast Marwanid architectural program that will be discussed further below exists, although in certain cases, epigraphy proves useful for identifying various Abbasid constructions. Finally, there is the imbalance in modern scholarship: to exaggerate the situation somewhat, it could be said that in recent decades, Umayyad Syria has primarily been the purview of archaeologists, while Abbasid Syria has been the province of historians. Copious evidence thus indicates that

3 See above, Ch. 4.

these two moments in the region's history have not been treated equally. Cobb has identified certain salient features in the Shām after the year 132/750[4] that remain to be described for the Marwanid era; at the same time, however, his conclusions exempt us from various developments when we shift our focus to the Abbasid period. The current state of the field explains the specific architecture of this chapter.

8.1 Patrimonialism and the Creation of a Caliphal Landscape

In 72/962, the Umayyad caliphate returned from the brink of destruction: it had nearly disappeared after several years of fierce combat against opposition from all sides. In order to restore their caliphal authority, everything needed to be rebuilt. The battle of Karbalāʾ had left lasting trauma and irreparable fractures; the shockwaves of the second *fitna* reverberated long after the confrontation of the two dominant tribal factions, Kalb and Qays, at the battle of Marj Rāhiṭ in 64–65/684. The southern Arabs' victory in no way calmed these elevated tribal tensions. This unrest proved fertile ground for Ibn al-Zubayr, who appeared as a rival during the fleeting caliphate of Marwān I (64–65/684–685) and continued to pose a threat throughout the reign of his son, ʿAbd al-Malik. Seven years would pass before ʿAbd al-Malik got the better of this foe – in addition to several other adversaries who tried to profit from the situation[5] – thus becoming the true caliph.[6] After his military victory, ʿAbd al-Malik needed to reassert Marwanid authority, reconstructing his networks of power and regaining control over vast regions of the empire that had long eluded the Umayyads' grasp. The caliph had to initiate ambitious programs in the face of these formidable challenges. Here, we will not analyse in detail all the caliphate's policies to this end, among them the Arabisation of the administration and fiscal reforms;[7] rather, we will examine the Syrian aspects of these projects. This reflection is essential, as these reforms inaugurated new practices of power.

---

4 Cobb, *White Banners*.

5 For an overview of the difficulties faced by ʿAbd al-Malik, see Robinson, *ʿAbd al-Malik*, 39–48. See also the classic studies of Rotter, *Die Umayyaden und der zweite Bürgerkrieg*, 162 ff., and Dixon, *The Umayyad Caliphate*, 121 ff., and finally Donner, *Muhammad and the Believers*, 177–224.

6 The traditional division, in which Ibn al-Zubayr is presented as an anti-caliph, has ʿAbd al-Malik's reign beginning upon the death of his father in 65/685. However, Robinson has recently argued that his caliphate did not actually start until 72/692, *ʿAbd al-Malik*, 31–48. This point has long been subject to debate; see, for example, al-Masʿūdī, *Murūj*, vol. V, 210, trans. Pellat vol. III, 785.

7 The bibliography on this subject is immense. See Robinson, *ʿAbd al-Malik*, in particular 59 ff.

8.1.1 *The Construction of an Islamic Caliphal Landscape*

Robinson has recently defended the idea that the year 72 of the *hijra* (691–692) marked the true "beginning of the [Islamic] state."[8] One of the major dimensions of this state construction lay in the development of a remarkable architectural program, with the Dome of the Rock, almost certainly completed in 72,[9] as its inception.[10] The goal was to create a caliphal and Islamic landscape, to define "a politico-cultural identity in visual terms."[11] Here, Islam truly entered the space: the Dome of the Rock affirmed the superiority of the new religion while simultaneously inscribing it in time both past and future in a place replete with memory. The al-Aqṣā Mosque completed this appropriation of the esplanade of the Temple and the Holy Sepulchre.[12] The policy was continued and amplified by al-Walīd,[13] and a veritable building frenzy took hold of the caliphate: mosques were expanded throughout the empire at the ruler's behest,[14] while the Shām was transformed into a vast open-air construction site. The efforts dedicated to sites of Muslim worship helped to define Islamic rituals.[15] The construction of the mosque of Damascus was undeniably a major point of pride in this architectural program.[16] The message, recorded in a conversation between a young al-Muqaddasī and his uncle, was clear:

8 Robinson, *'Abd al-Malik*, 6. An identical opinion from an archaeological perspective is espoused by Johns, "Archaeology and the History of Early Islam." See also Donner, "From Believers to Muslims" and *Muhammad and the Believers*.

9 Scholars disagree over the dating of this monument. The dedicatory inscription on the Dome of the Rock is in the name of al-Ma'mūn, but dated to the year 72 of the *hijra*! This chronological aberration can likely be explained by the substitution of the Abbasid caliph's name for that of 'Abd al-Malik. It remains uncertain, however, if this date corresponds to the beginning or the completion of construction work; most scholars prefer the latter interpretation. See Robinson, *'Abd al-Malik*, 1–9. For the opposite argument, see Blair, "What is the Date." See also Rabbat, "The Dome of the Rock."

10 On the other aspects of 'Abd al-Malik's reforms, see Robinson, *'Abd al-Malik*, especially 66–80.

11 Flood, *The Great Mosque*, 185. See also Straughn, *Materializing Islam*, 55 ff., and Genequand, "Formation et devenir."

12 On the organisation of this trebly holy space, see Elad, *Medieval Jerusalem*; Raby and Johns, *Bayt al-Maqdis*; Grabar, *The Shape of the Holy*; Grafman and Rosen-Ayalon, "The Two Great Syrian Umayyad Mosques;" Rosen-Ayalon, *Art et archéologie*, 26–43; Flood, *The Great Mosque*, 188.

13 On the artistic program developed in these places of worship and its significance, see Flood, *The Great Mosque*, in particular 196–206, 211–3.

14 Flood, *The Great Mosque*, 187.

15 On this question, see Donner, "Umayyad Efforts at Legitimation."

16 See Flood, *The Great Mosque*.

> One day, I said to my uncle: "Al-Walīd was wrong to spend so much of the Muslims' wealth on the mosque of Damascus.[17] He would have done far better had he used that [money] to build and maintain roads and cisterns or to repair fortresses." [My uncle replied:] Not so, my child! Al-Walīd was right to undertake such a significant project: the Shām, land of the Christians, contains many beautiful churches famous for their splendour, such as those at al-Qumāma, Ludd (Lydda), or al-Ruhā (Edessa); al-Walīd wanted similarly to provide for the Muslims, to give them a mosque that would draw much admiration and be one of the great wonders of the world. He followed in the footsteps of ʿAbd al-Malik [b. Marwān], who, upon seeing the imposing and magnificent dome [of the church] at al-Qumāma, constructed the Dome of the Rock, out of fear that the dome [at al-Qumāma] would leave too deep an impression in the hearts of Muslims.[18]

The intended goal was achieved, judging by the impression the edifice left on the Byzantine ambassadors who travelled to Damascus during ʿUmar II's caliphate:

> some Byzantine ambassadors presented themselves before ʿUmar II; they entered the mosque in order to see it. When they raised their heads toward the mosque, one of their leaders paled and lowered his eyes. When asked why, he replied: "We, the people of Byzantium (*ahl al-rūmiya*), declare that the Arabs will not endure. But having seen what they have built, I acknowledge that they are making good use of a period of time that they shall fill."[19]

This was said to be the reaction of several of the emperor's envoys, who had dissuaded ʿUmar b. ʿAbd al-ʿAzīz from undertaking a project to remove the mosque's ornamentation, the value of which seemed to him better used in the public treasury.[20] These religious edifices contributed to the definition

17 Slightly before this passage, al-Muqaddasī notes "that to complete this project, al-Walīd brought in Persian, Hindu, Maghribī and Byzantine artisans and levied a property tax throughout the Shām for seven years, the revenues from which were dedicated entirely to it [the mosque's construction]; this is to say nothing of the shipment of gold and silver brought in on eighteen boats from Cyprus, nor of the materials and mosaics provided by the Byzantine ruler," *Aḥsan*, 158, trans. 170.

18 Al-Muqaddasī, *Aḥsan*, 159, trans. 173–4.

19 Ibn al-Faqīh, *Mukhtaṣar*, 108, trans. 132–3.

20 Ibn al-Faqīh, *Mukhtaṣar*, 108, trans. 132–3.

of a "symbolic identity vis-à-vis Byzantium […] and at the same time a desire to demonstrate a separate identity in relation to the Christian subjects in the Caliphate."[21] The message of a triumphant Islam was addressed to these latter, even in the mosque's dedicatory inscription commemorating the destruction of the cathedral of Saint John.[22] While the inscription is lost today, Ibn ʿAsākir gives the following reading:

> There is no God but Allāh, alone, without equal, and we love no other but Him. Our Lord is Allāh, alone; our religion is Islam and our Prophet is Muḥammad […]. The construction of this mosque and the destruction of the church that was there were ordered by the servant of God, al-Walīd, Commander of the Faithful, in Dhū al-Qaʿda of the year 86/24 October–22 November 705.[23]

The inscriptions on the Dome of the Rock already bore a similar message for the Christians.[24] While they carried an explicit proclamation, these epigraphs also served as an Umayyad "visual language," defining the "decorative canon"[25] of gold letters on a background of lapis-lazuli blue.[26] This construction of "Umayyad power in visual terms" would also later provide an opportunity for

21 Cameron, commenting on Griffith's contribution, "Images, Islam and Christian Icons," 138.

22 Flood, *The Great Mosque*, 226.

23 TMD, vol. 2/1, ed. Munajjid, 37, trans. Élisséeff, 55–6. Al-Masʿūdī proposed a slightly different reading: "Al-Walīd had inscribed on the wall of the mosque, in gold letters on a background of lapis lazuli: Our Lord is Allāh, we love no other than Allāh. The order to build this mosque and to demolish the church that occupied this site was given by the servant of God, al-Walīd, Commander of the Faithful, in the month of Dhū al-ḥijja of the year 87/13 November–11 December 706. This inscription in gold characters can still be read in the mosque of Damascus in the present year 332/943," *Murūj*, vol. V, 362–3, trans. Pellat vol. III, 844. Disagreement over the date is found in the works of other authors, who cite the year 88/707–708; see Flood, *The Great Mosque*, 253. Al-Balādhurī corroborates the date of 86, *Futūḥ*, 126, trans. 193. See also Hoyland, *Seeing*, 701–2.

24 See Kessler, "ʿAbd al-Malik's Inscription;" Whelan, "Forgotten Witness;" Hoyland, *Seeing*, 696–9.

25 Flood, *The Great Mosque*, 190, 205.

26 Flood, *The Great Mosque*, 218, 245. This chromatic choice is attested for the Dome of the Rock, the mosques of Damascus and Aleppo, the *sūq* at Baysān, and even the mosque at Cordoba constructed by the Andalusian Umayyads. I must thank Sophie Makariou for drawing my attention to this point. The Umayyads did not have a monopoly on the use of this combination of gold and blue, which is also very well attested in Late Antiquity and later eras, as famously in the Blue Qurʾān. The cosmological dimension of the Dome of the Rock and its inscription of gold letters on a blue background has been emphasised by Nees, who proposed that this colour choice be interpreted as a reference to Solomon. See Nees, "Blue Behind Gold."

the dynasty's detractors to claim that the caliphate had been disfigured and transformed into a monarchy (*mulk*).[27] Beyond these prestigious structures in Damascus and Jerusalem, most of the cities in the Bilād al-Shām were endowed with mosques during the Marwanid era, from Aleppo to al-Ramla, ʿAnjar to Palmyra and al-Ruṣāfa.[28]

However, it is not these Muslim places of worship – durably inscribing Islam and the Umayyads into the landscape – that should retain our attention here; rather, our focus must be the other building projects that often accompanied them. Mosques were generally part of a broader architectural program that included other structures in older urban fabric, such as Jerusalem, Jarash, Palmyra or al-Ruṣāfa.[29] An identical program was carried out at the same time in the new cities erected by the caliphs, such as al-Ramla,[30] Qaṣr al-Ḥayr al-Sharqī,[31] ʿAnjar,[32] ʿAqaba,[33] and the famous "desert castles,"[34] of which more than thirty examples are known to us today, thanks to archaeology.[35] Still other establishments characterised this period of major works: hospitals,[36] systems of irrigation and water supply,[37] expansion or creation of roadways,[38] etc.

27 Flood, *The Great Mosque*, 216.

28 Sauvaget, *Alep*; Rosen-Ayalon, *Art et archéologie*; Hillenbrand, "ʿAnjar;" Genequand, "An Early Islamic Mosque in Palmyra" and *Les établissements*; Sack, *Resafa IV*. See also Jalabert, *Hommes et lieux*, 50–83.

29 On these sites, see Elad, *Medieval Jerusalem*; Rosen-Ayalon, *Art et archéologie*; Walmsley, "The 'Islamic City'" and *Early Islamic Syria*; Walmsley and Damgaard, "The Umayyad;" Sack, *Resafa IV*; Ulbert, "Ein umaiyadischer Pavillon;" Al-Asʿad and Stepniowski, "The Umayyad Sūq;" Foote, *Umayyad Markets*.

30 Rosen-Ayalon, *Art et archéologie*; Luz, "The Construction;" Sourdel, "La fondation;" Gibson and Vitto, *Ramla*.

31 Grabar et al., *City in the Desert*; Genequand, "From 'Desert Castle' to Medieval Town" and *Les établissements*, which lists the pertinent bibliography.

32 See Hillenbrand, "ʿAnjar" and Finster, "Researches in ʿAnjar."

33 Whitcomb, "The Misr of Ayla;" Northedge, "Archaeology and New Urban Settlement," 238.

34 Out of convenience, I will use the customary expressions "desert castles" or "Umayyad castles," despite the problems posed by this deceptive terminology.

35 On all of the sites mentioned in this paragraph, see Genequand, "Formation et devenir" and *Les établissements*. See also Northedge, *Entre Amman et Samarra* and "Archaeology and New Urban Settlement."

36 The medieval sources incorrectly attribute the foundation of the first Islamic hospitals to al-Walīd I. See Ibn al-Faqīh, *Mukhtaṣar*, 106, trans. 130, and Conrad, "Did al-Walīd I."

37 The Umayyads' water policies are the subject of an important study by Genequand, "Économie de production, affirmation du pouvoir et *dolce vita*." By the same author, see also *Les établissements*, and see Vibert-Guigue, "La question de l'eau."

38 This question is addressed further below.

ʿAbd al-Malik and his immediate successors, al-Walīd I foremost among them, "materialized Islam"[39] by inscribing it in the landscape. This architectural program, like the frescoes at Quṣayr ʿAmra or the presentation of lineage claimed by the caliph Yazīd III (126/744),[40] attests to a widespread concern for establishing the dynasty's place in the world and in history.[41] These elements were also aimed at defining the new social relations produced by the restoration of Umayyad authority.[42] Before we return to certain of these sites in greater detail, we must identify the complex political stakes surrounding them. This architectural explosion was not only a matter of creating a landscape to help affirm the new Marwanid authority; it was also and perhaps above all a process of establishing a structure of patrimonial power with which to define its nature vis-à-vis the need for mobility required to control an immense empire in the pre-modern era.

8.1.2 *Patrimonialism and Regionalisation of Powers*

While this newly reasserted power had to be situated with respect to the empire as a whole – a consequence of the schism created by the Zubayrid anti-caliphate – ʿAbd al-Malik also desperately needed to reaffirm his hold over the Syrian space in the wake of the deep division carved by the tribal conflict that had raged during his father's reign. To do so, the caliph relied primarily on his family. ʿAbd al-Malik's nominations for governors of the Syrian *jund*s are especially revealing in this respect, as the vast majority of these positions were given to his brothers, uncles, sons, and various other relatives.[43] The caliph's children also make for an interesting case study here; it would appear that they were assigned to specific regions within the Syrian space, in which they established an "architectural patronage."[44] These practices attest to a patrimonial

39 To borrow Straughn's expression, *Materializing Islam*.

40 To whom the Islamic sources attribute the following phrase: "I am the son of *Kisrā*; my father is Marwān. One grandfather is a *qayṣar*; the other a *khāqān*." See al-Ṭabarī, vol. II, 1874, trans. vol. XXVI, 243; al-Masʿūdī, *Murūj*, vol. VI, 31–2, trans. Pellat vol. IV, 909; Ibn al-Athīr, vol. III, 425. On the frescoes at Quṣayr ʿAmra, see below.

41 Flood, *The Great Mosque*, 216; al-Azmeh, *Muslim Kingship*, 67.

42 See Straughn's remarks, *Materializing Islam*, 58–9, and Flood, *The Great Mosque*, 216–7. This point was earlier discussed by MacAdam, "Some Notes," 541: "The raison d'être of the Umayyad 'palaces' in Jordan now makes more sense. Their prominent, even ostentatious, presence was a constant reminder to the Arab tribes of Azraq that the old order had changed."

43 See the list of these governors compiled by Crone, *Slaves*, 124–5.

44 Bacharach, "Marwanid Umayyad Building Activities," 28. As we shall see below, the general idea underpinning this article is both important and quite solid. However, it is

conception of power in the Shām, one that led to the development of a "patrimonial sovereignty."[45]

Décobert has recently discussed this subject, emphasising that the structure of Umayyad power must be understood as patrimonial in the Weberian sense of the concept. This "particular mode of traditional dominance" combined a form of "personal" – but not "charismatic" – "power" with "a practice of familial appropriation of the space in which power was exercised."[46] Authority founded on this basis depends on personal connections and loyalty. This system was established by Muʿāwiya but, after his reign, management of people and territory took on a new form. Under the Umayyad "imperial system," governors negotiated "their allegiance to the caliph against a portion of the province's revenue that had been allocated to them for themselves and their families;" this then became a sort of "rent" (*affermage*). At the same time, patrimonial practice also worked as a "process of caliphal appropriation of this imperial territory."[47]

This tendency emerged during the caliphate of Marwān I (64–65/684–685) in the troubled context of the second *fitna*. The *Byzantine-Arab Chronicle of 741* explicitly states that the caliph "distributed the provinces" between his sons. ʿAbd al-Malik (*Habdelmele*) was assigned Arabia, Syria, Mesopotamia, Osrhoene,[48] Armenia and Persia; ʿAbd al-ʿAzīz (*Habdellaziz*) inherited Egypt, Ethiopia and North Africa; and finally, Muḥammad was given control of the armies on land and sea who were destined to secure victory over the Byzantines.[49] ʿAbd al-Malik largely continued his father's program,[50] dividing the Shām among his relatives. Two major implications arose from this political

---

unfortunate that the argument is based on examples that are less firm, and the dubious attributions of certain sites should be viewed with caution.

45 This question was studied in detail by Décobert, "Notule sur le patrimonialisme omeyyade." See also Crone, *Slaves*, especially 37 ff.

46 Décobert, "Notule sur le patrimonialisme omeyyade," 229. It is precisely this "practice of familial appropriation of space in which power was exercised" that is the focus of the discussion in the pages below. However, it is well beyond the scope of this study to provide a comprehensive account of all the social and economic implications of this Weberian conception of patrimonialism. For a critical reading of the use of this model (as well as the Marxist model), see Hodgson, *The Venture of Islam*, vol. I, 105 ff., and more recently Mårtensson, "Discourse and Historical Analysis," 303–6. For more specific discussion of these subjects, see Matin-Asgari, "Islamic Studies and the Spirit of Max Weber" and Mårtensson, "The Power of the Subject."

47 Décobert, "Notule sur le patrimonialisme omeyyade," 231–2.

48 The region of Edessa.

49 *741*, § 31, trans. Hoyland, 621.

50 *741*, § 34, trans. Hoyland, 623.

choice: wielding power at the local level served as an educational experience for the Umayyad princes, while also further regionalising Marwanid authority.

Sulaymān b. ʿAbd al-Malik is perhaps the most instructive example of this caliphal formation. His father named him governor of Palestine, and he was then confirmed in this position by his brother al-Walīd,[51] whom he would later succeed as caliph. However, two of ʿAbd al-Malik's other sons, ʿAbd Allāh and Maslama, prove that obtaining a governorate did not guarantee accession to the highest level of power. Conversely, certain of ʿAbd al-Malik's sons who were never appointed governors of a Syrian *jund* – al-Walīd, Yazīd II and Hishām – would all become caliph. If governorship was neither a necessary prerequisite nor sufficient in itself as a condition for attaining the highest political power, it is due to the fact that the creation of caliphs was based on other criteria. Administrative status was generally not important, nor was the relegation of "the effective management of the provinces" to other people, since "sovereignty [...] belonged to the Umayyad family alone" in these regions.[52] This patrimonial conception was subject to profound "rationalization" efforts. While a man could change his status through conversion, territory could not; this effectively affirmed the existence of "a patrimonial sovereignty over conquered land, a sovereignty that would have been called into question if the convert had remained in control of this land."[53]

The system put in place by ʿAbd al-Malik that exclusively favoured his own offspring was only subject to two serious deviations in dynastic terms: ʿUmar b. ʿAbd al-ʿAzīz and Marwān b. Muḥammad. However, there was no shortage of attempts to upend the established order of succession, beginning with ʿAbd al-Malik's own wish to remove his brother from the line – as planned by Marwān – in order to replace him with his own son. ʿAbd al-ʿAzīz's death in 85/704 allowed these projects to unfold. Al-Walīd and Hishām's subsequent attempts to give their respective sons a similar advantage would prove futile. In fact, as mentioned above, only Sulaymān's succession and the accession of ʿUmar b. ʿAbd al-ʿAzīz were truly problematic, as Marwān II's rise to power took place in the context of the third *fitna*. We shall see that the logic behind this latter's strategy was identical to that initiated by the founder of the Dome of the Rock. The moment of caliphal succession was a critical one. It was an

---

51 Crone, *Slaves*, 124, 126.

52 Décobert, "Notule sur le patrimonialisme omeyyade," 233. Bacharach also noted that these zones assigned to Umayyad princes did not correspond to the limits of the *ajnād*, "Marwanid Umayyad Building Activities," 28.

53 Décobert, "Notule sur le patrimonialisme omeyyade," 237–8.

"uncertain time, incredibly tense and ambiguous, when world order was at stake," because the caliph was responsible for "the reproduction of [Islamic] order."[54]

ʿAbd al-Malik's initial choice led to a territorialisation of power in the Syrian space.[55] Regional dynamics then developed to their full extent following the prince's accession to the caliphate. However, these elements are more difficult to appreciate during shorter caliphal reigns. The Palestinian tropism attributed to Sulaymān b. ʿAbd al-Malik,[56] founder of the city of al-Ramla,[57] is also questionable to say the least after the year 96/715, given that the caliph spent a large portion of his rule at Dābiq and in Northern Syria during the major offensive launched against Constantinople. This is not to say that the privileged relationships established with the elites of Filasṭīn and al-Urdunn prior to his reign did not play a significant role in Sulaymān's caliphate; the influential figure Rajāʾ b. Ḥaywa is notable evidence of the importance of these connections. A similar problem plagued Yazīd b. ʿAbd al-Malik, who was closely associated with the region surrounding ʿAmmān, and also his son, the future al-Walīd II, who was present in that area as well, but whose caliphate essentially consisted of fleeing to al-Bakhrāʾ,[58] near Palmyra, where he would ultimately succumb beneath the blows of Yazīd III's supporters. Maslama's case is somewhat different, as he did not reach the pinnacle of power after having favoured the Shām's northern spaces, in particular those near Bālis[59] and Ḥiṣn Maslama/Madīnat al-Fār.[60] The most emblematic example is that of Hishām, who had deep roots in Palmyrena before gaining the throne and who then pushed the system's logic to its limits by making his primary residence in al-Ruṣāfa. We shall return below to the different networks established in Balqāʾ and Palmyrena. These same dynamics would later preside over Marwān II's choice of Ḥarrān, a city located in a region he had governed and one in which he could rely on firm tribal support.

54 Décobert, "Notule sur le patrimonialisme omeyyade," 240. On the succession, see Marsham, *Rituals*.

55 This shift to a predominantly territorial power system is characteristic of the Umayyad period, even beyond the Syrian context. See Décobert, "Notule sur le patrimonialisme omeyyade."

56 For example, see Bacharach, "Marwanid Umayyad Building Activities," 35.

57 See al-Balādhurī, *Futūḥ*, 143–4, trans. 220–1; Sourdel, "La fondation;" Rosen-Ayalon, *Art et architecture*, 53–60.

58 On this site, see Genequand, "Al-Bakhrāʾ" and *Les établissements*, 69–94.

59 Leisten, "Balis."

60 Haase, "Is Madinat al-Far," "Madīnat al-Fār," "Une ville des débuts de l'islam" and "The Excavations." On the sites associated with Maslama, see above, Ch. 5.

The regionalisation of power undoubtedly stimulated architectural and artistic competition among the Umayyad princes, who either agreed with the established order of succession or hoped to modify it. Ibn Shiḥna explains the splendor of the mosque of Aleppo, a symbol of the rivalry between al-Walīd and Sulaymān, in these terms, noting that the latter wanted to erect a masterpiece equal to that of his brother in Damascus.[61] These are perhaps the same reasons that shed light on Sulaymān's grandiose plans for the mosque of al-Ramla, again to prove himself the equal of his brother, al-Walīd; the dimensions of the mosque would be reduced by ʿUmar II.[62] However, as Hillenbrand has observed, while such rivalries are conceivable at the level of these lavish constructions, the problem is different with respect to the "desert castles" and the erection of new cities, both of which are better understood as part of a logic complementary to these networks rather than as part of a dialectic of concurrence.[63] The Marwanids' architectural munificence was thus the corollary of this patrimonial and territorialised power, yet its excess also had its fair share of detractors; it is almost certainly in this light that Yazīd III's pledge must be understood. During the conversation in which he announced that he had ordered the assassination of his cousin al-Walīd II, he promised not to dig canals or to place "stone upon stone nor brick upon brick."[64] This spate of monumental architecture was largely behind the accusation that the first Islamic dynasty had debased the institution of the caliphate and transformed it into a vulgar terrestrial *mulk*. In any case, it should be noted that, from the Umayyad perspective, this program was part of a patrimonialism that "was articulated with a religious and [divinely] inspired representation of power."[65]

Patrimonial sovereignty largely explains the creation of a caliphal landscape in the context of the affirmation of Marwanid authority. However, this power structure was not the only reason. Rather, it went in tandem with another

61 Sauvaget, "Les perles choisies," 56–7; Flood, *The Great Mosque*, 217. However, it should be noted that Ibn Shiḥna records another tradition attributing the completion of the mosque of Aleppo to al-Walīd himself. Bacharach saw in this confusion over the building's "patron" an argument for attributing it to Maslama b. ʿAbd al-Malik ("Marwanid Umayyad Building Activities," 34).

62 Al-Jahshiyārī, 48; al-Balādhurī, *Futūh*, 143, trans. 220. Sourdel has highlighted the astonishing similarities between the narratives dedicated to the construction of the mosques of Damascus and al-Ramla, "La fondation," 390. See also Flood, *The Great Mosque*, 219.

63 Hillenbrand, "ʿAnjar," 87.

64 Al-Ṭabarī, vol. II, 1834, trans. vol. XXVI, 194; *Kitāb al-ʿuyūn*, 150. The attack is clearly directed at al-Walīd II, who was often accused of excess and who may have proposed that the Jordan be diverted. See Braslavski, "Hat Welīd II."

65 Décobert, "Notule sur le patrimonialisme omeyyade," 244.

need, one inherent to exerting control over the immense space governed by an expanding caliphate: the exercise of power from a distance.

8.2 The Mobile Exercise of Power

The second/eighth century of Islamic history could be characterised as a period in which the caliphate was forced to define its relationship to space. In the final years of the Umayyad "century of conquest" and the decades that followed, the caliphs had to determine the most effective policies to solidify their authority over these vast territories. The caliphate's integrity and security – both internal and external – and even its economic viability were at stake. It was undoubtedly these spatial relations that gave rise to such opposing policies as those issued by ʿUmar II and Hishām b. ʿAbd al-Malik. Maslama, a unifying link between these two caliphs, also had the essential function of defining the *dār al-islām*. The early Abbasids' complex ties to Syria fell within the same logic.

Conquering new territory was one thing; ensuring that it remained in the caliphate's possession was quite another. Deciding how to exercise power and who should do so was thus highly consequential. Indeed, these spatial problems greatly surpass the context of Islamic history, as they were situated within the Braudelian *longue durée*. The caliphs faced many difficulties associated with exerting power over a vast geographic area, just like their Carolingian and Ottonian counterparts in the medieval West or the Tang in China.[66] In a pre-modern context, this relationship to space revolved primarily around the mobility of the agents of power. Paradoxically, however, these questions have not yet attracted the interest of specialists in medieval Islam,[67] although

66 The theme of "space and power" is the subject of a considerable bibliography; here, then, we shall limit ourselves to itinerant kingship. Beyond De Planhol's classic study (*Les fondements géographiques*), the works of Miquel (*La géographie humaine*), and Cornu (*Atlas*), those compiled by Harley and Woodward (*Cartography in the Traditional Islamic and South Asian Societies*) provide a more specific view of medieval geographers' perceptions of space. See also Mouton (*Le Sinaï*) and studies dedicated to borders, in particular those of Bonner (*Aristocratic Violence*), or, in the Muslim West, of Sénac (*La frontière et les hommes*) and Buresi (*Une frontière entre chrétienté et islam*). On this last subject, see *Castrum 4*, especially Toubert's valuable discussion ("Frontière et frontières") that retraces the historiography on the question since the pioneering works of Turner and Ratzel. All of these topics have been richly developed by scholars of the medieval West, a recent indication of which is Bourin and Zadora-Rio's "Analyses de l'espace."

67 The contingency of this mode of governance has sometimes been mentioned, but never truly studied in detail. The various theories proposed to interpret the functions of the "Umayyad castles" are discussed further below. The most relevant discussion on the

certain aspects have been briefly discussed in the broader context of the power relations between sedentary and nomadic populations.[68]

The years leading up to the restoration of Marwanid authority forced ʿAbd al-Malik to be constantly on the move, waging war on numerous fronts. His success and very survival depended on this relentless motion. As the situation calmed and peace returned after 72/692, a unique opportunity to renegotiate caliphal mobility presented itself.

8.2.1 *The Need for Mobility*

In the *Ansāb al-ashrāf*, al-Balādhurī transmits one of the very rare texts offering concrete evidence of the exercise of Marwanid power in the Syrian space:

> ʿAbd al-Malik spent the winter (*yashtū*) at al-Ṣinnabra in [the *jund*] of Jordan. When the winter had passed, he would go to al-Jābiya, where he ordered that hospitality be offered to his companions; [there,] he distributed cattle among these latter in fixed quantities according to their rank. After the first days of March (*ādhār*), ʿAbd al-Malik would make his entry into Damascus and reside at Dayr Murrān until the arrival of the summer heatwaves. He would then travel to Baalbek, where he would remain until the winds [heralding] winter arrived. He would then return to Damascus and, when the cold became too intense, he would leave once more for al-Ṣinnabra.[69]

---

mobile exercise of power is that of Gaube, who describes the "Umayyad castles" as sites of contact between caliphal and tribal authority. He also notes ʿAbd al-Malik's mobility, "Die syrischen Wüstenschlösser," 202. Helms has also insisted on the idea of an "architecture of diplomacy," *Early Islamic Architecture of the Desert*, 29–30. Spellberg emphasised the mobility of the Umayyad governors in the zone defined by numismatists as the "Umayyad North," and she noted the correlation between their movements and the mints, "The Umayyad North," 123–4. See also Bacharach, "Marwanid Umayyad Building Activities," or Hillenbrand, "ʿAnjar," 87 ff., and Marsham, *Rituals*, 125–8. Dakhlia's exemplary "Dans la mouvance du prince" is also very useful, although it deals with a much later era (Morocco in the seventeenth-eighteenth centuries).

68 Again, the bibliography on the subject is abundant, and it is impossible to present a comprehensive overview. Some of the most valuable works should be listed here, albeit in a somewhat arbitrary manner, beginning with Khazanov's exceptional *Nomads and the Outside World*. See also, for example, Lindholm, "Kinship structure," or Bonte et al., *Al-Ansâb*. Among the works most relevant for the area and time period of the present study, see Donner, "The Role of Nomads;" Khoury et al., *Tribes and State Formation*; Crone, "Tribes and States."

69 Al-Balādhurī, *Ansāb*, ed. Ahlwardt, 200.

This text has long been known to Orientalists, but has not been analysed in depth, and thus merits further scrutiny here. This extract precisely describes the modes of a mobile exercise of power conducted according to the rhythms of the changing seasons.[70] Before returning in detail to the information contained in this exceptional document, it is important to define the features of this form of government based on studies conducted on other regions so that we may evaluate the extent to which it clarifies practices of power in the Syrian space in the second/eighth century.

The idea of itinerant kingship is characteristic of a mode of governance in which the sovereign, possessed of all functional and symbolic representations of power, travels periodically or constantly through the territories under his authority.[71] This practice was common to a number of pre-modern societies, as attested by diverse examples, including nearly all the Germanic kingdoms that flourished after the fall of the Roman Empire in the West,[72] the kingdom of Ethiopia under the Solomonic dynasty beginning in 1270,[73] or Morocco in the nineteenth century until the death of Moulay Ḥasan in 1894.[74] Authority constructed on this basis is founded largely on personal connections strengthened by the monarch's visits; in this sense, mobile power is part of patrimonial sovereignty. The ruler also "took symbolic as well as actual possession of the realm."[75] The local elites, for their part, took advantage of their proximity to the king (*Königsnähe*) to solidify their positions. The royal itinerary was thus highly beneficial for both parties, as it determined "social interactions" and was a manifestation of the interdependence linking nobles and rulers in competition for control over this "interface between regional and regnal power." "Topographies of consensus" and "conflict" thus emerged,[76] revealing the complexity and changing nature of the power dynamics that were generated as a result.[77]

The different sites of royal power played a determining role in the sovereign's ability to garner support among local elites. Several spaces of power thus coexisted within the caliphate, and the ruler's task was to establish an equilibrium between the various levels at which these authorities operated. Caliphal

70 A similar practice is well-attested among the Sasanians. See Fiey, "Les résidences d'été."
71 Bernhardt, *Itinerant Kingship*, 45.
72 Bernhardt, *Itinerant Kingship*, 47.
73 Derat, *Le domaine des rois éthiopiens*.
74 Geertz, "Centers, Kings and Charisma," 162. See also Dakhlia, "Dans le mouvance du prince."
75 Bernhardt, *Itinerant Kingship*, 46.
76 Innes, "People, Places and Power," 398, 437, 426 ff.
77 See De Jong and Theuws (eds.), *Topographies of Power in the Early Middle Ages*.

mobility was essential to the construction of these networks of power, which simultaneously provided an indispensable foundation and represented a permanent threat. While these spatial aspects are often "invisible in the sources," they reveal themselves fully as soon as this equilibrium is broken and conflict erupts: "the geography of these events highlights the complexity of the spatial interaction between kings and elites." Exercising itinerant power is thus the condition of a power based on "mediation between regional elites and the [...] court." Mastery over spaces of power was therefore a central feature of the system and stimulated competition between the sovereign and the elites.[78]

The ruler generally developed rituals associated with this mobility aimed at organising the social sphere by opposing it with the magnificence of divinely-appointed royal authority. Ceremonies "locate the society's center and affirm its connection with transcendent things by stamping a territory with ritual signs of dominance."[79] The sovereign's movements throughout these journeys were part of a ritualistic program marked by processions and ceremonies.[80] The king's arrival was a deeply significant event, a powerful unifying factor that bound regional elites together. These spatial movements were accompanied by a temporal dimension that determined the political calendar and simultaneously integrated it with the religious calendar. Winter was the season of counsel, summer that of action,[81] as attested in the early centuries of Islam by the *ṣawāʾif*, the summer campaigns against the Byzantines. This mobility was also part of a sacred conception of power: always in motion, the sovereign could make an appearance anywhere at any time. As Geertz has noted, while the ruler could not in actuality be omnipresent, like God, he could try to give the impression that he was.[82] Other holy elements could also arise surrounding the figure of the king, in particular those connected with the notion of *baraka* in the Muslim world.[83] An illustration of this sacred dimension during the Umayyad period was the popular belief that caliphs were immune to the plague.[84]

78 Innes, "People, Places and Power," 426–34.
79 Geertz, "Centers, Kings and Charisma," 160, 153.
80 See Marsham, *Rituals*, 134–42.
81 Innes, "People, Places and Power," 423–4, 435.
82 Geertz, "Centers, Kings and Charisma," 163–4: "as long as he could keep moving, chastening an opponent here, advancing an ally there, the king could make believable his claim to a sovereignty as conferred by God."
83 Geertz, "Centers, Kings and Charisma," 162.
84 *Kitāb al-ʿuyūn*, vol. I, 101; al-Azmeh, *Muslim Kingship*, 78. However, Hishām also categorically refused to run the risk in the face of a looming epidemic; see al-Ṭabarī, vol. II, 1738, trans. vol. XXVI, 81.

This constant movement did not preclude the existence of a "capital" where the ruler would spend part of the year, a natural point of departure and return for all royal itineraries. Another option was multiple residences, where the sovereign would successively spend longer seasonal periods.[85] In each of these examples, however, the mobile exercise of power required the fulfillment of a certain number of practical conditions allowing it to function properly and ensuring its efficacy. The organisation of the king's circulation depended above all on the availability of resources and services en route. If the sovereign and his family did not possess the requisite goods, other networks must be sought and constructed to provide the necessary means. In Christian contexts, the construction of these itinerant spaces was based primarily on the monasteries, which were strategically situated along royal routes:[86] they represented the various stages of the journey and thus "organized space."[87] These monasteries were also directly linked to the ruling family, in some cases as a result of strategies of patronage.[88] Alongside the monasteries, palaces and royal residences made up the landscape of itinerancy. These edifices allowed movement between "a series of complementary centres."[89] This topic in particular has received much attention from German medievalists.[90] Notably, their research shows that royal residences permitted "interaction between the leader of the kingdom, who, ideally, covered the whole of this latter and temporarily crowned it with his itinerant presence, and each of his palaces, which were just as much buildings as local symbols of the mobile exercise of power."[91] To complete the phenomenon, it was thus important to "make the network of royal power visible in its variegated totality, no longer merely in its landmarks."[92] This mode of exercising power entailed strategies of occupying space, which spurred the development of large-scale architectural programs, either contributing to the creation of a "royal landscape"[93] or restructuring preexisting networks, like

85 Bernhardt, *Itinerant Kingship*, 47.

86 As attested primarily by the Ottonians and Ethiopians. See Bernhardt, *Itinerant Kingship*, in particular 291–2, and Derat, *Le domaine des rois éthiopiens*, 87 ff.

87 Derat, *Le domaine des rois éthiopiens*, 87.

88 Bernhardt, *Itinerant Kingship*, 292.

89 Innes, "People, Places and Power," 421.

90 A valuable synthesis of these works is found in Zotz, "L'étude des palais royaux en Allemagne," as well as "Präsenz und Repräsentation." See also Paravicini, "Cours et résidences;" Renoux, "Palais, cours et résidences;" and for the French side of this research, see Moeglin, "Les recherches françaises."

91 Zotz, "L'étude des palais royaux en Allemagne," 308.

92 Zotz, "L'étude des palais royaux en Allemagne," 312.

93 Innes, "People, Places and Power," 421.

the imperial cities of Morocco in the nineteenth century.[94] Mobility beyond these zones of patrimonial power was extremely difficult, even nearly impossible. Without such networks, or when the logistics necessary to facilitate such movement failed, mobile authority became particularly risky for the ruler.[95] For this reason as well, it was essential to respect geo-climatic conditions and seasonal rhythms.

Exerting power from a distance was the fundamental problem confronting both rulers and elites.[96] To be effective, itinerant kingship required a monopoly – or quasi-monopoly – on long-distance communication. Sovereigns therefore needed to construct routes with convenient rest-stops in reasonably secure locations.[97] If these conditions were not fulfilled, the balance of power was threatened. However, this mobility was not practiced throughout the entirety of the empire, but rather within a defined area;[98] the exercise of power was thus spatialised. Bernhardt has defined three types of zones: central (*Kernlandschaften*); remote (*Fernzonen*); and transitional (*Durchzugsgebiete*).[99] This spatial hierarchy invites an interrogation of "the local conditions of royal power,"[100] or the application of power to varying degrees in different places and the disparities that this practice established. There were economic repercussions, as the institution of these networks also resulted in the elevated status of certain regions, those containing monasteries, palaces and royal residences foremost among them. Although the sovereign did not retain direct control over the revenues generated from these domains, his regular presence *in situ* or his patronage signified that wealth sprung from his authority.[101] Thus, relationships with elites far surpassed the bounds of the merely political and encompassed a sizable financial dimension as well.

Approached over time, the general tendency was that "the mobile exercise of power evolved toward a power centered around a residence: residence, capital, and administrative center grew increasingly apart."[102] Rulers gradually came to frequent centres that offered the indispensable sacrality needed for the celebration of a divine royalty and the economic activity required to meet

94 Geertz, "Centers, Kings and Charisma," 162.
95 For an illustration of these risks, see Geertz, "Centers, Kings and Charisma," 165–6.
96 Innes, "People, Places and Power," 436.
97 Bernhardt, *Itinerant Kingship*, 56–7.
98 Derat, *Le domaine des rois éthiopiens*, 8; Innes, "People, Places and Power," 424.
99 Bernhardt, *Itinerant Kingship*, 61, adapting the typology defined by Müller-Mertens, *Die Reichsstruktur*.
100 Zotz, "L'étude des palais royaux en Allemagne," 308.
101 Bernhardt, *Itinerant Kingship*, 290 ff.
102 Paravicini, "Cours et résidences," 330.

the growing needs of the court.[103] However, the transition was a delicate one, as the "settling of the court" was not without consequences: other areas saw themselves deprived of royal visits, and this limited the ruler's regional control, while "a single region supported the economic burden of royal camp's presence, which exhausted subsistence resources and in turn required that taxes flow to the king's place of residence, whereas previously he had collected them on the spot."[104] This concludes our survey of the main lessons to be learned from a detailed analysis of the mobile exercise of power in various different contexts.

We shall now return to al-Balādhurī's text and the itinerary of ʿAbd al-Malik. Upon arriving at al-Jābiya, the caliph *ordered* that *hospitality* be offered to his companions. Here we see a classic aspect of the mobile exercise of power in other geographic areas: obligatory service to the court, the *servitium regis* of the authors of the medieval West.[105] In ʿAbd al-Malik's time, the caliph relied on a preexisting network to exert his mobile authority. The ruler's itinerary is quite telling in this regard. Al-Jābiya already occupied a central role during the Byzantine era, and it was there that Marwān I was named caliph in 64/684;[106] from a military point of view, it was a highly strategic location for ʿAbd al-Malik. It is probable that the campaigns devised against Constantinople spurred Sulaymān to transfer military functions to Dābiq, in Northern Syria.[107]

The convent of Dayr Murrān, on the slopes of Qāsiyūn, was the caliphs' preferred place of residence when staying in Damascus; it was there that al-Walīd I died.[108] Al-Walīd I's presence there is confirmed by Christian hagiography, as Saint Peter of Capitolias (d. 715) was brought there to the caliph before he was martyred: the monastery had been captured by the "tyrannical Arabs" and converted into a palace.[109] For ʿAbd al-Malik, beyond seasonal changes, other dating elements that might help us to determine his movements are few and far between. However, it should be noted that a biography of John of Daylam

103 Bernhardt, *Itinerant Kingship*, 296.
104 Derat, *Le domaine des rois éthiopiens*, 272.
105 See Bernhardt, *Itinerant Kingship*, 45 ff.
106 Yāqūt, *Muʿjam*, vol. II, 91–2; Sourdel-Thomine, "Djābiya."
107 Sourdel-Thomine, "Djābiya."
108 Al-Ṭabarī, vol. II, 1270, trans. vol. XXIII, 219; Yāqūt, *Muʿjam*, vol. II, 533–4. The subject of monasteries in early Islam is discussed by Fowden, "Monks" and "Christian Monasteries." On the importance of monasteries in classical Islamic culture, see Kilpatrick, "Monasteries Through Muslim Eyes."
109 Peeters, "La passion," 307; Hoyland, *Seeing*, 358.

(d. 738), a saint of the Church of the East, reports that this latter visited the court of the caliph "who was residing in Damascus at this time," likely around 701.[110]

ʿAbd al-Malik then travelled to Baalbek, the northernmost point on his itinerary.[111] The city was strategically located on the important route of the Bekaa between Damascus and Homs. Thanks to its imposing antique ruins, the site garnered the admiration of Muslim geographers and was associated with Solomon.[112] With his presence at Baalbek, ʿAbd al-Malik inscribed the caliphate in a continuity of great empires. The Umayyads' particular interest in linking themselves to the ancient king of Israel perhaps led to this "Solomonic direction."

Not one of these locations offers significant archaeological evidence to help identify the structures associated with ʿAbd al-Malik's stays. Al-Ṣinnabra, the beginning and endpoint of ʿAbd al-Malik's itineraries, is potentially the only site familiar to archaeology. The toponym, no longer in use today, was well-known to medieval authors[113] and clearly associated with several Umayyad caliphs starting with Muʿāwiya, who, according to Yāqūt, spent the winter there.[114] Al-Yaʿqūbī and al-Masʿūdī agree that Marwān I stayed at al-Ṣinnabra upon his return from Egypt, and it was there that he arranged his succession, designating ʿAbd al-Malik as his heir followed by his younger brother, ʿAbd al-ʿAzīz. Marwān I thereafter never left al-Ṣinnabra and eventually died there.[115] Beyond al-Balādhurī's account, the site reappears on the scene several decades later, as it was there that Yazīd b. al-Walīd received the *bayʿa* in 126/744.[116] Whitcomb has recently reinterpreted the earlier excavations of Khirbat al-Karak, on the banks of the Sea of Galilee, and proposed that it is actually al-Ṣinnabra.[117] The site contains a bath house and a *qaṣr*. The latter consists of an enclosure comprising four protruding square towers with a "basilical" reception hall that was once thought to be a church (see figs. 6 and 7). However, the ceramic and

110 Brock, "A Syriac Life," 27, p. 139, trans. 27, p. 148. The date of John of Daylam's visit is discussed in the appendix to Brock's translation, 180. See also Hoyland, *Seeing*, 203–5.

111 Our knowledge of Baalbek in early Islam is limited. See Gaube and von Gladiss, "Säulen unter dem arabischen Halbmond."

112 See above, Ch. 4.

113 And consequently known to modern scholars as well; see Musil, *Palmyrena*, 282; Lammens, "La Bâdia," 101; Sharon, "An Arabic Inscription;" Rotter, *Die Umayyaden*, 162; Gil, *A History*, index.

114 Yāqūt, *Muʿjam*, vol. III, 425. See also Le Strange, *Palestine*, 531 (who proposes the reading "al-Ṣannabra"); Marmardji, *Textes géographiques*, 118 (with the incorrect spelling "al-Ṣinnayra").

115 Al-Yaʿqūbī, *Taʾrīkh*, vol. II, 257; al-Masʿūdī, *Murūj*, vol. V, 205, trans. Pellat vol. III, 783.

116 Al-Ṭabarī, vol. II, 1833, trans. vol. XXVI, 192.

117 Whitcomb, "Khirbet al-Karak;" Genequand, "Umayyad Castles," 10.

numismatic evidence in addition to various different architectural parallels led Whitcomb to suggest that al-Ṣinnabra was in fact one of the "desert castles." The hypothesis is plausible, and would make al-Ṣinnabra the oldest "Umayyad castle" known today.[118] This early dating is crucial: it demonstrates that these sites were originally part of an itinerant exercise of power! Before returning to this essential point, the much larger project of which this route was but one part must be defined in greater detail.

The discovery of inscriptions and milestones erected on ʿAbd al-Malik's orders brings clarity to this dry text. Three of them, found near Afīq/Fīq not far from the Sea of Galilee, are particularly pertinent for the present study. The first, an inscription of very high quality, has been studied by Sharon.[119] It marks ʿAbd al-Malik's order, given in 73/692, for "the levelling of this difficult pass" (*bi-tashīl hadhihi al-ʿaqaba*),[120] here alluding to the ʿAqaba Afīq or ʿAqaba Fīq of the Arab geographers.[121]

The two other milestones, of lesser quality and dated 85/704, were analysed in detail by Elad.[122] They indicate the distance between them and Damascus, 52 and 53 miles respectively. The Umayyad mile is estimated to have been 2285 metres, which correctly places Fīq around 120 kilometres from Damascus.[123] More significantly, Elad was able to show that these two milestones represent ʿAbd al-Malik's creation of a new route, or perhaps more specifically, a new section of the route connecting Damascus and Tiberias in the Golan. On a larger scale, this section is situated on the road linking Damascus to Jerusalem,[124] one of the most important channels of communication in the Shām, connecting the two cities in which ʿAbd al-Malik and al-Walīd were most architecturally active.

118 Whitcomb, "Khirbet al-Karak," who notes that the form of the towers at al-Ṣinnabra, which were somewhat irregular for an "Umayyad castle," parallel those found at Bālis that were excavated by Leisten. See Leisten, "Balis," "The Umayyad Complex at Balis," and "For Prince and Country(side)." For an overview of the origins and architectural evolution of these sites, see Genequand, "Umayyad Castles" and *Les établissements*, in addition to Northedge, "The Umayyad Desert Castles."

119 Sharon, "An Arabic Inscription;" *CIAP*, vol. III, 206 ff.; Hoyland, *Seeing*, 700.

120 Sharon, "An Arabic Inscription," 368.

121 Yāqūt, *Muʿjam*, vol. I, 233 and vol. IV, 286. The site was also associated with eschatological traditions, see Elad, "The Southern Golan," 73–5.

122 Elad, "The Southern Golan;" *CIAP*, vol. III, 206 ff.

123 Elad, "The Southern Golan," 46. See also Sharon, *CIAP*, vol. III, 106.

124 Sharon, "An Arabic Inscription," 369, 372; *CIAP*, vol. III, 99–100. We know of other markers indicating the distance separating them not from Damascus, but from Jerusalem. See in particular *CIAP*, vol. I, 4.

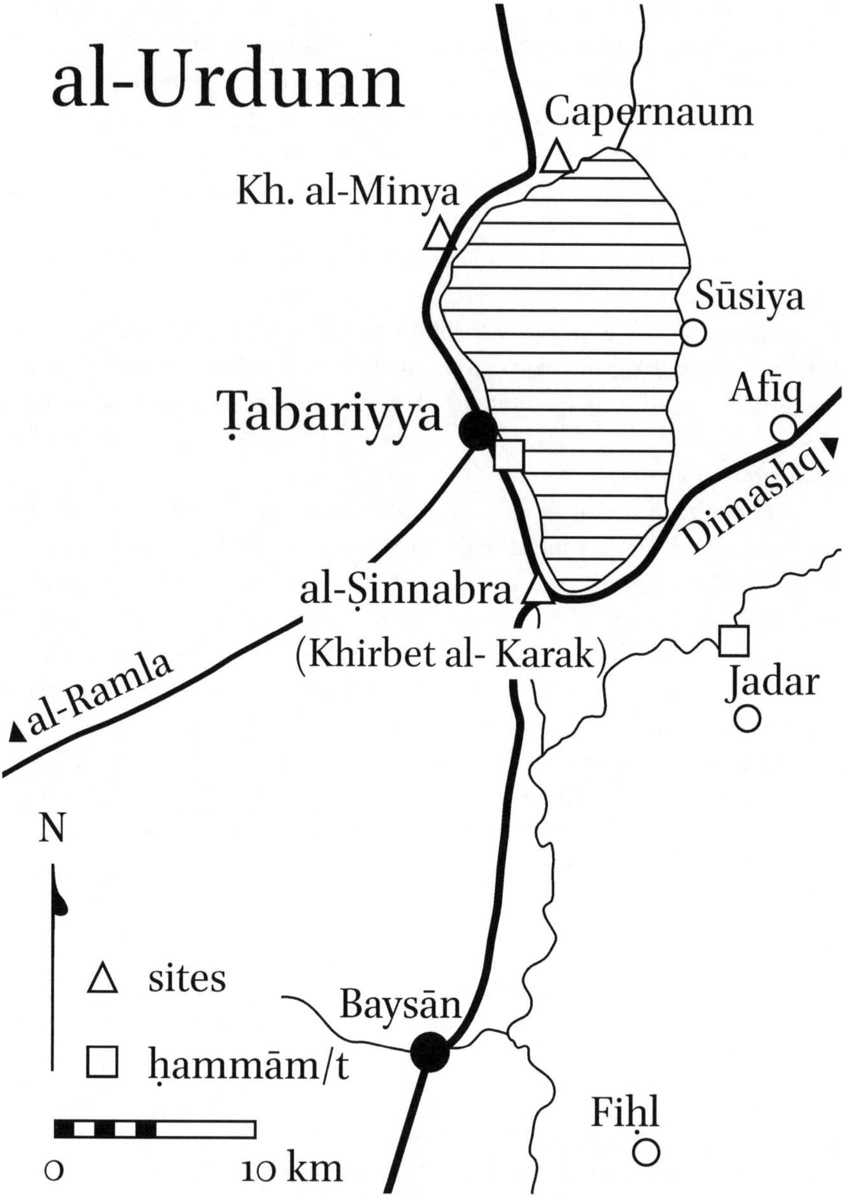

FIGURE 8.1 Location of al-Ṣinnabra / Khirbat al-Karak
© DONALD WHITCOMB, "KHIRBET AL-KARAK"

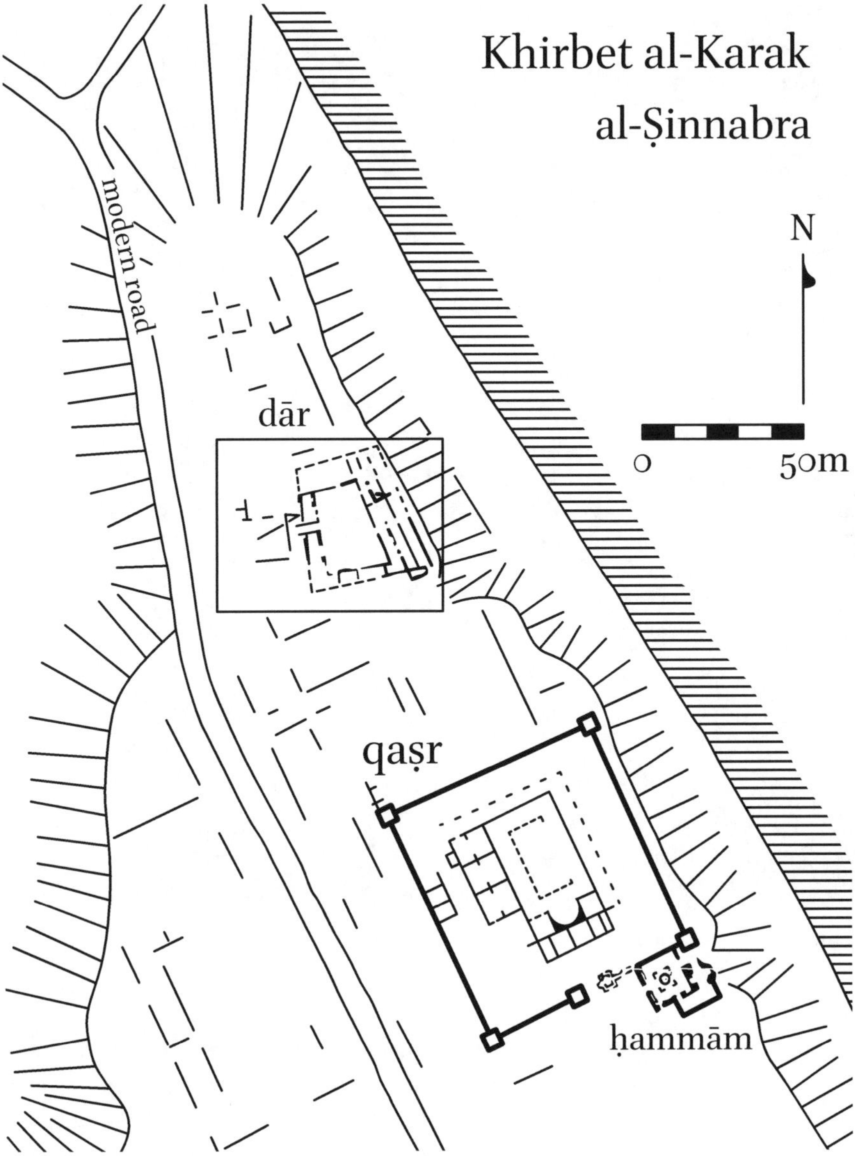

FIGURE 8.2 Al-Ṣinnabra / Khirbat al-Karak: site map
© DONALD WHITCOMB, "KHIRBET AL-KARAK"

FIGURE 8.3 Inscription of ʿAbd al-Malik (ʿAqaba Afīq / Fīq)
© MOSHE SHARON, *CIAP*, I, FIG. 48

Sharon hypothesised a route linking Damascus–Kiswa–Fīq–Baysān–Jericho and finally, Jerusalem.[125] However, we have the very rare advantage of being able to compare ʿAbd al-Malik's itinerary as reported by al-Balādhurī and these epigraphic indications in order to establish the stages of the route. It borrowed this new section of the road, identified by Elad, between al-Ṣinnabra, located at a strategic point for crossing the Jordan, and al-Jābiya (via Fīq/Afīq), where it rejoined the Roman road leading toward Kiswa and Damascus. This trajectory is perhaps a supplementary piece of evidence to refute van Berchem's

125 *CIAP*, vol. III, 99–100.

affirmation that ʿAbd al-Malik merely "repaired the roads crisscrossing his empire."[126]

If we look now to the northernmost portion of this route, between Damascus and Baalbek, one name immediately stands out: ʿAnjar. The site is not associated with ʿAbd al-Malik, nor is it mentioned by al-Balādhurī, yet this vast project – whose functions were clearly more extensive than a simple rest-stop – could perhaps at a later date have been part of the creation of other strategic transportation networks between Damascus and Northern Syria on the one hand, via the Bekaa, Baalbek and Homs, and Damascus, Beirut and the coastal areas on the other.[127] It is also possible that the construction of ʿAnjar was part of a massive development project undertaken in the southern part of the Bekaa valley, in particular aimed at draining the marshes.[128] ʿAnjar's strategic importance on the road linking Qinnasrīn – Homs – Damascus is confirmed by the battle that raged there between the future Marwān II and Sulaymān b. Hishām in 127/744–745. The former was victorious, thus opening the way for his own accession to the caliphate.[129]

Dating ʿAnjar divides scholars, but an Umayyad foundation is recognised today, even if the site remains insufficiently studied from an archaeological perspective.[130] The argument is based both on epigraphic evidence and Christian textual sources. Syriac inscriptions uncovered in the quarries of Kāmid al-Loz indicate that work began in 96/714–715 under the caliph (*amīrā*) al-Walīd I. The Nestorian quarrymen who inscribed these texts came from the Jazīra (Jazīra Ibn ʿUmar).[131] In ʿAnjar itself, Arabic graffiti provides other evidence, including one on the western wall dated to Rajab 123/May–June 741 that offers a *terminus ante quem* for the construction of the fortifying walls

126 Van Berchem, *Matériaux*, 22–3.

127 Hillenbrand suggests that the city could have played a significant logistical role in the preparations for Maslama's naval campaign against Constantinople, "ʿAnjar," 66.

128 Hillenbrand, "ʿAnjar," 68–9.

129 For a detailed account of Marwān's battles and winning strategy, see al-Yaʿqūbī, *Taʾrīkh*, vol. II, 337, and al-Ṭabarī, vol. II, 1876–9, trans. vol. XXVI, 249–53.

130 Sauvaget initially proposed this identification, "Les ruines omeyyades de ʿAndjar." Today, it has firm support among scholars, in particular Chehab, "On the Identification;" Northedge, "Archaeology and New Urban Settlement," 233–5 and *Entre Amman et Samarra*, 65 ff.; Hillenbrand, "ʿAnjar." For a discussion of Mouterde's earlier reservations and Grabar's more recent ones, see Hillenbrand, "ʿAnjar," 59, note 1.

131 On this corpus of inscriptions, see Yon's remarks in Kassis, Yon and Badwi, "Les inscriptions syriaques du Liban," 33–5. See also Mouterde's classic studies, "Inscriptions en syriaque dialectal" and "Trente ans après." Copts and Byzantine captives also participated in these works, see Chehab, "On the Identification," 46.

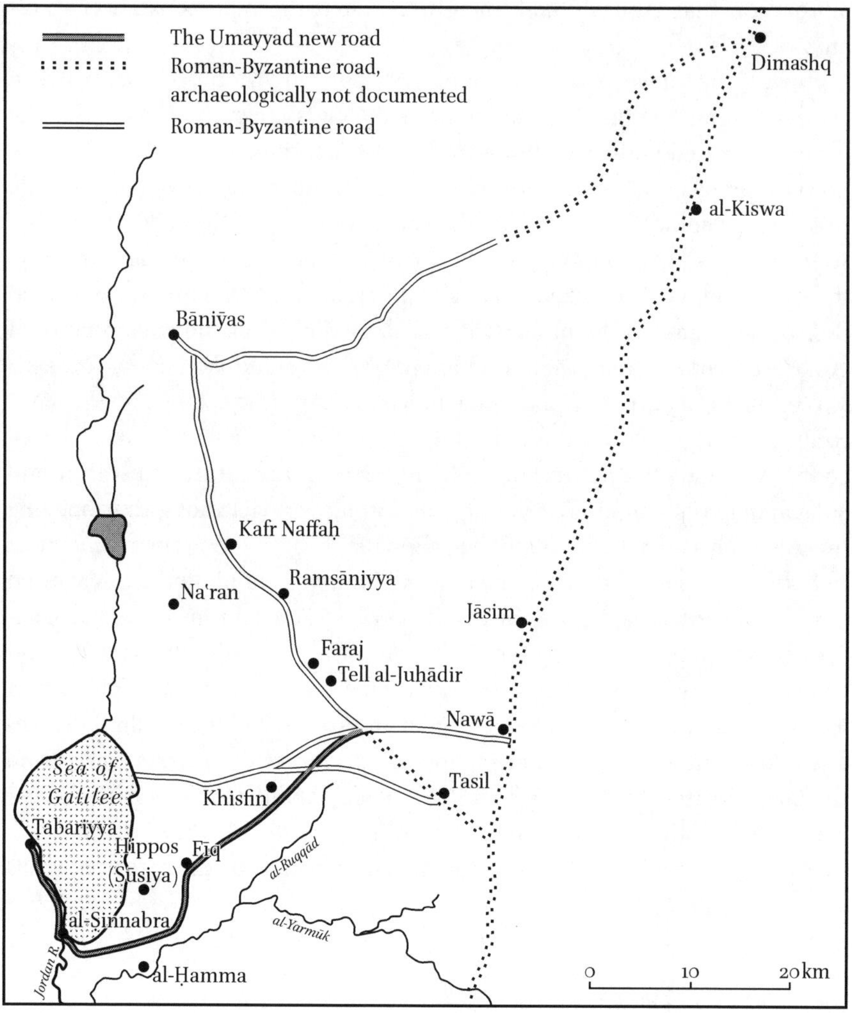

FIGURE 8.4 ʿAbd al-Malik's New Road in the Golan (based on Elad, "The Southern Golan," 64)

under Hishām's caliphate.[132] The anonymous Syriac chronicles of 819 and 846 mention al-Walīd I's foundation of a city (*mdīnātā*) named ʿAyn Gārā,[133] while Theophanes speculatively attributes[134] the city's paternity to the caliph's son

132 Ory, "Les graffiti omeyyades," 100.

133 *819*, 14, trans. 9; *846*, 232, Latin trans. 176, trans. Brooks, 581.

134 Theophanes's attribution of the construction of ʿAnjar to ʿAbbās is taken for granted by specialists, among them Chehab, "On the Identification," 44; Northedge, "Archaeology and New Urban Settlement," 234; Bacharach, "Marwanid Umayyad Building Activities," 34–5. See also Hillenbrand, "ʿAnjar." However, this passage in Theophanes is somewhat

and Maslama's brother-in-arms, ʿAbbās b. al-Walīd. Hillenbrand has suggested that ʿAnjar was a stage on the route between Damascus and Khirbat al-Minya constructed in response to the needs of a mobile court living a "semi-nomadic" lifestyle.[135] The crossroads at which the city is situated decidedly provides access to an array of much more extensive routes, notably toward the coast and central and northern Syria, but ʿAnjar fits perfectly within the logic of a mobile exercise of power, even if the scale of the site shows that it had other functions as well.

The Umayyad sites appear to have fulfilled the logistical requirements of an itinerant power. The case of the "desert castles," alongside al-Ṣinnabra, is exemplary in this respect, and thus we shall now turn our attention in this direction.

8.2.2 *The "Umayyad Castles" as an Expression of Mobile Power*

A recent work dedicated to topographies of power put the post-Roman East and West in fundamental opposition: the East perpetuated a power structure inherited from the Romans that centred around cities, while the medieval West opened itself up to a "plurality of locations of power."[136] This analysis perhaps led scholars to focus on the supposed transition between the *polis* and the *madīna*[137] while largely excluding any examination of questions related to the itinerant practices of a power that moved between multiple poles. The famous "desert castles" have been the subject of numerous studies, yet these studies have only scratched the surface of these questions without analysing them in depth or recognising the extent of their implications. While a comprehensive presentation of this scholarship is beyond the scope of the present inquiry, several recent works merit further attention here.[138] We shall briefly cover the dominant interpretative paradigms on the topic before discussing some of the main problems posed by these sites.

---

problematic, which has led Mango and Scott to prefer the hypothesis that the Byzantine chronicler intended to designate al-Walīd rather than his son. Theophanes, *Chronography*, 377, trans. 526.

135 Hillenbrand, "ʿAnjar," 87, 90. Nevertheless, it is important to note that ʿAnjar and Khirbat al-Minya were constructed on very different scales. As mentioned above, ʿAnjar was an urban development, and cannot be reduced to a mere rest-stop. For the latter, a much more modest installation was apparently quite sufficient.

136 Wickham, "Topographies of Power," 1, citing de Jong.

137 See Kennedy's classic article, "From *Polis* to *Madina*."

138 See Northedge, *Entre Amman et Samarra*, 40–54; Genequand, "Umayyad Castles" and *Les établissements*, which present an architectural typology of these sites.

8.2.2.1 Interpretations and Problems

The gradual discovery of these edifices throughout the nineteenth century has sustained lively interest from scholars.[139] At the beginning of the twentieth century, Lammens formulated the first major theory concerning these "desert castles." In a famous article on the *bādiya*, the Belgian Jesuit developed the idea of an Arab atavism for the desert that spurred the Umayyad caliphs, anxious to protect themselves against the plague, to retreat to the steppe.[140] This theory immediately sparked debate, as attested by the acerbic exchanges between Lammens and Musil, who discovered Quṣayr ʿAmra. The two men disagreed most notably on the rhythm of the caliphs' seasonal movements, a question related to itinerant power that unfortunately was largely forgotten thereafter.[141] This "romantic" vision has been widely rejected in modern scholarship. However, as Northedge has noted, "Lammens could cite numerous textual sources to support his arguments: it is always imprudent to completely reject a hypothesis that has the potential to be strongly confirmed by textual sources."[142] Indeed, the plague represented a very real threat to the cities of the Shām in the second/eighth century, infecting sedentary city residents en masse while leaving nomadic populations largely unscathed.[143]

Sauvaget then proposed a radically different explanation by analysing the sites in their environments. He developed the idea of the Umayyads' "agricultural colonization" of the Shām, a theory that fits well with certain information related to Hishām b. ʿAbd al-Malik in the Christian sources. However, Sauvaget died before completing his masterwork; the part that had been revised at the time of his death was later published posthumously by Dominique and Janine Sourdel. We can likely only arrive at a partial understanding of Sauvaget's broader project from this incomplete study.[144] However, many scholars then took up his economic interpretation, although it was criticised by Northedge, who suggested that for many of these sites, the "environmental conditions were too poor for the creation of lucrative large-scale agricultural projects."[145] Genequand arrived at a similar conclusion by examining the caliphs' water

139 See Genequand, *Les établissements*, in particular 379–99.

140 Lammens, "La Bâdia."

141 See Musil, *Palmyrena*, 277–84.

142 Northedge, *Entre Amman et Samarra*, 43.

143 Conrad, *The Plague*, "Ṭāʿūn and Wabāʾ" and "Die Pest." On the related question of the perception of the plague in Islamic territory and the Byzantine world, see Congourdeau and Melhaoui, "La perception de la peste."

144 Sauvaget, "Châteaux omeyyades de Syrie." See also Grabar, "Umayyad 'palace'."

145 Northedge, *Entre Amman et Samarra*, 44–5. See also Hillenbrand's reservations, "*La Dolce Vita*," 3–4.

policies: "if the Umayyads had a water policy aimed primarily at a production economy, it was not in the steppes but rather in traditional agricultural zones, such as the Euphrates valley, the valley of the Khabur or areas of western Syria that remain to be explored."[146]

Gaube then proposed an understanding of the "Umayyad castles" as places of contact between caliphal authority and the tribes, a model borrowed from a Ghassanid practice.[147] This crucial function has been widely accepted by specialists, and it is possible here to speak of an "architecture of diplomacy"[148] organised around an architectural element common to most of these Umayyad sites: the reception hall, where the *majlis* took place.[149] The notion of a hypothetical "Ghassanid model" (or, more appropriately, a Jafnid model) was problematic, however, and Gaube "likely gave too much weight to the princes of the Jafnid dynasty in developing a model of tribal political domination."[150]

The "desert castles" have also been interpreted as axes of communication, conveniently located along major routes.[151] These theories mainly arose from the fact that certain Umayyad sites were identified as caravanserais. Schlumberger presented one of the structures at Qaṣr al-Ḥayr al-Gharbī in this fashion, and Grabar preferred this interpretation for a small compound at Qaṣr al-Ḥayr al-Sharqī, its eastern counterpart.[152] This latter hypothesis has since been rejected: it was, in actuality, a palace facing the large enclosure.[153] The existence of a *khān* at Qaṣr al-Ḥayr al-Gharbī remains speculative.[154]

146 Genequand, "Économie de production, affirmation du pouvoir et *dolce vita*," 171. See also Genequand's exhaustive discussion of the economic functions of these sites, *Les établissements*, 251–378.

147 Gaube, "Die syrischen Wüstenschlösser."

148 Helms, *Early Islamic Architecture of the Desert*, 29–30. While Helms developed an ethnologic approach that corroborated Gaube's outline, it should nonetheless be noted that the purely archaeological section of his work (centred on the site of al-Risha) has been widely criticised by archaeologists. See the reviews of Kervran and Northedge, or Whitcomb's reservations, "Islam and the Socio-Cultural Transition of Palestine," 491.

149 Northedge, *Entre Amman et Samarra*, 51–2 and Genequand, *Les établissements*, 393–94.

150 Genequand, *Les établissements*, 390. On the problems associated with the use of the term "Ghassanid," see Genequand, "Some Thoughts."

151 King, "The Distribution of Sites and Routes" and "Settlement Patterns in Islamic Jordan;" MacAdam, "Some Notes;" Helms, *Early Islamic Architecture of the Desert*, 18 ff.; Brisch, "The Location."

152 Schlumberger, *Qasr el-Heir el-Gharbi*; Grabar et al., *City in the Desert*, 32. On Qaṣr al-Ḥayr al-Gharbī, see Genequand, "Some Thoughts," 64.

153 Northedge, "Archaeology and New Urban Settlement," 235–7; Genequand, "Châteaux omeyyades de Palmyrène," 7, and *Les établissements*, 95 ff.

154 See Northedge (*Entre Amman et Samarra*, 48 ff.), who notes that textual references to *khānāt* are rare for the Umayyad period and are generally connected with the eastern regions of the caliphate. However, Agapius of Manbij includes *khānāt* in his enumeration

According to this theory, the Umayyad castles functioned as rest-stops, in particular in the direction of the Hijaz on pilgrimage routes along desert roads.[155] Archaeologists have often rejected such interpretations, perhaps because they conjure up images of hotels for passing pilgrims. The main obstacle to this theory has to do with the *actors* of mobility: it is not an itinerant power structure that is proposed here, but rather that of movement facilitated by construction ordered by princes or caliphs. Northedge has emphasised that the *bayt*s characteristic of the internal arrangement of the palaces and "the partitioning of their layout into apartments [demonstrates] that they were destined for extended family members,"[156] although it is also possible that they were occupied by several different families. This organisation lends credence to the idea that a prince or caliph travelled with his entourage. Furthermore, Northedge notes that "the relationship between palace and route was real," especially because "resources are rare in the desert, and [people] are generally forced to build in the same places."[157]

Whitcomb, expanding his scope beyond the "desert castles" to include urban sites, has argued for the existence of a desire to affirm Umayyad authority within the Shām by instituting an urban model – one with roots in the Arabian peninsula – in new regions.[158] Other recent studies, concerned with distinguishing the specificities of each individual situation, attempt to define a typology of Umayyad sites based on three primary categories: old cities invested with new power; new cities; and "desert castles."[159]

However, it is admittedly impossible to reduce these "Umayyad castles" to a single function. In fact, the majority of the hypotheses mentioned above can coexist with ease.[160] The polyvalence of these constructions is also quite logical in the context of Umayyad patrimonialism:

---

of the buildings associated with Hishām and mentions that he earned substantial revenue from them. The text mainly covers the *Jazīra* and the *Shāmāt*, *Kitāb al-ʿunwān*, 505. See also Foote, *Umayyad Markets*, 195 ff. We shall see below that the site of Zīzāʾ, associated with the caliph al-Walīd II, is described as a stop for pilgrims returning from the *ḥajj*.

155 King, "The Distribution of Sites and Routes."

156 Northedge, *Entre Amman et Samarra*, 50.

157 Northedge, *Entre Amman et Samarra*, 49.

158 Whitcomb, "The Misr of Ayla;" "Umayyad and Abbasid Periods;" "Islam and the Socio-Cultural Transition of Palestine," in particular 495–6. On the relations between the "Umayyad castles" and the Arabian peninsula, see also Northedge, "The Umayyad Desert Castles."

159 Northedge, *Entre Amman et Samarra*; Genequand, "Formation et devenir" and *Les établissements*, 199–249.

160 For example, see Hillenbrand, *Islamic Architecture*.

> It is certainly thus that the existence of the famous Umayyad *quṣūr* must be understood, built in the desert regions of the Near East as palaces, cities, *bādiyya*, summer residences, caravanserais, and centers of tribal control all at once. They must without doubt be comprehended as *sites*, in the classical sense of the term, in the sense of configuration, that is, as architectural symbols of the process of patrimonial appropriation.[161]

This logic of appropriation is central to understanding the strategy that gave rise to the "Umayyad castles." To complete this assessment of an Umayyad land grab, caliphal mobility became integrated into this monumentality inscribed in the landscape while simultaneously confirming that these various edifices served numerous purposes. This caliphal architecture also ensured that power was asserted even when the sovereign or patron of the site was absent. German medievalists stressed this point as well: "in the monumental character of their architecture, they permanently embodied the empire's center in a particular place, and they preserved this memory during periods when the ruler and his court were absent."[162] It should similarly be noted that Conrad, discussing the terminological problems posed by the "desert castles," demonstrated that *qaṣr* fundamentally designated a permanent construction as opposed to a temporary structure.[163] Here, we return to the idea of inscribing architecture and its associated patron enduringly into the passage of time. Inscriptions commemorating the founder's name serve a similar purpose: "the Umayyad dynasty was conscious of the need to locate themselves physically on the landscape through these acts of monumentality."[164]

Before examining the networks developed through these processes, we must take certain precautions, as the undertaking is risky in more than one regard. First, our knowledge of Umayyad sites remains fragmentary and highly provisional. Today, we know of more than thirty "desert castles," but the representative nature of these latter is by no means certain, as some regions of the Bilād al-Shām have undergone extensive excavations while others have not yet been sufficiently studied. Kennedy has correctly noted that, archaeologically speaking, we now know much more about the margins of the steppes than, for example, the coastal regions.[165]

---

161 Décobert, "Notule sur le patrimonialisme omeyyade," 236.

162 Zotz, "L'étude des palais royaux en Allemagne," 308. See also Straughn, *Materializing Islam*, 60–9.

163 Conrad, "The *quṣūr*."

164 Straughn, *Materializing Islam*, 69.

165 His observation pertains to the Levant in the sixth century, although the question remains valid for the Islamic period as well. Kennedy, "Concluding Remarks," 270. See

Among the "Umayyad castles," Balqā' and Palmyrena have received the most archaeological attention. We may thus be victims of a distorting prism, and future archaeological developments are likely to modify the field only to a certain extent. In addition, these famous constructions are paradoxically poorly documented in the textual sources,[166] and the toponyms are often altered: from archaeology, we know a number of these sites by their modern names, while many of their medieval names are lost to us. Finally, the majority of these edifices are especially problematic when it comes to dating and attribution, as few can offer incontestable inscriptions of foundation. This is the case for Qaṣr al-Ḥayr al-Sharqī – which Genequand correctly categorises as a new Umayyad city rather than a "desert castle" – where an inscription that unfortunately is now lost described Hishām's foundation of a city (*madīna*). Elsewhere, other inscriptions that mention the name of an Umayyad prince or caliph do not necessarily mark an act of creation, but rather an act of appropriation. This is the case at Qaṣr Burquʿ, to which we shall return below.

Perhaps more than any other, one site in particular sheds light on these complex dating problems: Quṣayr ʿAmra. Since its discovery by Musil,[167] the baths adorned with magnificent paintings at this site have fascinated scholars.[168] The most famous of these frescoes, that of the six kings, is one such gem. Setting aside its artistic dimensions, this representation of six rulers of the world coming to pledge their allegiance to the caliph is the site's primary dating element. The six figures represented are designated by bilingual inscriptions in Arabic and Greek. Four names remain legible: Qayṣar, Kisrā, Najāshī and Lūdhrīq.[169] The identities of the first three are not difficult to determine;

---

also Genequand, *Les établissements*, 388–9, who notes in addition that the phenomenon was not limited to the Syrian space, as attested by the site of Tulūl al-Ukhayḍir (or Qaṣr Muqātil) in Iraq, near Karbalā'. On this site, see Finster and Schmidt, "Sasanidische und frühislamische Ruinen" and "The Origin of 'Desert Castles'." On the Umayyad sites in Iraq, see Northedge, *Entre Amman et Samarra*, 54–6. Northedge has also drawn scholarly attention to pre-Islamic Arabia, "The Umayyad Desert Castles."

166 See above, Ch. 4.

167 Musil, *Kusejr Amra*. On the chaotic conditions of this discovery, see Fowden, *Quṣayr ʿAmra*, 3 ff.

168 See Musil, *Kusejr Amra*; Almagro, *Qusayr Amra*; Fowden, *Quṣayr ʿAmra*; and Vibert-Guigue, *Les peintures de Qusayr ʿAmra*. Interest in these frescoes has long meant that research has focused almost entirely on the baths, to the neglect of other structures at the site, including a residence. Genequand has worked to partially overcome this deficit, and has most significantly offered information on the mosque. See Genequand, "Une mosquée à Quṣayr ʿAmra."

169 Or perhaps Rūdhrīq. For the last two figures on this fresco, whose names have disappeared, it has been proposed that they represent a Khāqān or a Chinese emperor as well as a Turkish or Indian prince. See Fowden, *Quṣayr ʿAmra*, 207.

they are the rulers of: Byzantium – the Caesar; Sasanian Iran – the Khosrow;[170] and Ethiopia – the Negus of Abyssinia. The fourth name poses some difficulty, as it may be read several different ways, but the Greek inscription clarifies the situation by offering the name *Rodorikos*.[171] This reading has long been associated with the last Visigoth ruler, Roderic, who was defeated by Muslim armies during the conquest of Spain in 92/711. This identification has served as a basis for dating the construction: it is undoubtedly an Umayyad edifice, and as such it must have been built between 92/711 and 132/750.[172] While Musil tried to link its construction to al-Walīd b. Yazīd, the baths have been almost unanimously attributed to al-Walīd b. ʿAbd al-Malik, during whose reign the decisive battle against the Visigoths took place.[173] Sauvaget, however, claimed that attribution to a specific caliph was not possible for epigraphic reasons. Indeed, one inscription painted at the top of the south wall of the eastern aisle of the reception hall, apparently describing the building's patron, merely designates him with the title *amīr*, rather than *amīr al-muʾminīn*, the standard titulature for caliphs.[174] On the basis of these observations, Grabar at one point suggested that Quṣayr ʿAmra be attributed to Yazīd b. al-Walīd, before seemingly abandoning this interpretation.[175]

Imbert's reading of an as-yet undeciphered inscription, which proposes that the expression *walī ʿahd al-muslimīn* is written on the baldachin atop the prince's head,[176] has led Northedge to theorise that the most likely "patron" for the site is Sulaymān b. ʿAbd al-Malik.[177] The significance of the paintings at Quṣayr ʿAmra lends credence to this hypothesis: could we not understand the

170 It seems indeed here that "Khosrow" is a title, rather than a proper name, as the defeated Sasanian sovereign was named Yazdagird.

171 See Fowden, *Quṣayr ʿAmra*, 204–5.

172 The selection of 92/711 as a *terminus post quem* nevertheless leaves certain questions unanswered, since knowledge of the name of the king of the Visigoths could easily have *preceded* the Muslim army's victory in al-Andalus, and even the conquest of the Iberian peninsula, given that Roderic acceded the throne in 709. For reasons that are difficult to justify, Fowden has proposed that the *terminus post quem* be fixed at 96/715, the year in which Mūsā b. Nuṣayr, conqueror of the Muslim West, returned to Damascus with his Andalusian prize. Fowden, *Quṣayr ʿAmra*, 144. It should also be noted that he had previously settled on the date 711, *Empire to the Commonwealth*, 144.

173 Van Berchem, "Aux pays de Moab," 367–70; Herzfeld, "ʿAmra," 338–9; Jaussen and Savignac, *Mission archéologique*, 111; Creswell, *Early Muslim*, 400–1.

174 Sauvaget, "Remarques sur les monuments," 13–5.

175 Grabar, "The Painting," 187 and "La place," 82.

176 Imbert, *Corpus*, 440–2 and "Note épigraphique."

177 Northedge, *Entre Amman et Samarra*, 57. Sulaymān was the heir designated by al-Walīd I, while the future al-Walīd II only reached this status under the caliphate of his father, Yazīd b. ʿAbd al-Malik.

fresco of the six kings as conveying hope for the achievement of Islam's universal calling and thus the conquest of the entire known world? Does this painting not constitute a memorial to Umayyad *victories*?[178] If this is indeed the case, the decisive protagonist is no longer the Visigoth king but rather Caesar, who seems, like his counterparts, destined for defeat. Could this representation really have occurred *after* the failed siege of Constantinople in 99/717? Who better than Sulaymān – he who, upon reaching the throne, would lead the largest offensive ever launched against the Byzantine capital – to illustrate Umayyad triumph on the walls of Quṣayr ʿAmra? This, however, is an impossible question to answer, since, as we saw in Chapter 5, a discourse proclaiming Maslama's symbolic victory had already been created. This example shows the difficulties of attribution associated with the "desert castles," even when they possess elements by which to date them.[179]

178 A Greek inscription on a fresco on the southern wall of the west wing may corroborate this theory: *NIKH*, 'victory' (or perhaps *CAPA NIKH*, "the victory of Sarah" or "victory to Sarah", or else *XAPIC NIKH*, "Grace" and "Victory"). The Arabic inscription accompanying the painting is unfortunately illegible, but it begins with the *basmala*. See Fowden, *Empire to Commonwealth*, 145–9 and *Quṣayr ʿAmra*, 175, 191 ff.; Cheddadi, *Les Arabes et l'appropriation de l'histoire*, 27–8. The idea of a monument commemorating Umayyad triumphs was first proposed in 1909 by van Berchem, who consequently suggested that the monument be associated with al-Walīd I, "*Aux pays du Moab*," 369.

179 It should also be noted that, of the four identifiable figures, three are only designated by their *titles*, not their *names*. Why, then, should Roderic be the only exception? While the text of the Greek inscription seemingly leaves little doubt as to this figure's identity, it should be added that people from the medieval West were subject to a certain fluidity in classical Islamic literature. In the *Murūj*, al-Masʿūdī presents the rulers of the world in the following manner: "the Persians [have their] Khosrows; the Rūm, their Caesars; the Abyssinians, their Negus; the Turks, their Khāqāns. The ruler […] of Spain [is called] *Lūdhrīq, which is a name common to all the kings of this country* […] *The last Lūdhrīq* was killed by Ṭāriq, *mawlā* of Mūsā b. Nuṣayr, when he conquered Spain and captured Toledo, the capital" (*Murūj*, vol. I, 359–60, trans. Pellat vol. I, 145–6). There was thus some confusion over a ruler's given name and that of his dynasty. Later in the *Murūj*, al-Masʿūdī also mentions the "court of the Visigoth kings (*ladhāriqa*)" (*Murūj*, vol. II, 37, trans. Pellat vol. I, 171). Elsewhere, however, he makes a clear distinction between the ruler's name (or that of his dynasty) and his titulature. He specifies that "the title Caesar became common to all the kings of Rūm" (*Murūj*, vol. II, 297, trans. Pellat vol. II, 270). These elements show that, at an unknown moment, the name *Lūdhrīq* designated the Visigoths, without further distinction (al-Masʿūdī also attributes the name *Lūdhrīq* to the Frankish kings, which may be the result of his confusion with the similar name *Lūdhwīq*, *Murūj*, vol. III, 70–1, trans. Pellat vol. II, 345). These uncertainties recall those of the Christian authors, who identified the caliphs as *Mirmumnus* (in the case of Hishām) – or some other distortion of *amīr al-muʾminīn* – which was generally considered a proper name rather than a title (for example, see Willibald's account of his pilgrimage, in which his companions left to see the "king of the Arabs named Mirmumnus," Wilkinson, *Jerusalem Pilgrims*, 245.

Returning to Musil's theses, Fowden has defended the attribution of Quṣayr ʿAmra to another heir to the throne, namely the future al-Walīd II, whose presence in the region is well documented, especially under the caliphate of Hishām.[180] This suggestion remains hypothetical, as it is based largely on the questionable identification of various other figures from several different frescoes depicting al-Walīd b. Yazīd's political projects.[181]

The situation is further complicated by the fact that, while multiple elements at Quṣayr ʿAmra may be presented as evidence that it was an Umayyad construction, this interpretation is far from assured for most of the other "desert castles." Indeed, while modern scholarship has more or less systematically associated a given edifice with a particular caliph or heir to the throne, it is only recently that a small number of works have addressed the possibility that these sites were built by elites rather than caliphs.[182] Bacharach's article is misleading in this respect, as his argument rests entirely on the identity of the sites' "patrons," whom he defines as individuals "who had primary responsibility for initiating a building project."[183] While the general vision of this study has a solid foundation,[184] based as it is on the notion of Umayyad patrimonialism, the idea that all site sponsors were Umayyad princes is less obvious. The sovereign's movements were a powerful incentive to begin new construction, but it was not necessarily the ruler himself – or even a member of his family – who "initiated" the building of a given structure. However, the general tendency in the scholarship is to follow Bacharach's thinking, even though this conception of patronage undoubtedly conceals the architectural initiatives of local elites trying to create structural networks designed to "attract" the caliphal itinerary to their areas. The *ashrāf* surely possessed the financial means to undertake these building projects, many of which could potentially figure into a strategy of local economic development.[185] The convergence of the interests of the Marwanid family and local elites is clear, although it simultaneously introduced an unavoidable competition whose consequences form an evolving

On the perception of the "Saracens" in the medieval West, see Tolan, *Les Sarrasins*). This confusion is not systematic in the Latin sources, however, as attested by the *Mozarabic Chronicle of 754*, which states that al-Walīd II's titulary was "*amir almuminim*" (*754*, § 71, trans. Hoyland, 628). This is the oldest extant reference to this terminology in a non-Muslim source, as Hoyland notes, *Seeing*, 628, note 96.

180 On the prince's presence in the region, see al-Ṭabarī, vol. II, 1743, 1795, trans. vol. XXVI, 91, 148.

181 Fowden, *Quṣayr ʿAmra*.

182 See Northedge, *Entre Amman et Samarra*, 56 ff.

183 Bacharach, "Marwanid Umayyad Building Activities," 27.

184 See Northedge, *Entre Amman et Samarra*, 57.

185 On the subject of the elites' financial resources, see Kennedy, "Elite Incomes."

map of the topographies of power. The current state of our knowledge, however, makes it impossible to illuminate the policies of these elites, and it is only their associations with Marwanid princes that are able to guide us through the twists and turns of these networks.

Despite these uncertainties, it is nevertheless interesting to try to sketch a general outline. Starting in 72/692, new circumstances forced ʿAbd al-Malik to initiate a "familial project" of immense magnitude. Beyond inscribing Islam into space, as evidenced by the erection of great mosques, one aspect of this project related to the caliph's ability to solidify his own authority vis-à-vis the primary agents of Syrian power. ʿAbd al-Malik responded to this need by instituting an itinerant exercise of power. In addition, given that he could not be in all four corners of the province at once, he *delegated* his mobility, first and foremost to his sons, in order to spatialise territory. The patrimonial sovereignty that developed was accompanied by the creation of networks that, at the local level, provided suitable conditions for this shared itinerance.

The strategy was immediately visible on the landscape: an inscription on a lintel at Qaṣr Burquʿ attributes the construction of the *buyūt* to the *amīr* al-Walīd, son of the Commander of the Faithful, and is dated to 81/700–701.[186] This inscription does not mark the foundation of the site, which had been occupied at least since the end of the Byzantine era, but rather its reorganisation. King noted that reusing the site of Qaṣr Burquʿ corresponded less to "a princely desire for solitude in the basalt wasteland [...] than with command of the route between northern Arabia and central Syria, and with the political relations of the tribes with the caliphate."[187] Other sites have been linked to al-Walīd on less certain evidence, including Jabal Says[188] and Qaryatayn.[189] It has been suggested that the appropriation of these three sites reveals al-Walīd's movements;[190] perhaps they are better seen as the establishment of a new itinerary for the exercise of mobile power, although the inclusion of Qaryatayn in this framework seems less assured. It would make more sense to add Khirbat al-Bayḍāʾ to this list, a site that Gaube attributed to the Ghassanids, although it

186 Gaube, "An Examination," 94, 97; Shboul, "On the Later Arabic Inscription." Robinson suggests that this inscription demonstrates that al-Walīd was henceforth named as heir in his father's line of succession instead of his uncle, ʿAbd al-ʿAzīz. See *ʿAbd al-Malik*, 27.

187 King, cited by MacAdam, "Settlements," 66.

188 Al-Bakrī, *Muʿjam*, ed. Wüstenfeld, 122. See also Brisch, "Le château omeyyade;" Sauvaget, "Les ruines omeyyades;" Northedge, *Entre Amman et Samarra*, 41; Bacharach, "Marwanid Umayyad Building Activities," 31–2.

189 *Kitāb al-Aghānī*, vol. XII, 32. See also Genequand, "Châteaux omeyyades de Palmyrène," 27–8.

190 Bacharach, "Marwanid Umayyad Building Activities," 32.

could in actuality date to the Umayyad period, when it would regardless have been subject to occupation.[191] If these theories are valid, al-Walīd would have been particularly active in the basalt deserts east of the Ḥawrān. This is an important point, as scholars often tend to associate the prince with the same locales frequented by his father, namely Damascus and Jerusalem.[192] These two cities may have had some sort of "caliphal prerogative," and al-Walīd, like his brothers, could have been assigned a particular area prior to his caliphate. In any case, we must not attempt to make our sketch too detailed, for, as we have seen, regions of patrimonial sovereignty did not correspond to any supposed administrative divisions,[193] and had fluid borders. It should also be noted that other sites, among them Khirbat al-Minya, Qaṣr al-Hallabat, Qaṣr Kharāna, and even ʿAnjar and Quṣayr ʿAmra, have been associated with al-Walīd, although the majority of these claims are contested today.[194] Two well-documented geographic areas, Balqāʾ and Palmyrena, permit further investigation.

8.2.2.2 Balqāʾ and Palmyrena: Elements of Historical Topography

The region of Balqāʾ, near Amman, offers a close-knit network of Umayyad sites.[195] The locations of these sites strongly suggest the existence of an itinerant mode of power, with numerous "castles" conveniently distributed at equal distances that almost certainly correspond to a short day's journey (see fig. 1). Yazīd b. ʿAbd al-Malik and his son, al-Walīd b. Yazīd, are the primary figures associated with this area, although Sulaymān was also active here. However, few concrete elements of attribution exist, and most of these sites do not clearly identify a specific patron. Al-Muwaqqar is an exception, as an inscription on a capital atop a graduated column which served as a gauge attributes the construction of the cistern adjacent to the "castle" to the caliph Yazīd II in 104/722–723.[196] It appears that this cistern was directly connected to the site

191 Gaube, *Ein arabischer Palast*. However, the author recently reconsidered the question and suggested that dating it to the period of ʿAbd al-Malik is also possible, "Wie ist Khirbat al-Bayḍāʾ." Northedge had already made this argument, *Entre Amman et Samarra*, 47.

192 See Bacharach, "Marwanid Umayyad Building Activities," 31–4.

193 On the older administrative division of the Shām, see Walmsley, *The Administrative Structure*; Haldon, "Seventh-Century Continuities;" Lilie, "Araber und Themen."

194 See Flood, *The Great Mosque*, 186–7, for a discussion of these different theories.

195 See MacAdam, "Settlements and Settlement Patterns," for a regional summary with a valuable bibliography, and Northedge, *Entre Amman et Samarra*, 57–60. On Amman, see Gaube, "ʿAmmān, Kharāne und Qasṭal;" Northedge, *Studies*; Almagro, *El Palacio*; Almagro et al., "El Palacio Omeyade;" Olavarri-Goioechea, *El Palacio Omeya*.

196 It has also been suggested that the site was connected with ʿAbd al-Malik based on a passage in Abū Zurʿa al-Dimashqī, in which the caliph leaves Jerusalem to take refuge at al-Muwaqqar to protect himself from the plague (*Taʾrīkh*, vol. 1, 409).

and operations of the domain rather than the road network.[197] The inscription confirms Yāqūt's similar assertion linking al-Muwaqqar to Yazīd b. ʿAbd al-Malik.[198] Per al-Ṭabarī, when relations between Hishām and al-Walīd b. Yazīd began to deteriorate,[199] the latter settled near al-Azraq[200] at a water source (*māʾ*) named al-Aghdaf.[201] Musil studied this topographic question and suggested that al-Aghdaf was at the site of Qaṣr Ṭūba,[202] around sixty kilometres south of the oasis at al-Azraq, a hypothesis that Sauvaget rejected.[203] According to al-Balādhurī, the future al-Walīd II took up residence at al-Azraq.[204]

Other constructions in the region pose problems of attribution similar to those previously mentioned at Quṣayr ʿAmra. Without giving an exhaustive presentation of these sites, it should be noted that an inscription dated Muḥarram 92 (29 October–27 November 710) was discovered at Qaṣr al-Kharāna.[205] This find corroborates the theory that a roadway was developed in the direction of the oasis at al-Azraq, one that undoubtedly began at Amman and passed through al-Muwaqqar. Qaṣr al-Mushāsh[206] was almost certainly part of the same project, as was Qaṣr al-Hallabat, albeit on a more northerly route.[207] Qaṣr al-Hallabat, connected to the baths at Ḥammām al-Sarākh,[208] must have allowed for greater circulation in the north, in the direction of the Ḥawrān. Some of these sites may have been founded by elites, and at several, the continuity of their occupation – despite the scarcity of nearby resources, especially water – attests to their powers of attraction. The region also benefited from a certain amount of constant activity, as evidenced by the repair work conducted on mosaics in a number of churches.[209]

---

197 Hamilton, "An Eighth-Century;" Genequand, "Économie de production, affirmation du pouvoir et *dolce vita*."

198 Yāqūt, *Muʿjam*, vol. V, 226.

199 On the conflict between the two men, see Judd, *The Third Fitna*, 68 ff.

200 The site, which consists of a Roman fort and a castle built from raw brick, remains to be studied. See MacAdam, "Settlements and Settlement Patterns," 67–8 and Genequand, "Projet implantations umayyades," 140–1.

201 Al-Ṭabarī, vol. II, 1743, 1795, trans. vol. XXVI, 91, 148.

202 Musil, *Palmyrena*, 285.

203 Sauvaget, "Remarques," 26–8; Gabrieli, "Al-Walīd b. Yazīd."

204 Derenk, *Leben*, 10.

205 Abbott, "The Kaṣr Ḫarāna;" Urice, *Qasr Kharana*; Jaussen and Savignac, *Mission archéologique*; Imbert, "Inscriptions et espaces d'écriture," 404–6.

206 Bisheh, "Qasr Mshash;" Genequand, "Projet implantations umayyades," 142–4.

207 Bisheh, "Excavations," "Qaṣr al-Hallabat;" Arce, "Qasr al-Hallabât," should be consulted with caution.

208 Bisheh, "Hammam al-Sarah."

209 These churches were interpreted as Umayyad-era constructions by Piccirillo ("The Umayyad Churches"), a claim later contested by Gatier ("Les mosaïques paléochrétiennes," 293), who was of the opinion that they were restorations.

South of Amman, the sheer concentration of structures is such that it has sustained scholarly interest. Genequand remarked that Umm al-Walīd,[210] al-Qasṭal, Mshattā and Zīzāʾ all exist "within a miniscule territory."[211] This aggregation of sites could indicate certain strategic reorientations toward the end of the Umayyad era. Al-Ṭabarī reports that al-Walīd II fed pilgrims and their animals returning from the *ḥajj* at Zīzāʾ, where he offered them hospitality for three days.[212] Mshattā has also been linked to this caliph,[213] and a passage in the *History of the Patriarchs of Alexandria* has been interpreted in support of this hypothesis. If we are to believe the author of the pertinent section, who, as noted above, was a contemporary of the period,[214] al-Walīd constructed a city in the steppe bearing his name (*madīna ʿalā ismihi fī al-bariyya*). The city was not conveniently located, as water had to be drawn from a well fifteen miles from the building site; this difficulty caused the death of numerous workers, even despite the use of two rotating teams of 600 camels to ensure a constant supply of water.[215] Topographic and environmental conditions remain ambiguous, however, making it impossible to confidently identify Mshattā as the site of this city. If Mshattā is indeed connected with al-Walīd II, it must be noted that al-Qasṭal is clearly a much earlier site. This castle, with its ornate mosaics crafted by artists from the school of Madaba,[216] is known to us from the Arabic sources. The poet Kuthayyir ʿAzza (d. 105/723) mentions it: "may God bless this family that resides from al-Muwaqqar to Qasṭal al-Balqāʾ, there where the reception hall (*maḥārib*) lies."[217] Given that these verses are addressed to Yazīd II, the patron of al-Muwaqqar, it has been proposed that his father, ʿAbd al-Malik, be associated with al-Qasṭal, rather than his brother and rival, al-Walīd b. ʿAbd al-Malik.[218]

---

210 Bujard and Genequand, "Umm al-Walīd."

211 Genequand, "Économie de production, affirmation du pouvoir et *dolce vita*."

212 Al-Ṭabarī, vol. II, 1754, trans. vol. XXVI, 103–4. Unfortunately, we do not possess any archaeological evidence for this site, which remains undiscovered to this day.

213 For more on the epigraphic and numismatic evidence in favour of an Umayyad dating for this site, see Bisheh, "Qaṣr al-Mshatta." Grabar proposed that Mshattā was an Abbasid construction, "The Date." See also Hillenbrand, "Islamic Art at the Crossroads" and Whitcomb, "Amman, Hesban, and Abbasid Archaeology."

214 On John of Wasīm, see above, Ch. 3.

215 *History of the Patriarchs*, PO, vol. V, 114–5.

216 Carlier and Morin, "Qastal al-Balqaʾ."

217 Kuthayyir ʿAzza, *Dīwān*, vol. II, 130. Here I have borrowed Sauvaget's translation, "Remarques," 20, note 2. See his discussion of this meaning of *maḥārib*, which he also suggests translating to "exedra," or the semi-circular room or alcove where the prince held court. On Kuthayyir, see ʿAbbās, "Kuthayyir."

218 Carlier and Morin, "Qastal al-Balqaʾ," 206.

These different networks may well overlap. The oldest of them, around al-Qasṭal in the direction of al-Muwaqqar or Umm al-Walīd, allowed for the mobile exercise of power south of Amman. Mshattā was part of an urban project initiated by al-Walīd II and thus distinct; Zīzāʾ was likely part of the road network developed throughout the Shām, here in the direction of the Hijaz, as attested by its use as a rest-stop for pilgrims. Al-Ṭabarī calls the site a *manzil*, which may be evidence of its more traditional function as a stopover residence. It should also be noted that other constructions connected to water resources are present in the region, always in relation to the development of *ḥajj* routes. The inscription of Rāmat Ḥāzim, south of Suwayda in the Ḥawrān, marks Hishām b. ʿAbd al-Malik's foundation of a *birka*.[219] Hishām's establishments of this sort are also mentioned by al-Masʿūdī, who notes that the caliph initiated "the digging of underground canals and reservoirs (*al-qunnā wa-al-birak*) on the route to Mecca."[220] Unlike the cistern at al-Muwaqqar connected to the "castle," the *birka* at Rāmat Ḥāzim was not tied to a specific edifice, but rather directly to the route itself, lending credence to the theory that different functional networks coexisted. As Genequand has noted, this inscription fits into a "caliphal policy concerning communications and pilgrimage," demonstrating the importance of associating a caliph with a "hydraulic monument."[221] We shall now turn to another significant site connected with Hishām: Palmyrena.

Although the region has suffered from archaeological comparisons to the Balqāʾ, which has long sustained more continuous interest from scholars, Genequand's recent studies are a welcome step toward overcoming this deficit (see fig. 1).[222] The area is closely linked to Hishām b. ʿAbd al-Malik. The two most famous sites, Qaṣr al-Ḥayr al-Gharbī and Qaṣr al-Ḥayr al-Sharqī, are effectively marked with the caliph's seal. For the former, an epigraph on the lintel of the entrance to the structure generally designated a "*khān*" attributes the site's construction to Hishām in 109/727.[223] For the latter, an inscription of foundation that is now unfortunately lost was located in the mosque and indicated that Hishām had ordered the construction of this city (*madīna*) in 110/728–729; the work was carried out by the *ahl Ḥimṣ*.[224] Despite these two

219 Rihaoui, "Découverte;" Genequand, "Économie de production, affirmation et *docle vita*," 158.

220 Al-Masʿūdī, *Murūj*, vol. V, 466, trans. Pellat vol. IV, 889.

221 Genequand, "Économie de production, affirmation du pouvoir et *dolce vita*," 158.

222 Genequand, "Châteaux omeyyades de Palmyrène" and *Les établissements*.

223 *RCEA*, vol. I, 23, n. 27; Schlumberger, *Qasr el-Heir el-Gharbi*; Genequand, "Châteaux omeyyades de Palmyrène" and "Some Thoughts."

224 Grabar et al., *City in the Desert*, 191 (with the history of the inscription's discovery and its previous publications).

epigraphic attestations, the toponymy associated with Hishām poses numerous problems. The two Qaṣr al-Ḥayr today bear names unknown to ancient authors,[225] who, for their part, associate other toponyms with Hishām. These questions have been subject to longstanding debates, which we shall briefly discuss below.

First, we must quickly address the question of Ruṣāfa Hishām, which Sauvaget suggested be identified as Qaṣr al-Ḥayr al-Sharqī[226] but which is now clearly recognised as the city of al-Ruṣāfa, formerly Sergiopolis.[227] Al-Ṭabarī expressly states that Hishām lived at al-Ruṣāfa, which he defined as a Byzantine city (*madīna rūmiyya*) in the region (*arḍ*) of Qinnasrīn. The caliph selected this site in the steppe (*al-barriyya*) as a precaution against the plague (*ṭāʿūn*) and had two castles (*qaṣrayn*) there.[228] It is tempting to think that here al-Ṭabarī is referencing certain palatial structures identified outside the southern walls of the old city.[229] German excavations may soon offer a clearer image of the situation, as have the results of archaeological work conducted within the walls of al-Ruṣāfa, on the mosque in particular.[230]

Al-Ruṣāfa is also mentioned in relation to Hishām's accession to the caliphate. Again according to al-Ṭabarī, ʿAbd al-Malik's son happened to be in al-Zaytūna, where he owned a house (*manzil*) on a small property (*duwayra*), when the scepter and seal (*al-ʿaṣā wa-al-khātm*) arrived by mail (*al-barīd*): in possession of these caliphal insignia, Hishām was recognised as the new ruler. He then left al-Ruṣāfa for Damascus.[231] This obscure passage led Sauvaget at one time to conclude that al-Zaytūna and al-Ruṣāfa were two names for a single location

225 It should be noted, however, that Qaṣr al-Ḥayr al-Gharbī was likely also that designated by the name 'al-Ḥayr' (as a postal station) in a Mamluk source. See Schlumberger, *Qasr el-Heir el-Gharbi*, 26; Genequand, "Some Thoughts."

226 Sauvaget, "Remarques," 1–13. Astonishingly, this is the interpretation that occurs in the relevant volume of Blankinship's translation of al-Ṭabarī, *The History of al-Ṭabarī*, vol. XXV, 2, note 7.

227 See Grabar et al., *City in the Desert*, 13; Fowden, *The Barbarian Plain*; Sack, *Resafa IV*.

228 Al-Ṭabarī, vol. II, 1737–8, trans. vol. XXVI, 80–1. See also *Kitāb al-ʿuyūn*, vol. I, 101.

229 Two of these exterior areas have been excavated: one, a palace briefly studied by Otto-Dorn ("Grabung"), the other a "pavilion" examined by Ulbert ("Ein umaiyadischer"). See also Sack et al., "Resafa-Umland" and Konrad, "Resafa-Rusafat Hisham," as well as Genequand, *Les établissements*, which confirms the identification of at least two "true castles, [while] other [edifices] offer plans that place them more clearly in the category of large residences," 234.

230 Sack, *Resafa IV*. For an overview of the archaeological projects conducted by Dorothée Sack at al-Ruṣāfa between 2006 and 2011, see http://bauforschung-denkmalpflege.de/resafa/ (consulted 10 December 2022).

231 Al-Ṭabarī, vol. II, 1467, trans. vol. XXV, 2.

(which he identified as Qaṣr al-Ḥayr al-Sharqī),[232] before later revising his earlier view and stating that al-Zaytūna should be sought in the vicinity of al-Raqqa on the eastern banks of the Euphrates.[233] Today, this hypothesis is the most probable one, taking into account a broader corpus of texts, notably including the *Chronicle of Zuqnīn*. This source indicates that Hishām had canals dug at Zaytūn and Hanī,[234] which corroborates al-Balādhurī's version mentioning the prince's undertakings at Wāsiṭ al-Raqqa.[235] Hishām's route between al-Zaytūna and Damascus thus logically would have passed by al-Ruṣāfa. Scholars have long been obsessed with identifying the site of al-Zaytūna, and multiple theories have been suggested, among them the ancient Zaytā – located on the Euphrates, south of Qarqīsiyya – and Qaṣr al-Ḥayr al-Gharbī.[236] The toponym was common, and thus could refer to many different homonymous locations, all of which merely adds to the confusion.[237]

In a perfect illustration of the patrimonial system developed by the Umayyads, Hishām, prior to his caliphate, received a parcel of land (*uqṭiʿ arḍan*) named Dūrayn.[238] The reading of this toponym is uncertain, and some prefer the reading Dawrīn[239] in reference to a canal of the same name located on the eastern bank of the Euphrates, south of the Khābūr.[240] The Nahr Dawrīn, however, is not known by this name in the textual sources; it may predate the Islamic period, although this point has sustained lively debates.[241] The reading Dūrayn is also hypothetical, even though similar names (Dūr, Dūrān)

232 Sauvaget, "Remarques," 4 ff.; Grabar rejects the identification of al-Ruṣāfa with Qaṣr al-Ḥayr al-Sharqī, instead linking al-Zaytūna with the latter site, *City in the Desert*, 13.

233 Sauvaget, "Notes de topographie," 103. See also Kellner-Heinkele, "Rusâfa in den arabischen Quellen." Ulbert suggests identifying Zaytūna as al-Khulla, "Die umaiyadische Anlage," 22.

234 *Zuqnīn*, 171, trans. Harrak, 160–1.

235 Al-Balādhurī, *Futūḥ*, 180; Meinecke, "Al-Raḳḳa." The sources prefer *al-Hanī wa-al-Marī* for these two canals, which further complicates the situation. Al-Marī and al-Zaytūn could be two names for the same installation, so caution must still be exercised.

236 For a detailed presentation of these different hypotheses, see Rousset, "La moyenne vallée de l'Euphrate," 565, note 7.

237 Genequand, "Économie de production, affirmation du pouvoir et *dolce vita*," 159.

238 Al-Ṭabarī, vol. II, 1735, trans. vol. XXVI, 77; al-Balādhurī, *Ansāb*, vol. VI B, 15.

239 This is Hillenbrand's solution adopted in the translation cited in the previous footnote. The two other occurrences of the word in the *Taʾrīkh al-rusul wa-al-mulūk* were both rendered as Dūrayn. See al-Ṭabarī, vol. II, 1433, 1895, trans. vol. XXIV, 163, vol. XXVII, 7. See also al-Balādhurī, *Ansāb*, vol. VI B, 15.

240 The canal has been subject to numerous excavations and digs led by Berthier, *Peuplement rural*, 32 ff.

241 Berthier, *Peuplement rural*, 32 ff., Rousset, "La moyenne vallée de l'Euphrate," 566; Genequand, "Économie de production, affirmation du pouvoir et *dolce vita*," 159.

occur more frequently in the texts; this is once more indicative of the inherent difficulties surrounding toponyms associated with Hishām. Be it Dūrayn or Dawrīn, Hishām found the site in ruins when he took possession of it and, in exchange for 400 dinar, he had some unscrupulous scribe add the phrase "Dūrayn and its villages (*qurā*)" to the *dīwāns*, which allowed him henceforth to collect substantial revenue on the land.[242]

The problems arising from the locations connected with Hishām do not permit us to form any precise ideas about his movements in Palmyrena. However, his undeniable ties to the two Qaṣr al-Ḥayr, al-Ruṣāfa, Wāsiṭ al-Raqqa, and various other sites in the Euphrates valley clearly demarcate the area of his mobility. Bacharach's suggestion that Arak and al-Sukhna be added to this list remains mere speculation in the absence of any definitive archaeological evidence.[243] Palmyra does not provide any more certainty, although it is tempting to connect the souk[244] uncovered along the *decumanus* with Hishām, whose investment in similar projects is known and attested in the epigraphy at Baysān.[245] It has been suggested that this market has ties to ʿAbd al-Malik,[246] who, through Hishām, could potentially have exercised patrimonial sovereignty in the region. The recent discovery of a mosque in the centre of Palmyra, likely from the Umayyad era, may reveal dating elements that can clarify the situation somewhat.[247] Other Umayyad sites, such as Qudaym[248] or Qaryatayn,[249] complement the coverage of Palmyrena,[250] although the sites are more widely scattered than in the Balqāʾ. Al-Bakhrāʾ, located around twenty kilometres south of Palmyra, is without question the most famous site after the two Qaṣr al-Ḥayr; indeed, al-Walīd II was assassinated there.[251]

Hishām's travels are only recorded when he left Palmyrena, including his aforementioned journey to Damascus after receiving the caliphal insignia. It

242 Hishām was hardly grateful to the scribe who had so contributed to his good fortune, and later, during his caliphate, even refused to give him a post as governor under the pretext that he had falsified the registers! Al-Ṭabarī, vol. II, 1735, trans. vol. XXVI, 77; al-Balādhurī, *Ansāb*, vol. VI B, 15.

243 Bacharach, "Marwanid Umayyad Building Activities," 31.

244 Al-Asʿad and Stepniowski, "The Umayyad Sûq;" Foote, *Umayyad Markets* and "Commerce." See also Genequand, "An Early Umayyad Mosque in Palmyra."

245 Khamis, "Two Wall Mosaic Inscriptions."

246 Foote, *Umayyad Markets*, 207.

247 Genequand, "An Early Islamic Mosque in Palmyra" and *Les établissements*, 52–67.

248 Genequand, "Châteaux omeyyades de Palmyrène," 11–2.

249 *Kitāb al-Aghānī*, vol. XII, 32; Genequand, "Châteaux omeyyades de Palmyrène," 27–8.

250 Genequand, "Châteaux omeyyades de Palmyrène," 28.

251 Al-Ṭabarī, vol. II, 1796–7, trans. vol. XXVI, 149–50, 156 ff.; Genequand, "Al-Bakhraʾ" and "Châteaux omeyyades de Palmyrène," 13–8.

may legitimately be supposed that this trip of capital importance, given the challenges accompanying every aspect of succession, was highly ritualised, especially the new caliph's entry into Damascus. The sources, unfortunately, have little to say on this subject,[252] just as they offer limited information on the details of the *ḥajj* completed by the caliph in 106/724–725 and again in 125/742–743.[253] Agapius of Manbij and the anonymous chronicler of *1234* report that the caliph stayed briefly in Malaṭiya, after which he returned to Damascus.[254] For a caliphate that lasted nearly twenty years, these few mentions seem meager indeed. The impression the sources give is that Hishām spent the majority of his time in or near al-Ruṣāfa,[255] an idea confirmed by the important constructions he undertook in the region. The Christian sources are especially prolix on the subject, and create the image of an administrative sovereign concerned with stimulating the economic production of the Euphrates valley (see Table 8.1).

The area in which these projects were concentrated explains the interest of the Syriac authors, who place particular emphasis on agriculture. They report the digging of canals around al-Raqqa to serve the needs of the many plantations in the region. Cities (*mdīnātā*), palaces (*ḥeṣnē*) and villages (*qūrīhā*) were also constructed,[256] and a bridge was built over the Euphrates at al-Raqqa.[257] Various commercial structures are also mentioned: *khānāt, ḥawānīt, ḥujar*.[258]

It is interesting to note that these references are older, as they occur in the historiographic layer that ends in 728 in the anonymous Syriac chronicles of *819* and *846*. It must thus be concluded that these ambitious policies were initiated at the latest during the first years of Hishām's caliphate. However, the program's scale would seem to indicate a much earlier starting date, perhaps at a time when the prince was exerting his patrimonial sovereignty over the zone. Maslama b. ʿAbd al-Malik also undertook major works in the neighboring region, near Bālis. At the insistence of the area's inhabitants, he also had a

252 On Umayyad ceremonial, see Grabar, *Ceremonial and Art*, and Marsham, *Rituals*, 81–180.

253 Al-Ṭabarī, vol. II, 1796–7, 1802 ff., trans. vol. XXVI, 149–50, 156 ff.; Genequand, "Al-Bakhra'" and "Châteaux omeyyades de Palmyrène," 13–8.

254 Agapius, *Kitāb al-ʿunwān*, 508; *1234*, vol. I, 312, Latin trans. 243.

255 As previously noted by Gabrieli, *Il Califfato*, 134. On the reasons behind his selection of al-Ruṣāfa, see Fowden, *The Barbarian Plain*, 174 ff.

256 *819*, 16, trans. 11; *846*, 235, Latin trans. 178, trans. Brooks, 584; *Zuqnīn*, 171, trans. Harrak, 160–1; Theophanes, *Chronography*, 403, trans. 557; Agapius, *Kitāb al-ʿunwān*, 505; Michael the Syrian, vol. II, 457, French trans. 490; *1234*, 309, Latin trans. 241.

257 *Zuqnīn*, 175, trans. Harrak, 165.

258 Such is the list provided by Agapius, *Kitāb al-ʿunwān*, 505. See also *819*, 16, trans. 11; *846*, 235, Latin trans. 178, trans. Brooks, 584. On these vocabulary issues, see Foote, *Umayyad Markets*, 168 ff.

TABLE 8.1 Main information related to Hishām's activities in the Christian sources

	Circuit of Theophilus of Edessa							Circuit of Qartamīn			
Information / Sources	Theophanes	Agapius	1234	Michael the Syrian	775	Zuqnīn	Łewond	819	846	Saʿīd b. Biṭrīq	Buṭrus b. Rāhib
Beginning of caliphate	X	X	X	X	X	X	X	X	X	X	X
Excessive taxation			X	X							
Construction of palaces, cities, etc.	X	X	X	X		X		X	X		
Development of agriculture/plantations	X	X	X	X		X		X	X		
Digging canals	X	X	X	X		X		X	X		
Canal (or bridge) near Raqqa		X	X	X		X		X	X		
Hishām appropriate the *ḍiyāʿ*		X									
Revenue from Hishām's domains exceeds the *kharāj*		X	X	X							
Miserly (*bakhīlan*)										X	X
Hoarding wealth										X	
Location of tomb (Ruṣāfa)										X	
Al-Walīd mistreats members of Hishām's entourage		X	X	X							

canal dug, the Nahr Maslama, in exchange for a third of the revenues (*ghullāt*), and then constructed a palace (*ḥeṣnē*).[259]

Here we touch upon an important economic question that, while largely beyond the scope of this study, is no less a significant part of the Umayyad patrimonial system. Problems of land status and, more precisely, the *ḍiyāʿ*, are what interest us here.[260] As Cahen has noted, these domains had a "social function," as they guaranteed the elites' means of subsistence.[261] Kennedy has recently reaffirmed the significant role played by these properties in creating revenue for the elites, as much under the Umayyads as the Abbasids.[262] The profitability of the system is clear when we consider Umayyad princes such as Sulaymān, Maslama, Saʿīd b. ʿAbd al-Malik, al-ʿAbbās b. al-Walīd, and others.[263] In Hishām's case, the success was such that, according to Agapius of Manbij and Michael the Syrian, the revenues he earned from these domains surpassed the entire *kharāj* of the empire![264] These impressive results would later inspire much admiration for Hishām's methods of governance,[265] while also undoubtedly serving to develop the image of a sovereign who amassed and hoarded great wealth, earning him the nickname "miserly" (*bakhīlan*).[266] While it is impossible here to devote more space to these aspects, we shall see below that they deeply conditioned how the entire system worked.

In sum: the "Umayyad castles" cannot be reduced to a single common function. To the contrary, the different functions proposed by modern scholarship are not mutually exclusive and point toward the reality of the situation. A given site could offer protection from epidemics, serve as a recreational hunting lodge or provide the pleasure of a verdant space in the steppe. Cultivation is necessary for human presence, without implying a systematic economic dimension outside traditional agricultural zones. By proposing a clearly identifiable architectural model, an Umayyad visual culture was created, inscribing Marwanid authority into the Syrian landscape. The location of certain sites with respect to roadways or paths, in addition to the possibilities for tribal contact

259 Al-Balādhurī, *Futūḥ*, 151, trans. 232; *Zuqnīn*, 171, trans. Harrak, 160–1. See also Kennedy, "Elite Incomes," 20–2. On the canals dug by ʿAbd al-Malik's sons, see Genequand, "Économie de production, affirmation du pouvoir et *dolce vita*."

260 On land status as a major affirmation of patrimonial sovereignty, see Décobert, "Du patrimonialisme omeyyade." On the *ḍiyāʿ*, see Cahen, "Ḍayʿa" and Kennedy, "Elite Incomes."

261 Cahen, "Ḍayʿa."

262 Kennedy, "Elite Incomes."

263 Blankinship, *The End of the Jihād State*, 82–3.

264 Agapius, *Kitāb al-ʿunwān*, 505; Michael the Syrian, vol. II, 457, French trans. 490.

265 Al-Ṭabarī, vol. II, 1732, trans. vol. XXVI, 75; Blankinship, *The End of the Jihād State*, 4.

266 See Saʿīd b. Biṭrīq, 46; al-Yaʿqūbī, *Taʾrīkh*, vol. II, 328 and *Mushākalat*, 20; Buṭrus b. Rāhib, *Taʾrīkh*, 57, trans. 63; and Blankinship, *The End of the Jihād State*, 79, note 19.

they offered, are of a different nature. However, the theory associating the "desert castles" with centres of circulation possesses a "fundamental truth,"[267] although it is deceptive in that it does not distinguish between the various protagonists of this Umayyad mobility. These elements respond first and foremost to the needs of an itinerant kingship that developed at the regional level in the context of patrimonial sovereignty. These policies were primarily initiated by ʿAbd al-Malik in order to assert control over the Shām. The solution adopted was to *delegate* caliphal mobility to the Marwanid princes, which led to an intense territorialisation of the Syrian space. Because this mobility was confided in others, the caliph could progressively establish himself in a preferred residence, as Hishām did. The rapid evolution of ʿAbd al-Malik's system was not without consequences. We shall now turn our attention to this question and the limitations of this form of government.

8.2.3 *Mobility Lost*

One of the primary effects of this mode of governance, which generated substantial resources, was to create strong rivalries and conflicts of interest. Hishām's aforementioned machinations to increase the size of the domain assigned to him is a testament to these economic stakes. Thus far, our discussion has focused on the Marwanids and, more specifically, on ʿAbd al-Malik's direct descendants. The potential for fierce competition between these claimants to the throne has already been discussed above. As often happens, the conflict served to bring actors who were otherwise lost to history to the fore. Umayyad patrimonialism must be understood in the broadest familial sense, to say nothing of the others who profited from this system. However, the clan is not limited to the Marwanids, nor even the Sufyanids, but includes other branches as well, in particular the Banū Muʿayṭ, the sons of Abū ʿAmr b. Umayya.

Al-Balādhurī reports that a descendant of Abū Muʿayṭ owned several mills (*arḥāʾ*)[268] and other holdings from which he derived revenue (*mustaghallāt*) at Acre.[269] Hishām tried in vain to persuade this man to cede these possessions; his refusal eventually motivated the caliph's decision to transfer the arsenal (*al-ṣināʿa*, for *dār al-ṣināʿa*), located until that point in Acre, to the city of

267 Northedge, *Entre Amman et Samarra*, 47.

268 This term could also indicate granaries or other storage facilities.

269 These could be cultivated fields, houses, shops, markets, etc. I have adopted the form *mustaghallāt* here rather than *mustaghillāt*, which more specifically means 'product' or 'revenue,' since the text seems to refer to agricultural and/or commercial structures. See Dozy, *Supplement*, vol. II, 220.

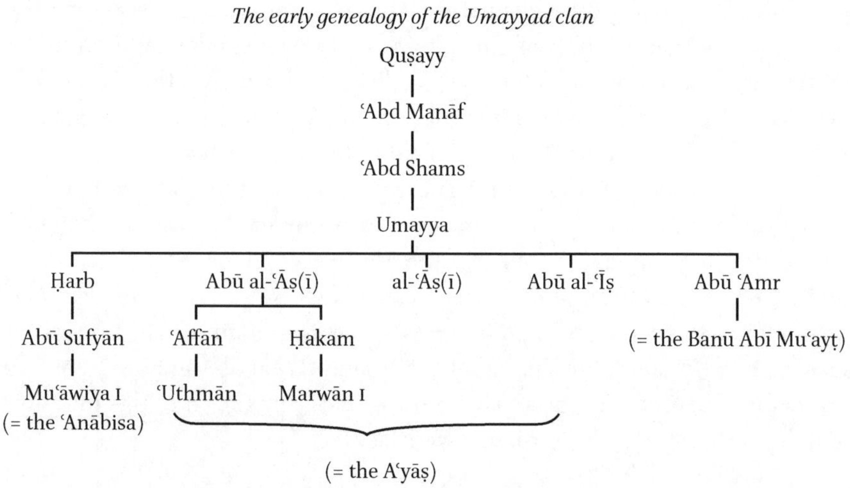

FIGURE 8.5 The Banū Umayya
© "UMAYYA," *ENCYCLOPAEDIA OF ISLAM, SECOND EDITION*

Tyre![270] Hishām's radical solution reveals the financial importance of controlling these installations. He also hastened to add a *funduq* and a *mustaghall* to the arsenal's new location. This example, while somewhat extreme, is illustrative of the fragility of the elites when confronted with the whims of a caliph or any other powerful prince.

Another observation arises in part from the previous one: if, during the period when he was still a potential heir to the throne, Hishām's actions were limited to the territory that had been granted him, his accession to the caliphate allowed him to extend his reach throughout the Shām and the rest of the empire. In addition to his aforementioned developments on the road to Mecca, the caliph "fortified the borders [...] and undertook other beneficial works that were destroyed by Dāwūd b. ʿAlī at the beginning of the Abbasids' reign."[271] He was especially supportive of commercial endeavours, as evidenced by the inscriptions in the market at Baysān,[272] in addition to his construction of souks in Homs, al-Ruṣāfa, and al-Raqqa.[273] Hishām, born in 72/691, is clearly a singular example. Out of all of ʿAbd al-Malik's successors, he (along with al-Walīd

270 Al-Balādhurī, *Futūḥ*, 117–8, trans. 181. See Borrut, "Architecture des espaces portuaires" and "L'espace maritime syrien."

271 Al-Masʿūdī, *Murūj*, vol. v, 466, trans. Pellat vol. IV, 889.

272 Khamis, "Two Wall Mosaic Inscriptions."

273 These souks were either built by Hishām or under his direct patronage. See Foote, *Umayyad Markets*, 210 ff., which also links Hishām to the souks in Medina, Fusṭāt, al-Ḥira, Baṣra and Kūfa.

b. Yazīd) is among those who spent the longest period of time as prince destined for the throne before assuming the caliphate for nearly twenty years. This remarkable longevity is itself a distorting prism, in that it is difficult to compare Hishām's achievements with those of caliphs who ruled for much shorter spans. However, at the same time, this long tenure in two different positions of power makes it easier to distinguish the prince's projects from the caliph's. While the first had only regional influence, it is interesting to note that the second, even after extending his architectural patronage at the level of the caliphate, remained fundamentally rooted in the area of his princely authority.

In Hishām's case, we return to an observation mentioned above: the ruler's presence progressively became more and more fixed in only one or a few different residences. Among the numerous references to works associated with the caliph, two particularly ambitious projects stand out: al-Ruṣāfa and Qaṣr al-Ḥayr al-Sharqī. However, these were clearly two *urban* projects. For the first, a very important edifice was constructed next to the city of al-Ruṣāfa, while the mosque was built within the city walls, attached to the basilica. Similarly, the foundation inscription at Qaṣr al-Ḥayr al-Sharqī identifies the site as a *madīna*, and the mosque is once again situated inside its walls. The very dimensions of these places of worship contrast with those of the mosques at the "desert castles," as they provided the caliphate with a necessary sacred space while also responding to the increasing needs of an urban population. Unfortunately, we know very little about the evolution of the religious aspects of court ceremonial. As Sauvaget noted, "a very complex ceremonial governing the relations between the Commander of the Faithful and his subjects from the early years of the dynasty on" is buried deep in the layers of both medieval and modern historiography.[274]

We do, however, have access to various indications of how life at the caliphal court developed,[275] including Hishām's penchant for luxury, especially silks and tapestries, and his love of horses, much celebrated by the poets. This passion led him to institute "races at which four thousand horses from his stables and [belonging] to others were gathered, which was unprecedented both in the Jāhiliyya and in Islam."[276] No racetrack has been discovered at al-Ruṣāfa,

274 Sauvaget, *La mosquée omeyyade de Médine*, 129.

275 See Gabrieli, *Il Califfato*, 120–1 and Grabar, *Ceremonial and Art*, 49 ff.

276 Al-Masʿūdī, *Murūj*, vol. v, 466, trans. Pellat vol. iv, 899. Hishām's passion for horses was shared by al-Walīd b. Yazīd, and the medieval authors used equestrian metaphors when describing the rivalry between the two men. Al-Masʿūdī echoes this tendency: "a passionate lover of horses, [al-Walīd b. Yazīd] enjoyed holding races. His horse, named al-Sindī, was the best of his day; however, in the races that took place under Hishām, he was beaten

which is not surprising insofar as the sources suggest sketchy installations.[277] In any case, the growing needs of the court almost certainly contributed to the development of economic activity, and the urban environment provided the most auspicious conditions for exchange. One of the economic implications of this situation was the need to conduct the flow of tax collection toward the region in which the caliph had chosen to reside. This phenomenon gave rise to recurring complaints, especially in the Christian sources, in response to taxation that seemed excessive.[278] These fiscal questions fit into the larger context of major reforms aimed at strengthening the central administration and affirming Umayyad control over the Shām as a whole. Bone's study of copper coins (*fulūs*) sheds light on this fiscal policy, initiated around 116/734, that encompassed the region stretching from Ḥarrān to Baysān.[279]

Another major aspect of these reforms concerns the desire to impose a religious orthodoxy. Although this project did not originate with Hishām, he did considerably expand the process and develop strategies against those who refused to comply: heretics.[280] To combat the heretics, the caliph relied on the *qāḍī*s, thus establishing a new network of power as part of the broader Umayyad development of a judicial system, a project Hishām strongly supported.[281] Reinforcing "the delegation of judicial power"[282] therefore became intertwined with the delegation of mobility. The *qāḍī*s became "religious representatives" of the caliph, and in this capacity could enter into conflict with governors and elites, whose competitors they now were.[283] Two networks of power thus vied with one another: that created by the dual forces of Umayyad patrimonialism and delegation of mobility; and that which arose from the definition of a religious orthodoxy. The famous *Risāla ilā walī al-ʿahd* – the *Epistle to the heir of the pact*, or the *épître au légataire du pacte*, to borrow Zakharia's French translation[284] – written by ʿAbd al-Ḥamīd al-Kātib is a good illustration of the importance of the *qāḍī*'s role at the end of the Marwanid period. In addition, it shows that "the *qāḍī* was not only an agent of the governor or caliph, but

by this latter's horse, named al-Dhāʾid; sometimes he finished in a tie, others he placed second," *Murūj*, vol. VI, 13, trans. Pellat vol. IV, 902.

277 On this subject, see Northedge, "The Racecourses."

278 Michael the Syrian, vol. II, 457, French trans. 490; *1234*, vol. I, 309, trans. 241.

279 Bone, *The Administration*, 311.

280 See Judd, *The Third Fitna*.

281 Judd, *The Third Fitna*, 156 ff.; on *qāḍī*s during the Umayyad and Abbasid eras, see Conrad, *Die Quḍāt Dimašq* and Tillier, *Les cadis d'Iraq*.

282 Tillier, *Les cadis d'Iraq*, ch. 1.

283 Judd, *The Third Fitna*, 157, 295.

284 ʿAbbās, *ʿAbd al-Ḥamīd*, 215–65. See Zakharia, "Le secrétaire et le pouvoir," 82, and Tillier, *Les cadis d'Iraq*, 74 ff.

also an agent of God."[285] This quote is reminiscent of one of the central questions in Islamic history related to the competition between the caliphs and the *ʿulamāʾ* for a monopoly over judicial and religious authority.[286] These policies thus represented potential contradictions with the patrimonial system, and created new power networks that served to limit the caliph's mobility.

Hishām also pursued a policy of expansion, one that Blankinship deemed not only anachronistic, but also ruinous for the caliphate, as it ultimately led to the Umayyads' downfall.[287] While this subject also surpasses the bounds of the present inquiry, we may glean an essential lesson therefrom: expansion meant that mobile power was projected to the empire's borders and entrusted to its soldiers. Maslama b. ʿAbd al-Malik was the perfect embodiment of this border mobility that eventually ensured Marwān II's victory. The phenomenon was not a new one, but it grew considerably under Hishām as a result of the policy of *jihād* erected as a "fundamental pillar of the state ideology."[288] Here we return to the deep opposition between ʿUmar II and Hishām, the caliph of reduction and the caliph of expansion. The two rulers did have one thing in common, however: both perceived the threat represented by the "soldier-princes" who were progressively usurping their mobility while simultaneously being able to claim valid rights to succession. It is perhaps for this reason that we must reexamine various elements related to Maslama that were mentioned previously in Chapter 5. When calling the general back from Constantinople, ʿUmar b. ʿAbd al-ʿAzīz was well aware of the risk he ran in so doing: thus, he begged Maslama not to revolt. Maslama complied,[289] although, according to certain traditions, he was distraught at the notion, "because the power had been transferred from the hands of [his] father's children to the children of [his] paternal uncle."[290] In 102/721, Yazīd II relieved Maslama of his brief term as governor of Iraq and the eastern provinces, claiming that he had failed to send the region's *kharāj* to Damascus.[291] This act was clearly intended to remove Umayyad princes from high-ranking administrative positions,[292] since they were simultaneously too difficult to control from the perspective of a centralised authority and

285 Tillier, *Les cadis d'Iraq*, 78.

286 The bibliography on this subject is massive. Among the more recent contributions, see those of Décobert, "L'autorité religieuse," Tillier, *Les cadis d'Iraq*. See also the essential works of Cook, *Commanding Right*, and Crone, *Medieval Islamic Political Thought*.

287 Blankinship, *The End of the Jihād State*. See Judd's reservations, *The Third Fitna*, 304.

288 Blankinship, *The End of the Jihād State*, 6.

289 Ibn Aʿtham al-Kūfī, vol. VII, 229–30; Balʿamī, 211.

290 See Ibn Abī al-Ḥadīd, *Sharḥ*, vol. VII, 137–8; Sharon, *Revolt*, 237.

291 Al-Ṭabarī, vol. II, 1416–7, 1432 ff., trans. vol. XXIV, 148, 162 ff.

292 Blankinship, *The End of the Jihād State*, 88.

represented a permanent threat due to their powerful military support. Finally, while certain texts report that Maslama, under Hishām, willingly abandoned his post as governor of Armenia and Azerbaijan to Marwān b. Muḥammad in order to tend to his land holdings in northern Syria,[293] al-Yaʿqūbī states that the caliph removed him from this position.[294] There is little ambiguity here: Maslama's changing fortunes are indicative of the various caliphal attempts to control their potential rivals.

An objection could be made that it was another Marwanid, Marwān b. Muḥammad, who was placed in charge of Maslama's former post in the Jazīra and the Caucasus. However, it is not clear that the future Marwān II was ever considered a true threat, as he was not a descendant of ʿAbd al-Malik. The "parenthesis" represented by ʿUmar II's caliphate, the only exception to the rule established by the founder of the Dome of the Rock, had been closed. A similar situation was supposed never to recur, and power was to remain in the hands of the Banū ʿAbd al-Malik. Marwān b. Muḥammad thus did not seem a natural candidate for the caliphate, and it was only thanks to the turbulent context of the third *fitna* that he was able to return to the fore. It should be noted that, during his uprising, Marwān II asserted that he was fighting in the name of the claims to the throne held by the sons of al-Walīd II, al-Ḥakam and ʿUthmān. The two had been imprisoned after their father's assassination and, following his victory at the battle of ʿAnjar over Sulaymān b. Hishām's forces, Marwān received the *bayʿa* in their names.[295] Dennett, in his pioneering study dedicated to Marwān II, demonstrated that al-Ṭabarī strove to present the general's strategy as a political calculation, using al-Walīd's sons as a simple pretext. He also highlighted the fact that some authors, such as al-Balādhurī, conversely argued that Marwān's intentions were sincere.[296] While Dennett found this hypothesis unlikely, it should be added that it is also present in the Christian sources derived from the circuit of Theophilus of Edessa, which offer the oldest historical information on the subject.[297] Judd has also presented other elements in support of this interpretation.[298] In any case, the conditions specific to the third *fitna* allowed Marwān II to harbor pretensions of his own, and it is quite probable that he never would have risen to the caliphate without the opportunity provided by these exceptional circumstances. Indeed, the

293 Ibn Aʿtham al-Kūfī, vol. VII, 288; Balʿamī, 248.
294 Al-Yaʿqūbī, *Taʾrīkh*, vol. II, 318.
295 Al-Ṭabarī, vol. II, 1877–8, trans. vol. XXVI, 250–2; al-Azdī, *Taʾrīkh*, 61.
296 Dennett, *Marwan*, 231.
297 Theophanes, *Chronography*, 418, trans. 580; Agapius, *Kitāb al-ʿunwān*, 512–3; *1234*, 317, Latin trans. 247; Hoyland, *Seeing*, 661.
298 Judd, *The Third Fitna*, 104. See also Hawting, "Marwān II."

conflict surrounding the assassination of al-Walīd II marked the breakdown of the "Umayyad program of establishing and imposing orthodoxy"[299] and balancing the powers that arose alongside it. ʿAbd al-Malik's desired "topography of consensus" was transformed into a "topography of conflict," and any caliphal attempts to control rival ambitions were thus destined for failure. Itinerant power passed to the hands of the "soldier-princes," while legal power was reinforced in the hands of the *qāḍīs*. The processes set in motion accelerated at a rapid pace, and the changes to older caliphal prerogatives resulted in an "immobile caliphate."[300]

Marwān II tried to stop this downward spiral by attempting to reinstate the equilibrium established under Hishām's reign.[301] The situation required increased mobility in order to assert his new authority, a task made all the more complicated by the fact that there were plenty of other claimants to the throne, beginning with the sons of Hishām b. ʿAbd al-Malik. It was, in fact, a natural move for the new ruler: he was a soldier, and mobility was an integral part of his mode of government. As such, he was the perfect embodiment of a war caliph, and he returned to the principles that had been the source of ʿAbd al-Malik's strength, illustrated by the coins minted with the "standing caliph" motif that represented the first stage of the latter's monetary reform.[302] Although he was not a descendant of ʿAbd al-Malik, Marwān II proceeded according to the logic of the regionalisation of Marwanid powers established by the founder of the Dome of the Rock. Marwān had served as governor of Armenia and Azerbaijan under Hishām, and later as governor of the Jazīra under Yazīd III. During the final stage of his administrative career prior to becoming caliph, the general took up residence at Ḥarrān, an important Qaysite centre at the time. This spatial anchoring was to prevail from the beginning of his caliphate, and Marwān II eventually transferred the treasury from Damascus to Ḥarrān.[303] He thus reproduced a classic framework, a "silent legacy"[304] from ʿAbd al-Malik. The regionalisation of power was pushed to its apogee, and for the first time, an Umayyad sovereign elected to govern from the eastern bank of the Euphrates.[305] The support of the *ahl al-Jazīra* was the determining factor in this decision, and was indicative of the military's growing role in the balance of power. Marwān II, precisely because he was a product of the military corps,

299 Judd, *The Third Fitna*, 303.
300 I borrow this expression from Martinez-Gros, *L'idéologie omeyyade*, 129.
301 Judd, *The Third Fitna*, 109.
302 See Robinson, *ʿAbd al-Malik*, 49 ff.
303 Michael the Syrian, 464, French trans. 505.
304 Borrowing Donner's idea, "Umayyad Efforts at Legitimation," 208.
305 Hawting, "Marwān II."

was able to reinvigorate the practice of itinerant power. Indeed, the oppositions that arose at the very start of his rule left him with few other options. The new caliph was forced to be active on multiple fronts, from Iraq to Syria. Homs revolted, while Sulaymān b. Hishām – who had obtained the caliph's *amān* and sworn allegiance following his military loss at ʿAnjar – allowed his troops to convince him to defend his claim. Sulaymān was defeated near Qinnasrīn, and Homs surrendered after a siege of several months that resulted in Marwān II's decision to raze the city's walls.[306] In Iraq, the Kharijites, led by al-Ḍaḥḥāk b. Qays, tried to profit from caliphate's weakness and occupied Mosul.[307] It was not until near the end of the year 129 AH (summer 747) that Marwān II was able to reestablish his authority over the empire's central provinces. In the same year, the *Hāshimiyya* had already been launched in Khurāsān, and a new threat loomed in the eastern region of the empire.

This new danger was not unconnected with the aforementioned limitations associated with the mobile exercise of power: it resulted primarily from the loss of the monopoly of mobility and long distance communication.[308] Communication relied on the postal system (*barīd*), which also functioned as an information network. This institution was essential for maintaining caliphal power throughout the empire and facilitated contact with distant provinces.[309] The bankruptcy of this system seems to have played an important role in the Umayyad regime's downfall. The sources paint a clear picture: an Umayyad functionary, interrogated by the Abbasids after their rise to power, confessed that "our ignorance of events was one of the primary causes of our empire's collapse."[310] An unpublished source studied by Silverstein, the *Siyāsat al-mulūk*, corroborates this account, stating that the Marwanids' ruin was caused by the "cessation of intelligence (*al-akhbār*)" networks.[311]

Despite Marwān II's best efforts, the general failure of the mode of governance inherited from ʿAbd al-Malik spelled the end for the dynasty. Confronted with the same situations and the same protagonists, the early Abbasids still took a great deal of inspiration from this model while simultaneously trying to

306 Al-Ṭabarī, vol. II, 1910, trans. vol. XXVII, 21. See also Agapius, *Kitāb al-ʿunwān*, 520; Michael the Syrian, vol. II, 464, French trans. 505.

307 On Kharijite activity in the Jazīra, see Robinson, *Empire and Elites*, in particular 109–26.

308 Bernhardt, *Itinerant Kingship*, 56–7.

309 See Silverstein, *Postal Systems*, as well as his articles "Documentary Evidence" and "On Some Aspects." The importance of the function of *Ṣāḥib al-khabar* is also emphasised by al-Naboodah, "*Ṣāḥib al-khabar*," although certain of the conclusions in this last work should be approached with caution.

310 Al-Masʿūdī, *Murūj*, vol. VI, 36, trans. Pellat vol. IV, 911.

311 Silverstein, "A New Source," 131, 134.

limit any structural weaknesses. The case of ʿAbd Allāh b. ʿAlī, analysed in the preceding chapter, sheds light on these shared practices, as his trajectory was similar to that of Marwān II in that he favoured the same groups and similar spaces of power.[312] The experiment was brief, but it did not seal the fate of all of al-Manṣūr's uncles, as the example of Ṣāliḥ b. ʿAlī would demonstrate.

8.3 Abbasid Reconfigurations

The imbalances in the available sources on Abbasid Syria, as mentioned in the introduction to this chapter, have significant implications for the remainder of this study. The archaeological evidence by which to evaluate the continuity of the occupation of these Umayyad sites under the early Abbasids remains fragmentary; the Islamic sources focus mainly on Iraq and Khurāsān from this point forward, while the Christian chroniclers henceforth are only marginally helpful as the eastern sources become silent.[313] More than ever, we must try to retrace a history steeped in oblivion, of which only quiet whispers reach us today. However, by a happy historiographic coincidence, recent works have become seriously engaged in this pursuit and offer a newly refreshed base of material.[314] Before we evaluate the extent to which the fruits of these labors can aid us in the present inquiry, a few preliminary remarks are necessary.

A methodological overview, mentioned in Chapter 4, must come first. The fundamentally negative treatment of Abbasid Syrian history that prevails in most modern historiography on the subject stems from a lasting confusion over the early Abbasids' anti-Umayyad policies and their Syrian ones. The amalgamation of the two has resulted in the neglect – and outright abnegation in older works – of the very principle of the second factor in this equation: beginning in 132/750, the Shām was destined to experience Abbasid resentment due to its ties to the previous dynasty. Conversely, the previous chapter demonstrated that the early Abbasids were confronted with the same situation and the same protagonists faced by the recently deposed Marwanids. These circumstances required that clear guidelines be established, *a fortiori* concerning the threat posed by ʿAbd Allāh b. ʿAlī's rebellion. The particularly virulent discourse unleashed against the Umayyads, following a program of *damnatio*

312 See above, Ch. 7.
313 See above, Ch. 3.
314 In particular, see Sourdel, "La Syrie;" Cobb, *White Banners* and "Community versus Contention;" Bonner, *Aristocratic Violence*; Kennedy, *The Early Abbasid Caliphate*; Whitcomb, "Archaeology of the ʿAbbāsid Period;" Genequand, "Formation et devenir;" Heidemann and Becker, *Raqqa II*; Daiber and Becker, *Raqqa III*.

memoriae, fit into the context of a "symbolic violence." However, these moves were not antithetical to a political project designed for a highly strategic province. One of al-Manṣūr's interlocutors emphasised this point when describing the *ahl al-Shām* as the "fortress of the Muslim community" (*ḥiṣn al-umma*).[315]

Ibn al-Muqaffaʿ himself remarked, at a very early date, that the new caliphal dynasty would need to define a Syrian policy. To this end, he suggested employing a specific group of Syrians to play along with the Abbasid regime:

> another question which should come to the attention of the Commander of the Faithful [concerns] the Syrians […] The Commander of the Faithful must neither reproach them for their hostility, nor expect that they will unanimously show him their affection. It would seem preferable, on their account, that the Commander of the Faithful favors a particular group (*khāṣṣa*) of them from whom he can expect approval or whose sincerity or fidelity he trusts. This group will soon detach itself from its compatriots through its ideas and feelings and play the game one wishes it to play.[316]

The formula is a familiar one: divide and conquer. Ibn al-Muqaffaʿ essentially advises that the Abbasids proceed along the very same lines as the Umayyads by relying on the support of a dominant tribal group![317] He later recommends as well that the Syrians not be deprived of the *fay'* owed to them and that they be treated justly.[318] It should be added that, alongside this argument proffered by ʿĪsā b. ʿAlī's secretary, the aforementioned inscription at Baysān shows that the first Abbasid caliph commissioned works in the city beginning in Dhū al-Qaʿda 135/9 May–7 June 753 in order to repair the damages wrought by the terrible earthquake that struck just before the Abbasid Revolution.[319] The Shām's maritime regions also received the Abbasid caliphs' attention.[320] Particular care was given to fortifying the borders, both on land and on the coast, beginning under the reigns of al-Manṣūr and al-Mahdī.[321] These precautions would increase under Hārūn al-Rashīd, to whom we shall return shortly.

315 Al-Ṭabarī, vol. III, 403, trans. vol. XXIX, 105.
316 Ibn al-Muqaffaʿ, *Risāla*, ed. and trans. 41.
317 See Crone, "Were the Qays and Yemen."
318 Ibn al-Muqaffaʿ, *Risāla*, ed. and trans. 42–3.
319 *CIAP*, vol. II, 214 ff.
320 On this space, generally seen as neglected under the Abbasids, see Borrut, "L'espace maritime syrien" and "Architecture des espaces portuaires."
321 Al-Balādhurī, *Futūḥ*, 163, trans. 251–2.

All of this is sufficient evidence to demonstrate that, from the moment they seized power, the Abbasids prioritised activities in the Bilād al-Shām, especially after the widespread destruction in the region caused by the earthquakes of 747–749, while their advisers strove to theorise the best way to implement and create new relationships with the Syrian space. This observation is even more critical since, as Cobb noted, the immediate implication of the coup d'état in 132/750 had been to reduce Syria to the rank of mere province. It was thus helpful to derive lessons from these events, both for the caliphs and those elites who hoped to maintain their status[322]

While ʿAbd Allāh b. ʿAlī's uprising prolonged the period of uncertainty regarding the province's new status, his defeat did not prevent his brother, Ṣāliḥ b. ʿAlī, from imposing himself as the new strongman in the Shām under al-Manṣūr. Thus, we must now shift our focus to the strategies employed by Ṣāliḥ and his descendants.

8.3.1 *The Banū Ṣāliḥ and Abbasid Syrian Patrimonialism*

Just as under the Umayyads, the structure of Abbasid power stemmed from a patrimonial logic. Although the Shām was no longer the seat of the caliphate, one problem remained: how to delegate provincial authority without creating a powerful rival who was liable to rebel. Marwanid precedent, in addition to ʿAbd Allāh b. ʿAlī's recent revolt, made this risk all the more palpable for al-Manṣūr. In response, the founder of Baghdad and his immediate successors experimented with various solutions. Despite these efforts, the "backgrounds of ʿAbbāsid governors" of the Shām would not evolve much until after the civil war that broke out following al-Rashīd's death.[323] Cobb has analysed these different strategies in detail. Relying primarily on Ibn ʿAsākir's (d. 571/1176)[324] *Taʾrīkh madīnat Dimashq*, he was able to study on the one hand the tactics used by the new rulers to assert their hold on the Syrian space while attempting to control their provincial governors (*umarāʾ*), and on the other hand the efforts employed by the Syrian *ashrāf* to preserve their high-ranking positions under the early Abbasids. To confront the danger represented by family members of equal rank and prestige who could potentially make valid claims on the caliphate, the general policy was to call as much as possible on the younger Abbasid generation and the *mawālī*. The young princes were not sufficiently

322 Cobb, *White Banners*, 125–6.

323 Cobb, *White Banners*, 21–2.

324 Sourdel ("La Syrie") has also gathered important evidence, in particular from Ibn al-ʿAdīm. On these two authors, see above, Ch. 3.

established to assert their own claims on the caliphal charge.[325] Despite the sovereigns' efforts, the Abbasid nobles had to maintain the upper hand on provincial power, at least until the reign of al-Maʾmūn.[326] On the Syrian front, Ṣāliḥ b. ʿAlī emerged not only as an unavoidable protagonist, but also succeeded in transferring his rights to his sons (see fig. 4). The Banū Ṣāliḥ's hold on the Shām was such that it led Kennedy to present the family as a "local sub-dynasty."[327]

During ʿAbd Allāh's rebellion, Ṣāliḥ, who was governor of Egypt at the time, clearly sided with al-Manṣūr. He fought in Palestine and the *jund* of al-Urdunn against troops loyal to his own brother, thus helping to affirm Mansurid authority in Syria, where he would henceforth resume his administrative functions. To do so, he relied primarily on the Qays and the *ahl al-Jazīra*, perpetuating ʿAbd Allāh's practice, which was itself an "inheritance" from Marwān II. Ṣāliḥ also took advantage of matrimonial strategies, wedding a widow of the last Umayyad caliph and marrying his daughter to al-Mahdī in 159/775–776.[328] He thus affirmed both his ties to the Syrian *ashrāf* and to the family who held the caliphate. Ṣāliḥ accumulated various Umayyad properties and also developed extensive architectural activity on the border zone, as at Malaṭiya;[329] this familial project was consistent throughout northern Syria, especially in the region of Salamiyya,[330] Aleppo and Qinnasrīn.[331] His authority in the area was such that Ṣāliḥ could stamp coins in his own name, a practice later imitated by his sons ʿAbd Allāh and Ibrāhīm.[332] The combination of these potentially dangerous factors worried al-Manṣūr, who saw him as a potential rival, capable at any moment of taking up where his brother ʿAbd Allāh had left off.[333] After Ṣāliḥ's death in 152/769, his son Faḍl succeeded him. Faḍl had been governor of Damascus when his father was alive, starting in 149/766, and he was also put

325 Cobb, *White Banners*, 22.

326 Cobb, *White Banners*, 27.

327 Kennedy, *The Early Abbasid Caliphate*, 74. Bonner contested this claim, *Aristocratic Violence*, 87–93. See also Cobb, *White Banners*, 30.

328 Al-Ṭabarī, vol. III, 466, trans. vol. XXIX, 177; Kennedy, *The Early Abbasid Caliphate*, 75.

329 Al-Ṭabarī, vol. III, 122, trans. vol. XXVIII, 49. On Ṣāliḥ's activities in the region, see Bonner, *Aristocratic Violence*, 58–61.

330 Al-Balādhurī associated the site with Ṣāliḥ b. ʿAlī, and reports information on its fortification works (*Futūḥ*, 134, trans. 205), while al-Yaʿqūbī linked it to ʿAbd Allāh b. Ṣāliḥ and mentions that a canal was dug there (*Kitāb al-buldān*, 324, trans. 170). See also Sourdel, "La Syrie," 160 and Daftary, "Salamiyya."

331 Cobb, *White Banners*, 30. Ibn al-ʿAdīm indicates that the Banū Ṣāliḥ put down lasting roots in Aleppo and Manbij, since some of their descendants still lived there in the seventh/thirteenth century, *Bughyat*, vol. I, 529.

332 Bresc, *Monuments numismatiques*, 406–8.

333 Kennedy, *The Early Abbasid Caliphate*, 75; Cobb, *White Banners*, 27.

in charge of the *jund* of Qinnasrīn after his father's death. In addition, he was at one time in charge of the Jazīra, and he accompanied the caliph al-Mahdī on his trip to Jerusalem in 163/779.[334] Ibrāhīm b. Ṣāliḥ also held several posts, including leadership of the *junds* of Damascus, al-Urdunn and Filasṭīn under al-Mahdī, to which the Jazīra was added under al-Hādī; at one time removed from his positions by al-Rashīd, he was once more assigned to Damascus by the latter. ʿAbd al-Malik b. Ṣāliḥ would later carry on the family name, having served as governor of Medina under al-Rashīd and led numerous campaigns against the Byzantines in northern Syria and Anatolia. He was also in charge of the *jund* of Qinnasrīn and the new zone of the *ʿAwāṣim*.[335]

Like al-Manṣūr before him, Hārūn al-Rashīd was concerned by the Banū Ṣāliḥ's considerable power. In order to better control them, the caliph tried to limit their field of activity to the single *jund* of Qinnasrīn, even though ʿAbd al-Malik b. Ṣāliḥ had been temporarily placed in charge of Damascus in 178/794 to restore order in the wake of Abū al-Haydhām al-Murrī's rebellion.[336] Following this intervention, the Banū Ṣāliḥ could no longer obtain posts outside their holdings in northern Syria.[337] However, even these strategies of isolation did not reassure al-Rashīd, who finally had ʿAbd al-Malik b. Ṣāliḥ arrested in 187/803, despite the fact that he had previously made him tutor to his son, al-Qāsim.[338] He remained in prison until the caliph's death six years later before regaining his freedom and taking al-Amīn's side in the conflict.[339] The causes of the strife between ʿAbd al-Malik and the caliph are unclear. Hārūn al-Rashīd accused him of plotting to seize the caliphate, while ʿAbd al-Malik claimed that he was the victim of a conspiracy hatched by one of his sons.[340] Among the multiple traditions that circulated regarding ʿAbd al-Malik, the son of Marwān II's widow, persistent rumors denied that Ṣāliḥ was his father, claiming that he was instead the offspring of the last Umayyad caliph![341] In any case, his arrest shows the constant risk posed by the powerful governors of the Shām during the reign of al-Rashīd.

Before adopting this radical solution, al-Rashīd tried to restore caliphal authority through other channels according to a strictly patrimonial logic.

334 Al-Ṭabarī, vol. III, 500, trans. vol. XXIX, 215; Cobb, *White Banners*, 28.
335 Cobb, *White Banners*, 28.
336 On this uprising and its consequences, see below.
337 Cobb, *White Banners*, 28.
338 Al-Ṭabarī, vol. III, 688 ff., 652, trans. vol. XXX, 230 ff., 181. Sourdel, *L'état impérial*, 74.
339 Al-Ṭabarī, vol. III, 688 ff., trans. vol. XXX, 230 ff.; Kennedy, *The Early Abbasid Caliphate*, 75; Cobb, *White Banners*, 29.
340 Cobb, *White Banners*, 29–30.
341 Al-Jahshiyārī, 263; Sourdel, *Le Vizirat*, vol. I, 168–9.

In 173/789–790, al-Amīn was designated as heir to the throne. Two years later, he was given the governorate of Syria and Iraq.[342] In 183/799–800, al-Maʾmūn was named second successor; al-Rashīd then put in him charge of the vast territory stretching from Hamadān to the eastern edges of the empire. This division between al-Amīn and al-Maʾmūn encompassed the topography of the conflict that would tear the caliphate apart after the death of their father.[343] The principle was not a new one: al-Rashīd himself had been named governor of Armenia, Azerbaijan and the Maghreb in 163/780.[344] However, Abbasid patrimonial sovereignty was diluted across these immense spaces and drained of its substance, in particular in the Shām, just as the Banū Ṣāliḥ's power was steadily increasing.

The version of the succession finalised by al-Rashīd and sealed in the Kaʿba during his famous pilgrimage to Mecca in 186/802 mentions the name of a third heir, his son al-Qāsim, who was slated to lead after his two brothers.[345] Al-Qāsim adopted the *laqab* al-Mu'taman and was given the provinces of the Jazīra, Thughūr and the ʿAwāṣim.[346] The precise date of this nomination divides scholars, but Bonner has argued convincingly that it took place in 187/803: al-Qāsim was selected in lieu of ʿAbd al-Malik b. Ṣāliḥ after the latter's dismissal.[347] While it was necessary to fill the vacancy left by this move, it was first and foremost a sign that the caliphate was taking action to firmly regain control of this strategic region.

In each of the final years of his reign, while trying to solve the question of his succession, Hārūn used grand strategies to eliminate those he perceived as enemies capable of thwarting his plans. Within the span of only a few months, the Barmakids and ʿAbd al-Malik b. Ṣāliḥ fell victim to these reorganisations. Although the disgrace and consequences of the former have long sustained scholarly interest,[348] the case of ʿAbd al-Malik is symptomatic of the problems

342 Al-Ṭabarī, vol. III, 652, trans. vol. XXX, 180.

343 Nicol, *Early Abbasid Administration*, 1.

344 Bonner, *Aristocratic Violence*, 73.

345 Al-Ṭabarī, vol. III, 653, trans. vol. XXX, 181. However, several different versions of al-Rashīd's organisation of his succession exist, none of which mention the place given to al-Qāsim. See Kennedy, *The Early Abbasid Caliphate*, 125 and Kimber, "Hārūn al-Rashīd's Meccan Settlement." Al-Masʿūdī only situates al-Qāsim's designation as an heir in 187/803, *Murūj*, vol. VI, 328, trans. Pellat vol. IV, 1030. Michael the Syrian also records this date for al-Qāsim's nomination as successor, vol. III, 489, French trans. 17.

346 Al-Ṭabarī, vol. III, 653, trans. vol. XXX, 181.

347 Bonner, *Aristocratic Violence*, 93.

348 Among recent works on the subject, see El-Hibri, *Reinterpreting*; Dakhlia, *L'empire des passions*.

provincial power posed for the Abbasid empire. The implications of this conflict of interests must now be evaluated.

8.3.2 *Competition for Mobility and Its Consequences*

While the early Abbasids, in particular with respect to the Banū Ṣāliḥ, may have used certain Umayyad "recipes" at first, the Syrian elites did not have this luxury. Cobb emphasised this "crisis of the *ashrāf*," who went from members of the imperial nobility to the more precarious status of the provincial elites. After 132/750, very few Syrians were appointed to governorates outside of the Shām.[349] Even within Syria, most governorships were taken by non-Syrians, except during the troubled periods immediately following the Abbasid Revolution and the civil war that erupted after al-Rashīd's death. By contrast, the elites of the Shām remained quite active on the military front, especially in the campaigns against the Byzantines, and Syrian troops accompanied Hārūn al-Rashīd on his expedition in 190/806.[350] Their military presence is largely explained by the fact that al-Manṣūr had reintegrated Syrian soldiers into the army by granting them amnesty in 136/754.[351] Indeed, what better way to avoid rebellion among the troops than keeping them at the front?

Under the early Abbasids, the patrimonialism that developed around the Banū Ṣāliḥ in the Syrian space attests to the continuity of Umayyad practices. The most notable difference was the fact that power in Syria rested in the hands of a branch of the family who were not in control of the caliphate. The system now created great Abbasid princes (and thus potential rivals for the throne) rather than caliphs. As a result, this patrimonial power structure would come into conflict with the caliphate's attempts to maintain control. Mobility was still delegated: the Banū Ṣāliḥ held a quasi-monopoly on movement throughout the Abbasid Shām. The method was a successful one: after ʿAbd Allāh b. ʿAlī's revolt, the sources make no further mention of uprisings in Syria until al-Rashīd's caliphate, with a few minor exceptions. This period of relative calm coincided precisely with the growing power of the Banū Ṣāliḥ, who maintained equilibrium between various rival factions.[352] However, the

349 With the notable exception of the Banū Khuraym, whose misadventures and eventual fall from grace under al-Rashīd may have played an important role in the outbreak of Abū al-Haydhām al-Murrī's revolt. See Cobb, *White Banners*, 79.

350 Cobb, *White Banners*, 78–80.

351 Cobb, *White Banners*, 78. These career continuities were discussed in the previous chapter. See also Bligh-Abramski, *From Damascus to Baghdad* and "Evolution vs. Revolution;" Elad, "Aspects of the Transition." On al-Manṣūr's strategies with respect to the troops in northern Syria, see Bonner, *Aristocratic Violence*, 65 ff.

352 Cobb, *White Banners*, 78–9.

attempt to sequester them in the *jund* of Qinnasrīn reduced their capabilities and spatialised their movement within limited areas, thus providing opportunities for new forces and actors in southern Syria. This strategy of isolation enacted to protect the caliphate endangered the existence of the system over which the Banū Ṣāliḥ presided, perpetuating a Marwanid practice. The fragile tribal balance that had been restored in the wake of the third *fitna* suffered as a result of this caliphal policy.

The revolt of the Qaysite Abū al-Haydhām al-Murrī that raged for months in Damascus and the Ghūṭa in 177/793 is a perfect illustration of the consequences of al-Rashīd's weakening of the Banū Ṣāliḥ. This complex event has been analysed in detail by Cobb through the lens of an important notice recorded in its entirety by Ibn ʿAsākir, who preserved the account given by al-Madāʾinī (d. *c.*235/850).[353] Although Abū al-Haydhām's motivations for inciting this rebellion remain uncertain, the conflict proceeded in three distinct stages. First, Abū al-Haydhām took up arms on behalf of the Qaysite villagers whose houses had been razed by the southern Arabs. The retaliatory operation was a success, and the Qaysites occupied Damascus, forbidding entry into the city to the governor – who lived in a palace outside city walls, Qaṣr al-Ḥajjāj – as well as to the Yemenites, who were located near Dayr Murrān. After several weeks of brutal fighting in the Ghūṭa, the Yemenite leaders called for a cessation of hostilities. The truce was short-lived, however, and the second phase of the revolt saw Abbasid troops dispatched to combat Abū al-Haydhām, who was henceforth deemed a rebel. The Yemenites and the Khurāsānīs then entered the fray, but an Umayyad notable, ʿAbd al-ʿAzīz al-ʿUmarī – a descendant of ʿUmar II – intervened to negotiate, and was able to broker an agreement. While he tried to have the terms of this peace recorded in writing, other Yemenite troops, unaware of the treaty that was in the process of being signed, attacked the Qaysites from behind and thus brought a swift end to the negotiations. As reinforcements arrived from Iraq to quash the rebellion, the Yemenites claimed that Abū al-Haydhām had gone back on his oath of allegiance to the caliph, which the Qaysites denied. A pact was negotiated that finally allowed

353 *TMD*, vol. XXVI, 62–87. See also Cobb, *White Banners*, 82–91, and "Community versus Contention," 112–26. Bianquis first drew scholarly attention to the importance of this text ("Deux révoltes bédouines"), and the subject was then studied by ʿAbbās (*Taʾrīkh Bilād al-Shām fī al-ʿaṣr al-ʿabbāsī*, 41–8). The vast complexity of the topographic elements of the revolution were analysed in detail and tentatively mapped by Guérin, "Les territoires." The episode is only briefly mentioned in the classical Islamic narrative sources. For example, see al-Ṭabarī, vol. III, 624–6, trans. vol. XXX, 131–4.

the Abbasids to regain direct control over Damascus, while Abū al-Haydhām returned to the Ḥawrān.[354]

However, the matter did not end there. These months of conflict had left many wounds unhealed, and the Yemenites wanted revenge. The arrival of a new governor in Damascus, Mūsā b. ʿĪsā b. ʿAlī, gave them occasion they needed. They persuaded the new governor to launch an expedition against the Ḥawrān and Lajā to capture Abū al-Haydhām. The attempt ended in failure, as Abū al-Haydhām was able to remain hidden in areas he knew well. Although they were unable to locate him in these hostile territories, those bent on destroying Abū al-Haydhām obtained the support of a Qaysite leader, Ibn Riyāḥ, who offered to deliver the rebel in return for his nomination as head of the region of Ḥawrān. Abū al-Haydhām was in Buṣrā at the time, and Ibn Riyāḥ launched an operation that was foiled. Mūsā b. ʿĪsā, assuming that the expedition would be successful, wrote too early to al-Rashīd that Abū al-Haydhām had been executed, and the caliph removed him from his post as a result. The end was now near. Sensing a change in the winds, Ibn Riyāḥ called for Abū al-Haydhām to be pardoned, but the meeting went sour, and Abū al-Haydhām killed the traitor. Abū al-Haydhām then immediately informed the authorities in Damascus that they no longer had anything to fear from him, and that he would return peaceably to the Ḥawrān. This appeasement did not prevent a final attempt to capture him on his journey back to the province. The skirmish was intense, and one of Abū al-Haydhām's sons was killed in the fighting, while his father disappeared and remained in hiding until his death of unknown causes in 182/798.[355]

There is much to be learned from this lengthy revolt. It reveals the existence of shaky accords that needed little prompting to break. It also underscores how difficult it was for the caliphate to restore order, and shows the mobilising abilities of charismatic leaders like Abū al-Haydhām. It is also important to note that it was a descendant of ʿUmar b. ʿAbd al-ʿAzīz who emerged as the most suitable person to negotiate the cessation of hostilities, and that ʿAbd al-Malik b. Ṣāliḥ was temporarily replaced as head of the *jund* of Damascus in the aftermath of the rebellion in 178/794. Only those who had perfectly mastered the Syrian context were able to maintain social peace in the province. However, this violent episode was localised around Damascus and in the Ḥawrān. Isolating the Banū Ṣāliḥ in the north came at a heavy price in the southern half of the Shām. Abū al-Haydhām's revolt was the first in a series of other uprisings and, following ʿAbd al-Malik b. Ṣāliḥ's death in 187/803, northern Syria was no longer

354 Cobb, *White Banners*, 82–6.
355 Cobb, *White Banners*, 86–8.

spared. In 190/806, the residents of Homs rebelled and Hārūn al-Rashīd had to march against them himself. The insurgents ultimately surrendered when the caliph reached Manbij.[356]

The year 187/803 marked a profound turning point in al-Rashīd's reign. The removal of both the Barmakids and ʿAbd al-Malik b. Ṣāliḥ gave the caliph political autonomy and a freedom unrivalled since the beginning of his rule. However, this liberty also exposed the sovereign. Confronted with this new situation, Hārūn pursued a strategy of affirming himself as the "*ghāzī*-caliph,"[357] using *jihād* and the ideology that accompanied it[358] to fill the void that had been created. The characterisation of the ʿAwāṣim as sacred territory developed as a result of this official policy. In so doing, the caliph sought to free himself from the grip of "intermediate powers within the Abbasid patrimonial state." The desire to make war on Byzantium a caliphal "prerogative"[359] was a strong message: mobility, or more precisely, a caliphal monopoly on mobility, was al-Rashīd's ultimate goal. The Syrian space would become the main stage for this power struggle.

The radical decisions that marked the end of his caliphate were only part of a long process that becomes fully comprehensible in light of the policies carried out in northern Syria. In Chapter 5, we noted that Hārūn was associated early on with campaigns against the Byzantines. In 163/779–780, he led an expedition that reached the Bosphorus, and then another in 165/781–2. It is therefore not surprising that Hārūn was particularly invested in the region from the very start of his caliphate. In 170/786, the very first year of his reign, he created a new district, the ʿAwāṣim, separate from the *jund* of Qinnasrīn.[360] Bonner has conducted a detailed study of the conditions that motivated this initiative. He notes that al-Rashīd used this undertaking as a means of inserting himself physically in the region while at the same time seeking to limit the influence of the "warlords of the frontier."[361] El-Hibri has also emphasised the symbolic dimension of al-Rashīd's campaigns, which employed "monarchal

356 Cobb, *White Banners*, 92.

357 I borrow this expression from Bosworth, from his introduction to the translation of volume 30 of al-Ṭabarī's *Taʾrīkh al-rusul wa-al-mulūk*, xvii. The phrase was later used and developed by Bonner, *Aristocratic Violence*, 99–106 and *Le jihad*, 156–60.

358 It is not possible to address these questions here; they have produced a lengthy bibliography. See Bonner, *Le jihad* and Cook, *Understanding Jihad*. See also Décobert, *Le mendiant et le combattant*, especially 52; Donner, "The Sources;" Picard, "Regards croisés."

359 Bonner, *Aristocratic Violence*, 69, 96, 99–106, and *Le jihad*, in particular 156 ff.

360 Al-Ṭabarī, vol. III, 99, trans. vol. XXX, 604. Bonner, *Aristocratic Violence*, 85.

361 Bonner, *Aristocratic Violence*, 87.

techniques" aimed at affirming the association between a space and a personal hegemony.[362]

In 190/806, Hārūn launched the most important campaign of his reign. The scale of this expedition was unprecedented in the Abbasid era: it was an expedition both on land and by sea. Cyprus was victim to the maritime attack, while the caliph himself took Heraclea and forced the emperor Nikephorus to sign a peace treaty.[363] The victory was celebrated with great pomp upon his return. The *ghāzī* champion of *jihād* achieved his architectural apogee with the construction of Hiraqla.[364] Erected several kilometres west of Raqqa, the monument proclaims the triumph of the leader of a righteous war. The site, designated as a *ḥiṣn* by Yāqūt,[365] comprises a square palace situated atop a terrace, enclosed within a circle 510 metres in diametre. While this circular form clearly echoes the arrangement of Baghdad, it seems it was constructed by Byzantine artisans in order to better proclaim "the superiority of the Muslim world over the Byzantine empire."[366] This logic accords perfectly with that already present during the Umayyad period.[367] Al-Rashīd's death in 193/809, however, prevented this edifice from being completed.[368]

This inscription of Abbasid success in a specific zone of the Syrian landscape invites us to turn our attention now to the locations of Abbasid power in the Syrian space. To conclude our inquiry, we must envision the changing dynamics of this authority that constantly sought to ensure its mobility.

8.3.3 *Between Damascus and Baghdad: Spaces of Caliphal Power*

This study has placed a great deal of emphasis on the opposition fabricated in both medieval and modern historiography between Umayyad and Abbasid spaces of power. In Chapter 4, we discussed this history that was recomposed in the mirror of the Euphrates. And yet, analysis of the spatial dynamics set in motion during the course of the second/eighth century conversely reveal

362 El-Hibri, *Reinterpreting*, 29.

363 Al-Ṭabarī, vol. III, 709–10, trans. vol. XXX, 262–3; Michael the Syrian, vol. III, 488–9, French trans. 16. See also al-Masʿūdī's detailed account, *Murūj*, vol. II, 340 ff., trans. Pellat vol. II, 286 ff.

364 Herzfeld was the first to identify this site's connection to Hārūn al-Rashīd. See Meinecke, *Patterns*, 16 ff.; Northedge, *Entre Amman et Samarra*, 85–6. See also Toueir et al., "Hiraqla."

365 Yāqūt, *Muʿjam*, vol. V, 398–9.

366 Meinecke, *Patterns*, 23. Toueir defended the inverse opinion, stating that "the workmen and sculptors were Arab Muslims." This claim is somewhat surprising, given that the argument is based on the discovery of an Arabic inscription near the western gate of the palace that was situated *backward* during construction, "L'Héraklia," 181.

367 Flood, *The Great Mosque*, 234.

368 Michael the Syrian, vol. III, 490, French trans. 21; Toueir, "L'Héraklia," 182–3.

a tropism deeply rooted in the Euphrates. This tendency is obvious under the Marwanids, the prime examples being those spaces of power preferred by Hishām and Marwān II. Al-Ruṣāfa and Ḥarrān are clear illustrations, corroborated by the numismatic evidence: the "administrative center of gravity" shifted toward the north.[369] In choosing al-Anbār, Abū al-ʿAbbās perpetuated an attachment to the Euphrates whose focus nonetheless remained somewhat further to the south. Al-Manṣūr's foundation of Baghdad seems to have sealed the fate of this union between caliphate and river to the benefit of its confluent, the Tigris. But even this is largely an optical illusion that the narrative sources tend to magnify. This distorting prism masks the significance of the Euphrates's constant power of attraction, one that materialised around two architectural projects: al-Rāfiqa and al-Raqqa.[370]

The first major project was at al-Rāfiqa, a new city constructed approximately 200 metres west of Raqqa. The sources betray a certain confusion surrounding its foundation. Al-Yaʿqūbī indicates that the plan was conceived by Abū Jaʿfar, who was then governor of the region under the caliphate of his brother, Abū al-ʿAbbās.[371] This is the only mention that situates the undertaking at such an early date, as the other sources all place the city's foundation under the caliphate of al-Manṣūr. Perhaps these attributions should be viewed as references to works that began later, after Abū Jaʿfar's accession to the caliphate, while the site itself had existed for some time prior. The project was met with hostility from the inhabitants of Raqqa, who feared that their economy would suffer from the proximity of this new rival city. A monk's prediction stating that Abū Jaʿfar was destined to build a city in this location nevertheless convinced the caliph to overcome his hesitations, and he constructed al-Rāfiqa. This passage, however, is dubious, as it is completely identical to the account of the foundation of Baghdad. Al-Ṭabarī recounts this monk's anecdote justifying the creation of al-Rāfiqa twice, first under the year 145/762 following the narrative on the foundation of Baghdad, and again on its own under the year 154/770–771.[372] The affirmation that Baghdad served as a model for the plan of al-Rāfiqa may be the source of this confusion. Al-Ṭabarī's two accounts may also differ with respect to the architectural parallels between the two cities. He first states that al-Rāfiqa was built in the image of the round city, "except[373] for the walls (*al-sūr*), iron gates (*abwāb al-ḥadīd*) and a moat (*khandaq*) at some

369 Bone, *The Administration*, 9.

370 On the history of these two interconnected cities, see Heidemann, "Die Geschichte von ar-Raqqa/ar-Rāfiqa" and Bosworth, "Ar-Raqqa: Geopolitical Factors and its History."

371 Al-Yaʿqūbī, *Taʾrīkh*, vol. II, 358.

372 Al-Ṭabarī, vol. III, 276 and 372, trans. vol. XXVIII, 244 and vol. XXIX, 67–8.

373 If we follow McAuliffe's translation (trans. vol. XXVIII, 245), although *siwan* (or *suwan*) could also signify that the list that follows is identical to the Baghdad model, rather than

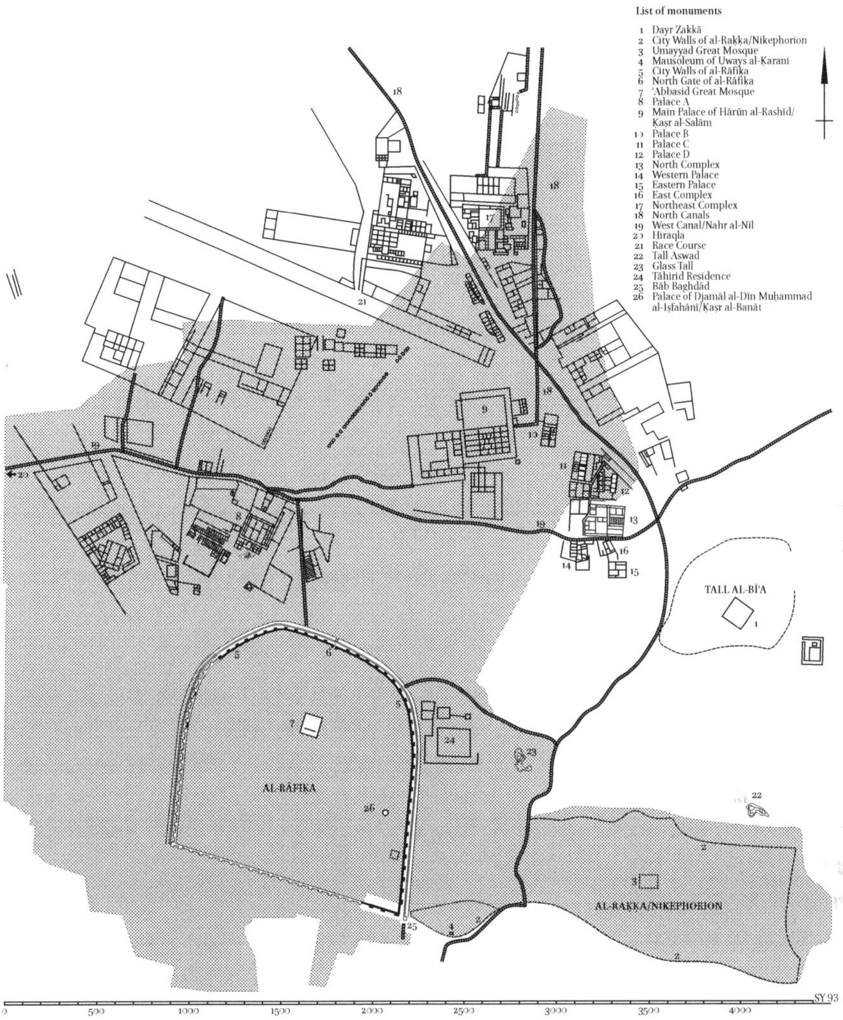

FIGURE 8.6 Plan of al-Raqqa / al-Rāfiqa
© "AL-RAḲḲA," *ENCYCLOPAEDIA OF ISLAM, SECOND EDITION*

distance."[374] Later, he indicates that in 155/771–772, al-Manṣūr sent al-Mahdī to build al-Rāfiqa, and the latter constructed gates, courtyards (*riḥāb*), and streets (*shawāriʿ*) identical to the Baghdad model, whose subdivisions (*fuṣūl*) he also adopted.[375] Al-Mahdī equipped the city with walls and dug a trench

different. This is what the second report recorded by al-Ṭabarī would seem to suggest, vol. III, 372, trans. vol. XXIX, 67–8.

374 Al-Ṭabarī, vol. III, 276, trans. vol. XXVIII, 245.

375 Al-Ṭabarī, vol. III, 373, trans. vol. XXIX, 69. Kennedy proposes translating *fuṣūl* as "arcades."

before returning. This insistence on imitating Baghdad perhaps belies a desire to oppose an Abbasid urbanist ideal with the Umayyad "visual culture" that had prevailed in the region until then. Based on al-Ṭabarī's text, it seems that the decision to build the city was made in 154 and that work began in 155. This last date is also cited by al-Balādhurī, who specifies that a *jund* of the *ahl Khurāsān* was located there under the authority of al-Mahdī.[376] The *Anonymous Syriac Chronicle of 813* also mentions the construction of a city by al-Manṣūr in the year 1080 of the Seleucid era.[377]

The site of al-Rāfiqa, associated with at least two of the three first rulers of the Abbasid empire, was undoubtedly part of a project to solidify caliphal power in the region, one with a strong military dimension. The plan of the city takes the shape of a "parallelogram surmounted by a half-circle"[378] approximately 1300 metres in size. A massive rampart nearly five kilometres long and guarded by 120 towers constitutes the most impressive part of the city's defense. The enclosure at first comprised three entrances; excavations conducted at the level of the northern gate have revealed its majestic dimensions.[379] A road led from this gate to the great mosque situated in the centre of the city. The palace was likely also located there, although no trace thereof has been uncovered.[380] The architectural program presiding over the construction of al-Rāfiqa is marked by an incontestable monumentality in the context of the Syrian space, for it nearly equaled Damascus in size; in conjunction with al-Raqqa, the dimensions of the two cities were surely second only to Baghdad, and surpassed all the cities of Syria and Mesopotamia as well.[381] While al-Rāfiqa was originally the "companion" to al-Raqqa, the cities eventually fused into one, and al-Manṣūr's city became the heart of al-Rashīd's Raqqa.[382]

Al-Rashīd's decision to settle here may seem logical, although the caliph also appears to have set his sights on other locales. The sources state that he had also planned to settle in Antioch; according to Ibn al-Faqīh, the inhabitants of the city did not approve of this project, and did not hesitate to inform him that it was not "his land" (*balād*).[383] It is impossible to know if this reproach

376 Al-Balādhurī, *Futūḥ*, 179; Ibn al-Faqīh, *Mukhtaṣar*, 132, trans. 159; Sourdel, "La Syrie," 160.

377 *813*, 247, Latin trans. 188. The Seleucid era began in the year 311 BC, so the above date corresponds to year 769.

378 Meinecke, "al- Raḳḳa." See also Miglus, *Raqqa I*; Heidemann and Becker, *Raqqa II*; Daiber and Becker, *Raqqa III*.

379 Meinecke, "al-Raḳḳa."

380 Northedge, *Entre Amman et Samarra*, 82.

381 Meinecke, "al-Raḳḳa."

382 Kennedy, *When Baghdad Ruled the Muslim World*, 66–7.

383 Ibn al-Faqīh, *Mukhtaṣar*, 116, trans, 141; Sourdel, "La Syrie," 167.

amounts to mere hostility from the region's natives in the face of Abbasid power, or if it is an indication of the Banū Ṣāliḥ's hold on the area. Al-Masʿūdī, who also mentions the caliph's aborted plan, simply cites reasons of climate as justification for al-Rashīd's decision not to settle there.[384] After these issues, the caliph ultimately decided on al-Raqqa, which he made his primary residence (*waṭān*) beginning in 180/796–797.[385] Kennedy also highlighted the irony of the fact that, thanks to the *Thousand and One Nights*, the name Hārūn al-Rashīd is linked perhaps more so than any other with Baghdad, despite the caliph's strenuous efforts to distance himself from this city he did not love.[386]

Settling on the banks of the Euphrates fit into al-Rashīd's broader political aims, as his decision to make al-Raqqa his home coincided precisely with his institution of the practice of starting his official edicts (*fī ṣudūr kutubihi*) with the phrase "*al-ṣalāt ʿalā Muḥammad ṣalā Allāh ʿalayhi wa-salam.*"[387] The city was home to the main governing bodies and the royal court; during his pilgrimage in 186/802, Hārūn left Ibrāhīm b. ʿUthmān b. Nahīk al-ʿAkkī in Raqqa in charge of the harem (*al-ḥaram*), the treasury and finances (*al-khazāʾin wa-al-amwāl*), and the army (*al-ʿaskar*).[388] The importance of this city was not lost on Michael the Syrian, who saw it as a "second Babylon," or, in other words, the equal of Baghdad. The patriarch also mentioned important works in the region, among them two canals dug to ensure the city's water supply – one derived from the Euphrates, the other from the Sarūj – whose banks boasted numerous lush gardens.[389] The canal connected to the Euphrates was almost certainly that known as the Nahr al-Nīl.[390]

German archaeological excavations at Raqqa have confirmed that al-Rashīd's installation there resulted in the development of massive agricultural programs. For these purposes, an important palatial zone was created north of the twin cities, covering a total surface area of nearly ten square kilometres. Twenty different palaces and palace complexes have been discovered thanks to these digs or through the use of aerial photography.[391] One castle with particularly monumental dimensions (approximately 350 × 300 metres), located in a central position, has been identified as the caliph's primary residence, or

384 Al-Masʿūdī, *Murūj*, vol. II, 284, trans. Pellat vol. II, 264–5.

385 Al-Ṭabarī, vol. III, 645, trans. vol. XXX, 162. See also Michael the Syrian, vol. III, 483, French trans. 10.

386 Kennedy, *When Baghdad Ruled the Muslim World*, 65–6.

387 Al-Ṭabarī, vol. III, 646, trans. vol. XXX, 166.

388 Al-Ṭabarī, vol. III, 654, trans. vol. XXX, 183.

389 Michael the Syrian, vol. III, 483, French trans. 10.

390 Meinecke, "al- Raḳḳa."

391 See Daiber and Becker, *Raqqa III*.

what Yāqūt called the Qaṣr al-Salām. Despite the lack of inscriptions associated with these structures,[392] numismatic evidence offers valuable information: for example, significant quantities of coins were struck in the caliph's name at al-Rāfiqa in 189/804–805.[393] Caliphal presence contributed to sustained economic activity in the area, as attested today both by the discovery of currency minted there[394] as well as by the production of pottery and glass.[395] The city occupied a strategic position, and the Euphrates was an important channel for communication, especially with Iraq. When setting out for Khurāsān on what would be his final journey, Hārūn al-Rashīd made the trip from Raqqa to Baghdad by boat (*sufun*).[396]

Al-Rashīd died at Ṭūs in Jumādā II 193/March 809. His son al-Amīn succeeded him and settled in Baghdad. His mother, Zubayda,[397] had the treasury transported from Raqqa to al-Manṣūr's city.[398] The site of Raqqa bears the marks of the court's rapid departure for Iraq: certain buildings were never completed, and the minting of coinage there decreased significantly.[399]

Scholars have long argued that these two projects at al-Rāfiqa and Raqqa served dual purposes: to strengthen control over Syria and to better ensure border security against Byzantium. Al-Ṭabarī reports that al-Rashīd told one of his officers that his main reasons for settling in Raqqa were the people in the region's (*nāḥiyya*) attachment to the Umayyads and their propensity to revolt; if not for these factors, he would never have left Baghdad, whose praises he then sings.[400] However, it has been shown above that the caliph tried hard to distance himself from this city, with which he was associated mainly thanks to the *Thousand and One Nights*. The caliph had also briefly envisioned settling in places other than Antioch and Raqqa; he had considered the Jibāl, Marj al-Qalaʿa, and later Bāqirdā, on the Tigris north of Mosul. Work was even begun in these locales, before the caliph renounced these projects and moved on.[401] Thus, it seems quite clear that Hārūn had no desire to reside in Baghdad.

---

392 Ibn Shaddād mentions an inscription in al-Rashīd's name near the Bāb al-Sibāl, the eastern gate of al-Rāfiqa. See Meinecke, "al- Raḳḳa."

393 Meinecke, "al Raḳḳa."

394 Although the coins produced appear to have been used in a relatively limited region surrounding the caliphal residence, see Heidemann, "Die Fundmünzen" and "Numismatische Quellen."

395 Meinecke, "al- Raḳḳa." The ceramics have been analysed in detail by Miglus, *Raqqa I*.

396 Al-Ṭabarī, vol. III, 730, trans. vol. XXX, 291.

397 On this influential figure, see Abbott's classic *Two Queens of Baghdad*.

398 Al-Ṭabarī, vol. III, 775, trans. vol. XXXI, 18; Michael the Syrian, vol. III, 490, French trans. 21.

399 Heidemann, "Numismatische Quellen."

400 Al-Ṭabarī, vol. III, 706, trans. vol. XXX, 256–7.

401 Al-Ṭabarī, vol. III, 606–7, 610, trans. vol. XXX, 103, 109–10.

Al-Ṭabarī's account, then, must be contextualised further. The scene he describes took place in Dhū al-Ḥijja 189/November 805: on the road to Raqqa, the caliph passed through Baghdad and ordered that the dismembered remains of Jaʿfar the Barmakid, which had been hung from the city's bridges, be burned.[402] Al-Rashīd's aforementioned defense of the city and this gruesome affair are in fact intrinsically connected: the praise al-Ṭabarī attributes to the caliph is undoubtedly less rooted in his appreciation for al-Manṣūr's city than in his pleasure at the Barmakids' defeat and the newly restored authority of his ancestors. It should also be noted that Hārūn addressed these remarks to a soldier, and it is certain that the *abnāʾ*, the soldiers from Khurāsān installed in Baghdad, did not look favourably upon the Barmakids' stranglehold on the Abbasid state. The hostility between the two camps was such that it was very likely one of the reasons behind al-Rashīd's decision to leave Baghdad.[403] The Barmakids' downfall was thus a means for the caliph to connect with his troops, who had assured the Abbasids' success. In Baghdad, the victory of the *abnāʾ* and the caliphate was displayed in particularly ostentatious ways, as witnessed by the pieces of Jaʿfar b. Yaḥyā's body suspended from the city's bridges. In these circumstances, the caliph would have been forced to oppose these two places of memory: Raqqa, synonymous with the Barmakids' rise to power, and Baghdad, which symbolised a return to order and caliphal authority. These associations required the caliph to sing the latter city's praises at this time; nevertheless, it should also be noted that Raqqa was not only Hārūn's favourite residence, but also the city in which the Barmakids Yaḥyā b. Khālid and his son Faḍl were imprisoned and died, without being subjected to the same unfortunate fate as Jaʿfar.[404]

In effect, contrary to the assertions found in much modern historiography on the subject, al-Rashīd's move to Raqqa cannot simply be described as a response to the existence of rebellious tendencies in Syria. The province was no more susceptible to uprisings than any other region under the Abbasid caliphate, Khurāsān foremost among them.[405] The Syrian space was not, therefore, exceptional in this regard, requiring the caliph's presence and intervention more than any other area. Indeed, between the rebellion of ʿAbd Allāh b. ʿAlī in 136/754 and that of Abū al-Haydhām in 177/793, the Shām witnessed a period of relative calm. Was this last uprising sufficient cause to justify al-Rashīd's

402 Al-Ṭabarī, vol. III, 706, trans. vol. XXX, 256–7. For more on the circumstances in which Jaʿfar's corpse was ostensibly exhibited in Baghdad, see al-Ṭabarī, vol. III, 683, trans. vol. XXX, 223.

403 Shaban, *Islamic History*, vol. II, 37; Kennedy, *The Early Abbasid Caliphate*, 120.

404 El-Hibri, *Reinterpreting*, 56.

405 Cobb, *White Banners*, 131.

decision to settle on the banks of the Euphrates? Unlikely: ʿAbd al-Malik b. Ṣāliḥ was almost certainly a greater motivating factor than Abū al-Haydhām. The previous pages have demonstrated that the caliph's choice of residence figured into a reaffirmation of caliphal authority over the provincial elites. The Abbasid patrimonialism enjoyed by Ṣāliḥ b. ʿAlī and his heirs provoked the caliphate's mistrust, especially given the unfortunate experience of Ṣāliḥ's brother, ʿAbd Allāh b. ʿAlī, who appeared as a rival to the future al-Manṣūr. However, limiting the Banū Ṣāliḥ's power by progressively isolating them in the *jund* of Qinnasrīn had destabilising consequences for the province.

The accent on northern Syria during al-Rashīd's caliphate was also tied to the region's proximity to the border and thus to the war effort against the Byzantines. Here again, as noted previously, *jihād* was an additional means of, rather than a purpose for, filling the void left by the respective downfalls of the Barmakids and ʿAbd al-Malik b. Ṣāliḥ. Without completely negating their importance – for the *ahl al-Shām* and the border both clearly required surveillance – these two reasons must be inscribed within the broader context of lasting continuities inherited from the Marwanid government in Syria. Al-Rāfiqa and Raqqa are also part of this context.

The continuation of a preexisting practice of power is illustrated by the evolution of sites commissioned by the Umayyads in the Syrian space. Although the archaeological evidence remains fragmentary, a recognisable tendency nevertheless emerges, a few examples of which will suffice to demonstrate its relevance. At Qaṣr al-Ḥayr al-Sharqī, the city founded by Hishām, two-thirds of the residences making up the "peripheral edifices" were abandoned before the end of the eighth century, while the other third were occupied at least through the first few decades of the ninth century. During this period, secondary structures were built within the small compound, both in the courtyard and in certain rooms; rubbish heaps accumulated inside the enclosure in the first half of the ninth century. These findings demonstrate that, by the first half of the ninth century at the latest, "the monument no longer served as a palace, but as a residential area."[406] Elsewhere, the "Umayyad castles" at al-Faddayn/Mafraq, Khirbat al-Minya and al-Bakhrāʾ evolved along similar lines, while others, such as al-Muwaqqar, seem to have been occupied for a slightly longer period, although no longer in a palatial capacity. Only al-Qasṭal appears as a notable exception to this rule, as the site remained a residence for elites until the late ninth century. This, at least, is the impression given by the inscriptions that have been studied at the site's necropolis – the only cemetery indisputably

406 Genequand, "Formation et devenir," 432.

connected to an "Umayyad castle" – although archaeology has not yet allowed us to confirm or refine this conception.[407]

This evidence led Genequand to argue in favour of a "continuous decline" at these sites in the wake of the Marwanids' downfall, which, over a period of approximately fifty to one hundred years, eventually led to their "complete abandonment or reduced occupation, without any memory of their previous states." This "ephemeral architectural landscape" thus lost "its primary function;"[408] it no longer responded to the needs that had made Syria the locus of patrimonial strategies and an exercise of mobile power aimed at preserving delicate balances throughout the long second/eighth century. The evolution of the sites commissioned by the Umayyads thus followed the rhythm of a history that anchored itself for a time along the banks of the Euphrates, before undergoing major transformations due to the political upheaval following al-Rashīd's death that would ultimately shift its focus firmly in the direction of Iraq and Iran.

The textual sources create an image of Marwanid mobility as strictly limited to the Syrian space, with the notable exceptions of the *ḥajj* and periods of unrest that required combat on all fronts. The early Abbasids, by contrast, appear much more mobile. Al-Manṣūr visited Jerusalem twice in 140/757–758, and then again in 154/771, accompanied by his son, al-Mahdī.[409] Al-Mahdī travelled again to Palestine in 163/779–780 after traversing the roads of northern Syria with his son, Hārūn, who was soon to march on Constantinople.[410] It may seem at first glance as though an Islamic mobility replaced a Syrian one. However, this impression is deceptive, as the movements of rulers throughout the Shām remained essentially tied to pilgrimages or campaigns against the Byzantines. Syria was first and foremost a transit zone (*Durchzugsgebiete*),[411] although Jerusalem remained a focal point of attraction.

407 Imbert, "La nécropole islamique;" Genequand, "Formation et devenir."

408 Genequand, "Formation et devenir," 444. The "ephemeral" dimension of these sites refers strictly to the nature of their occupation and in no way to the considerable influence these structures had on the history of Islamic architecture.

409 Al-Ṭabarī, vol. III, 129, 372, trans. vol. XXVIII, 60–1, vol. XXIX, 67; Sourdel, "La Syrie," 166. This voyage is the one associated with the inscription at Ascalon written in the name of al-Mahdī mentioned in the previous chapter. See *RCEA*, vol. I, n. 42; Sharon, *CIAP*, vol. I, 144–6. Al-Manṣūr's first trip to Jerusalem is also recorded by Elias of Nisibis (who dates it to 141 AH), 176, Latin trans. 83, trans. Delaporte, 108.

410 Al-Ṭabarī, vol. III, 500, trans. vol. XXIX, 215. On al-Mahdī and his son's itinerary in northern Syria, see above, Ch. 5. It should also be noted that al-Rashīd had a cistern constructed at al-Ramla in 172/789. See Rosen-Ayalon, *Art et architecture*, 56–7.

411 Preserving the typology of spaces of mobility proposed by Bernhardt, *Itinerant Kinship*, 61, adapted from that defined by Müller-Mertens, *Die Reichsstruktur*.

Al-Rashīd's caliphate brought significant developments in the form of the *jihād*, which led him to alternate military campaigns with the *ḥajj*. The reasons for this shift were analysed above: in the words of von Sievers, these Byzantine wars were used "as an instrument for a restructuring of the social hierarchy."[412] Hārūn al-Rashīd's efforts to become the "*ghāzī*-caliph," especially in the final years of his caliphate, were nullified by the conflict that erupted between his sons. The reappropriation of the war caliph's prerogatives thus gave way to the war of the caliphs.

Despite its deep impact on Abbasid society, the civil war did not alter the initial equation: governing from a distance remained the caliphate's most pressing problem. The solutions adopted after 197/813 were firmly part of an Iraqi context, without discounting the important "sequel" in which al-Mutawakkil tried to move the caliphate back to Damascus in 244/858.[413] The mobility question crystallised around Sāmarrāʾ, which became a sort of gilded cage for the caliphs, a space in which the Abbasid rulers' itinerance came to an irrevocable end. To borrow Dakhlia's expression, this limitation of caliphal movement was essentially a "political castration,"[414] as mobility would thereafter become the exclusive domain of the Turkish soldiers. The "Sāmarrāʾ moment" was thus a fundamental one, both politically and historiographically.

The patrimonial system underlying the exercise of power throughout the second/eighth century also changed dramatically after the fourth *fitna*. Cobb highlighted the profound implications of these transformations in Syria,[415] while Décobert has shed light on the progressive shift of a portion of patrimonial power from the hands of the caliphate to those of "the men of scriptural knowledge (*hommes du savoir scripturaire*)".[416] Kennedy has also shown how the economic policies at the base of these patrimonial developments changed over time: the *ḍiyāʿ* were increasingly incorporated into the caliphal domain, a phenomenon that took place under al-Rashīd's reign. Land ownership and agricultural development no longer constituted the primary sources of revenue for the elites, which henceforth derived from control over taxation.[417] The gradual accumulation of these elements sealed the fate of most of the sites commissioned by the Umayyads, which now failed to sufficiently respond to new needs. These transformations meant that the "desert castles" were

412 Von Sievers, "Military, Merchants and Nomads," 219.

413 On this episode, see Cobb, "Al-Mutawakkil's Damascus."

414 Dakhlia, *L'empire des passions*, 56.

415 Cobb, *White Banners*, 92–102.

416 Décobert, "Notule sur le patrimonialisme omeyyade," 247 ff.

417 Kennedy, "Elite Incomes," 28.

destined to quickly become the embodiment of an "ephemeral architectural landscape."[418]

These aspects together coincided to form the landscape of the Shām during a period in which it was important to define a relationship to space. In addition to the creation of an Umayyad "visual culture," its other salient characteristic was the detachment of the ʿAwāṣim and Thughūr, which attests to a recognition of the impossibility of ever taking Constantinople, experienced first-hand by Hārūn in 163/779–780.[419] The border was traditionally an area invested with a surplus of power: al-Rashīd offered a perfect illustration of this fact. Analysis of these factors allows us to better understand the complex image of Syria sketched by the geographers of the classical period:[420] the Shām they describe was the result of these successive spatial constructions.

Regional power dynamics under the late Umayyads and early Abbasids emerged more from a "continuity of change"[421] than a logic of opposition. The coherence of the period spanning 72/692 to 193/809 rests perhaps above all in the construction of a Syrian space, molded by a specific power practice, at once mobile and patrimonial, and accompanied by the desire to create a caliphal landscape.

418 Genequand, "Formation et devenir," 444.

419 The importance of al-Rashīd in the construction of the border landscape has been discussed by Straughn, *Materializing Islam*, 165–6. On the related question of the *ribāṭs*, see Borrut and Picard, "Râbata, ribât, râbita."

420 On the specific problems posed by the geographic sources, see above, Ch. 3.

421 Shboul and Walmsley, "Identity and Self-Image," 275. See also Eddé and Sodini, "Les villages de Syrie du Nord."

Conclusion

At the outset of our investigation, we discussed the methodological difficulties inherent to any study dedicated to the first centuries of Islam. These circumstances have led us on a winding path as we tried to disentangle the threads of these rewritten narratives. This Syrian history steeped in oblivion cannot be approached directly; it must be read through the shadows, passing swiftly from Umayyad clarity to Abbasid obscurity. We have tried to restore vibrant colour to an image faded in many places to a simple dichotomy of black and white. After such a meandering journey through the Syrian space, it will be helpful to conclude our voyage with a brief review of these many interwoven and often seemingly unrelated elements.

Older written history did indeed exist in the Shām, under the Marwanids as well as the early Abbasids. This historiography, however, fell victim to strategies of oblivion, and today only distant echoes of this production remain. These whispers are nevertheless important, because these initial narratives would condition the possibilities for later rewritings, as much for what they left unsaid – information thus practically irretrievable for the Abbasid scribes – as for what they recorded. In this sense, a series of Umayyad historiographic filters were put into place. This statement applies equally to the early Abbasids, who undertook a significant rewriting project aimed at affirming their superiority over their Alid cousins. These successive stages fundamentally shaped the compositional material available to subsequent generations of historians.

Two antithetical factors played a predominant role in ensuring that historical information survived the vagaries of transmission. The first was the exclusivity of certain facts, which perhaps translates to prior attempts at imposing a historiographic filter, as no other version of the past was accessible at the time that the new phase of writing was begun; the second, at the other extreme of the circulation of information, was the early diffusion of a broader corpus of texts that provided firm guarantees against strategies of silence. Elements that were already well-known could not be completely effaced.

These early recordings of history were likely even more important than is often acknowledged, as their task was a crucial one: they responded to the need for legitimation.[1] For this reason, writing necessitated rewriting according to the changing political winds. These successive recompositions read as so many consecutive historiographic filters, and we have tried to clarify the rhythms of these various ideological crystallisations. From the approach of a

1 Donner, *Narratives*, 114.

 | DOI:10.1163/9789004466326_011

history of meanings, analysing the *moments* of composition and recomposition allows us to illuminate the constant flow of new significations given to a past that had to be reshaped to conform with the needs of the present.

This series of orthodoxies resulted in the imposition of a historiographic canon that developed in Abbasid Iraq in the post-Sāmarrā' period. This vulgate was not the only attempt at doing so, but it was the one that ultimately prevailed, in part due to previous strategies of selection. New meaning was thus given to the recent Islamic past, which was enclosed within a rigid framework and reduced to a kernel of events that were destined to become common in nearly every source. Other interpretations were still possible, but the field of possible interpretations was henceforth limited. This "historiographic skeleton" has left an indelible mark: it is perhaps the greatest inheritance from this "age of writing."[2]

In order to free ourselves from these confines and fully comprehend their significance, it was necessary to situate the pertinent sources with respect to the historiographic canon. This point was essential to our approach. Other perspectives thus emerged, in particular from the non-Muslim sources. Traditionally deemed "external sources," they were, in fact, the products of dynamics at work in many historiographies throughout the Near East. Detailed examination of these intercultural exchanges opens myriad avenues for research, most of which have not yet been explored. Studying the transmission between these different corpora allows us to undertake an archaeology of the texts, which in some cases makes it possible to date a particular piece of historical information's entry into circulation and offers a critical perspective for a study whose goal is to seek out alternative pasts beneath the layers of constantly rewritten historiographies. The different *moments* of memory sedimentation reveal the many distinct *meanings* given to the past; they clearly demand to be situated within a history of memory.

The first stage in this voyage into the memory of the first centuries of Islam evoked the Umayyad *memoria* and the strategies of oblivion to which the first Islamic dynasty fell victim. Analysis of the Abbasids' attitudes when confronted with the memory of their adversaries reveals that the Umayyads slipped gradually from adversity to alterity, thus enabling the redemption of their memory, a step that was in fact necessary in order to affirm the political continuity of the caliphate. The unavoidable Umayyad "realms of memory" were also preserved in this manner. However, this obligatory historical rehabilitation of the Marwanids was not without consequences. Since they were unable to completely erase the traces of the first Islamic dynasty, the

2 Martinez-Gros, *L'idéologie omeyyade*, 321.

chronographers developed other strategies, especially regarding the spaces with which they had been associated. The Umayyad Shām was thus held up in fundamental opposition to Abbasid Iraq, the Euphrates acting as a mirror between the two. At the same time that Umayyad memory was being confined to a particular and exclusive space, the remnants of an Abbasid Syrian past were being erased, all as part of an ambiguous dialectic between oblivion that was not always possible and remembrance that was often necessary. This process may have been facilitated by the fact that the Syrian space played an important role in Umayyad ideology, as attested by the emphasis on forging Solomonic connections.

These many recompositions notwithstanding, certain positive Umayyad exceptions emerged in Abbasid historiography, even despite its reputation for hostility to the first Islamic dynasty. Two Marwanid figures in particular stand out: Maslama b. ʿAbd al-Malik and ʿUmar b. ʿAbd al-ʿAzīz. Many lessons can be learned from these two examples. They illustrate both the complexity of the processes of rewriting history underway at the time and reveal deep-seated historiographic competitions. Examining the images of these two figures also helps us understand their roles in the Umayyad pantheon as well as in Islamic historiography. They both had uniquely significant connections to space that conditioned the remainder of this study. Maslama, as a new Alexander the Great, represented the establishment of the definitive borders of the world, while the caliph ʿUmar II was the face of the empire's contraction. These interconnected functions explain the tenuous links between the two men, both of whom serve to show how Umayyad heroes were created.

Their redemption in Abbasid historiography was the result of a rapid diffusion, via numerous channels, of images constructed during their lifetimes or just after their deaths. To comprehend why the Abbasid chronographers were so interested in these enemy heroes, we must examine the roles assigned to them in Abbasid history and historiography. The answer to this question lies above all in the fact that the Umayyads had the essential function of preserving the potential for the Abbasids to accede to the caliphate. ʿUmar II fulfilled this role perfectly by sanctioning the marital union that produced Abū al-ʿAbbās, while Maslama postponed the conditions of the End of Days, thus allowing for the fulfilment of Abbasid time. Others, like Hishām, were held up as models of good governance.

Alongside these Umayyad figures who were fundamental to the realisation of the Abbasids' political aims, the Abbasid chronographers composed an origin myth primarily intended to minimise their masters' violent seizure of power in 132/750. A heavily standardised vulgate was circulated, and it henceforth came to dominate most medieval and modern historiography. When considered strictly in the context of Syria, the episode nevertheless exposes the traces of other histories and allows us to shed light on the methods of oblivion employed by these historians. The event was essentially created, thus imposing meaning upon it. The troublesome figure of ʿAbd Allāh b. ʿAlī fell victim to strategies of isolation, relegated to the rank of Syrian rebel; the manipulations even went so far as to confiscate his *laqab*, al-Saffāḥ, which classical historiography attributed instead to the first Abbasid caliph, Abū al-ʿAbbās. More broadly, *revolutionary time* was the true target of the chroniclers' efforts, concerned as they were with limiting the period of uncertainty in which Abbasid pretentions struggled against rival ambitions.

This fabrication of origins is also at the heart of the deeply contrasting image of Syrian history. The Abbasid Revolution, presented as a fundamental rupture, gave credence to the hypothesis that the Shām was in decline at the same time that Iraq was on the rise. Analysis of the historiographic constructions that produced this presentation of the facts has revealed that other readings of the period were also possible. This evidence pushed us in the direction of another *meaning* that could be assigned to the Syrian space in the second/eighth century. The theme of the exercise of power helped us retrace this Syrian history for a period in which the caliphate was obliged to define its relationship to the immense territories it had acquired through conquest. The portraits sketched in the preceding chapters reach their full significance here.

ʿAbd al-Malik's reforms after his victory over Ibn al-Zubayr were intended to restore Umayyad authority. Several strategies were thus employed to this end. Architecture and numismatics helped create an Islamic identity and a caliphal landscape while simultaneously affirming a Marwanid visual culture. The caliph gave his relatives sovereignty over a given portion of the Shām as an expression of patrimonial power. ʿAbd al-Malik also relied on a mobile practice of power that his sons would later imitate in the regions they had been granted. The famous "desert castles" were the product of this governing principle, providing concrete conditions for itinerance while also conveying the prince's authority in his absence. These elements offer new opportunities to illuminate the conditions that presided over the construction of a caliphal landscape, ensuring the *memoria* of a dynasty[3] whose primary function was

3 See Flood, *The Great Mosque*, 213: "The changes to the urban fabric of Damascus undertaken in the early eighth century constituted an Umayyadisation, or at least a memorialisation of Umayyad hegemony, as much as an Islamicisation."

to structure social relations,[4] while "the mobility of the king was thus a central element in his power."[5]

Although this system allowed the Marwanid restoration to take place, it gradually unravelled, as the example of Hishām b. ʿAbd al-Malik's caliphate demonstrates. The caliph restricted his mobility to a preferred area, one he had held authority over since his days as a prince and heir to the throne; to compensate for this loss, the ruler delegated his mobility more and more, and it was gradually usurped by the military. Competition between different power networks increased as a result: the desire for mobility and the imposition of an orthodoxy collided, leaving the path open for others to infiltrate the gaps created in the process. The Umayyads also lost their monopoly on long-distance mobility, an essential condition for maintaining stability in a system based on itinerant power.

Inheritors of a Syria wracked by long years of conflict in the wake of the third *fitna* and faced with the same protagonists as their predecessors, the Abbasids tried to slowly rebuild the foundations of Marwanid government. Patrimonialism remained the rule, in particular for the descendants of Ṣāliḥ b. ʿAlī. However, in trying to prevent the recurrence of situations as dangerous as ʿAbd Allāh b. ʿAlī's rebellion, the caliphs employed strategies of isolation to limit the influence of the people to whom they had delegated their authority. The Banū Ṣāliḥ were thus progressively marginalised, their sphere of influence restricted to northern Syria. This caliphal policy, however, simultaneously weakened their control over the province, providing ample opportunity for new revolts to arise. These new threats did not prevent Hārūn al-Rashīd from seeing this policy through to its end, achieved simply by evicting ʿAbd al-Malik b. Ṣāliḥ. To fill the void thus created and further widened by the Barmakids' downfall, the sovereign sought to portray himself as the "*ghāzī*-caliph,"[6] making northern Syria his preferred region of power. This dual effort to dictate Abbasid patrimonialism and develop the ideology of *jihād* favoured the Euphrates-based tropism of the caliphate under the early Abbasids, represented above all by al-Rāfiqa and Raqqa, where al-Rashīd would spend many long years.

The upheavals brought by the civil war that erupted after the caliph's death in 193/809 effectively broke the ties that had linked the caliphs to the Euphrates. Al-Rashīd marked the border between victory and defeat, between two eras and also two worlds, and thus he became the object of sweeping

4 Straughn, *Memorializing Islam*, 58.

5 Geertz, "Centers, Kings and Charisma," 163.

6 Bonner, *Aristocratic Violence*, 99–106 and *Le jihad*, 156–60.

narrative strategies thereafter.[7] New political stakes developed in a firmly Iraqi context, between Baghdad and Sāmarrā'. The sites commissioned in Syria as part of this practice of power, like the "Umayyad castles," became an "ephemeral architectural landscape"[8] because the function for which they had been created was slowly vanishing.

What we think we know about the Syrian space in the second/eighth century is above all the product of what the Abbasid historians themselves wanted to know and transmit. Narrative crystallisation took place in the post-Sāmarrā' period, a time when it was necessary to weave new threads in the direction of the past. As Geary has noted, "when traditional relationships between present and past break down, those most affected by this rupture respond by reshaping an understanding of that which unites past and present in terms of some new continuity in order to defend themselves from the effects of this rupture."[9] This construction of the past was not a complete written falsification, as some scholars have claimed, but rather shows that mastery over the past was of the utmost importance. The best illustration of this "need for writing"[10] is perhaps its *speed*, as noted throughout the preceding pages. From the walls of Constantinople to the gates of the Caucasus, from Medina to Damascus or the Great Zāb to the Nahr Abī Fuṭrūs, history was written almost in real time. The rapid pace at which it was recorded is evidence of how both the Umayyads and the Abbasids exploited "the potential of written culture."[11] Rewritings, which gave different meanings to these recomposed pasts, generated significant historiographic sedimentation.

These superimposed writings produced a history and a historiography full of paradoxes: a military hero who also represented defeat; a "holy" caliph given a cold welcome by the Banū ʿAbd al-Malik, who were then stripped of their power; a claimant to the throne – a designated heir – transformed into a rebel; and a bloodthirsty figure made a generous one. These apparent contradictions were deeply rooted in space, and derived their meaning from it: Syria was the land of Umayyad heroes and Abbasid anti-heroes. The period was also heavily inflected with messianic tendencies, as attested above all by a prolific apocalyptic production and numerous soteriological figures who gave order to the period and conditioned political and ideological choices. This concurrence

7 See El-Hibri, *Reinterpreting*.

8 Genequand, "Formation et devenir," 444.

9 Geary, *Phantoms of Remembrance*, 8. Geary's comments are based on Pocock's insights, "The Origins," 217.

10 Martinez-Gros, *L'idéologie omeyyade*, 27.

11 McKitterick, *History and Memory*, 22.

of histories and memories merged with other competitions, such as those for monumentality or mobility.

For Islamic history, the second/eighth century was a fundamental moment when relations of power were formed – between political authorities and the scholarly elite, between caliphs and military men – that left their mark on Islamic history thereafter. It was also the moment at which an Islamic memory was forged, made up of Muslim heroes and depicting a caliphal and sacred landscape, in addition to the geography of the caliphate. Syria, home of the first Islamic state, played a central role in these processes. The second century of the *hijra* is in some ways deeply Syrian, situated between the Dome of the Rock in Jerusalem and the commemorative monument at Hiraqla proclaiming the triumph of the "*ghāzī*-caliph."

This eighth Syrian century thus did not come to a close with the Abbasid Revolution in 132/750, as certain sources would have us believe; its history was written in the flow of the Euphrates. An Umayyad interregnum (*relais omeyyade*) existed, one that the Abbasids needed in order to affirm a *continuum* of the caliphate. From this perspective, Umayyad failures, more than any other factor, served the Abbasids' future success, and this fact meant that the Shām was fated to be caught between memory and power. The first/seventh century was that of memory of the Prophet, while the second century of the *hijra* was that of the memory of the caliphate and the Islamic state. The long eighth Syrian century was foundational, and for that reason, its appropriation was imperative.

Abbreviations

AAAS	*Annales archéologiques arabes syriennes*
ADAJ	*Annual of the Department of Antiquities of Jordan*
BASOR	*Bulletin of the American Schools of Oriental Research*
BEO	*Bulletin d'études orientales*
BSOAS	*Bulletin of the School of Oriental and African Studies*
CSCO	*Corpus Scriptorum Christianorum Orientalium*
DM	*Damaszener Mitteilungen*
IJMES	*International of Journal of Middle East Studies*
IOS	*Israel Oriental Studies*
IQ	*Islamic Quarterly*
JA	*Journal Asiatique*
JAL	*Journal of Arabic Literature*
JAOS	*Journal of the American Oriental Society*
JESHO	*Journal of Economic and Social History of the Orient*
JRAS	*Journal of the Royal Asiatic Society*
JSAI	*Jerusalem Studies in Arabic and Islam*
JSS	*Journal of Semitic Studies*
MUSJ	*Mélanges de l'Université Saint-Joseph*
OPSAS	*Occasional Papers of the School of Abbasid Studies*
PO	*Patrologia Orientalis*
REI	*Revue des études islamiques*
RSO	*Rivista degli Studi Orientali*
SHAJ	*Studies in the History and Archaeology of Jordan*
SI	*Studia Islamica*
ZDMG	*Zeitschrift der deutschen morgenländische Gesellschaft*

Sources

705 = Land, J. P. N. *Anecdota Syriaca*. vol. 2. Leiden: E. J. Brill, 1868. 11 (*addenda* to vol. I).

716 = Nau, F. "Un colloque du patriarche Jean avec l'émir des Agaréens et faits divers des années 712 à 716." *JA* 5 (1915): ed. 253–256, trans. 264–267.

724 = *Chronicon miscellaneum ad annum domini 724 pertinens*. Ed. E. W. Brooks. *Chronica Minora* II. CSCO vol. 3, Scriptores Syri t. 3. Leuven, 1904. 77–155.

– Latin trans. Jean-Baptiste Chabot. *Chronica Minora* II. CSCO vol. 4, Scriptores Syri t. 4. Leuven, 1955. 61–119.

775 = *Expositio quomodo se habeant generationes et familiae et anni ab Adamo usque hunc diem*. Ed. E. W. Brooks. *Chronica Minora* III. CSCO vol. 5, Scriptores Syri t. 5. Leuven, 1905. 337–349.

– Latin trans. E. W. Brooks. *Chronica Minora* III. CSCO vol. 6, Scriptores Syri t. 6. Leuven, 1960. 265–275.

813 = *Fragmenta chronici anonymi auctoris ad annum Domini 813 pertinentia*. Ed. E. W. Brooks. *Chronica Minora* III. CSCO vol. 5, Scriptores Syri t. 5. Leuven, 1905. 243–260.

– Latin trans. E. W. Brooks. *Chronica Minora* III. CSCO vol. 6, Scriptores Syri t. 6. Leuven, 1960. 185–196.

818 = Schoene, Alfred (ed.). *Eusebi chronicorum libri duo*. vol. 1, Appendix I. Berlin, 1875. 64–101.

819 = *Chronicon anonymum ad annum Domini 819 pertinens*. Ed. Aphram Barsaum in *Chronicon ad annum Christi 1234 pertinens* I. CSCO vol. 81, Scriptores Syri vol. 36. Leuven, 1920. 3–22.

– Latin trans. Jean-Baptiste Chabot. In *Chronicon ad annum Christi 1234 pertinens* I. CSCO 82, Scriptores Syri 37. Leuven, 1965 [1937]. 1–16.

846 = *Chronicon ad annum 846 pertinens*. Ed. E. W. Brooks. *Chronica Minora* II. CSCO vol. 3, Scriptores Syri t. 3. Leuven, 1904. 157–238.

– Partial English trans. E. W. Brooks. "A Syriac Chronicle of the Year 846." *ZDMG* 51 (1897): 569–588.

– Full Latin trans. Jean-Baptiste Chabot. *Chronica Minora* II. CSCO vol. 4, Scriptores Syri t. 4. Leuven, 1955. 121–180.

1234 = *Chronicon ad annum Christi 1234 pertinens*. Ed. Jean-Baptiste Chabot. 2 vol. CSCO vol. 81 and 82, Scriptores Syri vol. 36 and 37. Leuven, 1920 and 1916.

– Latin trans. vol. I Jean-Baptiste Chabot. CSCO vol. 109, Scriptores Syri t. 56. Leuven, 1965.

– French trans. vol. II Albert Abouna. CSCO 354, Scriptores Syri t. 154. Leuven, 1974.

Abū Dāwūd. *Sunan Abī Dāwūd*. 4 vol. Ed. M. M. ʿAbd al-Ḥamīd. Dār al-Fikr, n. p./n. d.

Abū al-Fidā'. *Taqwīm al-buldān*. Ed. J. T. Reinaud and W. M. de Slane. *Géographie d'Aboulfeda*. Paris 1840.

Abū Nuʿaym al-Iṣfahānī. *Ḥilyat al-awliyā' wa-ṭabaqāt al-asfiyā'*. 10 vol. Cairo: Maṭbaʿat al-Saʿāda, 1935.

Abū Yūsuf Yaʿqūb. *Kitāb al-kharāj*. Cairo: al-Maṭbaʿa al-Salafiyya, 1346 AH.

– *Le livre de l'impôt foncier*. Trans. Edmond Fagnan. Paris: Geuthner, 1921.

Abū Zurʿa al-Dimashqī. *Ta'rīkh*. 2 vol. Ed. S. A. al-Qujānī. Damascus: Majmaʿ al-lugha al-ʿarabiyya, 1980.

Aghānī = see al-Iṣfahānī.

Agapius of Manbij. *Kitāb al-ʿunwān*. Ed. and French trans. A. Vasiliev. *Patrologia Orientalis*, vol. VIII. Paris, 1911.

Akhbār al-dawla al-ʿabbāsiyya. Ed. A. A. Duri and A. J. al-Muṭṭalibī. Beirut, 1971.

Akhbār Majmūʿa = Ed. E. Lafuente y Alcántara, *Ajbar machmûa (Colección de tradiciones)*. Madrid, 1867. *A History of Early al-Andalus: the Akhbār Majmūʿa*. English trans. David James. London and New York: Routledge, 2012.

Akhbār ʿUbayd = see Ibn Hishām, *Kitāb al-tījān*.

Aḥmad b. Ḥanbal. *Al-Musnad*. 15 vol. Ed. A. M. Shākir. Cairo: Dār al-maʿārif, 1365–1375/1949–1956.

Al-Azdī. *Ta'rīkh al-Mawṣil*. Ed. ʿAlī Ḥabība. Cairo, 1967.

Baḥshal. *Ta'rīkh Wāsiṭ*. Ed. K. ʿAwwād. Baghdad, 1967.

Al-Bakrī. *Muʿjam mā istaʿjam min asmā' al-bilād wa-al-mawāḍiʿ*. Ed. Ferdinand Wüstenfeld. *Das geographische Wörterbuch*. Göttingen, 1876–1877; Ed. M. al-Saqa. Cairo, 1951.

Al-Balādhurī. *Ansāb al-ashrāf*.

– Vol. III. Ed. A. A. Duri. Wiesbaden: Franz Steiner Verlag, 1978.

– Vol. IV A. Ed. Max Schlössinger. Jerusalem, 1971.

– Vol. IV B. Ed. Max Schlössinger, 1938–1940.

– Vol. V. Ed. S. D. Goitein. 1936.

– Vol. VI B. Ed. Khalil Athamina. Jerusalem: The Max Schlössinger Memorial Series, The Hebrew University of Jerusalem, 1993.

– Vol. VII. Ed. M. al-Firdaws al-ʿAẓm. Damascus: Dār al-Yaqẓa al-ʿArabiyya, 2000.

– Vol. XI. Ed. W. Ahlwardt. *Anonyme arabische Chronik*. Greifswald, 1883.

Al-Balādhurī. *Kitāb futūḥ al-buldān*. Ed. M. J. de Goeje. Leiden: Brill, 1866.

– English trans. Philip K. Hitti and Francis Clark Murgotten. *The Origins of the Islamic State*. New York, 1968 [1916].

Balʿamī = al-Tabarī. *La chronique. Histoire des prophètes et des rois*, vol. II: *Mohammed, sceau des prophètes; Les quatre premiers califes; Les Omayyades; L'âge d'or des Abbassides*. Trans. Hermann Zotenberg. Paris: Thesaurus, Actes Sud/Sindbad, 2001 [1867–1874].

Bar Hebraeus. *Gregorii Barhebraei Chronicon Syriacum*. Ed. Paul Bedjan. Paris-Leipzig, 1890.
– English trans. Ernest W. Budge. *The Chronography of Gregory Abû'l-Faraj (1225–1286)*. Amsterdam: Apa-Philo Press, 1976 [1932].
Bible. The New Oxford Annotated Bible. New Revised Standard Version with the Apocrypha. 4th ed. Ed. Michael D. Coogan. New York: Oxford University Press, 2010.
Buṭrus b. Rāhib. *Ta'rīkh*. Ed. Louis Cheikho. CSCO vol. 45, Scriptores Arabici t. 1. Leuven, 1962 [1903].
– Latin trans. Louis Cheikho. CSCO vol. 46, Scriptores Arabici t. 2. Leuven, 1960 [1903].
Byzantine-Arabic Chronicle of 741 = *Byzantine-Arabic Chronicle of 741, Corpus Scriptorum Muzarabicorum*, I. Ed. Juan Gil. Madrid, 1973. 7–14.
– English trans. Robert G. Hoyland. In *Seeing Islam as Others Saw It*. Princeton: Darwin Press, 1997. 611–630.
Mozarabic Chronicle of 754 = *Mozarabic Chronicle of 754, Corpus Scriptorum Muzarabicorum*, I. Ed. Juan Gil. Madrid, 1973. 16–54.
Constantine Porphyrogenitus. *De administrando imperio*. Ed. Gyula Moravcsik and R. J. H. Jenkins. Dumbarton Oaks, 1967.
Constantine Porphyrogenitus. *Le livre des cérémonies*. Ed. J. J. Reiske. Bonn, 1829.
Al-Dīnawarī. *Al-Akhbār al-ṭiwal*. Ed. V. Guirgass. Leiden: Brill, 1910.
Elias of Nisibis. *Eliae Metropolitae Nisibeni, Opus Chronologicum*.
– Vol. I. Ed. E. W. Brooks, CSCO vol. 62*, Scriptores Syri t. 21. Leuven, 1910 and 1909.
– Vol. II. Ed. Jean-Baptiste Chabot, CSCO vol. 62**, Scriptores Syri t. 22. Leuven, 1910 and 1909.
– Vol. I. Latin trans. E. W. Brooks, CSCO vol. 63*, Scriptores Syri t. 23. Leuven, 1910 and 1954 [1910].
– Vol. II. Latin trans. Jean-Baptiste Chabot. CSCO vol. 63**, Scriptores Syri t. 24, Leuven, 1910 and 1954 [1910].
– French trans. Louis-Joseph Delaporte. *Chronographie de Mar Élie bar Šinaya métropolitain de Nisibe*. Paris: Bibliothèque de l'École des Hautes Études, Librairie H. Champion, 1910.
Al-Farazdaq. *Dīwān*. 2 vol. Beirut, 1960.
Al-Fasawī. *Al-Ma'rifa wa-al-ta'rīkh*. vol. I. Ed. A. D. al-'Umarī. Beirut: Mu'assasat al-risāla, 1981.
History of the Patriarchs = "History of the Patriarchs of the Coptic Church of Alexandria." Ed. and trans. B. Evetts. *PO* 5 (1910): 3–215 and *PO* 10 (1915): 359–547.
Ibn 'Abd al-Ḥakam. *Sīra 'Umar b. 'Abd al-'Azīz*. Ed. A. 'Ubayd. Cairo, 1983.
Ibn 'Abd Rabbih. *Al-'Iqd al-farīd*. 7 vol. Ed. M. al-Tawnajī. Beirut: Dār Ṣādir, 2001.
Ibn Abī al-Ḥadīd. *Sharḥ nahj al-balāgha*. Ed. A. al-Faḍl Ibrāhīm. Cairo, 1378–1383/1959–1964.

Ibn Abī Ṭāhir Ṭayfūr. *Kitāb Baghdād*. Ed. and trans. H. Keller. *Sechster Band des Kitâb Baġdâd von Ahmad Ibn Abî Tâhir Taifûr*. 2 vol. Leipzig: Harrassowitz, 1908.

Ibn al-ʿAdīm. *Bughyat al-ṭalab min taʾrīkh Ḥalab*. 11 vol. Ed. S. Zakkār. Damascus, 1988.

Ibn al-ʿAdīm. *Zubdat al-Ḥalab min taʾrīkh Ḥalab*. 3 vol. Ed. S. al-Dahhān. Damascus: IFD, 1951–68.

Ibn ʿAsākir. *Taʾrīkh madīnat Dimashq*. 80 vol. Ed. ʿUmar al-ʿAmrāwī. Beirut: Dār al-Fikr, 1995–1998; concurrent edition from the Arab Academy of Damascus, 10 vol. published since 1965.

– French trans. Nikita Elisséeff. *La description de Damas d'Ibn ʿAsākir*. vol. 1. Damascus, 1959.

Ibn Aʿtham al-Kūfī. *Kitāb al-futūḥ*. 8 vol. Ed. Dār al-Kutub al-ʿIlmiyya. Beirut, 1967.

Ibn al-Athīr. *Al-Kāmil fī al-taʾrīkh*. 13 vol. Ed. C. J. Tornberg. Beirut: Dār Ṣādir and Dār Bayrūt, 1965–1967.

Ibn al-Faqīh. *Mukhtaṣar kitāb al-buldān*. Ed. M. J. de Goeje. Leiden: Brill, 1885.

– French trans. Henri Massé. *Abrégé du livre des pays*. Damascus, 1973.

Ibn Ḥawqal. *Kitāb ṣūrat al-arḍ*. Ed. G. H. Kramers. Leiden: Brill, 1938–1939.

– French trans. G. H. Kramers and Gaston Wiet. *Configuration de la terre*. 2 vol. Paris: Maisonneuve et Larose, 2001.

Ibn Hishām. *Kitāb al-tījān*. Hyderabad, 1347/1928.

Ibn Hishām. *Sīra Rasūl Allāh*. Ed. Ferdinand Wüstenfeld. *Das Leben Muhammed's*. 2 vol. Göttingen, 1858–1860.

– English trans. Alfred Guillaume. *The Life of Muhammad. A Translation of Ibn Isḥāq's Sīrat Rasūl Allāh*. Oxford: Oxford University Press, 1955.

Ibn al-Jawzī. *Al-Ḥathth ʿalā ḥifẓ al-ʿilm wa-dhikr kibār al-ḥuffāẓ*. Beirut, 1985.

Ibn al-Jawzī. *Manāqib amīr al-muʾminīn ʿUmar b. al-Khaṭṭāb*. Ed. Z. I. Qārūt. Beirut: Dār al-kutub al- ʿilmiyya, 1980.

Ibn al-Jawzī. *Sīra (or manāqib) ʿUmar b. ʿAbd al-ʿAzīz*. Ed. M. b. al-Khaṭīb. Cairo: Maktabat al-Manār, 1331/1912–1913.

Ibn Kathīr. *Al-Bidāya wa al-nihāya fī al-taʾrīkh*. 14 vol. Ed. A. ʿAbd al-Wahhāb Fātiḥ. Cairo: Dār al-ḥadīth, 1994.

Ibn Khaldūn. *The Muqaddimah*. English trans. Franz Rosenthal. Princeton: Princeton University Press, 2015.

– French trans. Abdesselam Cheddadi. *Le livre des exemples, 1: Autobiographie, Muqaddima*. Paris: Gallimard (Bibliothèque de la Pléiade), 2002.

Ibn Khurradādhbih. *Kitāb al-masālik wa-al-mamālik*. Ed. and partial French trans. M. J. De Goeje. *Le livre des routes et des royaumes*. Leiden: E. J. Brill, 1967 [1889].

Ibn Manẓūr. *Lisān al-ʿarab*. 18 vol. Beirut: Dār Ṣādir, 2000.

Ibn Manẓūr. *Mukhtaṣar taʾrīkh Dimashq li-ibn ʿAsākir*. 29 vol. Ed. ʿAbd al-Ḥamīd Murād. Damascus: Dār al-fikr, 1984.

Ibn al-Munādī. *Kitāb al-malāḥim*. Qum: Dār al-Sīra, 1418/1997.

Ibn al-Muqaffaʿ. *Risāla fī al-ṣaḥāba*. Ed. and French trans. Charles Pellat. *Ibn al-Muqaffaʿ (mort vers 140/757) « conseilleur » du calife*. Paris: Publications du département d'islamologie de l'Université de Paris-Sorbonne, Maisonneuve et Larose, 1976.

Ibn al-Nadīm. *Al-Fihrist*. Ed. Gustav Flügel. Leipzig, 1871.

Ibn Qutayba. *Kitāb al-maʿārif*. Ed. T. ʿUkāsha. Cairo: Maṭbaʿat dār al-kutub, 1960.

Ibn Qutayba. *ʿUyūn al-akhbār*. Ed. M. A. Al-Dīnawarī. Cairo: Maktabat dār al-kutub al-miṣriyya, 1965 [1925].

Ibn Rustah. *Kitāb al-aʿlāk al-nafīsa*. Ed. M. J. de Goeje. Leiden: Brill, 1967 [1892].

– French trans. Gaston Wiet. *Les atours précieux*. Cairo, 1947.

Ibn Saʿd. *Kitāb al-ṭabaqāt al-kabīr*. 9 vol. Ed. Eduard Sachau. Leiden, 1904–1940; ed. Iḥsān ʿAbbās. 9 vol. Beirut: Dār Ṣādir, 1998 [1957].

Ibn Shaddād. *Al-Akhlāq al-khaṭīra fī dhikr umarāʾ al-Shām wa-al-Jazīra*.

– Partial ed. S. Dahhān. *Description de Damas*. Damascus, 1956.

– Partial ed. S. Dahhān. Damascus, 1962.

– Partial ed. S. Dahhān. *Liban, Jordanie, Palestine*. Damascus, 1963.

– Partial ed. Dominique Sourdel. *Description d'Alep*. Beirut, 1953.

– Partial ed. Anne-Marie Eddé. *BEO*, XXXII–XXXIII, 1980–1981.

– French trans. Anne-Marie Eddé. *Description de la Syrie du Nord*. Damascus, 1984.

Irshād = see Yāqūt.

Al-Iṣfahānī. *Kitāb al-Aghānī*. 20 vol. Ed. Būlāq. Al-maṭbaʿa al-amīrīya, 1868; 16 vol. Cairo: Dār al-kutub al-miṣriyya, 1927–1961.

Al-Iṣṭakhrī. *Kitāb al-masālik wa-al-mamālik*. Ed. M. J. De Goeje. Leiden: Brill, 1927.

Al-Jāḥiẓ. *Kitāb Faḍl Hāshim ʿalā ʿAbd Shams*. In *Rasāʾil al-Jāḥiẓ*. Ed. H. Al-Sandūbī. Cairo, 1352/1933.

Al-Jāḥiẓ. *Kitāb al-ḥayawān*. 7 vol. Ed. A. M. Hārūn. Cairo, 1948.

Al-Jahshiyārī. *Kitāb al-wuzarāʾ wa-al-kuttāb*. Ed. M. al-Ṣafa et al. Cairo, 1938.

John Bar Penkāyē = Brock, S. P. "North Mesopotamia in the Late Seventh Century. Book XV of John Bar Penkāyē's Rīš Mellē." *JSAI* 9 (1987): 51–75.

Khalīfa b. Khayyāṭ al-ʿUṣfūrī. *Ṭabaqāt Khalīfa b. Khayyāṭ*. Ed. S. Zakkār. Damascus, 1967.

Khalīfa b. Khayyāṭ al-ʿUṣfūrī. *Taʾrīkh*. 2 vol. Ed. A. D. al-ʿUmarī. Najaf: Maṭbaʿat al-ādāb, 1967.

Al-Khaṭīb al-Baghdādī. *Taʾrīkh Baghdād*. 14 vol. Cairo: Dār al-Saʿāda, 1931.

Al-Khawlānī. *Taʾrīkh Dārayyā wa-man nazala bihā min al-ṣaḥāba wa-al-tābiʿīn wa-tābiʿī al-tābiʿīn*. Ed. S. al-Afghānī. Damascus: Maṭbaʿat al-taraqqī, 1950.

Kitāb al-ʿuyūn = *Fragmenta Historicorum Arabicorum*. 2 vol. Ed. M. J. De Goeje. Leiden: Brill, 1869.

Kuthayyir ʿAzza. *Dīwān*. Ed. Henri Pérès. *Koṯayyir ʿAzza, Dîwân, accompagné d'un commentaire arabe*. Algiers, 1928–30.

Łewond. *Histoire des guerres et des conquêtes des Arabes en Arménie par l'éminent Ghévond, Vardabed arménien*. French trans. G. V. Chahnazarian. Paris, 1856.

Machiavelli, Niccolò. *The Prince*. Ed. Peter Bondanella. Oxford: Oxford World's Classics, 2008.

Mālik b. Anas. *Kitāb al-Muwaṭṭa'*, in the recension of Yaḥyā b. Yaḥyā al-Laythī. Ed. A. R. ʿArmūsh. Beirut, 1971.

Al-Maqdisī. *Kitāb al-bad' wa-al-ta'rīkh*. 6 vol. Ed. C. Huart. Paris, 1899–1919.

Al-Maqrīzī. *Kitāb fī dhikr mā warada fī Banī Umayya wa-Banī al-ʿAbbās*. MS 342b. Codex Vindobonensis Palatinus, Alter Fond. Österreichische Nationalbibliothek, Vienna.

Al-Maqrīzī. *Kitāb al-nizāʿ wal-al-takhāṣum fīmā bayna Banī Umayya wa-Banī Hāshim*. Ed. G. Vos. *Die Kämpfe und Streitigkeiten zwischen den Banū Umajja und den Banū Hāšim*. Leiden, 1888.

– English trans. C. E. Bosworth. *Al-Maqrīzī's "Book of Contention and Strife Concerning the Relations Between the Banū Umayya and the Banū Hāshim"*. Manchester: Journal of Semitic Studies Monographs, University of Manchester, 1980.

Al-Masʿūdī. *Murūj al-dhahab wa-maʿādin al-jawhar*. 7 vol. Ed. Charles Pellat. Beirut: al-Jāmiʿa al-lubnāniyya, 1965–1979.

– French trans. Charles Pellat. *Les prairies d'or*. 5 vol. Paris: Société Asiatique, 1965–1989.

Al-Masʿūdī. *Kitāb al-tanbīh wa-al-ishrāf*. Ed. M. J. De Goeje. Leiden: Brill, 1894.

– French trans. Bernard Carra de Vaux. *Le livre de l'avertissement et de la révision*. Paris: Imprimerie nationale, 1896.

Al-Māwardī. *Al-Aḥkām al-sulṭāniyya*. Beirut: Dār al-kitāb al-ʿarabī, 1990.

– English trans. Wafaa H. Wahba. *The Ordinances of Government*. Reading: Garnet Publishing, 1996.

Michael the Syrian. *Chronique de Michel, patriarche jacobite d'Antioche 1166–1199*. Ed. and trans. Jean-Baptiste Chabot. Paris, 1899–1905.

Muʿaffa b. Zakariyya al-Jarīrī. *Jalīs al-ṣāliḥ al-kāfī wa-al-anīs al-nāṣiḥ al-shāfī*. 2 vol. Ed. M. M. al-Khūlī. Beirut: ʿAlām al-kutub, 1981–1983.

Al-Muqaddasī. *Aḥsan al-taqāsīm fī maʿrifat al-aqālīm*. Ed. M. J. de Goeje. Leiden: Brill, 1906.

– French trans. André Miquel. *La meilleure répartition pour la connaissance des provinces*. Damascus, 1963.

Muslim. *Ṣaḥīḥ*. 18 vol. Ed. M. M. ʿAbd al-Laṭīf. Dār al-fikr, n. p., 1401/1981.

Nicephorus. *Short History* = Mango, Cyril. *Nikephoros Patriarch of Constantinople. Short History*. Dumbarton Oaks, 1990.

Nuʿaym b. Ḥammād. *Kitāb al-fitan*. Ed. S. Zakkār. Beirut: Dār al-fikr, 2003.

– English trans. David Cook. *The Book of Tribulations: The Syrian Muslim Apocalyptic Tradition*. Edinburgh: Edinburgh University Press, 2017.

Qudāma b. Ja'far. *Kitāb al-kharāj wa-ṣināʿat al-kitāba*. Ed. and partial trans. M. J. De Goeje. Leiden: Brill, 1967 [1889].

Qur'ān. *The Koran Interpreted*. Trans. A. J. Arberry. London: Oxford University Press, 1964.

Al-Qushayrī. *Ta'rīkh al-Raqqa*. Damascus, 1998.

Al-Rabaʿī. *Kitāb faḍā'il al-Shām wa-Dimashq*. Ed. Ṣalāḥ al-Dīn al-Munajjid. Damascus: Maṭbaʿat al-Tarraqī, 1950.

Al-Sadūsī. *Kitāb ḥadhf min nasab Quraysh*. Ed. Ṣalāḥ al-Dīn al-Munajjid. Cairo, 1960.

Al-Ṣafadī. *Kitāb umarā' Dimashq fī al-islām*. Ed. Ṣalāḥ al-Dīn Al-Munajjid. Beirut: Dār al-kitāb al-jadīd, 1983.

Saʿīd b. Biṭrīq = Eutychii Patriarchae Alexandrini. *Annales*. Ed. Louis Cheikho, Bernard Carra de Vaux and Habib Zayyat. CSCO vol. 50 and 51, Scriptores Arabici 6 and 7. Beirut and Paris: Otto Harrassowitz, 1909.

Sayf b. ʿUmar al-Tamīmī. *Kitāb al-Ridda wa'l-futūḥ and Kitāb al-Jamal wa masīr ʿĀ'isha wa ʿAlī, A facsimile edition of the fragments preserved in the University Library of Imām Muḥammad Ibn Saʿūd Islamic University in Riyadh, Saʿudi Arabia*. 2 vol. Ed. Qāsim al-Sāmarrā'ī. Leiden: Smitskamp Oriental Antiquarium, 1995.

Step'anos Asołik. *The Universal History of Step'anos Tarōnec'i*. Ed. and trans. Tim Greenwood. Oxford: Oxford University Press, 2017.

– French trans. E. Dulaurier. *Étienne Açoghic de Daron, Histoire universelle*. Paris, 1883.

Al-Suyūṭī. *Ḥāwī li-al-fatāwā*. Beirut, n.d.

Al-Suyūṭī. *Itḥāf al-akhiṣṣā bi-faḍā'il al-masjid al-Aqṣā*. 2 vol. Ed. A. R. Aḥmad. Cairo, 1984.

Al-Suyūṭī. *Kashf al ṣalṣala ʿan wasf al-zalzala*. Ed. A. Saʿdānī. Fez, 1971.

– French trans. S. Al-Najjar. Rabat: Cahiers du Centre Universitaire de la Recherche Scientifique, 1974.

Al-Suyūṭī. *Ta'rīkh al-khulafā'*. Ed. I. Ṣāliḥ. Beirut and Damascus: Dār Ṣādir – Dār al-Bashā'ir, 1997.

Al-Ṭabarānī. *Al-Muʿjam al-kabīr* [*ʿalā asmā' al-ṣaḥāba*]. 10 vols. Beirut, 1983.

Al-Ṭabarī. *Ta'rīkh al-rusul wa-al-mulūk*. 15 vols. Ed. M. J. de Goeje. Leiden: Brill, 1879–1901.

– English trans. *The History of al-Ṭabarī*. 39 vol. Albany: Bibliotheca Persica, State University of New York Press, 1985–2002.

Ta'rīkh al-khulafā'. Ed. P. A. Gryaznevich. Moscow, 1967.

The Continuatio = Levy-Rubin, Milka. *The "Continuatio" of the Samaritan chronicle of Abū l-Fatḥ al-Sāmirī al-Danafī*. Princeton: Darwin Press, 2002.

Theodoret of Cyrrhus. *Histoire des moines de Syrie*. 2 vol. "Histoire Philothée" I–XIII. Ed. and trans. Pierre Canivet and Alice Leroy-Molinghen. Paris, 1977.

Theophanes, *Chronography* = *Theophanis chronographia*. Ed. Carolus de Boor, B. G. Teubner. Leipzig, 1883.

- English trans. Cyril Mango and Roger Scott. *The Chronicle of Theophanes Confessor.* Oxford: Oxford University Press, 1997.

TMD = see Ibn ʿAsākir.

ʿUmar b. ʿAbd al-ʿAzīz (attributed to). *Musnad.* Ed. M. ʿAwwāma. Aleppo, 1397/1977.

Al-Wāqidī. *Kitāb al-maghāzī.* 3 vol. Ed. Marsden Jones. London: Oxford University Press, 1966.

Yaḥyā ibn Saʿīd of Antioch. *Histoire de Yaḥyā ibn Saʿīd d'Antioche.* Ed. I. Kratchkovsky and A. Vasiliev. *PO* XVIII: 701–833; XXIII: 349–520. Paris, 1924 and 1932.

Yaḥyā ibn Saʿīd of Antioch. Ed. and French trans. F. Micheau and Gérard Troupeau. *Histoire de Yaḥyā ibn Saʿīd d'Antioche. PO* XLVII (1997): 373–539.

Al-Yaʿqūbī. *Kitāb al-buldān.* Ed. M. J. de Goeje. Leiden, 1892, re-edition 1967.

- French trans. Gaston Wiet. *Le livre des pays.* Cairo, 1937.

Al-Yaʿqūbī. *Mushākalat al-nās li-zamānihim.* Ed. William G. Millward. Beirut, 1972.

- English trans. William G. Millward. "The adaptation of men to their times. An historical essay by al-Yaʿqūbī." *JAOS* 84 (1964): 329–44.

Al-Yaʿqūbī. *Taʾrīkh.* 2 vol. Beirut: Dār Ṣādir, 1960.

Yāqūt. *Irshād al-arīb ilā maʿrifa al-adīb* [*Muʿjam al-udabāʾ*]. 7 vol. Ed. D. S. Margoliouth. Leiden, 1907–1927; 20 vol. Ed. A. F. Rifāʿī. Cairo: Dār al-Maʾmūn, 1936–1938.

Yāqūt. *Muʿjam al-buldān.* 5 vol. Beirut: Dār Bayrūt, 1988.

Al-Zuhrī. *Kitāb al-jughrāfiyā.* Ed. M. Hajj Sadock. *BEO* 2 (1968).

Zuqnīn = *Chronicon Pseudo-Dionysianum vulgo dictum.* 2 vol. Ed. Jean-Baptiste Chabot. CSCO vol. 91 and 104, Scriptores Syri vol. 43 and 53. Leuven, 1927 and 1933 [repr. 1965].

- Vol. I. Latin trans. Jean-Baptiste Chabot. CSCO vol. 121, Scriptores Syri vol. 66. Leuven, 1949.
- Vol. II. French trans. R. Hespel. CSCO vol. 507, Scriptores Syri vol. 213. Leuven, 1989.
- English trans. Amir Harrak. *The Chronicle of Zuqnīn, Part III and IV, A.D. 488–775.* Toronto: Pontifical Institute of Medieval Studies, 1999.
- Partial English trans. Andrew Palmer. *The Seventh Century in the West Syrian Chronicles.* Liverpool: Liverpool University Press, 1993. 53–70.

Bibliography

Reference Works

ʿAbbās, Iḥsān. *ʿAbd al-Ḥamīd b. Yaḥyā al-Kātib wa-mā tabaqqā min rasāʾilihi wa-rasāʾil Sālim Abī al-ʿAlāʾ*. Amman: Dār al-Sharq, 1988.

ʿAbbās, Iḥsān."Kuthayyir b. ʿAbd al-Raḥmān." *EI*².

ʿAbbās, Iḥsān. *Shiʿr al-khawārij*. Dār al-Thaqāfa, n.d.

ʿAbbās, Iḥsān. *Taʾrīkh Bilād al-Shām fī al-ʿaṣr al-ʿAbbāsī, 132–255 H / 750–870 M*. Amman: Lajnat taʾrīkh Bilād al-Shām, 1993.

Abbott, Nabia. "Arabic papyri of the reign of Jaʿfar al-Mutawakkil (AH 232–247/AD 847–861)." *ZDMG* 92 (1938): 88–135.

Abbott, Nabia. "The Kasr Kharāna inscription of 92 H. (710 AD), a new reading." *Ars Islamica* XI–XII (194): 190–195.

Abbott, Nabia. *The Qurrah Papyri from Aphrodito in the Oriental Institute*. Chicago: University of Chicago Press, 1938.

Abbott, Nabia. *Studies in Arabic Literary Papyri. I: Historical Texts*. Oriental Institute Publications. Chicago: University of Chicago Press, 1957.

Abbott, Nabia. *Studies in Arabic Literary Papyri. II: Qurʾānic commentary and tradition*. Oriental Insitute Publications. Chicago: University of Chicago Press, 1967.

Abbott, Nabia. *Two Queens of Baghdad: Mother and Wife of Hārūn al-Rashīd*. Chicago: University of Chicago Press, 1946.

Abd al-Haqq, S. and N. Salibi. "Rapport préliminaire sur les campagnes de fouilles à Raqqa." *AAAS* 1 (1951): 111–121.

Abel, Armand. "Changements politiques et littérature eschatologique dans le monde musulman médiéval." *SI* 2 (1954): 23–43.

Abiad, Malak. *Culture et éducation arabo-islamiques au Šām pendant les trois premiers siècles de l'islam d'après le "Tārīḫ Madīnat Dimašq" d'Ibn ʿAsākir (499/1105–571/1176)*. Damascus: PIFD, 1981.

Abiad, Malak. "Origine et développement des dictionnaires biographiques arabes." *BEO* XXXI (1979): 7–15.

Abramowski, Rudolf. *Dionysius von Tellmahre, jakobitischer Patriarch von 818–845. Zur Geschichte der Kirche unter dem Islam*. Leipzig: F. A. Brockhaus, 1940.

Afsaruddin, Asma. *Excellence and Precedence: Medieval Islamic Discourse on Legitimate Leadership*. Leiden: Brill, 2002.

Agha, S. S. and Tarif Khalidi. "Poetry and Identity in the Umayyad Age." *Al-Abhath* 50–51 (2002–2003): 55–120.

Agha, S. S. "Abū Muslim's Conquest of Khurasan: Preliminaries and Strategy in a Confusing Passage of the *Akhbār al-Dawlah al-ʿAbbāsiyyah*." *JAOS* 120/3 (2000): 333–347.

Agha, S. S. "The Arab Population in Ḫurāsān During the Umayyad Period. Some Demographic Computations." *Arabica* 46 (1999): 211–229.

Agha, S. S. *The Revolution which Toppled the Umayyads: Neither Arab nor ʿAbbāsid*. Leiden: Brill, 2003.

Aigle, Denise (ed.). *Barhebraeus et la renaissance syriaque (Actes du colloque, Paris, décembre 2007)*. *Paroles de l'Orient* 33 (2008).

Aigle, Denise. "Bar Hebraeus et son public, à travers ses chroniques en arabe et en syriaque." *Le Muséon* 118/1–2 (2005): 83–106.

Aigle, Denise (ed.). *Figures mythiques de l'Orient musulman. Thème sous la responsabilité de Denise Aigle*. *Revue des mondes musulmans et de la Méditerranée* 89–90 (2000).

Aigle, Denise. "L'histoire sous forme graphique en arabe, persan et turc ottoman: origines et fonctions." *BEO* LVIII (2008–2009): 11–49.

Aigle, Denise. "Les inscriptions de Baybars dans le Bilād al-Šām. Une expression de la légitimité du pouvoir." *SI* 98.

Albert, Jean-Pierre. "Du martyr à la star. Les métamorphoses des héros nationaux." In P. Centlivres, D. Fabre, F. Zonabend, *La Fabrique des héros*. Paris: Maison des sciences de l'homme, 1998. 11–32.

Alexander, Paul J. "Medieval apocalypses as historical sources." *American Historical Review* 73/4 (1968): 997–1018; repr. in *Religious and Political Thought in the Byzantine Empire*. London: Variorum, 1987.

Alexander, Paul J. "The Medieval Legend of the Last Roman Emperor and its Messianic Origin." *Journal of the Warburg and Courtauld Institutes* 41 (1978): 1–15.

Ali, Samer M. *Ardor for Memory: Mythicizing the Patricide of al-Mutawakkil in Court Poetry*. Ph. D. diss. Indiana University, 2002.

Almagro, Antonio and Emilio Olavarri. "A new Umayyad Palace at the Citadel of Amman." *SHAJ* I (1982): 305–321.

Almagro, Antonio, Pedro Jiménez and Julio Navarro. "El Palacio Omeya de ʿAmman III." Grenada, 2000.

Almagro, Antonio. "Building Patterns in Umayyad Architecture in Jordan." *SHAJ* IV (1992): 351–356.

Almagro, Antonio. "Origins and Repercussions of the Architecture of the Umayyad Palace in Amman." *SHAJ* III (1987): 181–192.

Almagro, Antonio. *El Palacio Omeya de Amman I. La Arquitectura*. Madrid, 1983.

Almagro, Martin, Luis Caballero, Juan Zozaya and Antonio Almagro. *Qusayr ʿAmra. Residencia y baños omeyas en el desierto de Jordania*. 2nd ed. Grenada: El Legado Andalusí, 2002 [1975].

Althoff, Gerd, Johannes Fried and Patrick J. Geary (eds.). *Medieval Concepts of the Past. Ritual, Memory, Historiography*. Publications of the German Historical Institute. Cambridge: Cambridge University Press, 2002.

Amélineau, Émile. "Les derniers jours et la mort du khalife Merouân II, d'après l'histoire des Patriarches d'Alexandrie." *JA* 4 (1914): 421–449.

Amiran, David H. K. "Location Index for Earthquakes in Israel since 100 B.C.E." *Israel Exploration Journal* 46/1–2 (1996): 120–130.

Amitai-Preiss, Nitzan. "Umayyad Coin Hoards from the Beth Shean Excavations of the Hebrew University." *Israel Numismatic Journal* 14 (2000–2002): 224–238.

Amitai-Preiss, Nitzan, Ariel Berman, and Shraga Qedar. "The Coinage of Scythopolis-Baysān and Gerasa-Jerash." *Israel Numismatic Journal* 13 (1994–1999): 133–151.

Arazi, A. "Périodisation, oralité et authenticité de la poésie arabe préislamique." *JSAI* 29 (2004): 377–412.

Arazi, A. "*Al-Šiʿru ʿilmu al-ʿarabi wa-dīwānuhā* (La poésie est la science des anciens Arabes et leurs archives). Étude de poétique classique." In R. G. Khoury (ed.), *Urkunden und Urkundenformulare im Klassischen Altertum und in den orientalischen Kulturen*. Heidelberg, 1999. 203–220.

Arce, Ignacio. "Qasr al-Hallabât (Jordan) Revisited: Reassessment of the Material Evidence." In Hugh Kennedy (ed.), *Muslim Military Architecture in Greater Syria. From the Coming of Islam to the Ottoman Period*. Leiden: Brill, 2006. 26–44.

Arjomand, S. A. "ʿAbd Allah Ibn al-Muqaffaʿ and the ʿAbbasid Revolution." *Iranian Studies* 27 (1994): 9–36.

Al-Asʿad, Khaled and Franciszer M. Stepniowski. "The Umayyad Sūq in Palmyra," *Damaszener Mitteilungen* 4 (1989): 205–223.

Assier-Andrieu, Louis. "Penser le temps culturel du droit. Le destin anthropologique du concept de coutume." *L'Homme* 160 (2001): 67–90.

Assmann, Jan. *Ägypten. Eine Sinngeschichte*. Munich and Vienna, 1996.

Assmann, Jan. *Cultural Memory and Early Civilization*. Cambridge: Cambridge University Press, 2012.

Assmann, Jan. *La mémoire culturelle. Écriture, souvenir et imaginaire politique dans les civilisations antiques*. Paris: Aubier, 2010.

Assmann, Jan. "Introduction: What is 'Cultural Memory'?" In Jan Assmann, *Religion and Cultural Memory*. Stanford, CA: Stanford University Press, 2006. 1–30.

Assmann, Jan. *Moïse l'égyptien*. Paris: Flammarion, 2001.

Assmann, Jan. *Moses the Egyptian*. Cambridge, MA: Harvard University Press, 1997.

Assmann, Jan. *Stein und Zeit, Mensch und Gesellschaft im alten Ägypten*. Munich, 1991.

Athamina, Khalil. "The sources of al-Balādhurī's *Ansāb al-Ashrāf*." *JSAI* 5 (1984): 237–262.

Auchterlonie, Paul. *Arabic Biographical Dictionaries: a Summary Guide and Bibliography*. Durham, 1987.

Al-Azmeh, Aziz. "Chronophagous Discourse: A Study of Clerico-Legal Appropriation of the World in an Islamic Tradition." In Frank E. Reynolds and David Tracy (eds.),

Religion and Practical Reason. New Essays in the Comparative Philosophy of Religions. Albany: State University of New York Press, 1994. 163–211.

Al-Azmeh, Aziz. "Histoire et narration dans l'historiographie arabe." *Annales E.S.C.* 2 (1986): 411–431.

Al-Azmeh, Aziz. *Muslim Kingship. Power and the Sacred in Muslim Christian and Pagan Polities.* London and New York: Tauris, 2001.

Bacharach, Jere L. "*Laqab* for a Future Caliph: The Case of the Abbasid al-Mahdī." *JAOS* 113/2 (1993): 271–274.

Bacharach, Jere L. "Al-Mansur and Umayyad Dirhams." *Yarmouk Numismatics* 4 (1992): 7–17.

Bacharach, Jere L. "Marwanid Umayyad Building Activities: Speculations on Patronage." *Muqarnas* 13 (1996): 27–44.

Bacqué-Grammont, Jean-Louis, François De Polignac and Georges Bohas. "Monstres et murailles, Alexandre et bicornu, mythes et bon sens." In Denise Aigle (ed.), *Figures mythiques de l'Orient musulman. Thème sous la responsabilité de Denise Aigle. Revue des mondes musulmans et de la Méditerranée* 89–90 (2000): 109–127.

Al-Bakhit, Muḥammad A. and Iḥsān ʿAbbās. *Proceedings of the Second Symposium on the History of Bilad al-Sham During the Early Islamic Period up to 40 A.H./640 A.D. The Fourth International Conference on the History of Bilad al-Sham.* 2 vols. Amman: University of Jordan Press, 1987.

Al-Bakhit, Muḥammad A. and Robert Schick. *Bilād al-Shām during the Abbasid period (132 AH/750 AD–451 AH/1059 AD): Proceedings of the Fifth International Conference on the History of Bilād al-Shām.* Amman: Lajnat taʾrīkh Bilād al-Shām, 1992.

Al-Bakhit, Muḥammad A. and Robert Schick. *Bilād al-Shām during the Umayyad period. The fourth international conference on the history of Bilad al-Sham.* Amman, 1989.

Balty-Guesdon, Marie-Geneviève. "Le *Bayt al-Ḥikma* de Baghdad." *Arabica* 39/2 (1992): 131–150.

Baramki, Dimitri C. "Excavations at Khirbet el Mefjer. III." *The Quarterly of the Department of Antiquities in Palestine* III (1939): 51–53.

Barthold, W. W. "The Caliph ʿUmar II and the Contradictory Information about his Personality." *I.Q.* 15 (1971).

Bartl, Karin. "Balīḫ Valley Survey. Settlements of the Late Roman/Early Byzantine and Islamic Period." In Karin Bartl and Stefan R. Hauser (eds.), *Continuity and Change in Northern Mesopotamia from the Hellenistic to the Early Islamic Period.* Berliner Beiträge zum Vorderen Orient 17. Berlin: Dietrich Reimer Verlag, 1996. 333–348.

Bartl, Karin. "Einige frühislamische Glasfunde aus Madīnat al-Fār (Nordsyrien)." *Archéologie Islamique* 7 (1997): 7–26.

Bartl, Karin. "Tell Sheikh Hasan. A Settlement of the Roman-Parthian to the Islamic Period in the Balikh Valley/Northern Syria." *Archéologie Islamique* 4 (1994): 5–17.

Bartl, Karin and Stefan R. Hauser (eds.). *Continuity and Change in Northern Mesopotamia from the Hellenistic to the Early Islamic Period.* Berliner Beiträge zum Vorderen Orient 17. Berlin: Dietrich Reimer Verlag, 1996.

Bartl, Karin and Abd al-Razzaq Moaz (eds.). *Residences, Castles, Settlements. Transformation Processes from Late Antiquity to Early Islam in Bilad al-Sham. Proceedings of the International Conference held at Damascus, 5–9 November 2006.* Rahden: Verlag Marie Leidorf GmbH, 2009.

Bashear, Suliman. "Apocalyptic and Other Materials on Early Muslim-Byzantine Wars: A Review of Arabic Sources." *JRAS* 1/2 (1991): 173–207.

Bashear, Suliman. "Muslim Apocalypses and the Hour: a Case-Study in Traditional Reinterpretation." *IOS* 13 (1993): 75–99.

Bashear, Suliman. "The Title "Fārūq" and its association with ʿUmar I." *SI* 72 (1990): 47–70.

Bates, Michael L. "The Arab-Byzantine Coinage of Syria: An Innovation by ʿAbd al-Malik." In *A Colloquium in Memory of George Carpenter Miles.* New York: American Numismatic Society, 1976. 16–27.

Bates, Michael L. "Byzantine Coinage and its Imitations, Arab Coinage and its Imitations: Arab-Byzantine coinage." *Aram* 6 (1994): 381–403.

Bates, Michael L. "The Dirham Mint of the Northern Provinces of the Umayyad Caliphate." *American Numismatic Journal* 15 (1989): 89–111.

Bates, Michael L. "History, Geography and Numismatics in the First Century of Islamic Coinage." *Revue Suisse de Numismatique* 65 (1986): 231–261.

Bates, Michael L. "Khurāsānī Revolutionaries and al-Mahdī's Title." In Farhad Daftary and Josef W. Meri (eds.), *Culture and Memory in Medieval Islam. Essays in Honour of Wilferd Madelung.* London: Tauris, 2003. 279–317.

Becker, C. H. "Eine Neue christliche Quelle zur Geschichte des Islam." *Der Islam* 3 (1912): 295–296.

Becker, C. H. "Das Reich der Ismaeliten im koptischen Danielbuch." *Nachrichten der Königlichen Gesellschaft der Wissenschaft zu Göttingen, Philologisch-historische Klasse*, 1916. 7–57.

Becker, C. H. "Studien zur Omajjadengeschichte. ʿUmar II" *Zeitschrift für Assyriologie* 15 (1900).

Beeston, A. F. L. (ed.). *Arabic Literature to the End of the Umayyad Period.* Cambridge: Cambridge University Press, 1983.

Beeston, A. F. L. and Lawrence I. Conrad. "On Some Umayyad Poetry in the History of al-Ṭabarī." *JRAS* 3/3/2 (1993): 191–206.

Bellamy, James A. "Pro-Umayyad Propaganda in Ninth-Century Baghdad in the Works of Ibn Abī 'l-Dunyā." In George Makdisi, Dominique Sourdel and Janine Sourdel-Thomine (eds.), *Prédication et propagande au Moyen Age. Islam, Byzance, Occident.* Paris: PUF, 1983. 71–86.

Ben Dov, M. *In the Shadow of the Temple*. Jerusalem, 1982.

Ben Dov, M. *The Omayyad Structures near the Temple Mount*. Jerusalem, 1971.

Benkheira, M. H. "L'analyse du *ḥadīṯ* en question. À propos de A.-L. de Prémare et G. H. A. Juynboll." *Arabica* 52/2 (2005): 294–306.

Benoist, Jocelyn and Fabio Merlini (eds.). *Une histoire de l'avenir: Messianité et Révolution*. Paris: Vrin, 2004.

Benoist, Jocelyn and Fabio Merlini. "Révolution et messianité: l'Histoire et les figures de l'au-delà." In Jocelyn Benoist and Fabio Merlini (eds.), *Une histoire de l'avenir: Messianité et Révolution*. Paris: Vrin, 2004. 7–12.

Berchem, Max van. *Corpus inscriptorum arabicarum* II: Northern and Southern Syria. Cairo, 1920–1949.

Berchem, Max van. "Inscriptions arabes de Syrie." *Mémoires présentées à l'institut d'Égypte* III (1897).

Berchem, Max van. *Matériaux pour un corpus inscriptionum arabicarum* II: Southern Syria. Cairo, 1922.

Berchem, Max van. "Aux pays de Moab et d'Edom." *Journal des savants* nouvelle série – 7e année (1909): 363–372.

Berchet, Jean-Claude. *Le voyage en Orient, Anthologie des voyageurs français dans le Levant au XIXe siècle*. Paris: Robert Laffont, 1985.

Berg, Herbert. "The Implications of, and Opposition to, the Methods and Theories of John Wansbrough." *Method and Theory in the Study of Religion* 9/1 (1997): 3–22.

Berg, Herbert (ed.). *Method and Theory in the Study of Islamic Origins*. Leiden: Brill, 2003.

Berger, Klaus. *Die griechische Daniel-Diegese. Eine altkirchliche Apokalypse*. Leiden, 1976.

Bernhardt, John W. *Itinerant Kingship & Royal Monasteries in Early Medieval Germany (c. 936–1075)*. Cambridge: Cambridge University Press, 2002 [1993].

Berthier, Sophie (dir.). *Peuplement rural et aménagements agricoles dans la moyenne vallée de l'Euphrate, fin VIIe–XIXe siècle*. Damascus: PIFD, 2001.

Bianquis, Thierry. "Damas." In Jean-Claude Garcin (ed.), *Grandes villes méditerranéennes du monde musulman médiéval*. École Française de Rome. Rome, 2000. 37–55.

Bianquis, Thierry. *Damas et la Syrie sous la domination Fatimide (969–1076)*. 2 vol. Damascus, 1986–1989.

Bianquis, Thierry. "Deux révoltes bédouines en Syrie méridionale au Moyen-Age." *The Third International Conference on Bilād al-Šām: Palestine, 19–24 April 1980. Vol. III: History of Palestine*. Amman: Lajnat ta'rīkh Bilād al-Shām, 1984. 11–15.

Biddle, David W. *The Development of the Bureaucracy of the Islamic Empire During the Late Umayyad and Early Abbasid Period*. Ph. D. diss. University of Texas, 1972.

Bijovsky, Gabriela. "A Hoard of Byzantine Solidi from Bet She'an in the Umayyad Period." *Revue Numismatique* (2002): 161–227.

Bisheh, Ghazi. "Excavations at Qasr al-Hallabat 1979." ADAJ 24 (1980): 69–78.

Bisheh, Ghazi. "From Castellum to Palatium: Umayyad Mosaic Pavements from Qaṣr al-Hallabat in Jordan." *Muqarnas* 10 (1993): 49–56.

Bisheh, Ghazi. "Hammam al-Sarah in the Light of Recent Excavations." DM 4 (1989): 225–30.

Bisheh, Ghazi. "Qaṣr al-Hallabat: an Umayyad Desert Retreat or Farm-Land." SHAJ II (1985): 263–265.

Bisheh, Ghazi. "Qasr Mshash and Qasr ʿAyn al-Sil: Two Umayyad Sites in Jordan." In Muḥammad A. al-Bakhit and Robert Schick (eds.), *The Fourth International Conference on the History of Bilad al-Sham during the Umayyad period.* Amman, 1989. 81–103.

Bisheh, Ghazi. "Qaṣr al-Mshatta in the Light of a Recently Found Inscription." SHAJ III (1987): 193–197.

Blair, Sheila. "What is the Date of the Dome of the Rock?" In Julian Raby and Jeremy Johns (eds.), *Bayt al-Maqdis: ʿAbd al-Malik's Jerusalem* I. Oxford, 1992. 59–87.

Blankinship, Khalid Y. *The End of the Jihād State: The Reign of Hishām Ibn ʿAbd al-Malik and the Collapse of the Umayyads*. Albany: State University of New York Press, 1994.

Blankinship, Khalid Y. "The Tribal Factor in the ʿAbbāsid Revolution: the Betrayal of the Imam Ibrāhīm b. Muḥammad." JAOS 108/4 (1988): 589–603.

Blau, Joshua. *A Grammar of Christian Arabic Based Mainly on South-Palestinian Texts from the First Millennium*. 2 vol. Leuven, 1966.

Blau, Joshua. "The Importance of Middle Arabic Dialects for the History of Arabic." *Scripta Hierosolymitana* 9 (1961): 206–228.

Bligh-Abramski, Irit I. *From Damascus to Baghdad: the ʿAbbasid Administrative System as a Product of the Umayyad Heritage (41/661–320/932)*. Ph. D. diss. Princeton University, 1982.

Bligh-Abramski, Irit I. "Evolution Versus Revolution: Umayyad Elements in the ʿAbbāsid Regime 133/750–320/932." *Der Islam* 65 (1988): 226–243.

Bone, Harry J. *The Administration of Umayyad Syria: The Evidence of the Copper Coins.* Ph. D. diss. Princeton University, 2000.

Bonner, Michael. *Aristocratic Violence and Holy War. Studies in the Jihad and the Arab-Byzantine Frontier*. New Haven, CT: American Oriental Society, 1996.

Bonner, Michael. "Jaʿāʾil and Holy War in Early Islam." *Der Islam* 68/1 (1991): 45–64.

Bonner, Michael. *Le jihad. Origines, interprétations, combats.* Paris: Téraèdre, 2004.

Bonner, Michael. "Al-Khalīfa al-Marḍī: the Accession of Hārūn al-Rašīd." JAOS 108/1 (1988): 79–91.

Bonner, Michael. "The Mint of Hārūnābād and al-Hārūniyya, 168–171 H." *American Journal of Numismatics* (2nd series) 1 (1989): 171–193.

Bonner, Michael. "The Naming of the Frontier: ʿAwāṣim, Thughūr and the Arab Geographers." BSOAS LVII/1 (1994): 17–24.

Bonner, Michael. "Some Observations Concerning the Early Development of *Jihad* on the Arab-Byzantine Frontier." *SI* 75 (1992): 5–31.

Bonte, Pierre, Edouard Conte, Constant Hamès, and Abdel Wedoud Ould Cheikh (eds.). *Al-Ansâb, la quête des origines. Anthropologie historique de la société tribale arabe*. Paris: Éditions de la maison des sciences de l'Homme, 1991.

Borgolte, Michael. "*Memoria*. Bilan intermédiaire d'un projet de recherche sur le Moyen Age." In Jean-Claude Schmitt and Otto G. Oexle (dir.), *Les tendances actuelles de l'histoire du Moyen Âge en France et en Allemagne. Actes des colloques de Sèvres (1997) et Göttingen (1998) organisés par le C.N.R.S. et le Max-Planck-Institut für Geschichte*. Paris: Publications de la Sorbonne, 2003. 53–69.

Borrut, Antoine. "Architecture des espaces portuaires et réseaux défensifs du littoral syro-palestinien dans les sources arabes (VIIe–XIe s.)." *Archéologie Islamique* 11 (2001): 21–46.

Borrut, Antoine. "La circulation de l'information historique entre les sources arabo-musulmanes et syriaques: Élie de Nisibe et ses sources." In Muriel Debié (ed.), *Historiographie syriaque*. Paris: Geuthner (Études syriaques 6), 2009. 137–159.

Borrut, Antoine. "Entre tradition et histoire: genèse et diffusion de l'image de ʿUmar II." *MUSJ* 58 (2005): 329–378.

Borrut, Antoine. "L'espace maritime syrien au cours des premiers siècles de l'Islam (VIIe–Xe siècle): le cas de la région entre Acre et Tripoli." *Tempora. Annales d'histoire et d'archéologie de l'Université Saint-Joseph* 10–11 (1999–2000): 1–33.

Borrut, Antoine. "La *memoria* omeyyade: les Omeyyades entre souvenir et oubli dans les sources narratives islamiques." In Antoine Borrut and Paul M. Cobb (eds.), *Umayyad Legacies: Medieval Memories from Syria to Spain*. Leiden: Brill, 2010. 25–61.

Borrut, Antoine. "La Syrie de Salomon: l'appropriation du mythe salomonien dans les sources arabes." *Pallas* 63 (2003): 107–120.

Borrut, Antoine and Paul M. Cobb (eds.). *Umayyad Legacies: Medieval Memories from Syria to Spain*. Leiden: Brill, 2010.

Borrut, Antoine and Paul M. Cobb. "Introduction: Toward a History of Umayyad Legacies." In Antoine Borrut and Paul M. Cobb (eds.), *Umayyad Legacies: Medieval Memories from Syria to Spain*. Leiden: Brill, 2010. 1–22.

Borrut, Antoine and Christoph Picard. "Râbata, ribât, râbita: une institution à reconsidérer." In Philippe Sénac and Nicolas Prouteau (eds.), *Chrétiens et Musulmans en Méditerranée Médiévale (VIIIe–XIIIe s.): échanges et contacts*. Civilisation Médiévale XV, Poitiers, 2003. 33–65.

Bosworth, C. E. "Administrative Literature." In M. J. L. Young, J. D. Latham and R. B. Serjeant (eds.), *Religion, Learning and Science in the ʿAbbasid Period. The Cambridge History of Arabic Literature*. Cambridge: Cambridge University Press, 1990. 155–167.

Bosworth, C. E. "The City of Tarsus and the Arab-Byzantine Frontiers in Early and Middle ʿAbbāsid Times." *Oriens* 33 (1992): 268–286.

Bosworth, C. E. "An Early Arabic Mirror for Princes: Ṭāhir Dhū l-Yamīnain's Epistle to His Son ʿAbdallāh (206/821)." *JNES* 29/1 (1970): 25–41.

Bosworth, C. E. *Al-Maqrīzī's Book of Contention and Strife Concerning the Relations Between the Banū Umayya and the Banū Hāšim*. Manchester, 1980.

Bosworth, C. E. "Al-Maqrīzī's Epistle Concerning What Has Come Down to Us about the Banu Umayya and the Banu l-ʿAbbās." In Wadād al-Qāḍī (ed.), *Studia Arabica et Islamica, Festschrift for Iḥsān ʿAbbās on his Sixtieth Birthday*. Beirut: American University of Beirut, 1981. 39–45.

Bosworth, C. E. "Rajāʾ ibn Ḥaywa al-Kindī and the Umayyad caliphs." *IQ* 16 (1972): 36–80.

Bosworth, C. E. "Ar-Raqqa: Geopolitical Factors and Its History Under the Caliphs." In S. Heidemann and A. Becker (eds.), *Raqqa II. Die islamische Stadt*. Mainz: Philipp von Zabern, 2003. 57–61.

Bosworth, C. E. "Umayya b. ʿAbd Shams." *EI*².

Bourdieu, Pierre. *Esquisse d'une théorie de la pratique*. Paris: Droz, 1972.

Bourin, Monique and Élisabeth Zadora-Rio. "Analyses de l'espace." In Jean-Claude Schmitt and Otto G. Oexle (dir.), *Les tendances actuelles de l'histoire du Moyen Âge en France et en Allemagne. Actes des colloques de Sèvres (1997) et Göttingen (1998) organisés par le C.N.R.S. et le Max-Planck-Institut für Geschichte*. Paris: Publications de la Sorbonne, 2003. 493–510.

Bowersock, G. W., Peter Brown and Oleg Grabar (eds.). *Late Antiquity: A Guide to the Post-Classical World*. Cambridge, MA and London: The Belknap Press of Harvard University Press, 1999.

Braslavski, I. "Hat Welīd II den Jordan ablenken wollen?" *Journal of the Palestine Oriental Society* 13/1–2 (1933): 97–100.

Braudel, Fernand. *La Méditerranée et le monde à l'époque de Philippe II*. 3 vol. Paris: Armand Colin, 1990 [1949].

Bray, Julia. "Lists and Memory: Ibn Qutayba and Muḥammad b. Ḥabīb." In Farhad Daftary and J. W. Meri (eds.), *Culture and Memory in Medieval Islam: Essays in Honour of Wilferd Madelung*. London: Tauris, 2003. 210–231.

Bresc, Cécile. *Monuments numismatiques du Bilād al-Šām médiéval: monnaies, politique et circulation (132–368/750–978)*. Ph. D. diss. Université Paris Sorbonne-Paris IV, 2008.

Breydy, Michael. "Das Chronikon des Maroniten Theophilus ibn Tuma." *Journal of Oriental and African Studies* (Athens) 2 (1990): 34–46.

Breydy, Michael. *Études sur Saʿīd ibn Biṭrīq et ses sources*. Leuven: Peeters, 1983.

Briquel-Chatonnet, Françoise, Muriel Debié and Alain Desreumaux (eds.). *Les inscriptions syriaques*. Paris: Geuthner (Études syriaques 1), 2004.

Brisch, Klaus. "Le château omeyyade du Djebel Seis. Rapport préliminaire de la première campagne de fouilles entreprises avec les fonds de "Deutsche Forschungsgemeinschaft" (April–June 1962)." AAAS XIII (1963): 135–158.

Brisch, Klaus. "The Location of the Umayyad Residences in Greater Syria as Indicators of the Geopolitical Conditions of the Time." *Proceedings of the First International Conference on Bilad al-Sham*. Amman, 1984. 29–70.

Brock, Sebastian P. "North Mesopotamia in the Late Seventh Century. Book XV of John Bar Penkāyē's Rīš Mellē." *JSAI* 9 (1987): 51–75.

Brock, Sebastian P. "Syriac Historical Writing: a Survey of the Main Sources." *Journal of the Iraqi Academy* 5 (1979–1980): 1–30.

Brock, Sebastian P. "A Syriac Life of John of Dailam." *Parole de l'Orient* 10 (1981–1982): 123–189.

Brock, Sebastian P. "Syriac Sources for the Seventh Century History." *Byzantine and Modern Greek Studies* 2 (1976): 17–36.

Brock, Sebastian P. "Syriac Views on Emergent Islam." In G. H. A. Juynboll (ed.), *Studies on the First Century of Islamic Society*. Carbondale and Edwardsville, IL: Southern Illinois University Press, 1982. 9–22.

Brooks, E. W. "The Arabs in Asia Minor (641–750), from Arabic Sources." *The Journal of Hellenic Studies* 18 (1898): 182–208.

Brooks, E. W. "The Campaign of 716–718, from Arabic Sources." *The Journal of Hellenic Studies* 19 (1899): 19–31.

Brooks, E. W. "The Chronological Canon of James of Edessa." ZDMG 53 (1899): 261–327.

Brooks, E. W. "Notes on the Syriac Chronicle of 846." ZDMG 51 (1897): 416–417.

Brooks, E. W. "The Sources of Theophanes and the Syriac Chroniclers." *Byzantinische Zeitschrift* 15 (1906): 578–587.

Brooks, E. W. "A Syriac Chronicle of the Year 846." ZDMG 51 (1897): 569–588.

Brooks, E. W. "A Syriac Fragment." ZDMG 54 (1900): 195–230.

Brown, Jonathan. *The Canonization of al-Bukhārī and Muslim*. Leiden: Brill, 2007.

Brown, Peter. *The World of Late Antiquity AD 150–750*. London: W. W. Norton & Company, 1971.

Brühl, C. "Remarques sur les notions de "capitale" et de "résidence" pendant le Haut Moyen Âge." *Journal des savants* (1967): 193–215.

Bujard, Jacques and Denis Genequand. "Umm al-Walid et Khan az-Zabib, deux établissements omeyyades en limite du désert jordanien." In B. Geyer (ed.), *Conquête de la steppe et appropriations des terres sur les marges arides du Croissant fertile*. Lyon, 2001. 189–218.

Burckhardt, Titus. *Art of Islam: Language and Meaning*. London: World of Islam Festival Pub. Co., 1976.

Buresi, Pascal. *Une frontière entre chrétienté et Islam dans la péninsule Ibérique (XIe–XIIIe siècle)*. Paris: Publibook, 2004.

Busse, H. "'Omar b. al-Ḫaṭṭāb in Jerusalem." *JSAI* 5 (1984): 73–119.
Busse, H. "'Omar's Image as the Conqueror of Jerusalem." *JSAI* 8 (1986): 149–168.
Cabrol, Cécile. "Une étude sur les secrétaires nestoriens sous les Abbassides (762–1258) à Bagdad." *Parole de l'Orient* 25 (2000): 407–491.
Caetani, Leone. *Annali dell'Islam*. Milan: U. Hoepli, 1905–1926.
Caetani, Leone. *Chronographia Islamica*. Paris, 1912.
Cahen, Claude. "Ḍay'a." *EI*².
Cahen, Claude. "Fiscalité, propriété, antagonismes sociaux en Haute Mésopotamie au temps des premiers Abbassides, d'après Denys de Tell-Mahré." *Arabica* 1 (1954): 136–152.
Cahen, Claude. "Points de vue sur la "Révolution ʿabbāside"." In Claude Cahen, *Les peuples musulmans dans l'histoire médiévale*. Damascus, 1977. 105–160.
Cahen, Claude. *La Syrie du Nord à l'époque des Croisades et la principauté franque d'Antioche*. Paris: Geuthner, 1940.
Calder, Norman. *Studies in Early Muslim Jurisprudence*. Oxford: Clarendon Press, 1993.
Cameron, Averil and Lawrence I. Conrad (eds.). *The Byzantine and Early Islamic Near East I: Problems in Literary Source Material*. Princeton: Darwin Press, 1992.
Cameron, Averil and Lawrence I. Conrad. "Introduction." In Averil Cameron and Lawrence I. Conrad (eds.), *The Byzantine and Early Islamic Near East I: Problems in Literary Source Material*. Princeton: Darwin Press, 1992. 1–24.
Cameron, Averil (ed.). *The Byzantine and Early Islamic Near East III: States, Resources and Armies*. Princeton: Darwin Press, 1995.
Cameron, Averil. "Ideologies and Agendas in Late Antique Studies." In Luke Lavan and William Bowden (eds.), *Theory and Practice in Late Antique Archaeology*. Leiden: Brill, 2003. 3–21.
Cameron, Averil. "Texts as Weapons: Polemic in the Byzantine Dark Ages." In Alan K. Bowman and Greg Woolf (eds.), *Literacy and Power in the Ancient World*. Cambridge, 1994. 198–215.
Cameron, Marianne E. "Sayf at First: the Transmission of Sayf ibn ʿUmar in al-Ṭabarī and Ibn ʿAsākir." In James E. Lindsay (ed.), *Ibn ʿAsākir and Early Islamic History*. Princeton: Darwin Press, 2001. 62–77.
Campbell, Sandra Sue. *Telling Memories: The Zubayrids in Islamic Historical Memory*. Ph. D. diss. University of California, 2003.
Canard, Marius. "Al-Baṭṭāl." *EI*².
Canard, Marius. *Byzance et les musulmans du Proche-Orient*. London: Variorum reprints, 1973.
Canard, Marius. "Delhemma, épopée arabe des guerres arabo-byzantines." *Byzantion* 10 (1935): 283–300.
Canard, Marius. "Ḏū al-Himma ou Ḏāt al-Himma." *EI*².

Canard, Marius. "Les expéditions des Arabes contre Constantinople dans l'histoire et dans la légende." JA 208 (1926): 61–121.

Canard, Marius. *Histoire de la dynastie des Hamdanides de Jazîra et de Syrie*. Algiers, 1951.

Canard, Marius. "Les principaux personnages du roman de chevalerie arabe Ḏāt al-Himma wa-l-Baṭṭāl." *Arabica* 8 (1961): 158–173.

Canard, Marius. "La prise d'Héraclée et les relations entre Hârûn al-Rashîd et l'empereur Nicéphore Ier." *Byzantion* XXXII (1962): 345–379.

Canivet, Pierre and Jean-Paul Rey-Coquais. *La Syrie de Byzance à l'Islam: VIIe–VIIIe siècles, Actes du colloque international, Lyon et Paris, 11–15 septembre 1990*. Damascus: PIFD, 1992.

Cardaillac, Denise. *La polémique anti-chrétienne du manuscrit aljamiado N 4944 de la bibliothèque nationale de Madrid*. 2 vol. Ph. D. diss. Université Paul Valéry, Montpellier, 1972.

Carlier, Patricia and Frederic Morin. "Qastal al-Balqa': mosaïques omeyyades civiles (685/705 apr. J.-C.)." In Noël Duval (ed.), *Les églises de Jordanie et leurs mosaïques*. Beirut: BAH 168, 2003. 199–206.

Carruthers, Mary. *Le livre de la mémoire. La mémoire dans la culture médiévale*. Paris: Macula, 2002.

Carruthers, Mary. *Machina Memorialis. Méditation, rhétorique et fabrication des images au Moyen Âge*. Paris: Gallimard, 2002.

Caskel, Werner. "Al-Uḫaiḍir." *Der Islam* 39 (1964): 27–37.

Caskel, Werner. *Ǧamharat an-Nasab. Das Genealogische Werk des Hišam ibn Muḥammad al-Kalbī*. 2 vols. Leiden: Brill, 1966.

Castrum 4. Frontière et peuplement dans le monde méditerranéen au Moyen Âge. Madrid, 1992.

Cattenoz, Henri Georges. *Tables de concordance des ères chrétienne et hégirienne*. Rabat, 1954.

Centlivres, Pierre, Daniel Fabre and Françoise Zonabend (eds.). *La fabrique des héros*. Paris: Maison des sciences de l'homme, 1998.

Centlivres, Pierre, Daniel Fabre and Françoise Zonabend. "Introduction." In Pierre Centlivres, Daniel Fabre, Françoise Zonabend (eds.), *La fabrique des héros*. Paris: Maison des sciences de l'homme, 1998. 1–8.

Chabbi, Jacqueline. "La représentation du passé aux premiers âges de l'historiographie califale. Problèmes de lecture et de méthode." *Itinéraires d'Orient. Hommages à Claude Cahen, Res Orientales* 6. Bures-sur-Yvettes, 1994. 21–46.

Chabbi, Jacqueline. *Le seigneur des tribus. L'islam de Mahomet*. Paris: Noêsis, 1997.

Chamberlain, Michael. *Knowledge and Social Practice in Medieval Damascus, 1190–1350*. Cambridge: Cambridge University Press, 1994.

Cheddadi, Abdesselam. *Les Arabes et l'appropriation de l'histoire. Émergence et premiers développements de l'historiographie musulmane jusqu'au* IIe/VIIIe *siècle*. Paris: Sindbad-Actes Sud, 2004.

Cheddadi, Abdesselam. "À l'aube de l'historiographie islamique: la mémoire islamique." *SI* LXXIV (1991): 29–41.

Chehab, Hafez K. "On the identification of ʿAnjar (ʿAyn al-Jarr) as an Umayyad foundation." *Muqarnas* 10 (1993): 42–48.

Chehab, Hafez K. "Les palais Omeyyades d'Anjar. Résidences princières d'été." *Archéologia* 87 (1975): 18–25.

Chehab, Maurice. "The Umayyad palace at Anjar." *Ars Orientalis* V (1963): 18–26.

Cheikh-Moussa, Abdallah. "L'historien et la littérature arabe médiévale." *Arabica* 43/1 (1996): 152–188.

Chiffoleau, Jacques. *La comptabilité de l'au-delà. Les hommes, la mort et la religion dans la région d'Avignon à la fin du Moyen Age (vers 1320–vers 1480)*. Rome: École Française de Rome, 1980.

Chiffoleau, Jacques. "Pour une histoire de la religion et des institutions médiévales. Présentation des recherches de J. Chiffoleau à l'occasion de son habilitation." *Cahiers d'Histoire* (1991): 3–21.

Chiffoleau, Sylvia. "Le pèlerinage à La Mecque à l'époque coloniale: matrice d'une opinion publique musulmane?" In Sylvia Chiffoleau and Anna Madœuf (eds.), *Les pèlerinages au Maghreb et au Moyen-Orient: espaces publics, espaces du public*. Damascus: IFPO, 2005. 131–163.

CIAP = see Moshe Sharon.

Clanchy, Michael. *From Memory to Written Record: England, 1066–1307*. Oxford, 1993 [1979].

Clausewitz, Carl von. *On War*. New York: Modern Library, 1943.

Clover, F. M. and R. S. Humphreys. *Tradition and Innovation in Late Antiquity*. Madison, WI: Wisconsin University Press, 1989.

Cobb, Paul M. "Community versus Contention: Ibn ʿAsākir and ʿAbbāsid Syria." In James E. Lindsay (ed.), *Ibn ʿAsākir and Early Islamic History*. Princeton: Darwin Press, 2001. 100–126.

Cobb, Paul M. "The Empire in Syria, 705–763." In Chase F. Robinson (ed.), *The New Cambridge History of Islam, vol. 1: The Formation of the Islamic World, Sixth to Eleventh Centuries*. Cambridge: Cambridge University Press, 2010. 226–268.

Cobb, Paul M. "Al-Maqrīzī, Hashimism, and the Early Caliphates." *Mamlūk Studies Review* VII/2 (2003): 69–81.

Cobb, Paul M. "Al-Mutawakkil's Damascus: a New ʿAbbāsid Capital?" *JNES* 58/4 (1999): 241–257.

Cobb, Paul M. "A note on ʿUmar's visit to Ayla in 17/638." *Der Islam* 71/2 (1994): 283–288.

Cobb, Paul M. "Scholars and Society at Early Islamic Ayla." *JESHO* 38/4 (1995): 417–428.

Cobb, Paul M. "'Umar (II) b. 'Abd al-'Azīz." *EI*².

Cobb, Paul M. "Virtual Sacrality: Making Muslim Syria Sacred Before the Crusades." *Medieval Encounters* 8/1 (2002): 35–55.

Cobb, Paul M. *White Banners: Contention in 'Abbasid Syria 750–880*. Albany: SUNY Press, 2001.

Congourdeau, Marie-Hélène and Mohammed Melhaoui. "La perception de la peste en pays chrétien byzantin et musulman." *Revue des Études Byzantines* 59 (2001): 95–124.

Conrad, Gerhard. *Abū 'l-Ḥusain al-Rāzī (347/958) und seine Schriften. Untersuchungen zur frühen Damaszener Geschichtsschreibung*. Stuttgart: Franz Steiner, 1991.

Conrad, Gerhard. "Zur Bedeutung des *Ta'rīḫ madīnat Dimašq* als historische Quelle." In Werner Diem and Abdoldjavad Falaturi (eds.), *XXIV Deutscher Orientalistentag. Ausgewählte Vorträge, ZDMG Supplement VIII*. Stuttgart, 1990. 271–282.

Conrad, Gerhard. "Das Kitab al-Tabaqat des Abu Zur'a al-Dimasqi (-281 H.): Anmerkungen zu einem unbekannten frühen rigal-Werk." *Die Welt des Orients* 20–21 (1989–1990): 167–226.

Conrad, Gerhard. *Die Quḍāt Dimašq und der Madhab al-Auzā'ī. Materialen zur syrischen Rechtsgeschichte*. Beirut: Komission bei Franz Steiner Verlag Stuttgart, 1994.

Conrad, Lawrence I. "Abraha and Muḥammad: Some Observations Apropos of Chronology and Literary *Topoi* in the Early Arabic Historical Tradition." *BSOAS* L/2 (1987): 225–240.

Conrad, Lawrence I. "The Arabs and the Colossus." *JRAS* 6 (1996): 165–187.

Conrad, Lawrence I. "Al-Azdī's History of the Arab Conquests in Bilād al-Shām: Some Historiographical Observations." In Muḥammad A. al-Bakhit and Iḥsān 'Abbās (eds.), *Proceedings of the Second Symposium on the History of Bilad al-Sham During the Early Islamic Period up to 40 A.H./640 A.D. The Fourth International Conference on the History of Bilad al-Sham*. Amman, 1987. 28–62.

Conrad, Lawrence I. "The Conquest of Arwād: a Source-Critical Study in the Historiography of the Early Medieval Near East." In Averil Cameron and Lawrence I. Conrad (eds.), *The Byzantine and Early Islamic Near East I: Problems in Literary Source Material*. Princeton: Darwin Press, 1992. 317–401.

Conrad, Lawrence I. "Did al-Walīd I Found the First Islamic Hospital?" *Aram* 6 (1994): 225–244.

Conrad, Lawrence I. "Epidemic Disease in Central Syria in the Late Sixth Century: Some New Insights from the Verse of Ḥassān ibn Thābit." *Byzantine and Modern Greek Studies* 18 (1994): 12–58.

Conrad, Lawrence I. "Heraclius in Early Islamic Kerygma." In G. J. Reinink and B. H. Stolte (eds.), *The Reign of Heraclius (610–641): Crisis and Confrontation*. Leuven: Peeters, 2002. 113–156.

Conrad, Lawrence I. "Historical Evidence and the Archaeology of Early Islam." In S. Seikaly, R. Baalbaki, P. Dodd (eds.), *Quest for Understanding: Arabic and Islamic*

Studies in Memory of Malcolm H. Kerr. Beirut: American University of Beirut, 1991. 263–282.

Conrad, Lawrence I. "Ibn A'ṯam al-Kūfī." In Julie Scott Meisami and Paul Starkey (eds.), *Encyclopedia of Arabic Litrature, Volume 1: A–K*. London: Routledge, 1998. 314.

Conrad, Lawrence I. "Notes on al-Ṭabarī's History (vol. XXV)." *JRAS* 3/3/1 (1993): 1–31.

Conrad, Lawrence I. "On the Arabic Chronicle of Bar Hebraeus: His Aim and Audience." *Parole de l'Orient* 19 (1994): 319–378.

Conrad, Lawrence I. "Die Pest und ihr soziales Umfeld im Nahen Osten des frühen Mittelalters." *Der Islam* 73 (1996): 81–112.

Conrad, Lawrence I. *The Plague in the Early Medieval Near East*. Ph. D. diss. Princeton University, 1981.

Conrad, Lawrence I. "The *quṣūr* of Medieval Islam: Some Implications for the Social History of the Near East." *Al-Abhath* 29 (1981): 7–23.

Conrad, Lawrence I. "Recovering Lost Texts: Some Methodological Issues." *JAOS* 113/2 (1993): 258–263.

Conrad, Lawrence I. "Seven and the Tasbīʿ: On the Implications of Numerical Symbolism for the Study of Medieval Islamic History." *JESHO* 31/1 (1988): 42–73.

Conrad, Lawrence I. "Syriac Perspectives on Bilād al-Shām During the Abbasid Period." In Muḥammad A. Al-Bakhit and Robert Schick (eds.), *Bilād al-Shām During the Abbasid Period (132 AH/750 AD–451 AH/1059 AD): Proceedings of the Fifth International Conference on the History of Bilād al-Shām*. Amman: Lajnat ta'rīkh Bilād al-Shām, 1992. 1–44.

Conrad, Lawrence I. "Ṭāʿūn and Wabā', Conceptions of Plague and Pestilence in Early Islam." *JESHO* 25 (1982): 268–307.

Conrad, Lawrence I. "Theophanes and the Arabic Historical Tradition: Some Indications of Intercultural Transmission." *Byzantinische Forschungen* 15 (1988): 1–44.

Conrad, Lawrence I. "Varietas Syriaca: Secular and Scientific Culture in the Christian Communities of Syria after the Arab Conquest." In G. J. Reinink and A. C. Klugkist (eds.), *After Bardaisan. Studies in Continuity and Change in Honour of Professor Han J. W. Drijvers*. Leuven: Peeters, 1999. 85–105.

Constable, Olivia Remie. "Perceptions of the Umayyads in Christian Spanish Chronicles." In Antoine Borrut and Paul M. Cobb (eds.), *Umayyad Legacies: Medieval Memories from Syria to Spain*. Leiden: Brill, 2010. 105–130.

Conte, Gian Biagio. *The Rhetoric of Imitation: Genre and Poetic Memory in Virgil and Other Latin Poets*. Trans. Charles Segal. Ithaca, NY: Cornell University Press, 1986.

Cook, David. "An Early Muslim Daniel Apocalypse." *Arabica* 49/1 (2002): 55–96.

Cook, David. "Messianism and Astronomical Events During the First Four Centuries of Islam." In Mercedes García-Arenal (dir.), *Mahdisme et Millénarisme en Islam, Revue des Mondes Musulmans et de la Méditerranée*, 91–92–93–94 (2000): 29–52.

Cook, David. "Muslim Apocalyptic and *Jihād*." *JSAI* 20 (1996): 66–104.

Cook, David. *Studies in Muslim Apocalyptic*. Princeton: Darwin Press, 2002.
Cook, David. "A Survey of Some of the Muslim Sources on Comets and Meteors." *Journal for the History of Astronomy* 30 (1999): 131–160.
Cook, David. *Understanding Jihad*. Berkeley, CA: University of California Press, 2005.
Cook, Michael A. *Commanding Right and Forbidding Wrong in Islamic Thought*. Cambridge: Cambridge University Press, 2000.
Cook, Michael A. "An Early Islamic Apocalyptic Chronicle." *JNES* 52 (1993): 25–29.
Cook, Michael A. *Early Muslim Dogma*. Cambridge: Cambridge University Press, 1981.
Cook, Michael A. "Eschatology and the Dating of Traditions." *Princeton Papers in Near Eastern Studies* 1 (1992): 23–47.
Cook, Michael A. "The Opponents of the Writing of Tradition in Early Islam." *Arabica* 44 (1997): 437–530.
Cook, Michael A. and Patricia Crone. *Hagarism. The Making of the Islamic World*. Cambridge: Cambridge University Press, 1977.
Cooperson, Michael. *Classical Arabic Biography. The heirs of the Prophet in the Age of al-Maʾmūn*. Cambridge: Cambridge Studies in Islamic Civilization, 2000.
Cooperson, Michael. "The Grave of al-Maʾmūn in Tarsus: a Preliminary Report." In James E. Montgomery (ed.), *ʿAbbasid Studies, Occasional Papers of the School of ʿAbbasid Studies, Cambridge, 6–10 July* 2002. Leuven: Peeters, 2004. 47–60.
Cooperson, Michael. "Ibn al-Muqaffaʿ." In Michael Cooperson and Shawkat M. Toorawa (eds.), *Arabic Literary Culture, 500–925*. Detroit, MI: Thomson Gale, 2005. 150–163.
Cooperson, Michael. *Al-Maʾmun*. Oxford: Oneworld, 2005.
Cornette, Joël. *Le roi de guerre. Essai sur la souveraineté dans la France du Grand Siècle*. Paris: Payot, 2000.
Cornu, Georgette. *Atlas du monde arabo-islamique à l'époque classique* (*IX*^{e}–*X*^{e} *siècles*). Leiden: Brill, 1983.
Costaz, Louis. *Dictionnaire Syriaque-Français, Syriac-English Dictionary*. Beirut: Imprimerie Catholique, 1963.
Creswell, K. A. C. *Early Muslim Architecture*. 2 vol. Oxford, 1969.
Creswell, K. A. C. *A Short Account of Early Muslim Architecture*. Rev. by J. W. Allan. Cairo: The American University in Cairo Press, 1989.
Crone, Patricia and Martin Hinds. *God's Caliph. Religious Authority in the First Centuries of Islam*. Cambridge: Cambridge University Press, 1986.
Crone, Patricia. "The ʿAbbāsid Abnāʾ and Sāsānid Cavalrymen." *JRAS* 8/3 (1998): 1–19.
Crone, Patricia. "Islam, Judeo-Christianity and Byzantine Iconoclasm." *JSAI* 2 (1980): 59–96.
Crone, Patricia. *Meccan Trade and the Rise of Islam*. Princeton: Princeton University Press, 1987.
Crone, Patricia. *Medieval Islamic Political Thought*. Edinburgh: Edinburgh University Press, 2004.

Crone, Patricia. "Muhallabids." *EI*².

Crone, Patricia. "On the Meaning of the ʿAbbāsid Call to al-Riḍā." In C. E. Bosworth et al. (eds.), *The Islamic World from Classical to Modern Times, Essays in Honour of Bernard Lewis*. Princeton: Darwin Press, 1989. 95–111.

Crone, Patricia. "Review of M. Sharon, *Black Banners from the East: The Establishment of the ʿAbbāsid State – Incubation of a Revolt*." *BSOAS* 1 (1987): 134–136.

Crone, Patricia. "The Significance of Wooden Weapons in al-Mukhtār's Revolt and the ʿAbbāsid Revolution." In Ian R. Netton (ed.), *Studies in Honour of Clifford Edmund Bosworth*, vol. 1: *Hunter of the East: Arabic and Semitic Studies*. Leiden: Brill, 2000. 174–187.

Crone, Patricia. *Slaves on Horses: The Evolution of the Islamic Polity*. Cambridge: Cambridge University Press, 1980.

Crone, Patricia. "Tribes and States in the Middle East." *JRAS* 3/3 (1993): 353–376.

Crone, Patricia. "Were the Qays and Yemen of the Umayyad Period Political Parties?" *Der Islam* 71 (1994): 1–57.

Cubitt, Geoffrey. *History and Memory*. Manchester and New York: Manchester University Press, 2007.

Daftary, Farhad. "Salamiyya." *EI*².

Dahan, Sami. "The Origin and Development of the Local Histories of Syria." In Bernard Lewis and P. M. Holt (eds.), *Historians of the Middle East*. London: Oxford University Press, 1962. 108–117.

Daiber, Verena and Andrea Becker (eds.). *Raqqa III. Baudenkmäler und Paläste I*. Mainz: Philipp von Zabern, 2004.

Dakhlia, Jocelyne. "Collective Memory and the Story of History" = "Le sens des origines: comment on raconte l'histoire dans une société maghrébine." *Revue Historique* 277 (1987): 401–427.

Dakhlia, Jocelyne. "Dans la mouvance du prince: la symbolique du pouvoir itinérant au Maghreb." *Annales. Histoire, Sciences Sociales* 43/3 (1988): 735–760.

Dakhlia, Jocelyne. "Des prophètes à la nation: la mémoire des temps anté-islamiques au Maghreb." *Cahiers d'études africaines* 27 (1987): 241–267.

Dakhlia, Jocelyne. *Le divan des rois. Le politique et le religieux dans l'islam*. Paris: Aubier, 1998.

Dakhlia, Jocelyne. *L'empire des passions. L'arbitraire politique en Islam*. Paris: Aubier, 2005.

Dakhlia, Jocelyne. "New Approaches in the History of Memory? A French Model." In Angelika Neuwirth and Andreas Pflitsch (eds.), *Crisis and Memory in Islamic Societies, Proceedings of the third Summer Academy of the Working Group Modernity and Islam held at the Oriental Institute of the German Oriental Society in Beirut*. Beirut: Ergon Verlag Würzburg in Kommission, 2001. 59–74.

Dakhlia, Jocelyne. *L'oubli de la cité: la mémoire collective à l'épreuve du lignage dans le Jérid tunisien*. Paris: La Découverte, 1990.

Dakhlia, Jocelyne. "Sous le vocable de Salomon. L'exercice de la "justice retenue" au Maghreb." *Annales Islamologiques* 27 (1993): 169–180.

Daniel, Elton L. "The "Ahl al-Taqādum" and the Problem of the Constituency of the 'Abbāsid Revolution in the Merv Oasis." *Journal of Islamic Studies* 7 (1996): 150–179.

Daniel, Elton L. "The Anonymous History of the Abbasid Family and its Place in Islamic Historiography." IJMES XIV/4 (1982): 419–432.

Daniel, Elton L. "Arabs, Persians and the Advent of the Abbasids Reconsidered." JAOS 117/3 (1997): 542–548.

Daniel, Elton L. "Balʿamī's Account of Early Islamic History." In Farhad Daftary and J. W. Meri (eds.), *Culture and Memory in Medieval Islam. Essays in Honour of Wilferd Madelung*. London: Tauris, 2003. 163–189.

Daniel, Elton L. *The Political and Social History of Khurasan under Abbasid Rule, 747–820*. Minneapolis and Chicago: Bibliotheca Islamica, 1979.

Daniel, Elton L. "Review of M. Sharon, *Black Banners from the East: The Establishment of the 'Abbāsid State – Incubation of a Revolt*; J. Lassner, *Islamic Revolution and Historical Memory: An Inquiry into the Art of 'Abbāsid Apologetics*." IJMES 21 (1989): 578–583.

Daniel, Elton L. "Al-Yaʿqūbī and Shiʿism Reconsidered." In James E. Montgomery (ed.), *'Abbasid Studies, Occasional Papers of the School of 'Abbasid Studies, Cambridge, 6–10 July* 2002. Leuven: Peeters, 2004. 209–231.

Darkazally, B. *Al-Ḥajjāj ibn Yūsuf al-Thaqafī: The Consolidation of Umayyad Authority in Iraq (75–95 A.H./694–714 A.D.)*. Ph. D. diss. University of Toronto, 1977.

Darley-Doran, Robert. "Wāsiṭ." EI².

Debié, Muriel. *L'écriture de l'histoire en syriaque: transmission interculturelle et construction identitaire entre hellénisme et islam*. Leuven: Peeters, 2015.

Debié, Muriel. (ed.). *Historiographie syriaque*. Paris: Geuthner (Études syriaques, 6), 2009.

Décobert, Christian. "L'ancien et le nouveau: à propos de l'enfance de l'islam." *L'arabisant* 26 (1987): 45–57.

Décobert, Christian. "L'autorité religieuse aux premiers siècles de l'islam." *Archives de Sciences Sociales des Religions* 125 (2004): 23–44.

Décobert, Christian. "La mémoire monothéiste du Prophète." SI 72 (1990): 19–46.

Décobert, Christian. *Le mendiant et le combattant. L'institution de l'islam*. Paris: Seuil, 1991.

Décobert, Christian. "Notule sur le patrimonialisme omeyyade." In Antoine Borrut and Paul M. Cobb (eds.), *Umayyad Legacies: Medieval Memories from Syria to Spain*. Leiden: Brill, 2010. 213–253.

De Jong, Mayke and Frans Theuws (eds.). *Topographies of Power in the Early Middle Ages*. Leiden: Brill, 2001.

Den Heijer, J. Mawhūb ibn Manṣūr. *Ibn Mufarrig et l'historiographie Copto-Arabe. Étude sur la composition de l'histoire des Patriarches d'Alexandrie*. Leuven: Peeters, 1989.

Dennett, Daniel C. *Marwan ibn Muhammad: The Passing of the Umayyad Caliphate*. Ph. D. diss. Harvard University, 1939.

Derat, Marie-Laure. *Le domaine des rois éthiopiens (1270–1527). Espace, pouvoir et monachisme*. Paris: Publications de la Sorbonne, 2003.

Derenk, Dieter. *Leben und Dichtung des Omaiyadenkalifen al-Walīd ibn Yazīd*. Freiburg im Breisgau, 1974.

DeShazo, Alan S. and Michael L. Bates. "The Umayyad governors of al-ʿIraq and the Changing Annulet Patterns on their Dirhems." *Numismatic Chronicle* 14 (1974): 110–118.

Diem, Werner and Marco Schöller. *The Living and the Dead in Islam. Studies in Arabic Epitaphs. I. Epitaphs as Texts. II. Epitaphs in Context. III. Indices*. Wiesbaden: Harrassowitz Verlag, 2004.

Dixon, A. A. *The Umayyad Caliphate 65–86/684–705*. London: Luzac, 1971.

Djaït, H. "L'Islam ancien récupéré à l'histoire." *Annales E.S.C.* 4 (1975): 900–914.

Donner, Fred M. *The Early Islamic Conquests*. Princeton, 1981.

Donner, Fred M. "From Believers to Muslims: Confessional Self-Identity in the Early Islamic Community." *Al-Abhath* 50–51 (2002–2003): 9–53.

Donner, Fred M. "Maymūn b. Mihrān." *EI*².

Donner, Fred M. *Muhammad and the Believers: At the Origins of Islam*. Cambridge, MA and London: The Belknap Press of Harvard University Press, 2010.

Donner, Fred M. *Narratives of Islamic Origins. The Beginnings of Islamic Historical Writing*. Princeton: Darwin Press, 1998.

Donner, Fred M. "The Problem of Early Arabic Historiography in Syria." In Muḥammad A. al-Bakhit and Iḥsān ʿAbbās (eds.), *Proceedings of the Second Symposium on the History of Bilad al-Sham During the Early Islamic Period up to 40 A.H./640 A.D. The Fourth International Conference on the History of Bilad al-Sham*. Amman, 1987. 1–27.

Donner, Fred M. "La question du messianisme dans l'islam primitif." In Mercedes García-Arenal (ed.), *Mahdisme et millénarisme en Islam*, REMMM, 91–92–93–94 (2000): 17–28.

Donner, Fred M. "Review of H. Kennedy, *The Prophet and the Age of the Caliphates*." *Speculum* 65 (1990): 182–184.

Donner, Fred M. "The Role of Nomads in the Near East in Late Antiquity (400–800 C. E.)." In F. M. Clover and R. S. Humphreys (eds.), *Tradition and Innovation in Late Antiquity*. Madison, WI: Wisconsin University Press, 1989. 73–85.

Donner, Fred M. "The Sources of Islamic Conceptions of War." In John Kelsay and James Turner Johnson (eds.), *Just War and Jihad. Historical Perspectives on War and Peace in Western and Islamic Traditions*. New York: Greenwood Press, 1991. 31–69.

Donner, Fred M. "Umayyad Efforts at Legitimation: The Umayyads' Silent Heritage." In Antoine Borrut and Paul M. Cobb (eds.), *Umayyad Legacies: Medieval Memories from Syria to Spain*. Leiden: Brill, 2010. 187–211.

Donner, Fred M. "ʿUthmān and the Rāshidūn Caliphs in Ibn ʿAsākir's *Taʾrīḫ madīnat Dimashq*: a Study in Strategies of Compilation." In James E. Lindsay (ed.), *Ibn ʿAsākir and Early Islamic History*. Princeton: Darwin Press, 2001. 44–61.

Dozy, R. *Dictionnaire détaillé des noms de vêtements chez les Arabes*. Amsterdam: Jean Müller, 1845.

Dozy, R. *Supplément aux dictionnaires arabes*. Leiden and Paris: Maisonneuve, 1927.

Drijvers, H. J. W. "Christians, Jews and Muslims in Northern Mesopotamia in Early Islamic Times: the Gospel of the Twelve Apostles and Related Texts." In Pierre Canivet and Jean-Paul Rey-Coquais, *La Syrie de Byzance à l'Islam: VIIe–VIIIe siècles, Actes du colloque international, Lyon et Paris, 11–15 septembre 1990*. Damascus: IFD, 1992. 67–74.

Drijvers, H. J. W. "The Gospel of the Twelve Apostles: a Syriac Apocalypse from the Early Islamic Period." In Averil Cameron and Lawrence I. Conrad (eds.), *The Byzantine and Early Islamic Near East I: Problems in Literary Source Material*. Princeton: Darwin Press, 1992. 189–213.

Drijvers, H. J. W. et al. *IV Symposium Syriacum 1984*. Orientalia Christiana Analecta 229. Rome: Pont. Institutum Studiorum Orientalium, 1987.

Drory, Rina. "The Abbasid Construction of the Jahiliyya: Cultural Authority in the Making." *SI* 83 (1996): 33–49.

Duby, Georges. *Le dimanche de Bouvines, 27 juillet 1214*. Paris: Gallimard, 1985 [1973].

Duby, Georges. *The Legend of the Bouvines*. Trans. Catherine Tihanyi. Cambridge: Polity Press, 1990.

Dunlop, Douglas M. "Balʿamī." *EI*².

Duri, A. A. "Bait al-Maqdis in Islam." *SHAJ* I (1982): 351–355.

Duri, A. A. "Ḍawʾ jadīd ʿalā al-daʿwa al-ʿabbāsiyya." *Majallat kulliyat al-ādāb wa-al-ʿulūm* 2 (1957): 64–82.

Duri, A. A. "Al-Fikra al-mahdiyya bayna al-daʿwa al-ʿabbāsiyya wa-al-ʿaṣr al-ʿabbāsī al-awwal." In Wadād al-Qāḍī (ed.), *Studia Arabica et Islamica. Festschrift for Iḥsān ʿAbbās*. Beirut, 1981. 123–132.

Duri, A. A. "Ibn al-Naṭṭāḥ." *EI*².

Duri, A. A. "The Iraq School of History in the Ninth Century – A Sketch." In Bernard Lewis and P. M. Holt (eds.), *Historians of the Middle East*. London: Oxford University Press, 1962. 46–53.

Duri, A. A. *The Rise of Historical Writing Among the Arabs*. Ed. and trans. Lawrence I. Conrad. Princeton: Princeton University Press, 1983.

Duri, A. A. "Al-Zuhrī: A Study on the Beginnings of History Writing in Islam." BSOAS 19/1 (1957): 1–12.

Dussaud, René. *Topographie historique de la Syrie antique et médiévale*. Paris: Librairie orientaliste Paul Geuthner (Bibliothèque archéologique et historique, tome 4), 1927.

Dutton, Yasin. "ʿAmal v. Ḥadīth in Islamic Law: the Case of Sadl al-Yadayn (Holding one's Hands by One's Sides) when Doing the Prayer." *Islamic Law and Society* 3/1 (1996): 13–40.

Dutton, Yasin. "Review of *Studies in Early Muslim Jurisprudence* by N. Calder." *Journal of Islamic Studies* 5 (1994): 102–108.

Dutton, Yasin. *The Origins of Islamic Law. The Qur'an, the Muwaṭṭa' and Madinan ʿAmal*. London and New York: RoutledgeCurzon, 1999.

Duval, Noël (ed.). *Les Églises de Jordanie et leurs mosaïques*. Actes de la journée d'études organisée le 22 février 1989 au musée de la Civilisation gallo-romaine de Lyon, (Bibliothèque archéologique et historique, tome 168). Beirut: IFPO, 2003.

Eddé, Anne-Marie. "Alep." In Jean-Claude Garcin (ed.), *Grandes villes méditerranéennes du monde musulman médiéval*. Rome: École Française de Rome, 2000. 157–175.

Eddé, Anne-Marie. *La principauté ayyoubide d'Alep (579/1183–658/1260)*. Stuttgart: Freiburger Islamstudien, XXI, 1999.

Eddé, Anne-Marie. "Sources arabes des XIIe et XIIIe siècles d'après le dictionnaire biographique d'Ibn al-ʿAdîm (Bughyat al-talab fî ta'rîkh Halab)." *Res Orientales* 6 (1994): 293–308.

Eddé, Anne-Marie. "Les sources de l'histoire omeyyade dans l'œuvre d'Ibn al-ʿAdīm." In Antoine Borrut and Paul M. Cobb (eds.), *Umayyad Legacies: Medieval Memories from Syria to Spain*. Leiden: Brill, 2010. 131–166.

Eddé, Anne-Marie. "Les sources d'Ibn al-ʿAdīm sur le règne de Sayf al-Dawla en Syrie du Nord (333–356/944–967)." In Chase F. Robinson (ed.), *Texts, Documents and Artefacts: Islamic Studies in Honour of D. S. Richards*. Leiden: Brill, 2003. 121–156.

Eddé, Anne-Marie and Jean-Pierre Sodini. "Les villages de Syrie du Nord du VIIe au XIIIe siècle." In Jacques Lefort, Cécile Morrisson and Jean-Pierre Sodini (eds.), *Les villages dans l'Empire byzantin (IVe–XVe siècles)*. Paris: Buchet-Chastel, 2005. 465–484.

Effros, Bonnie. "Monuments and Memory: Repossessing Ancient Remains in Early Medieval Gaul." In Mayke De Jong and Frans Theuws (eds.), *Topographies of Power in the Early Middle Ages*. Leiden: Brill, 2001. 93–118.

Eisener, Reinhard. *Zwischen Faktum und Fiktion. Eine Studie zum Umayyadenkalifen Sulaimān b. ʿAbdalmalik und seinem Bild in den Quellen*. Wiesbaden, 1987.

El-Acheche, Taïeb. *La poésie šiʿite des origines au IIIe siècle de l'hégire*. Damascus: IFPO, 2003.

Elad, Amikam. “Aspects of the Transition from the Umayyad to the ʿAbbāsid Caliphate.” *JSAI* 19 (1995): 89–132.

Elad, Amikam. “The Beginning of Historical Writing by the Arabs: The Earliest Syrian Writers on the Arab Conquests.” *JSAI* 28 (2003): 65–152.

Elad, Amikam. “The Caliph Abū’l-ʿAbbās al-Saffāḥ, The First ʿAbbāsid Mahdī: Implications of an Unknown Inscription from Bet-Shean (Baysān).” In E. Fleischer et al. (eds.), *Mas’at Moshe: Studies in Jewish and Islamic Culture Presented to Moshe Gil*. Jerusalem: Bialik Institute, 1998. [article in Hebrew with an English abstract].

Elad, Amikam. “Community of Believers of “Holy Men” and “Saints” or Community of Muslims? The Rise and Development of Early Muslim Historiography.” *JSS* XLVII/1 (2002): 241–308.

Elad, Amikam. “The Ethnic Composition of the ʿAbbāsid Revolution.” *JSAI* 24 (2000): 246–326.

Elad, Amikam. *Medieval Jerusalem and Islamic Worship*. Leiden: Brill, 1995.

Elad, Amikam. “The Rebellion of Muḥammad b. ʿAbd Allāh b. al-Ḥasan (Known as al-Nafs al-Zakīya) in 145/762.” In James E. Montgomery (ed.), *ʿAbbasid Studies. Occasional Papers of the School of ʿAbbasid Studies, Cambridge 6–10 July 2002*. Leuven: Peeters, 2004. 147–198.

Elad, Amikam. “The Siege of al-Wāsiṭ (132/749): Some Aspects of ʿAbbāsid and ʿAlīd Relations at the Beginning of ʿAbbāsid Rule.” In Moshe Sharon (ed.), *Studies in Islamic History and Civilization in Honour of Professor David Ayalon*. Leiden: Brill, 1986. 59–90.

Elad, Amikam. “The Southern Golan in the Early Muslim Period. The Significance of Two Newly Discovered Milestones of ʿAbd al-Malik.” *Der Islam* 76 (1999): 33–88.

Elad, Amikam. “Why did ʿAbd al-Malik Build the Dome of the Rock? A Re-Examination of the Muslim Sources.” In Julian Raby and Jeremy Johns (eds.), *Bayt al-Maqdis (Part 1): ʿAbd al-Malik’s Jerusalem*. Oxford, 1992. 33–58.

El-Cheikh, Nadia M. “Byzantine Leaders in Arabic-Muslim Texts.” In John Haldon and Lawrence I. Conrad (eds.), *Elites Old and New in the Byzantine and Early Islamic Near East*. Princeton: Darwin Press, 2004. 109–131.

El-Cheikh, Nadia M. *Byzantium Viewed by the Arabs*. Cambridge, MA and London: Harvard University Press (Harvard Middle Eastern Monographs, 36), 2004.

El-Hibri, Tayeb. “The Redemption of Umayyad Memory by the ʿAbbāsids.” *JNES* 61:4 (2002): 241–265.

El-Hibri, Tayeb. “The Regicide of the Caliph al-Amīn and the Challenge of Representation in Medieval Islamic Historiography.” *Arabica* 42 (1995): 334–364.

El-Hibri, Tayeb. *Reinterpreting Islamic Historiography. Hārūn al-Rashīd and the Narrative of the ʿAbbāsid Caliphate*. Cambridge: Cambridge Studies in Islamic Civilization, 1999.

Élisséeff, Nikita. *La description de Damas d’Ibn Asakir*. Damascus, 1959.

Élisséeff, Nikita. *Nūr al-Dīn, un grand prince musulman de Syrie au temps des Croisades (511–569H./1118–1174)*. 3 vol. Damascus, 1967.

EI[1] = *Encyclopaedia of Islam, First Edition*. Leiden: Brill, 1913–1938.

EI[2] = *Encyclopaedia of Islam, Second Edition*. Leiden: Brill, 1960–2005.

EI[3] = *Encyclopaedia of Islam, Third Edition*. Leiden: Brill, 2007–.

Ende, Werner. *Arabische Nation und islamische Geschichte. Die Umayyaden im Urteil arabischer Autoren des 20 Jahrunderts*. Beirut, 1977.

Esch, Arnold. "Chance et hasard de transmission. Le problème de la représentativité et de la déformation de la transmission historique." In Jean-Claude Schmitt and Otto G. Oexle (dir.), *Les tendances actuelles de l'histoire du Moyen Âge en France et en Allemagne. Actes des colloques de Sèvres (1997) et Göttingen (1998) organisés par le C.N.R.S. et le Max-Planck-Institut für Geschichte*. Paris: Publications de la Sorbonne, 2003. 15–29.

Ettinghausen, Richard. *La peinture arabe*. Les trésors de l'Asie. Geneva: A. Skira, 1962.

Fabre, Daniel. "L'atelier des héros." In Pierre Centlivres, Daniel Fabre and Françoise Zonabend (eds.), *La fabrique des héros*. Paris: Maison des sciences de l'homme, 1998. 237–318.

Fathi-Chelhod, Jean. "L'origine du nom Bar 'Ebroyo: une vieille histoire d'homonymes." *Hugoye* 4/1 (2001).

Fattal, Antoine. *Le statut légal des non-musulmans en pays d'Islam*. Beirut: Imprimerie Catholique, 1958.

Fentress, James and Christopher Wickham. *Social Memory*. Oxford and Cambridge, MA: Blackwell, 1992.

Fiey, Jean-Maurice. *Chrétiens syriaques sous les Abbassides surtout à Bagdad. 749–1258*. C.S.C.O. 420. Leuven, 1980.

Fiey, Jean-Maurice. "Les chroniqueurs syriaques avaient-ils le sens critique?" *Parole de l'Orient* 12 (1984–1985): 253–264.

Fiey, Jean-Maurice. "Les résidences d'été des rois perses d'après les actes syriaques des martyrs." *Parole de l'Orient* 20 (1995): 325–336.

Fiey, Jean-Maurice. "The Umayyads in Syriac Sources." In Muḥammad A. al-Bakhit and Robert Schick (eds.), *Bilād al-Shām during the Umayyad period, The fourth international conference on the history of Bilad al-Sham*. Amman, 1989. 11–25.

Finkelstein, Israel and Silberman, Neil A. *La Bible dévoilée. Les nouvelles révélations de l'archéologie*. Paris: Gallimard, 2002.

Finkelstein, Israel and Silberman, Neil A. *Les rois sacrés de la Bible. À la recherche de David et Salomon*. Paris: Bayard, 2006.

Finster, Barbara. "Researches in 'Anjar. I, Preliminary Report on the Architecture of 'Anjar." *Baal* 7 (2003): 209–244.

Finster, Barbara and Jürgen Schmidt. "The Origin of 'Desert Castles': Qasr Bani Muqatil near Karbala, Iraq." *Antiquity* 79 (2005): 339–349.

Finster, Barbara and Jürgen Schmidt. “Sasanidische und frühislamische Ruinen im Iraq, Tulul al Uhaidir, Erster vorläufiger Grabungsbericht.” *Baghdader Mitteilungen* 8 (1976): 57–150.

Flood, Finbarr B. *The Great Mosque of Damascus. Studies on the Makings of an Umayyad Visual Culture*. Leiden: Brill, 2000.

Foote, Rebecca. “Commerce, Industrial Expansion, and Orthogonal Planning: Mutually Compatible Terms in Settlements of Bilad al-Sham During the Umayyad Period.” *Mediterranean Archaeology* 13 (2000): 25–38.

Foote, Rebecca. *Umayyad Markets and Manufacturing: Evidence for a Commercialized and Industrializing Economy in Early Islamic Bilād al-Shām*. Ph. D. diss. Harvard University, 1999.

Foss, Clive. “Syria in Transition, AD 550–750: An Archaeological Approach.” *Dumbarton Oaks Papers* 51 (1997): 189–269.

Foss, Clive. “A Syrian Coinage of Muʿawiya.” *Revue numismatique* (2002): 353–365.

Foss, Clive. *Arab-Byzantine Coins. An Introduction, with a Catalogue of the Dumbarton Oaks Collection*. Dumbarton Oaks Research Library and Collection (Distributed by Harvard University Press). Washington D.C., 2008.

Fowden, Garth. *Empire to Commonwealth: Consequences of Monotheism in Late Antiquity*. Princeton: Princeton University Press, 1993.

Fowden, Garth. *Quṣayr ʿAmra: Art and the Umayyad Elite in Late Antique Syria*. Berkeley, CA: University of California Press, 2004.

Fowden, Garth and Elizabeth K. Fowden. *Studies on Hellenism, Christianity and the Umayyads*. Athens: Research Centre for Greek and Roman Antiquity/National Hellenic Research Foundation, 2004.

Fowden, Elizabeth K. *The Barbarian Plain: Saint Sergius Between Rome and Iran*. Berkeley, CA: University of California Press, 1999.

Fowden, Elizabeth K. “Christian Monasteries and Umayyad Residences in Late Antique Syria.” In Garth Fowden and Elizabeth K. Fowden, *Studies on Hellenism, Christianity and the Umayyads*. Athens: Research Centre for Greek and Roman Antiquity/National Hellenic Research Foundation, 2004. 175–192.

Fowden, Elizabeth K. “Monks, Monasteries and Early Islam.” In Garth Fowden and Elizabeth K. Fowden, *Studies on Hellenism, Christianity and the Umayyads*. Athens: Research Centre for Greek and Roman Antiquity/National Hellenic Research Foundation, 2004. 149–174.

Fried, Johannes. “Le passé à la merci de l’oralité et du souvenir. Le baptême de Clovis et la vie de Benoît de Nursie.” In Jean-Claude Schmitt and Otto G. Oexle (dir.), *Les tendances actuelles de l’histoire du Moyen Âge en France et en Allemagne. Actes des colloques de Sèvres (1997) et Göttingen (1998) organisés par le C.N.R.S. et le Max-Planck-Institut für Geschichte*. Paris: Publications de la Sorbonne, 2003. 71–104.

Frye, Richard N. "The ʿAbbasid Conspiracy and Modern Revolutionary Theory." *Indo-Iranica* 5 (1952–1953): 9–14.

Frye, Richard N. "The Role of Abu Muslim in the ʿAbbasid Revolution." *Muslim World* 37 (1947): 28–38.

Furet, François. *Penser la Révolution française*. Paris: Gallimard, 2001 [1978].

Gabrieli, F. "ʿAdjam" EI².

Gabrieli, F. "Il califfato di Hishâm." *Mémoires de la Société Royale Archéologique d'Alexandrie*, t. VII, 1935.

Gabrieli, F. "L'eroe omayyade Maslama ibn ʿAbd al-Malik." *Rend. Accad. Lincei* ser. 8, 5, (1950–1951): 22–39.

Gabrieli, F. *Al-Ma'mun e gli ʿAlidi*. Leipzig: Verlag Eduard Pfeiffer, 1929.

Gabrieli, F. "L'Opera di Ibn al-Muqaffaʿ." RSO 13 (1932): 196–247.

Gabrieli, F. "La poesia Ḫārigita nel secolo degli Omayyadi." RSO 20 (1943): 331–372.

Gabrieli, F. "La rivolta dei Muhallabiti nel ʿIrāq e il nuovo Balāḏurī." *Rendiconti della Classe di Scienze morali, storiche e filologiche*. Ser. VI, vol. XIV, fasc. 3–4, 1938. 199–236.

Gabrieli, F. "La Successione di Hārūn al-Rashīd e la guerra fra al-Amīn e al-Ma'mūn: Studio storico su un periodo del califfato ʿAbbāside." RSO 11 (1926–1928): 341–397.

Gabrieli, F. "Al-Walīd b. Yazīd, il califfo e il poeta." RSO 15 (1935): 1–64.

GAL = Brockelmann, Carl. *Geschichte der arabischen Literatur*. 2 vol. and 3 supplements. Leiden: E. J. Brill, 1937–1949.

García-Arenal, Mercedes. "Introduction." In Mercedes García-Arenal (dir.), *Mahdisme et Millénarisme en Islam, REMMM*, 91–92–93–94 (2000): 7–16.

García-Arenal, Mercedes (dir.) *Mahdisme et Millénarisme en Islam, REMMM*, 91–92–93–94 (2000).

Garcin, Jean-Claude (ed.). *Grandes villes méditerranéennes du monde musulman médiéval*. Rome: École Française de Rome, 2000.

Gardet, L. "Dhikr." EI².

Garsoïan, Nina G. "Reality and Myth in Armenian History." *The East and the Meaning of History, International Conference (23–27 November 1992)*. Bardi, Rome, 1994. 117–145.

GAS = Sezgin, Fuat. *Geschichte des arabischen Schrifttums*. 9 vol. Leiden: E. J. Brill, 1967–1984.

Gatier, Pierre-Louis. "Les inscriptions grecques d'époque islamique (VIIᵉ–VIIIᵉ siècles) en Syrie du Sud." In Pierre Canivet and Jean-Paul Rey-Coquais (eds.), *La Syrie de Byzance à l'Islam: VIIᵉ–VIIIᵉ siècles, Actes du colloque international, Lyon et Paris, 11–15 septembre 1990*. Damascus: PIFD, 1992. 145–157.

Gatier, Pierre-Louis. "Les mosaïques paléochrétiennes de Jordanie et l'histoire de l'Arabie byzantine." In Noël Duval (ed.), *Les églises de Jordanie et leurs mosaïques*. Beirut: IFPO (BAH 168), 2003. 289–295.

Gatier, Pierre-Louis. "Villages du Proche-Orient protobyzantin (4ème–7ème s.). Étude régionale." In G. D. R. King and Averil Cameron (eds.), *The Byzantine and Early*

Islamic Near East II: Land Use and Settlement Patterns. Princeton: Darwin Press, 1994. 17–48.

Gaube, Heinz. "ʿAmmān, Ḫarāne und Qasṭal. Vier frühislamische Bauwerke in Mitteljordanien." *Zeitschrift des Deutschen Palästina-Vereins* 93 (1977): 52–86.

Gaube, Heinz. *Ein arabischer Palast in Südsyrien, Hirbat el-Baiḍa*. Beirut and Wiesbaden: Orient-Institut der Deutschen Morgenländischen Gesellschaft and F. Steiner, 1974.

Gaube, Heinz. "An Examination of the Ruins of Qaṣr Burquʿ." *ADAJ* 19 (1974): 93–100.

Gaube, Heinz. "Die syrischen Wüstenschlösser. Einige wirtschaftliche und politische Gesichtspunkte zu ihrer Entstehung." *Zeitschrift des Deutschen Palästina-Vereins* 95 (1979): 182–209.

Gaube, Heinz. "Wie ist Ḫirbat al-Bayḍāʾ Chronologisch Einzuordnen?" *Oriente Moderno* 23/2 (2004): 449–467.

Gaube, Heinz and Almut von Gladiss. "Säulen unter dem arabischen Halbmond." In Margarete van Ess and Thomas Weber (eds.), *Baalbek. Im Bann römischer Monumentalarchitektur*. Mainz: Philipp von Zabern, 1999. 72–87.

Gaudeul, Jean-Marie. "The Correspondence Between Leo and ʿUmar. ʿUmar's Letter Re-Discovered?" *Islamochristiana* 10 (1984): 109–157.

Gawlikowski, M. "Installations Omayyades à Jérash." *SHAJ* IV (1992): 357–361.

Gawlikowski, M. "Jerash in Early Islamic Times." *Oriente Moderno* 23/2 (2004): 469–476.

Geary, Patrick J. "Land, Language and Memory in Europe 700–1100." *Transactions of the Royal Historical Society* 9 (1999): 169–184.

Geary, Patrick J. "Oblivion Between Orality and Textuality in the Tenth Century." In Gerd Althoff, Johannes Fried and Patrick J. Geary (eds.), *Medieval Concepts of the Past: Ritual, Memory, Historiography*. Cambridge: Publications of the German Historical Institute, Cambridge University Press, 2002. 111–122.

Geary, Patrick J. *Phantoms of Remembrance: Memory and Oblivion at the End of the First Millennium*. Princeton: Princeton University Press, 1994.

Geertz, Clifford. "Centers, Kings, and Charisma: Reflections on the Symbolics of Power." In Joseph Ben-David and Terry N. Clark (eds.), *Culture and its Creators: Essays in Honor of Edward Shils*. Chicago: Chicago University Press, 1977. 150–171.

Genequand, Denis. "Al-Bakhraʾ (Avatha), from the Tetrarchic Fort to the Umayyad Castle." *Levant* 36 (2004): 225–242.

Genequand, Denis. "Châteaux omeyyades de Palmyrène." *Annales islamologiques* 38 (2004): 3–44.

Genequand, Denis. *Les élites omeyyades en Palmyrène: contribution à l'étude des aspects fonctionnels et économiques des établissements aristocratiques omeyyades du Bilād al-Shām*. 2 vol. Ph. D. diss. Université de Lausanne and Université de Paris I Panthéon-Sorbonne, 2010.

Genequand, Denis. *Les établissements des élites omeyyades en Palmyrène et au Proche-Orient*. Beirut: IFPO (Bibliothèque archéologique et historique, tome 200), 2012.

Genequand, Denis. "Formation et devenir du paysage architectural omeyyade: l'apport de l'archéologie." In Antoine Borrut and Paul M. Cobb (eds.), *Umayyad Legacies: Medieval Memories from Syria to Spain*. Leiden: Brill, 2010. 417–473.

Genequand, Denis. "From 'Desert Castle' to Medieval Town: Qasr al-Hayr al-Sharqi (Syria)." *Antiquity* 79/304 (2005): 350–361.

Genequand, Denis. "Une mosquée à Quṣayr 'Amra." *Annual of the Department of Antiquities of Jordan* 46 (2002): 583–589.

Genequand, Denis. "Projet "Implantations umayyades de Syrie et de Jordanie". Rapport sur une campagne de prospection et reconnaissance." *SLSA-Jahresbericht 2001*, 2002. 131–161.

Genequand, Denis. "Rapport préliminaire de la campagne de fouille 2004 à Qasr al-Hayr al-Sharqi (Syrie)." *Schweizerisch-Liechtensteinische Stiftung für Archäologische Forschungen im Ausland* (*SLSA/FSLA/SLFA*) – *Jahresbericht 2004*. Zürich, 2005. 143–166.

Genequand, Denis. "Some Thoughts on Qasr al-Hayr al-Gharbi, its Dam, its Monastery and the Ghassanids." *Levant* 38 (2006): 63–84.

Genequand, Denis. "Umayyad Castles: The Shift from Late Antique Military Architecture to Early Islamic Palatial Building." In Hugh Kennedy (ed.), *Muslim Military Architecture in Greater Syria. From the Coming of Islam to the Ottoman Period.* Leiden: Brill, 2006. 3–25.

Genequand, Denis. "Wadi al-Qanatir (Jordanie): un exemple de mise en valeur des terres sous les Omeyyades." *SHAJ* VII (2001): 647–654.

Gibb, H. A. R. "The Fiscal Rescript of Umar II." *Arabica* 2/1 (1955) 1–16.

Gibb, H. A. R. *Studies on the Civilisation of Islam*. London, 1962.

Gibson, Shimon and Fanny Vitto. *Ramla: the Development of a Town from the Early Islamic to the Ottoman Periods*. Jerusalem, 1999.

Gil, Moshe. *A History of Palestine, 634–1099*. Trans. Ethel Broido. Cambridge: Cambridge University Press, 1992.

Gilliot, Claude. *Exégèse, langue et théologie en Islam. L'exégèse coranique de Tabari (m. 311/923)*. Paris: Vrin, 1990.

Gilliot, Claude. "La formation intellectuelle de Tabari (224/5–310/839–923)." *JA* 276/3–4 (1988): 203–244.

Gilliot, Claude. "Une leçon magistrale d'orientalisme: l'*opus magnum* de J. Van Ess." *Arabica* 45 (1993): 345–402.

Gilliot, Claude. "Récit, mythe et histoire chez Ṭabarī. Une vision mythique de l'histoire universelle." *MIDEO* 21 (1993): 277–289.

Given-Wilson, Chris. *Chronicles: The Writing of History in Medieval England*. London: Hambledon and London, 2004.

Gjuzelev, Vasil. "La participation des Bulgares à l'échec du siège arabe de Constantinople en 717–718." In *Medieval Bulgaria, Byzantine Empire, Black Sea, Venice, Genoa*. Villach, 1988. 91–113.

Goitein, S. D. "The Historical Background of the Erection of the Dome of the Rock." *JAOS* 70 (1950).

Goitein, S. D. "Jerusalem in the Arab Period (638–1099)." *The Jerusalem Cathedra* 2 (1982): 168–195.

Goitein, S. D. "A Plea for the Periodization of Islamic History." *JAOS* 88/2 (1968): 224–228.

Goitein, S. D. "The Sanctity of Jerusalem and Palestine in Early Islam." In S. D. Goitein, *Studies in Islamic History and Institutions*. Leiden: E. J. Brill, 1968 [1966]. 135–148.

Goitein, S. D. *Studies in Islamic History and Institutions*. Leiden: E. J. Brill, 1968 [1966].

Goldziher, Ignaz. *Le dogme et la loi de l'islam*. Paris: Geuthner, 1973.

Goldziher, Ignaz. *Muhammedanische Studien*. 2 vol. Halle: Max Niemeyer, 1890; trans. C. R. Barber and S. M. Stern, *Muslim Studies*. 2 vol. London: Allen and Unwin, 1967–1971; partial French trans. Léon Bercher, *Etudes sur la tradition islamique*. Paris: A. Maisonneuve, 1952.

Gordon, Matthew S. *The Breaking of the Thousand Swords: A History of the Turkish Military of Sāmarrā*. Albany: SUNY Press, 2001.

Görke, Andreas and Gregor Schœler. *Die ältesten Berichte über das Leben Muhammads. Das Korpus 'Urwa ibn Az-Zubair*. Princeton: Darwin Press, 2008.

Grabar, Oleg. *Ceremonial and Art at the Umayyad Court*. Ph. D. diss. Princeton University, 1955.

Grabar, Oleg. "The Date and Meaning of Mšattā." *Dumbarton Oaks Papers* 41 (1987): 243–247.

Grabar, Oleg. "The Earliest Islamic Commemorative Structures, Notes and Documents." *Ars Orientalis* 6 (1966): 7–46.

Grabar, Oleg. *La Formation de l'art islamique*. Paris: Flammarion, 1987.

Grabar, Oleg. "Al-Mushatta, Baghdād and Wāsiṭ." In James Kritzeck and R. Bayly Winder, *The World of Islam: Studies in honour of Philip K. Hitti*. London: Macmillan & Co., 1960. 99–108.

Grabar, Oleg. "The Painting of the Six Kings at Quṣayr 'Amrah." *Ars Orientalis* 1 (1954): 185–187.

Grabar, Oleg. "La place de Qusayr Amrah dans l'art profane du Haut Moyen Age." *Cahiers Archéologiques* 36 (1988): 75–83.

Grabar, Oleg. "Qasr al-Hayr al-Sharqi, Preliminary Report." *AAAS* 15 (1965): 108–120.

Grabar, Oleg. *The Shape of the Holy: Early Islamic Jerusalem*. Princeton: Princeton University Press, 1996.

Grabar, Oleg. "Three Seasons of Excavations at Qaṣr al-Ḥayr al-Šarqī." *Ars Orientalis* 8 (1970): 65–85.

Grabar, Oleg. "The Umayyad Dome of the Rock in Jerusalem." *Ars Orientalis* 3 (1959): 33–62.

Grabar, Oleg. "Umayyad 'Palace' and the 'Abbasid 'Revolution'." *SI* 18 (1963): 5–18.

Grabar, Oleg, Reneta Holod, James Knustad and William Trousdale. *City in the Desert: Qasr al-Hayr East*. 2 vol. Harvard, 1978.

Graf, Georg. *Geschichte der christlich-arabischen Literatur*. 5 vol. Vatican: Biblioteca Apostolica Vaticana, 1944–1953.

Grafman, Rafi and Myriam Rosen-Ayalon. "The Two Great Syrian Umayyad Mosques: Jerusalem and Damascus." *Muqarnas* 16 (1999): 1–15.

Grégoire, Henri. "Comment Sayyid Baṭṭâl, martyr musulman du VIIIe siècle, est-il devenu, dans la légende, le contemporain d'Amer († 863)?" *Byzantion* 11 (1936): 571–575.

Gregory, Shelagh and David Kennedy (eds.). *Sir Aurel Stein's Limes Report*. BAR International Series 272. Oxford, 1985.

Grierson, Philip. "The Monetary Reforms of Abd al-Malik. Their Metrological Basis and their Financial Repercussions." *JESHO* 3 (1960): 241–264.

Griffith, Sidney H. "Images, Islam and Christian Icons. A Moment in the Christian/Muslim Encounter in Early Islamic Times." In Pierre Canivet and Jean-Paul Rey-Coquais, *La Syrie de Byzance à l'Islam: VIIe–VIIIe siècles, Actes du colloque international, Lyon et Paris, 11–15 septembre 1990*. Damascus: PIFD, 1992. 121–138.

Griffith, Sidney H. "Michael, the Martyr and Monk of Mar Sabas Monastery, at the Court of the Caliph 'Abd al-Malik; Christian Apologetics and Martyrology in the Early Islamic Period." *Aram* 6 (1994): 115–148.

Grohmann, Adolf. *Arabic Papyri from Hirbat el-Mird*. Bibl. Muséon, vol. 52. Leuven, 1963.

Grohmann, Adolf. *Arabic Papyri in the Egyptian Library*. Cairo: Egyptian Library Press, 1934.

Grumel, V. "Homélie de Saint Germain sur la délivrance de Constantinople." *Revue des études byzantines* 16 (1958): 183–205.

Grumel, V. *Traité d'études Byzantines I: La chronologie*. Paris: PUF, 1958.

Guenée, Bernard. "Les grandes chroniques de France." In Pierre Nora (dir.), *Les lieux de mémoire*. vol. I. Paris: Gallimard, 1997. 189–214.

Guenée, Bernard. *Histoire et culture historique dans l'Occident médiéval*. Paris: Aubier, 1991.

Guenée, Bernard. "Temps de l'histoire et temps de la mémoire au Moyen Âge." *Annuaire Bulletin de la Société d'Histoire de France* (1976–1977): 25–35.

Guérin, Alexandrine. "L'occupation abbasside de Nasibin. Typologie et chronologie préliminaires de la céramique prospectée en surface." In Karin Bartl and Stefan R. Hauser (eds.), *Continuity and Change in Northern Mesopotamia from the Hellenistic to the Early Islamic Period.* Berlin: Berliner Beiträge zum Vorderen Orient 17, Dietrich Reimer Verlag, 1996. 377–400.

Guérin, Alexandrine. "Les territoires de la ville de Damas à la période Abbasside." *BEO* LII (2000): 221–241.

Guérin, Alexandrine. *Terroirs, territoires et peuplement en Syrie méridionale à la période islamique* (*VIIe siècle–XVIe siècle*). Ph. D. diss. Université Lumière Lyon II, 1998.

Goffman, Erving. *The Presentation of Self in Everyday Life.* New York: Anchor Books, 1959.

Guessous, Azeddine. "Le rescrit fiscal de ʿUmar b. ʿAbd al-ʿAzīz: une nouvelle appréciation." *Der Islam* 73 (1996): 113–137.

Geuenich, Dieter and Otto G. Oexle (eds.). *Memoria in der Gesellschaft des Mittelalters.* Göttingen: Veröffentlichungen des Max-Planck-Institus für Geschichte, 1994.

Guidi, Ignazio. *Tables alphabétiques du Kitâb al-Aġânî.* Leiden: Brill, 1900.

Guidoboni, Emanuela. *Catalogue of Ancient Earthquakes in the Mediterranean up to the 10th Century.* Trans. Brian Phillips. Rome: Instituto nazionale di Geofisica, 1994.

Guilland, Rodolphe. "L'expédition de Maslama contre Constantinople (717–718)." *Al-Machriq* 49 (1955): 89–112.

Günther, Sebastian. "Due Results in the Theory of Source-criticism in Medieval Arabic Literature." *Al-Abhath* 42 (1994): 3–15.

Gutas, Dimitri. *Greek Thought, Arabic Culture: The Graeco-Arabic Translation Movement in Baghdad and Early ʿAbbāsid Society* (*2nd–4th/8th–10th centuries*). London and New York: Routledge, 1998.

Haase, Claus-Peter. "The Excavations at Madinat al-Far/Hisn Maslama on the Balikh Road." In Hugh Kennedy (ed.), *Muslim Military Architecture in Greater Syria: From the Coming of Islam to the Ottoman Period.* Leiden: Brill, 2006. 54–60.

Haase, Claus-Peter. "Is Madinat al-Far, in the Balik region of northern Syria, an Umayyad foundation?" *Aram* 6 (1994): 245–257.

Haase, Claus-Peter. "Madīnat al-Fār. The Regional Late Antique Tradition of an Early Islamic Foundation." In Karin Bartl and Stefan R. Hauser (eds.), *Continuity and Change in Northern Mesopotamia from the Hellenistic to the Early Islamic Period.* Berlin: Berliner Beiträge zum Vorderen Orient 17, Dietrich Reimer Verlag, 1996. 165–171.

Haase, Claus-Peter. *Untersuchungen zur Landschaftsgeschichte Nordsyriens in der Umayyadenzeit.* Kiel, 1975.

Haase, Claus-Peter. "Une ville des débuts de l'Islam d'après les fouilles effectuées à Madinat al-Far (Syrie du Nord). Les premières fondations urbaines umayyades." *Archéologie Islamique* 11 (2001): 7–20.

Habermas, Jürgen. *Logique des sciences sociales et autres essais.* Paris: PUF, 1987.

Halbwachs, Maurice. *Les cadres sociaux de la mémoire.* Paris: Alcan, 1925.

Halbwachs, Maurice. *La Mémoire collective.* Paris: PUF, 1950.

Haldon, John and Lawrence I. Conrad (eds.). *Elites Old and New in the Byzantine and Early Islamic Near East.* Princeton: Darwin Press (The Byzantine and Early Islamic Near East VI), 2004.

Haldon, John F. *Byzantium in the Seventh Century. The Transformation of a Culture.* Cambridge: Cambridge University Press, 1990.

Haldon, John F. "Seventh-Century Continuities: the Ajnād and the "Thematic Myth"." In Averil Cameron (ed.), *The Byzantine and Early Islamic Near East III: States, Resources and Armies.* Princeton: Darwin Press, 1995. 379–423.

Halevi, Leor. *Muhammad's Grave: Death Rites and the Making of Islamic Society.* New York: Columbia University Press, 2007.

Hamidullah, Muhammad. "La lettre du Prophète à Héraclius et le sort de l'original." *Arabica* 2/1 (1955): 97–110.

Hamidullah, Muhammad. "Le livre des généalogies d'al-Baladhûrî." *BEO* XIV (1952–1954).

Hamidullah, Muhammad. *Six originaux des lettres du prophète de l'islam.* Paris, 1985.

Hamilton, R. W. "An Eighth-Century Water-Gauge at al-Muwaqqar." *Quarterly of the Department of Antiquities of Palestine* 12 (1946): 70–72.

Hamilton, R. W. *Khirbat al-Mafjar: An Arabian Mansion in the Jordan Valley.* Oxford, 1959.

Hamilton, R. W. *Walid and his Friends: An Umayyad Tragedy.* Oxford: Oxford University Press, 1988.

Hansen, Inge L. and Christopher Wickham (eds.). *The Long Eighth Century: Production, Distribution and Demand.* Leiden: Brill, 2000.

Harley, J. B. and David Woodward (eds.). *Cartography in the Traditional Islamic and South Asian Societies, The History of Cartography.* vol. 2/1. Chicago and London: University of Chicago Press, 1992.

Harrak, Amir. "Ah! The Assyrian is the Rod of my Hand!: Syriac View of History after the Advent of Islam." In J. J. Van Ginkel et al., *Redefining Christian Identity: Cultural Interaction in the Middle East since the Rise of Islam.* Leuven: Peeters, 2005. 45–65.

Harrak, Amir. "La victoire arabo-musulmane selon le chroniqueur de Zuqnin (VIIIe siècle)." In Muriel Debié (ed.), *L'historiographie syriaque.* Paris: Geuthner, 2009. 89–105.

Hartmann, Angelika. *Geschichte und Erinnerung im Islam.* Göttingen: Vandenhoeck and Ruprecht, 2004.

Hartmann, Angelika. "Rethinking Memory and Remaking History: Methodological Approaches to "Lieux de mémoire" in Muslim Societies." In Antonino Pellitteri (ed.), *Maǧāz: culture e contatti nell'area del Mediterraneo. Il ruolo dell'Islam. Atti 21. Congresso UEAI, Palermo, 2002.* Palermo: Università di Palermo, 2003. 51–61.

Hartmann, Angelika, Sabine Damir-Geilsdorf and Beatrice Hendrich (eds.). *Mental Maps – Raum – Erinnerung Kulturwissenschaftliche Beiträge zum Verhältnis von Raum und Erinnerung.* Münster, 2004.

Hartmann, Richard. "Der Sufyānī." In F. Hvidberg (ed.), *Studia Orientalia Ioanni Pedersen Septuagenario. A. D. VII Id. Nov. Anno MCMLIII a Collegis Discipulis Amicis Dicata.* Copenhagen: E. Munksgaard, 1953. 141–151.

Haverkamp, Anselm and Renate Lachmann (eds.). *Memoria. Vergessen und Erinnern.* Munich, 1993.

Hawting, Gerald R. *The First Dynasty of Islam: the Umayyad Caliphate, AD 661–750.* Carbondale, IL: Southern Illinois University Press, 2000 [1987].

Hawting, Gerald R. *The Idea of Idolatry and the Emergence of Islam.* Cambridge: Cambridge University Press, 1999.

Hawting, Gerald R. "Khālid b. ʿAbd Allāh al-Qasrī." EI^2.

Hawting, Gerald R. "Marwān II b. Muḥammad b. Marwān b. Ḥakam." EI^2.

Hawting, Gerald R. "Umayyads." EI^2.

Hawting, Gerald R. "The Umayyads and the Ḥijāz." *Proceedings of the 5th Seminar for Arabian Studies.* London, 1972.

Heck, Paul. *The Construction of Knowledge in Islamic Civilization: Qudāma b. Jaʿfar and his* Kitāb al-kharāj wa ṣināʿat al-kitāba. Leiden: Brill, 2002.

Heidemann, Stefan. "Al-ʿAqr, das islamische Assur: Ein Beitrag zur historischen Topographie in Nordmesopatamien." In Karin Bartl and Stefan R. Hauser (eds.), *Continuity and Change in Northern Mesopotamia from the Hellenistic to the Early Islamic Period.* Berlin: Berliner Beiträge zum Vorderen Orient 17, Dietrich Reimer Verlag, 1996. 259–285.

Heidemann, Stefan. "Die Fundmünzen von Ḥarrān und ihr Verhältnis zur lokalen Geschichte." *BSOAS* 65/2 (2002): 267–299.

Heidemann, Stefan. "Die Geschichte von ar-Raqqa/ar-Râfiqa – ein Überblick." In Stefan Heidemann and Andrea Becker (eds.), *Raqqa II. Die islamische Stadt.* Mainz: Philipp von Zabern, 2003. 9–56.

Heidemann, Stefan. "The Merger of Two Currency Zones in Early Islam. The Byzantine and Sasanian Impact on the Circulation in Former Byzantine Syria and Northern Mesopotamia." *Iran* XXXVI (1998): 95–112.

Heidemann, Stefan. "Numismatische Quellen." In Stefan Heidemann and Andrea Becker (eds.), *Raqqa II. Die islamische Stadt.* Mainz: Philipp von Zabern, 2003. 113–196.

Heidemann, Stefan and Andrea Becker (eds.). *Raqqa II. Die islamische Stadt.* Mainz: Philipp von Zabern, 2003.

Helms, S. *Early Islamic Architecture of the Desert: A Bedouin Station in Eastern Jordan.* Edinburgh: Edinburgh University Press, 1990.

Herzfeld, E. "ʿAmra." EI^1.

Herzfeld, E. "Die Könige der Erde." *Der Islam* 21 (1933): 233–236.

Hill, Donald R. "Mathematics and Applied Science." In M. J. L. Young, J. D. Latham and R. B. Serjeant (eds.), *Religion, Learning and Science in the ʿAbbasid Period, The*

Cambridge History of Arabic Literature. Cambridge: Cambridge University Press, 1990. 248–273.

Hill, Donald R. *The Termination of Hostilities in the Early Arab Conquests, A.D. 634–656*. London: Luzac, 1971.

Hillenbrand, Robert. "ʿAnjar and Early Islamic Urbanism." In G. P. Brogiolo and Bryan Ward-Perkins, *The Idea and Ideal of the Town between Late Antiquity and the Early Middle Ages*. Leiden: Brill, 1999. 59–98.

Hillenbrand, Robert. "La *Dolce Vita* in Early Islamic Syria: the Evidence of Later Umayyad Palaces." *Art History* 5/1 (1982): 1–35.

Hillenbrand, Robert. *Islamic Architecture: Form, Function, and Meaning*. Edinburgh: Edinburgh University Press, 2000.

Hillenbrand, Robert. "Islamic Art at the Crossroads: East Versus West at Mshattā." In Abbas Daneshvari (ed.), *Essays in Islamic Art and Architecture in Honor of Katharina Otto-Dorn*. Malibu: Undena Publications, 1981. 63–86.

Hinz, Walther. *Islamische Masse und Gewichte*. Leiden: Brill, 1955.

Hitti, Philip K. *History of Syria including Lebanon and Palestine*. London: Macmillan & Co., 1951.

Hodgson, M. G. S. *The Venture of Islam: Conscience and History in a world civilization*. 3 vol. Chicago, 1974.

Hopkins, J. F. P. "Geographical and Navigational Literature." In M. J. L. Young, J. D. Latham and R. B. Serjeant (eds.), *Religion, Learning and Science in the ʿAbbasid Period, The Cambridge History of Arabic Literature*. Cambridge: Cambridge University Press, 1990. 301–327.

Howard-Johnston, James. "The Two Great Powers in Late Antiquity: a Comparison." In Averil Cameron (ed.), *The Byzantine and Early Islamic Near East III: States, Resources and Armies*. Princeton: Darwin Press, 1995. 157–226.

Hoyland, Robert G. *Arabia and the Arabs: From the Bronze Age to the Coming of Islam*. London and New York: Routledge, 2001.

Hoyland, Robert G. "Arabic, Syriac and Greek Historiography in the First Abbasid Century: an Inquiry into Inter-Cultural Traffic." *Aram*. 3 (1991): 211–233.

Hoyland, Robert G. "The Content and Context of Early Arabic Inscriptions." *JSAI* 21 (1997): 77–102.

Hoyland, Robert G. "The Correspondence of Leo III (717–741) and ʿUmar II (717–720)." *Aram* 6 (1994): 165–177.

Hoyland, Robert G. "History, Fiction and Authorship in the First Centuries of Islam." In Julia Bray (ed.), *Writing and Representations in Medieval Islam: Muslim Horizons*. London and New York: Routledge, 2006. 16–46.

Hoyland, Robert G. "New Documentary Texts and the Early Islamic State." *BSOAS* 69/3 (2006): 395–416.

Hoyland, Robert G. *Seeing Islam as Others Saw it: A Survey and Evaluation of Christian, Jewish and Zoroastrian Writings on Early Islam.* Princeton: Darwin Press, 1997.

Hrbek, I. "Bulghār." *EI*².

Humphreys, R. S. *Islamic History: A Framework for Inquiry.* Princeton: Princeton University Press, 1991.

Humphreys, R. S. *Mu'awiya ibn Abi Sufyan: From Arabia to Empire.* Oxford: Oneworld, 2006.

Humphreys, R. S. "Qur'anic Myth and Narrative Structure in Early Islamic Historiography." In F. M. Clover and R. S. Humphreys (eds.), *Tradition and Innovation in Late Antiquity.* Madison, WI: University of Wisconsin Press, 1989. 271–290.

Humphreys, R. S. "Syria." In Chase F. Robinson (ed.), *The New Cambridge History of Islam, vol. I: The Formation of the Islamic World, Sixth to Eleventh Centuries.* Cambridge: Cambridge University Press, 2010. 508–542.

Humphreys, R. S. "Ta'rīkh." *EI*².

Ḥusayn, Ṭāhā. *Fī al-shi'r al-jāhilī.* Cairo: Maṭba'at Dār al-Kutub al-Miṣriya, 1926.

Illisch, Lutz. *Sylloge Numorum Arabicorum Tübingen, Palästina. IVa Bilād aš-Šām I.* Tübingen, 1993.

Imbert, Frederic and Sylvie Bacquey. "Sept graffiti arabes au palais de Mušattā." *ADAJ* 33 (1989): 259–267.

Imbert, Frederic. *Corpus des inscriptions arabes de Jordanie du Nord.* Ph. D. diss. Université de Provence, Aix-Marseille 1, 1996.

Imbert, Frederic. "Inscriptions et espaces d'écriture au Palais d'al-Kharrâna en Jordanie." *SHAJ* V (1995): 403–416.

Imbert, Frederic. "Inscriptions et graffiti arabes de Jordanie: quelques réflexions sur l'établissement d'un récent corpus." *Quaderni di Studi Arabi* 16 (1998): 45–58.

Imbert, Frederic. "La nécropole islamique de Qasṭal al-Balqā' en Jordanie." *Archéologie Islamique* 3 (1992): 17–59.

Imbert, Frederic. "Note épigraphique et paléographique. L'inscription peinte sur le baldaquin." In Claude Vibert-Guigue, *Les peintures de Qusayr 'Amra. Un bain omeyyade dans la bâdiya jordanienne.* Beirut: IFPO/Department of Antiquities of Jordan, 2007. 45–46.

Innes, Matthew. "Keeping it in the Family: Women and Aristocratic Memory, 700–1200." In Elisabeth van Houts (ed.), *Medieval Memories: Men, Women and the Past, 700–1300.* New York: Pearson Education Limited, 2001. 17–35.

Innes, Matthew. "Memory, Orality and Literacy in an Early Medieval Society." *Past and Present* 158 (1998): 3–36.

Innes, Matthew. "People, Places and Power in the Carolingian World: a Microcosm." In Mayke De Jong and Frans Theuws (eds.), *Topographies of Power in the Early Middle Ages.* Leiden: Brill, 2001. 397–437.

Ishaq, Y. M. "The Significance of the Syriac Chronicle of Pseudo-Dionysius of Tel Maḥrē. A Political, Economical and Administrative Study of Upper Mesopotamia in the Umayyad and Abbasid Ages." *Orientalia Suecana* XLI–XLII (1992–1993): 106–118.

Jacobi, Renate. "Al-Mufaḍḍaliyyāt." *EI*².

Jalabert, Cyrille. "Comment Damas est devenue une métropole islamique." *BEO* 53–54 (2001–2002): 13–42.

Jalabert, Cyrille. *Hommes et lieux dans l'islamisation de l'espace syrien (Ier/VIIe–VIIe/XIIIe siècles)*. Ph. D. diss. Université de Paris I, 2004.

Jaussen, Antonin and Raphael Savignac. *Mission archéologique en Arabie. III. Les châteaux arabes de Qeseir 'Amra, Haraneh et Tuba*. Paris, 1922.

Jayyusi, Salma K. "Umayyad Poetry." In A. F. L. Beeston (ed.), *Arabic Literature to the End of the Umayyad Period*. Cambridge: Cambridge University Press, 1983. 387–432.

Jeffery, Arthur. "Ghevond's Text of the Correspondence between 'Umar II and Leo III." *Harvard Theological Review* 37 (1944): 277–330.

Jeffreys, Elizabeth. "Notes Towards a Discussion of the Depiction of the Umayyads in Byzantine Literature." In John Haldon and Lawrence I. Conrad (eds.), *Elites Old and New in the Byzantine and Early Islamic Near East*. Princeton: Darwin Press, 2004. 133–147.

Johns, Jeremy. "Archaeology and the History of Early Islam: The First Seventy Years." *JESHO* 46/4 (2003): 411–436.

Johns, Jeremy (ed.). *Bayt al-Maqdis. 'Abd al-Malik's Jerusalem*. Oxford Studies in Islamic Art, vol. 9, part 2. Oxford: Oxford University Press, 1999.

Johns, Jeremy. "Islamic Settlement in Arḍ al-Karak." *SHAJ* 4 (1992): 363–368.

Judd, Steven C. "Character Development in al-Ṭabarī's and al-Balādhurī's Narratives of Late Umayyad History." In Sebastian Günther (ed.), *Insights into Arabic Literature and Islam: Ideas, Concepts and Methods of Portrayal*. Leiden: Brill, 2005. 209–26.

Judd, Steven C. "Competitive Hagiography in Biographies of al-Awzāʿī and Sufyān al-Thawrī." *JAOS* 122/1 (2002): 25–37.

Judd, Steven C. "Ghaylan al-Dimashqi: the Isolation of an Heretic in Islamic Historiography." *IJMES* 31 (1999): 161–184.

Judd, Steven C. "Ibn 'Asākir's Sources for the Late Umayyad Period." In James E. Lindsay (ed.), *Ibn 'Asākir and Early Islamic History*. Princeton: Darwin Press, 2001. 78–99.

Judd, Steven C. "Medieval Explanations for the Fall of the Umayyads." In Antoine Borrut and Paul M. Cobb (eds.), *Umayyad Legacies: Medieval Memories from Syria to Spain*. Leiden: Brill, 2010. 89–104.

Judd, Steven C. "Reinterpreting al-Walīd b. Yazīd." *JAOS* 128/3 (2008): 439–458.

Judd, Steven C. *The Third Fitna: Orthodoxy, Heresy and Coercion in Late Umayyad History*. Ph. D. diss. University of Michigan, 1997.

Juynboll, G. H. A. *Muslim Tradition: Studies in Chronology, Provenance and Authorship of Early Ḥadīth*. Cambridge: Cambridge University Press, 1983.

Kaegi, Walter E. *Byzantium and the Early Islamic Conquests*. Cambridge: Cambridge University Press, 1992.

Karcz, Iaakov. "Implications of Some Early Jewish Sources for Estimates of Earthquake Hazard in the Holy Land." *Annals of Geophysics* 47/2–3 (2004): 759–792.

Karev, Y. "La politique d'Abū Muslim dans le Māwarā'annahr. Nouvelles données textuelles et archéologiques." *Der Islam* 79/1 (2002): 1–45.

Kassis, Antoine, Jean-Baptiste Yon and Abdo Badwi. "Les inscriptions syriaques du Liban: bilan archéologique et historique." In Françoise Briquel-Chatonnet, Muriel Debié and Alain Desreumaux (eds.), *Les inscriptions syriaques*. Paris: Geuthner, 2004. 29–43.

Kaufhold, Hubert. "Notizen zur späten Geschichte des Barsaumô-Klosters." *Hugoye* 3/2 (2000).

Kazimirski, Albert de Biberstein. *Dictionnaire Arabe-Français*. 2 vol. Cairo, 1875.

Keaney, Heather N. *Remembering Rebellion: 'Uthmān b. 'Affān in Medieval Islamic Historiography*. Ph. D. diss. University of California, 2003.

Kellner-Heinkele, Barbara. "Rusâfa in den arabischen Quellen." In Dorothée Sack (ed.), *Resafa IV. Die Grosse Moschee von Resafa- Ruṣāfat Hišām*. Mainz, 1996. 133–154.

Kennedy, E. S. and David Pingree. *The Historical Astrology of Māshā'allāh*. Cambridge, MA: Harvard University Press, 1971.

Kennedy, Hugh. *The Armies of the Caliphs: Military and Society in the Early Islamic State*. London and New York: Routledge, 2001.

Kennedy, Hugh. "Caliphs and their chroniclers in the Middle Abbasid period (third/ninth century)." *Texts Documents and Artefacts: Islamic Studies in Honour of D. S. Richards*. Ed. Chase F. Robinson. Leiden: Brill, 2003. 17–35.

Kennedy, Hugh. "Central Government and Provincial Élites in the Early 'Abbasid Caliphate." *BSOAS* 44 (1981): 26–38.

Kennedy, Hugh. "Concluding Remarks." In G. D. R. King and Averil Cameron (eds.), *The Byzantine and Early Islamic Near East II: Land Use and Settlement Patterns*. Princeton: Darwin Press, 1994. 267–270.

Kennedy, Hugh. *The Early Abbasid Caliphate: A Political History*. London: Croom Helm, 1981.

Kennedy, Hugh. "Elite Incomes in the Early Islamic State." In John Haldon and Lawrence I. Conrad (eds.), *Elites Old and New in the Byzantine and Early Islamic Near East*. Princeton: Darwin Press, 2004. 1–28.

Kennedy, Hugh. "From Oral Tradition to Written Record in Arabic Genealogy." *Arabica* 44/4 (1997): 531–544.

Kennedy, Hugh. "From Polis to Madina: Urban Change in Late Antique and Early Islamic Syria." *Past and Present* 106 (1985): 3–27.

Kennedy, Hugh. *An Historical Atlas of Islam, Atlas historique de l'Islam*. Leiden: Brill, 2002.

Kennedy, Hugh. "Islam." In G.W. Bowersock, Peter Brown and Oleg Grabar (eds.), *Late Antiquity: A Guide to the Post-Classical World*. Cambridge, MA and London: The Belknap Press of Harvard University Press, 1999. 219–237.

Kennedy, Hugh. *The Prophet and the Age of the Caliphates: the Islamic Near East from the Sixth to the Eleven Century*. New York, 2004 [1987].

Kennedy, Hugh. "Succession Disputes in the Early Abbasid Caliphate (132/749–193/809)." In Robert Hillenbrand (ed.), *Union européenne des arabisants et islamisants, 10th Congress, Edinburgh 1980: Proceedings*. Edinburgh, 1982.

Kennedy, Hugh. (ed.). *Al-Ṭabarī. A Medieval Muslim Historian and his Work*. Princeton: Darwin Press, 2008.

Kennedy, Hugh. "Al-Walīd II." *EI*².

Kennedy, Hugh. *When Baghdad Ruled the Muslim World: The Rise and Fall of Islam's Greatest Dynasty*. Cambridge: Da Capo Press, 2005.

Kessler, Christel. "ʿAbd al-Malik's Inscription in the Dome of the Rock: a Reconsideration." *JRAS* (1970): 2–14.

Khalidi, Tarif. *Arabic Historical Thought in the Classical Period*. Cambridge: Cambridge University Press, 1994.

Khalidi, Tarif. *Islamic Historiography: The Histories of al-Masʿūdī*. Albany: State University of New York Press, 1975.

Khamis, Elias. "Two Wall Mosaic Inscriptions from the Umayyad Market Place in Bet Shean/Baysān." *BSOAS* 64/2 (2001): 159–176.

Khazanov, Anatoly M. *Nomads and the Outside World*. Madison, WI: University of Wisconsin Press, 1994 [1983].

Khoury, Nuha N.N. "The Dome of the Rock, the Kaʿba, and Ghumdan: Arab Myths and Umayyad Monuments." *Muqarnas* 10 (1993): 57–65.

Khoury, R.G. "Kalif, Geschichte und Dichtung: Der jemenitische Erzähler ʿAbīd Ibn Šarya am Hofe Muʿāwiyas." *Zeitschrift für arabische Linguistik* 25 (1993): 204–218.

Khoury, R.G. *Wahb b. Munabbih*. Wiesbaden: Harrassowitz, 1972.

Khoury, Philip S. and Joseph Kostiner (eds.). *Tribes and State Formation in the Middle East*. Berkeley: University of California Press, 1990.

Kilpatrick, Hilary. *Making the Great Book of Songs: Compilation and the Author's Craft in Abū l-Faraj al-Isbahānī's* Kitāb al-aghānī. London: RoutledgeCurzon, 2003.

Kilpatrick, Hilary. "Monasteries Through Muslim Eyes: the Diyārāt Books." In David Thomas (ed.), *Christian at the Heart of Islamic Rule. Church Life and Scholarship in ʿAbbasid Iraq*. Leiden: Brill (The History of Christian-Muslim Relations), 2003. 19–37.

Kilpatrick, Hilary. "ʿUmar ibn ʿAbd al-ʿAzīz, al-Walīd ibn Yazīd and their Kin: Images of the Umayyads in the Kitāb al-Aghānī." In Antoine Borrut and Paul M. Cobb (eds.), *Umayyad Legacies: Medieval Memories from Syria to Spain*. Leiden: Brill, 2010. 63–87.

Kimber, R. A. "Hārūn al-Rashīd's Meccan Settlement of AH 186/AD 802." *OPSAS* 1 (1986): 55–79.

Kimber, R. A. "The Succession to the Caliph Mūsā al-Hādī." *JAOS* 121/3 (2001).

Kimber, R., and C. Vazquez. "Al-Ma'mun and Baghdad: the nomination of 'Ali al-Rida." *Actas XVI Congreso UEAI, Salamanca: Agencia Espanola de Cooperacion Internacional, Consejo Superior de Investigaciones Cientificas, Union Europeenne d'Arabisants et d'Islamisants*. 1995. 275–280.

King, David A. "Astronomy." In M. J. L. Young, J. D. Latham and R. B. Serjeant (eds.), *Religion, Learning and Science in the 'Abbasid period, The Cambridge History of Arabic literature*. Cambridge: Cambridge University Press, 1990. 274–289.

King, G. D. R. "The Distribution of Sites and Routes in the Jordanian and Syrian Deserts in the Early Islamic Period." *Proceedings of the Twentieth Seminar for Arabian Studies*. London, 1987. 91–105.

King, G. D. R. "Settlement Patterns in Islamic Jordan: the Umayyads and their Use of the Land." *SHAJ* 4 (1992): 369–375.

King, G. D. R. and Averil Cameron (eds.). *The Byzantine and Early Islamic Near East II: Land Use and Settlement Patterns*. Princeton: Darwin Press, 1994.

Kister, Meir J. "The Battle of Ḥarra: Some Socio-Economic Aspects." In Myriam Rosen-Ayalon (ed.), *Studies in Memory of Gaston Wiet*. Jerusalem: Hebrew University of Jerusalem, 1977. 33–49.

Kister, Meir J. "The Seven Odes: Some Notes on the Compilation of the Muʿallaqāt." *RDSO* 44 (1970): 27–36.

Kohlberg, Etan. "Muḥammad b. 'Alī, dit Al-Bāqir." *EI*².

Kohlberg, Etan. "Al-Rāwandiyya." *EI*².

Kohlberg, Etan. "Some Imāmī Shīʿī Interpretations of Umayyad History." In G. H. A. Juynboll, *Studies on the First Century of Islamic Society*. Carbondale and Edwardsville, IL: Southern Illinois University Press, 1982. 145–159.

Konrad, Christoph. "Resafa-Rusafat Hisham (Syrien), Archäologische Untersuchungen I. Das Gebäude [FP 220], ein umaiyadischer Qasr." *Jahrbuch MSD 2006–08* (Technische Universität Berlin) (2008): 37. (Accessible at the following address: http://bauforschung-denkmalpflege.de/resafa/ [consulted 10 December 2022]).

Kooper, Erik (ed.). *The Medieval Chronicle. Proceedings of the 1st International Conference on the Medieval Chronicle, Driebengen/Utrecht 13–16 July 1996*. Amsterdam and Atlanta: Rodopi, 1999.

Kooper, Erik. *The Medieval Chronicle II. Proceedings of the 2nd International Conference on the Medieval Chronicle, Driebengen/Utrecht 16–21 July 1996*. Amsterdam and New York: Rodopi, 2002.

Koren, Judith and Yehuda D. Nevo. *Crossroads to Islam: The Origins of the Arab Religion and the Arab State*. New York: Prometheus Books, 2003.

Kraemer, C. J. *Excavations at Nessana: Non-literary papyri*. Princeton, 1958.

Kränzle, Andreas. "Der abwesende König. Überlegungen zur Ottonischen Königsherrschaft." *Frühmittelalterliche Studien* 31 (1997): 120–157.

Krenkow, Fritz. "The Two Oldest Books on Arabic Folklore." *Islamic Culture* II (1928): 55–89, 204–236.

Kurat, Akdes N. "Abū Muḥammad Aḥmad b. Aʿthām al-Kūfī's *Kitāb al-Futūḥ* and its Importance Concerning the Arab Conquest in Central Asia and the Khazars." Ankara Universitesi, *Dil ve Tarih-Cografiya Fakultesi Dergisi* 8 (1949): 274–282.

Kurd ʿAlī, Muḥammad. *Kitāb khiṭaṭ al-Shām*. 6 vol. Damascus: Maṭbaʿa al-ḥadīth, 1925.

Lammens, Henri. "L'ancienne frontière entre la Syrie et le Ḥidjâz (Notes de géographie historique)." *Bulletin de l'IFAO* 14 (1918): 69–96.

Lammens, Henri. "La "Bâdia" et la "Hîra" sous les Omaiyades. Un mot à propos de Mshattâ." *Mélanges de la faculté orientale de Beyrouth* IV (1910): 91–112.

Lammens, Henri. "Le chantre des Omiades," *JA* 9/4 (1894): 94–176, 193–241, 381–459.

Lammens, Henri. *Études sur le siècle des Omayyades*. Beirut, 1930.

Lammens, Henri. "Maslama b. ʿAbd al-Malik." *EI*[1].

Lammens, Henri. "Le "Sofiânî" héros narional des Arabes syriens." *Bulletin de l'IFAO* 21 (1923): 131–144.

Lammens, Henri. *La Syrie. Précis historique*. 2 vol. Beirut: Imprimerie Catholique, 1921.

Lancaster, William. *The Rwala Bedouin Today*. Cambridge: Cambridge University Press, 1981.

Landau-Tasseron, Ella. "The "Cyclical Reform": A Study of the *Mujaddid* Tradition." *SI* 70 (1989): 79–117.

Landau-Tasseron, Ella. "On the Reconstruction of Lost Sources." *Al-Qanṭara* 25 (2004): 45–91.

Landau-Tasseron, Ella. "Sayf Ibn ʿUmar in Medieval and Modern Scholarship." *Der Islam* 67/1 (1990): 1–26.

Lang, Katherine. *Awāʾil in Early Arabic Historiography: Beginnings and Identity in the Middle Abbasid Empire*. Ph. D. diss. University of Chicago, 1997.

Langlamet, F. "Pour ou contre Salomon? La rédaction pro-salomonienne de I Rois I–II." *Revue Biblique* 83 (1976): 321–379 and 481–528.

Laoust, Henri. "Ibn al-Djawzī." *EI*[2].

Laoust, Henri. "Ibn Kathīr." *EI*[2].

Laoust, Henri. "Ibn Kaṯīr historien." *Arabica* 2/1 (1955): 42–88.

Laoust, Henri. *Les schismes dans l'islam*. Paris: Payot, 1965.

Lapidus, Ira. "The Separation of the State and Religion in the Development of Early Islamic Society." *IJMES* 6 (1975): 363–385.

Lassner, Jacob. "The ʿAbbasid *Dawla*: An Essay on the Concept of Revolution in Early Islam." In F. M. Clover and R. S. Humphreys (ed.), *Tradition and Innovation in Late Antiquity*. Madison, WI: Wisconsin University Press, (1989): 247–270.

Lassner, Jacob. "Did the Caliph Abu Jaʿfar al-Manṣūr Murder his Uncle ʿAbdallāh b. ʿAlī, and other Problems within the Ruling House of the ʿAbbasids." In Myriam Rosen-Ayalon (ed.), *Studies in Memory of Gaston Wiet*. Jerusalem: Hebrew University of Jerusalem, 1977. 69–99.

Lassner, Jacob. *Islamic Revolution and Historical Memory: An Inquiry into the Art of ʿAbbāsid Apologetics*. New Haven: American Oriental Society, 1986.

Lassner, Jacob. *The Middle East Remembered: Forged Identities, Competing Narratives, Contested Spaces*. Ann Arbor: University of Michigan Press, 2000.

Lassner, Jacob. *The Shaping of Abbasid Rule*. Princeton: Princeton University Press, 1980.

Laurens, Henry. *La bibliothèque orientale de Barthélemi d'Herbelot*. Paris, 1978.

Lavenant, René (ed.). *V Symposium Syriacum 1988*. Rome: Pont. Institutum Studiorum Orientalium, 1990.

Lauwers, Michel. *La mémoire des ancêtres, le souci des morts: morts, rites et société au Moyen Âge (diocèse de Liège, XIe–XIIIe siècles)*. Paris: Beauchesne, 1997.

Lauwers, Michel. "*Memoria*. À propos d'un objet d'histoire en Allemagne." In Jean-Claude Schmitt and Otto G. Oexle (dir.), *Les tendances actuelles de l'histoire du Moyen Âge en France et en Allemagne. Actes des colloques de Sèvres (1997) et Göttingen (1998) organisés par le C.N.R.S. et le Max-Planck-Institut für Geschichte*. Paris: Publications de la Sorbonne, 2003. 105–126.

Lebecq, Stéphane. *Les origines franques Ve–IXe siècle*. Paris: Points, Éditions du Seuil, 1990.

Lecker, Michael. "Bibliographical Notes on Ibn Shihāb al-Zuhrī." *JSS* 41 (1996): 26–63.

Lecker, Michael. "Review of Sayf b. ʿUmar al-Tamīmī (m.180/796), *Kitāb al-Ridda wa'l-futūḥ and Kitāb al-Jamal wa masīr ʿĀʾisha wa ʿAlī, A Facsimile Edition of the Fragments Preserved in the University Library of Imām Muḥammad Ibn Saʿūd Islamic University in Riyadh, Saʿudi Arabia*, ed. Q. al-Samarrai, 2 vol. Smitskamp Oriental Antiquarium, Leiden, 1995." *JAOS* 119/3 (1999): 533.

Lecker, Michael. "Al-Zuhrī." *EI*².

Lecomte, Gérard. *Ibn Qutayba. L'homme, son œuvre, ses idées*. Damascus: PIFD, 1965.

Lecomte, Gérard. "Ibn Qutayba." *EI*².

Leder, Stefan. "Authorship and Transmission in Unauthored Literature. The Akhbār Attributed to al-Haytham ibn ʿAdī." *Oriens* 31 (1988): 67–81.

Leder, Stefan. "Conventions of Fictional Narration in Learned Literature." In Stefan Leder (ed.), *Story-Telling in the Framework of Non-Fictional Arabic Literature*. Wiesbaden, 1998. 34–60.

Leder, Stefan. "Features of the Novel in Early Historiography – the Downfall of Xālid al-Qasrī." *Oriens* 32 (1990): 72–96.

Leder, Stefan. "Heraklios erkennt den Propheten. Ein Beispiel für Form und Entstehungsweise narrativer Geschichtskonstruktionen." *ZDMG* 151/1 (2001): 1–42.

Leder, Stefan. *Das Korpus al-Haiṯam ibn ʿAdī (st. 207/822). Herkunft, Überlieferung, Gestalt früher Texte der Ahbar Literatur*. Frankfurt: Vittorio Klostermann, 1991.

Leder, Stefan. "The Literary Use of the *Khabar*: A Basic Form of Historical Writing." In Averil Cameron and Lawrence I. Conrad (eds.), *The Byzantine and Early Islamic Near East I: Problems in the Literary Source Material*. Princeton: Darwin Press, 1992. 277–315.

Leder, Stefan. "al-Ṣūlī." *EI*².

Leder, Stefan. "al-Wāqidī." *EI*².

Le Goff, Jacques. *Histoire et mémoire*. Paris: Gallimard, 1988.

Le Goff, Jacques. *History and Memory*. Trans. Steven Rendall and Elizabeth Claman. New York: Columbia University Press, 1992.

Le Goff, Jacques. *Saint Louis*. Paris: Gallimard, 1996.

Leisten, Thomas. "Balis. Preliminary Report on the Campaigns 1996 & 1998." *Berytus* 44 (1999–2000): 35–57.

Leisten, Thomas. "For Prince and Country(side) – the Marwanid Mansion at Balis on the Euphrates." In Karin Bartl and Abd al-Razzaq Moaz (eds.), *Residences, Castles, Settlements. Transformation Processes from Late Antiquity to Early Islam in Bilad al-Sham. Proceedings of the International Conference held at Damascus, 5–9 November 2006*. Rahden: Verlag Marie Leidorf GmbH, 2009. 377–394.

Leisten, Thomas. "The Umayyad Complex at Balis. Scientific Report Regarding the activities of the Cooperative Project of the Syrian Directorate of Antiquities and Princeton University in the Summer of 2002." *AAAS* 47–48 (2004–2005): 251–270.

Lellouch, Benjamin and Stéphane Yerasimos. *Les traditions apocalyptiques au tournant de la chute de Constantinople*. Actes de la Table ronde d'Istanbul (13–14 April 1996). Paris: L'Harmattan, 1996.

Le Strange, Guy. *Palestine under the Moslems: A description of Syria and the Holy Land from A.D. 650 to 1500*. Boston and New York; 1890, repr. Beirut: Khayats (Oriental Reprints), 1965.

Lévi, Israël. "Une apocalypse judéo-arabe." *Revue des études juives* 67 (1914): 178–182.

Lewinstein, Keith. "The Azāriqa in Islamic heresiography." *BSOAS* 54 (1991): 251–268.

Lewinstein, Keith. "Making and Unmaking a Sect: The Heresiographers and the Ṣufriyya." *SI* 76 (1992): 75–96.

Lewis, Bernard and P. M. Holt. *Historians of the Middle East*. London: Oxford University Press, 1962.

Lewis, Bernard. "ʿAlī al-Riḍā." *EI*².

Lewis, Bernard. "An Apocalyptic Vision of Islamic History." *BSOAS* 13/2 (1950): 308–338.

Lewis, Bernard. *Les Arabes dans l'histoire*. Paris: Aubier, 1993.

Lewis, Bernard. *Islam*. Paris: Quarto, Gallimard, 2005.

Lewis, Bernard. "Islamic Concepts of Revolution." In P. J. Vatikiotis (ed.), *Revolution in the Middle East*. London, 1972. 30–40.

Lewis, Bernard. "On Revolutions in Early Islam." *SI* 32 (1970): 215–231.

Lewis, Bernard. "Perceptions musulmanes de l'histoire et de l'historiographie." *Itinéraires d'Orient. Hommage à Claude Cahen, Res Orientales* VI (1994): 77–81.

Lewis, Bernard. "The Regnal Titles of the First Abbasid Caliphs." *Dr. Zaki Husain Presentation Volume*. New Delhi, 1968.

Lilie, Ralph-Johannes. "Araber und Themen. Zum Einfluss der arabischen Expansion auf die byzantinische Militärorganisation." In Averil Cameron (ed.), *The Byzantine and Early Islamic Near East III: States, Resources and Armies*. Princeton: Darwin Press, 1995. 425–460.

Lilie, Ralph-Johannes. *Die byzantinische Reaktion auf die Ausbreitung der Araber: Studien zur Strukturwandlung des byzantinischen Staates im 7. und 8. Jhd.* Munich: Institüt für Byzantinistik und neugriechische Philogie der Universität, 1976.

Lindholm, Charles. "Kinship Structure and Political Authority: The Middle East and Central Asia." *Comparative Studies in Society and History* 28/2 (1986): 334–355.

Lindsay, James E. "Caliphal and Moral Exemplar? ʿAlī Ibn ʿAsākir's Portrait of Yazīd b. Muʿāwiya." *Der Islam* 74/2 (1997): 250–278.

Lindsay, James E. "Damascene Scholars During the Fāṭimid Period: an Examination of ʿAlī b. ʿAsākir's *Taʾrīkh Madīnat Dimashq*." *Al-Masāq* 7 (1994): 35–75.

Lindsay, James E. (ed.) *Ibn ʿAsākir and Early Islamic History*. Princeton: Darwin Press, 2001.

Lorenz, Chris. "Comparative Historiography: Problems and Perspectives." *History and Theory* 38/1 (1999): 25–39.

Luz, Nimrod. "The Construction of an Islamic City in Palestine. The Case of Umayyad al-Ramla." *JRAS* 3.7.1 (1997): 27–54.

Lyons, Jonathan. *The House of Wisdom: How the Arabs Transformed Western Civilization*. New York: Bloomsbury Press, 2009.

Lyons, M. C. *The Arabian Epic: Heroic and Oral Story-Telling*. 3 vol. Cambridge: University of Cambridge Oriental Publications, 1995.

Macadam, Henry I. "Settlements and Settlement Patterns in Northern and Central Transjordania, ca 550–ca 750." In G. D. R. King and Averil Cameron (eds.), *The Byzantine and Early Islamic Near East II: Land Use and Settlement Patterns*. Princeton: Darwin Press, 1994. 49–94.

Macadam, Henry I. "Some Notes on the Umayyad Occupation of North-East Jordan." In Philip Freeman and David Kennedy (eds.), *The Defence of the Roman and Byzantine East. Proceedings of a Colloquium held at the University of Sheffield in April 1986*. II, 1986. 531–547.

Macler, Frédéric. "Les apocalypses apocryphes de Daniel." *Revue d'histoire des religions* 33 (1896): 37–53, 163–176 and 288–319.

Madelung, Wilferd. "ʿAbd Allāh b. al-Zubayr and the Mahdi." *JNES* 40 (1981): 291–305.

Madelung, Wilferd. "Abū'l-ʿAmayṭar the Sufyānī." *JSAI* 24 (2000): 327–342.

Madelung, Wilferd. "Apocalyptic Prophecies in Ḥimṣ in the Umayyad Age." *JSS* 31/2 (1986): 141–185.

Madelung, Wilferd. "al-Mahdī." *EI*².

Madelung, Wilferd. "New Documents Concerning al-Maʾmūn, al-Faḍl b. Sahl and ʿAlī al-Riḍā." In Wadād al-Qāḍī (ed.), *Studia Arabica et Islamica: Festschrift for Iḥsān ʿAbbās on his Sixtieth Birthday*. Beirut: American University of Beirut, 1981. 333–346.

Madelung, Wilferd. "The Sufyānī between Tradition and History." *SI* 63 (1984): 5–48.

Madelung, Wilferd. "Zayd b. ʿAlī." *EI*².

Mahé, J.-P. "Entre Moïse et Mahomet: réflexions sur l'historiographie arménienne." *Revue des études arméniennes* 23 (1992): 121–153.

Marín, Manuela. "Constantinopla en los geografos arabes." *Erytheia* 9/1 (1988): 49–60.

Marin-Guzman, Roberto. "The ʿAbbasid Revolution in Central Asia and Khurāsān: An Analytical Study of the Role of Taxation, Conversion, and Religious Groups in its Genesis." *Islamic Studies* 33 (1994): 227–252.

Marin-Guzman, Roberto. *Popular Dimensions of the ʿAbbasid Revolution: A Case Study of Medieval Islamic Social History*. Cambridge, MA: Fulbright-Laspau, 1990.

Marmardji, A. S. *Textes géographiques arabes sur la Palestine*. Paris, 1951.

Marmorstein, Arthur. "Les signes du Messie." *Revue des études juives* 52 (1906): 176–186.

Marquet, Yves. "Le šīʿisme au IXᵉ siècle à travers l'histoire de Yaʿqūbī." *Arabica* 19/1 (1972): 1–45; 19/2 (1972): 101–138.

Marsham, Andrew. "The Early Caliphate and the Inheritance of Late Antiquity (c. ad 610–c. ad 750)." In Philip Rousseau (dir.), *A Companion to Late Antiquity*. Chichester: Wiley-Blackwell, 2009. 479–492.

Marsham, Andrew. *Rituals of Islamic Monarchy: Accession and Succession in the First Muslim Empire*. Edinburgh: Edinburgh University Press, 2009.

Marsham, Andrew and Chase F. Robinson. "The Safe-Conduct for the Abbasid ʿAbd Allāh b. ʿAlī (d. 764)." *BSOAS* 70/2 (2007): 247–281.

Mårtensson, Ulrika. "Discourse and Historical Analysis: The Case of al-Ṭabarī's History of the Messengers and the Kings." *Journal of Islamic Studies* 16/3 (2005): 287–331.

Mårtensson, Ulrika. "The Power of the Subject: Weber, Foucault and Islam." *Critique: Critical Middle Eastern Studies* 16/2 (2007): 97–136.

Martinez-Gros, Gabriel. "Le califat omeyyade selon Ibn Khaldūn: revanche des impies ou fondation de l'Empire?" In Antoine Borrut and Paul M. Cobb (eds.), *Umayyad Legacies: Medieval Memories from Syria to Spain*. Leiden: Brill, 2010. 167–183.

Martinez-Gros, Gabriel. *Ibn Khaldûn et les sept vies de l'islam*. Paris: Sindbad-Actes Sud, 2006.

Martinez-Gros, Gabriel. *Identité andalouse*. Arles: Sindbad-Actes Sud, 1997.

Martinez-Gros, Gabriel. *L'idéologie omeyyade. La construction de la légitimité du Califat de Cordoue (Xᵉ–XIᵉ siècles)*. Madrid: Bibliothèque de la Casa de Velázquez, 8, 1992.

Martinez-Gros, Gabriel. "Le passage vers l'Ouest: remarques sur le récit fondateur des dynasties omeyyade de Cordoue et Idrisside de Fès." *Al-Masāq* 8 (1995): 21–44.

Marzolph, Ulrich. "Islamische Kultur als Gedächtniskultur. Fachspezifische Überlegungen anhand des Fallbeispiels Iran." *Der Islam* 75/2 (1998): 296–317.

Matin-Asgari, Afshin. "Islamic Studies and the Spirit of Max Weber: A Critique of Cultural Essentialism." *Critique: Critical Middle Eastern Studies* 13/3 (2004): 293–312.

Mattock, J. N. "History and Fiction." *OPSAS* 1 (1986): 80–97.

Mayer, Tobias. "Neue Aspekte zur Nominierung 'Umars II. durch Sulaimān b. 'Abdalmalik (96/715–99/717)." *Die Welt des Orients* 25 (1994): 109–115.

Mayeur-Jaouen, Catherine. "Lieux sacrés, lieux de culte, sanctuaires en islam. Bibliographie raisonnée." In André Vauchez (dir.), *Lieux sacrés, lieux de culte, sanctuaires. Approches terminologiques, méthodologiques, historiques et monographiques*. Rome: École française de Rome, 2000. 149–170.

Mayeur-Jaouen, Catherine (dir.). *Saints et héros du Moyen-Orient contemporain*. Paris: Maisonneuve et Larose, 2002.

McAuliffe, Jane D. (ed.). *The Cambridge Companion to the Qur'ān*. Cambridge: Cambridge University Press, 2006.

McDonald, Michael V. "A Minor Early Abbasid Poet: Muḥammad b. Kunāsa." *JAL* 25 (1994): 107–115.

McKitterick, Rosamond. *The Carolingians and the Written Word*. Cambridge, 1989.

McKitterick, Rosamond. *History and Memory in the Carolingian World*. Cambridge: Cambridge University Press, 2004.

McKitterick, Rosamond. *Perceptions of the Past in the Early Middle Ages*. Notre Dame, IN: University of Notre Dame Press, 2006.

McKitterick, Rosamond (ed.). *The Uses of Literacy in Early Medieval Europe*. Cambridge, 1990.

McNicoll, Anthony and Alan Walmsley. "Pella/Fahl in Jordan during the Early Islamic Period." *SHAJ* 1 (1982): 339–345.

Meinardus, Otto. "A Commentary on the XIVth Vision of Daniel According to the Coptic Version." *Orientalia Christiana Periodica* 32 (1966): 3949–449.

Meinardus, Otto. "New Evidence on the XIVth Vision of Daniel from the History of the Patriarchs of the Egyptian Church." *Orientalia Christiana Periodica* 34 (1968): 281–309.

Meinecke, Michael. "Die Frühislamischen Kalifenresidenzen: Tradition oder Rezeption?" In Karin Bartl and Stefan R. Hauser (eds.), *Continuity and Change in Northern Mesopotamia from the Hellenistic to the Early Islamic Period*. Berlin: Dietrich Reimer Verlag, 1996. 139–164.

Meinecke, Michael. *Patterns of Stylistic Changes in Islamic Architecture: Local Traditions versus Migrating Artists*. New York: New York University Press, 1996.

Meinecke, Michael. "Al-Raḳḳa." *EI*².

Melchert, Christopher. *Ahmad Ibn Hanbal*. Oxford: Oneworld, 2006.

Melchert, Christopher. *The Formation of the Sunni Schools of Law, 9th–10th Centuries C.E.* Leiden: Brill, 1997.

Mélikoff, I. "Al-Baṭṭāl." *EI*².

Meyer, Carol. "Byzantine and Umayyad Glass from Jerash: Battleship Curves." *ADAJ* 33 (1989): 235–243.

Micheau, Françoise. "Bagdad." In Jean-Claude Garcin (ed.), *Grandes villes méditerranéennes du monde musulman médiéval*. Rome: École Française de Rome, 2000. 86–112.

Micheau, Françoise. "Le *Kāmil* d'Ibn al-Aṯīr, source principale de l'histoire des Arabes dans le *Muḫtaṣar* de Bar Hebraeus." *MUSJ* 58 (2005): 425–439.

Miglus, Peter A. *Ar-Raqqa I. Die frühislamische Keramik von Tall Aswad*. Mainz: Philipp von Zabern, 1999.

Miquel, André. *La géographie humaine du monde musulman*. 4 vol. Paris: Mouton, 1967–1988.

Moeglin, Jean-Marie. "Les recherches françaises sur les cours et les résidences au bas Moyen Age." In Jean-Claude Schmitt and Otto G. Oexle (dir.), *Les tendances actuelles de l'histoire du Moyen Âge en France et en Allemagne. Actes des colloques de Sèvres (1997) et Göttingen (1998) organisés par le C.N.R.S. et le Max-Planck-Institut für Geschichte*. Paris: Publications de la Sorbonne, 2003. 357–362.

Monnet, Pierre. "Conclusions." In Jean-Claude Schmitt and Otto G. Oexle (dir.), *Les tendances actuelles de l'histoire du Moyen Âge en France et en Allemagne. Actes des colloques de Sèvres (1997) et Göttingen (1998) organisés par le C.N.R.S. et le Max-Planck-Institut für Geschichte*. Paris: Publications de la Sorbonne, 2003. 625–644.

Morabia, Alfred. *Le ǧihâd dans l'Islam médiéval*. Paris: Albin Michel, 1993.

Mordtmann, A. D. "Nachrichten über Taberistan aus dem Geschichtswerke Taberi's." *ZDMG* 2 (1848): 285–314.

Mordtmann, J. H. "Al-Ḳusṭanṭīniyya" *EI*².

Moreland, John "Concepts of the Early Medieval Economy." In Inge L. Hansen and Christopher Wickham (eds.), *The Long Eighth Century*. Leiden: Brill, 2000. 1–34.

Morony, Michael G. "Apocalyptic Expressions in the Early Islamic World." *Medieval Encounters* 4/3 (1998): 175–177.

Morony, Michael G. "Bayn al-Fitnatayn: Problems in the Periodization of Early Islamic History." *JNES* 40/3 (1981): 247–251.

Morony, Michael G. *Iraq after the Muslim Conquest*. Princeton Studies on the Near East. Princeton: Princeton University Press, 1984.

Morony, Michael G. "Land Use and Settlement Patterns in Late Sasanian and Early Islamic Iraq." In G. D. R. King and Averil Cameron (eds.), *The Byzantine and Early Islamic Near East II: Land Use and Settlement Patterns*. Princeton: Darwin Press, 1994. 221–230.

Morony, Michael G. "Michael the Syrian as a Source for Economic History." *Hugoye* 3/2 (2000).

Morray, David. *An Ayyūbid Notable and His World: Ibn al-ʿAdīm and Aleppo as Portrayed in his Biographical Dictionary of People Associated with the City*. Leiden: Brill, 1994.

Moscati, Sabatino. "Le califat d'al-Hâdî." *Studia Orientalia* 13/4 (1946): 3–28.

Moscati, Sabatino. "Le massacre des Umayyades dans l'histoire et dans les fragments poétiques." *Archiv Orientální* 18 (1950): 88–115.

Moscati, Sabatino. "Nuovi Studi storici sul califfato di al-Mahdī." *Orientalia* 15 (1946): 155–179.

Moscati, Sabatino. "Studi storici sul Califfato di al-Mahdī." *Orientalia* 14 (1945): 300–345.

Mottahedeh, Roy. *Loyalty and Leadership in an Early Islamic Society*. Princeton: Princeton University Press, 1980.

Motzki, Harald. "Der Fiqh des Zuhrī: die Quellenproblematik." *Der Islam* 68/1 (1991): 1–44.

Motzki, Harald. "The Prophet and the Cat: On Dating Mālik's Muwaṭṭaʾ and Legal Traditions." *JSAI* 22 (1998): 18–83.

Mourad, Suleiman A. "On Early Islamic Historiography: Abū Ismāʿīl al-Azdī and his *Futūḥ al-Shām*." *JAOS* 120/4 (2000): 577–593.

Mourad, Suleiman A. "Publication History of TMD." In James E. Lindsay (ed.), *Ibn ʿAsākir and Early Islamic History*. Princeton: Darwin Press, 2001. 127–133.

Mouterde, Paul. "Inscriptions en Syriaque dialectal à Kāmed (Beqʿa)." *MUSJ* 22/4 (1939): 73–106.

Mouterde, Paul. "Trente ans après, les inscriptions de Kamed (complément)." *MUSJ* 44 (1968): 23–29.

Mouton, Jean-Michel. *Damas et sa principauté sous les Saljoukides et les Bourides*. Cairo, 1994.

Mouton, Jean-Michel. *Le Sinaï médiéval. Un espace stratégique de l'Islam*. Paris: PUF, 2000.

Müller-Mertens, Eckhard. *Die Reichsstruktur im Spiegel der Herrschaftspraxis Ottos des Großen*. Berlin, 1980.

Al-Munajjid, Ṣalāh al-Dīn. *Madīnat Dimashq ʿinda al-jughrāfiyīn wa-al-raḥḥālīn al-muslimīn*. Beirut: Dār al-kitāb al-jadīd, 1967.

Al-Munajjid, Ṣalāh al-Dīn. *Muʿjam banī umayya*. Beirut: Dār al-kitāb al-jadīd, 1970.

Murad, M. Q. "ʿUmar II's View of the Patriarchal Caliphs." *Hamdard Islamicus* 10/1 (1987): 31–56.

Musil, Alois. *Kusejr Amra*. 2 vol. Vienna, 1907.

Musil, Alois. *Palmyrena: A Topographical Itinerary*. Published under the Patronage of the Czech Academy of Sciences and Arts and of Charles R. Crane. New York, 1928.

Al-Naboodah, Hasan M. "*Ṣāḥib al-khabar*: Secret Agents and Spies During the First Century of Islam." *Journal of Asian History* 39/2 (2005): 158–176.

Nadler, Rajaa. *Die Umayyadenkalifen im Spiegel ihrer zeitgenössischen Dichter*. Inaugural dissertation, Friedrich-Alexander Universität, Erlangen-Nuremberg, 1990.

Nau, F. "Un colloque du patriarche Jean avec l'émir des Agaréens et faits divers des années 712 à 716." *JA* 11/5 (1915): 225–279.

Nawas, John Abdallah. "Toward Fresh Directions in Historical Research: an Experiment in Methodology using the Putative "Absolutism" of Hârûn al-Rashîd as a Test Case." *Der Islam* 70/1 (1993): 1–51.

Nees, Lawrence. "Blue Behind Gold: The Inscription of the Dome of the Rock and its Relatives," in J. Bloom and S. Blair (eds.), *And Diverse Are Their Hues: Color in Islamic Art and Culture*. New Haven [Conn.] & London: Yale University Press, 2011. 152–73.

Neuwirth, Angelika. "Qur'an and History. A Disputed Relationship. Some Reflections on Qur'anic History and History in the Qur'an." *Journal of Qur'anic Studies* 5/1 (2003): 1–18.

Neuwirth, Angelika, Birgit Embaló, Sebastian Günther and Maher Jarrar. *Myths, Historical Archetypes and Symbolic Figures in Arabic Literature: Towards a New Hermeneutic Approach. Proceedings of the International Symposium in Beirut, June 25th–June 30th, 1996*. Beirut: In Kommission bei Franz Steiner Verlag Stuttgart, 1999.

Neuwirth, Angelika and Andreas Pflitsch (eds.). *Crisis and Memory in Islamic Societies, Proceedings of the third Summer Academy of the Working Group Modernity and Islam held at the Oriental Institute of the German Oriental Society in Beirut*. Beirut: Ergon Verlag Würzburg in Kommission, 2001. 59–74.

Nicol, Norman D. *Early Abbasid Administration in the Central and Eastern Provinces, 132–218 AH / 750–833 A.D.* Ph. D. diss. University of Washington, 1979.

Nora, Pierre. *Les lieux de mémoire*. vol. I. Paris: Gallimard (Quarto), 1997.

Nora, Pierre. *Realms of Memory*. Ed. Lawrence D. Kritzman. Trans. Arthur Goldhammer. New York: Columbia University Press, 1996.

Northedge, Alastair. "Archaeology and New Urban Settlement in Early Islamic Syria and Iraq." In G. R. D. King and Averil Cameron (eds.), *Studies in Late Antiquity and Early Islam II: Settlement Patterns in the Byzantine and Early Islamic Near East*. Princeton: Darwin Press, 1994. 231–265.

Northedge, Alastair. *Entre Amman et Samarra: l'archéologie et les élites au début de l'islam (VIIe–IXe siècle)*. Synthesis of work submitted for authorization to direct research, Université de Paris I, 2000.

Northedge, Alastair. *The Historical Topography of Samarra, Samarra Studies I*. London: British School of Archaeology in Iraq, 2005.

Northedge, Alastair. "The Racecourses at Samarra." *BSOAS* 53 (1990): 31–56.

Northedge, Alastair. *Studies on Roman and Islamic 'Ammān*, vol. 1. *History, Site and Architecture*. Oxford: British Academy Monographs in Archaeology no. 3, 1993.

Northedge, Alastair. "Ukhaydir." *EI*².

Northedge, Alastair. "The Umayyad Desert Castles and Pre-Islamic Arabia." In Karin Bartl and Abd al-Razzaq Moaz (eds.), *Residences, Castles, Settlements: Transformation Processes from Late Antiquity to Early Islam in Bilad al-Sham. Proceedings of the International Conference held at Damascus, 5–9 November 2006*. Rahden: Verlag Marie Leidorf GmbH, 2009. 243–259.

Noth, Albrecht. "Fiktion als historische Quelle." In Stefan Leder (ed.), *Story-Telling in the Framework of Non-Fictional Arabic Literature*. Wiesbaden, 1998. 472–487.

Noth, Albrecht. "Futūḥ-History and Futūḥ-Historiography. The Muslim Conquest of Damascus." *Al-Qanṭara* X/2 (1989): 453–462.

Noth, Albrecht. *Quellenkritische Studien zu Themen, Formen und Tendenzen frühislamischer Geschichtsüberlieferung*. Bonn, 1973.

Noth, Albrecht. "Zum Verhältnis von Kalifaler Zentralgewalt und Provinzen in Umayyadischer Zeit: Die "Ṣulḥ" – "ʿAnwa" Traditionen für Ägypten und den Iraq." *Die Welt des Islams* XIV/1–4 (1973): 150–162.

Noth, Albrecht and Lawrence I. Conrad. *The Early Arabic Historical Tradition: A Source-Critical Study*. Trans. Michael Bonner. Princeton: Darwin Press, 1994.

Oexle, Otto G. "Die Gegenwart der Toten." In Herman Braet and Werner Verbeke (eds.), *Death in the Middle Ages*. Leuven, 1983. 19–77.

Oexle, Otto G. "L'historicisation de l'histoire." In Jean-Claude Schmitt and Otto G. Oexle (dir.), *Les tendances actuelles de l'histoire du Moyen Âge en France et en Allemagne. Actes des colloques de Sèvres (1997) et Göttingen (1998) organisés par le C.N.R.S. et le Max-Planck-Institut für Geschichte*. Paris: Publications de la Sorbonne, 2003. 31–41.

Oexle, Otto G. *Memoria als Kultur*. Göttingen: Veröffentlichungen des Max-Planck-Instituts für Geschichte, 121, 1995.

Oexle, Otto G. "Memoria und Memorialüberlieferung im früheren Mittelalter." *Frühmittelalterliche Studien* 10 1976. 70–95.

Olavarri-Goicoechea, Emilio. *El Palacio Omeya de Amman II. La Arqueología*. Valencia, 1985.

Oleson, John Peter. "The Ḥumayma Hydraulic Survey: Preliminary Report of the 1986 Season." *ADAJ* 30 (1986): 253–260.

Oleson, John Peter. "Landscape and Cityscape in the Hisma: the Resources of Ancient al-Humayma." *SHAJ* VI (1997): 175–188.

Oleson, John Peter. "The Water-Supply System of Ancient Auara: Preliminary Results of the Humeima Hydraulic Survey." *SHAJ* IV (1992): 269–275.

Oleson, John Peter, Khairieh ʿAmr, Rebecca Foote and Robert Schick. "Preliminary Report of the Humayma Excavation Project, 1993." *ADAJ* 39 (1995): 317–354.

Oleson, John Peter, Khairieh ʿAmr, Rebecca Foote, Judy Logan, M. Barbara Reeves and Robert Schick. "Preliminary Report of the al-Humayma Excavation Project, 1995, 1996, 1998." *ADAJ* 43 (1999): 411–450.

Oleson, John Peter, Greg Baker, Erik de Bruijn, Rebecca Foote, Judy Logan, M. Barbara Reeves and Andrew N. Sherwood. "Preliminary Report of the al-Humayma Excavation Project, 2000, 2002." ADAJ 47 (2003): 37–64.

Omar, Farouk. *The ʿAbbāsid Caliphate 132/750–170/786*. Baghdad: National Printing and Publishing Co., 1969.

Omar, Farouk. *ʿAbbāsiyyāt: Studies in the History of the Early ʿAbbāsids*. Baghdad: University of Baghdad, 1976.

Omar, Farouk. "Ibrāhīm b. Muḥammad." EI².

Omar, Farouk. "A Note on the *laqabs* (i.e. epithet) of the Early ʿAbbasid Caliphs." In Farouk Omar, *ʿAbbāsiyyāt: Studies in the History of the Early ʿAbbāsids*. Baghdad: University of Baghdad, 1976. 141–147.

Omar, Farouk. "Some Aspects of the ʿAbbāsid-Ḥusaynid Relations During the Early ʿAbbāsid Period 132–193 A.H./750–809 A.D." *Arabica* 22/2 (1975): 170–179.

Omar, Farouk. "Some Observations on the Reign of the ʿAbbāsid Caliph al-Mahdī 158/775–169/785." *Arabica* 21/2 (1974): 139–150.

Orthmann, Eva. *Stamm und Macht. Die arabische Stämme im 2. und 3. Jahrhundert der Hiǧra*. Wiesbaden: Dr. Ludwig Reichert Verlag, 2002.

Ory, Solange. "Les graffiti omeyyades de ʿAyn al Garr." *Bulletin du musée de Beyrouth* 20 (1967): 97–148.

Otto-Dorn, Katharina. "Grabung in umayyadischen Rusafah." *Ars Orientalis* 2 (1957): 119–33.

Palmer, Andrew. "Les chroniques brèves syriaques." In Muriel Debié (ed.), *L'historiographie syriaque*. Paris: Geuthner, 2009. 57–87.

Palmer, Andrew. "The Messiah and the Mahdi: History Presented as the Writing on the Wall." In Hero Hokwerda, Edmé R. Smits and Marinus M. Woesthuis (eds.), *Polyphonia Byzantina: Studies in Honour of Willem J. Aerts*. Groningen, 1993. 45–84.

Palmer, Andrew. *Monk and Mason on the Tigris Frontier*. Cambridge: Cambridge University Press, 1990.

Palmer, Andrew. *The Seventh Century in the West-Syrian Chronicles*. Liverpool: Liverpool University Press, 1993.

Paravicini, Werner. "Cours et résidences du Moyen Age tardif. Un quart de siècle de recherches allemandes." In Jean-Claude Schmitt and Otto G. Oexle (dir.), *Les tendances actuelles de l'histoire du Moyen Âge en France et en Allemagne. Actes des colloques de Sèvres (1997) et Göttingen (1998) organisés par le C.N.R.S. et le Max-Planck-Institut für Geschichte*. Paris: Publications de la Sorbonne, 2003. 327–350.

Patton, Walter M. *Ahmad Ibn Hanbal and the Mihna*. Leiden: E. J. Brill, 1897.

Payne, Jessie Smith. *A Compendious Syriac Dictionary*. Oxford: Clarendon Press, 1903.

Payne, Robert Smith. *Thesaurus Syriacus*. Oxford: Clarendon Press, 1879–1901.

Peacock, Andrew C. S. *Medieval Islamic Historiography and Political Legitimacy. Balʿamī's Tārīkhnāma*. London and New York: Routledge, 2007.

Peeters, Paul. "La passion de S. Pierre de Capitolias († 13 janvier 715)." *AB* 57 (1939): 299–333.

Pellat, Charles. "Le culte de Muʿāwiya au IIIe siècle de l'hégire." *SI* 7 (1956): 53–66.

Pellat, Charles. "Un document important pour l'histoire politico-religieuse de l'Islâm. La "Nâbita" de Djâhiz." *Annales de l'Institut d'Études Orientales* 10 (1952): 302–325.

Pellat, Charles. "Ḳāṣṣ." *EI*².

Pellat, Charles. *Langue et littérature arabes*. Paris: A. Colin, 1952.

Pellat, Charles. *Le milieu Basrien et la formation de Ǧāḥiẓ*. Paris: Librairie d'Amérique et d'Orient Adrien-Maisonneuve, 1953.

Pérès, Henri. *Koṯayyir ʿAzza, Dîwân, accompagné d'un commentaire arabe*. Algiers, 1928–30.

Périer, J. *Vie d'al-Ḥadjdjâj ibn Yousof (41–95 de l'Hégire = 661–714 de J.-C.) d'après les sources arabes*. Paris, 1904.

Petersen, Erling L. *ʿAlī and Muʿāwiya in Early Arabic Traditions*. Copenhagen, 1964.

Piacentini, Valeria F. "Madīna/Shahr, Qarya/Deh, Nāḥiya/Rustāq. The City as Political-Administrative Institution: the Continuity of a Sasanian Model." *JSAI* 17 (1994): 85–107.

Picard, Christophe. "Regards croisés sur l'élaboration du jihad entre Occident et Orient musulman (VIIIe–XIIe siècle): perspectives et réflexions sur une origine commune." In Daniel Baloup and Philippe Josserand (eds.), *Regards croisés sur la guerre sainte. Guerre, religion et idéologie dans l'espace méditerranéen latin (XIe–XIIIe siècle)*. Toulouse: Méridiennes, 2006. 33–66.

Piccirillo, Michele. "The Umayyad Churches of Jordan." *ADAJ* 28 (1984): 333–341.

Piccirillo, Michele and Taysir Aṭṭiyat. "The Complex of Saint Stephen at Umm er-Rasas – Kastron Mafaa. First Campaign, August 1986." *ADAJ* 30 (1986): 341–351.

Pinggera, Karl. "Nestorianische Weltchronistik: Johannes Bar Penkaye und Elias von Nisibis." In Martin Wallraf (ed.), *Julius Africanus und die christliche Weltchronistik*. Berlin: De Gruyter, 2006. 263–283.

Pingree, David. "Abū Sahl b. Nawbaḫt." *Encyclopaedia Iranica* I, 1985. 369.

Pingree, David. "From Alexandria to Baghdād to Byzantium. The Transmission of Astrology." *International Journal of the Classical Tradition* 8/1 (2001): 3–37.

Pingree, David. "Māshāʾallāh." In Charles Coulson Gillispie (ed.), *Dictionary of Scientific Biography*, 9. New York, 1974. 159–162.

Planhol, Xavier de. *Les fondements géographiques de l'histoire de l'Islam*. Paris, 1968.

Pocock, J. G. A. "History and Theory." *Comparative Studies in Society and History* 4/4 (1962): 525–535.

Pocock, J. G. A. "The Origins of Study of the Past: A Comparative Approach." *Comparative Studies in Society and History* 4/2 (1962): 209–246.

Polignac, François de. "Alexandre entre ciel et terre: invitation et investiture." *SI* 84/2 (1996): 135–144.

Polignac, François de. "Alexandre maître des seuils et des passages: de la légende grecque au mythe arabe." In *Alexandre le Grand dans les traditions médiévales occidentales et proche-orientales*. Nanterre, Université de Paris X, 1999.

Polignac, François de. "Cosmocrator. L'islam et la légende antique du souverain universel." In Margaret Bridges and J. Christoph Bürgel (eds.), *The Problematics of Power: Eastern and Western Representations of Alexander the Great*. Bern: Peter Lang, 1996. 149–164.

Polignac, François de. "L'image d'Alexandre dans la littérature arabe." *Arabica* 29 (1982): 296–306.

Polignac, François de. "L'imaginaire arabe et le mythe de fondation légitime." In Robert Ilbert (dir.), *Alexandrie entre deux mondes*. REMMM 46 (1987): 55–62.

Polignac, François de. "Un "nouvel Alexandre" mamelouk al-Malik al-Ashraf Khalīl et le regain eschatologique du XIIIe siècle." In Denise Aigle (dir.), *Figures mythiques de l'Orient musulman*. REMMM 89–90 (2000): 73–87.

Prémare, Alfred-Louis de. "ʿAbd al-Malik b. Marwān et le processus de constitution du Coran." In Karl-Heinz Ohlig and Gerd-Rüdiger Puin (eds.), *Die dunklen Anfänge. Neue Forschungen zur Entstehung und frühen Geschichte des Islam*. Berlin: Verlag Hans Schiler, 2005. 179–210.

Prémare, Alfred-Louis de. *Les fondations de l'islam. Entre écriture et histoire*. Paris: Seuil, 2002.

Prémare, Alfred-Louis de. *Aux origines du Coran. Questions d'hier, approches d'aujourd'hui*. Paris: Téraèdre, 2004.

Prémare, Alfred-Louis de. "Wahb b. Munabbih, une figure singulière du premier islam." *Annales. Histoire, Sciences Sociales* 3 (2005): 531–549.

Al-Qāḍī, Wadād. "Biographical Dictionaries: Inner Structure and Cultural Significance." In George N. Atiyer (ed.), *The Book in the Islamic World: The Written Word and Communication in the Middle East*. Albany: State University of New York Press, 1995. 93–122.

Al-Qāḍī, Wadād. "A Documentary Report on Umayyad Stipends Registers (*Dīwān al-ʿAṭāʾ*) in Abū Zurʿa's *Tārīkh*." *Quaderni di Studi Arabi* 4 (2009): 7–44.

Al-Qāḍī, Wadād. "The Earliest "Nābita" and the Paradigmatic Nawābit." *SI* 78 (1993): 27–61.

Al-Qāḍī, Wadād. "Early Islamic State Letters: The Question of Authenticity." In Averil Cameron and Lawrence I. Conrad (eds.), *The Byzantine and Early Islamic Near East I: Problems in the Literary Source Material*. Princeton: Darwin Press, 1992. 215–275.

Al-Qāḍī, Wadād. "Madkhal ilā dirāsat ʿuhūd al-ṣulḥ al-islāmiyya zaman al-futūḥ." In Muḥammad A. al-Bakhit and Iḥsān ʿAbbās (eds.), *Proceedings of the Second Symposium on the History of Bilad al-Sham During the Early Islamic Period up to 40 A.H./640 A.D. The Fourth International Conference on the History of Bilad al-Sham*. Amman, 1987. 193–269.

Al-Qāḍī, Wadād. "The Religious Foundation of Late Umayyad Ideology and Practice." *Saber Religioso y Poder Político en el Islam. Actas del Simposio Internacional (Granada, 15–18 octubre 1991)*. Madrid: Agencia Española de Cooperación Internacional, 1994. 231–273.

Al-Qāḍī, Wadād. (ed.) *Studia Arabica et Islamica. Festschrift fot Iḥsān 'Abbās*. Beirut: American University of Beirut, 1981.

Al-Qāḍī, Wadād. "The Term "Khalīfa" in Early Exegetical Literature." In Axel Havemann and Baber Johansen, *Gegenwart als Geschichte. Islamwissenschaftliche Studien – Fritz Steppert zum fünfundsechzigsten Geburtstag*. Leiden: Brill, 1988. 392–411.

Qedar, S. "Copper Coinage in Syria in the Seventh and Eighth Century AD." *Israel Numismatic Journal* 10 (1988–1989): 27–39.

Rabbat, Nasser "The Dome of the Rock Revisited: Some Remarks on al-Wasiti's Accounts." *Muqarnas* 10 (1993): 67–75.

Raby, Julian and Jeremy Johns (eds.). *Bayt al-Maqdis: 'Abd al-Malik's Jerusalem*. Oxford Studies in Islamic Art, vol. 9, part 1. Oxford: Oxford University Press, 1993.

Rada, W. S. and F. R. Stephenson. "A Catalogue of Meteor Showers in Medieval Arab Chronicles." *Quarterly of the Journal of the Royal Astronomical Society* 33 (1992): 5–16.

Radtke, Bernd. "Towards a Typology of Abbasid Universal Chronicles" *OPSAS* 3 (1990): 1–18.

Raghib, Yusuf. "Lettres nouvelles de Qurra b. Šarīk." *JNES* 40/3 (1981): 173–187.

RCEA = Etienne Combe et al. *Répertoire chronologique d'épigraphie arabe*. Paris, 1931.

Rebenich, Stefan. "Late Antiquity in Modern Eyes." In Philip Rousseau (dir.), *A Companion to Late Antiquity*. Chichester: Wiley-Blackwell, 2009. 77–92.

Reinink, G. J. "The Beginnings of Syriac Apologetic Literature in Response to Islam." *Oriens Christianus* 77 (1993): 164–187.

Renoux, Annie. "Palais, cours et résidences." In Jean-Claude Schmitt and Otto G. Oexle (dir.), *Les tendances actuelles de l'histoire du Moyen Âge en France et en Allemagne. Actes des colloques de Sèvres (1997) et Göttingen (1998) organisés par le C.N.R.S. et le Max-Planck-Institut für Geschichte*. Paris: Publications de la Sorbonne, 2003. 351–356.

Retsö, Jan. *The Arabs in Antiquity: Their History from the Assyrians to the Umayyads*. London: RoutledgeCurzon, 2003.

Rice, David S. "Medieval Ḥarrān: Studies on its Topography and Monuments, I." *Anatolian Studies* 2 (1952): 36–84.

Riché, Pierre. *Les Carolingiens. Une famille qui fit l'Europe*. Paris: Pluriel, 1997.

Ricœur, Paul. *La mémoire, l'histoire, l'oubli*. Paris: Seuil, 2003.

Rigney, Ann. "Time for Visions and Revisions: Interpretative Conflict from a Communicative Perspective." *Storia della Storiografia* 22 (1992): 85–92.

Rihaoui, A. K. "Découverte de deux inscriptions arabes." *AAAS* 12–13 (1961–1962): 206–212.

Robinson, Chase F. *ʿAbd al-Malik*. Oxford: Oneworld, 2005.
Robinson, Chase F. "The Conquest of Khūzistān: A Historiographical Reassessment." BSOAS 67/1 (2004): 14–39.
Robinson, Chase F. *Empire and Elites after the Muslim Conquest: the Transformation of Northern Mesopotamia*. Cambridge: Cambridge University Press, 2000.
Robinson, Chase F. "Ibn al-Azraq, his Taʾrīkh Mayyāfāriqīn, and Early Islam." JRAS 3/6/1 (1996): 7–27.
Robinson, Chase F. *Islamic Historiography*. Cambridge: Cambridge University Press, 2003.
Robinson, Chase F. "A Local Historian's Debt to al-Ṭabarī: the Case of al-Azdī's *Taʾrīkh al-Mawṣil*." In Hugh Kennedy (ed.), *Al-Ṭabarī: A Medieval Muslim Historian and His Work*. Princeton: Darwin Press, 2008. 299–318.
Robinson, Chase F. "Al-Muʿāfā b. ʿImrān and the Beginnings of the Ṭabaqāt Literature." JAOS 116 (1996): 114–120.
Robinson, Chase F. "Neck-Sealing in Early Islam." JESHO 48/3 (2005): 401–441.
Robinson, Chase F. "Reconstructing Early Islam: Truth and Consequences." In Herbert Berg (ed.), *Method and Theory in the Study of Islamic Origins*. Leiden: Brill, 2003. 101–134.
Robinson, Chase F. "Review of Andrew Palmer, *The Seventh Century in the West-Syrian Chronicles* (Liverpool University Press, Liverpool, 1993)." JRAS 3/5 (1995): 97–101.
Robinson, Chase F. "The Study of Islamic Historiography: A Progress Report." JRAS 7/2 (1997): 199–227.
Robinson, Chase F. "Tribes and Nomads in Early Islamic Northern Mesopotamia." In Karin Bartl and Stefan R. Hauser (eds.), *Continuity and Change in Northern Mesopotamia from the Hellenistic to the Early Islamic Period*. Berlin: Berliner Beiträge zum Vorderen Orient 17, Dietrich Reimer Verlag, 1996. 429–452.
Robson, J. [Wensinck A. J.]. "Anas b. Mālik Abū Ḥamza." EI².
Rosen-Ayalon, Myriam (ed.). *Art et archéologie islamiques en Palestine*. Paris: PUF, 2002.
Rosen-Ayalon, Myriam. *Studies in memory of Gaston Wiet*. Jerusalem: Hebrew University of Jerusalem, 1977.
Rosenthal, Franz. "General Introduction." *The History of al-Ṭabarī*. vol. I. Albany: State University of New York Press, 1989. 3–154.
Rosenthal, Franz. *A History of Muslim Historiography*. Leiden: Brill, 1968.
Rosenthal, Franz. "Ibn ʿAbd al-Ḥakam." EI².
Rosenthal, Franz. "Ibn ʿĀʾidh." EI².
Rosenthal, Franz. "Ibn Sharya." EI².
Rosenthal, Franz. "The Influence of the Biblical Tradition on Muslim Historiography." In Bernard Lewis and P. M. Holt (eds.), *Historians of the Middle East*. London: Oxford University Press, 1962. 35–45.

Rotter, Gernot. "Abu Zurʿa al-Dimašqī (st. 281/894) und das Problem der frühen arabischen Geschichtsschreibung in Syrien." *Die Welt des Orients* 6/1 (1971): 80–104.

Rotter, Gernot. "Maslama b. ʿAbd al-Malik b. Marwān." *EI*².

Rotter, Gernot. "Zur Überlieferung einiger Historischer Werke Madāʾinīs in Ṭabarīs Annalen." *Oriens* 23–24 (1974): 103–133.

Rotter, Gernot. *Die Umayyaden und der zweite Bürgerkrieg (688–692)*. Wiesbaden, 1982.

Rousseau, Philip (dir.). *A Companion to Late Antiquity*. Chichester: Wiley-Blackwell, 2009.

Rousset, Marie-Odile. *L'Archéologie islamique en Iraq: bilan et perspectives*. Damascus: Institut français de Damas, 1992.

Rousset, Marie-Odile. "La moyenne vallée de l'Euphrate d'après les sources arabes." In Sophie Berthier (dir.), *Peuplement rural et aménagements agricoles dans la moyenne vallée de l'Euphrate, fin VIIe–XIXe siècle*. Damascus: PIFD, 2001. 554–571.

Rubin, Uri. "Apocalypse and Authority in Islamic Tradition: the Emergence of the Twelve Leaders." *Al-Qanṭara* 18 (1997): 11–42.

Rubin, Uri. "Prophets and Caliphs: the Biblical Foundations of the Umayyad Authority." In Herbert Berg (ed.), *Method and Theory in the Study of Islamic Origins*. Leiden: Brill, 2003. 73–99.

Rüsen, Jörn. "Some Theoretical Approaches to Intercultural Comparative Historiography." *History and Theory* 35/4 (1996): 5–22.

Russell, Kenneth W. "The Earthquake Chronology of Palestine and Northwest Arabia from the 2nd through the Mid-8th Century A.D." *BASOR* 260 (1985): 37–59.

Rydving, Hakan (ed.). *Al-Ṭabarī's History: Interpretations and Challenges*. Uppsala: Uppsala Universitet, 2007.

Sack, Dorothée. *Damaskus: Entwicklung und Struktur einer orientalisch-islamischen Stadt*. Mainz, 1989.

Sack, Dorothée. *Resafa IV. Die Grosse Moschee von Resafa-Ruṣāfat Hišām*. Mainz, 1996.

Sack, Dorothée, Helmut Becker, Manfred Stephani and Faris Chouker. "Resafa-Umland: Archäologische Geländebegehungen, geophysikalische Untersuchungen und Digitale Geländemodelle zur Prospektion in Resafa-Rusâfat Hisham. Bericht über die Kampagnen 1997–2001." *Damaszener Mitteilungen* 14 (2004): 207–232.

Ṣafwat, Ahmad Zaki. *Jamharat rasāʾil al-ʿarab*. 4 vol. Cairo: Muṣṭafā al-Ḥalabī, 1937.

Sakly, Mondher. "Wāsiṭ." *EI*².

Saliba, George. *Islamic Science and the Making of the European Renaissance*. Cambridge, MA and London: MIT Press, 2007.

Al-Sāmarrāʾī, Qāsim. "A Reappraisal of Sayf b. ʿUmar as a Historian in the Light of the Discovery of his *Kitāb al-Ridda wa al-Futūḥ*." In *Essays in Honour of Ṣalāḥ al-Dīn al-Munajjid*. London: Al-Furqān Islamic Heritage Foundation, 2002. 531–557.

Samir, Khalil. "Date de la mort d'Élie de Nisibe." *Oriens Christianus* 72 (1988): 124–132.

Sarre, Friedrich and Ernst Herzfeld. *Archäologische Reise im Euphrat- und Tigris-gebiet.* Berlin: D. Reimer, 1920.

Sauer, James A. "The Pottery of Jordan in the Early Islamic Periods." *SHAJ* I (1982): 329–337.

Sauvaget, Jean. *Alep, essai sur le développement d'une grande ville syrienne des origines au milieu du XIXe siècle.* Paris: Geuthner, 1941.

Sauvaget, Jean. "Châteaux omeyyades de Syrie. Contribution à l'étude de la colonisation arabe aux Ier et IIe siècles de l'hégire." *REI* 35 (1967): 1–52.

Sauvaget, Jean. "Les Ghassanides et Sergiopolis." *Byzantion* 14 (1939): 115–130.

Sauvaget, Jean. *Introduction à l'histoire de l'Orient musulman: éléments de bibliographie* (*édition refondue et complétée par Cl. Cahen*). Paris: A. Maisonneuve, 1961.

Sauvaget, Jean. *La mosquée omeyyade de Médine.* Paris, 1947.

Sauvaget, Jean. "Notes de topographie omeyyade." *Syria* 24 (1944–1945): 96–112.

Sauvaget, Jean. *Les perles choisies d'Ibn ach-Chihna, Matériaux pour servir à l'histoire de la ville d'Alep*, t. 1. Beirut: Institut français de Damas, 1933.

Sauvaget, Jean. "Le plan de Laodicée sur mer." *BEO* 4 (1934): 81–115.

Sauvaget, Jean. "Remarques sur les monuments omeyyades. I Châteaux de Syrie." *JA* 231 (1939): 1–59.

Sauvaget, Jean. "Les ruines omeyyades de 'Andjar." *Bulletin du Musée de Beyrouth* 3 (1939): 5–11.

Sauvaget, Jean. "Les ruines omeyyades du Djebel Seis." *Syria* 20 (1938): 239–256.

Savage, Elizabeth. "Early 'Abbāsid Coinage, Traces of the Past?" In Karin Bartl and Stefan R. Hauser (eds.), *Continuity and Change in Northern Mesopotamia from the Hellenistic to the Early Islamic Period.* Berlin: Berliner Beiträge zum Vorderen Orient 17, Dietrich Reimer Verlag, 1996. 173–184.

Savage-Smith, Emilie. "Memory and Maps." In Farhad Daftary and J. W. Meri (eds.), *Culture and Memory in Medieval Islam: Essays in Honour of Wilferd Madelung.* London: Tauris, 2003. 109–127.

Sbeitani, M. R., R. Darawcheh and M. Mouty. "The Historical Earthquakes of Syria: An Analysis of Large and Moderate Earthquakes from 1365 B.C. to 1900 A.D." *Annals of Geophysics* 48/3 (2005): 347–435.

Schacht, Joseph. "Mālik b. Anas." *EI*².

Schacht, Joseph. "On Mūsā b. 'Uqba's *Kitāb al-Maghāzī*." *Acta Orientalia* 21/4 (1953): 288–300.

Schacht, Joseph. *The Origins of Muhammadan Jurisprudence.* Oxford: Clarendon Press, 1950.

Schacht, Joseph. "A Revaluation of Islamic Traditions." *JRAS* (1949): 143–154.

Schacht, Joseph. "Sur l'expression "Sunna du Prophète"." In *Mélanges d'Orientalisme offerts à Henri Massé.* Tehran, 1963. 361–365.

Schick, Robert. *The Christian Communities of Palestine from Byzantine to Islamic Rule: A Historical and Archeological Study*. Princeton: Darwin Press, 1995.

Schick, Robert. "Palestine in the Early Islamic Period. Luxuriant Legacy." *Near Eastern Archaeology* 61/2 (1998): 74–108.

Schlumberger, Daniel. "Deux fresques omeyyades." *Syria* 25 (1946): 86–102.

Schlumberger, Daniel. "Les fouilles de Qasr el-Heir el-Gharbi (1936–1938). Rapport préliminaire." *Syria* 20 (1939): 195–238 and 324–373.

Schlumberger, Daniel. *Qasr el-Heir el Gharbi*. Paris: Geuthner, 1986.

Schmid, Karl and Joachim Wollasch (eds.). *Memoria. Der geschichtliche Zeugniswert des liturgischen Gedenkens im Mittelalter*. Munich, 1984.

Schmitt, Jean-Claude and Otto G. Oexle (dir.). *Les tendances actuelles de l'histoire du Moyen Âge en France et en Allemagne. Actes des colloques de Sèvres (1997) et Göttingen (1998) organisés par le C.N.R.S. et le Max-Planck-Institut für Geschichte*. Paris: Publications de la Sorbonne, 2003.

Schmitt, Jean-Claude. "L'appropriation du futur." In Jean-Claude Schmitt, *Le corps, les rites, les rêves, le temps. Essais d'anthropologie médiévale*. Paris: Gallimard, 2001. 416–435.

Schmitt, Jean-Claude. "Une réflexion nécessaire sur le document." In Jean-Claude Schmitt and Otto G. Oexle (dir.), *Les tendances actuelles de l'histoire du Moyen Âge en France et en Allemagne. Actes des colloques de Sèvres (1997) et Göttingen (1998) organisés par le C.N.R.S. et le Max-Planck-Institut für Geschichte*. Paris: Publications de la Sorbonne, 2003. 43–46.

Schmitt, Jean-Claude. "Le Temps. "Impensé" de l'histoire ou double objet de l'historien?" *Cahiers de civilisation médiévale* 48 (2005): 31–52.

Schœler, Gregor. *Écrire et transmettre dans les débuts de l'islam*. Paris: Islamiques, PUF, 2002.

Schœler, Gregor. *The Genesis of Literature in Islam: From the Aural to the Read*. Edinburgh: Edinburgh University Press, 2009.

Schœler, Gregor. "Foundations for a New Biography of Muḥammad: The Production and Evaluation of the Corpus of Traditions from 'Urwah b. al-Zubayr." In Herbert Berg (ed.), *Methods and Theory in the Study of Islamic Origins*. Leiden: Brill, 2003. 21–28.

Schœler, Gregor. "Mündliche Thora und Hadīṯ: Überlieferung, Schreibverbot, Redaktion." *Der Islam* 66 (1989): 213–251.

Schœler, Gregor. "Writing and Publishing. On the Use and Function of Writing in the First Centuries of Islam." *Arabica* 44 (1997): 423–435.

Schönig, Hannelore. *Das Sendschreiben des 'Abdalhamid b. Yahya (gest. 132/750) an den Kronprinzen 'Abdallah B. Marwan II. Ein Beitrag zur Kenntnis der frühen arabischen Prosaliteratur*. Stuttgart, 1985.

Sears, Stuart D. "An 'Abbasid Revolution Hoard from the Western Jazīra (al-Raqqa?)." *American Journal of Numismatics* 12 (2000): 171–193.

Sears, Stuart D. "Umayyad Partisan or Khārijite Rebel?: The Issue of 'Abd al-'Azīz b. MDWL?" *Studia Iranica* 31 (2002): 71–78.

Segal, J.-B. "Ibn al-'Ibrī." *EI*².

Seidensticker, Tilman. "Al-Akhṭal." *EI*³.

Sellheim, Rudolf. "Prophet, Chalif und Geschichte. Die Muhammed-Biographie des Ibn Isḥāq." *Oriens* 18/19 (1965/1966): 33–91.

Sellheim, Rudolf. "Al-Sam'ānī." *EI*².

Sellheim, Rudolf. *Der zweite Bürgerkrieg im Islam (680–692). Das Ende der Mekkanisch-Medinensischen Vorherrschaft*. Wiesbaden: Franz Steiner Verlag, 1970.

Sénac, Philippe. *La frontière et les hommes (VIII*ᵉ*–XII*ᵉ *siècle): le peuplement musulman au nord de l'Ebre et les débuts de la reconquête aragonaise*. Paris: Maisonneuve et Larose, 2000.

Serjeant, R. B. "Early Arabic Prose." In A. F. L. Beeston (ed.), *Arabic Literature to the End of the Umayyad Period*. Cambridge: Cambridge University Press, 1983. 114–153.

Shaban, M. A. *The 'Abbāsid Revolution*. Cambridge: Cambridge University Press, 1970.

Shaban, M. A. "Ibn A'tham." *EI*².

Shaban, M. A. *Islamic History: A New Interpretation*. 2 vol. Cambridge: Cambridge University Press, 1976.

Shacklady, H. "The 'Abbasid Movement in Khurāsān." *OPSAS* 1 (1986): 98–112.

Sharon, Moshe. "The Abbasid *Da'wa* Re-examined on the Basis of the Discovery of a New Source." In J. Mansur (ed.), *Arabic and Islamic Studies*. Ramat Gan: University of Bar Ilan, 1973. XXI–XLI.

Sharon, Moshe. "An Arabic Inscription from the Time of the Caliph 'Abd al-Malik." *BSOAS* 29/2 (1966): 367–372.

Sharon, Moshe. *Black Banners From the East*. Jerusalem and Leiden: The Magnes Press and E. J. Brill, 1983.

Sharon, Moshe. *Corpus inscriptionum arabicarum Palaestiniae* (*CIAP*). Leiden: Brill, 1997–.

Sharon, Moshe. "The Development of the Debate Around the Legitimacy of Authority in Early Islam." *JSAI* 5 (1984): 121–141.

Sharon, Moshe. "Qaḥṭaba b. Šabīb." *EI*².

Sharon, Moshe. *Revolt: The Social and Military Aspects of the 'Abbāsid Revolution*. Jerusalem: The Hebrew University, 1990.

Sharon, Moshe (ed.). *Studies in Islamic History and Civilization in Honour of Professor David Ayalon*, Leiden: Brill, 1986.

Sharon, Moshe. "The Umayyads as *Ahl al-Bayt*." *JSAI* 14 (1991): 115–152.

Shboul, Ahmad and Alan Walmsley. "Identity and Self-Image in Syria-Palestine in the Transition From Byzantine to Early Islamic Rule: Arab Christians and Muslims." *Mediterranean Archaeology* 11 (1998): 255–287.

Shboul, Ahmad. "On the Later Arabic Inscription in Qasr Burquʿ." *ADAJ* 20 (1975): 95–98.

Shoshan, Boaz. *Poetics of Islamic Historiography: Deconstructing Ṭabarī's History*. Leiden: Brill, 2004.

Sievers, Peter von. "Military, Merchants and Nomads: The Social Evolution of the Syrian Cities and Countryside During the Classical Period, 780–969/164–358." *Der Islam* 56 (1979): 212–244.

Sievers, Peter von. "Taxes and trade in the ʿAbbāsid Thughūr, 750–962/133–351." *JESHO* 25/1 (1982): 71–99.

Sijpesteijn, Petra. *Shaping a Muslim State: Papyri Related to a Mid-Eighth-Century Egyptian Official*. Ph. D. diss. Princeton University, 2004.

Sijpesteijn, Petra and Lennart Sundelin (eds.), *Papyrology and the History of Early Islamic Egypt*, Brill, Leiden, 2004.

Sijpesteijn, Petra, Lennart Sundelin, Sofia Torallas Tovar and Amalia Zomeño (eds.). *From al-Andalus to Khurasan: Documents from the Medieval Muslim World*. Leiden: Brill, 2007.

Silverstein, Adam. "Documentary Evidence for the early Barīd." In Petra Sijpesten and Lennart Sundelin (eds.), *Papyrolgy and the History of Early Islamic Egypt*. Leiden: Brill, 2004. 153–161.

Silverstein, Adam. "A New Source on the Early History of the Barīd." *Al-Abhath* 50–51 (2002–2003): 121–134.

Silverstein, Adam. "On Some Aspects of the Abbasid Barīd." In James E. Montgomery (ed.), *Abbasid Studies*. Leuven, 2004. 23–32.

Silverstein, Adam. *Postal Systems in the Pre-Modern Islamic World*. Cambridge: Cambridge University Press, 2007.

Snoek, J. A. M. "Canonization and Decanonization. An Annotated Bibliography." In Arie Van der Kooij and Karel Van der Toorn (eds.), *Canonization and Decanonization. Papers Presented to the International Conference of the Leiden Institute for the Study of Religions (LISOR), Held at Leiden 9–10 January 1997*. Leiden: Brill, 1998. 435–506.

Sourdel, Dominique and Janine. *La civilisation de l'Islam classique*. Paris: Arthaud, 1983 [1968].

Sourdel, Dominique and Janine. "Notes d'épigraphie et de topographie sur la Syrie du Nord." *Annales Archéologiques de Syrie* 3 (1953): 83–88.

Sourdel, Dominique. "Al-ʿAmq" *EI²*.

Sourdel, Dominique. "Appels et programmes politico-religieux durant les premiers siècles de l'islam." In George Makdisi, Dominique Sourdel and Janine Sourdel-Thomine (eds.), *Prédication et propagande au Moyen Age. Islam, Byzance, Occident*. Paris: PUF, 1983. 111–131.

Sourdel, Dominique. "La biographie d'Ibn al-Muqaffaʿ d'après les sources anciennes." *Arabica* 1/3 (1954): 307–323.

Sourdel, Dominique. "Dābiq." *EI²*.

Sourdel, Dominique. *L'état impérial des califes Abbassides* (*VIII*e–*X*e *siècle*). Paris: Islamiques, PUF, 1999.

Sourdel, Dominique. "La fondation umayyade d'al-Ramla." *Studien zur Geschichte und Kultur des vorderen Orients* (Festschrift B. Spuler). Leiden: Brill, 1981. 387–395.

Sourdel, Dominique. "Un pamphlet musulman anonyme d'époque 'Abbāside contre les Chrétiens." *REI* 34 (1966): 1–33.

Sourdel, Dominique. "La politique religieuse du calife 'abbaside al-Ma'mûn." *REI* XXX (1962): 27–60.

Sourdel, Dominique. "La Syrie au temps des premiers califes abbassides." *REI* 48/2 (1980): 155–175.

Sourdel, Dominique. *Le vizirat abbasside de 749 à 936* (*132 à 324 de l'Hégire*). 2 vol. Damascus: PIFD, 1959–1960.

Sourdel-Thomine, Janine. "Djābiya." *EI*².

Soucek, Priscilla Parsons. "Solomon's Throne/Solomon's Bath: Model or Metaphor?" *Ars Orientalis* 23 (1993): 109–134.

Soucek, Priscilla Parsons. "The Temple of Solomon in Islamic Legend and Art." In Joseph Gutmann, *The Temple of Solomon: Archaeological Fact and Medieval Tradition in Christian, Islamic and Jewish Art*. 1976.

Spellberg, Denise A. "The Umayyad North: Numismatic Evidence for Frontier Administration." *American Numismatic Society Museum Notes* 33 (1988): 119–127.

Spiegel, Gabrielle M. "Genealogy: Form and Function in Medieval Historical Narratives." *History and Theory* 22 (1983): 43–53.

Spiegel, Gabrielle M. "History, Historicism and the Social Logic of the Text in the Middle Ages." *Speculum* 65 (1990): 59–86.

Spiegel, Gabrielle M. "Political Utility in Medieval Historiography: A Sketch." *History and Theory* 14 (1975): 314–325.

Spiegel, Gabrielle M. *Romancing the Past: The Rise of Vernacular Prose Historiography in Thirteenth-Century France*. Berkeley and Los Angeles: University of California Press, 1993.

Spiegel, Gabrielle M. "Social Change and Literary Language: The Textualization of the Past in Thirteenth-Century Old French Historiography." *Journal of Medieval and Renaissance Studies* 17 (1987): 129–148.

Spiegel, Gabrielle M. "Theory into Practice: Reading Medieval Chronicles." In Erik Kooper (ed.), *The Medieval Chronicle. Proceedings of the 1st International Conference on the Medieval Chronicle, Driebengen/Utrecht 13–16 July 1996*. Amsterdam and Atlanta: Rodopi, 1999. 1–12.

Stern, Henri. "Notes sur l'architecture des châteaux umayyades." *Ars Islamica* 11–12 (1946): 72–97.

Stern, Henri. "Quelques œuvres sculptées en bois, os et ivoire de style omeyyade." *Ars Orientalis* I (1954): 119–131.

Stetkevych, Suzanne P. *The Poetics of Islamic Legitimacy: Myth, Gender and Ceremony in Classical Arab Ode*. Bloomington, IN: Indiana University Press, 2002.

Stetkevych, Suzanne P. "Umayyad Panegyric and the Poetics of Islamic Hegemony: al-Akhṭal's "Khaffa al-Qaṭīnu" ("Those That Dwelt with You Have Left in Haste")." *JAL* 28/2 (1997): 89–122.

Stock, Brian. *The Implications of Literacy: Written Language and Models of Interpretation in the Eleventh and Twelfth Centuries*. Princeton: Princeton University Press, 1983.

Straughn, Ian B. *Materializing Islam: an Archaeology of Landscape in Early Islamic Period Syria (c. 600–1000 CE)*. Ph. D. diss. University of Chicago, 2006.

Suermann, H. "Notes concernant l'apocalypse copte de Daniel et la chute des Omayyades." *Parole de l'Orient* 11 (1983): 329–348.

Takahashi, Hidemi. *Barhebraeus. A Bio-Bibliography*. Piscataway, NJ: Gorgias Press, 2005.

Tate, Georges. *Les campagnes de la Syrie du Nord du IIe au VIIe siècle*. Paris, 1992.

Tchalenko, Georges. *Villages antiques de la Syrie du nord*. Paris, 1958.

Tellenbach, Gerd. "Erinnern und Vergessen. Geschichtsbewusstein und Geschichtswissenschaft." *Saeculum* 46 (1995): 317–329.

Thompson, Martyn P. "Reception Theory and the Interpretation of Historical Meaning." *History and Theory* 32/3 (1993): 248–272.

Thompson, Robert W. "L'historiographie arménienne." In Muriel Debié (ed.), *L'historiographie syriaque*. Paris: Geuthner, 2009. 197–209.

Tillier, Mathieu. *Les cadis d'Iraq et l'état Abbasside (132/750–334/945)*. Damascus: IFPO, 2009.

Todt, Susanne R. "Die Syrische und die arabische Weltgeschichte des Bar Hebraeus – ein Vergleich." *Der Islam* 65/1 (1988): 60–80.

Togan, Zeki V. "Ibn Aʿtham al-Kufi." *Islamic Culture* 44/4 (1970): 249–252.

Tolan, John V. *Les Sarrasins. L'islam dans l'imagination européenne au Moyen Âge*. Paris: Aubier, 2003.

Töllner, Helmut. *Die türkischen Garden am Kalifenhof von Samarra, ihre Entstehung und Machtergreifung bis zum Kalifat al-Muʿtaḍids*. Bonn, 1971.

Toomer, G. J. "Al-Khwārizmī, Abū Jaʿfar Muḥammad ibn Mūsā." In Charles Coulson Gillispie (ed.), *Dictionary of Scientific Biography*, vol. 7. New York, 1973. 358–365.

Toorawa, Shawkat M. *Ibn Abī Ṭāhir Ṭayfūr and Arabic Writerly Culture: A Ninth-Century Bookman in Baghdad*. London and New York: RoutledgeCurzon, 2005.

Tor, D. G. "An Historiographical Re-examination of the Appointment and Death of ʿAlī al-Riḍā." *Der Islam* 78/1 (2002): 103–128.

Touati, Houari. *L'armoire à sagesse: bibliothèques et collections en Islam*. Paris: Aubier, 2003.

Touati, Houari. *Islam et voyage au Moyen Âge*. Paris: Le Seuil, 2000.

Toubert, Pierre. "Frontière et frontières: un objet historique." In *Castrum 4. Frontière et peuplement dans le monde méditerranéen au Moyen Âge*. Madrid, 1992. 9–17.

Toueir, K. "L'Héraklia de Hārūn al-Rachīd à Raqqa, réminiscences byzantines." In Pierre Canivet and Jean-Paul Rey-Coquais (eds.), *La Syrie de Byzance à l'Islam: VIIe–VIIIe siècles, Actes du colloque international, Lyon et Paris, 11–15 septembre 1990*. Damascus: PIFD, 1992. 179–186.

Toueir, K., Sergeij Chmelnizkij and Udo Becker. "Hiraqla." In Verena Daiber and Andrea Becker (eds.), *Raqqa III. Baudenkmäler und Paläste I*. Mainz: Philipp von Zabern, 2004. 135–156.

Trombley, Frank R. "The Documentary Background to the *History of the Patriarchs* of Pd.-Sawīrus ibn al-Muqaffaʿ." In Petra Sijpesteijn, Lennart Sundelin, Sofia Torallas Tovar and Amalia Zomeño (eds.), *From al-Andalus to Khurasan: Documents from the Medieval Muslim World*. Leiden: Brill, 2007. 131–152.

Troupeau, Gérard. "La connaissance des chrétiens syriaques chez les auteurs arabo-musulmans." *Orientalia Christiana Analecta Roma* 221 (1983): 273–280.

Troupeau, Gérard. "De quelques apocalypses conservées dans des manuscrits arabes de Paris." *Parole de l'Orient* 18 (1993): 75–87.

Tsafrir, Yoram and Gideon Foerster. "The Dating of the 'Earthquake of the Sabbatical Year' of 749 C. E. in Palestine." *BSOAS* 55/2 (1992): 231–235.

Tuqan, Fawwaz Ahmad. "'Abdallāh Ibn 'Alī: A Rebellious Uncle of al-Manṣūr." *Studies in Islam* 6 (1969): 1–26.

Ulbert, Thilo. "Die umaiyadische Anlage." In Michaela Konrad (ed.), *Resafa V. Der spätrömische Limes in Syrien*. Mainz: Phillip Von Zabern, 2001. 19–22.

Ulbert, Thilo. "Ein umaiyadischer Pavillon in Resafa-Ruṣāfat Ḥišām." *Damaszener Mitteilungen* 7 (1993): 213–231.

Urice, Stephen K. *Qasr Kharana in the Transjordan*. Durham, 1987.

Al-ʿUsh, M. A. F. "Inscriptions arabes inédites à Djabal Usays." *AAAS* 13 (1963): 225–237.

Valensi, Lucette. *Fables de la mémoire: la glorieuse bataille des rois*. Paris: Éditions du Seuil, 1992.

Van Der Kooij, Arie and Karel Van Der Toorn (eds.). *Canonization and Decanonization. Papers Presented to the International Conference of the Leiden Institute for the Study of Religions (LISOR), Held at Leiden 9–10 January 1997*. Leiden: Brill, 1998.

Van Ess, Joseph. *Anfänge muslimischer Theologie*. Beirut and Wiesbaden, 1977.

Van Ess, Joseph. "Les Qadarites et la Ġailānīya de Yazīd III." *SI* 41 (1970): 269–286.

Van Ess, Joseph. "Qadariyya." *EI*².

Van Ess, Joseph. "The Qadariyya in Syria: A Survey." *Proceedings of the First International Conference on Bilad al-Sham*. Amman, 1984. 53–59.

Van Ess, Joseph. *Theologie und Gesellschaft im 2. und 3. Jahrhundert Hidschra. Eine Geschichte des religiösen Denkens im frühen Islam*, I. Berlin: Walter de Gruyter, 1991.

Van Ess, Joseph. "Umar II and his Epistle against the Qadariya." *Abr-nahrain* 12 (1971–1972): 19–26.

Van Houts, Elisabeth. "Introduction: Medieval Memories." In Elisabeth Van Houts (ed.), *Medieval Memories: Men, Women and the Past, 700–1300*. Pearson Education Limited, Harlow, 2001. 1–16.

Van Lent, Jos. "Les apocalypses coptes de l'époque arabe: quelques réflexions." *Études Coptes V*. Leuven and Paris: Cahiers de la bibliothèque copte. 181–195.

Van Lent, Jos. "The Nineteen Muslim Kings in Coptic Apocalypses." *Parole de l'Orient* 25 (2000): 643–693.

Van Vloten, Gerlof. *De Opkomst der Abbasiden in Chorasan*. Leiden: E.J. Brill, 1890.

Van Vloten, Gerlof. "Recherches sur la domination arabe, le chiitisme, et les croyances messianiques sous le Khalifat des Omayades." *Verhandelingen der Koninklijke Akademie van wetenschappen te Amsterdam; Afdeling Letterkunde*, 1/3. Amsterdam: J. Muller, 1894.

Varisco, Daniel Martin. "Making "Medieval" Islam Meaningful." *Medieval Encounters* 13 (2007): 385–412.

Vasiliev, A. A. "Medieval Ideas of the End of the World: West and East." *Byzantion* 16 (1942–1943): 462–502.

Vernet, J. "al-Khʷārazmī." *EI*².

Vibert-Guigue, Claude. *Les peintures de Qusayr ʿAmra. Un bain omeyyade dans la bâdiya jordanienne*. Beirut: IFPO / Department of Antiquities of Jordan, 2007.

Vibert-Guigue, Claude. "La question de l'eau à l'époque omeyyade en Jordanie: approches iconographique et architecturale." *Aram* 13–14 (2001–2002): 533–567.

Vogts, Matthias. *Figures de califes entre histoire et fiction. Al-Walīd b. Yazīd et al-Amīn dans la représentation de l'historiographie arabe de l'époque ʿabbāside*. Beirut: Ergon Verlag, 2006.

Vries, Bert de. "Continuity and Change in the Urban Character of the Southern Hauran from the 5th to the 9th Century: The Archaeological Evidence at Umm al-Jimal." *Mediterranean Archaeology* 13 (2000): 39–45.

Vries, Bert de. "Urbanization in the Basalt Region of North Jordan in Late Antiquity: The Case of Umm el-Jimal." *SHAJ* 2 (1985): 249–256.

Walmsley, Alan G. *The Administrative Structures and Urban Geography of the Jund of Filastin and the Jund of al-Urdunn*. Ph. D. diss. University of Sydney, 1987.

Walmsley, Alan G. *Early Islamic Syria: An Archaeological Assessment*. London: Duckworth, 2007.

Walmsley, Alan G. "Fiḥl (Pella) and the Cities of North Jordan during the Umayyad and Abbasid Periods." *SHAJ* 4 (1992): 377–384.

Walmsley, Alan G. "The Friday Mosque of Early Islamic Jarash in Jordan." *Journal of the David Collection* 1 (2003): 110–131.

Walmsley, Alan G. "The 'Islamic City': The Archaeological Experience in Jordan." *Mediterranean Archaeology* 13 (2000): 1–9.

Walmsley, Alan G. "Production, Exchange and Regional Trade in the Islamic East Mediterranean: Old Structures, New Systems?" In Inge L. Hansen and Christopher Wickham (eds.), *The Long Eighth Century*. Leiden: Brill, 2000. 265–343.

Walmsley, Alan and Kristoffer Damgaard. "The Umayyad Congregational Mosque of Jarash in Jordan and its Relationship to Early Mosques." *Antiquity* 79/304 (2005): 362–378.

Wansbrough, John. *Quranic Studies: Sources and Methods of Scriptural Interpretation, Foreword, Translations, and Expanded Notes by Andrew Rippin*. New York: Prometheus Books, 2004 [1977].

Wansbrough, John. *The Sectarian Milieu: Content and Composition of Islamic Salvation History. Foreword, Translations, and Expanded notes by Gerald Hawting*. Amherst: Prometheus Books, 2006 [1978].

Ward-Perkins, Bryan. "Re-Using the Architectural Legacy of the Past." In G. P. Brogiolo and Bryan Ward-Perkins, *The Idea and Ideal of the Town between Late Antiquity and the Early Middle Ages*. Leiden: Brill, 1999. 225–244.

Watt, W. Montgomery. *Free Will and Predestination in Early Islam*. London: Luzac & Co, 1948.

Watt, W. Montgomery. "The Materials Used by Ibn Isḥāq." In Bernard Lewis and P. M. Holt (eds.), *Historians of the Middle East*. London: Oxford University Press, 1962. 23–34.

Wellhausen, Julius. *The Arab kingdom and its fall*. Trans. M. G. Weir. Calcutta: University of Calcutta, 1927.

Wellhausen, Julius. *Das arabische Reich und sein Sturz*. Berlin, 1960 [1902].

Wellhausen, Julius. "Die Kämpfe der Araber mit den Romäern in der Zeit der Umaijaden." *Nachrichten G. W. Gött.*, 1901.

Wellhausen, Julius. *The Religio-Political Factions in Early Islam*. Ed. and trans. Robin Clayton Ostle. Oxford, 1975.

Wellhausen, Julius. *Die religiös-politischen Oppositionsparteien im alten Islam*. Berlin, 1901.

Wellhausen, Julius. "Die religiös-politischen Oppositionsparteien im alten Islam." *Abh. G. W. Gött.* 5 (1901).

Wellhausen, Julius. *Skizzen und Vorarbeiten*, vol. 6. Berlin and New York: W. de Gruyter, 1985 [1899].

Weltecke, Dorothea. *Die «Beschreibung der Zeiten» von Mor Michael dem Grossen (1126–1199): eine Studie zu ihrem historischen und historiographiegeschichtlichen Kontext*. CSCO 594, Subsidia 110. Leuven: Peeters, 2003.

Weltecke, Dorothea. "Originality and Function of Formal Structures in the Chronicle of Michael the Great." *Hugoye* 3/2 (2000).

Weltecke, Dorothea. "Les trois grandes chroniques syro-orthodoxes des XIIe et XIIIe siècles." In Muriel Debié (ed.), *L'historiographie syriaque*. Paris: Geuthner, 2009. 107–135.

Weltecke, Dorothea. "The World Chronicle by Patriarch Michael the Great (1126–1199): Some reflections." *Journal of Assyrian Academic Studies* 11/2 (1997): 6–30.

Wensinck, A. J. *Concordance et indices de la tradition musulmane*. 8 vol. Leiden, 1936–1988.

Whelan, Estelle. "Forgotten Witness: Evidence for the Early Codification of the Quran." *JAOS* 118/1 (1998): 1–14.

Whitcomb, Donald S. "Amman, Hesban, and Abbasid Archaeology in Jordan." In Lawrence E. Stager, Joseph A. Green and Michael D. Coogan (eds.), *The Archaeology of Jordan and Beyond: Essays in Honor of James A. Sauer*. Winona Lake, IN: Eisenbrauns, 2000. 505–515.

Whitcomb, Donald S. "Archaeology of the 'Abbāsid Period: The Example of Jordan." *Archéologie Islamique* 1 (1990): 75–85.

Whitcomb, Donald S. "Islam and the Socio-Cultural Transition of Palestine – Early Islamic Period (638–1099 CE)." In Thomas E. Levy (ed.), *The Archaeology of Society in the Holy Land*. New York: Fact on Files, 1994. 489–501.

Whitcomb, Donald S. "Khirbet al-Karak Identified with Sinnabra." *Al-ʿUsur al-Wusta: The Bulletin of the Middle East Medievalists* 14/1 2002. 1–6.

Whitcomb, Donald S. "Mahesh Ware: Evidence of Early Abbasid Occupation from Southern Jordan." *ADAJ* 33 (1989): 269–285.

Whitcomb, Donald S. "The Misr of Ayla: New Evidence for the Early Islamic City." *SHAJ* V (1995): 277–288.

Whitcomb, Donald S. "Reassessing the Archaeology of Jordan of the Abbasid Period." *SHAJ* IV (1992): 385–390.

Whitcomb, Donald S. "Umayyad and Abbasid Periods." In Burton MacDonald, Russell Adams and Piotr Bienkowski (eds.), *The Archaeology of Jordan*. Sheffield, 2001. 503–513.

Whittow, Mark. "Decline and Fall? Studying Long-Term Change in the East." In Luke Lavan and William Bowden (eds.), *Theory and Practice in Late Antique Archaeology*. Leiden: Brill, 2003. 404–423.

Wickham, Christopher. *Framing the Early Middle Ages: Europe and the Mediterrean, 400–800*. Oxford: Oxford University Press, 2005.

Wickham, Christopher. *The Inheritance of Rome: A History of Europe from 400 to 1000*. New York: Viking, 2009.

Wickham, Christopher. "Topographies of Power: An Introduction." In Mayke De Jong and Frans Theuws (eds.), *Topographies of Power in the Early Middle Ages*. Leiden: Brill, 2001. 1–8.

Wiet, Gaston. "Būṣīr." *EI*².

Wilkinson, John. *Jerusalem Pilgrims Before the Crusades*. Warminster: Aris & Phillips, 2002 [1977].

Witakowski, Witold. *The Syriac Chronicle of Pseudo-Dionysius of Tell-Mahrē: A Study in the History of Historiography*. Uppsala: Almqvist and Wiksell, 1987.

Witakowski, Witold. "Elias Barshenaya's Chronicle." In W. Van Bekkum, J. W. Drijvers and A. C. Klugkist (eds.), *Syriac Polemics. Studies in Honour of Gerrit Jan Reinink*. Leuven: Peeters, 2007. 219–237.

Yanoski, Jean and Jules David. *Syrie ancienne et moderne*. Univers pittoresque, Asie, tome VII. Paris: Firmin Didot, 1848.

Yates, Frances A. *L'art de la mémoire*. Trans. Daniel Arass. Paris: Gallimard, 1975.

Yates, Frances A. *The Art of Memory*. London: Routledge and Kegan Paul, 1966.

Yerushalmi, Yosef H. *Zakhor. Histoire juive et mémoire juive*. Paris: Gallimard, 1991.

Young, M. J. L. "Arabic Biographical Writing." In M. J. L. Young, J. D. Latham and R. B. Serjeant (eds.), *Religion, Learning and Science in the 'Abbasid Period, The Cambridge History of Arabic Literature*. Cambridge: Cambridge University Press, 1990. 301–327.

Yucesoy, Hayrettin. "Between Nationalism and the Social Sciences: An Examination of Modern Scholarship on the 'Abbāsid Civil War and the Reign of al-Ma'mūn." *Medieval Encounters* 8/1 (2002): 56–78.

Yucesoy, Hayrettin. *Messianic Beliefs & Imperial Politics in Medieval Islam: The 'Abbāsid Caliphate in the Early Ninth Century*. Columbia, SC: University of South Carolina Press, 2009.

Zakeri, Mohsen. *Sāsānid Soldiers in Early Muslim Society: the Origins of 'Ayyārān and Futuwwa*. Wiesbaden: Harrasowitz, 1995.

Zakharia, Katia. "Le secrétaire et le pouvoir: 'Abd al-Ḥamīd Ibn Yaḥyā al-Kātib." In Floréal Sanagustin (ed.), *Les Intellectuels en Orient musulman*. Cairo: IFAO, 1998.

Zakkar, S. "Ibn Khayyāṭ al-'Uṣfurī." *EI*².

Zaman, Muhammad Qasim. "The Caliphs, the 'Ulamā', and the Law: Defining the Role and Function of the Caliph in the Early 'Abbāsid Period." *Islamic Law and Society* 4/1 (1997): 1–36.

Zaman, Muhammad Qasim. "Maghāzī and the Muḥaddithūn: Reconsidering the Treatment of "Historical" Materials in Early Collections of Ḥadith." *IJMES* 28 (1996): 1–18.

Zaman, Muhammad Qasim. "The Nature of Muḥammad al-Nafs al-Zakiyya's Mahdiship: A Study of Some Reports in Iṣbahānī's *Maqātil*." *Hamdard Islamicus* 13 (1990): 59–65.

Zaman, Muhammad Qasim. *Religion and Politics under the Early 'Abbāsids: The Emergence of the Proto-Sunnī Elite*. Leiden: Brill, 1997.

Zaman, Muhammad Qasim. "Al-Ya'qūbī." *EI*².

Zayyāt, Ḥ. "al-Tashayyu' li-Mu'āwiya fī 'ahd al-'Abbāsiyyīn." *Al-Mašriq* 26 (1928): 410–415.

Zettерstéen, Karl Vilhelm. "'Abd al-'Azīz b. Marwān." *EI*².

Zetterstéen, Karl Vilhelm. [C. E. Bosworth]. "Al-Muhtadī bi 'llāh, Abū, 'Abd Allāh Muḥammad b. Hārūn al-Wāthiḳ." *EI*².

Zimmermann, F. "The Particle Ḥattā, God's Knowledge of What We Shall Do and the Caliph 'Umar b. 'Abd al-'Azīz." In Alan Jones (ed.), *Arabicus Felix: Luminosus Britannicus. Essays in Honour of A. F. L. Beeston on his Eightieth Birthday*. Oxford: Ithaca Press Reading, 1991. 163–180.

Zolondek, Leon. "An Approach to the Problem of the Sources of the *Kitāb al-Agānī*." *JNES* 19/3 (1960): 217–234.

Zotz, Thomas. "L'étude des palais royaux en Allemagne." In Jean-Claude Schmitt and Otto G. Oexle (dir.), *Les tendances actuelles de l'histoire du Moyen Âge en France et en Allemagne. Actes des colloques de Sèvres (1997) et Göttingen (1998) organisés par le C.N.R.S. et le Max-Planck-Institut für Geschichte*. Paris: Publications de la Sorbonne, 2003. 307–326.

Zotz, Thomas. "Präsenz und Repräsentation. Beobachtungen zur königlichen Herrschaftspraxis im hohen und späten Mittelalter." In Alf Lüdtke (dir.), *Herrschaft als soziale Praxis. Historische und sozial-anthropologische Studien*. Göttingen: Veröffentlichungen des Max-Planck-Institut für Geschichte, 91, 1991. 168–194.

Index

ʿAbbās, I. 97, 324
Abbasid Revolution
actors' identities 289–290, 292–295, 324–327
and messianism 329–338
Christian sources 299–311, 300–301f
continuities with Umayyad era 297–299, 399
key episode 284–287, 310–311
legitimation 67, 68–73, 189, 245–247, 304–305, 312–314, 333–335
modern interpretations 298–299, 336–337
see also Abū Muslim; *dawla*; historiographic phases; key episodes; Khurāsān
ʿAbd Allāh b. ʿAbbās 183, 188
ʿAbd Allāh b. ʿAlī 304
campaign against the Byzantines 304, 315
death 288, 304, 320–321, 323
governor of the Shām 304
massacre of the Umayyads 162–164, 165–169
pretentions to the caliphate 288, 314–321
Syrian rebel 321–327
see also laqab (attribution)
ʿAbd Allāh b. Marwān 171
ʿAbd al-ʿAzīz al-ʿUmarī 400–401
ʿAbd al-Ḥakam b. Aʿyan b. al-Layth al-Aylī 278
ʿAbd al-Ḥamīd al-Kātib 23, 66, 97, 195, 293–294, 298, 388
ʿAbd al-Malik b. Marwān
and ʿAlī b. ʿAbd Allāh 183
and Solomon 193–195
and the Umayyad state 5, 34–36, 60, 142, 157–158, 341
and writing history 58–61
and al-Zuhrī 40
architectural program 176–177, 346
mobile exercise of power 352–353, 357–363, 374–375
patrimonialism 346–351, 374–375
see also al-Ḥajjāj; Ibn al-Zubayr
ʿAbd al-Malik b. Ṣāliḥ 397, 398, 401–402, 409–410, 418
ʿAbd al-Ṣamad b. ʿAlī 318
Abū al-ʿAbbās
designation by Ibrāhīm al-Imām 184, 303, 312–314
first Abbasid caliph 288, 304–305
massacre of the Umayyads 164–165
residence at al-Anbār 303, 314
succession 307, 312, 314–317
see also laqab (attribution)
Abū ʿAbd al-Raḥmān Khālid b. Hishām al-Umawī 51
Abū Ayyūb Sulaymān b. Makhlad al-Muryānī al-Khūzī 297
Abū al-Azhar al-Muhallab b. Abī ʿĪsā 320
Abū Bakr b. Muḥammad b. ʿAmr b. Ḥazm 274
Abū al-Faraj al-Iṣfahānī 102–103, 165, 251, 255
Abū Ḥamza al-Khārijī 117, 273
Abū Hāshim b. Muḥammad b. al-Ḥanafiyya 322
Abū al-Haydhām al-Murrī 400–402
Abū Ismāʿīl al-Azdī 31
Abū Jaʿfar. *See* al-Manṣūr
Abū Maʿshar Najīḥ 50
Abū Mikhnāf 29, 50, 73, 228–232
Abū Muḥammad al-ʿAbdī 162
Abū Mushir al-Ghassānī 33, 47–48
Abū Muslim
and ʿAbd Allāh b. ʿAlī 304, 318, 321
and ʿĪsā b. Mūsā 315, 317–318
and al-Manṣūr 318, 325
and the Shām 325
assassination 304
Khurāsān rebellion 287, 288, 289, 293, 302
Abū Nuʿaym al-Iṣfahānī 254
Abū Nukhayla 245
Abū Saʿīd b. Yūnus 90
Abū ʿUbayd Allāh Muʿāwiya b. ʿUbayd Allāh b. Yassār 297

Abū ʿUbayda b. al-Jarrāḥ 205
Abū Yūsuf Yaʿqūb 44, 73
Abū Zurʿa al-Dimashqī 32–33, 48, 49, 324
Agapius of Manbij
  Abbasid Revolution 302–304
  ʿAbd Allāh b. ʿAlī 325
  as a source 126–127
  Hishām 382, 384
  massacre of the Umayyads 166–167
  ʿUmar II 269
Agha, S. S. 290, 293
al-Aghdaf 376
ahl al-Jazīra. *See* Jazīra
ahl Khurāsān. *See* Khurāsān
ahl al-Shām. *See* Shām
ʿajam (definition) 294–295
  see also Persians
Akhbār al-dawla al-ʿAbbāsiyya. *See* Anonymous History of the Abbasids
Akhbār Majmūʿa 328
akhbāriyūn 21
al-Akhṭal 59–60, 101
Albert, Jean-Pierre 203, 250, 283
Aleppo 106, 128–129, 315, 345, 350, 396
Alexander the Great. *See* Dhū al-Qarnayn
ʿAlī b. ʿAbd Allāh b. ʿAbbās 183–184, 185–188, 317, 328, 335, 337
ʿAlī b. Abī Ṭālib,
  and the Umayyads 157, 166, 169, 181, 309, 311
  cursing of 252–253, 267
  ignored caliphate 49, 130, 132–133, 138, 142
  succession of the Prophet 70
ʿAlī b. Mujāhid 51
ʿAlī al-Riḍā 74
Alids
  ʿAbd Allāh b. ʿAlī 162–163, 168–169
    in Abbasid historiography 414
  al-Maʾmūn's policies 75
  Muḥammad al-Nafs al-Zakiyya 332, 335–336
  rivalry with the Abbasids 67, 69, 115–116, 166, 175, 177, 303, 337
  sources 83, 89, 335–336
ʿamal 73, 275
al-Aʿmāq (cycle of) 239
al-Amīn 74, 141, 179, 331, 397–398, 408
Amman (region) 376–378
ʿAmmūriyya 212, 239–240
Anas b. Mālik Abū Ḥamza 274
al-Anbār 303, 314, 315, 318, 404
al-Andalus 113, 175, 261
Andalusian sources 113, 222
ʿAnjar 345, 363–365, 375, 390–392
Anonymous History of the Abbasids 82, 184, 188, 257, 280–281, 287–288, 328, 335
Antichrist 267, 331
Antioch 406
Antipatris. *See* Nahr Abī Fuṭrus
apocalypse of Shenute 141, 330
apocalypses 113–116, 139–143, 194, 238–240, 330–332
  see also messianism
archives 85
Arjomand, S. A. 291, 317, 319
Amorium. *See* ʿAmmūriyya
archaeological sites
  ʿAnjar 363–365
  Baysān 381, 394
  al-Ḥumayma 99, 188
  in the Balqāʾ 375–378
  in Palmyrena 378–385
  Khirbat al-Mafjar 195–196, 197f
  Qaṣr al-Ḥayr al-Gharbī 367, 378
  Qaṣr al-Ḥayr al-Sharqī 181, 370, 378, 410
  Qaṣr al-Kharāna 376
  al-Qasṭal 377, 410
  al-Ṣinnabra 358–361
  see also architectural evidence
archaeological sources 22, 55–56, 98–100, 159, 181–183, 189, 369–370, 378
  see also archaeological sites; architectural evidence
architectural evidence
  And memory 154, 157–159, 159, 176–177
  dating 370–372
  Dome of the Rock 195, 342
  Hiraqla 403
  Khirbat al-Mafjar 195–196, 197f
  milestones 359–363
  mosque of al-Aqṣā 342
  mosque of Damascus 343–344
  mosque of al-Ramla 349–350
  mosques 342–344, 349–350
  Quṣayr ʿAmra 370–372

architectural evidence (*cont.*)
source of knowledge 98–99, 157–159, 340–341
symbolic spaces 195–196, 342–346
see also archaeological sites; Umayyad castles
Armenian sources 128, 135–136
Arnold of Regensburg 18
al-Aṣbagh (brother of ʿUmar II) 257
Ascalon 333
Assmann, Jan 4, 57, 152, 153–155, 250
ʿAwāna b. al-Ḥakam 50
ʿawāṣim 4, 397–398, 402, 413
al-Awzāʿī 46, 62
Ayla 187–188, 278
al-Azraq 376

Baalbek 190, 352, 358, 363
Bāb al-Abwāb 232–236
Bāb al-Lān 232
Bacharach, Jere L. 332, 373, 381
Badā 187–188
Baghdad
and writing history 68–88
architectural model 403, 404–405
caliphal residence 51, 80–81, 83–84, 408
fitna 74–75
foundation 67, 70–71, 181, 404–405
Hishām b. al-Ghāz 46
intellectual life 76–78, 124
military value 116, 409
Baḥshal (al-Wāsiṭī) 106
al-Bakhrāʾ 381
Bakhtarī b. al-Ḥasan 216
Bakkār b. Muslim al-ʿUqaylī 298
al-Balādhurī
ʿAbd al-Malik 352–353, 357–358
and Syrian memory 104
Banū Abī Muʿayṭ 385–386
Ibn al-Muqaffaʿ 317
massacre of the Umayyads 162
prosopography 81
al-Rāfiqa 406
reading framework 89
al-Saffāḥ 327
use of Syrian sources 30, 81
al-Walīd II 376
Yazīd b. al-Muhallab 228–232
Balʿamī 80, 85, 89, 208, 211–214, 215
Bālis 349, 382
Balqāʾ 183
Banū Abī Muʿayṭ 385–386
Baqī b. Makhlad al-Qurṭubī 48
al-Bāqir (Muḥammad b. ʿAlī) 257–258
Bar Hebraeus 128–129
Barmakids 73, 298, 398, 402, 409–410, 418
Barthold, W. W. 251, 274, 281
Bashear, S. 256, 258
Baṣra 12, 29, 230, 288, 304, 317, 318
Bates, Michael L. 115, 333
al-Baṭṭāl 203–204, 211, 212, 213
Baysān 72, 381, 394
Bayt al-Ḥikma 76
Bernhardt, John W. 356
Bible (references)
Daniel 134, 257, 308
David and Goliath 326
Isaiah 307, 331
Solomon 189–198
see also apocalypses; messianism
biographical dictionaries 103–106
biography 109–110
Blankinship, Khalid Y. 290, 312, 389
Bligh-Abramski, Irit I. 293, 297–298
Bone, H. J. 388
Bonner, Michael 398, 402
Bukhārā 116, 332
al-Bukhārī 47, 92
Būṣīr 285
Buṭrus b. Rāḥib 167

Cahen, Claude 134, 289, 337, 384
Calder, Norman 275
caliphal residences (movement)
al-Anbār 303
Baghdad 67, 83, 174
Byzantine proximity 73
Ḥarrān 66, 198, 309
Raqqa 73, 407, 408
al-Ruṣāfa 63–64
Sāmarrāʾ 77
see also al-Ḥumayma
caliphs and writing history
ʿAbd al-Malik 60
Hishām 63–64
al-Mahdī 72
al-Maʾmūn 74–78

caliphs and writing history (*cont.*)
- al-Manṣūr 70–71 174
- Marwān II 66
- al-Mutawakkil 77
- al-Rashīd 72–73
- al-Saffāḥ 72
- Sulaymān 61–62
- ʿUmar II 61–62, 270
- *see also* historiographic filter; historiographic phases; writing layers

Campbell, Sandra S. 148–149
Canard, M. 203–205, 210, 215–216
Carruthers, Mary 153
Cheddadi, Abdesselam 19, 24–25, 28, 86, 148
Chiffoleau, J. 163
Chinese sources 51*n*238, 143, 305
Christian sources
- Abbasid Revolution 399–311, 300f
- apocalypses 139–143
- campaign in the Caucasus 236–237
- chronicles 132–140
- echoing Umayyad sources 200–201, 270–271
- Hishām 382–385
- importance 56–57, 134–139
- siege of Constantinople 215–228, 217f, 219f–221f
- Theophilus of Edessa 123–132
- ʿUmar II 262–271, 263f, 264f

Chronicle of 705 132
Chronicle of 716 133, 262
Chronicle of 724 132, 267
Chronicle of 741
- as a source 129–130
- regionalisation of powers 347
- siege of Constantinople 222
- ʿUmar II 269

Chronicle of 754
- Abbasid Revolution 304–305
- as a source 129–130
- siege of Constantinople 222

Chronicle of 775 132, 267, 305
Chronicle of 813 133, 406
Chronicle of 818 138, 306
Chronicle of 819
- Abbasid Revolution 306–307, 309–310
- ʿAnjar 364
- as a source 130–131
- Hishām 382
- rampart in the Caucasus 236
- siege of Constantinople 217–218
- ʿUmar II 269–270

Chronicle of 846
- Abbasid Revolution 306–307, 309–310
- ʿAnjar 364
- as a source 130–131
- Hishām 382
- rampart in the Caucasus 236
- siege of Constantinople 217–218
- ʿUmar II 269–270

Chronicle of 1234
- Abbasid Revolution 302–303
- as a source 124–125, 128
- massacre of the Umayyads 167
- siege of Constantinople 216
- ʿUmar II 269

Chronicle of Zuqnīn
- Abbasid Revolution 307–308
- as a source 133–135
- campaign in the Caucasus 236–237
- dating 243
- definition of history 17–18
- natural disasters 266
- siege of Constantinople 216, 223–227

chronographies
- areas of production 10–11, 29–31
- chronological gap 10, 306
- divergences 31, 90, 207, 230, 236, 310
- emergence 32–35, 42–43
- establishing a vulgate 53–54, 83–89
- first Syrian authors 34–43

chronology of Qartamīn 131
Clausewitz, Carl von 201
Cobb, Paul M.
- Abbasid Shām 286, 292, 324, 341, 395, 399, 412
- historiography 107, 179

Conrad, Lawrence I. 79–80, 369
Constantine (VII) Porphyrogenitus 205, 306
Constantinople
- caliphal objectives 206–207
- mosque of 203–206, 214–215, 241
- symbolic possession 206, 213–214, 227
- under the Prophet's protection 241–242
- *see also* year 100 AH; key episodes; Maslama b. ʿAbd al-Malik

Continuatio of the Samaritan Chronicle 137–138, 267
Cook, David 85, 114–115, 240–241, 243, 259
Cook, Michael 12, 31, 119, 255
Coptic apocalypse of Daniel 140–141, 330
Cornette, J. 244
colours. *See* symbolism of colours
Crone, Patricia 117–118, 119, 254, 255, 271–272, 290, 324

Dābiq 131, 206, 208–209, 212, 333, 349, 357
al-Ḍaḥḥāk b. Qays 392
al-dajjāl. *See* Antichrist
Dakhlia, Jocelyne 412
Damascus
  Abbasid capital 80, 188, 325–326
  and Hishām 379, 381–382
  mosque 190–191, 342–344
  Qaysite revolt 400–402
  space of Umayyad memory 158
  Umayyad capital 182, 352, 358
Daniel, Elton L. 290
daʿwa 168–169, 184, 229, 281, 290, 291, 320, 336
  see also Abbasid Revolution; year 100 AH
dawla (definition) 295–296, 336, 338
  see also Abbasid Revolution
Dawrīn. *See* Dūrayn
Daylam 242–243
Dayr Murrān 270, 352, 357, 400
Dayr Simʿān 269–270
Décobert, Christian
  Islamic historiography 3
  Mālik b. Anas 275
  patrimonialism 347–349, 369, 412
  prophetic memory 148
Dennet, Daniel C. 390
Derat, M.-L. 353, 355, 357
Dhāt al-Himma 204
Dhū al-Qarnayn 232–236
Digenis Akritas 204
Dionysius of Tell-Maḥrē 124–125
documentary sources
  epigraphy 96–97
  letters 97
  numismatics 96–7
  papyri 96
  various documents 97–98

Dome of the Rock
  and Solomon 194–195
  construction 37
  inscriptions 43, 176–177, 344
  political and religious message 97, 342, 344–345
  symbolism 158, 176–177, 344–345
Donner, Fred M.
  messianism 255
  al-Ṭabarī 55, 91
  writing history 19–20, 24–33, 43, 45, 49
Duby, Georges 284
Dulūk 315
Dūrayn 380–381
Duri, A. A. 29, 39, 82
Dutton, Yasin 274–275

Egypt
  ʿAbd al-ʿAzīz 267
  and ʿUmar II's image 278–279
  Continuatio of the Samaritan Chronicle 137
  History of the Patriarchs of Alexandria 136, 267
  Ibn ʿAbd al-Ḥakam 109, 278
  Marwān I 358
  Marwān II's flight and death 130, 285, 288, 299, 303, 305, 326, 336
  massacre of the Umayyads 165
  papyri 95–96
  regionalisation of powers 347
  Ṣāliḥ b. ʿAlī 317–318, 396
  siege of Constantinople 222
  al-Ṭabarī 86, 90
  al-Yaʿqūbī 83
El-Hibri, Tayeb 68, 86, 149, 179, 402–403
Elad, Amikam 291, 292–294, 297–298, 359
Elias of Nisibis 76, 138–139
Eliezer (*Pirqē*) 331
epigraphic sources 96–97, 328, 344–345, 370–372, 381
epistolary sources 97, 194–195, 232, 252, 262–263, 293–294
Esch, Arnold 9–11, 94, 104, 143, 337
Euphrates
  and caliphal power 403–408
  caliphal residence at al-Anbār 303
  Hishām's works 381–384

Euphrates (*cont.*)
- site of al-Zaytūna 379–380
- symbolic border 181, 199, 309

faḍāʾil 108, 175
Faḍl b. Ṣāliḥ 396–397
al-Farazdaq 101–102, 117, 192, 194
Fentress, James 151
fitna
- ʿAbd Allāh b. ʿAlī 318–319
- and Islamic memory 157
- and revolution 311
- and writing history 49, 59, 60–61, 179–180, 311
- first *fitna* 25, 49, 112, 169, 181, 309, 311
- fourth fitna 74–80, 412
- in opposition to the dawla 296, 311
- second fitna 51, 58–61, 341, 347
- third *fitna* 65–68, 292, 296, 348, 388–391, 418–419
- *see also* Abbasid Revolution; Ibn al-Zubayr; key episodes; Qadarites

Fōrsāyē. *See* Persians
Fowden, Garth 373
Fried, Johannes 155
Frye, Richard N. 289
Furet, François 175, 310

García-Arenal, Mercedes 280
Gaube, Heinz 367, 374–375
Geary, Patrick J.
- creation of the past 182
- creative oblivion 68
- historical continuity 84, 180, 298–299, 419
- memory 150–153
- oral vs. written 153
- relation to the past 8, 18, 84–86, 145–146, 281–282

Geertz, Clifford 339, 353–354, 418
Genequand, Denis
- ephemeral landscapes 412–413, 419
- Qaṣr al-Ḥayr al-Sharqī 370
- Quṣayr ʿAmra 370
- sites in the Balqāʾ 377
- sites at Palmyrena 378
- Umayyad agriculture 366–367
- *see also* Umayyad castles

geographic sources 107–108, 149
Ghaylān al-Dimashqī 38, 47, 64
Ghūṭa 267, 400–401
Gil, Moshe 278
Gilliot, Claude 92
Goeje, M. J. de 91
Gog and Magog 234, 237–238, 238, 242, 282
Goitein, S. D. 292, 294, 297
Grabar, Oleg 181, 294, 367, 371
Greek apocalypse of pseudo-Daniel 141–142
Griffith, Sidney H. 308
Gryaznevitch, P. A. 82
Günther, S. 153

ḥadīth
- and codification 43–44, 62
- and messianism 258–260
- and capturing Constantinople 241–242
- dictated to al-Zuhrī 40–41
- Syrian transmitters 36–49
- ʿUmar II 271–273

al-Ḥafṣ b. Nuʿmān al-Umawī 328
al-Ḥajjāj 36, 60–61, 112, 157, 183, 251, 274
Ḥajjī Khalīfa 91
Halbwachs 151–152
Ḥammām al-Sarākh 376
Harrak, Amir 134–135
Ḥarrān
- and ʿAbd Allāh b. ʿAlī 316, 318, 327
- and the *Chronicle of 846* 131
- death of Ibrāhīm al-Imām 164, 184, 287, 303, 312–314
- Qaysite context 66
- Umayyad capital 66, 112, 198, 296, 309, 349, 391, 404

al-Ḥārith b. Surayj al-Tamīmī 294
Hārūn al-Rashīd
- and ʿAbd al-Malik b. Ṣāliḥ 397
- and jihād 402–403, 412
- and Maslama b. ʿAbd al-Malik 246–247
- and the Shām 397–398
- Antioch 406
- Byzantine campaigns 402–403, 410
- death and succession 73–77, 178–180, 408, 418
- patrimonialism 397–398
- Raqqa 407–408
- siege of Constantinople 245–247

al-Ḥasan b. ʿAlī 260
Hawting, G. R. 7, 12, 91
Heraclius 241–242
Herbelot (Barthélemi d') 91
heroisation 200–201, 202–203, 227–228, 231–232, 249–250, 271–272
  see also Maslama b. ʿAbd al-Malik; ʿUmar II
Hillenbrand, Robert 350, 365
Hinds, Martin 117, 254, 271–273
Hiraqla 403
Hishām b. ʿAbd al-Malik
  and al-Manṣūr 172–173
  and Maslama b. ʿAbd al-Malik 231–232
  and Palmyrena 349, 378–384
  and Solomon 192
  and ʿUmar II 270, 282–283
  and al-Walīd II 41–42
  and al-Zuhrī 63–65
  mobile exercise of power 379–385
  see also Qaṣr al-Ḥayr al-Gharbī; Qaṣr al-Ḥayr al-Sharqī; al-Ruṣāfa; al-Zaytūna
Hishām b. al-Ghāz 46
Ḥiṣn Maslama 349
historians
  Abbasid period 46–49, 73
  and Bayt al-Ḥikma 76
  and memory 150–152, 155–157
  and poetry 100–103
  conditions of knowledge 57
  definition of the Abbasid Revolution 287–299
  messianic context 116–117
  search for continuity 84
  al-Ṭabarī's influence 88–92
  ties to power 59–61, 71–73
  Umayyad period 34–43
historical conscience
  emergence 23–28
  first chronographies 32–35
historical material
  and memory 145–146, 155
  apocalypses 113–116
  architectural evidence 154
  common kernel 55, 168–169, 227
  exclusivity 55
  geography 107–108, 149
  heresiographies 116–118
  khabar 18–22, 82
  transmission as 22
historical sources. *See* archaeological sources; architectural evidence; documentary sources; epigraphic sources; narrative sources; numismatic sources
historicity
  and Muslim identity 26–28, 59–60, 85–86
  and the Qurʾān 23–26
historiographic filter
  Abū Mikhnāf 73
  and external sources 122
  and memory sedimentation 177
  definition 53–54
  al-Madāʾinī 78
  Sayf b. ʿUmar 73
  al-Ṭabarī 87, 88–92, 215
  al-Wāqidī 78
  al-Zuhrī 64–65
  see also caliphs and writing history; historiographic phases; writing layers
historiographic phases
  Abbasid legitimation 69–73, 167–169, 173–174, 280–283, 296–297, 320–321, 326, 334–335
  Hishām's caliphate 63–65, 218, 236, 243, 270–271, 383–384
  Marwanid affirmation 58–61
  Marwanid reforms 61–63
  al-Mutawakkil's caliphate 80–83
  post-Sāmarrāʾ 83–88, 179–180, 214–215
  al-Rashīd's succession 74–80, 179–180
  third fitna 65–66
  see also Abbasid Revolution
History of the Patriarchs of Alexandria 136–137, 267, 299, 326, 377
Hitti, Philip K. 286
Homs
  and axes of communication 358, 363
  and Hishām 386
  apocalyptic traditions 114
  narrative subject 106
  rebellion 392, 402
  sources 31, 37, 42, 45, 126

Hoyland, Robert G. 120, 129–130, 134, 136, 141, 262
al-Ḥumayma 99, 108, 183–189, 285–287, 312–314, 321–323, 335, 340
Humphreys, R. Stephen 84–85, 289
al-Ḥusayn b. ʿAlī 116, 157, 163, 164–166, 169
hypomnēma 14, 149

Ibn ʿAbd al-Ḥakam 78, 273, 274, 277–278
Ibn Abī al-Ḥadīd 316
Ibn Abī Ṭāhir Ṭayfūr 76
Ibn al-ʿAdīm 104–106
Ibn ʿĀʾidh al-Dimashqī 33, 48, 81
Ibn ʿAsākir
  ʿAbd Allāh b. ʿAlī 323
  Abū al-Haydhām al-Murrī 400
  and ʿUmar II 255
  as a source 104–105, 395, 400
  mosque of Damascus 190, 344
  Taʾrīkh madīnat Dimashq 104–105
  transmitter of Sayf b. ʿUmar 16
Ibn Aʿtham al-Kūfī 79–80
  siege of Constantinople 211–214, 215, 223
  Yazīd b. al-Muhallab 229–232
Ibn al-Athīr 255
Ibn al-Faqīh 108
  mosque of Constantinople 205
  mosque of Damascus 191–192, 343
Ibn Ḥajar al-ʿAsqalānī 333
Ibn Ḥanbal 47, 259
Ibn Ḥawqal 108, 158, 233
Ibn Hishām
  and Ibn Isḥāq 34
  authenticity 71
Ibn Isḥāq
  at al-Manṣūr's court 71
  Medina school 29, 31
  works 50, 71
Ibn al-Jawzī 254
Ibn Kathīr 109–110
Ibn Khaldūn
  reading framework 111–113
  role of history 44–45
  Solomon and Islam 191
  Solomon and Umayyads 192–194
  ʿUmar II 253, 260
Ibn Manẓūr 105, 187
Ibn al-Muqaffaʿ 44, 174, 317, 319, 394
Ibn al-Nadīm 33, 50
Ibn Qutayba 17, 37, 161, 257
Ibn Saʿd 78, 105, 271
Ibn Shiḥna 350
Ibn al-Zubayr
  and the Abbasids 183, 322–323
  and the *Anonymous History of the Abbasids* 188
  consequences of revolt 20, 40, 58–59
  in the Syriac sources 138, 309
  legitimate caliph 138, 339–341
  Zubayrid memory 148
Ibrāhīm b. Ṣāliḥ b. ʿAlī 397
Ibrāhīm b. ʿUthmān b. Nahīk al-ʿAkkī 407
Ibrāhīm al-Imām 164, 184, 287–288, 302–303, 312–313, 317, 320, 321
Imbert, F. 371
inscription of Ehnesh 333
Iraq
  and spaces of memory 178–183
  and writing history 9–12, 30–33, 68–88, 336–337, 414–415
  Iraqi-Abbasid *memoria* 180–183, 189, 198–199, 416
  forgotten Umayyad space 182–183
  see also Abbasid Revolution; Baghdad; caliphal residences; Euphrates; al-Ḥajjāj; Maslama b. ʿAbd al-Malik; Sāmarrāʾ; vulgate
ʿĪsā b. ʿAlī 317–318
ʿĪsā b. Mūsā
  and ʿAbd Allāh b. ʿAlī 320–321
  caliphal pretentions 315–321
al-Iṣfahānī 102–103
Isḥāq b. Muslim al-ʿUqaylī 298
isnād
  authenticity 20–21
  chain of transmission 78, 147
  collective *isnād* 54–55
  emergence 19–20
  isnād/khabar pair 18–22, 82, 106
  loss of importance 86
  manipulation 255
  memorisation 147, 149
  siege of Constantinople 207–209
  ʿUmar II 271–273, 274

Jabal Says 374
al-Jābiya 352, 357, 362
al-Jāḥiẓ 111
Jarīr 101–102, 194, 251
al-Jarrāḥ b. ʿAbd Allāh al-Ḥakamī 237
Jazīra
  ʿAbd Allāh b. ʿAlī 315, 318, 324–325, 337
  ahl al-Jazīra 315, 324–325, 337, 391, 396
  al-Azdī 106
  and Syriac sources 122, 278–279
  Banū Ṣāliḥ 397
  Euphrates as border 181
  Isḥāq b. Muslim al-ʿUqaylī's revolt 298
  al-Manṣūr 298, 304
  Marwān II 196–198, 389–390, 391
  Marwanid administrative entity 4, 244–245
  Maslama b. ʿAbd al-Malik 217–218, 232–233, 244–245
  Maymūn b. Mihrān 38
  monasteries 122
  Ṣāliḥ b. ʿAlī 396
  see also Euphrates
Jazīra ibn ʿUmar 363
Jerusalem
  and mobile exercise of power 359, 411
  and Solomon 190
  and Umayyad caliphs 375
  al-Mahdī 252, 397, 411
  al-Manṣūr 411
  al-Muqaddasī 108
  Thawr b. Yazīd al-Kalāʿī 45
  ʿUmar I 256
  Umayyad architectural program 345
  vs. Mecca 40
  see also Dome of the Rock; Palestine
John of Daylam 357–358
John of Wasīm 136, 299
Judd, Steven C. 89, 390
Juynboll, G. H. A. 272

Kalb 89, 158, 341
  see also Yemenites
Kallinikos. *See* Raqqa
Keaney, Heather N. 88
Kennedy, Hugh 369, 384, 396, 407, 412
key episodes
  Abū al-ʿAbbās's succession 306–307
  Abū al-Haydhām al-Murrī's revolt 400–401
  and history of the Shām 339
  assassination of al-Walīd II 302, 381
  battle of al-Ḥarra 58–59
  battle of Marj Rāhiṭ 60, 341
  battle of Ṣiffīn 132, 157, 169, 181
  battle of Zāb 157, 285, 288, 303, 336–337
  al-Ḥumayma as Abbasid stronghold 183–189, 287–288
  Ibn al-Zubayr's anti-caliphate 58–59
  al-Manṣūr's caliphate 169–173
  massacre of the Umayyads 160–170
  miḥna 57, 179
  al-Rashīd's death 179–180, 408, 419
  siege of Constantinople 141–142, 202–228, 239–240, 261–262
  siege of Mecca 157
  Umayyad downfall 115, 140, 285
  Umayyad memoria 157–159
  year 100 AH 114–115, 184
  see also Abbasid Revolution; Abū Muslim; Khurāsān
khabar
  isnād/khabar pair 18–22, 82, 106
Khālid b. Maʿdān al-Kalāʿī al-Ḥimṣī 37, 244
Khālid al-Qasrī 186
Khalidi, Tarif 20, 25, 27, 89, 101
Khalīfa b. Khayyāṭ
  and Ibn ʿĀʾidh 48
  and al-Khwārizmī 76
  first chronography 28, 81
  massacre of the Umayyads 161–162
  prosopography 81
  siege of Constantinople 215
  use of Syrian sources 30, 81
al-Khawlānī 106
Khazars 201–202, 228, 230, 232–236, 242
Khirbat al-Bayḍāʾ 374–375
Khirbat al-Mafjar 195–196, 197f
Khirbat al-Minya 365
Khunāṣira 252
Khurāsān
  Abbasid Revolution 287–288, 289–290, 291, 293, 302–303, 336, 391–392
  ahl Khurāsān 166–167, 293, 315, 324, 406, 409
  and narrative sources 285, 305, 393

Khurāsān (*cont.*)
governors 74, 112, 212, 229, 230, 244, 293, 333
Hārūn al-Rashīd 408
messianic expectations 333
theory of schools 25–26
al-Khwārizmī 76, 83, 139, 235
King, G. D. R. 374
kitāb (definition) 14
Kitāb al-Aghānī. *See* Abū al-Faraj al-Iṣfahānī
Kitāb al-Fitan. *See* Nuʿaym b. Ḥammād
Kitāb al-ʿUyūn 210–211
Kohlberg, E. 116–117
Kūfa
and Abū al-ʿAbbās 82, 288, 304, 313
and Abū Jaʿfar al-Manṣūr 304
theory of schools 29, 31
Kuthayyir ʿAzza 377
kuttāb 60

Lammens, Henri 7, 8, 101, 183, 286, 366
Landau-Tasseron, Ella 14–17, 59, 279 *n*171
laqab (attribution)
al-Hādī 334
al-Mahdī 115–116, 329, 332–334
al-Manṣūr 332
al-Marḍī 334
al-Mu'taman 398
al-Rashīd 334
al-Saffāḥ 165, 327–329, 417
Lassner, Jacob 149, 291, 317, 320
Lauwers, Michel 176
Le Goff, Jacques 155, 279
Lecker, Michael 39, 187–188
Leder, Stefan 22
Leo III
correspondence with ʿUmar II 135–136, 261–262, 267
siege of Constantinople 203–232
Lewis, Bernard 142, 295, 297, 331
Łewond
as a source 135–136
campaign in the Caucasus 236
correspondence between ʿUmar II/Leo III 261
siege of Constantinople 224–228
ʿUmar II 267
libraries 27, 65–66, 76, 90
licitness of writing 12–14, 59
literary sources 203–205
see also poetry
literate administration 60–61

Maʿān 158
al-Madā'inī
Abū al-Haydhām al-Murrī 400
and Ibn Aʿtham al-Kūfī 80
historiographic filter 78
siege of Constantinople 208–209, 215
madīnat al-Fār. *See* Ḥiṣn Maslama
madīnat al-Qahr 212–214
mahdī 115, 256–262, 279–280
al-Mahdī
messianic dimension 72, 115–116
al-Rāfiqa 405
Umayyad memory 69–70, 176–177
Malaṭya 396
Mālik b. Anas 39, 42–43, 45, 64, 193, 273–278, 280
al-Ma'mūn 74–78, 121, 139, 175–177, 179–180, 331, 398
man with forty cubits 210
Manbij 402
al-Manṣūr
and Umayyad memory 169–173, 176
caliphal pretentions 288, 318–319
elimination of ʿAbd Allāh b. ʿAlī 320–322
laqab 331–332
legitimacy 321–324
messianic dimension 331–332
patrimonialism 395–397
al-Rāfiqa 403–407
Umayyad downfall 304
see also Abū Muslim; Alids; Baghdad
al-Maqrīzī 110–111
Martinez-Gros, Gabriel 111–112
Marwān II
and Solomon 198
caliphal pretentions 390–391
flight and death 303, 305, 306, 326
governor 390
Ḥarrān 349
Ibrāhīm al-Imām's death 184, 288, 312–314
mobile exercise of power 391–392
rise to power 302–303
see also key episodes
al-Masīḥiyya 213–214

Maslama b. ʿAbd al-Malik
  administrator 244–245, 349, 383–384, 390
  against Yazīd b. al-Muhallab 229–230
  and Dhū al-Qarnayn 232–234
  and Hishām 230, 231–232, 245, 282
  and ʿUmar II 247–248, 249–250, 281, 282
  combat hero 201–202, 231–232, 238–248
  in the Caucasus 230–238, 242
  messianic dimension 238
  siege of Constantinople 202–228
Maslama b. Hishām 41, 323
al-Masʿūdī
  Abū al-ʿAbbas's succession 322–323
  Antioch 406
  assassination of ʿAbd Allāh b. ʿAlī 319–320
  al-Ḥumayma 186–187
  al-Manṣūr 169–173, 334
  massacre of the Umayyads 161
  rampart in the Caucasus 235
  al-Saffāḥ 328
  siege of Constantinople 212
  al-Ṣinnabra 358
  sources 50–51, 82, 106, 113, 127
  ʿUmar II 252, 270
Maymūn b. Mihrān 38, 81
McKitterick, Rosamond 152, 178, 419
Mecca
  Abū Jaʿfar al-Manṣūr 288, 315, 322
  Hishām 117, 378, 386
  Hārūn al-Rashīd 398
  Ibn al-Zubayr 36, 40
  al-Maqrīzī 110
  Muḥammad b. al-Ḥanafiyya 188
  siege of 157
  Thawr b. Yazīd al-Kalāʿī 45
  vs. Jerusalem 40
Medina
  ʿAbd al-Malik b. Ṣāliḥ 397
  and the Umayyads 111
  al-Mahdī 96, 176, 335
  Mālik b. Anas 42, 275, 276
  mosque of 69, 176, 335
  Samhūdī 187
  theory of schools 29–32
  Thawr b. Yazīd al-Kalāʿī 45
  ʿUmar II 257, 273–274, 276, 278–279
  ʿUrwa b. al-Zubayr 36
  al-Zuhrī 39
memory
  and Islam 147–150, 169, 272
  collective 150–152
  cultural 153–155
  historical material 155
  memorial competition 159
  memorial culture 147–149
  social 103–104, 146, 151
  see also key episodes; memoria; architectural evidence; remembrance; oblivion
memoria
  Abbasid 180–181, 188–189, 280–283
  as culture 151
  as research subject 147–155
  as social phenomenon 151, 153–154
  reuse 173–174, 175–176, 189, 199
  Shām 105, 108, 198–199
  Umayyad 155–156, 189–199, 246–248, 278–283, 345–346
  see also key episodes; memory; architectural evidence
memorial culture 147–149
  see also memoria
Merv 74, 77, 114
Mesopotamia (Upper). *See* Jazīra
messianic dimension
  Abbasids 71, 183–185, 326, 326–338
  al-Hādī 334
  al-Mahdī 72, 115–116, 332–333
  al-Manṣūr 331–332
  Maslama b. ʿAbd al-Malik 238
  Muḥammad al-Nafs al-Zakiyya 70
  al-Rashīd 334
  ʿUmar b. al-Khaṭṭāb 255–256
  ʿUmar II 256–262, 280–281
  see also laqab (attribution)
messianic expectations 62, 72, 85, 113–116, 158–159, 238–239, 262–266, 279–280
  (*see also* messianism)
messianism
  and Islam 255–256
  context 76, 114–117, 142, 258–261, 329–330

messianism (*cont.*)
use 327–328
see also year 100 AH; apocalypses; messianic expectations; messianic dimension; Sufyānī; myth of return
methodology
comparative historiography 123
interpretation of the Abbasid Revolution 289–299
search for lost sources 53–54, 57–58, 340–341
transmission as a historical object 21–22
use of external sources 56–57
use of memory 146
Michael the Sabaite 308
Michael the Syrian
as a source 124–125, 125–128
Hishām 384
natural disasters 262–266
Raqqa 407
ʿUmar II 261, 268–269
miḥna 75, 77–78
mobile exercise of power
Abbasid 395–403
and patrimonialism 353–354, 374–375, 385, 395, 411–413
definition 353–358
pre-modern era 353–358
territorial control 352–358, 395–403, 410–413
Umayyad 357–365, 374–375, 378, 384–385, 392–393
Umayyad castles 359, 365, 365–385, 378, 410–411
Morony, Michael G. 297
Mordtmann, A. D. 91
Moscati, Sabatino 160
Mosul (Mawṣil) 106, 129, 315, 392, 408
Motzki, Harald 20, 275
Mshattā 377–378
al-Muʾarrij b. ʿAmr al-Sadūsī 72
Muʿāwiya
and Solomon 192–194
and ʿUbayd b. Sharya 33–34
and Umayyad *memoria* 85, 157–159, 175, 252, 260
first fitna 169, 181, 309, 311
in the sources 46, 49, 50, 331
patrimonialism 347
siege of Constantinople 241
al-Ṣinnabra 358
Syrian coast 45
writing layers 101
Muʿāwiya II 259
Muḍarites. *See* Qaysites
Muḥammad b. ʿĀʾidh al-Dimashqī. *See* Ibn ʿĀʾidh
Muḥammad b. ʿAlī b. ʿAbd Allāh b. al-ʿAbbās 186, 246, 281, 287
Muḥmmad b. al-Ḥanafiyya 188
Muḥammad b. Ṣāliḥ b. al-Nattāḥ 81–82
Muḥammad b. al-Walīd b. ʿĀmir al-Zubaydī al-Ḥimṣī 42
Muḥammad al-Nafs al-Zakiyya 70, 332, 335, 337
al-Muhtadī 281
mujaddid 114, 251, 256, 280
al-Muqaddasī 108, 205, 342–343
Muqātil al-ʿAkkī 316
Muqātil b. Sulaymān 20–21, 234
Murad, M. Q. 255
Mūsā b. ʿĪsā b. ʿAlī 401
Musil, Alois 366, 370–373, 376
al-Mutawakkil 80–81, 180, 188, 325, 412
Mutiʿ b. Iyās 333
al-Muwaqqar 376, 410

Nahr Abī Fuṭrus 161
narrative sources
and orality 13–14
and Qurʾān 23–24
authenticity 251–252
caliphal control 55, 68
chronological gap 10, 310–311
common kernel 55–56, 168, 227–228, 278, 280–281
concurrent versions 32–33, 89, 94, 160–161, 164–165, 223, 228–232, 310–311
dating 215–216, 243, 270–271, 275, 282–283
distortions 11–12, 14–15, 17–18, 49–50, 68, 312–314
external sources 118–120
gaps 11–12, 23
historical material 55–56

narrative sources (*cont.*)
  intercultural transmission 121–123, 215–216
  licitness of writing 13–14
  oblivion 14–15, 68, 310
  representativity 11–12
  transmission 9–10, 14, 51–52, 53–56
Naṣr b. Sayyār 293
Nisibis 138, 288, 304, 318, 337
Nora, Pierre 149, 152, 157
Northedge, Alastair 366, 368, 371
Nuʿaym b. Ḥammād 114, 239, 242, 336
numismatic sources 96–97, 116, 332, 404, 408
numismatics. *See* numismatic sources

oblivion
  and orality 152
  as social revenge 154–155
  of narrative sources 14–15, 51–52, 309–310, 325–326
  prior to historiography 146–147
  strategy of compilers 51–52, 145–146, 160–162, 168, 320–321
  see also memory; memoria
Oexle, O. G. 57, 153–154
Omar, Farouk 289
orality
  and oblivion 152
  and transmission 13–14
  coexistence with writing 152–154

Palestine
  and al-Mahdī 411
  and Ṣāliḥ b. ʿAlī 396
  and Sulaymān b. ʿAbd al-Malik 348–349
  Continuatio of the Samaritan Chronicle 137–138
  sources 72, 106, 115, 308
  see also key episodes; Nahr Abī Fuṭrus
Palmyra
  and Marwān II 198
  and Solomon 190
  Umayyad architectural projects 345, 381
  see also Umayyad castles
papyri 13, 23, 28, 95–96
Paravicini, Werner 356
patriarch Germanus's homily
  as a source 216
  siege of Constantinople 216, 224–227
patrimonialism
  Abbasid 395–399, 411
  and mobile exercise of power 352–353, 374–375, 384–385, 395, 411–413
  definition 346–348
  al-Manṣūr 395–397
  regionalisation of powers 346–351, 411
  Umayyad 346–351, 382–385
  see also Umayyad castles
Persians 293–295, 306–308, 309
poetry 59–60, 86, 100–103, 176, 254, 295, 328
practice 73, 275
Prémare, A.-L. de 21, 25
prosopography 81–82

Qabīṣa b. Dhuʾayb 36
Qadarites 37, 45–46, 47, 48, 63, 66, 272, 277
al-Qāḍī, Wadād 37, 97, 195, 293
Qaḥṭaba b. Shabīb al-Ṭāʾī 303, 313
Qaryatayn 374, 381
al-Qāsim 398
Qaṣr Burquʿ 374
Qaṣr al-Hallabat 375–376
Qaṣr al-Ḥayr al-Gharbī 367, 378
Qaṣr al-Ḥayr al-Sharqī 181, 370, 378, 387, 410
Qaṣr al-Kharāna 375–376
Qaṣr al-Mushāsh 376
Qaṣr Ṭūba 376
al-Qasṭal 377, 410
Qaysites 66, 298, 303, 396, 400–402
al-Qifṭī 91
Qinnasrīn 38, 244, 363, 392, 396, 400, 402, 410
Qudaym 381
Qurʾān
  and ʿAbd al-Malik 60
  and al-Ḥajjāj 36, 60
  and historicity 23–26
  and licitness of writing 12–13
  and narrative sources 23
  and political legitimation 169
Qurra b. Sharīk 96
Quṣayr ʿAmra 99, 195, 346, 366, 370–373
al-Qushayrī 106

al-Rabaʿī (ʿAlī b. Muḥammad) 108, 177
al-Rāfiqa 340, 403–408, 405f
Rajāʾ b. Ḥaywa al-Kindī 37–38, 349
al-Ramla 161, 345, 349–350
Raqqa 73, 158, 340, 380, 382, 403–408, 405f
Rāwandiyya 332–333
Rayṭa bt. ʿUbayd Allāh al-Ḥārithī 281
al-Rāzī (Abū al-Ḥusayn) 105
realms of memory
  Abbasids 183–189
  and Umayyad memoria 159
  definition 157
  Dhū al-Qarnayn 237–238
  al-Ḥumayma 183–189
  importance 149
  Khirbat al-Mafjar 195
  of Maslama b. ʿAbd al-Malik 205–206
  Umayyads 157–159, 182–183, 196–199
  see also key episodes; architectural evidence
remembrance
  and poetry 100, 103
  and political legitimation 163–167
  as historical material 154–155
  memorial images 57
  search for meaning 57
rewriting history
  concurrent versions 169, 310
  geographic justifications 64, 66, 67, 73, 83
  justifying assassination 65–66, 74, 179–180
  key moments 53–54, 60–61, 173–174, 198–199, 278–283, 284–287, 310–311, 336–337
  legitimation by history 43–45, 113
  messianic expectations 62, 62–63, 85, 258–259
  methodological approach 56–57
  search for continuity 84–85, 179–180
  social logic 84
Robinson, Chase F.
  Abbasid Revolution 161, 188–189
  historiography 18–19, 27, 49, 98, 109
  Islamic state 342
  methodology 1
  non-Muslim sources 132
  transmission 153
role of history
  appropriation of the past 84–87, 178, 179–180
  educational virtues 43–45
  legitimation of power 43–45, 178, 285–286, 337–338
al-Ruṣāfa
  and Hishām's memory 172
  Hishām's accession to the caliphate 379
  Hishām's residence 66, 349, 382, 387, 404
  identifying Ruṣāfa Hishām 379–380
  mobile exercise of power 381, 387
  Muḥammad b. al-Walīd ʿĀmir al-Zubaydī al-Ḥimṣī 42
  Sulaymān b. Mūsā 38
  Umayyad architectural program 345, 379–380, 386
  al-Zuhrī and Hishām 30–31, 40–41, 63–64
Ruṣāfa Hishām. *See* al-Ruṣāfa

Sābiq al-Khwārizmī 313
al-Ṣafadī 105
al-Saffāḥ. *See* ʿAbd Allāh b. ʿAlī; Abū al-ʿAbbās; *laqab* (attribution)
al-Ṣaḥṣāḥ 204
Saʿīd b. Biṭrīq 136, 267
Saʿīd b. Musayyab 257
Saʿīd b. ʿUmar b. Jaʿda b. Ḥubayra al-Makhzūmī 316
Saʿīd b. al-Ḥarāshī 230–231
Saʿīd al-Tanūkhī 31
Saint Peter of Capitolias 357
Salamiyya 396
Ṣāliḥ b. ʿAlī
  and the Abbasid Revolution 285, 288, 304–305
  and the Syrian space 188, 337, 393, 395–396
  governor of Egypt 317
  massacre of the Umayyads 166
  patrimonialism 396–397, 410, 418–419
Sāmarrāʾ
  abandonment 83–84
  anarchy 81
  capital 77–78, 296–297, 412, 418–419
  al-Ṭabarī 86
  see also historiographic phases

Samhūdī 187
Samuel of Qalamūn 141, 330
Sauvaget, Jean 119, 294, 366, 371, 376, 379–380, 387
Sayf b. ʿUmar
historiographic filter 73
Kūfa school 29
"reliable" transmitter 16–17
writing history 73
Schacht, J. 277
Schlumberger, Daniel 367
Schmitt, Jean-Claude 15, 22
Schoeler, Gregor 13–14, 23, 27, 42, 102, 149, 153
sedimentation of memory 58, 159, 177
Sergiopolis. *See* al-Ruṣāfa
Shaban, M. A. 289
Shacklady, H. 291
Shaghb wa-Badā 41, 187–188
Shām
Abbasid space 182–189, 198–199, 285–287, 339–341, 395–403, 410–413
ahl al-Shām 37, 174, 186, 229, 315, 318, 323–325, 337, 394, 410
and spaces of memory 178–183
Arab space 309
East of the Syriac authors 309
historical continuity 339–340, 399, 412–413
Islamic space 106, 107, 110, 113, 174–175, 179
land of revolt 313–314, 314–327, 395–403
memorial stakes 180–199
messianic space 335–336
sources 29–31, 80–81, 103–108, 270–271, 340–341
Umayyad space 174–177, 189–199, 244, 248, 270–271, 278–283, 311, 339–341
see also mobile exercise of power
al-Sharāt 184
Sharon, M. 289–290, 317, 333, 359, 362
Shuʿayb b. Abī Ḥamza 41, 42
Ṣiffīn. *See* key episodes
Silverstein, Adam 392
Simon ben Yōḥai 142, 330
al-Ṣinnabra 352, 358–359, 360f, 361f
Solomon 190–199
Sourdel, Dominique 269, 286, 366
Sourdel, Janine 269, 366
Spiegel, Gabrielle M. 87, 90
Stetkevych, Suzanne P. 59–60
Straughn, Ian B. 369
Sudayf b. Maymūn 162*n*103, 164
Sufyān b. al-Thawrī 30
Sufyānī
curse 175–176
myth of return 115, 158–159, 256 *n*47, 335
Sulaymān b. ʿAbd al-Malik
and Palestine 347–349
and siege of Constantinople 206, 206–208, 212–214, 217–218, 222, 240–242
and Solomon 194
and ʿUmar II 251–252
Quṣayr ʿAmra 371–373
regionalisation of powers 347–350
Sulaymān b. ʿAlī 288, 304, 317, 319
Sulaymān b. Dāwūd 42, 190–198
Sulaymān b. Hishām 164, 363, 392
Sulaymān b. Muʿādh 210–211, 215–217, 218
Sulaymān b. Mūsā 38–39, 280
sunna 271–273, 280
al-Suyūṭī 242–243
symbolism of colours
black 74–75, 132, 135, 181–182, 294, 302–304, 322–323, 325–326
gold and blue 344–345
green 74
white 181–182, 213
yellow 229
syngramma 14, 149
Syria. *See Shām*

al-Ṭabarānī 240
al-Ṭabarī
Abbasid Revolution 288
and ʿUmar II 251, 261
assassination of ʿAbd Allāh b. ʿAlī 320–321
al-Azraq 376
campaign in the Caucasus 232–235
Hishām 380–381
historiographic filter 87, 88–92
al-Ḥumayma 184–185
al-Manṣūr 334

al-Ṭabarī (*cont.*)
- al-Manṣūr's caliphate 172–173
- massacre of the Umayyads 160–161
- personal observations 86
- popularity 90–92
- al-Rāfiqa 406
- Raqqa 407–409
- reading framework 89
- al-Ruṣāfa 380–381
- al-Saffāḥ 327
- siege of Constantinople 207–211, 211, 215
- Solomon and the Umayyads 194
- spread to the East 91–92
- *sunna* 272
- transmitter of Sayf b. ʿUmar 16
- use of Syrian sources 29–30
- al-Walīd II 377
- Yazīd b. al-Muhallab 229–232

Ṭaha Ḥusayn 101
al-Ṭāʾif 188
takbīr
- siege of Constantinople 213, 239–240
- topos (Islamic literature) 240

al-Tanūkhī (Saʿīd b. ʿAbd al-ʿAzīz) 32, 47, 49
taʾrīkh
- definition 27–28

Tarsus 75
Ṭawāna 212
Ṭayyāyē 307–308
Thawr b. Yazīd al-Kalāʿī 45, 81
Theophanes
- Abbasid Revolution 302–305
- chronicler 125–126
- al-Mahdī 333
- massacre of the Umayyads 166
- siege of Constantinople 216, 222
- ʿUmar II 268

Theophilus of Edessa
- Abbasid Revolution 302–305
- as a source 123–131
- siege of Constantinople 222
- ʿUmar II 268
- *see also* transmission

theory of schools 29–32
thughūr 4, 398, 413
topos (Islamic literature)
- book burning 58
- dying while reading the Qurʾān 169
- grandeur 170
- licitness of writing 58
- piety 170
- *takbīr* 239–240
- walls and ramparts 190–191, 239–240
- writing 12–13

transmission
- and memory 147–150
- and writing history 15, 49–51, 85–87
- as a historical object 22
- between Muslim/Christian sources 131–133, 166–167, 201, 269–271
- Christian sources 131, 166–167
- codification 22
- dating information 131, 215, 215–216, 243, 277–278
- intercultural 121–123, 215–216
- manipulation 255, 312–314
- narrative sources 9–10, 14, 51–52, 53–56
- predominance of certain authors 54
- reliability of authors 15–18
- selectivity 169
- variety of sources 143
- *see also* isnād

Turks
- Maslama's enemies 201–202, 205, 228–229, 232–233, 234–237, 242
- rise 77, 80, 87, 180
- *see also* Gog and Magog; Sāmarrāʾ

ʿUbāda b. Nusayy al-Kindī 38, 81
ʿUbayd b. Sharya al-Jurhumī 33–34
Ukhaydir 183
ʿUmar b. ʿAbd al-ʿAzīz. *See* ʿUmar II
ʿUmar (I) b. al-Khaṭṭāb
- and ʿUmar II 253–256
- messianic dimension 255–256

ʿUmar b. Hubayra 208, 210, 216
ʿUmar II
- and Abbasids 280–281
- and Hishām 282
- and Mālik b. Anas 273–278
- and Maslama b. ʿAbd al-Malik 246–247, 249–250, 281
- and mosque of Damascus 344
- and siege of Constantinople 209–211, 214, 218–222, 218–224, 228, 261–262
- and Solomon 192

ʿUmar II (*cont.*)
and Sulaymān b. ʿAbd al-Malik 250, 250–251, 261
and ʿUmar b. al-Khaṭṭāb 253–256
biography 109, 278–279
correspondence with Leo III 135–136, 261, 266–267
fifth orthodox caliph 250–253
governor of Medina 257–258, 273–274, 276
"holy" caliph 249–283
legislator 273–278
messianic dimension 255–283
musnad attributed to 272
religious policies 267–268, 276–277
scar 256–257
tomb 163, 269–270
Umayyad castles
Biblical references 195
in the Balqāʾ 375–378
in Palmyrena 378–385
interpretations 365–375
mobile exercise of power 359, 365, 365–385, 377–378
multiple functions 368–369, 382–385
Qaṣr al-Ḥayr al-Sharqī 181, 370, 378–379, 387, 410
Quṣayr ʿAmra 370–373
al-Ṣinnabra 358–359
spaces of memory 99, 159
see also ʿAnjar; patrimonialism
Umayyad sources
and the Shām 103–108, 113, 243, 244, 270–271, 340
architectural evidence 100, 176–177, 340–341
echoes in Christian sources 200–201, 243, 270
poetry 100–103
Umm al-Walīd 377
ʿUrwa b. al-Zubayr
and al-Zuhrī 36, 39, 64
as a source 36
destruction of works 58–59

Van Berchem, Max 362–363
Van Vloten, G. 289
Von Sievers, Peter 412

vulgate
and Abbasid Shām 180, 285–288
and messianism 336
and other Islamic sources 94–95
and persistent divergences 89–90
characteristics 88, 287–288
conditions of development 53–54, 83–88, 285–288, 304–305, 336
see also rewriting history

Wādī al-Qurā 187
al-Waḍīn b. ʿAṭāʾ al-Dimashqī 46
Wahb b. Munabbih 190
al-Walīd b. Muslim al-Umawī al-Dimashqī 47, 48, 81
al-Walīd (I) b. ʿAbd al-Malik
and ʿAlī b. ʿAbd Allāh 185
and Solomon 190–191, 194
mobile exercise of power 374–375
mosque of Damascus 190, 343–344
al-Walīd (II) b. Yazīd
and Hishām 41
and al-Zuhrī 41, 65
assassination 65, 157, 169, 296, 302, 390
al-Bakhrāʾ 381
image 89, 157, 195
in the Balqāʾ 376
mobile exercise of power 349–350, 377
Quṣayr ʿAmra 373
al-Wāqidī
and Ibn Aʿtham al-Kūfī 80
historiographic filter 78, 82
library 76
school of Medina 29
siege of Constantinople 207–208, 215
Wāsiṭ 106, 112, 182–183, 183, 230, 285, 303
Wāsiṭ al-Raqqa 380–381
Wellhausen, J. 16, 29–30, 32, 91, 290, 293, 295–296
Whitcomb, Donald 358–359, 360f, 361f, 368
Wickham, Chris 151, 365
writing history. *See* rewriting history
writing layers
and caliphal legitimacy 60–61, 61–62, 69–70, 76
and cultural turning points 60
and orthodoxy 64, 65–66

writing layers (*cont.*)
and political changes 58–59, 62–63, 66, 282–283
and transfer of caliphal residence 64, 66, 67–68, 73, 76–77, 83, 173–174
early Abbasids 68–89, 160–169, 160–174, 183–189, 281, 306–307, 336–338
Marwanids 58–68, 278–281, 382–384
al-Ṭabarī 88–92
see also caliphs and writing history; historiographic filter; historiographic phases

Yaḥyā b. Saʿīd al-Umawī 47
al-Yaʿqūbī
ʿAbd Allāh b. ʿAlī 319
and Christian sources 167
legitimate revenge 166
al-Manṣūr 319
massacre of the Umayyads 162
al-Rāfiqa 404
siege of Constantinople 215
al-Ṣinnabra 358
ʿUmar II 252–253
works 83
Yāqūt
Hiraqla 403
massacre of the Umayyads 161
al-Muwaqqar 376
Raqqa 408
Shaghb 188
al-Ṣinnabra 358
Yazīd b. al-Muhallab 212, 228–232, 272–273
Yazīd (II) b. ʿAbd al-Malik
and Maslama 231–232, 389
and Yazīd b. al-Muhallab 229
and al-Zuhrī 40
Chronicle of 724 133
Chronicle of 741 130
historiographic phases 63, 218
Łewond 224
mobile exercise of power 375–376, 375–377
patrimonialism 348
Yazīd (III) b. al-Walīd
and assassination of al-Walīd II 350
and Quṣayr ʿAmra 371
architectural program 350
laqab 133, 138
Qadarism 46, 66, 89
al-Ṣinnabra 358
year 100 AH 85, 114–115, 184, 239, 256–261, 262–266, 279–280, 337
Yemenites 290, 303, 400

Zāb. *See* key episodes
Zayd b. ʿAlī 164, 168
al-Zaytūna 379–380
Zīzāʾ 377–378
Zotz, Thomas 355–356
al-Zuhrī
ʿAlī b. ʿAbd Allāh 187
and ʿAbd al-Malik 40
and Hishām 63–65
and political ruptures 63–66
and ʿUrwa b. al-Zubayr 36, 39, 65
and al-Walīd II 42, 65–66
domains 42, 187
historiographic filter 64–65
passage to writing 13–14
ties to the Umayyads 39–42, 50